LINGVA LATINA

A Companion to
Roma Aeterna

Based on Hans Ørberg's *Instructions*, with Vocabulary and Grammar

LINGVA LATINA

A Companion to
Roma Aeterna

Based on Hans Ørberg's *Instructions*, with Vocabulary and Grammar

Jeanne Marie Neumann

focus an imprint of
Hackett Publishing Company, Inc.
Indianapolis/Cambridge

In memoriam
David Morgan
1960–2013
excepto quod non simul esses, cetera laeta

A Focus book
Focus an imprint of
Hackett Publishing Company

10 19 18 17   1 2 3 4 5 6 7

For further information, please address

Hackett Publishing Company, Inc.

P.O. Box 44937

Indianapolis, Indiana 46244-0937

www.hackettpublishing.com

Cover design by Brian Rak

Interior design by Elizabeth L. Wilson

Composition by Integrated Composition Systems

Library of Congress Cataloging-in-Publication Data

Names: Neumann, Jeanne Marie, author. | Oerberg, Hans H. (Hans Henning),
    1920–2010. Instructions. | Oerberg, Hans H. (Hans Henning), 1920–2010.
Lingua Latina per se illustrata. Pars II, Roma Aeterna.
Title: Lingua latina : a companion to Roma aeterna : based on Hans Ørberg's
Instructions, with vocabulary and grammar / Jeanne Marie Neumann.
Description: Indianapolis ; Cambridge : Hackett Publishing Company, Inc., 201y. |
    "A Focus book."
Identifiers: LCCN 2016032292 | ISBN 9781585108411 (pbk.)
Subjects: LCSH: Latin language—Grammar. | Latin language—Textbooks.
Classification: LCC PA2080.2 .N48 2016 | DDC 478.2/421—dc23
LC record available at http://lccn.loc.gov/2016032292

∞

Table of Contents

PARS ALTERA

Introduction

Overview of *Rōma Aeterna*

In the second book of his work *On Oratorical Education* (*Īnstitūtiō Ōrātōria*), Quintilian (*Mārcus Fabius Quintiliānus*, first century AD) suggests narratives for those beginning their rhetorical education:

> I, in fact, would like [students] to read the best authors—both as first authors and for the rest of their lives, but further still, of those best authors I'd have them read all those most straightforward and particularly lucid: for example, I'd have them read Livy in their boyhood rather than Sallust. Although Sallust is the greater writer of history, one needs to be already advanced in order to understand him. Cicero, as it seems to me at least, is both delightful for those just starting out and is also fairly clear; he can not only advance their understanding but also become a favorite. Next, as Livy advises, I would choose authors based on resemblance of each to Cicero.

> *Ego optimōs quidem et statim et semper, sed tamen eōrum candidissimum quemque et maximē expositum velim, ut Līvium ā puerīs magis quam Sallustium (et hic historiae maior est auctor, ad quem tamen intellegendum iam prōfectū opus sit). Cicerō, ut mihi quidem vidētur, et iūcundus incipientibus quoque et apertus est satis, nec prōdesse tantum sed etiam amārī potest: tum, quem ad modum Līvius praecipit, ut quisque erit Cicerōnī simillimus.*

Hans Ørberg's *Rōma Aeterna* follows Quintilian's plan. The book begins with Ørberg's own admirable prose (Caps. XXXVI to XL). Cap. XXXVI helps the instructor assess student strengths and weaknesses. This chapter effortlessly brings students back to their Latin after the inevitable break from Latin over summer or winter vacations. It also introduces critical new syntax. Students first learn, for example, about subordinate clauses in *indirect discourse* in Cap. XXXVI.

Caps. XXXVII–XL offer a prose retelling of the early books of Vergil's (*Pūblius Vergilius Marō*) *Aeneid*. These chapters are a good bridge from FAMILIA RŌMĀNA to the unadapted selections in RŌMA AETERNA. A prose narrative, instead of verse, is prudent: although students are often enticed into reading more Latin through the offer of poetry, without a solid foundation in Latin prose, they will not be able to appreciate the special voice that Latin verse offers. The prose is in part closely modeled on Vergil's language, interspersed with verse excerpts from the *Aeneid*.

Caps. XLI–XLV introduce the Roman historian Livy's (*Titus Līvius*) *ab Urbe Conditā*. Ørberg's adaptation enables the student to become gradually accustomed to Livy's prose style. The Latin grows increasingly less adapted until Cap. XLV.222, after which the student reads unadapted—although not unabridged—Livy. Cap. XLV is the transitional chapter, and, if one chapter is to introduce students to unadapted ancient texts, it is a good place to start.

While the predominant author for Caps. XLI to LI is Livy—either in his own words, Ørberg's adaptation, or the *periochae* (later summaries of the lost books of Livy's history)—we are also introduced to other authors who have contributed to our understanding of Roman history: *Eutropius* (Caps. XLVI and LIII), *Aulus Gellius* (Cap. XLVII), *Cornēlius Nepōs* (Cap. XLIX). While the styles of these writers differ from Livy's, the change from chapter to chapter will not present any obstacle to the reader.

At the end of Cap. LI, however, we are introduced to Sallust (*Sallustius Crīspus*), presented, as Quintilian advised, after the reader has a good amount of experience with Latin prose. Sallust is, as Quintilian warned, more difficult to understand. Some rudimentary remarks, not only about individual style but also about generic expectations, can be found in the section on style at the end of this introduction as well as in the Points of Style sections in individual chapters.

KEY FOUNDATIONS OF THE *RŌMA AETERNA* TEXT

Marginalia

The instructor might need to remind (read: hound) students about the *marginalia*, truly a *sine quā nōn* of reading the text as well as an invaluable aid to the mastery of Latin vocabulary. Synonyms in the margins connect new words with familiar ones and encourage students to absorb Latin as a genuine language instead of a lot of unrelated morphemes. The information in the margins also keeps the reader focused on Latin and not English translation.

Grammatica Latīna

The GRAMMATICA LATĪNA that conclude the chapters in RŌMA AETERNA differ from those of FAMILIA RŌMĀNA. The first GRAMMATICA LATĪNA section does not occur until Cap. XLVIII, in which it offers a synopsis of verb themes (*verbī themata*) of the principal parts;[1] Cap. XLIX, a synopsis of syncopation (*dē verbīs contractīs*);[2] and Cap. L, *ōrātiō oblīqua et recta*, indirect and direct speech).[3] From Cap. LI onward, the sections offer useful information about the vocabulary formation (*dē vocābulīs faciendīs*):

- prefixes (*praeverbia*, Cap. LI)
- suffixes and verbs from nouns (*suffīxa, verba ē nōminibus*, Cap. LII)
- adjectives from nouns (*adiectīva ē nōminibus*, Cap. LIII)
- nouns from verbs (*nōmina ē verbīs*, Cap. LIV)
- feminine abstract nouns from adjectives (*nōmina fēminīna ex adiectīvīs*, Cap. LV)
- inchoative verbs (*verba inchoātīva*, Cap. LVI)

This last GRAMMATICA LATĪNA section also contains an explanation of the Sapphic stanza, further explained here in the companion; a review of Cap. XXXIV of FAMILIA RŌMĀNA would be helpful to students.

The value of the GRAMMATICA LATĪNA lies not only in the useful information provided but also in its efficacy in showing students how to talk about Latin *Latīnē*. While the Companion has its own value, moving students toward the target language remains the essential objective of LINGUA LATINA PER SE ILLUSTRATA (LLPSI). The excerpt from Dōnātus's *Ars Minor* in Cap. XXXV of FAMILIA RŌMĀNA affords one model for the target language; the GRAMMATICA LATĪNA, however, remain the most important resource.

THE COMPANION

Format of the Companion

This book comprises two main parts: RĒS GRAMMATICAE for all chapters, followed by the reading helps, or AUXILIA LEGENDĪ, which are preceded by an INTRODUCTION to the chapter. As in the *Companion to FAMILIA RŌMĀNA*, a vocabulary concludes each chapter. A full vocabulary concludes the book.

---

1. See Cap. XXII of the *Companion to FAMILIA RŌMĀNA*.
2. See also Cap. XLII of this companion.
3. See also Cap. XLII of this companion.

Pars Prīma: Rēs Grammaticae

Students learned a great deal of Latin grammar in *Familia Rōmāna*. There is still quite a bit to be introduced in *Rōma Aeterna*. Some of the material fine-tunes what students have already learned; many concepts critical to the under-standing of Latin are introduced here for the first time. The material in each chapter has been organized into five categories (note: not all chapters contain all five categories):

I. Rēs Grammaticae Novae: new syntax.

II. Rēs Grammaticae Fūsius Explicātae: expansion and refinement of syntax introduced elsewhere.

III. Dēmonstrātiō Verbōrum: explanation of words and phrases at the lexical level.

IV. Recēnsiō: review material.

V. Points of Style: information about the language of the author under consideration.

Pars Prima and Pars Altera both contain new syntax. Pars Altera puts syntax into a larger context by referring students to what else they have learned else-where about, e.g., *cum* clauses (Cap. XXXVII). Although they will learn in Cap. XXXVII more about *cum* plus the subjunctive (which is "new" syntax), putting this in the context of what they already know about *cum* plus the indic-ative will foster a sense of larger perspective on how Latin works. Categorizing material has been, at times, difficult, and some may disagree with my decisions.

Pars Altera: Introduction and Auxilia Legendī

The introductions to each chapter come from Hans Ørberg. They have been in places altered and/or supplemented. The Auxilia Legendī aim to be faithful to the spirit of the book. Historical and stylistic notes are limited to those that facilitate reading and expedite mastery of the language. Information contained in the marginalia is generally not repeated in the reading helps. In other words, the reading notes are just that: help in reading the text. The commentary is not scholarly and brings in contextual information only where it seemed necessary to understanding what is going on in the Latin text.

Vocābula can be found at the end of the reading notes for individual chap-ters (as well as a full vocabulary at the end of the book).

Notes on vocabulary presentation:

Nouns

- Gender is given for all 3rd declension nouns; for other declensions (since their gender is fairly regular), gender is given only if other than the norm (e.g., 1st declension masculine) or the noun is plural.

- Nouns that are substantives from the adjective are generally placed with adjectives, with a footnote giving their alternative status as nouns.

Verbs

- The principal parts of 1st and 4th conjugation verbs are quite regular. The full four parts are listed only when they deviate from the norm.

- For compound verbs, the root verb is given when needed to guide the formation of the secondary system (e.g., *circumdare* (< *dare*):

  ▷ Principal parts will follow the root, with stem changes (e.g., *adigere* from *ad-agere*; *redimere* from *red-emere*).

  ▷ Principal parts are given for compounds from an unfamiliar root.

  ▷ An arbitrary exception has been made for the compounds from *cadere* (*-cidere*) and *caedere* (*-cīdere*).

PACING FOR *RŌMA AETERNA*

RŌMA AETERNA was composed as a continuation of *FAMILIA RŌMĀNA*. Although some readers will want—and have the necessary time—to read the text cover to cover, the companion is designed to facilitate selection. A good deal of repetition in the reading notes is one result: the companion does not take for granted that everyone has read and remembered everything that went before, and the notes will generally reference the chapter (of *RŌMA AETERNA* or *FAMILIA RŌMĀNA*) where a concept is discussed. Since the two parts of *Lingua Latina* (*FAMILIA RŌMĀNA* and *RŌMA AETERNA*) were written sequentially, chapters are referred to by number alone. For example, in the following, XIII.52 means *FAMILIA RŌMĀNA*, Cap. XIII, line 52:

> *Lūna 'nova' esse dīcitur* (XIII.52): "the moon is said to be 'new.'"

Caps. I–XXXV can be found in part one, *Familia Rōmāna*, while Caps. XXXVI–LV are found in part two, *Rōma Aeterna*.

When the reference is to chapter alone, more clarity is needed, e.g.:

- *dignus* + ablative (Cap. XIX)

- You learned the ablative of comparison in Cap. XXIV.

- *rēgnī rērumque tuārum*: genitive with *oblītōs* (Caps. XXV, XXXII): i.e., Caps. XXV *and* XXXII

References to line numbers in the chapter under review appear without the chapter number. For example, if you are reviewing Cap. XXXVI in this volume, line references to *Rōma Aeterna* Cap. XXXVI will appear as, e.g., "l.105," for line 105 whereas line references to other chapters will include chapter number. For example, *Familia Rōmāna* Cap. XXV, line 88 will appear as "XXV.88" and *Rōma Aeterna* XL, line 50 will appear as "XL.50."

Rōma Aeterna can be approached in several ways. Ideally, the reader will make his or her way through the book at a comfortable pace, absorbing the Latin in the way Ørberg intended. This approach makes the most sense for an independent learner or for homeschooling. At the high school level, *Rōma Aeterna* could provide material for Latin III (Caps. XXXVI–XLV/XLVI) and IV (Caps. XLVI/XLVII–LVI), complementing Latin I and II (*Familia Rōmāna*). Those chapter breaks are somewhat arbitrary, but Cap. XXXVI provides an excellent review to begin the school year, as do either Cap. XLVI (Eutropius) or Cap. XLVII (Aulus Gellius). A two-year reading of *Rōma Aeterna* provides a rigorous program of Latin.

Using *Rōma Aeterna* for Review

In addition to the valuable Pensa at the close of each chapter, *Rōma Aeterna* supplies much material in itself to help students review. Sentences can be chosen and manipulated to remind students of the knowledge that might not be currently active in their minds. Here are some examples, for the sake of review, of different ways of construing a sentence:

> *At puer Ascanius ācrī equō vectus iam eōs praeterit aprum aut leōnem quaerēns.* (Cap. XL.51–53)

- Participle → relative clause

  ▷ *At puer Ascanius, qui ācrī equō vehebatur, iam eōs praeterit aprum aut leōnem quaerēns.*

- Participle → independent clause

  ▷ *At puer Ascanius ācrī equō vectus iam eōs praeterit <u>et</u> aprum aut leōnem <u>quaerit</u>.*

- Participle → causal clause

  ▷ *At puer Ascanius ācrī equō vectus iam eōs praeterit <u>quia</u>* (or *quod, propterea quod) aprum aut leōnem <u>quaerit</u>.*

- Participle → purpose (final) clause

  ▷ *At puer Ascanius ācrī equō vectus iam eōs praeterit ut aprum aut leōnem quaerat.*[4]

- Direct statement → indirect statement

  ▷ *Vergilius narrat puer<u>um</u> Ascan<u>ium</u> ācrī equō vect<u>um</u> <u>tum</u> eōs <u>praeterīre</u> aprum aut leōnem quaer<u>entem</u>.*

- Direct statement → indirect question

  ▷ *Nescīmus cur puer Ascanius ācrī equō vectus ~~iam~~ eōs <u>praetereat</u> aprum aut leōnem quaerēns.*

- Direct statement → indirect command

  ▷ *Pater Aeneas puer<u>um</u> Ascan<u>ium</u> <u>monet</u> <u>nē</u> ācrī equō vectus <u>sē</u> ~~iam~~ <u>praetereat</u> aprum aut leōnem quaerēns.*

  ▷ *Pater Aeneas puer<u>ō</u> Ascani<u>ō</u> <u>imperat</u> <u>nē</u> ācrī equō vectus <u>sē</u> ~~iam~~ <u>praetereat</u> aprum aut leōnem quaerēns.*

Students can be asked to find syntax covered in *FAMILIA RŌMĀNA*, either singly or in groups.

ABRIDGING *RŌMA AETERNA*

RŌMA AETERNA is clearly not a book that can be read in one course. For those who must abridge the book, there are a variety of ways in which *RŌMA AETERNA* can be adapted. A selection might prove to be most useful for various environments, especially at the college level. The instructor will be able to pick and choose from the great wealth of material suitable for the intermediate level.

If *RŌMA AETERNA* is to be used following *FAMILIA RŌMĀNA* in a course of unadapted Latin, some important syntax from the early chapters needs to be mastered. The full reading of the early chapters can be omitted, and the com-

---

4. Sequence of tense after the historic present (as here in *praeterit*) sometimes follows the primary sequence (as above), sometimes the secondary.

panion can be used, in conjunction with the text, to teach the essential grammar. Cap. XXXVII, for example, can be used to review temporal clauses in addition to the new grammar. In teaching new grammar, it is helpful to use the examples in the Companion to go back to the text and read not only the sentence containing the new grammar but the context as well.

The instructor can choose an early chapter featuring necessary syntax as an introduction to the course and to essential grammar not found in FAMILIA RŌMĀNA. The instructor can manipulate sentences to introduce concepts not found in the chapter. For example, in Cap. XXXVI we read the following about the gates of the temple of Janus (ll.101–105):

> *Illa aedēs duās iānuās vel portās habet, quae tum dēmum clauduntur cum per tōtum imperium populī Rōmānī terrā marīque pāx facta est—id quod per septingentōs annōs inter Rōmulum et Augustum bis tantum ēvenit.*

To demonstrate a few possibilities:

- *cum* circumstantial (Cap. XXXVII): The sentence above, as written, shows *cum* temporal with the indicative. Changed to circumstantial, it could read: *Cum Rōmānī bella gerant, iānuae aedis Iānī patent.*

- Descriptive relative clause (Cap. XXXIX): *Nēmō est quī velit portās aedis Iānī aperīrī.*

- Wishes (Cap. XXXIX): *Utinam pax fiat et portae aedis Iānī claudantur!*

Instead of, or in addition to, manipulating sentences, the instructor could pick out illustrative examples of the grammar to be mastered from the text. Of course, the instructor could just use the Companion to find sentences, but it is more natural to see the sentences in context, perhaps looking at what precedes and follows. For example, the first part of the sentence above could be used to demonstrate *cum* temporal with the indicative:

> *Illa aedēs duās iānuās vel portās habet, quae <u>tum</u> dēmum clauduntur <u>cum</u> per tōtum imperium populī Rōmānī terrā marīque pāx <u>facta est</u>.*

And compared to the following sentences from Cap. XXXVII:

> *Graecī enim, <u>cum</u> urbem vī expugnāre nōn <u>possent</u>, dolō ūsī sunt*
> (ll.23–24)

> *Trōiānī vērō, <u>cum</u> Graecōs Argōs in patriam suam āvectōs esse*
> <u>*arbitrārentur,*</u> *tum dēmum post tot annōs portās aperuērunt*
> *atque exīre ausī sunt.* (ll.30–32)

Another approach to abridging chapters uses excerpts from them in class as reading comprehension exercises. For example, Cap. XLI begins:

> *Iam prīmum omnium cōnstat Troiā captā Aenēam domō pro-*
> *fugum prīmō in Macedoniam vēnisse, inde in Siciliam dēlātum*
> *esse, ab Siciliā classe ad Laurentem agrum tenuisse. Ibi ēgressī*
> *Troiānī, quibus ab immēnsō prope errōre nihil praeter arma*
> *et nāvēs supererat, cum praedam ex agrīs agerent, Latīnus rēx*
> *Aborīginēsque quī tum ea tenēbant loca, ad arcendam vim*
> *advenārum armātī ex urbe atque agrīs concurrunt.*

One way of approaching this passage without translating is to have students respond to questions. Projecting the text on a screen so that all are looking up and looking at it at the same time makes the exercise easier and quicker (and also saves you from seeing only the tops of students' heads). One way of doing this is:

1. Instructor reads aloud, slowly.

2. Student reads aloud, with (minimum) pronunciation correction from instructor.

3. Instructor reads aloud in a natural reading voice (that is, inflected for meaning).

Here is a sampling of questions to give a sense of things the instructor can ask (more examples, of course, can be gleaned from PENSUM C):

- *Versū secundō, quid significat "cōnstat?"*

  ▷ *(īnspice marginālia)*

- *Cur Aenēas profugus est?*

- *Quis Trōiam cēpit?*

  ▷ (must be remembered from previous chapters)

- *Quo prīmō vēnit Aenēas?*

- *Ad quōs aliōs locōs vēnit Aenēas?*

- *Versū quintō quid significat tenēre? Quod vocābulum subaudītur?*

  ▷ *(īnspice marginālia)*

- *Quid (versū quintō/sextō) significat 'immēnsus error'?*

  ▷ *Idem est ac 'magnum iter,' id est, Trōiānī errābant.*

- *Quid supererat iter/error?*

- *Quid significat 'praeda'?*

- *Quis est Latīnus?*

- *Dīc (vv. 8–9) 'ad arcendam vim' aliō modō.*

  ▷ *(īnspice marginālia)*

- *Dīc (v. 8) 'loca tenēbant' aliō modō.*

  ▷ e.g., *in illīs locīs habitābant*

- *Advena est nōmen commūne (id est: et masculīnum et femināinum). De quibus duōbus vocābulīs venit?*

  ▷ *ad + venīre*

- *Dīc 'virī armātī' aliīs verbīs.*

  ▷ *virī quī arma gerunt/portant,* etc.

PARTITIONING THE BOOK AND THEMATIC READINGS

At over four hundred pages, RŌMA AETERNA seems a formidable tome. The following lists are offered as samples of how one might selectively approach the book.

Review and New Grammar

Five chapters (XXXVI–XL)

    Cap. XXXVI: The City of Rome

    Cap. XXXVII: Vergil, *Aeneid* II

    Cap. XXXVIII: Vergil, *Aeneid* III

    Cap. XXXIX: Vergil, *Aeneid* I

    Cap. XL: Vergil, *Aeneid* IV

Introduction to Livy

Five chapters (XLI–XLV)

Cap. XLI: Livy, *ab Urbe Conditā* I/Ovid, *Fāstī*

Cap. XLII: Livy, *ab Urbe Conditā* I

Cap. XLIII: Livy, *ab Urbe Conditā* I/Cicero, *dē Inventiōne*

Cap. XLIV: Livy, *ab Urbe Conditā* I/Ovid, *Fāstī* VI

Cap. XLV: Livy, *ab Urbe Conditā* I/Ovid, *Fāstī* II

The Punic Wars: Hannibal

Two chapters (XLVIII–XLIX)

Cap. XLVIII: Livy, *ab Urbe Conditā* XXI–XXX

Cap. XLIX: Cornelius Nepos, *Hannibal* (unadapted)

Rome in the East

Three chapters (L–LII)

Cap. L: Livy, *ab Urbe Conditā* XXXI–XLV

Cap. LI: Livy, *ab Urbe Conditā* XLV

Cap. LII: Sallust, *Bellum Iugurthīnum*

Later Latin

Three+ chapters (XLVI, XLVII, LIII, LIV)

Cap. XLVI: Eutropius, *Breviārum Historiae Rōmānae/Aeneid* VI

Cap. XLVII: Aulus Gellius, *Noctēs Atticae* I, XI

Caps. LIII and LIV: Eutropius, *Breviārum Historiae Rōmānae*

Cicero

Three chapters (LIV–LVI)

Cap. LIV: Cicero, *prō Lēge Mānīliā*

Cap. LV: Cicero, *dē Rē Pūblicā*

Cap. LVI: Cicero, *Somnium Scīpiōnis*

Comparative Historical Style

Cap. XLVIII: Livy, *ab Urbe Conditā*

Cap. LII: Sallust, *Bellum Iugurthīnum*

Comparative Genres

Cap. XLVIII/L: History

Cap. XLIX: Biography

Cap. LIV: Oratory

Cap. LV/LVI: Political Philosophy

The chapters on Hannibal and the Second Punic War (Caps. XLVIII and XLIX) could be treated as a separate book or combined with the three chapters on the Romans in the East (L–LII). The three chapters on Cicero, with or without additional passages, would make a great reader.

The late Latin writers might be kept on their own or compared to earlier prose. When we have both Livy and the *periochae*, students can learn much about Livy's style by comparing the two—as well as get a sense of how much a tragedy the lost books of Livy presents.

The presentation of history offers a good sweep of the events of the foundation and growth of Rome during the Republic. RŌMA AETERNA brings us from the mythological foundations (Aeneas) to Cicero's remarkable ideal of the *rēs pūblica* and his vision of the men who contributed to the state's flourishing. This scope cannot be achieved without abridging several books of Livy and at times focusing on a not particularly lively string of great men and their battles. An additional problem is the reliance on the *periochae* of Livy, the writing style of which is decidedly inferior to that of the historian himself. By presenting those chapters first and adding some extended passages (some of the highlights), the book would accomplish the goal of an overview of history while still engaging students in some interesting narratives. Supplementing the *periochae* in Cap. L with notable passages from Livy (perhaps in English) would enrich the narrative, for example:

Book XXXI.1: Livy on the long narrative of the war with Carthage and the transition to Macedon.

Book XXXI.7: Publius Sulpicius' speech on why the Romans should fight Philip (refers both to Hannibal and Pyrrhus).

Book XXXII.24: Flamininus attacks Elatia.

Book XXXIII.12: Quinctius and the safety of Greece (how to keep Greece strong enough after the Romans leave—good for thinking about political ramifications of intervention/imperialism).

Book XXXIII.21: Death (and eulogy) of Attalus.

Book XXXIII.32–33: Flamininus announces freedom for Greece at the Isthmian Games.

TO THE STUDENT: READING LONG SENTENCES

Consider the following sentence (Cap. XXXVI.10–15):

> *Palātium prīmum mūnītum est, sed ea moenia quadrāta,*
> *quibus Rōmulus, prīmus rēx Rōmānōrum, Palātium mūnīvisse*
> *dīcitur iam prīdem periērunt, neque ūlla casa restat ex illā*
> *urbe antīquissimā, quae ā fōrmā moenium 'Rōma quadrāta'*
> *appellābātur, praeter 'casam Rōmulī' strāmentō tēctam.*

What might seem daunting at first becomes simpler with rereading and compartmentalizing. Read through the sentence, taking note of <u>endings</u> and <u>structure markers</u>, such as:

- coordinating conjunctions (*et, atque/ac, sed, neque/nec, vel,* etc.)
- subordinating conjunctions (*antquam/postquam, cum, dum, si,* etc.)
- relative pronouns/relative clauses
- prepositional phrases
- words/phrases in apposition

Looking at endings and markers will help you determine the relationship of words to each other and the structure of the sentence. A single underline indicates subject (and its modifiers, including predicate nominatives and adjectives); a double marks the verb; words in **bold** are conjunctions and relative pronouns; parentheses mark prepositional phrases; and brackets mark off relative clauses:

> <u>Palātium</u> prīmum <u>mūnītum est</u>, **sed** <u>ea</u> <u>moenia quadrāta</u>, [**quibus** <u>Rōmulus</u>, <u>prīmus rēx</u> Rōmānōrum, Palātium <u>mūnīvisse dīcitur</u>] iam prīdem <u>periērunt</u>, **neque** <u>ūlla casa restat</u> (ex illā urbe antīquissimā), [**quae** (ā fōrmā moenium) '<u>Rōma quadrāta' appellābātur</u>], (praeter 'casam Rōmulī' strāmentō tēctam).

With practice you will be able to "mark" (parse) sentences in your head as you read. By reading through even a very long and complex sentence carefully several times, you can arrive at its meaning without translating. A few more suggestions:

- Latin sentences are not random—they are designed to move as they do, expressing meaning in the order the author chooses.

- Focus at first on structure and endings, *before* English meaning of the word. Often students will go through and identify vocabulary and then make up a meaning that seems to fit the context.

- Do not fret about relative pronouns that are not nominative or accusative (e.g., *quibus* above—you won't know that it's an ablative until you understand the rest of the clause). It is often impossible to determine what their role in the sentence is until you have reviewed the rest of the clause.

- Do <u>not</u> write out an English translation!

  ▷ Time consuming!

  ▷ You will make mistakes. Once you have written out your translation, it will make sense to you, and you will have a harder time understanding how it can be wrong.

  ▷ You will be tempted to look at your English instead of the Latin.

  ▷ You won't learn Latin by writing out and memorizing translations. You will learn Latin only by continuing to read Latin!

- Do <u>not</u> write the English meaning of a Latin word in your text! Your eye will go to the English, and you will learn nothing.

The following lengthy and complex sentence comes from Cicero's speech in Cap. LIV.56–64:

> *Quī posteā cum māximās aedificāsset ōrnāssetque classēs*
> *exercitūsque permagnōs quibuscumque ex gentibus potuisset*
> *comparāsset et sē Bosporānīs fīnitimīs suīs bellum īnferre*
> *similāret, usque in Hispāniam lēgātōs ac litterās mīsit ad eōs*
> *ducēs quibuscum tum bellum gerēbāmus, ut, cum duōbus in*
> *locīs disiūnctissimīs māximēque dīversīs ūnō cōnsiliō ā bīnīs*
> *hostium cōpiīs bellum terrā marīque gererētur, vōs ancipitī*
> *contentiōne districtī dē imperiō dīmicārētis.*

This complex period[5] can be made easier by separating out the subordinate clauses; the following dissection of the period is offered as an example, in which there are parentheses around phrases, brackets around clauses; the subject is underlined once and the verb twice; important reading signals are bolded. The order has been changed to reflect levels of subordination:

- *Quī* **posteā**

  ▷ **cum** *māximās aedificāsset ōrnāsset**que** classēs exercitūs**que** permagnōs comparāsset*
     - *[quibuscumque (ex gentibus) potuisset]*

  ▷ **et** *similāret*
     - *sē Bosporānīs fīnitimīs suīs bellum īnferre*

- *usque (in Hispāniam) lēgātōs **ac** litterās mīsit*

  ▷ *(ad eōs ducēs)*
     - *[quibuscum tum bellum gerēbāmus]*

- **ut** *vōs ancipitī contentiōne districtī (dē imperiō) dīmicārētis*

  ▷ **cum** *(duōbus in locīs disiūnctissimīs māximē**que** dīversīs) ūnō cōnsiliō (ā bīnīs hostium cōpiīs) bellum (terrā marī**que**) gererētur.*

Here is a rewritten simplification of the sentence:

> *Mithradātēs maximās classēs aedificāvit ōrnāvitque; exercitusque permagnōs quibuscumque ex gentibus poterat comparāvit; simulāvit sē Bosporānīs fīnitimīs suīs bellum īnferre. Deinde (i.e., posteā) usque in Hispāniam lēgātōs ac litterās mīsit ad eōs ducēs quibuscum tum bellum gerēbāmus. [Hoc fēcit] ut, cum duōbus in locīs disiūnctissimīs maximēque dīversīs ūnō cōnsiliō ā bīnīs hostium cōpiīs bellum terrā marīque gererētur, vōs ancipitī contentiōne districtī dē imperiō dīmicārētis.*

STYLE

RŌMA AETERNA offers chronological glimpses into the history of the Roman Republic. The readings, however, fall into various genres: history (Livy, Sallust), historical epitome (Eutropius, *periochae*), oratory (Cicero), biography (Nepos), political philosophy (Cicero), and miscellany (Aulus Gellius).

---

5. A period signifies a long, carefully constructed sentence, often marked by several subordinate clauses, that generally does not complete the full thought until it has reached the end.

"Genre" stems from *genus*, "type"; genres are different categories of literature with particular stylistic expectations. The requirements of each genre differ, but each has its foundations in the principles of rhetoric. "Every speech, moreover," wrote Quintilian, "consists of content and words: discovery (*inventiō*) must focus on the matter at hand, expression (*ēlocūtiō*) in the choice of words, arrangement (*conlocātiō*) in both, which memory (*memoria*) holds in its grasp (and) the delivery (*āctiō*) distinguishes."[6] Although Quintilian was writing about oratory, his words are broadly applicable. Each writer devises an argument from his sources, picks what he wants to say (*inventiō*), and arranges the material (*conlocātiō* or *distribūtiō*). Each must then choose the best way of phrasing his thoughts (*ēlocūtio*, which also involves *conlocātiō*). Authors gave public readings of their works, and so, like the orator, the author needed to express himself not only with vocal intonation but also with appropriate gesture. Delivery was physically strenuous.

Despite public readings, some genres are directed more toward a listening audience and others toward readers. Livy's style, for example, is very different from that of Sallust. Quintilian calls Livy's smooth abundance "milky richness" (*illa Līuī lactea ūbertās*). He labels Sallust's style compressed and choppy—"*illa Sallustiāna brevitās et abruptum sermōnis genus*"—a style that would sail over the heads of listeners but be less likely to trip up a reader with plenty of time to digest his meaning ("*quod ōtiōsum fortasse lēctōrem minus fallat, audientem trānsuolat*"). You can notice for yourself the difference between works primarily meant to be heard instead of read when you read Cicero's speech for Pompey in Cap. LIV.

We should look for variation of style within a genre, even within the work of one author. Livy's books, for example, are usually talked about in "decades," referring not to time but to groups of books. Caps. XLI–XLV in your reading come from the first decade (indeed, from the first book) and are considered more poetic in style than the later books. You can decide what that might mean by comparing the styles for yourself.

Livy and Sallust differ in the goal of their history as well. Livy's continuous history begins from the foundation of the city (*ab Urbe Conditā*), while Sallust's history of the war with Jugurtha focuses on a political narrative of Rome's war against Numidia (111–105 BC). In contrast to both, Eutropius's fourth-century *Breviārium Historiae Rōmānae* aims to narrate the greatest amount of history as succinctly as possible (the *periochae* are brief, like the *Breviārium*, but their aim is to summarize Livy's *ab Urbe Conditā*).

---

6. *Īnstitūtiō Ōrātōria* 8.preface: *Ōrātiōnem porrō omnem constāre rēbus et verbīs: in rēbus intuendam inventiōnem, in verbīs ēlocūtiōnem, in utrāque conlocātiōnem, quae memoria complecteretur, āctiō commendāret.*

All of our authors received training in rhetoric, sound principles applicable not only to speeches but to any kind of composition. Consider Cicero's statement (a bit fuller than that of Quintilian above) in a youthful work on rhetoric, *dē Inventiōne*: *inventiō* is the "thinking out" of things that are true or very like the truth, which can make the case credible; *dispositiō* is the orderly arrangement of those things that have been "thought out"; *ēlocūtiō* is the adapting of words and sentences to the material as thought out; *memoria* is the mind's solid grasp of the arguments and words pertaining to the material as thought out; *prōnuntiātiō* is the physical adaptation of the body to the voice in accordance with the dignity of the arguments and words.[7]

Sometimes we have other ancient sources with which to compare our texts and thus get some idea of the *inventiō* and *dispositiō* of our authors. For the most part, however, a narrower scope confines our evaluation of prose style: the *dispositiō* of material within a section of a work (What does the author include? What might he have included that he did not? What other ways might he have arranged it?) and the *ēlocūtiō*, or choice and arrangement of words and expression of ideas. As for performance, we have only our imaginations to help us. When reading, consider the arrangement of the material: How does Livy, for example, present episodes from early Roman history for their greatest dramatic effect? What details does he include, and in what order? How does he embellish the narrative? What view of Roman history does his work present?

You know by experience that, although Latin word order is much more fluid than that of English, there are definite patterns. The subject and its modifiers tend to come first (S), then the object and its modifiers (O), while the verb and its modifiers tend to come last (V). Latin word order can express emphasis in a way similar to that of the human voice. The emphatic parts of a sentence are the beginning and the end. A variety of ways of transposing natural word order, known as *hyperbaton* (Greek: ὑπερβατόν) or *trānsgressiō* (Latin), renders Latin flexible and pleasing. As Quintilian says, it's important to find the place in the sentence where words fit most effectively (*Īnstitūtiō Ōrātōria* 8.62).

Writers also made use of various figures of expression that call attention to language by altering accustomed usage. There were many handbooks of figures (*figūrae*, Latin; σχῆμα, Greek). The enumeration and elucidation of figures lie beyond the scope of this introduction, but some of them you can notice without formal training. For example, you will be able to mark in your reading lists

---

7. *Inventiō est excōgitātiō rērum vērārum aut vērī similium, quae causam probābilem reddant; dispositiō est rērum inventārum in ōrdinem distribūtiō; ēlocūtiō est idōneōrum verbōrum [et sententiārum] ad inventiōnem accommodātiō; memoria est firma animī rērum ac verbōrum ad inventiōnem perceptiō; prōnūntiātiō est ex rērum et verbōrum dignitāte vōcis et corporis moderātiō.*

without conjunctions (asyndeton) or lists with an abundance of conjunctions (polysyndeton).

The best way to determine the prose style of an author is to, first, pay attention to the way each author expresses himself and then compare the mode of one with another. And the best way to know how an author expresses himself is to ask questions. Professor Timothy J. Moore, the John and Penelope Biggs Distinguished Professor of Classics at Washington University in St. Louis, kindly has permitted me to reprint his checklist for considering Latin prose style (below).

Rōma Aeterna gives you a variety of prose styles that will greatly enhance your appreciation of Latin verse: once you are familiar with the way prose authors tend to write, you will be able to see how much word order contributes to the beauty of poetry, whose word choice and word order is more varied than that of prose.

STYLISTIC ANALYSIS OF LATIN PROSE: A CHECKLIST

I. Morphology and Orthography

- What choices has the author made between alternate forms and spelling (e.g., *ere* or *erunt* in the 3rd plural perfect active indicative; *is* or *es* in the accusative plural 3rd declension)?

- Are any forms or spelling used which you might not expect in a prose author of this period (e.g., *quum* for *cum*, *qui* for *quo*)?

II. Diction

- Are words or phrases used here which are rare elsewhere in this author? in this period? in this genre? in prose? in Latin?

- Are there words or phrases which seem to reflect the formulaic language of law, diplomacy, government, or religion?

- Are there words or phrases which seem archaic, poetic, or colloquial?

- Are any words or phrases repeated in the passage, or is diction deliberately varied?

- To what extent does the author use metaphorical expressions?

- Are any expressions particularly effective in their imagery?

- What words does the author choose to make transitions from one sentence to another?

- Does the author prefer abstract or concrete nouns?
- What choices has the author made between synonyms?

III. Syntax

- What syntactical features stand out (e.g., historical infinitives, impersonal passives, repeated grammatical elements)?
- Which sentences are long, which short?
- How are the longer sentences constructed?
    - ▷ Are clauses strung along paratactically, or hypotactically?
    - ▷ How are clauses subordinated (e.g., with participles, or with conjunctions)?
    - ▷ Which thoughts occur in the main clauses, which in subordinate clauses?
    - ▷ Do the clauses follow one another by an easily comprehensible logic, or must the reader work to piece the sentences together?
    - ▷ Are the sentences "periodic," i.e., longer, carefully constructed sentences whose full meaning is kept somewhat in suspense until the end of the sentence?
    - ▷ How are clauses arranged according to rhythm and length?
    - ▷ Has the author placed the longest clauses last?
    - ▷ Does the author show concern for the rhythm of phrases, especially the last phrase of each sentence (clausula)?
    - ▷ Does the author use pairs, tricola, or other numbers of clauses?
    - ▷ To what extent does the author use parallelism in arranging his clauses?
- Word order
    - ▷ How are words, phrases, and clauses arranged for emphasis? Remember that the first and last positions in the sentence are most emphatic.
    - ▷ What other effects has the author produced through manipulation of the order of words (e.g., juxtaposition of contrasting words, hyperbaton, chiasmus)?

IV. General

- Does the passage provide echoes of previous authors in diction or phraseology? Do these echoes seem to be deliberate or unconscious?

- Has the author said only what is necessary to make his point (*brevitas*), or are unnecessary words, phrases, and sentences added (*copia*)?

- Reported speech

  ▷ Which speeches in the passage are reported indirectly, which directly?

  ▷ To what extent are the syntax and diction of the speeches manipulated to characterize speakers?

- Aside from reported speeches, does the author provide the perspective of anyone besides himself (e.g., through descriptions of reactions)?

- Does the author use any rhetorical tropes (e.g., anaphora, apostrophe, asyndeton, zeugma)?

V. What Is the Effect of All This?

Some passages for comparison:

1. Second Punic War vs. War with Jugurtha
   a. Livy: Cap. XLVIII.1–11
   b. Sallust: Cap. LII.1–6

2. Comparison of Character
   a. Livy on Hannibal: Cap. XLVIII.43–58
   b. Sallust on Jugurtha: Cap. LII.24–31

3. Military Qualities
   a. Sallust representing the speech of C. Marius: Cap. LII.457–518
   b. Cicero on Pompey: Cap. LIV.286–345

4. Livy vs. Periochae
   a. Periochae: Cap. XLVIII.274–275
   Hannibal, per continuās vigiliās in palūdibus oculō āmissō, in Etrūriam vēnit.

b. Livy: Book XXII.2.10

Ipse Hannibal aeger oculīs ex vernā prīmum intemperiē variante calōrēs frīgoraque, elephantō, quī ūnus superfuerat, quō altius ab aquā exstāret, vectus, vigiliīs tamen et noctūrnō ūmōre palustrīque caelō gravante caput et quia medendī nec locus nec tempus erat alterō oculō capitur.

Vocabulary

vernus, -a, -um: springtime (< *ver, veris* (n.))

intemperies, -ēi (f.): inclemency

variāre: to change, to vary (*varius*)

ex-stāre: stand above

ūmor, -ōris (m.): liquid, moisture

paluster, -tris, -tre: swampy

gravāre: to burden, oppress (*gravis*)

PARS PRIMA

XXXVI: TRICESIMVM SEXTVM: *RŌMA AETERNA*[1]

I. Rēs Grammaticae Novae: New Syntax

Subordinate Clauses in Indirect Discourse

When an indirect discourse (known as *ōrātiō oblīqua*)[2] contains a subordinate relative clause, the verb in that clause will be in the subjunctive,[3] following the rule you learned in Cap. XXVIII, repeated here.

> If the main verb is <u>primary</u> (present, future, sometimes perfect),[4] the verb in the subordinate subjunctive clause will be either <u>present</u> (incomplete action) or <u>perfect</u> (completed action).

> If the main verb is <u>secondary</u> (imperfect, perfect, pluperfect), the verb in the subordinate subjunctive clause will be either <u>imperfect</u> (incomplete action) or <u>pluperfect</u> (completed action). Secondary sequence is also called historical, that is, referring to the past.

---

1. For an explanation of the line number references convention, see p. xxvi.

2. That is, an indirect statement, which you first learned as the accusative and infinitive construction.

3. The verb can be in the indicative even in indirect statement, when the speaker wishes to stress the factual basis of the clause or when the clause just explains something in the indirect statement (so doesn't really belong to the indirect statement).

4. When the perfect tense emphasizes the current state resulting from the action, it is a primary tense; e.g., *fenestra clausa est*: the window has been closed (secondary) the window is closed (primary).

In table form:

Main Clause Verb(s)	Subordinate Clause Verb(s)	
	Incomplete Action	Completed Action
Primary Tense	Present Subjunctive	Perfect Subjunctive
Secondary Tense	Imperfect Subjunctive	Pluperfect Subjunctive

E.g.:

> [Augustus] glōriātus sit 'marmoream sē relinquere urbem
> quam latericiam accēpisset' (ll.229–230)

Accēpisset is

subjunctive because:

- it is the verb in a subordinate clause in indirect statement introduced
  by *glōriātus sit.*

pluperfect because:

- the main verb *glōriātus sit* is perfect.

- the action of the subordinate verb (*accēpisset*) is prior (completed) to
  the action of the main verb.

Dative of Purpose (*datīvus fīnālis*)

Latin can combine two datives, a dative of purpose (*datīvus fīnālis*) and a dative
of reference, into a construction called "double dative." Most often the double
dative is found with a form of the verb *esse*. In this chapter, we see it with *venīre*:

> [*Castor et Pollux*] saepius <u>Rōmānīs</u> in proeliīs <u>auxiliō</u> vēnērunt.
> (ll.139–140)

The dative *auxiliō* shows for what <u>purpose</u> Castor and Pollux have come, and
the dative *Rōmānīs* shows the people <u>for whom</u> they have come. *Auxiliō* is one
of the words commonly found in the double dative. Some other examples of
the double dative are:

> *cui bonō est?*: for whom (*cui*: reference) is it good/an advantage
> (*bonō*: purpose)?

> *praesidiō exercituī esse*: to be a source of protection (*praesidiō*:
> purpose) to the army (*exercituī*: reference)

II. Rēs Grammaticae Fūsius Explicātae: Expansion and Refinement of Syntax Introduced Elsewhere

Gerund/Gerundive

You first met the <u>gerund</u>, or verbal noun, in Cap. XXV:

> *Ibi nāvis mea parāta est ad nāvigandum* (XXV.93–94): "for sailing"

> *Parāta sum ad fugiendum* (XXV.97)

In addition to *ad* + the accusative of the gerund to express purpose (as above), the gerund is found in the genitive, dative,[5] and as an ablative of cause or, as below, of means:

> *Rōmānī cotīdiē in thermās illās celebrēs lavātum eunt atque ibīdem corpora exercent natandō, currendō, luctandō* (ll.247–249): "…They exercise by swimming, running, wrestling."[6]

You first met the <u>gerundive</u>, or verbal adjective, in Cap. XXXI. There you learned that the gerundive is a pass<u>ive</u> adject<u>ive</u> that expresses an action that the noun is suited for or fit for, e.g.:

> *Vīvant omnēs fēminae amandae* (XXXI.172–173): *amandae* here means "lovable," "fit to be loved."

The gerundive can also be joined with a form of the verb "to be," a construction which indicates something that is to be done. This construction, often called the passive periphrastic, can be impersonal (the first example below) and personal (the second example):

> *In summā Sacrā viā īnfrā clīvum Palātīnum est arcus Titī, dē quō mox <u>dīcendum</u> <u>erit</u>* (ll.171–172):
>
> > *dīcendum est* is impersonal: literally the relative clause means, "about which there <u>will</u> soon <u>have</u> <u>to</u> <u>be</u> <u>a</u> <u>speaking</u>."

---

5. The gerund is rare in the dative case.

6. In the example above, *lavātum* is a **SUPINE** (Cap. XXII). *Lavātum eunt* means (literally) "they go for the purpose of washing" or, in better English, "they go to wash."

> *Inter cētera Domitiānī opera memorandum est stadium in campō Mārtiō factum* (ll.318–319):
>
>> "Among the rest of Domitian's works, the <u>running track</u> made in the Campus Martius <u>must</u> <u>be</u> <u>mentioned</u> (*stadium memorandum est*)."

We also see the gerundive used in this way—expressing what is to be done to something—when used with the object of certain verbs. In this chapter, we see several examples of the gerundive used with the object of *cūrāre*:

> *Pompēius…theātrum aedificandum cūrāvit* (ll.196–197): Pompey "attended to a theatre which was to be built" conveys roughly the same idea as *Pompeius cūrāvit ut theātrum aedificārētur.*
>
> *viam Appiam mūniendam cūrāvit* (l.253)
>
> *novum forum faciendum cūrāvit* (l.325)

In Cap. XXXVII, you'll see the same construction with the verbs *dare* and *offerre*:

> *[Euandrō] Faunus…arva colenda dedit.* (ll.12–14)
>
> *Tum subitō māter Venus…fīliō sē videndam obtulit.* (ll.186–187)

Dīcitur and *nārrātur* with Nominative + Infinitive Perfect

In Cap. XIII, you learned that with passive verbs of speaking, hearing, etc.,[7] we find nominative and infinitive instead of accusative and infinitive:

> *Lūna 'nova' esse dīcitur* (XIII.52, "the moon is said to be 'new'")

In this chapter, we find the same construction with the perfect infinitive. The passives *dīcitur* and *nārrātur* with nominative and infinitive perfect state what is reported to have taken place, e.g.:

> *Rōmulus…Palātium mūnīvisse dīcitur* (ll.11–12): "Romulus…is said to have fortified the Palatine."
>
> *quī sē…praecipitāvisse nārrātur* (ll.65–66)
>
> *ōlim rēgēs Rōmānī habitāvisse dīcuntur* (ll.117–118)

---

7.   That is, the verbs that will introduce an accusative and infinitive construction.

> *Aedēs Concordiae antīqua eō tempore aedificāta esse dīcitur.*
> (ll.147–148)

> *gēns Iūlia ā Venere orta esse dīcitur* (ll.209–210)

> *Nerō...dīcitur iniisse domesticam scaenam et cecinisse Trōiae incendium.* (ll.266–269)

The same construction is seen with other verbs that introduce indirect statement:

> *Templum Mārtis Ultōris nōminātum est, quod ille deus mortem Caesaris ultus esse pūtābatur.* (ll.221–223)

Ablative of Place

Although place where is usually expressed by the ablative with a preposition, in a few phrases in Latin, the preposition *in* is not used. One of these phrases is:

> *terrā marīque* (l.103, "on land and sea")

Ablative of Separation (*ablātīvus sēparātiōnis*)

The ablative of separation[8] is generally found with a preposition. There are many instances, however, when the ablative alone (without a preposition) is used for separation:

> *Mēdus surgere cōnātur, nec vērō sē loco movēre potest.*
> (XVI.140–141)

> *Īnfāns neque somnō neque cibō carēre potest* (XX.5–6)

> *Iūlia dīcit "sē patre suō carēre nōlle."* (XX.140–141)

> *servīs meīs imperābō ut tē agrīs meīs pellant* (XXVII.89)

> *servitūte līberābantur* (XXXII.6)

In this chapter, we find more examples of the ablative of separation without a preposition:

> *...tōta vallis...domibus vacua facta esset* (ll.277–278)

> *Iuppiter, arce suā cum tōtum spectat in orbem* (l.362): "from his citadel."

---

8. Caps. VI, XVI, XX, XXVII, XXXII.

Comparison of Adjectives

In this chapter, we meet adjectives whose comparatives and/or superlatives deviate from the general rule.[9] These forms follow rules as well (which are given only when of practical use):

> *Magnificus, -a, -um:*
>> comparative: *magnificentior* (ll.44, 245)
>> superlative: *magnificentissimus* (l.19)
>
> *vetus* (stem *veter-*):[10]
>> superlative: *veterrimus* (l.100)

Adjectives in *-eus, -ius,* and *-uus* (except *-quus*) are compared using *magis* and *māximē*:

> *magis necessārius*
> *māximē idōneus*
> *māximē arduus* (l.27)

III. Dēmonstrātiō Verbōrum: Explanation of Words and Phrases at the Lexical Level

Vēnīre, vēndĕre ‖ perīre, perdĕre

The verb *vēn-īre* ("to be sold") serves as passive of *vēn-dere* ("to sell"). The two verbs are compounds of *īre* and *dare* with *vēnum*, "sale," so *vēnīre*[11] means "to go to sale" or "be sold" and *vēndere* means "to give to sale" or "sell."

> *Nunc autem mercēs in vīcīs et in aliīs forīs vēneunt* (ll.75–76):
> "Now however, merchandise is sold in the streets (i.e., neighborhoods) and in other squares."

> *...bovēs aliaeque pecudēs vēneunt* (ll.177–178): "are sold"

---

9. Caps. XII, XIII, XVIII (including Rēcēnsiō), XIX, XXIV.

10. *Vetus* ("old") is a 3rd declension adjective (Cap. XXXI) of one termination (Cap. XIX).

11. *Vēnīre*, "to sell," is distinguished from *vĕnīre*, "to come," by the long vowel in the present system. (In the perfect system, *vĕnīre* also has a long vowel in the stem [*vēnisse*], but context easily gives the sense.)

You have met another pair of verbs that works the same way: *perdere* (Cap. XXIII) and *perīre* (Cap. XXVII). *Perīre*, "to be destroyed," is the passive of *perdere*, "to destroy":

> *Nōnne tibi satis fuit vestem tuam novam perdere?* (XXIII.72–73)

> *Nōlō pecūniam meam perdere!* (XXIII.146–147)

> *"Pereat quī nescit amāre! Bis tantō pereat quisquis amāre vetat!"* (XXXI.196–197)

> *Nec omnēs īnfantēs expositī pereunt* (XXXI.148)

Fierī potest

The regular way in Latin to say "is possible" is *fierī potest*, literally "it is able to become/happen":[12]

> *tantīs dīvitiīs exōrnāvit ut nihil magnificentius fierī posset* (ll.43–44)

> *neque vērō id sine auxiliō deōrum, praecipuē Mārtis, fierī posse arbitrābātur* (l.213)

Both of these sentences are completed by a direct object (*nihil*, *id*), but *fierī posse* can also be completed by a noun clause:

> *fierī potest ut*: "it is possible (that)"
> *non fierī potest ut*: "it is impossible (that)"

1st Declension Dative/Ablative in *-ābus*

In Cap. XIV, you learned that the dative and ablative plural of *duo, duae, duo* is *duōbus, duābus, duōbus*. The ending *-ābus* also distinguishes the gender of two easily confused nouns: *deus/dea* and *fīlius/fīlia*. The ending *-ābus* in dative and ablative plural of *dea* and *fīlia* makes it possible to distinguish between the feminine and masculine:

> *Iūnōnī et Minervae, <u>duābus</u> māximīs <u>deābus</u>* (ll.39–40)

> *Sex virginēs Vestālēs ex <u>fīliābus</u> Rōmānōrum illūstrium* (ll.111–112)

> *porticus duodecim diīs et <u>deābus</u> cōnsecrāta* (ll.160–161)

---

12. *Possibilis, possibile* first appears in Quintilian (first century AD) to translate the Greek δυνατόν; it does not, in classical Latin, replace *fierī posse*.

Summus, medius, infimus

The adjectives *summus* ("top of"), *medius* ("middle of"), and *īnfimus* ("bottom of") agree with their noun:

> *medius*
>> *in mediō marī*: "in the middle of the sea"
>> *in mediō forō* (ll.63, 329)

> *summus*
>> *summum Iāniculum* (l.26): "the top of Janiculum"
>> *in summā Arce* (l.53)
>> *in summā Sacrā viā* (l.171)
>> *in summā columnā* (l.336)

> *īnfimus*
>> *in īnfimō Capitōliō* (ll.55–56): "at the foot of the Capitol"
>> *ad īnfimum Argīlētum* (l.100)

IV. Recēnsiō: Review Material

Genitive of Description (*genetīvus quālitātis*)

You met the genitive of quality/description in Cap. XIX. A noun and adjective in the genitive case add a qualifying description, often giving details of number or measurement:

> *Quīntus est puer septem annōrum.* (XIX.33–34)
>
> *adulēscēns vīgintī duōrum annōrum erat* (XIX.39–40)

In this chapter, we meet more examples, also detailing measurement:

> *opus arcuātum passuum sexāgintā* (ll.257–258)
>
> *...habet longitūdinem passuum quadrāgintā sex mīlium quadringentōrum sex* (ll.260–261)

Ut Clauses

The two-letter *ut* offers several interpretative possibilities, three included in this chapter:

Adverb of manner (Cap. IX) (see also *ut…ita*: Cap. XIX)

> *Nec vērō 'arx' nōmen huius montis proprium est, nam aliī quoque montēs arduī nātūrā et opere mūnītī 'arcēs' dīcuntur,* **ut** *summum Iāniculum, quod trāns Tiberim situm est.* (ll.23–26)

> *Caesar enim,* **ut** *plērīque prīncipēs Rōmānī, post mortem in deōrum numerō habētur et 'dīvus' vocātur.* (ll.123–124)

> *Hoc templum antīquissimum SENATVS POPVLVSQVE RO-MANVS INCENDIO CONSVMPTVM RESTITVIT,* **ut** *in fronte īnscrīptum est.* (ll.134–137)

> *Multae viae ex omnibus urbis partibus in forum ferunt,* **ut** *Argīlētum, Sacra via, Nova via* (ll.166–167)

> *…***ut** *versibus nārrat Ovidius* (l.184)

> *…***ut** *suprā dictum est* (ll.317–318)

Purpose clauses (Cap. XXVIII)

> *Ad hoc templum imperātor victor post triumphum ascendit,* **ut** *Iovī Optimō Māximō sacrificium faciat.* (ll.48–50)

> *Multī ōrātōrēs illūstrēs in Rōstra ascendērunt,* **ut** *ōrātiōnēs ad populum habērent.* (ll.91–93)

Result clauses (Cap. XXIX)

> *Postrēmō Domitiānus templum Iovis Capitōlīnī incendiō cōnsūmptum refēcit atque* **tantīs** *dīvitiīs exōrnāvit* **ut** *nihil magnificentius fierī posset* (ll.42–44).

> *…***tot et tanta** *nova opera marmorea aedificāvit* **ut** *iūre glōriātus sit 'marmoream sē relinquere urbem quam latericiam accēpisset'* (ll.228–230).

*...quae **ita** aurō atque gemmīs splendēbat **ut** iūre 'domus aurea' nōminārētur* (ll.280–281).

*Nerō ipse domum suam perfectam **ita** probāvit **ut** 'se' dīceret 'quasi hominem tandem habitāre coepisse!'* (ll.287–289)

*Videāmus nunc quōmodo haec urbs mīrābilis ā parvā orīgine ad **tantam** magnitūdinem **tantam**que glōriam pervēnit **ut** caput orbis terrārum appellētur* (ll.335–338).

Meter

There is a good amount of original verse in this and the following chapters. You should review Cap. XXXIV before proceeding. Here, to assist you in learning to read two common Latin meters, are some of the lines scanned:

ll.164–165: dactylic hexameter

Iūnō, Vĕstă, Mĭnērvă, Cĕrēs, Dīānă, Vĕnūs, Mārs, Mērcŭrĭūs, Iŏvĭ', Nēptūnŭs, Vulcānŭs, Ăpōllō.[13]

ll.182–183: elegiac couplet

cōnstĭtŭĭtquĕ sĭbī quæ 'Māxĭmă' dīcĭtŭr ārām (hexameter)
hīc ŭbĭ pārs ūrbĭs ‖ dē bŏvĕ nōmĕn hăbĕt (pentameter)

V. Points of Style: Information about the Language of the Author under Consideration

Accumulation of Genitives

A genitive can depend on another genitive. A good example can be seen in the expression:

cum multitūdine <u>omnis generis</u> <u>pecudum</u> ac <u>ferārum</u> (ll.286–287)

The genitive of description *omnis generis* qualifies *pecudum ac ferārum*, which are partitive genitives: a great number of farm animal and wild animals (partitive) of every type (quality/description).

---

13. Although *Iūppiter* is the usual nominative, *Iovis* is also occasionally found. At the time that Ennius was writing (turn of the third to the second century BC), the final *s* was often unpronounced if the next word began with a consonant.

XXXVII: TRICESIMVM SEPTIMVM: TROIA CAPTA (Vergil)[1]

I. Rēs Grammaticae Novae

Historical Present

In an account of past or "historical" events, the verbs are normally in the past tense or preterite (whether perfect, imperfect, or pluperfect). Occasionally, the present tense (called the "historical present") is used in main clauses to make the description more vivid and dramatic. The tense in dependent clauses is often past (and always past when the conjunction is *cum*). English conversation often employs a vivid present as well, switching from the past to the present for vivid and dramatic narration: "We were finished eating when we heard a noise. So I go outside to see what is happening. And I hear more noises. And then I see…"

The narration of the serpents attacking *Lāocoōn* in line 53 and those following opens with a perfect tense (*turbātī sunt*) but then moves to the historical present: *natant, prōspiciunt, petunt, edunt*, etc. Note that the preterite returns in the dependent clauses, an acknowledgment that the action takes place in the past:[2]

> *Cum terram attigissent…Trōiānōs perterritōs prōspiciunt* (ll.57–58)

> *…tum patrem ipsum, quī miserīs fīliīs auxiliō veniēbat, corripiunt* (ll.60–61)

---

1. For an explanation of the line number references convention, see p. xxvi.

2. The use of secondary tenses (imperfect and pluperfect subjunctive), does not, therefore, break the rule for the Sequence of Tense as outlined in Cap. XXXVI.

Origin (*ablātīvus orīginis*)

The ablative of source or origin is a subset of the ablative of separation.

> <u>Anchīsā</u> et <u>Venere</u> deā nātus (l.91): "born 'from' Anchises and
> Venus"

> nāte <u>deā</u> (l.99): "born of/from a goddess"

Origin (*ablātīvus causālis*)

The ablative of cause is used without a preposition, often with verbs of emotion; it is a subset of the ablative of means.[3]

> īrā permōtus (l.169): "moved by anger"

II. Rēs Grammaticae Fūsius Explicātae

Temporal Conjunctions

Dum

The conjunction *dum* (first introduced in Cap. X) generally takes the present tense (indicative),[4] even if the main clause is in the preterite:

> <u>Dum</u> Latīnus in Italiā in pāce diūturnā <u>rēgnat</u>, Trōia seu Īlium,
> clārissima Asiae urbs, post bellum decem annōrum tandem
> ā Graecīs <u>capta est</u>. (ll.21–23)

> Ita <u>dum</u> populus incertus in contrāriās sententiās <u>dīviditur</u>,
> Lāocoōn, Neptunī sacerdōs, ab summā arce dēcurrēns cīvēs
> suōs <u>monuit</u> nē Danaīs cōnfīderent. (ll.41–43)

> <u>Dum</u> Lāocoōn ad āram taurum <u>immolat</u>, subitō duo anguēs
> ingentēs ab īnsulā Tenedō per mare tranquillum ad lītus
> <u>natant</u>. (ll.54–56)

> <u>Dum</u> haec <u>aguntur</u>, Trōiānī sine cūrā <u>dormiēbant</u>. (l.90)

> Ergō parte mūrōrum dēstrūctā māchina illa hostibus armātīs
> plēna magnō labōre in urbem trahitur fūnibus, <u>dum</u> puerī

---

3.   Cf. Cap. XXVI: the gerund can be used as an ablative of means or emotion: *fessus sum ambulāndō*, XXVI.24.

4.   In Cap. XLI, you will learn that the conjunction *dum* can also take the subjunctive, when it looks toward a future action that it anticipated ("until," "long enough for").

> *puellaeque carmina sacra <u>canunt</u> et fūnem manū contingere*
> *<u>gaudent</u>.* (ll.72–75)

> *Quā rē perturbātus <u>dum</u> Aenēās celeriter ē nōtā viā <u>discēdit</u>,*
> *Creūsa incerta <u>cōnstitit</u> neque marītum aberrantem sequī*
> *<u>potuit</u>.* (ll.251–253)

> *Tālia dīcēns fixus eōdem locō <u>haerēbat</u>, <u>dum</u> fīlius et parvus*
> *nepōs omnisque domus multīs cum lacrimīs eī <u>suādent</u> 'nē*
> *omnēs suōs sēcum perderet'* (ll.199–202)[5]

Ubi

We have already seen *ubi* as a temporal conjunction with the indicative in the combination *ubi prīmum* (= *cum prīmum*, "as soon as"):

> <u>*Ubi*</u> <u>*prīmum*</u> *redēmptus est, ipse nāvēs armāvit.*
>   (XXXII.175–177)

> *sed <u>ubi</u> <u>prīmum</u> equum ligneum in lītore collocātum vīdērunt,*
> *stupentēs cōnstitērunt et mōlem equī mīrābantur.* (ll.34–36)

Ubi by itself can also mean "when," as we see in this chapter:

> <u>*Ubi*</u> *iam ad antīquam domum patriam pervēnit, Anchīsēs*
>   *pater…ex patriā captā fugere recūsāvit.* (ll.193–195)

> *Haec <u>ubi</u> dicta dedit, lacrimantem et multa volentem / dīcere*
> *dēseruit, tenuēsque recessit in aurās.* (ll.276–277)

Ut

The conjunction *ut* and *ut prīmum* may be used in the same way as *ubi* and *ubi prīmum*:

> *Rēx Priamus senex, <u>ut</u> <u>prīmum</u> forēs frāctās et hostēs in mediīs*
>   *aedibus vīdit, manibus īnfirmīs arma capit.* (ll.150–151)

> *Ut Aenēam cōnspexit venientem et arma Trōiāna agnōvit,*
>   *rē incrēdibilī exterrita palluit animusque eam relīquit.*
>   (XXXVIII.83–85)

---

5. In this last example, the verb in the indirect command (*perderet*) is in secondary sequence, even though *suādent* is in the present. The main verb (*haerēbat*) is past, and the sequence follows the main verb (instead of the subordinate *dum* clause).

Priusquam and *antequam*[6]

You first met *priusquam* in Cap. XXXI. There it was used with the future perfect indicative:

> *Profectō eum verberābō atque omnibus modīs cruciābō, sī eum invēnerō <u>priusquam</u> Italiam <u>relīquerit</u>.* (XXXI.63–65)

> *Neque enim mihi fās est rēs sacrās tangere <u>priusquam</u> manūs caede cruentās flūmine vīvō <u>lāverō</u>.* (XXXVII.238–240)

Like *postquam*, however, *priusquam* is often found with the perfect, just like *antequam*:[7]

> *Caesar autem, <u>priusquam</u> ita <u>necātus est</u>, nōn sōlum vetera opera refēcerat, sed etiam nova cōnstituerat.* (XXXVI.204–205)

> *Ergō Mārtī deō templum vōvit <u>priusquam</u> proelium <u>commīsit</u> cum Brūtō et Cassiō.* (XXXVI.213–215)

> *<u>Antequam</u> illae basilicae <u>exstrūctae sunt</u>, tabernae in forō erant...* (XXXVI.72–73)

Priusquam, *antequam*, and *postquam* are often split:

> *Nec <u>prius</u> respexit <u>quam</u> ad tumulum templumque Cereris pervēnit.* (XXXVII.253–255)

> *...tum omnem gregem in silvam ēgit, nec <u>prius</u> dēstitit <u>quam</u> septem ingentia corpora humī iacēbant.* (XXXIX.71–72)

> *Sed velim <u>prius</u> terra mē dēvoret vel Iuppiter mē fulmine percutiat, <u>quam</u> pudōrem solvō aut fidem fallō.[8]* (XL.15–17)

Cum

The conjunction *cum* (Cap. XXIX) is both temporal and causal and merits a fuller explanation than the conjunctions above.

Cum is followed by the **indicative** when it:

> refers to the present or future and means "when" (often almost the same as "if"):

---

6. In Cap. XLII you will learn that *antequam* and *priusquam* also take the subjunctive.

7. Cap. XV. Note that *antequam* and *priusquam* can also take the present tense in positive sentences (i.e., those without a negative).

8. The present tense with *antequam/priusquam* is rare.

Cum avis volat, ālae moventur. (X.15)

Cum syllabae iunguntur, vocābula fiunt. (XVIII.29)

Cum vocābula coniunguntur, sententiae fiunt.
   (XVIII.29–30)

refers strictly to "the time when"; you will sometimes find temporal markers in the sentence as well (e.g., *eō tempore, tum, tunc, iam,* etc.):

Quī nūper Athēnās vēnerat neque ibi fuerat <u>cum</u> urbs ā rēge Mīnōe expugnāta est. (XXV.52–53)

Aedēs Concordiae antīqua <u>eō</u> <u>tempore</u> aedificāta esse dīcitur <u>cum</u> post longam discordiam quae populum Rōmānum dīvīserat in duās factiōnēs. (XXXVI.147–149)

refers to repeated action (*cum iterātīvum*) and means "when" in the sense of "whenever" (Cap. XXIX):

Semper gaudeō <u>cum</u> dē līberīs meīs cōgitō. (XXIX.47)

...tū numquam mē salūtābās, <u>cum</u> mē vidēbās (XIX.99–100)

signals that the focus of the sentence is the *cum* clause, not the main clause; the *cum* clause in this construction, called *cum inversum*, follows the main clause and often marks a sudden occurrence:[9]

Tālia exclāmāns omnem domum gemitū complēbat—<u>cum</u> subitō mīrābile prōdigium vīsum est. (ll.218–219)

Iam portīs appropinquābant atque salvī esse vidēbantur, <u>cum</u> Anchīsēs per umbram prōspiciēns "Fuge, mī fīlī!" exclāmat. (ll.248–250)

Cum is followed by the **subjunctive** when it refers to:

the circumstances (*cum* circumstantial): the clause tells us what took place at the same time as (imperfect) or previous to (pluperfect) something else, as in this example:

<u>Cum</u> iam sōl <u>occidisset</u> et nox obscūra terram <u>tegeret</u>, Trōiānī fessī somnō sē dedērunt. (ll.83–84)

---

9.   Compare the force of the two English sentences: "When I was reading, the phone rang," and "I was reading when the phone rang." In both sentences, the focus of the sentence is on the phone ringing.

Occidisset shows prior time—the sun <u>had</u> <u>set</u>—while *tegeret* shows the night <u>was</u> <u>covering</u> the earth at the same time as the Trojans went to sleep.

the cause (*cum causāle*): when the *cum* clause explains the reason (can take any tense of the subjunctive):

> *Graecī enim, <u>cum</u> urbem vī expugnāre nōn <u>possent</u>, dolō*
> *ūsī sunt.* (ll.23–24)

> *nunc omnis aura, omnis sonus terret, <u>cum</u> pariter fīliō*
> *patrīque <u>timeat</u>* (l.247)

concessive/adversative: when *cum* means "although" (often *tamen* is found in the main clause). Otherwise, context will show whether *cum* is adversative.

Noun Clauses of Result

In Cap. XXVII, you learned about subjunctive noun clauses with *verba cūrandī*, such as *facere ut* and *efficere ut*. These clauses are consecutive and explanatory: they grow out of and explain their introductory words. *Mōs est ut* will also introduce a noun clause of result:

> <u>mōs</u> Rōmānōrum <u>est</u> <u>ut</u> mēnse Decembrī diēbus fēstīs quī
> dīcuntur Sāturnālia servī in convīviīs cum dominīs <u>discumbant</u>.
> (XXXVII.6–8)

The clause *ut discumbant* explains what the custom (*mōs*) is. Some other examples of phrases that are followed by these clauses are:

> *accidit ut*: "it happens that" (perfect: *accīdit ut*, "it happened that")
> *ēvenit ut*: "it turns out, results that" (perfect: *evēnit ut*, "it turned out that")
> *fit ut*: "it happens that"
> *fierī potest ut*: "it is possible that"

Alternate 2nd Person Singular Ending *-re* = *-ris*

The 2nd person singular passive has an alternate ending *-re* instead of *-ris*. Hecuba ends her summons to Priam to take refuge by the altar with these words:

> *Haec āra tuēbitur omnēs—aut moriēre simul!* (ll.158–159)

The *ē* of *moriēre* is long because *moriēre* is the future tense of the deponent verb *morī*, while *moriĕre* would be the present tense.

Possibilities for a verb ending in *-ēre* (remember to check for contextual clues!):

>   All conjugations
>>   3rd person plural perfect active indicative (alternate ending: see Cap. XXXIX, XLII):
>>   - *conticuēre* (XXXIX.304) = *conticuērunt* (syncopated ending)

>   2nd conjugation
>>   present active infinitive:
>>   - *habēre*: "to have"
>>   - *movēre*: "to move"

>>   2nd person singular present passive/deponent:
>>   - *habēre*: "you are considered"[10] = *habēris*
>>   - *cōnfitēre*: "you confess" (deponent: *cōnfitērī*) = *cōnfitēris*

>>   present passive/deponent imperative, singular:
>>   - *cōnfitēre*: "confess!"

>   3rd conjugation
>>   2nd person singular future passive/deponent:
>>   - *sequēre*: "you will follow" = *sequēris*
>>   - *moriēre*: "you will die" = *moriēris*
>>   - *amplectēre*: "you will embrace" = *amplectēris*

Possibilities for a verb ending in *-ere* (3rd conjugation)

>   present active infinitive:
>>   *īnspicere*: "to examine"
>>   *corripere*: "to seize"

>   2nd person singular present passive/deponent:
>>   *corripere*: "you are being seized" = *corriperis*
>>   *sequere*: "you are following" = *sequeris*
>>   *moriere*: "you are dying" = *morieris*
>>   *amplectere*: "you are embracing" = *amplecteris*

---

10. Remember that *habērī* (Cap. XXVIII) often means "be held," "be considered." Cf. XXXVI.30, 125.

present passive/deponent imperative, singular:

sequere: "follow!"

amplectere: "embrace!"

Greek Names

1. In *-ās* (e.g., *Aenēās*), most follow the 1st declension in Latin:

acc.	*-am* or *-an*	*Aenēam* (or *Aenēan*)
gen./dat.	*-ae*	*Aenēae*
abl.	*-ā*	*Aenēā*
voc.	*-ā*	*Aenēā*

In *-ēs*

Most (e.g., *Herculēs, Achillēs, Ulixēs*—Greek *Hēraklēs, Achilleus, Odysseus*) follow the 3rd declension:

acc.	*-em* or *-ēn*	*Herculem* (or *Herculēn*)
gen.	*-is*	*Herculis*
dat.	*-ī*	*Herculī*
voc.	*-ē*	*Herculē*

Some (e.g., *Anchīsēs*) follow the lst declension

acc.	*–ēn* or *-am*	*Anchīsēn* (or *Anchīsan*)
gen./dat.	*–ae*	*Anchīsae*
abl.	*-ā* or *-e*	*Anchīsā* (or *Anchīse*)

Dative with Compound Verbs

Compound verbs (i.e., verbs that consist of a stem and a prefix) often take a dative. This is true of both transitive and intransitive verbs.

Intransitive verbs (like *superesse*, "survive") will take the dative alone:

superesse: *Nōlō <u>urbī</u> <u>captae</u> superesse*, "I refuse to outlive a captured city." (l.198)

prōdesse: *Nihil enim <u>vīneīs</u> magis prōdest quam sōl et calor.* (XXVII.121–122)

praeesse: Agricola...ipse nōn sum, sed multīs agricolīs praesum.
(XXX.32–33)

deesse: Certus ac vērus amīcus est quī numquam amīcō suō
deest. (XXXII.115–116)

Transitive verbs (like *circumdare*, "surround") take an accusative (the object of the transitive verb) and a dative:

circumdare: [*anguēs*] *collō longa corpora sua circumdant* (1.63):
"the snakes wrap their long bodies [accusative] around his
neck [dative]."[11]

Praeficere[12] ("put *x* [accusative] in charge of *y* [dative]"):
[*Mīlitēs armātī*] *quibus praefectī erant Ulixēs et Pyrrhus.*
(ll.26–27)

Pontifex māximus...cēterīs omnibus sacerdōtibus Rōmānīs
praefectus est. (XXXVI.118–120)

addere: Si tibi certum est Trōiae peritūrae tē tuōsque addere.
(XVIII.204–205)

Dative of Interest/Reference

The dative case shows that someone or something has a stake in the sentence. Grammar books have many subcategories for the dative case, but if you keep in mind the idea that the verb concerns or affects the person invoked in the dative case, you can work out the best relationship. For example:

...cum pariter fīliō patrīque timeat (1.247): "...because he fears
equally *for* his son and father."

Aeneas is afraid, and his father and son are the people *for whom* he is afraid. Compare Laocoon's words:

Quidquid id est, timeō Danaōs—et dōna ferentēs! (1.49)

In this sentence, *timēre* takes an accusative: Laocoon fears the Greeks; were the case dative (i.e., *timeo Danaīs*), he would fear *for* them.

---

11. With the ablative, the same idea would be expressed differently: *collum longis corporibus* (ablative of means) *suis circumdant*: "they wrap around his neck with their long bodies."

12. In the examples from our text, there is no accusative because the verb is passive.

III. Dēmonstrātiō Verbōrum

Iuvāre

Iuvāre can mean "to help," as you have already seen:

> *Diīs iuvantibus spērō eum brevī sānum fore.* (XXXIV.9–10)

When *iuvāre* means "to be of use" and "to please," it is generally used impersonally:

> *Quid iuvat deōs invocāre.* (XXVI.32)
> *Quid iuvat mē lūgēre, ō dulcis coniūnx.* (1.268)
> *Sī pereō, hominum manibus periisse iuvābit.* (XXXVIII.174)
> *Sīc, sīc iuvat īre sub umbrās.* (XL.263)

Verbs Formed from the Adjective *plēnus*

You have already learned (Cap. VII) that the adjective *plēnus* can take either the genitive or the ablative, e.g.:

> *māchina...hostibus armātīs plēna* (ll.72–73)
> *hic saccus plēnus mālōrum est* (VII.43–44)

Verbs formed from *plēnus* can also take a genitive or an ablative, e.g., *complēre* (Cap. XXX), *supplēre* (Cap. XLIII), *implēre* (Cap. XVI):

> *mīlitibus armātīs complēvērunt* (ll.25–26)
> *rēgia tōta hostibus armātīs complētur* (ll.148–149)

Poenās dare

The noun *poena* denotes the penalty paid for an offense; the plural is used in the phrase *poenās dare* (+ dative: "pay the penalty to") which is equal to the passive *pūnīrī* (+ *ab*..."be punished by"), e.g.:

> *servus fugitīvus dominō poenās dat*
>   = *servus fugitīvus ab dominō pūnītur.*

> 'Lāocoontem poenās meritās Minervae dedisse' dīcunt (1.69)
>   'poenās Minervae dedisse' = ā Minervā pūnītum esse.

Fās

The indeclinable neuter *fās* denotes what is right by divine law, the will of the gods; it occurs mainly in the impersonal phrase *fās est* ("it is right/fitting"), which introduces an accusative + infinitive construction like that of indirect discourse.

> *Neque enim mihi f̲ā̲s̲ e̲s̲t̲ rēs sacrās tangere priusquam manūs caede cruentās flūmine vīvō lāverō.* (ll.238–240)

> *Nōn sine nūmine deōrum haec ēveniunt, nec f̲ā̲s̲ e̲s̲t̲ tē hinc comitem portāre Creūsam.* (ll.268–270)

Dative with the Impersonal *certum*

Certum est = "it is decided" + dative ("by whom"). In the phrase *certum mihi est* + infinitive ("I have decided"), the dative shows who made the decision:

> *Sī t̲i̲b̲i̲ certum est Trōiae peritūrae tē tuōsque addere.* (ll.204–205)

IV. RECĒNSIŌ

Dative with Adjectives

The same principle (the dative indicating reference) can be seen with some adjectives: many of the Latin adjectives with the dative are coupled with *to* or *for* in English as well.

You are already familiar with the following adjectives that take the dative:

> *amīcus* ("friendly to")
> *inimīcus* ("hostile to")
> *necessārius* ("necessary to/for")
> *nōtus* ("known to")
> *ignōtus* ("unknown to")
> *grātus* ("pleasing to/grateful to")
> *proximus* ("near to/next to")
> *cārus* ("dear to")

In this chapter, we see more examples:

> *mātūrus: sōla in rēgiā erat fīlia, nōmine Lāvīnia, iam mātūra virō.* (ll.16–17)

> *benignus: Minervae, deae Trōiānīs benignae.* (ll.36–37)

> *gravis: nec mihi grave erit hoc onus.* (ll.233–234)

> *sacer: In mediō marī Aegaeō est īnsula Apollinī sacra, nōmine Dēlos.* (XXXVIII.18)

Summary of Temporal Conjunctions

Conjunction	Meaning	Usual tense of the indicative[13]
antequam	before	perfect, future perfect
cum prīmum	as soon as	perfect
dum	while	present
postquam	after	perfect
priusquam	before	perfect, future perfect
simul atque	as soon as	perfect
ubi	when	perfect
ubi prīmum	as soon as	perfect
ut	when	perfect
ut prīmum	as soon as	perfect

Alter...alter and *alius...alius*

You first met the idiom *alius...alius* in Cap. X, where you learned that the idiom means "some...others" as in this chapter, where *aliī...aliī...aliī* offers several sets of reactions to the same situation:

> *Aliī eum ut dōnum Minervae, deae Trōiānīs benignae, sacrātum intrā mūrōs dūcī et in arce locārī iubēbant, aliī dōnum Graecōrum suspectum in mare praecipitandum et flammīs ūrendum esse cēnsēbant, aliī interiōrem equī partem īnspicere volēbant.* (ll.36–40)

---

13.   *antequam, priusquam,* and *dum* also take the subjunctive (Cap. XLI: *dum,* and Cap. XLII: *antequam, priusquam*).

Alter, altera, alterum (Cap. XIV) ("one...the other") can be used, as in this chapter, to mean "one another":

> *Ascanium puerum et patrem meum uxōremque <u>alterum</u>*
> *in <u>alterīus</u> <u>sanguine</u> trucīdātōs.* (ll.210–211)

Aeneas does not want to see his son, father, and wife killed, *one in the blood of another.*[14]

Indirect Commands

You encountered *verba postulandī* (verbs that require or command) in Cap. XXVII:

> *Ille graviter gemēns Aenēam <u>monuit</u> 'ut deōs Penātēs urbis*
> *Trōiae <u>caperet</u> atque ex urbe incēnsā <u>fugeret</u>'* (ll.96–98)

> *Hōc audītō Aenēās iuvenēs audācēs, quōs pugnandī cupidōs*
> *videt, paucīs verbīs <u>hortātur</u> <u>ut</u> sē arment <u>et</u> strictīs gladiīs*
> *in media hostium arma moritūrī sē <u>praecipitent</u>.* (ll.115–118)

> *...eīque <u>suāsit</u> ut celeriter domum ad suōs <u>fugeret</u>* (ll.187–188)

> *Lāocoōn, Neptunī sacerdōs, ab summā arce dēcurrēns cīvēs suōs*
> *<u>monuit</u> <u>nē</u> Danaīs <u>cōnfīderent</u>.* (ll.41–42)

These noun clauses, introduced by *ut* or *nē* and completed by the subjunctive (present or imperfect, as the clause represents incomplete action), are signaled by a word of asking, requiring, or demanding. The case depends on the verb used. It is helpful to memorize the constructions as phrases:

- Dative (intransitive verbs): *imperāre eī ut; persuādēre eī ut*

- Ablative + *ab* (the following verbs suggest "seek from"): *quaerere ab eō ut; petere ab eō ut; postulāre ab eō ut*

- Accusative: *rogāre eum ut; ōrāre eum ut; monēre eum ut; hortārī eum ut*

---

14.   As you learned in Cap. XIV, *alter* refers to one of two options; although three are listed here, it translates "one in the blood of the other."

V. Points of Style

The Latin "sandwich": Latin word order helps you to read phrases for meaning, often enclosing words that go together with a clause in the middle. This creates bookends or, in a different image, a kind of sandwich effect. A new thought does not start until the current one closes.

> *Aliī eum ut (dōnum Minervae, deae Trōiānīs benignae, sacrātum) intrā mūrōs dūcī et in arce locārī iubēbant, aliī (dōnum Graecōrum suspectum) in mare praecipitandum et flammīs ūrendum esse cēnsēbant, aliī interiōrem equī partem īnspicere volēbant.* (ll.36–40)

Everything between *dōnum* and *sacrātum* belongs to the same thought and forms the subject of *dūcī* and *locārī*; similarly, *Graecōrum* falls between *dōnum* and *suspectum* (the subject of *praecipitandum* and *ūrendum*) because it is part of the same thought.

> <u>*parva*</u> *duōrum fīliōrum* <u>*corpora*</u> *complexī* (l.59)

The object of *complexī* is *parva corpora*; putting *duōrum fīliōrum* between the noun and the adjective facilitates the sense.

> *Ergō (<u>parte</u> mūrōrum <u>dēstrūctā</u>) (<u>māchina illa</u> hostibus armātīs <u>plēna</u>) magnō labōre in urbem trahitur fūnibus.* (ll.72–73)

> *Cassandra, fīlia Priamī virgō (cui rēs futūrās praedīcentī) nēmō umquam crēdēbat.* (l.78)

The relative pronoun and present participle enclose the object of the participle and complete a thought (l.78).

XXXVIII: DVODEQVADRAGESIMVM: PIVS AENEAS (Vergil)[1]

II. Rēs Grammaticae Fūsius Explicātae

Reflexive Pronouns in Indirect Questions

You learned about indirect questions in Cap. XXIX. In indirect questions, as in indirect commands, a reflexive pronoun refers to the subject of the main verb (the person asking):

> *Māter interrogat 'cūr sē vocet fīlia sua?'* = Māter: *"Cūr mē vocat fīlia mea?"*

> *Aeneas...quaesivit 'quae perīcula sibi vitanda essent?'* (ll.101–103) = *Quae perīcula mihi vitanda sunt?*

Dative of Separation/Disadvantage

The dative of reference when used with verbs that mean "take away" such as *adimere* (l.69), can mean "from":

> *...clipeum, quem <u>cuidam hostī</u> <u>adēmerat</u>*: "the shield, which he had taken away *from* a certain enemy"

---

1. For an explanation of the line number references convention, see p. xxvi.

III. Dēmonstrātiō Verbōrum

Verbs That Take an Ablative of Means

There are five deponent verbs that are completed by an ablative of means. In Caps. XXVII and XXX, you learned two of them, *ūtī* and *fruī*:

> *Quī arat <u>arātrō</u> ūtitur; quī metit <u>falce</u> ūtitur; quī serit manū suā ūtitur.* (XXVII.20–22)

> *Orontēs…vītā rūsticā nōn fruitur.* (XXX.35)

In this chapter, you find two more deponent verbs with the ablative, *potīrī* ("take possession of") and *vescī* ("feed on"):

> *Polydōrum obtruncāvit et <u>aurō</u> vī <u>potītus est</u>.* (l.14)

> *Helenum, Priamī fīlium, <u>rēgnō</u> Ēpīrī <u>potītum esse</u>* (l.76–77)

> *Helenum <u>Chāoniā</u>, parte Ēpīrī extrēmā, <u>potītum esse</u>* (l.95)

> *Polyphēmus, quī <u>carne</u> et <u>sanguine</u> hominum miserōrum <u>vescitur</u>* (l.181)

The fifth, *fungī* ("discharge," "complete"), you will meet in Cap. XLIII (in a compound, *dēfungī*) and XLIV:

> *Et ille <u>dēfungī</u> <u>proeliō</u> festīnat* (XLIII.106–107).

> *Māiōrem partem aetātis eius quā <u>cīvīlibus</u> <u>officiīs fungantur</u>.* (XLIV.152–153)

Summary:

ūtor, ūtī, ūsum esse	use, enjoy
fruor, fruī, frūctum esse	enjoy
fungor, fungī, functum esse	discharge, complete
potior, potīrī, potītum esse	take possession of
vescor, vescī	feed (on), eat

Praestāre

Like *iuvāre* (Cap. XXXVII), *praestāre* can also be used personally and impersonally:

Personally:

> *Officium meum praestābō sīcut cēterī mīlitēs Rōmānī*
> (XXXIII.80–81): "I will fulfill my duty just as the rest of
> the Roman soldiers."

> *...ex tribus prīmīs generibus longē praestat...rēgium* (LIV.217–
> 218): "Monarchy is by far the best of the three types."

When used impersonally, *praestāre* means "it is preferable/better":

> *Praestat tōtam Siciliam longō cursū circumīre quam semel*
> *Scyllam īnfōrmem vidēre et saxa illa resonantia experīrī.*
> (ll.118–120)

Verbal Nouns

Instead of *postquam sōl occidit*, you find *post sōlis occāsum* (ll.132–133), and instead of *antequam sōl ortus est*, you find *ante sōlis ortum* (l.163). The sense is the same, but *occāsus, -ūs* and *ortus, -ūs* are 4th declension nouns formed from the supine stems of the verbs *occidere* and *orīrī*. These nouns look like the perfect passive participle; for example, *metus, -ūs* (fear) looks like the participle of *metuere* (to fear).

In this way, many verbal nouns are formed, e.g.:

> *cantus, -ūs < canere*: "singing," "music"
> *cursus, -ūs < currere*: "running," "race," "course"
> *cāsus, -ūs < cadere*: "fall," "chance," "accident"
> *exitus, -ūs < exīre*: "exit," "end"
> *rīsus, -ūs < rīdēre*: "laughter," "laugh"
> *ductus, -ūs < dūcere*: "leadership," "command"
> *gemitus, -ūs < gemere*: "groan"
> *ululātus, -ūs < ululāre*: "howling"
> *lūctus, -ūs < lūgēre*: "grief, mourning"
> *flētus, -ūs < flēre* (l.169): "weeping"
> *versus, -ūs < vertere* ("line," i.e., a "turn" in writing): "verse"

Greek Names in Latin

The Latin ending *-us* (2nd declension) corresponds to Greek *-os* (ος). Usually Greek names in *-os* have *-us* in Latin and follow the 2nd declension. The gender of the following Greek *places* is *feminine*, of the Greek men's *names*, *masculine*:

> *Olympus, -ī* (f.)
> *Rhodus, -ī* (f.)
> *Ēpīrus, -ī* (f.)
> *Daedalus, -ī* (m.)
> *Īcarus, -ī* (m.)
> *Priamus, -ī* (m.)

Sometimes *-os* is retained in Latin, as we have seen in the names of some Greek islands. When the *-os* is retained, the accusative also has the Greek ending *-on*. Note that the gender of these nouns is *feminine*:

> *Samos, -ī* (f.)
> *Chios, -ī* (f.)
> *Lesbos, -ī* (f.)
> *Lēmnos, -ī* (f.)
> *Tenedos, -ī* (f.)
> *Dēlos, -ī* (f.) (l.19)
> *Zacynthos, -ī* (f.) (l.63)

Most Latinized Greek names of islands, towns, and countries ending in *-us* and *-os* are feminine:

> *Dēlō relictā* (l.23)

Greek nouns in Latin may end in *-a* (1st declension), e.g.:

> *Eurōpa*
> *Crēta*
> *Ariadna*
> *Helena*

Or in -ē, e.g.:

> *Samē*
> *Andromachē*

Greek nouns in *-ē* have the following endings:

> genitive in *-ēs*: *Samēs, Andromachēs*
> accusative in *-ēn*: *Samēn, Andromachēn*
> ablative in *-ē*: *Samē, Andromachē*

Prōnōmen *-cumque*

Adding *-cumque* to *quī, quae,* and *quod* makes the pronoun (or adjective) indefinite:

> In *quāscumque terrās mē abdūcite!* (ll.170–171): "Take me away to whatever lands you want!…to any lands whatever!"
>
> *Quaecumque es, sīs nōbīs fēlīx* (l.104): "Whoever you are…"
>
> *Quīcumque es, dīs caelestibus cārus esse vidēris.* (l.143)

Prōnōmen *-met*

The ending *-met* can be added to personal pronouns for emphasis, e.g.:

> *Egomet vīdī eum in mediō antrō iacentem.* (l.182)
>
> *Dūrāte, et vōsmet rēbus servāte secundīs!* (XXXIX.86)
>
> *et ipsa mēmet super eōs iēcissem* (XL.232)

Adjectives with the Genitive

Of adjectives that take the genitive, you know *plēnus* (Cap. VII), *cupidus* (Cap. XXV), and *studiōsus* (Cap. XXVI). Now you find the genitive with:

> *potēns* ("powerful," "having power over," "having control of"):
> *dī maris et terrae tempestātumque potentēs* (l.141)
>
> *ignārus* ("ignorant of"): *ignārī viae* (l.156)
>
> *memor* ("remembering," "mindful of"): *memor veteris bellī*
> (XXXIX.7)

Certiōrem facere/certiōr fierī

The idiom *certiōrem facere/certiōr fierī* means "to inform/to be informed"; some of the common constructions that complete *certiōrem facere aliquem* (*aliquem* = person informed) are:

> absolutely (by itself):
>> *mē certiōrem faciet*: "he will inform me."

> *dē* + the ablative:
>> *patrem suum dē rē <u>certiōrem facit</u>* (l.43): "he informed his father about (*dē* + ablative) the matter."

> *alicuius reī* (genitive):
>> *certiorem me sui consilii fēcit*: "He informed me of his intention." (Cicero, *Ad Atticum* 9.2)

> accusative and infinitive:
>> *Iūlia patrem suum <u>certiōrem</u> facit sē domī esse*: "Julia informed her father that she was home."

Remember (Cap. XXVI) that the passive of *facere* is *fierī*:

> *cum ā virō ipsō <u>certior fierī</u> cuperet classe in portū relictā ad urbem prōgrediēbātur.* (l.79)

XXXIX: VNDEQVADRAGESIMVM: KARTHAGO (Vergil)[1]

I. Rēs Grammaticae Novae

Relative Clauses with the Subjunctive (To Be Continued in Further Chapters)

There is a good reason why you learned relative clauses so early in your study of Latin (Cap. III): they are ubiquitous in Latin; in order to read Latin well, you might as well get used to them early! In relative clauses, the verb is normally in the indicative, but the subjunctive is used in relative clauses in several circumstances. For example, relative clause can further explain:

> *purpose* (relative clauses of purpose)
> *reason* (relative causal clauses)
> *result or tendency* (relative clauses of result/tendency)

Relative Clauses of Purpose: *Quī = ut is*

You have learned that the meaning of *quī, quae,* and *quod* can carry more weight than just "who" or "that." At the beginning of a sentence, *quī* acts as a connective and a demonstrative (*quī = et is,* Cap. XXV):

> *Quī postquam ad rēgīnam adductī sunt, Īlioneus, māximus eōrum, sīc ōrsus est* (l.203) = "And after they…"

---

1. For an explanation of the line number references convention, see p. xxvi.

Quī can also mean *ut is* ("who" = "so that he"); when *quī* = *ut is*, the verb is in the subjunctive, just as it is in "regular" purpose clauses. In the following sentence, for example, *quī* does not describe Achates; it tells us Aeneas's <u>purpose</u> in sending him ahead to the ships:

> *Aenēās autem ad nāvēs praemittit Achātēn, <u>quī</u> Ascaniō haec <u>nūntiet</u> eumque in urbem <u>dūcat</u>.* (ll.263–264)
>
> = *ut Ascaniō haec nuntiet…dūcat*

Relative Causal Clauses: *Quī* = *cum is*

When a relative clause gives the reason (*quī* = *cum is*) behind the main clause, the verb is in the subjunctive.[2]

> *…dīs caelestibus cārus esse vidēris, quī ad urbem Karthāginem advēneris* (ll.144–145): "…you seem to be dear to the heavenly gods, since you have come to the city of Carthage" (*quī… advēneris = quoniam…advenistī*).

Descriptive Relative Clauses

The subjunctive is also found in a relative clause referring to the general character of the antecedent. Such clauses are also called Generic Clauses, Relative Clauses of Characteristic, and Relative Clauses of Tendency.[3]

This type of clause is especially common with indefinite or negative antecedents, as in Cap. XXXVI.363: *nīl nisi Rōmānum quod tueātur habet.*

Other triggers for generic descriptive clauses:

est quī/sunt quī:
> *Ille est quī hoc dicit*: "That is the man who is saying this" (states the fact: indicative).
>
> *Est quī hoc dīcat*: "There is the kind of man who would say this" (states a tendency: subjunctive).

nēmō est quī:
> *nēmō est quī hoc dīcat*: "There is no one who would say this."

---

2. Compare the causal use of *cum*, which also takes the subjunctive (see Cap. XXXVII).

3. These are originally derived from the potential subjunctive, about which you will learn in Cap. XLI.

Notā bene:

Indirect questions can *look* like a relative clause with the subjunctive. In both examples below, the clauses represent questions:

> *Posterō diē, ut prīmum lūx orta est, pius Aenēās exīre cōnstituit et nova loca explōrāre atque quaerere quī hominēs incolerent.* (ll.92–94): "Aeneas decided…to find out what people lived there" ("What people live here?").

> *Quaecumque es…doceās nōs quō sub caelō et quibus in ōrīs versēmur.* (ll.104–105)

Ut as an Interrogative Adverb

Ut may be used as an interrogative adverb (= *quōmodo*, e.g., *ut valēs?* "how are you?"), chiefly in indirect questions explaining how something has happened— or just stating the fact that it has happened, e.g.:

> *(Aenēās) nārrāvit quae ipse vīderat: ut Graecī Trōiam īnsidiīs cēpissent atque incendissent, ut ipse…fūgisset et…errāvisset* (ll.311–314): "…how the Greeks had taken Troy by artifice and set it afire, how he himself had fled…and wandered."

II. RĒS GRAMMATICAE FŪSIUS EXPLICĀTAE

Wishes

The present subjunctive is used to express wishes for the future:

> *Vīvat fortissimus quisque! Vīvant omnēs fēminae amandae!* (XXXI.172–173): We would say, "Long live every very brave man! Long live all lovable women!"

> *Quisquis amat valeat! Pereat quī nescit amāre! Bis tantō pereat quisquis amāre vetat!* (XXXI.196–197)

> *sīs nōbīs fēlīx* (l.104): "May you be propitious to us!"

Wishes are often introduced by *ut* or *utinam*:

> *Utinam aliquandō līber patriam videam!* (XXXII.157)
>
> *Utinam salvī in Graeciam perveniant!* (XXXII.223)
>
> *Utinam nē pīrātae mē...occīdant!* (XXXII.179–180)

The imperfect subjunctive is used to express an unfulfilled wish (one that didn't come true) in the present (as you learned in Cap. XXXIII):

> *Atque utinam rēx ipse...afforet Aenēās!* (ll.227–228)[4]
>
>> "And I wish that King Aeneas himself...were here" (but he isn't).
>>
>> "Would that King Aeneas himself...were here."

The pluperfect subjunctive indicates a wish that didn't come true in the past (Cap. XXXIII):

> *Utinam ego quoque in campīs Īliacīs animam prō patriā effūdissem!* (ll.36–37)
>
>> "I wish that I too had poured out my life for my fatherland on the fields of Troy" (but I didn't)."
>>
>> "Would that I had," etc.

In the next chapter (XL), you will see that *velle ut* can also express a wish (or act of will).

Accusative of Exclamation

You learned the accusative of exclamation in *FAMILIA RŌMĀNA*:

> *Exclāmat magister: "Ō, discipulōs improbōs...!"* (XV.23)
> *Mē miseram!* (XXXIV.74)

---

4.   The imperfect subjunctive of *esse* (i.e.: *essem, essēe, esset*, etc.) has an alternate form, shown here in the compound *afforet* (= *ad* + *foret*: *forem, forme, foret*, etc.). *Fore* (without endings) = *futūrum esse* (Cap. XXXIII).

The accusative + infinitive can be used in the same way. The wounded and vindictive goddess Juno, who has seen Minerva sink the ships of Ajax because he raped Cassandra in her temple, exclaims:

> *"Mēne rēgem Teucrōrum ab Italiā āvertere nōn posse?"* (ll.16–17):
> "Am I not able…?!"

Ablative of Respect

You are already familiar with the ablative of respect:

> *Nec modo <u>pede</u>, sed etiam <u>capite</u> aeger est.* (XI.55)
> *Ille vir pessimus <u>tē</u> dignus nōn erat!* (XIX.110)
> *Nympham suam <u>fōrmā</u> pulcherrimam* (ll.25–26)
> *Dīdō rēgīna, <u>fōrmā</u> pulcherrima* (l.193)

The ablative of respect points to the specific point in which the adjective is true. It can also be used with verbs:

> *(Hannibal) <u>praestitisse</u> cēterōs imperātōrēs <u>prūdentiā</u>* (XLIX.4–5):
> "Hannibal surpassed all other generals in intelligence."

One important use of the ablative of respect is with the supine, familiar to you from Cap. XXII:

> *Nōmen meum nōn est facile <u>dictū</u>* (XXII.43) = "My name
>   is not easy to say."
>
> *mīrābile <u>dictū</u>!* (l.167) = "miraculous to tell about!"

Ablative of Comparison

You learned the ablative of comparison in Cap. XXIV:

> *Nunc pēs dexter māior est <u>pede</u> <u>laevō</u>.* (XXIV.30)
> *<u>dictō</u> citius* (l.56): "sooner than spoken"

The ablative of comparison can be used, as in the examples below, as a different way of giving a superlative:

> <u>Aeneā</u> nēmō fortior fuit ("no one was braver than Aeneas") = Aenēās omnium fortissimus fuit.

> Aenēās, <u>quō</u> nēmō iūstior fuit nec...fortior = quī omnium iūstissimus fuit et fortissimus. (ll.210–211)

> Fāma <u>quā</u> nōn aliud malum ūllum vēlōcius est (XL.62–63)

III. Dēmonstrātiō Verbōrum

Obviam īre

Obviam (ob viam) is an adverb ("toward") frequently used with forms of īre:

> Cui māter Venus in media silvā obviam iit (ll.96–97)

Ablative with comitātus

Comitārī is a deponent verb meaning "to accompany." The participle comitātus, -a, -um can be used in a passive sense with the ablative to mean "accompanied by":

> ipse <u>ūnō</u> <u>Achātē</u> comitātus graditur (l.95)
> <u>magnā</u> iuvenum <u>catervā</u> comitāta (l.194)

XL: QVADRAGESIMVM: INFELIX DIDO (Vergil)[1]

II. Rēs Grammaticae Fūsius Explicātae

Impersonal Passive of Intransitive Verbs

Intransitive verbs, like *venīre*, *pugnāre*, and *tacēre*, as you know, are not completed by an accusative direct object. Therefore, they are not normally found in the passive voice, unless, as in the examples below, they are being used impersonally (Cap. XXXIII):

> *Cum complūrēs hōrās...pugnātum esset* (XXXIII.119–121):
> "When there had been fighting for many hours (literally: it had been fought)."

> *Hīc vērō ācerrimē pugnābātur* (XXXVII.135): "But here there was very fierce fighting" (literally: "It was being very vehemently fought").

> *Postquam in altōs montēs ventum est...* (l.50)

The impersonal passive is also found in the gerundive, e.g., the passive periphrastic:

> *Tacendum est* (XXXI.178)

---

1. For an explanation of the line number references convention, see p. xxvi.

Impersonal Verbs

You have learned (Cap. XXIII) the impersonal verb *pudēre*, one of a small group of verbs (see below for list) that are used impersonally and construed with the accusative and either the genitive or infinitive. In other words, we find:

> 3rd person singular verb + accusative of person concerned (or "subject") and either:
> > a genitive of person/thing affected (or "object")
> > an infinitive that completes the thought

With the accusative of person and infinitive:

> *Nōnne tē pudet hoc fēcisse? Profectō mē pudet hoc ā meō fīliō factum esse.* (XXIII.79–80)

> *Nōnne tē pudet pauperī magistrō mercēdem negāre?* (XXIII.138–139)

With the accusative of person and genitive of thing:

> *Puerum pudet factī suī.* (XXIII.82)

Other verbs that follow the pattern of *pudet* are:

> *taedet* (expressing disgust)
> > *Taedet eam vītae* (l.167) = *taedet eam vīvere*: "she is tired of life."
> > *Fēminae Trōiānae, cum eās longī errōris taedēret, nāvēs incendērunt.* (ll.281–282)

> *paenitet* (expressing regret)
> > *nec tē paenitēbit nōbīs auxilium tulisse* (XXXIX.212–213): "it will not cause you regret to have brought us aid."
> > *Numquam, rēgīna...mē paenitēbit tuī meminisse* (*tuī* here is the objective genitive with *meminisse*, not *paenitēbit*) (ll.123–124)
> > *Aenēās plērāsque fēminās, quamquam eās iam factī suī paenitēbat, in Siciliā relīquit...* (ll.283–286)

piget (expressing revulsion or displeasure)

> *Sī vōs piget cōnūbiī inter vōs, in nōs vertite īrās.*
> (XLII.155–156)

(see also example under *miseret*)

miseret (expressing pity)[2]

> *mea mater, tuī mē miseret; meī piget*: "My mother, I pity
> you, I am chagrined at myself" (Cicero, quoting the
> poet Ennius in *de Divinatione*, Book I.66).

Although we don't find the impersonal *miseret* in our book, we do find the verb *miserērī* ("have pity on").[3] Like *oblīvīscī* (Cap. XXV) and *meminisse* (Cap. XXXII), *miserērī* is followed by an objective genitive:

> "*miserēre meī*" (l.112): "Take pity on me!"

Dubitāre (nōn dubitō quīn)

You are accustomed to seeing *dubitāre* used as both an intransitive and a transitive verb:

> *Iūlius, quī Mārcum discipulum pigerrimum esse scit, iam*
> *dē verbīs eius <u>dubitāre</u> incipit. Aemilia vērō nihil <u>dubitat</u>,*
> *sed omnia crēdit!* (XXI.129–131)

> *Hoc nōn dubitō* (XXV.69)

And with indirect questions:

> *dubitō num haec fābula vēra sit* (XXIX.116–117)
>
> > original question: *num haec fābula vēra est?*

> *Dubitō num ego tam diū famem ferre possim.* (XXX.45–46)
> *valdē dubitō num pecūniā suā mē redimere velint* (XXXII.98–99)
> *Ego quoque dubitāre coeperam num nūntius vērum dīxisset.*
> (XXXIII.112–113)

---

2. Only the active *misereor, miserērī*, occurs in *FAMILIA RŌMĀNA* or *RŌMA AETERNA*, not the impersonal *miseret*.

3. See above on the impersonal use of the active form *miseret*, which also takes the genitive.

In this chapter, you see a different construction, *nōn dubitō + quīn*[4] and an indirect question:

> *Equidem nōn dubitō quīn deā nātus sit* (l.8): "Indeed, I have no doubt that he is born of a goddess."

Taken as separate clauses, you can see how the construction arose:

> *quīn deā nātus sit?*: "why shouldn't he be born of a goddess?"
>
> *equidem nōn dubitō*: "I am certainly not in doubt."

Summary:

- *Dubitō num* suggests *nōn crēdō*; *num* tells you that the original interrogative (see first example above) was "*num,*" expecting a "no" answer.

- *Dubitō an*, like *haud sciō an* and *nesciō an* (XXXII.84), suggests "I am inclined to think." *An* is a disjunctive conjunction, meaning it states or implies two choices ("is the story true or false?"). If we are given only one option instead of two, that is probably the option the speaker thinks is the case, e.g.:

  ▷ *dubitō num haec fābula vēra sit* = "This story isn't true is it?" "I doubt that it is true."

  ▷ *dubitō an haec fābula vēra sit* = "I am inclined to think that it is true."

  ▷ *Nōn dubitō quīn* is equivalent to *crēdō*.

Posse

The subjunctive can be used to signal possibility (as you will learn in Cap. XLI). But because *posse* ("to be able") has the force of possibility in its meaning, we often find it in the indicative where we might expect the subjunctive. So, for example, in the present contrafactual condition in lines 10–12:

> *Nisi certum mihi esset nūllī virō coniugiō mē iungere, postquam prīmus amor mē morte fefellit, huius ūnīus amōrī forsitan succumbere potuī!*

---

4.   For *quīn*, see Cap. XXII and below, under adverbs.

We might expect the imperfect subjunctive *possem* (instead of the perfect indicative *potuī*) to complete the contrafactual thought. Because *potuī* means "I could have," it implies "I could have (but in fact I didn't)."

We saw a similar example of this use of *posse* in the indicative instead of subjunctive in Cap. XXIV:

> *Mīror tē crūs nōn frēgisse. Facile os frangere potuistī.* (ll.32–33)

While an English translation would run "I am amazed that you did not break your leg. You could have easily broken a bone," the Latin actually says, "You were able to break a bone." The implication is that, although there was the possibility of breaking a bone in the past, it didn't happen.

Wishes

The Recēnsiō at the end of Cap. XXXIX reviewed wishes. In this chapter, you see another way of expressing a wish: the subjunctive of *velle* with the subjunctive (with or without the conjunction *ut*):

> *Sed velim prius terra mē dēvoret vel Iuppiter mē fulmine percutiat, quam pudōrem solvō aut fidem fallō.* (ll.15–17)

Personal Pronouns: Genitives

In Cap. XXIX, you learned that the personal pronouns show two forms for the genitive plural:

> *nostrum, vestrum*: partitive
> *nostrī, vestrī*: objective

Whether partitive (Cap. XII) or objective (Cap. XXV), we use the same form for the singular: *meī, tuī*. You have already seen that the genitive of personal pronouns is used for the partitive:

> *quis vestrum?* "Who of you?"
>
> …*vīta omnium nostrum servāta est*: "the life of all of us"
>   (XXIX.37–38)
>
> *nēmō nostrum periit*: "no one of us" (XXIX.39)

But the genitive of the personal pronouns is mostly used in the objective sense:

> *memoriam <u>tuī</u>*: "memory of you" (l.119)
>
> *<u>meī</u>...imāgō*: "an image (i.e., ghost) of me" (l.257)

Remember that instead of a possessive genitive, Latin uses the possessive adjectives *meus, tuus, noster, vester*.

Quīn

The adverb *quīn*:

> With the 2nd person of the present indicative, *quīn* expresses a request or order (= *age, cur nōn?*):
> > *Quīn aperiēs? = aperī!* (XXII.29)

> When followed by an imperative, *quīn* is emphatic (= *cur nōn?*), as when Dido bids herself:
> > *Quīn morere, ut merita es.* (l.197)
> > *Quīn mē admittis?* (XXII.32)

> With *etiam*, *quīn* shows emphasis ("indeed"):
> > *Quīn etiam hībernō tempore classem ōrnās et per mediōs Aquilōnēs nāvigāre properās!* (ll.108–109)
> > *Quīn etiam clāmāre ausus est maestusque 'Creūsam' iterum iterumque vocāvit.* (XXXVII.264–265)

> As a conjunction (meaning "but that, but"), *quīn* occurs after negative expressions of doubt and is followed by the subjunctive, e.g.:
> > *Equidem nōn dubitō quīn deā nātus sit.* (l.8, see above on *dubitāre*)

Dum + the Subjunctive

Cap. XXXVII reviewed the syntax of the conjunction *dum* with the indicative, meaning "when" in the sense of "while." The subjunctive, not the indicative, follows the conjunction *dum* when the clause indicates what is expected or intended. Here it means "when" in the sense of "until," "long enough for":

> *Quid moror? an dum frāter Pygmaliōn mea moenia dēstruat aut Iarbās, rēx Gaetūlōrum, captam mē abdūcat?*: "What am I waiting for? Or (should I wait) until my brother Pygmalion destroys my walls or Iarbas, the king of the Gaetuli, leads me away captured?" (ll.115–117)

> *Moram brevem petit 'dum fortūna sē dolēre doceat'*: not "while" but "until" (l.162)

In these examples, *dum* looks toward an anticipated event rather than focusing on an event going on at the same time as another event (as it does with the indicative).

Dum with the subjunctive can also mean "as long as," "provided that." In this sense, *dum* is frequently accompanied by *modo*: *dummodo*. You will meet this construction in Cap. XLIV:

> *Tanaquīl…oblītaque amōris patriae, dummodo virum honōrātum vidēret* (XLIV.109–111): "Tanaquil…forgetful of her love of fatherland, provided that she might see her husband honored."

III. Dēmonstrātiō Verbōrum

Compounds of *stāre*

At the end of the chapter, you will notice that the principal parts for compounds do not always follow the same pattern of orthography. You will find:

> *(obstō) obstāre, obstitisse, obstātum*
> *(circumstō) circumstāre, circumstetisse*

The difference is in the preposition that compounds the verbs. Disyllabic prepositions, like *circum*, will have a third principal part in *-stetī* while monosyllabic prepositions, like *ob*, will have a third principal part in *-stitī*. These differences stem from natural Latin speech patterns.

IV. Recēnsiō

Locative

Remember that for names of cities, towns, and small islands, as well as for *domus*, *rūs*, and *humus*, instead of *in* + the ablative, Latin uses the locative. A review of the locative endings:

Declension	Singular	Plural	Examples
1st	*ae*	*īs*	*Rōmae, Athēnīs*
2nd	*ī*	*īs*	*Tūsculī, humī*
3rd	*ī, ĕ*	*ibus*	*rūrī, Karthāgine, Gādibus*
4th			*domī*

Interrogative Pronouns in Exclamations

In Cap. VIII, you learned that *quam* used in exclamations means "how." In Cap. XXVI and Cap. XXXVII, you saw that the interrogative pronouns and adjectives beginning with *qu-* may also be used in exclamations:

> "*Ō, quot parvae īnsulae in marī ingentī sunt!*" (XXVI.91–92)

> *Ecce eī in somnō appāruit maestissimus Hector, fīlius Priamī mortuus—sed quālis erat, quantum mūtātus ab illō Hectore quī ex tot proeliīs victor redierat!* (XXXVII.92–94)

This chapter offers more examples:

> "*Quālis hospes tēctīs nostrīs successit, quam nōbilis, quam fortis!...quam ille fātīs iactātus est! Quae bella exhausta nārrābat!*" (ll.7–10)

> "*Quanta erit potentia Poenōrum, quanta glōria tua, soror, si cum duce Trōiānōrum tē coniūnxeris!*" (ll.29–30)

> *Quō tum dolōre Dīdō afficiēbātur...Quōs gemitūs dabat!* (ll.156–157)

V. Points of Style

Understanding Participles

Remember you can adapt the way you interepret participles to fit the way your own language works:

> *Dum…rēx Gaetūlōrum, captam mē abdūcat:*
>> Literally: "Until the king of the Gaetuli leads me, having been captured, away"
>>
>> "Until the king of the Gaetuli leads me away as a captive"
>>
>> "Until the king of the Gaetuli captures me and leads me away"

XLI: VNVM ET QVADRAGESIMVM: ORIGINES (Livy)[1]

I. Rēs Grammaticae Novae

Potential Subjunctive (Negative: *nōn*)

Another important use of the independent subjunctive is the **potential subjunctive**. While the volitive subjunctive expresses will and the optative expresses desire, the potential subjunctive denotes possibility (what might or could happen).

Indefinite Potential Subjunctive

The potential subjunctive can be used to make a general statement not tied to any particular person. English generalizes by saying either "one" (e.g., "One needs to see the pyramids to appreciate how big they are") or "you" (e.g., "you really had to be there" means "anyone who was not there wouldn't get it").

The generalizing potential in Latin is chiefly 2nd person singular and imperfect:

> *hīc ubi nunc fora sunt, lintrēs errāre vidērēs* (1.207): "you/one might have seen…"

> [*eōs*] *sēnsisse putārēs* (1.221): "you/one would have thought…"

The imperfect tense above suggests "you would have seen/thought had you been there"; that is, it refers to what might or could have been/happened.

Further uses of the potential subjunctive are introduced in Cap. XLVIII.

---

1. For an explanation of the line number references convention, see p. xxvi.

II. Rēs Grammaticae Fūsius Explicātae

Subjunctive in Conditions

You have already seen the subjunctive in contrafactual, or unreal, conditions (Cap. XXXIII), referring to the present (imperfect subjunctive) or the past (pluperfect subjunctive):

> *Sī Mercurius essem ālāsque habērem…in Italiam volārem!*
> (XXXIII.73–75): "If I were Mercury and I had wings,
> I would fly into Italy!"

> *Sī iam tum hoc intellēxissem, certē patrem audīvissem nec ad*
> *bellum profectus essem* (XXXIII.181–182): "If I had at that
> time understood this, I would certainly have listened to my
> father and I would not have set out for war."

The present subjunctive in a condition is potential and refers to a vague future, what might or could happen. Such conditions are variously labeled "future less vivid," "ideal," and, from their usual English translation, "should-would" conditions:

> *Ō dea, sī ā prīmā orīgine repetēns labōrēs nostrōs nārrem, ante*
> *vesperum fīnem nōn faciam!* (XXXIX.133–135): "if I should
> tell…I would not make an end."

III. Dēmonstrātiō Verbōrum

Cōnstat (Impersonal)

In Cap. VIII, you learned one meaning of *cōnstāre*: to cost:

> *Hic ānulus centum nummīs cōnstat.* (VIII.59)

The verb *cōnstāre* can also be used impersonally; *cōnstat* followed by accusative + infinitive states a fact: "it is certain," "it is an established fact that…":

> *cōnstat Trōiā captā Aenēam domō profugum prīmō in Macedo-*
> *niam vēnisse.* (ll.2–3)

Convenit (Impersonal)

You met *convenit* as "fit" in Cap. VIII:

> *Tanta gemma ad tam parvum ānulum nōn* <u>*convenit*</u> (VIII.81–
> 82): "Such a big jewel does not fit such a small ring" ("is not
> suitable for")

> *...sciēbat et tempus quō ipse eōs sustulisset ad id tempus*
> <u>*convenīre*</u> (ll.120–121)

Also note the impersonal use of *convenīre* about an agreement between two
people:

> *inter frātrēs* <u>*convēnit*</u> *ut* (l.145): "it was agreed between the
> brothers," "the brothers agreed that..."

That which is agreed upon may be the subject of *convenīre*, e.g.:

> *Pāx ita* <u>*convēnerat*</u> *ut Etrūscīs Latīnīsque fluvius Albula, quem
> nunc Tiberim vocant, fīnis esset* (ll.66–68): "peace had been
> agreed on in such a way that..."

Both of the examples given show the construction as *convenit ut*, but, as is true
of many Latin verbs, *convenit* will be found with more than one construction
(e.g., accusative and infinitive).

> *lacrimāre puerō Rōmānō nōn convenit* (XV.63–64): "it is not
> fitting/suitable, for a Roman boy to cry."

4th Declension Verbal Nouns (Continued)

This chapter introduces more 4th declension verbal nouns (see Cap. XXXVIII):

> *discessus < discēdere*
> *adventus < advenīre*
> *partus < parere*
> *vāgītus < vāgīre*

Some 4th declension verbal nouns are found only in the ablative (ablative of cause, Cap. XXXVII) with a genitive or possessive pronoun: for example, *iussū*:

> *iussū rēgis* (l.119)
> *iussū meō*

IV. Recēnsiō: Uses of the Subjunctive

In Independent Clauses

You have already learned several uses for the independent subjunctive.

- Deliberative questions (Cap. XXIX); negative: *nōn*

  > *Quid faciam? Quid spērem?* (XXIX.22–23): "what should I do? What can I hope for?"

  > *Quid facerem?* = "What was I to do?"

- Negative commands (Cap. XXXII); negative: *nē*

  > *Nē timueris! Nē timueritis!!* (XXXII.215, 199 = *nōlī/nōlīte timēre*): "Don't be afraid!"

- Volitive subjunctive:[2] act of will; negative: *nē*

  Hortatory subjunctive (Cap. XXX)

  > *Triclīnium intrēmus!* (XXX.86–87): "Let's go into the dining room!"

  > *Gaudeāmus atque amēmus* (XXXI.173): "Let us rejoice and let us love"

  Jussive subjunctive (Cap. XXXI)

  > *Quisquis fēminās amat, pōculum tollat et bibat mēcum!* (XXXI.176–177): "Whoever loves women, let him lift his cup and drink with me!"

- Optative subjunctive: wish/desire (Cap. XXXI); negative: *nē*

  > *Vīvat fortissimus quisque! Vīvant omnēs fēminae amandae!* (XXXI.172–173)

---

2.   Jussive and hortatory are both *volitive* subjunctives; they express an act of will (hortatory in 1st person, jussive in 3rd).

Utinam salvī in Graeciam perveniant! (XXXII.223): "I hope
they arrive safe into Greece!"/"May they arrive safe into
Greece."

Utinam nē pīrātae mē...occīdant! (XXXII.179–180): "May the
pirates not kill me"/"I hope the pirates don't kill me."

Utinam ego Rōmae essem! (XXXIII.67): "I wish I were at Rome"/
"Would that I were at Rome."

Utinam patrem audīvissem! (XXXIII.66): "I wish I had listened
to my father"/"Would that I had listened to my father."

Rhetorical Questions

In Cap. XXIX, you learned about **deliberative** questions. **Rhetorical** questions
are also usually in the subjunctive; the subjunctive here is potential and the
assumed answer is "no" or "no one," i.e., "Who could ____?" "No one."

Quis enim rem tam veterem prō certō affirmet? (ll.53–54): "For
who could confirm such an old affair for certain?"

Quis crēdat puerīs nōn nocuisse feram? (l.228): "Who would believe that a wild beast did not harm the boys?"

Quis genus Aenĕadum, quis Trōiae nesciat urbem?
(XXXIX.219): "Who could not know the family of the Ae-
neadii, who could not know the city of Troy?"

Summary of Conditions

Conditions refer to the present, past, or future. When they refer to facts, they
take the indicative; otherwise they take the subjunctive. The difference between
the indicative and the subjunctive in a condition can be seen in the excerpt
from Ovid's *Fāstī* that concludes the book (ll.213–216). When the slaves bring
the newborns Romulus and Remus to the bank of the Tiber, one exclaims
(ll.397–400):

Sī genus arguitur vultū, nisi fallit imāgō,
    nescioquem in vōbīs suspicor esse deum.

At sī quis vestrae deus esset orīginis auctor
    in tam praecipitī tempore ferret opem.

The first sentence is a statement of fact and uses the indicative: based on their appearance, the slave suspects the children have some sort of divine parentage. In the second (present contrafactual), the slave expresses doubt about the divinity of Romulus and Remus: if they were the children of a god, that god would bring help.

Conditions can be summarized as follows:

Type	Time	Mood and Tense of Conditional Clauses	Translation helps
General	present	present indicative *Sī hunc librum legit, multa cognoscit.*	"is…is" If she is reading this book, she is learning many things.
	past	imperfect or perfect indicative a. *Sī hunc librum lēgit, multa cognōvit.* b. *Sī hunc librum lēgēbat, multa cognoscēbat.*	"was…was" a. If she read this book, she learned many things. b. If she was reading this book, she was learning many things.
	future	future (protasis often future perfect) indicative a. *Sī hunc librum lēgerit, multa cognoscet.* b. *Sī hunc librum leget, multa cognoscet.*	"(present)…will" a. If she reads/will have read this book, she will learn many things. b. If she reads this book, she will learn many things.
Ideal	future	present subjunctive in both *Sī hunc librum legat, multa cognoscat.*	"should…would" If she should read this book, she would learn many things.
Contrary-to-fact	present	imperfect subjunctive a. *Sī hunc librum legeret, multa cognosceret.*	"were…would be" If she were reading this book, she would be learning many things.
	past	pluperfect subjuctive *Sī hunc librum lēgisset, multa cognōvisset.*	"had…would have" If she had read this book, she would have learned many things.

Conditions in *ōrātiō oblīqua* (Indirect Discourse)

In Cap. XXXVI you learned that in indirect discourse the verb in a subordinate clause will be in the subjunctive according to sequence of tense. When conditions are reported, they generally follow this same rule:

- The apodosis (the "then" clause) is a main clause so it changes to subject accusative and verb infinitive.
- The protasis (the "if" clause) is a subordinate clause and the verb goes into the subjunctive.

Sequence of Tense

Main Verb	Subordinate Verb	
	incomplete action	completed action
present & future tense	present subjunctive	perfect subjunctive
past tense	imperfect subjunctive	pluperfect subjunctive

Examples

Let's look at some examples, based on a line from the Roman poet Horace:[3] *Rēx est sī rectē facit*: "he is a king if he behaves correctly."

Indicative Conditions

Present: The tense of the verb in the protasis depends on the main verb:

Rēx est sī rectē facit → Putō eum rēgem esse sī rectē faciat.
Rēx est sī rectē facit → Putābam eum rēgem esse sī rectē faceret.

Past: The tense of the verb in the protasis depends on the main verb.

Rēx erat sī rectē fēcit → Putō eum rēgem fuisse sī rectē fēcerit.
Rēx erat sī rectē fēcit → Putābam eum rēgem fuisse sī rectē fēcisset.

Future:

- Future in both clauses
    Rēx erit sī rectē faciet → Putō eum rēgem fore/futūrum esse sī rectē faciat.
    Rēx erit sī rectē faciet → Putābam eum rēgem fore/futūrum esse sī rectē faceret.

---

3. Horace *Epistles* I.1.59–60: *Rēx eris sī rectē faciēs.*

- Protasis future perfect/apodosis future (Cap. XLI):

  > *Rēx erit sī rectē fēcerit → Putō eum rēgem fore/futūrum esse sī rectē fēcerit.*

  > *Rēx erit sī rectē fēcerit → Putābam eum rēgem fore/futūrum esse sī rectē fēcisset.*

Notā bene: A protasis in the future perfect represents something that will happen before the action in the apodosis (Cap. XXX); in *ōrātiō oblīqua* it becomes:

- perfect subjunctive in primary sequence
- pluperfect subjunctive in secondary sequence

Subjunctive Conditions

Ideal ("should…would"): present subjunctive in both clauses becomes:

> *Rēx sit sī rectē faciat → Putō eum rēgem fore/futūrum esse sī rectē faciat*
>
> *Rēx sit sī rectē faciat → Putābam eum rēgem fore/futūrum esse sī rectē faceret*

Notā bene: In *ōrātiō oblīqua*, future indicative and future ideal conditions look the same.

Contrafactual Present ("were…would be"): imperfect subjunctive in both clauses becomes:

> *Rēx esset sī rectē faceret → Putō eum rēgem futūrum fuisse sī rectē faceret*
>
> *Rēx esset sī rectē faceret → Putābam eum rēgem futūrum fuisse sī rectē faceret*

Contrafactual Past ("were…would be"): pluperfect subjunctive in both clauses becomes:

> *Rēx fuisset sī rectē fēcisset → Putō eum rēgem futūrum fuisse sī rectē fēcisset*
>
> *Rēx fuisset sī rectē fēcisset → Putābam eum rēgem futūrum fuisse sī rectē fēcisset*

Notā bene:

- The form *futūrum fuisse* is used only here: in the apodoses of contrafactual conditions in *ōrātiō oblīqua*.

- The rules for sequence of tense are violated in these conditions:
  - ▷ Present contrafactual keeps imperfect subjunctive in the protasis regardless of leading verb.
  - ▷ Past contrafactual keeps pluperfect subjunctive in the protasis regardless of leading verb.

- These oddities make recognizing a reported contrafactual condition quite easy.

Iterative Subjunctive: in general conditions, the imperfect and pluperfect subjunctive can be found in the protasis of a condition when the action is habitual or recurrent; the apodosis is indicative, e.g., Cap. LI.199–201:

> *Quem mīlitem extrā ōrdinem dēprehendit, sī Rōmānus esset, vītibus, sī extrāneus (sc. esset), virgīs cecīdit.*

V. Points of Style

Variātiō (Variation of Expression)

The 3rd person plural can be used in a general sense, as *vocant* here:

> *...fluvius Albula, quem nunc Tiberim <u>vocant</u>, fīnis esset* (ll.66–68): "...the river Albula, which they now call the Tiber"

"They (i.e., people) call" (cf. *ut āiunt*, XXIV.61). We do the same in English, e.g., "they say that..." when we don't have anyone in particular in mind. The following are different ways of saying the same thing in Latin:

- *Priōrī Remō auspicium vēnisse dīcitur* (l.147): "The bird sign is said to have come to Remus first" = *Priōrī Remō auspicium vēnisse dicunt*: "They say that the bird sign came to Remus first."

- *quem nunc Tiberim vocant = qui nunc Tiberis vocātur* (l.67)

- *Ea...mītis fuisse dīcitur = eam mītem fuisse nārrant* (ll.100–101)

- *Aenēam Trōiā vēnisse dīcitur/nārrātur = Aenēam Trōiā vēnisse dīcunt/nārrant*

XLII: ALTERVM ET QVADRAGESIMVM: BELLVM ET PAX (Livy)[1]

II. Rēs Grammaticae Fūsius Explicātae

Implied Indirect Discourse/Subjunctive of Reported Reason

Indirect discourse (*ōrātiō oblīqua*) does not always have a clear "signal" telling readers that a sentence is reporting another's words or thoughts. We have already seen many examples of extended indirect discourse and examples where the reader needs to pay attention to the leading verb.

The subjunctive is frequently employed in causal clauses that would otherwise take the indicative to indicate that the writer offers someone else's reason. In other words, the causal clause becomes a virtual indirect statement:

> *Īdem nefāstōs diēs fāstōsque fēcit, quia aliquandō nihil cum*
> *populō agī ūtile futūrum esset.* (ll.323–324)

Livy is reporting Numa's reason for dividing the days into *fāstī* and *nefāstī*. Were Livy giving his *own* reason, he would have used the indicative (*futūrum est* or simply *erit*).

Descriptive Relative Clauses (Continued from Cap. XXXIX)

When relative clauses state facts about the antecedent, they are followed by the indicative. But as we have seen with both purpose and result clauses (Cap. XXXIX), *quī* can sometimes be the equivalent of *ut is*. Such clauses describe something about the nature of the antecedent, and, like result clauses, have their origin in the potential subjunctive. Descriptive relative clauses, like result clauses, do not describe a fact, but rather a tendency, quality, or design.

The best way to understand these clauses is to look at examples.

---

1. For an explanation of the line number references convention, see p. xxvi.

In some relative clauses, the subjunctive indicates result or quality, as in:

> *sōlī centum cīvēs nōbilēs erant quī senātōrēs creārī possent* (l.17,
> virtually the same as *tam nōbilēs...ut...possent*)

> *Invēnī ratiōnem, Anna, quae mihi reddat eum aut amōre eius*
> *mē solvat* (XL.175–177)
>> *not* "a way of thinking that is either returning Aeneas
>> to me or freeing me from love of him"
>> *but* "a way of thinking that could return...or free"
>> (*ratiōnem ut*)

After the adjective *dignus*, such a relative clause is common, as it describes the natural consequence of being worthy (or unworthy: *indignus*) (for natural consequence, see Recēnsiō below):

> *sī rēgem* <u>*dignum*</u> <u>*quī*</u> *secundus ab Rōmulō* <u>*numerētur*</u> *creāveritis,*
> *auctōrēs fient* (ll.276–278): "worthy to be numbered second after
> Romulus"

As you saw in Cap. XXXIX, descriptive relative clauses are especially common after indefinite antecedents:

> *Fuisse crēdō tum quoque aliquōs quī 'rēgem ā patribus*
> *interēmptum esse' clam arguerent.* (ll.241–242)

Priusquam/antequam with Subjunctive

You have already learned the temporal conjunctions *postquam*, *antequam*, and *priusquam* with the present or future perfect indicative (Cap. XXXI) and with the perfect indicative (Cap. XXXVII) to express what actually will happen or has happened before the action of the main clause. The conjunctions *priusquam* and *antequam* may be followed by the subjunctive to indicate what is anticipated; there is an element of <u>purpose</u> to the clause.

Prius/ante quam with the

Indicative →

- present/future perfect: what will happen before the action of the
  main verb

- perfect: what actually *did* happen before the action of the main verb

Subjunctive →

- present (primary sequence) or imperfect (secondary sequence) subjunctive: what *could* happen before the expected or anticipated action of the main verb occurs

Examples:

> *Fidēnātēs...priusquam (urbs) tam valida esset quam futūra esse vidēbātur, properant bellum facere* (ll.184–186): "The people of Fidenae, before the city could become as strong as it seemed it would be, hasten to make war."
>
> > Note here, as usual, the subjunctive is in secondary sequence because the present *properant* is historical (Cap. XXXVII).

> *Fidēnātēs, prius paene quam Rōmulus equitēsque quī cum eō erant circumagerent equōs, terga vertērunt atque oppidum repetēbant* (ll.201–203): "The people of Fidenae, almost before Romulus and the cavalry who were with him could turn their horses around, turned their backs and were returning to the town."

> *priusquam forēs portārum oppōnerentur, Rōmānī velut ūnō agmine in oppidum irrūpērunt.* (ll.205–206)

> *Prius igitur quam alter—nec procul aberat—cōnsequī posset, et alterum Cūriātium cōnficit.* (XLIII.107–109)

> *Priusquam inde dīgrederentur, Tullus Mettiō imperat...* (XLIII.123)

III. DĒMONSTRĀTIŌ VERBŌRUM

Indefinite Pronouns

In addition to the indefinite pronouns *quīcumque, quaecumque,* and *quodcumque,* "whoever, whatever" (Cap. XXXVIII), the pronouns *quī-quae-quod/quid* can combine with other words as well to form other indefinite pronouns. These pronouns are variations on a theme and mean essentially the same thing: "whoever/whatever you please/want, anyone/anything":

> *quīlibet, quaelibet, quodlibet/quidlibet = quī-quae-quod/quid + libet*

> *libet*: "it is pleasing"

quīvīs, quaevīs, quodvīs/quidvīs = quī-quae-quod/quid + vīs

vīs: "you will/want"

As with the *-cumque* pronouns, *quīcumque, quaecumque*, and *quodcumque*, only the *quī, quae, quod/quid* declines:

> *quīlibet homō* (l.13): "any person you will" = "anyone at all"
>
> *cuilibet fīnitimārum cīvitātum bellō par* (ll.21–22): "equal in war to whichever of the neighboring states."

Cum…tum

The conjunctions *cum…tum* join two items, underscoring the second:

> *Cum vestem purpuream induit, tum līctōrēs duodecim sūmpsit, quī fascēs et secūrēs gerentēs rēgī anteīrent.* (ll.6–8)
>
> *Movet rēs cum multitūdinem, tum ducēs.* (l.160)

IV: Recēnsiō

Result vs. Purpose

- *Purpose* clauses are also called "final" clauses because the clause indicates the *end* (*fīnis*) in sight for the action in the main clause. Purpose clauses are related to the volitive subjunctive (e.g., jussive and hortatory).

- *Result* clauses are also called "consecutive" clauses because the clause indicates what *follows* (*cōnsequī*) either actually or naturally from the action in the main clause. Result clauses come originally from the potential subjunctive (Cap. XLI); the clause states the natural potential of the main clause.

Notice that in purpose and result clauses the sequence is incomplete:

- A present/future tense main verb is followed by a present subjunctive.

- A past tense main verb is followed by an imperfect subjunctive.

Purpose clauses are negated by *nē*; result by *ut nōn*:

	Negative Purpose	**Negative Result**
that...not	*nē*	*ut...nōn*
that...no one	*nē quis*	*ut...nēmo*
that...nothing	*nē quid*	*ut...nihil*
that...never	*nē umquam*	*ut...numquam*

Words that signal result clauses:

tantus, -a, -um	so great	adjective of magnitude, quantity
tālis, tāle	of such a sort	adjective of quality
eius modī	of such a sort	descriptive genitive
tot	so many	adjective of quantity
sīc	in this way	adverb
ita	so, in such a way	adverb
adeō	so far, to such an extent	adverb
tam	so	adverb: only w/adjs. & advs.

A Note on Sequence of Tense in Result Clauses

We tend to think of a result clause as showing something that did happen as a result of the activity in the main clause—e.g., "I studied so hard that I got an A," where "I got an A" is what actually happened. Latin often sees the relationship differently—e.g., "I studied so hard that the natural result was an A." That is, the stress is not on the achievement of the result, but that the result was a natural potential or outgrowth of the activity of the verb or adverb. The leading verb is the *cause* of the *result*. Hence, the sequence in result clauses is usually the same as purpose clauses: uncompleted action.

Look at each of the following examples from this chapter:

> *Ab illō vīribus datīs, <u>tantum</u> <u>valuit</u> urbs Rōma <u>ut</u> in quadrāgintā deinde annōs tūtam pācem habēret* (ll.223–224): "The city grew *so strong* (*tantum valuit*) that the natural consequence was peace."

> *Cum hoc sēnsissent patrēs, populō concēdendum esse cēnsuērunt—<u>ita</u> tamen <u>ut</u> <u>nōn</u> plūs iūris <u>darent</u> quam <u>retinērent</u>* (ll.269–271): "The senators voted to concede in such a way (*ita...ut*) that they could retain power."

> *Iam rēs Rōmāna <u>adeō</u> erat <u>valida</u> <u>ut</u> cuilibet fīnitimārum*
> *cīvitātum bellō pār <u>esset</u>* (ll.21–22): "Rome was *so strong*
> (*adeō valida*) that the inevitable outcome was its equality
> in war."

The perfect subjunctive can be used in result clauses when the speaker wishes
to stress the result as something completed, as a fact, e.g. Cap. LI. 7881:

> *Masinissa…adeō…in senectā viguit ut post sextum and*
> *ocōgēsimum annum fīlium genuerit*: "Masinissa was *so vigorous*
> in his old age that he fathered a son after his 86th year."

Summary of Expressions of Purpose

Latin expresses purpose in a variety of ways:

    1. an *ut/nē*-clause with the subjunctive, e.g.,

- *<u>Ut</u> hominēs agrestēs novum rēgem <u>verērentur</u>, ipse sē augustiōrem fēcit īnsignibus imperiī.* (ll.4–5)

- *<u>nē</u> vāna urbis magnitūdō <u>esset</u>…* (l.10)

- *<u>ut</u> arx potius vī quam dolō capta esse <u>vidērētur</u>* (ll.106–107)

- *<u>ne</u> quis impūne patriam suam <u>prōderet</u>* (l.108)

- *<u>Ut</u> Sabīnīs tamen aliquid <u>darētur</u>, cīvēs Rōmānī 'Quirītēs' ā Curibus appellātī sunt.* (l.164)

- *Vēientēs…ēgressī sunt, <u>ut</u> potius aciē <u>certārent</u> quam inclūsī dē tēctīs moenibusque <u>dīmicārent</u>.* (ll.213–215)

- *<u>Nē</u> huic fāmae plēbs <u>crēderet</u>, Proculus Iūlius, senātor nōbilissimus, in contiōnem prōdiit.* (ll.242–243)

- *…putābat itūrōsque ipsōs ad bella, <u>nē</u> rēge absente sacra <u>neglegerentur</u>* (ll.328–329)

- *hīs, <u>ut</u> assiduae templī sacerdōtēs <u>essent</u>, stipendium dē pūblicō statuit* (ll.332–333)

- *Cētera quoque omnia pūblica prīvātaque sacra pontificī mandāvit, <u>ut</u> <u>esset</u> quem plēbs cōnsuleret, <u>nē</u> rītus neglegerentur.* (ll.340–342)

2. a relative clause with subjunctive (where *quī = ut is*, Cap. XXXIX), e.g.,

- *Rōmulus ex cōnsiliō patrum lēgātōs ad vīcīnās gentēs mīsit, quī societātem cōnūbiumque nōvō populō peterent.* (ll.24–26)

- *līctōrēs duodecim sūmpsit, quī fāscēs et secūrēs gerentēs rēgī anteīrent.* (ll.6–7)

- *Rōmulus ex cōnsiliō patrum lēgātōs ad vīcīnās gentēs mīsit, quī societātem cōnūbiumque nōvō populō peterent.* (ll.24–26)

- *Iānum ad īnfimum Argīlētum fēcit, quī apertus bellum, clausus pācem esse indicāret.* (ll.306–307)

3. *Quō* + comparative + subjunctive: relative purpose clause (introduced in Cap. XLIX)

4. the supine in *-um* (accusative) (Caps. XXII, XXXVI), e.g.,

- *Huius fīlia virgō forte aquam petītum extrā moenia ierat.* (ll.103–104)

- *Eā clāde coāctī Vēientēs pācem petītum legātōs Rōmam mittunt.* (ll.219–220)

5. *ad* + gerund/gerundive (Caps. XXVI, XXXVI), e.g.,

- *Hodiē plūs temporis ad nārrandum nōn habeō.* (XXVI.10–11)

- *Haud longum tempus nōbīs reliquum est ad vīvendum.* (XXVI.28)

- *Ūna via nōbīs patet ad fugiendum.* (XXVI.36)

- *signō datō iuventūs Rōmāna ad rapiendās virginēs* (ll.41–42)

- *Inde ad foedus faciendum dūcēs prōdeunt.* (l.161)

- *ad turbandam omnium pācem* (l.346)

- *ad arcendam vim* (XLI.8)

6. *causā, grātiā* + a preceding genitive of gerund/gerundive (Cap. XXVI), e.g.:

- *lēgātōs mīsit pācis petendae causā/grātiā*

- *lēgātōs mīsit pācem petendī causā/grātiā*

7. future participle after verbs of motion:

- *Ille in Italiam trāiēcit bellum cīvīle gestūrus adversus Norbānum et Scīpiōnem cōnsulēs* (LIII.114–116)

V. POINTS OF STYLE

Perfect Tense 3rd Person Plural

Instead of the ending *-ērunt* in the past perfect (3rd pers. plur.), you sometimes find the older form *-ēre*, both in poetry and in prose. Book II of the *Aeneid* begins *Conticuēre omnēs...* (XXXIX.304). Livy is fond of this form, as the many examples from this chapter show:

> *convēnēre = convēnērunt* (1.34)
> *necāvēre = necāvērunt* (1.106)
> *tenuēre = tenuērunt* (1.114)
> *subiēre = subiērunt* (1.118)
> *restitēre = restitērunt* (1.135)
> *ēripuēre = ēripuērunt* (1.205)
> *rediēre = rediērunt* (1.210)
> *audīvēre = audīvērunt* (1.213)

The alternate form can be very useful for writing verse, as these two lines in the meter of the elegiac couplet from Ovid show:

> *sīc īllae tĭmŭērĕ |vĭrōs sĭnĕ lēgĕ rŭēntēs = illae timuērunt* (1.364, a hexameter line)

> *(raptae) īn tērrām pŏsĭtō ‖ prōcŭbŭērĕ gĕnū = prōcubuērunt* (1.385, a pentameter line)

-um = *-ōrum*

Other archaic forms are *-um* for *-ōrum* in *deum*:

> *pater deum hominumque = pater deōrum hominumque* (1.128)

> *X mīlia sēstertium = mīlia sēstertiōrum*[2]

---

2. Cf. 1.32: *X mīlia sēstertium = X mīlia sēstertiōrum*: 10 thousand sesterces. With *mīlia* you will regularly find *sēstertium*, not *sēstertiōrum*.

Perfect Participles

In Ablative Absolute

The perfect participle is a passive form and states what has or had been done (in English rendered by a clause beginning "after…" or "when…" or "because"). Livy often uses an ablative absolute with the perfect participle, and there are thirty examples of ablative absolutes in this chapter alone, e.g.:

> *rēbus dīvīnīs rīte factīs* (l.2)
> *vocātāque ad concilium multitūdine* (l.2)
> *cīvitāte ita auctā* (l.15)
> *plērīsque rogitantibus* (l.29)
> *turbātō per metum lūdicrō* (l.43)
> *duce hostium occīsō* (ll.71–72)

Of Deponent Verbs

Livy also uses the nominative of the perfect participle of deponent verbs (passive form with active meaning) agreeing with the subject in order to tell what someone has or had done (or does/did), e.g.:

> *(Rōmulus) ēgressus* (l.192): "Romulus, having gone out"
>
> *ipse cum parte māiōre atque omnī equitātū profectus* (ll.193–194): "he himself, having set out with the larger part [of the soldiers] and all the cavalry"
>
> *subitō exortī Rōmānī* (l.199): "the Romans, having suddenly sprung up"
>
> *persecūtus* (l.217): "having pursued" or "after pursuing"
>
> *locūtus* (l.251): "after he said [these things]"
>
> *ausī* (l.287): "daring"
>
> *deōs…precātus* (l.295): "having invoked the gods," "after he invoked the gods"
>
> *rēgnō potītus* (l.303): "having gained mastery of the kingdom"
>
> *ratus* (l.305): perfect participle of *rērī*, "thinking" or "as he thought"

Uti/utī for *ut*

Uti/utī instead of *ut* is found mostly in elevated style, as in the augur's prayer:

> *Iuppiter pater,…<u>uti</u> tū signa nōbīs certa dēclārēs inter eōs fīnēs quōs fēcī.* (ll.298–301)

> *…exercitus inclāmat Cūriātiīs <u>uti</u> opem ferant frātrī*
> (XLIII.103–104)

> *…Tullus Mettiō imperat <u>uti</u> iuventūtem in armīs habeat*
> (XLIII.123–124)

XLIII: QVADRAGESIMVM TERTIVM: ROMA ET ALBA (Livy)[1]

II. Rēs Grammaticae Fūsius Explicātae:

Posse, oportēre, dēbēre

You have met the past tense of *posse* with a present infinitive:

> *Miror te crus non fregisse. Facile os frangere potuisti* (XXIV.32–33): "I'm amazed you did not break your leg. You could easily have broken a bone."

Notice that Latin uses the past tense of *posse* with a present infinitive, the marker that shows the action of the verb as ongoing and incomplete (see Cap. XL). This is the usual construction with verbs that show what is fitting, necessary, or possible. We find the same construction at the end of this chapter:

> *Tamen ā frātre indemnātam necārī nōn oportuit.* (ll.353–354)

For such verbs in contrafactual conditions, see Cap. XLVI.

Fore/forem (esse)

The verb *esse* has an alternate imperfect subjunctive:

> *forem = essem*
> *forēs = essēs*
> *foret = esset*
> *forent = essent*

---

1. For an explanation of the line number references convention, see p. xxvi.

No alternate form is found for *essēmus* and *essētis*.

This form looks a good deal like the alternate future active infinitive, *fore*, which you met in Cap. XXXIII:

> *aciēs spectāculō <u>fore</u> Etrūscīs* (ll.59–60)
> *'ibi imperium <u>fore</u> unde victōria fuerit'* (ll.70–71)

Conditions in *Ōrātiō oblīqua*

In Cap. XXXVI you learned that in indirect discourse the verb in a subordinate clause will be in the subjunctive according to sequence of tense. When conditions are reported, they generally follow this same rule:

- The apodosis (the "then" clause) is a main clause so it changes to subject accusative and verb infinitive.

- The protasis (the "if" clause) is a subordinate clause and the verb goes into the subjunctive.

Sequence of Tense

Main Verb	Subordinate Verb	
	incomplete action	completed action
present & future tense	present subjunctive	perfect subjunctive
past tense	imperfect subjunctive	pluperfect subjunctive

Here we consider the three examples in *ōrātiō oblīqua* from this chapter:

- "Mixed condition" in *ōrātiō oblīqua*: protasis future, apodosis present-perfect, primary sequence (ll.22–25):

  > *Illī prīmum sē pūrgāre cōnantur: 'sē invītōs aliquid quod displiceat Tullō dictūrōs esse: rēs repetītum sē vēnisse; nisi reddantur, bellum indīcere iussōs esse.'*

  > Direct statement: *Invītī aliquid quod displicet Tullō dīcēmus: rēs repetītum vēnimus; nisi reddentur, bellum indīcere iussī sumus.*

  - ▷ *Notā bene*: the future of the protasis comes from context: a present (*redduntur*) would, in *ōrātiō oblīqua*, also go into the present subjunctive.

- Future condition in *ōrātiō oblīqua*, historical present, with the indirect command (*imperat uti…habeat*) in primary sequence to continue the vividness of the historical present, *foret* and *dīgrederentur* in secondary sequence (ll.123–125):

  > *Priusquam inde dīgrederentur, Tullus Mettiō imperat uti iuventūtem in armīs habeat: 'sē eōrum operā ūsūrum, sī bellum cum Vēientibus foret.'*

  > Direct statement: *eōrum operā ūtar, sī bellum cum Vēientibus erit.*

- Protasis of a future condition in *ōrātiō oblīqua*, secondary sequence, with the apodosis implied (ll.328–331):

  > *Iam hominēs eum statum rērum quī sub Numā rēge fuerat dēsīderantēs, ūnam opem aegrīs corporibus relictam esse crēdēbant: sī veniam ā dīs impetrāvissent.*

  > Direct statement: *sī veniam ā dīs impetrāverimus* [*opem aegrīs corporibus habēbimus*: i.e., the apodosis must be supplied from "they believed that one resource was left for their sick bodies"].

Ablative of Degree of Difference

The ablatives *multō* and *paulō* can be used before a comparative to indicate the degree of difference (Cap. XVI), for example, *multō melior*: "much better" ("better by much").

We have already seen *tantus* and *quantus* used alone or as correlatives (Cap. VIII); they are also used as ablatives of degree of difference either alone (*tantō melior*: "so much the better"), or combined with *quantō*:

> *quantō longior, tantō melior* ("the longer the better")

Other correlative ablatives of degree of difference:

> *eō* and *quō*

> *quō propior es, eō magis scīs* (ll.57–58): "to the degree that you are closer, the better you know"

Other examples:

> <u>*eō māiōre cum gaudiō*</u> *quod prope metum rēs fuerat* (l.117):
> "with so much the greater joy because the situation had
> been close to fear"

> *eo magis* (XLIV.143)

Pronoun Change from Direct to Indirect Discourse

When a statement is reported, the perspective changes, just as it does in
English.

> Julia: "I'd like to read this book now" = *mihi placet hunc librum*
> *nunc legere.*

> "She said she would like to read that book at that time (then)" =
> *dīxit sibi placēre illum librum eō tempore (tunc) legere.*

Note the shift of pronouns from direct to indirect statement, and vice versa:

> Direct Statement:
> > *"Diī patriī, patria ac parentēs omnēsque cīvēs vestra arma*
> > *nunc, vestrās manūs intuentur."*

> Indirect Statement: *vestra, vestrās* changes to *illōrum* (ll.26–28)
> > '*deōs patriōs, patriam ac parentēs omnēsque cīvēs illōrum*
> > *tunc arma, illōrum intuērī manūs!*' (ll.78–80)

> Indirect Statement (ll.124–125)
> > '*sē eōrum operā ūsūrum, sī bellum cum Vēientibus foret*'

> Direct Statement:
> > '*vestrā operā ūtar, sī bellum cum cum Vēientibus erit*'

III. Dēmōnstrātiō Verbōrum

Superlatives in *-limus, -a, -um*

In addition to *facilis* and *difficilis* there are four other adjectives that form superlatives in *-limus, -a, -um*:

> *cīvīlī bellō simillimum* (l.30)

facilis, -e	*facilior, facilius*	*facillimus, -a, -um*	easy
difficilis, -e	*difficilior, difficilius*	*difficillimus, -a, -um*	difficult
similis, -e	*similior, similius*	*simillimus, -a, -um*	similar, like (+ dat.)
dissimilis, -e	*dissimilio, dissimilius*	*dissimillimus, -a, -um*	dissimilar, unlike (+ dat.)
gracilis, -e	*gracilior, gracilius*	*gracillimus, -a, -um*	slender
humilis, -e	*humilior, humilius*	*humillimus, -a, -um*	low, lowly (*humus*)

Uter, uterque

You learned the pronouns *uter* and *uterque* in Cap. XIV. Like *neuter* and *alter*, *uter* and *uterque* are used about two things or people taken separately. Normally these pronouns are singular, e.g.:

> *uter...populus* (ll.26–27)
> *utrīusque populī* (l.63)

When plural forms occur, they refer to two groups of persons or things, "both parties." Such plurals are quite common in referring to two contending peoples, e.g.:

> *utrī utrīs imperent* (l.64)
> *cum utrīque suōs adhortārentur* (l.78)
> *utrīque suōs mortuōs sepeliunt* (l.118)
> *cum bellum utrīque summā ope parārent* (l.304)

Utrimque

From *uterque* is formed the adverb *utrimque* ("from/on both sides"). This adverb occurs frequently when fighting is described, e.g.:

> *utrimque lēgātī...missī sunt* (ll.13–14): "envoys were sent from both sides."

> *bellum utrimque omnibus vīribus parābatur* (ll.29–30): "war was being prepared on both sides with all their force."

> *instrūctī utrimque stābant* (l.51)

> *cōnsēderant utrimque prō castrīs duo exercitūs* (ll.81–82)

Velut

Velut (Cap. XXVIII) means "as, as if" and is here used in two different contexts:

Modifying a single word:

> *īnfēstīsque armīs velut aciēs ternī iuvenēs* (ll.84–85): "the young men like (as) a battle line"

> *pulvisque velut nūbe omnia implēverat* (ll.278–279): "dust, as if by a cloud, had filled everything"

> *Velut* working in similes: *velut captōs relinquerent deōs* (l.285)

Modifying an ablative absolute:

> *velut dīs quoque simul cum patriā relictīs* (l.316)

Rēs repetere

Rēs repetere: to seek reparations or compensation:

> *Utrimque lēgātī eōdem ferē tempore ad rēs repetendās missī sunt.* (ll.13–14)

> *Iniūriae et rēs nōn redditae, quae ex foedere repetītae sunt.* (ll.52–54)

IV. POINTS OF STYLE

Variātiō

For the sake of variation, Latin writers sometimes replace an adjective-noun combination with an abstract noun combined with a genitive. Horatius Senior first refers to *tam dēfōrme spectāculum* (adjective/noun, 1.170) and later to *tantā foeditāte suppliciī* (noun + noun, 1.178); the description of Mettius's horrifying punishment ends: *āvertēre omnēs ab tantā foeditāte spectāculī oculōs* (noun + noun, 1.265).

XLIV: QVADRAGESIMVM QVARTVM: REGES ET REGINAE (Livy)[1]

I. Rēs Grammaticae Novae

Historical Infinitive

In vivid narration, the present indicative is often substituted for the past (Cap. XXXVII). The present infinitive can be employed in the same way, and this historical infinitive also has the force of the indicative (imperfect 3rd person). The subject of the historical infinitive is nominative, not accusative. Livy uses the historical infinitive frequently:

> (Tullia) *alterum Tarquinium <u>admīrārī</u>, 'eum virum esse'*
> *<u>dīcere</u> 'ac rēgiō sanguine ortum'; <u>spernere</u> sorōrem quod*
> *virō audācī nūpta ipsa audāciā carēret; nūllīs verbōrum*
> *contumēliīs <u>parcere</u>. (ll.374–377)*

> *ab scelere ad aliud scelus <u>spectāre</u> mulier. Nec nocte nec interdiū*
> *virum conquiēscere <u>patī</u> (ll.383–385)*

> *Hōc muliebrī furōre īnstīnctus Tarquinius <u>circumīre</u> et <u>conci-</u>*
> *<u>liāre</u> sibi patrēs. <u>Admonēre</u> Tarquiniī Prīscī beneficiī ac prō*
> *eō grātiam <u>repetere</u>. <u>Allicere</u> dōnīs iuvenēs. Cum ingentia*
> *pollicendō, tum rēgis crīminibus, omnibus locīs <u>crēscere</u>.*
> *(ll.402–406)*

Notā bene: Because the historical infinitive has the force of an *imperfect* indicative, subordinate clauses follow secondary, not primary sequence. In the first example above, note:

> *...admīrārī...dīcere...spernere sorōrem quod virō audācī nūpta*
> *ipsa audāciā <u>carēret</u>*

---

1. For an explanation of the line number references convention, see p. xxvi.

Historical infinitives (nominative + infinitive: vivid narration) often shift into indirect speech (accusative + infinitive: reported speech). In your text, such shifts are marked by single quotes ('). **Such punctuation is not usual in Latin texts; you'll need to pay attention to the shift**. Study the passage below (383–389):

> *Iam enim ab scelere ad aliud scelus spectāre mulier. Nec nocte nec interdiū virum conquiēscere patī, nē grātuīta praeterita parricīdia essent: 'nōn sibi dēfuisse marītum cum quō tacita servīret—dēfuisse virum quī sē rēgnō dignum esse putāret, quī meminisset sē esse Prīscī Tarquiniī fīlium, quī habēre quam spērāre rēgnum māllet!'*

- *Iam enim ab scelere ad aliud scelus spectāre mulier*:

    ▷ historical narration: nominative subject + infinitive verb

    ▷ = *Iam enim ab scelere ad aliud scelus <u>spectābat</u> mulier.*

- *Nec nocte nec interdiū virum conquiēscere patī, nē grātuīta praeterita parricīdia essent*:

    ▷ historical narration: subject left unstated, followed by a negative purpose clause in secondary sequence (because the historical infinitive represents the imperfect)

    ▷ = *Nec nocte nec interdiū virum conquiēscere <u>patiebātur</u>, nē grātuīta praeterita parricīdia essent.*

- *'nōn sibi dēfuisse marītum cum quō tacita servīret—dēfuisse virum quī sē rēgnō dignum esse putāret, quī meminisset sē esse Prīscī Tarquiniī fīlium, quī habēre quam spērāre rēgnum māllet!'*:

    ▷ indirect statement representing what she was saying to her husband, containing:

    　　a purpose clause (*cum…servīret*)

    　　three relative clauses of character or tendency
    　　　　(Cap. XXXIX/XLII): not "I lack a husband who thinks…" but "I lack the kind of husband who would think himself worthy of the kingdom."

    ▷ = (in the original present tense) *'nōn <u>mihi·dēest</u> <u>marītus</u> cum quō tacita <u>serviam</u>—<u>dēest·vir</u> quī sē rēgnō dignum esse putet, quī meminerit sē esse Prīscī Tarquiniī fīlium, quī habēre quam spērāre rēgnum mālit.'*

II. Rēs Grammaticae Fūsius Explicātae

Omission of *esse*

The auxiliary verb *esse* is often omitted in the future infinitive and in the perfect infinitive passive, e.g.:

> *sē...habitūrum* (ll.20–21) = *sē...habitūrum esse*
>
> *in novō populō...futūrum locum* (ll.112–114) = *futūrum esse*
>
> *Tatium...rēgem factum, et Numam...in rēgnum accītum* (148–151) = *factum esse...accītum esse*

In the 3rd person of the perfect passive, *est, sunt* are apt to be left out by Livy, e.g.:

> *Aventīnum novae multitūdinī datum* (ll.71–72) = *datum est*
>
> *Quibus...in valle Murciā datae sēdēs. Iāniculum quoque urbī adiectum* (ll.78–79) = *datae sunt...adiectum est*
>
> *totidem centuriae factae. Quīnta classis aucta* (l.324) = *factae sunt...aucta est*

Partitive Genitive with Neuter Pronoun

The partitive genitive may depend on certain neuter pronouns but only in the nominative or accusative, such as *multum* and *paulum* (Cap. XVI), *aliquid, nihil, quid* (Cap. XXIX), e.g.:

> *Mettiō nōn plūs animī erat quam fideī* (XLIII.202)
> *quid reī esset* (ll.266–267)
> *quid hoc...reī est?* (l.424)
> *quidquid agrī* (l.198)

Dative by Attraction

When a dative of possession (Cap. XII) is used with a name (i.e., *nōmen eī est*), the name itself is usually dative, not predicate nominative, because the name has been "attracted to" (or drawn into) the dative of possession. We see two examples in this chapter:

puerō egentī post avī mortem nātō ab inopiā 'Egeriō' nōmen datum est (ll.103–104):[2]

> = *Egerius nōmen datum est*; the dative *'Egeriō'* agrees with the dative *puerō*

cui Serviō Tulliō fuit nōmen (l.226)

> = *cui Servius Tullius fuit nōmen*; the dative *Serviō Tulliō* agrees with the dative of possession *cui*

Locative/Ablative of Plural Place Names

The name of the Etruscan town *Tarquiniī* is plural. Therefore the ablative *Tarquiniīs* can mean both "from Tarquinii" (l.93, ablative of separation) and "at Tarquinii" (l.95, locative)—context will make it clear. Sometimes for clarity Livy puts *ab* before a town name, e.g.:

> *cōnsilium migrandī ab Tarquiniīs* (l.111)
> *Nōn...ab Corinthō nec ab Tarquiniīs* (l.391)

III. DĒMONSTRĀTIŌ VERBŌRUM

Quam prīmum

As you learned in *FAMILIA RŌMĀNA* (Cap. XXVII), *quam* + superlative (with or without *posse*) denotes the highest possible degree. As *prīmum* is the superlative of *prius*, the phrase *quam prīmum* means "as soon as possible":

> *Tarquinius postulābat ut quam prīmum comitia rēgī creandō fierent.* (ll.143–144)

Ferre

To describe the "handing down" (or "tradition"), we are accustomed to seeing *dīcitur* (Cap. XIII) and *nārrātur* (Cap. XXXVI), in addition to *dīcunt* and *nārrant* (Cap. XLI); the verbs *trāditur* ("is handed down," "is reported") and *fertur* (= *nārrātur*) are used in the same way:

> *accēpisse id augurium laeta dīcitur Tanaquīl* (l.122)
>
> *ōrātiōnem dīcitur habuisse* (l.146)

---

2. Egerius was the name given to Lucumo's nephew because he was *egēns* ("indigent").

> *Foedum inhūmānumque inde <u>trāditur</u> scelus: Tullia per patris corpus carpentum ēgisse <u>fertur</u>* (ll.445–447)
>
> *caput ārsisse <u>ferunt</u>* (ll.226–227)
>
> *fāma <u>ferēbat</u>* (l.351)

IV. Recēnsiō

Ablative Absolute

The ablative absolute is widely used with the perfect participle (forty examples in this chapter), but it also occurs frequently with the present participle, e.g., when stating during whose reign something happened (Cap. XVI):

> *Tullō rēgnante* (l.13): "while Tullus was reigning"
>
> *Ancō rēgnante* (l.92)
>
> *Spernentibus Etrūscīs* (l.108): "when the Etruscans were saying in scorn that..."
>
> *ventōque iuvante* (l.184): "with the wind helping"
>
> *necessitāte iam et ipsā cōgente ultima audēre* (l.432): "now that even necessity itself was compelling him to do the most daring things"

Impersonal Passive (Cap. XL): Examples

> *bellum fierī erat cōnsēnsum* (l.50)
>
> *aliquamdiū ibi variā victōriā pugnātum est* (l.73)
>
> *Ad Iāniculum forte ventum erat* (l.118)
>
> *Prīmō dubiā victōriā, magnā utrimque caede pugnātum est* (ll.174–175)
>
> *Additae huic classī duae fabrum centuriae, quae sine armīs stipendia facerent* (ll.317–318)
>
> *ad fīnēs eōrum vēnit unde rēs repetuntur* (ll.25–26)

XLV: QVADRAGESIMVM QVINTVM: ROMA LIBERATA (Livy)[1]

II. Rēs Grammaticae Fūsius Explicātae

Gerund/Gerundive

In this chapter there are some examples of the gerund in the genitive or ablative with an object in the accusative:

> *mōrem...senātum cōnsulendī* (l.16): "the custom of consulting the Senate"
>
> *interrogandō exspectandōque respōnsum nūntius fessus* (l.144): "the messenger, tired of asking and waiting for an answer"
>
> *āvertendō noxam* (l.266): "by turning away the guilt"
>
> *auctorque arma capiendī* (l.293): "and who prompted them to take up arms"

In most cases, however, the construction is altered so that the noun is in the genitive or ablative and the verb form, now a gerundive, agrees with the noun as an adjective, e.g.:

> *vēndendā praedā* (ll.94–95) = *vēndendō praedam*
>
> *libīdō Lucrētiae stuprandae* (l.226) = *libīdō Lucrētiam stuprandī*

---

1. For an explanation of the line number references convention, see p. xxvi.

In this chapter we also find the gerundive construction in the dative with the adjective *intentus*:

> *fundāmentīs templī iaciendīs aliīsque urbānīs operibus intentum*
>   (l.100)

> *intentus perficiendō templō* (l.160)

Only the gerundive, never the gerund with an object, is found with a preposition (*ad, de, in*):

> *dē renovandō foedere* (ll.78–79)

> *ad forōs in circō faciendōs cloācamque Māximam agendam*[2]
>   (ll.166–167)

> *in fossās cloācāsque exhauriendās dēmersae* (ll.311–312):
>   "submerged in the digging of ditches and sewers"

The gerund is, of course, found without objects as well:

> *cupīdō scīscitandī* (l.185): gerund without an object

Supine

As you learned in Cap. XXIII, the accusative supine occurs with verbs of motion like *īre, venīre*, and *mittere*:

> *praedātum īret* (l.128)
> *mittit scīscitātum* (ll.138–139)
> *exsulātum…iērunt* (ll.334–335)

In the above examples the verb itself expresses the motion, but motion can also be implied, as in the accusative supine of *nūbēre* in this example:

> *fīliam nūptum dat* (l.24)

Giving one's daughter away to be married includes the sense of her leaving her father's house for her husband's, that is, motion.

---

2.   That is, Latin will always have *ad cloacam maximam agendam* (gerundive) and **not** *ad cloacam maximam agendum* (gerund).

Futūrum esse ut/fore ut

In *Familia Romāna* (Cap. XXXII) you learned the future passive infinitive, which is formed from the supine and *īrī* (the present passive infinitive of *īre*):

> *Ego eum nec mūtātum esse nec posthāc mūtātum īrī crēdō*
> (ll.118–119)

Latin writers, however, tend to avoid the future passive infinitive, instead using *futūrum* (*esse*) *ut* or its equivalent, *fore ut*, plus the subjunctive. For example:

> '*brevī futūrum ut ā portīs Gabīnīs sub Rōmāna moenia bellum trānsferātur*' (ll.118–120)

That is, writers often prefer *futūrum ut...bellum trānsferātur* instead of the future passive *bellum trānslātum īrī*. The same line could have been written with *fore ut*:

> '*fore ut bellum transferātur*'

III. DĒMONSTRĀTIŌ VERBŌRUM

Opus est + ablative

The impersonal phrase *opus est* means "there is need of"; the thing needed is in the ablative:

> '*opus esse colloquiō*' (Caps. XLIII, XLVI–XLVII)
>
> *ita factō mātūrātōque opus esse* (l.251): the ablative perfect participles of *fierī* and *mātūrāre* are equivalent to neuter abstract nouns.

Difficulter

The irregular adverb *difficulter* is formed from *difficilis*:

> *Haud difficulter persuāsit Latīnīs...* (ll.79–80)

IV. RECĒNSIŌ

Historical Infinitive (Cap. XLIV): Examples

Notice these further examples of the historical infinitive with subject nominative (see Cap. XLIV):

> *Ibi, cum 'dē aliīs rēbus assentīre sē veteribus Gabīnīs' dīceret, identidem bellī <u>auctor</u> <u>esse</u> et in eō sibi praecipuam prūdentiam <u>assūmere</u>...* (ll.122–124)

> *tum <u>ūniversī</u> Gabīnī Sextum Tarquinium dīvīnitus sibi missum ducem <u>crēdere</u>* (l.133)

> *Apud mīlitēs vērō, cum pariter perīcula obīret ac labōrēs tolerāret praedamque benignē largīrētur, tantā cāritāte <u>esse</u> ut nōn pater Tarquinius potentior Rōmae quam fīlius Gabiīs esset.* (ll.134–137)

> *Suam <u>quisque</u> <u>laudāre</u> mīrīs modīs* (l.211)

> *Cum pavida ex somnō mulier nūllam opem, prope mortem imminentem vidēret, tum <u>Tarquinius</u> <u>fatērī</u> amōrem, <u>ōrāre</u>, <u>miscēre</u> precibus minās, <u>versāre</u> in omnēs partēs muliebrem animam.* (ll.239–242)

Ablative Absolute: Examples

There are several examples of the ablative absolute (Cap. XVI) with the present participle:

> *illō adiuvante* (l.118)

> *sequente nūntiō* (ll.141–142)

> *pōtantibus hīs* (ll.208–209)

> *sōle parante* (l.347)

> *exsecrantibus quācumque incēdēbat invocantibusque parentum Furiās virīs mulieribusque* (ll.325–326): "men and women cursing her wherever she walked and invoking the Furies who avenge parents"

We also find the ablative absolute with

> adjectives:

- *īnsciā multitūdine* (l.130)
- *rē imperfectā* (l.144)
- *īnsciō Collātīnō* (l.230)
- *illīs lūctū occupātīs* (l.275)

> nouns:

- *auctōribus patribus* (l.8)
- *duce Brūtō* (l.298)

Adjectives with Genitive: Examples

As you learned in Cap. XXV, when a noun or an adjective has a verbal force, the genitive that follows it is called the "objective genitive" (the genitive used as an object). This chapter has several examples:

> *ignārus respōnsī expersque imperiī* (l.190)
>
> *īnscia rērum* (l.350)
>
> *perītus* (*perītus ūtilitātis dignitātisque cīvīlis*, LV.448–449)

XLVI: QVADRAGESIMVM SEXTVM: POST REGES EXACTOS (Eutropius)[1]

I. Rēs Grammaticae Novae

Genitive of the Charge

The genitive is used with judicial expressions: accusations, condemnations, and acquitals:

> *Ob quam rem ā dictātōre <u>capitis</u> damnātus* (ll.190–191): "he was condemned with the loss of his head."

II. Rēs Grammaticae Fūsius Explicātae

Indicative in Contrafactual Conditions

Indicative in the apodosis: In Cap. XXIV, you learned that the past tense of *posse* could express what might have happened (but didn't):

> *Miror tē crūs nōn frēgisse. Facile os frangere potuistī.*
> (XXIV.32–33)

Facile os frangere potuistī is a contrafactual statement, even though *posse* is in the indicative: "you could easily have broken a bone (but didn't)." *Oportēre* and *dēbēre* (Cap. XLIII) function the same way. The past tense of the following verbs

> *oportēre*
> *dēbēre*

---

1. For an explanation of the line number references convention, see p. xxvi.

> *posse*
> *necesse esse*
> *opus esse*

implies what was necessary, possible, or due in the past, suggesting lack of ful-fillment. Thus, when such verbs are part of a contrafactual condition, they are in the indicative instead of the subjunctive:

> [*Pyrrhus dīxit*] '*sē tōtīus orbis dominum esse <u>potuisse</u>, sī tālēs sibi mīlitēs contigissent.*' (ll.233–234)

In this contrafactual condition in indirect discourse, *potuisse* stands for an original indicative, completely normal for a verb of possibility. This is the usual construction with such verbs, as well as with future participles and gerundives with a past tense of *esse*:

> *Quod sī Rōmae Cn. Pompēius prīvātus esset hōc tempore,*
> *tamen ad tantum bellum is erat dēligendus atque mittendus:*
> "Even if Cn. Pompey were at this time in Rome as a private
> citizen, he would have to be chosen and sent to such a great
> war" (XLIV.528–530).

Indicative in the apodosis: If the protasis is negative, the apodosis of a contra-factual condition is in the indicative when the action of the verb is interrupted (imperfect indicative) or when the apodosis seems a forgone conclusion.

In the example below from the reading, the protasis itself is in the indicative:

> *Et <u>subācta</u> Āfrica tunc <u>fuisset</u>, nisi quod tanta famēs <u>erat</u>*
> *ut diūtius exercitus exspectāre nōn posset.* (ll.361–362)

Fuisset marks the apodosis of a past contrafactual condition; but *nisi quod* ("except for the fact that") cuts off the possibility of the Romans conquering. *Nisi quod* is followed by the indicative (unless in *ōrātiō oblīqua*): They would have conquered except for the fact that there was a famine.

V. Points of Style

Indirect Commands: Resolutions of the Senate

Resolutions of the Senate are indirect commands expressed by the phrase (*patribus*) *placet* followed by:

> *ut/nē* + subjunctive
>
> > Et <u>placuit</u> <u>nē</u> imperium longius quam annuum habēret, <u>nē</u>
> > per diūturnitātem potestātis īnsolentiōrēs redderentur, sed
> > cīvīlēs semper essent, quī sē post annum scīrent futūrōs
> > esse prīvātōs (ll.4–7)
> >
> > <u>placuerat</u> enim '<u>nē</u> quisquam in urbe manēret quī Tarquinius
> > vocārētur.' (ll.11–13)

> or by accusative + infinitive
>
> > nūllōs placuit fierī (l.140)
> >
> > Omnibus igitur patribus placēbat aliquod caput cīvitātis
> > esse (XLII.260–261)

The Language of Eutropius

The language of Eutropius, writing in the fourth century AD, differs slightly from that of Livy, who lived from the middle of the first century BC to the beginning of the first century AD. The features of his Latin that depart from earlier Latin are noted below.

Tamquam/quasī

In late Latin *tamquam* and *quasī* can introduce clauses of reported reason:

> tamquam ā senātū atque cōnsulibus premerētur (ll.49–50)
>
> quasi praedam male dīvīsisset (ll.108–109)

Perfect/Pluperfect Passive

The perfect passive is formed with the auxiliary verb *esse* in the present: *laudātus (-a, -um) est/sit.* The pluperfect passive has the auxiliary verb *esse* in the imperfect: *laudātus (-a, -um) erat/esset.* One finds, however, the auxiliary verb in the perfect or pluperfect: *laudātus fuit/fuerit* (perfect passive) *fuerat/*

fuisset. Although using the perfect or pluperfect instead of the present or imperfect is found in all periods of Latin, it is more frequent in later Latin. In Eutropius you find several examples:

Perfect passive:
> *īnfrāctus fuit* instead of *īnfrāctus est* (l.369)

Pluperfect passive:
> *fuerat expulsus* (l.17)
> *datum fuerat* (l.120)
> *datus fuisset* (l.204)
> also: ll.197, 350, 362, 394, 437

Other features of later Latin that you'll encounter in Eutropius:

diēs is always feminine (Cap. XIII)
> *eā diē* (l.282)
> *ex illā diē* (l.388)

ipse often stands for *is* or *ille*
> *contrā ipsōs* (l.104)
> *...quae sub ipsīs agēbant...ipsum Praeneste agressus* (l.136)
> *triumphusque ipsī dēcrētus* (l.138)
> *cum ipsīs* (l.197)
> *plūrima ipsōrum oppida cēpit* (l.205)
> *contrā ipsum* (l.411)

Some of his numerals are worth noticing:

> *decem et octō* for *duodēvīgintī* (ll.343, 344)
> *octāvō decimō* for *duodēvīcēsimō* (ll.56, 99)
> *quadrāgintā novem* for *ūndēquīnquāgintā* (ll.208–209)

Gerundive for Future Passive Infinitive

In Cap. XLV you learned that *fore ut/fūtūrum esse* is often used instead of the rare future passive infinitive (Cap. XXI). The gerundive can also be used instead of the future infinitive passive.

Thus, the following three constructions (future passive infinitive, *fore ut/ futūrum esse ut*, gerundive) are different ways of saying "They undertook the war promising the senate and the people that the whole contest would be fulfilled by them":

future passive infinitive:

> *bellum...suscēpērunt promittentēs senātuī et populō 'per sē omne certāmen <u>implētum īrī</u>'*

gerundive instead of future passive infinitive:

> *bellum...suscēpērunt promittentēs senātuī et populō 'per sē omne certāmen implendum (esse)'* (1.70)

fore ut/futūrum esse ut instead of future passive infinitive:

> *bellum...suscēpērunt promittentēs senātuī et populō <u>fore ut</u> 'per sē omne certāmen implērētur'*

> *bellum...suscēpērunt promittentēs senātuī et populō <u>futūrum esse ut</u> 'per sē omne certāmen implērētur'*

XLVII: QVADRAGESIMVM SEPTIMVM: GRAECI ET ROMANI (Aulus Gellius)[1]

III. Dēmonstrātiō Verbōrum

Impersonal *cōnstat*

The impersonal verb *cōnstat* (Cap. XLI) is here in the perfect: *cōnstitit*, "it is established/an established fact":

> *inter omnēs ferē scrīptōrēs cōnstitit* (l.18)
>
> *per eās tempestātēs decemvirōs lēgibus scrībundīs creātōs cōnstitit* (ll.60–62)
>
> *Sed eam mulierem tunc ā Tarquiniō dīgressam posteā nusquam locī vīsam cōnstitit* (ll.188–190)

Idioms

Note the following idiomatic expressions:

> The verb *est* can be used with an infinitive to mean "it is possible."
>
> > *Nusquam...scrīptum invenīre est...aut 'mehercle' fēminam dīcere aut...* (ll.202–204): "it is not possible anywhere to find written either a woman saying 'by Hercules' or..."
>
> The verb *obīre* ("go to meet") combined with the objects *diem* or *mortem* means "to die."
>
> > *quī...mortem obiit* (ll.43–45)
> >
> > *obiit mortis diem* (ll.113–115)

---

1. For an explanation of the line number references convention, see p. xxvi.

Libra/pondus

Libra means

1. scales, balance (see Cap. XIII, top)

2. a unit of weight: a Roman pound (327 g)

pondus -eris (neuter) means "weight" and is the word from which we get the English "pound." Although it is a 3rd declension noun, *pondus* has a 2nd declension ablative *pondō* ("in/by weight"), which may be added to *libra,* e.g.:

> *decem pondō librae* (l.132): "ten pounds by weight"

pondō is often used with the ellipsis of *librae:*

> *pondō CXXIII mīlia* (Cap. XLVIII.863)

Comparative: "Too"

Gellius begins by saying that he will limit himself to the time before the Second Punic War. So when he comes to mention writers who flourished after this war, he says *prōgressī longius sumus.* Here the comparative *longius* means "too far" (= *nimis longē*).

V. POINTS OF STYLE

Gerund/Gerundive: Archaic Spelling

The oldest Latin text mentioned by Aulus Gellius is *Leges XII tabulārum,* "The Laws of the Twelve Tables," which were written in 451–449 BC by a board of ten, *Decemvirī lēgibus scribundīs creātī* (l.61; cf. XLVI.88): "a board of ten created for the purpose of writing laws." *Lēgibus scrībundīs* (= *ad lēgēs scrībendās*) is dative of purpose; it is written with the archaic spelling of the gerund/gerundive *scrībundīs* instead of the more common *scrībendīs* (with *-und-* instead of *-end-* in the 3rd and 4th conjugations). This older form can be seen in:

> *gerere: gerundum*
> *eundum* from *īre*

The same ending is retained in the old Latin phrase about the purpose of marrying: *līberum* (= *-ōrum*) *quaerundōrum causā,* "for the sake of acquiring children" (ll.154–155).

Ablative: Examples

Two ablatives related to time occur frequently in this text:

ablātīvus temporis: ablative of time when or within which
note the use of *tempestāte* in addition to *tempore*:

▷ *quibus temporibus* (l.8)

▷ *iīsdem ferē temporibus* (l.19)

▷ *quā tempestāte* (l.67)

▷ *iīsdemque fermē tempestātibus* (ll.116–117)

ablātīvus mensūrae an differentiae ablative of (degree of) difference with *ante* and *post* stating "how long before or after," e.g.:

ante/post as prepositions:

▷ *annīs post bellum Trōiānum plūs CLX* (ll.22–26)

▷ *ante Rōmam autem conditam annīs circiter CLX* (ll.22–26)

post as an adverb (= *posteā*):

▷ *post…paucīs annīs* (l.52)

▷ *paucīsque annīs post* (ll.81, 107)

▷ *aliquot…annīs post* (l.98)

▷ *post aliquantō* (l.116)

▷ *post nōn longō tempore* (l.84)

▷ *brevī post tempore* (l.100)

▷ *post aliquantō tempore* (l.109)

posteā with:

▷ *neque multō posteā* (l.87)

▷ *neque magnō intervāllō posteā* (l.160)

▷ *annīs deinde posteā paulō plūribus quam vīgintī* (l.139)[2]

With comparative alone:

▷ *aliquantō antīquiōrem* (l.20)

---

2.   *paulo* + comparative is another ablative of difference.

Euphemisms

Like other languages Latin has many indirect terms and euphemisms for the idea of dying. Instead of *morī*, we have seen phrases like:

> *occidere*
> *lūcem relinquere*
> *ē vītā excēdere*
> *dēcēdere*
> *exspīrāre*
> *obīre mortem* (l.45)
> *obīre mortis diem* (ll.114–115)
> *vītā fungī* (l.116)

Variātiō

Gellius describes the handing down of historical events in various ways:

> *scrīptum relinquere* (ll.23, 94)
> *(memoriae) trādere* (ll.38, 42)
> *memoriae mandāre* (ll.65, 96–97)
> *prōdere: In antīquīs annālibus memoria super librīs Sibyllīnīs*
>   *haec prōdita est.* (l.171)

XLVIII: DVODEQVINQVAGESIMVM: BELLVM PVNICVM SECVNDVM (Livy)[1]

I. RēS GRAMMATICAE NOVAE

Clauses of Hindering

Verbs of preventing, forbidding, refusing, etc., may be followed by a clause with *nē* or *quōminus* explaining what is being blocked:

> *ea modo ūna causa, nē extemplō trānsīrent flūmen dīrigerentque aciem, tenuerit Rōmānōs; tenēre nē* (ll.432–433): "held them back lest they"

> *quōminus = ut eō minus*: literally: "by which (*quō*) the less (*minus*)" = "that not, lest"

These clauses can take *quīn* when negative.

II. RēS GRAMMATICAE FŪSIUS EXPLICĀTAE

Potential Subjunctive (Negative, *nōn*)

You met the potential subjunctive in Cap. XLI. Potential subjunctives refer to what the speaker thinks is possible. The present and perfect subjunctive refers to the future (either the immediate future or futher off), while the imperfect considers what was likely or possible in the past. The following are the most common uses.

---

1. For an explanation of the line number references convention, see p. xxvi.

<u>2nd</u> <u>Person</u> <u>Singular</u>: You learned in Cap. XLI that the generalizing potential in Latin is 2nd person singular:[2]

> *haud facile discernerēs utrum imperātōrī an exercituī cārior esse* (1.48): "you could not easily have decided…"

> *variōs vultūs dīgredientium ab nūntiīs cernerēs* (1.365): "you would have seen different expressions on the faces of those walking away from the messengers."

<u>1st</u> <u>Person</u> <u>Singular</u>: The potential subjunctive can be used to express oneself in a cautious or mild way:

> *quaerendum cēnseam* (1.242): "I should think"

> *Respondeam Himilcōnī…* (1.648): "I might answer…"

> *velim seu Himilcō seu Māgō respondeat…* (1.665): "I would like H. or M. to answer…"

> *scīre velim* (1.671): "I would like to know"

The imperfect is also used and expresses an unfulfilled desire in the present[3] particularly in verbs of wishing:

> *vellem eum adesse*: "I would like him to be here" (but he's not)

> *mallem crustula quam pānem:* "I would prefer cookies rather than bread" (but this is clearly bread)

> *nōllem*

> *cuperem*

The potential subjunctive, both present and imperfect, is common in questions.

> Cap. XXIX: deliberative questions:
> *Quid faciam? Quid spērem?* (XXIX.22–23)
> *Ō dī bonī! Quid faciāmus* (XXIX.198–199)

---

2. The examples in *Rōma Aeterna* are all imperfect, but the present is also found.

3. Because of something that has not proven to be true. Cf. the apodosis of contrafactual conditions (Cap. XLI) and wishes (Cap. XXXIX, Recēnsiō).

Cap. XLI: Rhetorical Questions:

> *Quis enim rem tam veterem prō certō affirmet?*
> (XLI.53–54)

The potential subjunctive occurs in all persons and numbers to express what is, in the speaker's opinion, credible:

aliquis dīcat: "someone might say"

aliquis dīxerit: "someone might say"[4]

nīl ego contulerim iūcundō sānus amīco (Horace, *Satires* 1.5.44): "While I am in my right mind, I would compare nothing to a pleasant friend."

Relative Comparative Clauses:

Descriptive (generic) relative clauses (Caps. XXXIX, XLII) can be found after a comparative, introduced by *quam ut* or *quam quī.*

> *Hannibalī nimis laeta rēs est vīsa* <u>*māiorque*</u> <u>*quam*</u> <u>*ut*</u> *eam statim capere animō* <u>*posset*</u> (ll.534–535): "greater than he could grasp with his mind," or "too great to grasp"

IV. Recēnsiō

Fear Clauses

Clauses expressing a fear (Cap. XXXII) that something will or will not happen grew out of two paratactic wishes: "I am afraid! May this not happen!" This statement expresses a fear that it *will* happen = I am afraid that this will happen. When the two independent (paratactic) clauses became subordinated (hypotactic), the original syntax was maintained.

> *Vereor! Nē hoc fiat!*: "I am afraid! May this not happen!"
>
> *Vereor nē hoc fiat*: "I am afraid that this might happen."
>
> *vereor nē haec quoque laetitia vāna ēvādat* (ll.656–657)
>
> *Antiochum* <u>*timor*</u> <u>*incessit*</u> <u>*nē*</u> *quās per imminentia iuga callēs invenīret ad trānsitum Rōmānus.* (L.176–177)

---

4. There is no difference between the present and the perfect subjunctive: both refer to the future.

Conversely, an expression of fear followed by *ut* suggests something desired that might not happen.

> *Timeō! Ut* (*utinam*) *vincāmus*: "I am afraid! May we be victorious (conquer)" expresses a fear that we will not win. So *timeō ut vincāmus* means "I am afraid that we may not be victorious."

V. Points of Style

Technical Vocabulary: *Referre, cēnsēre, sententia, senātūs cōnsultum*

The verb *referre* can mean that an issue is submitted to the Senate for deliberation, and can be used with an accusative or *dē* + the ablative:

> *rem ad senātum referre* (l.101)
> *dē rē referre* (ll.95–96)

During the debate each senator is asked, *"Quid cēnsēs?"* (Caps. XLIV–XLVI), and he gives his opinion, *sententia*, by answering *"Cēnseō"* followed by the accusative + infinitive with the gerundive:

> *"terrā marīque rem gerendam (esse) cēnseō."*

The final decision of the Senate is called *senātūs cōnsultum.*

Note on Style

The readings in this chapter offer an opportunity to compare the style of Livy with that of other, later authors, albeit in a limited way, since the later authors composed abbreviated histories. For the Battle of Lake Trasumenae, we have the *periochae* of the same event; for the Battle of Cannae, there is the *Breviārium* of Eutropius.

XLIX: VNDEQVINQVAGESIMVM: HANNIBAL (Nepos)[1]

II. Rēs Grammaticae Fūsius Explicātae

Quō + Comparative + Subjunctive: Relative Purpose Clause

You learned in Cap. XXXIX that *quī* can be the equivalent of *ut is* when a relative clause expresses purpose, e.g.:

> *Ad quem cum lēgātī vēnissent Rōmānī, quī dē eius voluntāte explōrārent darentque operam...* (ll.19–21)

The ablative of the relative pronoun (*quō*) can be the equivalent of *ut eō*. When there is a comparative adjective or adverb within a relative clause of purpose, *quō* is the equivalent of *ut eō*; in the following example, *valentior* triggers *quō* = *ut eō*:

> [Hannibal] *cupīvit impraesentiārum bellum compōnere, quō valentior posteā congrederētur* (l.112): "in order that he could meet him afterward (so much) the stronger"

Syncopated Forms

In verbs the *-v-* of the perfect is often dropped. These contractions are called syncopated forms. Syncopation can happen:

1. before *-is-*, e.g.:
   - *–āvisse* to *-āsse*
   - *–īvisse* to *-iisse/īsse*

2. before *-er-/-ēr-*, e.g.:
   - *–āverat* to *-ārat*
   - *–āvērunt* to *-ārunt*

---

1. For an explanation of the line number references convention, see p. xxvi.

The complete rules are given after the chapter in the section Grammatica Latina.

In Cornelius Nepos there are many examples of such contractions (noted below in the reading helps).

III. Dēmonstrātiō Verbōrum

Dōnum/dōnāre/dōnō dare

Mūnerī dare (l.228) is a dative of purpose (Caps. XXXVI, XL). Like *mūnerī*, *dōnō* can be combined with *dare* in the phrase *dōnō dare* ("to give for the purpose of a gift/to give as a gift"), where *dōnō* is dative of purpose.

From the noun *dōnum* comes the verb *dōnāre* ("to give as a gift," "to bestow"), which is construed either:

> like *dare* with dative and accusative, e.g.,
> > *Mēdus Lȳdiae anulum dōnat.*

> Or with ablative of the thing given and accusative of the recipient, e.g.,
> > *Mēdus Lȳdiam ānulō dōnat* (cf. English "presents her with...")

In this chapter we see the latter construction used in a relative clause of purpose:

> *Lēgātī Kathāginiēnsēs Rōmam vēnērunt, quī...corōnā aureā eōs dōnārent.* (l.129)

Operam dare

Operam dare means "to give attention to something" (+ dative), "to take care to/endeavor to" (+ the subjunctive with *ut, nē*):

> *darentque operam cōnsiliīs clandestīnīs ut*: "they took care by secret counsels to..."

Verba Dare: *verba* here means "just words," so "to give just words, only words" means "to trick, to deceive":

> *Hic, clausus locōrum angustiīs, noctū sine ūllō dētrīmentō exercitūs sē expedīvit, Fabiōque, callidissimō imperātōrī, dēdit verba.* (ll.88–90)

Ūsū venīre means, as in the margins, roughly the same as *ēvenīre*: "to occur in the course of events":

> *scīlicet verēns nē ūsū venīret quod accidit.* (ll.229–230)

L: QVINQVAGESIMVM:
GRAECIA LIBERATA (Livy)

II. Rēs Grammaticae Fūsius Explicātae

Genitive of Possession: Characteristic

The genitive of possession (Cap. II) can be used as a predicate to suggest a characteristic of somone or something:

> *convīvium īnstruere et lūdōs parāre <u>eiusdem</u> esse* (ll.599–601): characteristic of/part of the same person

LI: VNVM ET QVINQVAGESIMVM: SCIPIO AEMILIANVS (Livy/Sallust)[1]

III. DĒMONSTRĀTIŌ VERBŌRUM

Dē vocābulīs faciendīs

When studying Latin vocabulary it is easy to see that a great many words are derived from others. From now on each chapter is followed by a GRAMMATICA LATINA section on derivation or word formation (*dē vocābulīs faciendīs*). In Cap. LI this section shows the formation of new verbs by means of prefixes (in Latin *praeverbia*). Most of these prefixes are prepositions, e.g.:

> *ab-*
> *ad-*
> *de-*
> *con- = cum*
> *dis-* denotes separation or dispersal
> *re-* denotes movement back or repetition

Some prefixes are often changed by assimilation before certain consonants, e.g.:

> *ad-* to *af-* before *f*
> *in-* and *con-* to *im-* and *com-* before *m* and *p*

The addition of a prefix causes a change in the verbal stem:

> *a* to *i* or *e*
> *e* to *i*

---

1. For an explanation of the line number references convention, see p. xxvi.

For example:

> from *rapere*: *abripere, abreptum*
> from *tenēre*: *retinēre, retentum*

The rules governing the changes are found in lines 339–383; you will need to know them when doing PENSVM A.

V. POINTS OF STYLE

The language of the inscription at the beginning of the chapter differs considerably from classical Latin; the differences are explained in the margin. Note, e.g.:

> archaic ablative ending *od* which later became *ō*
> > CNAIVOD (*Cnaiuod* = *Gnaeō*)

> diphthongs instead of single vowels:
> > *ei* for *ī*
> > > VIRTVTEI (*virtutei* = *virtutī*)
> > > QVEI (*quei* = *quī*)
> > *ou* for *ū*
> > > LOVCANA (*loucana* = *lūcāna*)
> > > ABDOVCIT (*abdoucit* = *abdūcit*)
> > *ai* for *ae*
> > > AIDILIS (*aidilis* = *aedīlis*)
> > > CNAIVOD (*Cnaiuod* = *Gnaeō*)

LII: ALTERVM ET QVINQVAGESIMVM: IVGVRTHA (Sallust)[1]

III. Dēmonstrātiō Verbōrum

Potīrī

The deponent verb *potīrī* ("become/be master of") usually takes the ablative (Cap. XXXVIII) but it can take the genitive, as it often does in Sallust:

> *fore uti sōlus imperiī Numidiae potīrētur* (l.65)
> *postquam omnis Numidiae potiēbātur* (ll.172–173)

Impersonal *rĕferre*

The impersonal verb *rē-ferre rē-tulisse* (as opposed to *rĕferre*, Cap. XLVIII) is a compound of *rē* (ablative of *rēs*) and *ferre*: *rē-fert* means "it matters," "it is of importance"; the person to whom it is of importance is expressed by a genitive or by *meā, tuā, suā…* (ablative feminine of passive pronoun agreeing with the *rē* of the verb), e.g.:

> *quid meā rēfert? = quid meā rē fert?*

> *Faciundum eī aliquid quod illōrum magis quam suā rētulisse*
>   *vidērētur* (ll.684–685): "he had to do something that would
>   seem to be of more importance to them than to him."

---

1.   For an explanation of the line number references convention, see p. xxvi.

Dē vocābulīs faciendīs

The Grammatica Latina sections in this and the following chapters deal with suffixes, i.e., endings used to derive new words:

> verbs from nouns (Cap. LII)
> adjectives from nouns (Cap. LIII)
> nouns from verbs (Cap. LIV)
> nouns from adjectives (Cap. LV)
> inchoative verbs (Cap. LVI)

IV. Recēnsiō

Quam + Superlative: Examples

In this chapter you find several examples of *quam* before a superlative (with or without *potest*) denoting the highest possible degree (Cap. XXVII):

> *quam māximās potest cōpiās armat* (ll.164–165)
> *quam ōcissimē ad prōvinciam accēdat* (l.336)
> *quam occultissimē potest* (l.560)
> *quam māximum silentium habērī iubet* (l.618)
> *quam prīmum* (l.592)

V. Points of Style

Features of Sallust's Latin

Archaisms

There are many archaisms in Sallust's work, e.g.:

> *uti* for *ut* (ll.26, 65 etc.)
> *quīs* for *quibus* (dative/ablative plural, ll.177, 332, 647)
> *foret* for *esset* (ll.285, 597)
> *duum* for *duōrum* (ll.560, 662)
> *huiusce* for *huius* (ll.5, 91, 477, 519)
> *-que...-que* for *et...et* (ll.97, 293, 500, 512, 679)

Other Features of Sallust's Latin:

Sallust's Latin shows a preference for the:

> perfect 3rd person plural original ending *-ēre* to *-ērunt*
> gerund/gerundive *-und* to *-end-*, e.g.:
>> *mittundum, subveniundum* (ll.326, 327)

> ablative rather than genitive of description
>> *decōrā faciē* (l.24)
>> *impigrō atque ācrī ingeniō* (l.53)
>> *placidō ingeniō* (l.253)
>> *animō ingentī* (l.583)

> genitive of description is also found:
>> *gentis paticiae nōbilis* (l.581)

The ablative of separation is used freely without the prepositions *ex, ab, dē*:

> *expellere: rēgnō fortūnīsque omnibus; Āfricā* (ll.192, 596)
> *ēicere: fīnibus* (l.192)
> *ēgredī: Cūriā, castrīs, oppidō* (ll.218, 557, 563)
> *prohibēre: moenibus* (ll.283–284)
> *dēcēdere: Āfricā, Italiā* (ll.246, 313, 366, 432)
> *dēterrēre: proeliō* (l.614)

The dative of purpose or final dative, *datīvus fīnālis* (Cap. XXXVI):

> *dōnō dēdit* (l.15)
> *praesidiō missum* (l.653)
> *glōriae fore* (l.33)
> *terrōrī esset* (l.59)
> *gaudiō esse* (l.78)
> *lūdibriō habitus* (l.408)

LIII: QVINQVAGESIMVM TERTIVM: MARIVS ET SVLLA (Evtropivs/Cicero)[1]

II. Rēs Grammaticae Fūsius Explicātae

Locative Ablative

We have seen the ablative (locative) without *in* denoting "place where" in:

> *terrā marīque*
> *eō locō*
> *multīs locīs*

The preposition is often missing in combinations with

> *tōtus:*
>> *tōtō marī* (Cap. LIV.332)[2]

> *cūnctus*
>> *cūnctā Asiā et Graeciā* (Caps. LIV, XXXVI)

III. Dēmonstrātiō Verbōrum

Nouns in *-ennium*

Latin has neuter nouns in *-ennium* to denote a number of years:

> *Biennium*: "two years," "a two-year period" (l.344)

> *triennium*: "three years," "a three-year period" (*intrā triennium*, l.181)

---

1. For an explanation of the line number references convention, see p. xxvi.
2. *In* with these adjectives is also found: *tōtā in Asiā* (l.358 and LIV.36).

quadriennium: "four years," "a four-year period" (*quadrienniō*, l.45)

quinquennium: "five years," "a five-year period" (l.393)

Nouns in *-duum*

Similarly the noun:

bīduum: "two days"
trīduum: "three days"
quadrīduum: "four days"

The case of these nouns changed over time. Although these nouns were normally in the accusative when describing "how long" something lasts, later a tendency arose to use the ablative instead of the accusative to express time "how long." See Cicero's usage with the accusative:

cum essem biennium versātus in causīs... (l.344)

Cum igitur essem in plurīmīs causīs et in prīncipibus patrōnīs quīnquennium ferē versātus... (l.393)

Eutropius uses both accusative and ablative for temporal duration:

Nam post aliquantum nūllōs placuit fierī, et quadriennium in urbe ita flūxit ut potestātēs ibi māiōrēs nōn essent. (XLVI.141)

Praesūmpsērunt tamen tribūnī mīlitārēs cōnsulārī potestāte iterum dignitātem, et triennium persevērāvērunt. (XLVI.143)

Quadrienniō cum grāvī tamen calamitāte hoc bellum tractum est (l.45): "for four years"

...Archelāus ipse trīduō nūdus in palūdibus latuit (l.95): "for three days"

Numerical Adverbs

The form of the adverb from ordinals also changed over time. Classical Latin prefers the accusative ending -*um:*

> *Deinde idem templum* <u>*iterum*</u> *et* <u>*tertium*</u> *sacrātum est.* (XXXVI.40–41)
>
> > *iterum*: for the second time
> >
> > *tertium*: for the third time
> >
> > *quārtum*: for the fourth time
> >
> > *quīntum*: for the fifth time

The ablative is also used to form adverbs in *ō* from ordinals, a feature found especially in later Latin:

> *secundō*: for the second time (l.10)
> *tertiō*: for the third time (l.12)
> *quārtō*: for the fourth time
> *quīntō*: for the fifth time (l.18)

LIV: QVINQVAGESIMVM QVARTVM: CN. POMPEIVS MAGNVS (Cicero)[1]

I. Rēs Grammaticae Novae

Heteroclitic Nouns

While you have met heteroclitic nouns before, the term is first used here. A noun is called heteroclitic if its declension varies. You met the heteroclitic *domus*, whose declension varies between the 2nd and the 4th, in Cap. XIX:

nom.	*domus*	*domūs*
acc.	*domum*	*dom<u>ōs</u>*
gen.	*domūs*	*dom<u>ōrum</u>* (or *dom<u>uum</u>*)
dat.	*domuī*	*domibus*
abl.	*dom<u>ō</u>*	*domibus*

Some nouns have declensions in both the 1st and 5th. *Māteria* (Caps. XVIII, XLIII) belongs to the 5th as well as the 1st declension (*māteriēs, -eī* as well as *māteria, -ae*). In this chapter you meet *pecus*, which in the singular means one animal out of a flock or herd and in the plural refers to the herd itself. *Pecus* has both 3rd and 4th declension forms (only attested forms are given):

nom.	*pecus/pecū*	*pecua/pecuda*
gen.	*pecoris*	*pecuum*
dat.	*pecuī*	
acc.		*pecua/pecuda*
abl.	*pecū*	*pecubus*

---

1. For an explanation of the line number references convention, see p. xxvi.

II. Rēs Grammaticae Fūsius Explicātae

Rhetorical Questions

In Cap. XLII, you learned about rhetorical questions, often in the subjunctive but also in the indicative, depending on whether the question is potential (subjunctive) or statement of fact (indicative):

> *Quis igitur hōc homine scientior umquam aut fuit aut esse*
> *dēbuit?* (ll.289–290)

There are several rhetorical questions in this speech; they are noted in the *auxilia legendī*.

III. Dēmonstrātiō Verbōrum

Agitur dē, rēs agitur

Agere plays a role in many idiomatic expressions, among which is *rēs agitur* and *agitur dē* plus the ablative: "is at stake, is about":

> *agitur populī Rōmānī glōria* (l.23): "the glory of the Roman people
>   is at stake."
> *agitur salūs sociōrum atque amicōrum* (ll.25–26)
> *aguntur certissima populī Rōmānī vectīgālia* (ll.27–28)
> *aguntur bona multōrum cīvium* (ll.29–30)

Extrēmus

Just like *medius* ("middle of," Cap. XXXIII), *summus* ("top of," Cap. XXXVI), *īnfimus* ("bottom of," Cap. XXXVI), and *prīmus* ("beginning of," Cap. XXXVIII), *extrēmus* can mean "end of."

Cōnsulere + Dative

The verb *cōnsulere* is related to *consilium* and *consul* and, by itself, means "to deliberate, reflect." When *cōnsulere* is used with the accusative, it means "to ask the advice of." With the dative it usually means "take care of, to consult for," as here:

> *bona...quibus est ā vōbīs et ipsōrum causā et reī pūblicae*
> *cōnsulendum* (ll.30–31)

LV: QVINQVAGESIMVM QVINTVM: DE RE PVBLICA (Cicero)[1]

II. Rēs Grammaticae Fūsius Explicātae

Velle + Subjunctive

The verb *velle* is often followed by the subjunctive (without *ut/nē*) to express will (as in the first example) or a wish (as in the second):

> *Vīsne igitur hoc prīmum…videāmus…?* (l.31)
>
> *Quam vellem Panaetium nostrum nōbīscum habērēmus!*
>   (ll.35–36 = *utinam…habērēmus!*)

Oportēre, necesse est + Subjunctive

Oportēre (Cap. XVII) and *necesse est* (Cap. X) are impersonal and take an accusative and infinitive construction; they can also be followed by a subjunctive, without *ut*:

> *At tū vērō animum quoque relaxēs oportet* (l.26) = *At tē vērō animum quoque <u>relaxāre</u> oportet.*
>
> *Hīc tū…ostendās oportēbit…* (LVI.46 = *tē ostendere*)
>
> *…vīvendī finem habeat necesse est* (LVI.263–264)
>
> *vel concidat omne caelum omnisque nātūra et cōnsistat necesse est* (LVI.275–276)

---

1. For an explanation of the line number references convention, see p. xxvi.

Ethical Dative

As you have learned, the dative is often used to show to whom the action in the clause refers; a particular form of the dative of reference, called the "ethical dative," is used only with personal pronouns and signals the particular interest or involvment of the person in the dative:

> *quid enim mihi L. Paulī nepōs…quaerit* (ll.118–120): "Why, I ask you (*mihi*), is the grandson of Lucius Paulus…asking."

The ethical dative is a feature of colloquial speech.

III. DĒMONSTRĀTIŌ VERBŌRUM

Semi-deponents

Besides *audēre* (see XXXI.169), a few other verbs are semi-deponent:

> *soleō, solēre, solitum esse* (l.150): "to be accustomed"
>
> *gaudeō, gaudēre, gavīsum esse*: "to rejoice, be glad"
>
> *fīdo, fīdere, fīsum esse*: "to trust" (+ dat.)
>
> *cōnfīdo, cōnfīdere, cōnfīsum esse*: "to trust" (+ dat.; LII.345, *cōnfīsī*)
>
> *diffīdo, diffīdere, diffīsum esse*: "to distrust" (+ dat.)

Placēre, used impersonally, may be semi-deponent:

> *placitum est = placuit* (l.74)
> cf. *placitus*, "pleasing" (XL.24)

LVI: QVINQVAGESIMVM SEXTVM: SOMNIVM SCIPIONIS (Cicero/Horace)[1]

I. Rēs Grammaticae Novae

Epexegetical Genitive

Latin poets sometimes imported Greek syntax, among which is the genitive that explains an adjective (epexegisis = "explanatory"). We find two of these epexegetical infinitives in the first line of Horace's poem:

> *integer vītae* (cf. "integrity")
> *sceleris pūrus* ("pure of crime," "guiltless")

III. Dēmonstrātiō Verbōrum

Quaesō

The verb *quaesō* (1st person singular present indicative) is used in combination with a request or a question: "I ask you," "please (tell me)":

> *Quaesō, pater sānctissimē atque optimē... quid moror in terrīs?*
> (ll.81, 115)

Quaesō can also be used with the subjunctive (= *ōrō ut...*), with or without *ut/nē*:

> *St! quaesō nē mē ē somnō excitētis...* (l.58)

> *...tamen paucīs quaesō sinātis mē cum pūblicā fēlīcitāte*
> *comparāre eō quō dēbeō animō prīvātam meam fortūnam.*
> (l.630)

---

1. For an explanation of the line number references convention, see p. xxvi.

Impersonal Verb Interest

The impersonal verb *inter-est*, "it makes a difference," "it is of interest/importance," is construed like *rē-fert* (Cap. LII) with the genitive or with *meā, tuā, suā*:

> *meā māximē interest tē valēre*
>
> *Quid autem interest ab iīs quī posteā nāscentur sermōnem fore*
>   *dē tē?* (ll.214–215)

In this example we should understand *quid tuā interest*: "Why is it important to you? Why do you care?"

V. Points of Style

Neuter for Adverb

In the last stanza of Horace's poem, the neuter form *dulce* is used as an adverb (= *dulciter*; cf. *facile*).

PARS ALTERA

Introductions adapted from Hans H. Ørberg's *Lingva Latina Per Se Illvs-trata Pars II Instructions*. © Hans H. Ørberg 2005.

XXXVI: TRICESIMVM SEXTVM: ROMA AETERNA[1]

I. Ørberg's Introduction

Part II of Lingva Latina Per Se Illvstrata opens with a chapter on the Eternal City, *Rōma Aeterna*, as it looked in the second century AD. You read about its location on the banks of the Tiber on and around the Seven Hills as well as about the splendid buildings and historic monuments found in the capital of the Roman Empire. The illustrations will give you an idea of what some of these monuments looked like in ancient times. The chapter also gives a sense of the progression of Roman history from the time of the kings (753–510 BC) to the republic (510–31 BC) to the second century AD and concludes with a very useful table coordinating buildings, dates, and historical personages.

Posterity has not been kind to the remains of ancient Rome. Several medieval and Renaissance churches and palaces were built with materials taken from the ruins of ancient temples and public buildings. Nevertheless, some buildings have been preserved because they were transformed into churches. In the forum, for example, the Senate-House, or *Curia*, was rebuilt on the old foundations after a fire in the late third century AD and became a church in the seventh century AD. The original bronze doors adorn the main entrance of St. John Lateran (Rome). The Temple of Faustina, also in the Forum, became a church in the seventh or eighth century AD. The front row of columns of the temple of Saturn is still standing, as are a few columns of the Temple of Vespasian and the Temple of Castor. The temple of Vesta was partly restored in 1930. The other Forum buildings mentioned in this chapter have all but disappeared: all that remains of most of them is their foundations. Despite this, archaeological

---

1. For an explanation of the line number references convention, see p. xxvi.

explorations and computer-generated reconstructions enable us to envision—
and marvel at—the architectural splendors of ancient Rome.

Among the more or less preserved monuments elsewhere in the city that are
worthy of mention are: the Flavian Amphitheater, which was later named the
Colosseum (completed 80 AD); the Arch of Titus with its reliefs showing Titus's
triumph after the capture of Jerusalem in 70 AD; the Pantheon, a round temple
with a huge dome (rebuilt during the reign of Emperor Hadrian, 117–38 AD);
Trajan's column (completed AD 113), which now bears a statue of Saint Peter;
and the tomb of Emperor Hadrian, which was converted into a medieval castle
called Castel Sant'Angelo. The best-preserved Roman baths, those of Caracalla
and Diocletian, were built in the third century AD, but ruins remain of the
thermae Trāiānī on the Esquiline Hill above the Colosseum.

Sometimes inscriptions on the monuments give us some information of
their origin and function, but it is only by combining the archaeological finds
with the frequent references to localities in Rome found in the works of Roman
writers that we obtain factual knowledge about the topographical history of
Rome. As far as most of the major buildings are concerned, we know both
when and by whom they were constructed, and we are familiar with a great
many historical events that are connected with the individual monuments.

Be sure to make full use of the maps. In addition to the map of ancient Rome
on the inside of the cover of RŌMA AETERNA and detailed maps of the Forum
and its surroundings on pp. 6 and 10. Here you will find all the names of buildings and localities mentioned in the text. The chronological survey on pp. 24–
25 provides further support. The acquaintance with ancient Rome that you
obtain by studying this chapter will stand you in good stead in later chapters
when you come to read about historical events that have taken place in and
around the metropolis of the Roman world.

II. Auxilia Legendī

Palātium et Capitōlium: 1–57

2–3:	*vīgintī mīlia*: accusative of extent of space with partitive genitive *passuum*.
9:	*patet*: "lies open" (Cap. XXV).
11–12:	*quibus*: ablative of means; *Rōmulus…mūnīvisse dīcitur*: nominative and infinitive with passive verb.
22:	*ad septentriōnēs*: "to the north" (Cap. XVI).
30:	*habētur*: "is considered" (Cap. XXVIII).
38–39:	*Iovī…deābus*: datives with *cōnsecrāvit*.

Forum Rōmānum: 58–184

63–65:	Livy tells the story of the Lacus Curtius (*ab Urbe Conditā*, 7.6): an enormous chasm mysteriously opened up in the forum; consulting the gods, the seers proclaimed that the spot would have to be consecrated if Rome were to realize its power. The young Marcus Curtius, believing Rome's greatest potential lay in its valor and weapons, armed himself and, astride his horse, leapt into the chasm, making himself a votive offering on behalf of his city.
76:	See note on *vēnīre* vs. *vĕnīre* in grammar section above.
88:	*verba faciunt*: "make a speech," so too *ōrātiōnēs...habērent* (ll.91–92).
89–91:	At the Battle of Antium (modern Anzio on the southwest Italian coastline above Naples) in 338 BC, the Romans took the ships' prows (*rōstra*, named from their visual similarity to a bird's beak) to decorate the speakers' platform.
78:	*quō*: adverb of place to which (Cap. XXV); cf. *unde* (l.93): adverb of place from which.
101–103:	*Illa aedēs duās iānuās vel portās habet, quae <u>tum</u> dēmum clauduntur <u>cum</u> per tōtum imperium populī Rōmānī terrā marīque pāx facta est*: *cum* here is purely temporal, as shown by the *tum* (Caps. XXIX and XXXVII).
104–105:	*bis tantum*: "only twice" (Cap. IV); in fact, Augustus boasted that the gates had been closed three times in his lifetime, for a total of five times.
113:	*cūrant nē*: *verba cūrandī* (Cap. XXVII).
117–118:	*rēgēs...habitāvisse dīcuntur*: nominative and infinitive with passive verb.
119–120:	*cēterīs omnibus sacerdōtibus Rōmānīs praefectus est*: *praeficere* + dative.
125:	*habētur*: see note for line 30.
140:	*vēneunt*: see note on *vēnīre* vs. *vĕnīre* above.
147–148:	*cum*: with indicative because it points to specific time: *eō tempore...cum*.

162:            Ennius lived from about 239 to 169 BC. He had a great influ-
               ence on Roman verse; he is sometimes called the Father of
               Latin poetry.

Urbs marmorea: 185–263

Urbis incendium et domus aurea Nerōnis: 264–295

213:            *fierī posse*: see grammar notes above.

230:            *accēpisset*: pluperfect subjunctive in a subordinate clause in
               indirect statement in secondary sequence.

247–249:   *lavātum*: accusative supine of purpose (Cap. XXII); *natandō,
               currendō, luctandō*: gerunds, ablative of means (Cap. XXVI).

266–268:   *Nerō…dīcitur iniisse*: for the nominative and infinitive with a
               passive verb, see Cap. XIII; *iniisse* = *inīvisse* (Cap. XLIX).

274:            *funditus*: adverb, "from the bottom/foundation," "totally"
               (cf. l.299).

Imperātōrēs Flāviī: 296–320

304:            *rēs sacrae quās Titus Iūdaeīs victīs adēmit*: *adimere* + a dative
               of disadvantage (see Cap. XXXVIII), "take away from."

Trāiānus et Hadriānus: 321–352

325:            *forum faciendum cūrāvit* = *cūrāvit ut forum facerētur*.

339:            *templum praeclārum*: the prefix *prae-* before adjectives and
               adverbs has intensive force ("very…"); cf. *carmine praeclārō*
               (l.366).

342–343:   *ad…versus* = *adversus* + accusative: to, toward (Cap. XX).

Orbis caput: 353–370

363:            *nīl nisi Rōmānum quod tueātur habet*: "he has nothing that he
               can see that is not Roman (i.e., part of Rome)"; *quod tueātur*:
               relative clause of tendency/descriptive relative clause, see
               Cap. XXXIX.

III. Vocābula

Nōmina

1st

āra, -ae	altar
balneae, -ārum (*pl.*)	public baths
basilica, -ae	basilica
bibliothēca, -ae	library
casa, -ae	cottage, hut
cloāca, -ae	sewer
concordia, -ae	concord
cūria, -ae	curia (division of the people, Senate-House)
discordia, -ae	disagreement, discord
flamma, -ae	flame
prōra, -ae	prow
rēgia, -ae	royal palace
statua, -ae	statue
thermae, -ārum (*pl.*)	public baths
tuba, -ae	trumpet

2nd

aerārium, -ī	state treasury
candēlābrum, -ī	candelabrum
clīvus, -ī	slope, sloping street
focus, -ī	hearth
laurus, -ī	laurel
mausōlēum, -ī	mausoleum
metallum, -ī	metal
monumentum, -ī	memorial, monument
morbus, -ī	disease, illness
plēbēiī, -ōrum (*pl.*)	plebians
prōmunturium, -ī	headland, promontory
rōstrum, -ī	beak, beaked prow
sacrificium, -ī	sacrifice
simulācrum, -ī	image, statue
stadium, -ī	running track

stāgnum, ī	pool, pond
strāmentum, ī	straw
triumphus, ī	triumph
vestibulum, ī	forecourt
vīcus, ī	street, village

3rd

aedēs, -is (*f.*)	temple, *pl.* house
aes, aeris (*n.*)	copper, bronze, money
arx, arcis (*f.*)	hilltop, citadel
cōnsul, -is (*m.*)	consul
factiō, -ōnis (*f.*)	party, faction
genetrīx, -īcis (*f.*)	mother
later, -eris (*m.*)	brick
longitūdō, -inis (*f.*)	length
magnitūdō, -inis (*f.*)	size, greatness
odor, -ōris (*m.*)	smell
ōrātor, -ōris (*m.*)	speaker, orator, envoy
orīgō, -inis (*f.*)	beginning, origin
palūs, -ūdis (*f.*)	fen, swamp
pecus, -udis (*n.*)	farm animal, sheep
pōns, pontis (*m.*)	bridge
pontifex, -icis (*m.*)	high priest
sēdēs, -is (*f.*)	seat, abode, dwelling
senātor, -ōris (*m.*)	senator
ultor, -ōris (*m.*)	avenger
vetustās, -ātis (*f.*)	age, old age, long existence

4th

ductus, -ūs	leadership, command
porticus, -ūs (*f.*)	portico, colonnade
senātus, -ūs	senate, assembly, sitting

VERBA

-āre

(collocō) collocāre	place
(cōnsecrō) cōnsecrāre	consecrate

(cremō) cremāre	burn, cremate
(dēdicō) dēdicāre	dedicate
(glōriōr) glōriārī	boast
(incohō) incohāre	start work on, begin
(locō) locāre	place
(praecipitō) praecipitāre	throw, fall, rush headlong
(probō) probāre	approve of, prove
(renovō) renovāre	renew, resume
(restō) restāre	remain, be left
(sacrō) sacrāre	consecrate
(siccō) siccāre	dry, drain
(superō) superāre	cross, surpass, overcome, defeat, remain
(triumphō) triumphāre	celebrate a triumph

-ēre

(ārdeō) ārdēre, arsisse, arsum	burn
(ēmineō) ēminēre, ēminuisse	stick out, project, emit, utter
(exerceō) exercēre, -cuisse, -citum	exercise, practice, worry
(splendeō) splendēre	shine
(voveō) vovēre, vōvisse, vōtum	promise, vow

-ere

(absūmō) absūmere (< sūmere)	consume, waste, destroy
(adimō) adimere (< emere)	take away (from), steal
(collābor) collābī (< lābī)	fall down, collapse
(dēdūcō) dēdūcere (< dūcere)	lead/bring down, launch
(dēpōnō) dēpōnere (< pōnere)	put/lay down, deposit
(dēstruō) dēstruere (< struere)	demolish
(expellō) expellere (< pellere)	drive out, expel
(exstinguō) exstinguere, -tinxisse, -stinctum	extinguish, put out, kill, annihilate
(exstruō) exstruere (< struere)	erect, build
(incendō) incendere, -cendisse, -censum	set on fire, inflame
(indūcō) indūcere (< dūcere)	lead, bring (in), introduce
(praeficiō) praeficere (< facere)	put in charge of

(reficiō) reficere (< facere)	restore, repair
(restituō) restituere, -tuisse, -tutum	rebuild, restore, reinstate
(tegō) tegere, tetigisse, tactum	cover, conceal
(ulcīscor) ulcīscī, -ultum	revenge, avenge

-īre

(ēveniō) ēvenīre (< venīre)	happen, fall by lot

irregular

(ineō) inīre (< īre)	enter (upon), begin
(vēneō) vēnīre	be sold

ADIECTĪVA

1st/2nd

aereus, -a, -um	of bronze/copper
aeternus, -a, -um	eternal, everlasting
amplus, -a, -um	large, big
anniversārius, -a, -um	annual
arcuātus, -a, -um	arched
augustus, -a, -um	venerable, majestic
aurātus, -a, -um	gilded
dīvīnus, -a, -um	divine
dīvus, -a, -um	divine, (*m.*) god
domesticus, -a, -um	domestic, household
firmus, -a, -um	strong, stable, firm
īnsānus, -a, -um	mad, insane
interiectus, -a, -um	situated between
latericius, -a, -um	of brick
marmoreus, -a, -um	made of marble, marble
praeclārus, -a, -um	splendid, excellent
quadrātus, -a, -um	square
rotundus, -a, -um	round
sacer, -cra, -crum	holy, sacred
splendidus, -a, -um	shining, splendid
subterrāneus, -a, -um	underground
vīcēsimus, -a, -um	twentieth

3rd

celeber, -bris, -bre	crowded, well-known
illūstris, -re	brilliant, illustrious
interior, interius	interior, inner (part of)
triumphālis, -e	triumphal

ADVERBIA

ibīdem	in the same place
tertium	for the third time

XXXVII: TRICESIMVM SEPTIMVM: TROIA CAPTA (Vergil)[1]

[Ex Vergiliī Aenēidis librō II, solūtīs versibus]

I. ØRBERG'S INTRODUCTION

The introductory chapter on the city of Rome is now followed by an account of the history of Rome as told by the Romans themselves. The origins of Rome are lost in conjecture, so here poetic imagination has full scope. From a wish to link the prehistory of Rome with the city that had once fought so bravely against the Greek heroes arose the legend of the Trojan hero *Aeneas*, who after his flight from Troy and seven years' wanderings finally made his way to Latium and there prepared the eventual foundation of Rome.

This theme was treated by the poet Vergil (*Pūblius Vergilius Marō*, 70–19 BC) in his famous poem the *Aeneid* (Latin *Aenēis*). As Vergil tells the story, Aeneas had been chosen by the gods themselves to lay the foundations of the later Roman Empire, as it had been prophesied in divine revelations.

To a certain extent, Vergil had the *Iliad* and the *Odyssey* of Homer as his models. The first six books (*librī*) of the *Aeneid*, in which he tells of Aeneas's wanderings, are related to the *Odyssey*, which deals with the wanderings of Odysseus (Ulysses), and books VII–XII, in which the wars in Latium are described, can be compared with the Trojan War as described in the *Iliad*.

Like its Greek models, the *Aeneid* is written in hexameters, the usual meter for epic poems in Greek and Latin. Although you are not yet able to read Vergil's verses in their original form, Ørberg has composed a prose version based on the wording and style of Vergil, and some important passages (printed in *italics*) have been left unchanged. This prose version of the first part of the *Aeneid*, which takes up the next four chapters, can form the basis for a later study of Vergil. That is, Caps. XXXVII–XL present a prose version of the narrative in *Aeneid* I–IV.

---

1. For an explanation of the line number references convention, see p. xxvi.

Cap. XXXVII corresponds with the second book (*liber secundus*) of the *Aeneid*. It contains a description of the fall of Troy (*Trōia*) and the flight of Aeneas, as told by the hero himself to queen *Dīdō*, who offered him hospitality in Carthage (*Karthāgō* or *Carthāgō*). The chapter begins with a brief mention of the legendary kings of Latium from *Sāturnus* (whose reign was called the "golden age": *'aetās aurea' quae vocātur*) to *Latīnus*. Then we are told how the Greeks succeeded in entering Troy hidden in a huge wooden horse and about the heroic fight of the Trojans against the invaders. When king Priam (*Priamus*) is killed and the battle lost, Aeneas flees from the burning city with his old father *Anchīsēs*, his son *Ascanius*, and his wife *Creūsa*. Creusa gets lost during the flight; the others, however, reach a safe spot outside the city together with many other fugitives.

A note on the reading

On p. 31, you will find two sets of numbers: the line numbers of the frame narrative in RŌMA AETERNA and the verse numbers for the six original verses of the *Aeneid*. The numbers in italics indicate verse numbers in the *Aeneid*, Book II. RŌMA AETERNA follows this procedure throughout: italicized numbers refer to the line in the *Aeneid*, while plain numbers refer to the line of the chapter's narrative.

II. AUXILIA LEGENDĪ

Aborīginēs: 1–19

2–4:   *tantā iūstitiā fuisse dīcitur ut nec servīret…nec habēret…sed… essent*: result clause (Cap. XXVIII).

6–7:   *mōs Rōmānōrum est ut* + subjunctive: noun clause of result (see grammar section above): "it is the custom of the Romans to…"; *mēnse Decembrī, diēbus fēstīs*: both ablatives of time.

12–14:   [*Euandrō*] *Faunus…arva colenda dēdit*: see section on gerund/gerundive in Cap. XXXVI.

Equus Trōiānus: 20–88

36–40:   *aliī…iubēbant…aliī cēnsēbant*: both enclosing indirect statements; *aliī…volēbant* + complementary infinitive.

43:    *monuit nē*: indirect command.

45–46:   *ūlla putātis/dōna carēre dolīs Danaum*: ablative of separation with the intransitive *carēre*.

49:	*et = etiam*: even.
53:	*Paulō post*: ablative of degree of difference: "a little later (later by a little)."
56–57:	*capitibus ērēctīs oculīsque ārdentibus*: ablative absolute; *Trōiānōs perterritōs*: the prefix *per-* has intensive force ("very..."); cf. *perturbantur* (l.67).
59:	*complexī*: nominative of deponent perfect participle, sc. *anguēs*; object is *parva corpora*.
62–63:	*bis collō longa corpora sua circumdant*: see grammar section on dative with compound verbs (above).
69:	*quod...laeserit*: perfect subjunctive in a subordinate clause inside indirect discourse (*ōrātiō oblīqua*) (Cap. XXXVI).
72:	*machina illa*: i.e., the horse.
78:	*Etiam tunc Cassandra, fīlia Priamī virgō cui rēs futūrās praedīcentī nēmō umquam crēdēbat, fātum Trōiae cīvibus suīs praedīxit*: see above, POINTS OF STYLE; *cui...praedīcentī*: dative with *crēdēbat*.

Somnium Aenēae: 89–124

96–98:	*monuit ut...caperet atque...fugeret*: indirect command (see section on indirect commands above).
99:	*tēque hīs...ēripe flammīs*: ablative of separation.
102:	*Hīc*: adverb: "at this point."
103–104:	*unde...vidērent*: adverbial purpose clause.

Priamus: 125–180

126:	*nē...quidem*: "not even" (Cap. XXVI).
133:	*Trōiānī ab hostibus numerō superiōribus occīsī sunt*: ablative of respect (Cap. XI).
135:	*pugnābātur*: intransitive verb used impersonally in the passive (Cap. XXXIII).

140–141:   *cupidus…auxilium ferendī*: objective genitive of gerund (and accusative object) with *cupidus* (Cap. XXV).

150:    *ut prīmum*: "as soon as."

152:    *moritūrus*: future active participle: "intending to die."

156–157:   *Iam nōn tēlīs egēmus, sed auxiliō deōrum*: ablative of separation.

160:    Polītes is trying to reach the altar (where his family is) because altars are places of sanctuary (but Pyrrhus ignores the right of suppliants to safety at an altar).

169:    *īrā permōtus*: ablative of cause (Cap. XXV); *permōtus*: see note on line 57, above.

Anchīsēs: 181–240

184:    *vēnit eī in mentem*: a very frequent idiom.

187:    *fīliō sē videndam obtulit*: "she offers herself to her son to be seen (in order that he might see her)": see section on gerund/gerundive in Cap. XXXVI.

196–198:   *Dī caelestēs, sī mē vītam prōdūcere voluissent, hanc patriam mihi servāvissent*: Contrafactual condition in past time (Cap. XXXIII).

    Nōlō urbī captae superesse: see section on compound verbs + dative case, above.

199–202:   The verb in the indirect command (*perderet*) is in secondary sequence, as the main verb (*haerēbat*) determines the sequence; when *dum* signals continuous action in the past, it takes the present (*suādent*).

223:    *ā laevā (parte)*: thundering on the left was propitious.

Creūsa: 241–285

271:    *navigandum est*: see section on gerund/gerundive in Cap. XXXVI.

III. Vocābula

NŌMINA

1st

aura, -ae	breeze, wind
barba, -ae	beard
coma, -ae	hair
īnsānia, -ae	madness
iūstitia, -ae	justice
māchina, -ae	machine

2nd

arvum, -ī	(plowed) field
clipeus, -ī	round shield
dolus, -ī	guile, deceit, cunning
famulus, -ī	servant, slave
prōdigium, -ī	prodigy
rēgnum, -ī	kingship, kingdom, reign
socius, -ī	companion, partner, ally
somnium, -ī	dream
tēlum, -ī	spear, weapon
vinculum, -ī	bond, chain

3rd

aedēs, -ium (*f. pl.*)	house
anguis, -is (*m./f.*)	snake, serpent
crīnis, -is (*m.*)	hair
culmen, -inis (*n.*)	summit, top, peak, roof
cūstōs, -ōdis (*m./f.*)	guardian, guard
dēfēnsor, -ōris (*m.*)	defender
fragor, -ōris (*m.*)	crash
frōns, -ondis (*f.*)	foliage, leaves
fūnis, -is (*m.*)	rope
horror, -ōris (*m.*)	dread, horror
iuventūs, -ūtis (*f.*)	youth, young men
lūmen, -inis (*n.*)	light
mōlēs, -is (*f.*)	mass, bulk, effort
nepōs, -ōtis (*m./f.*)	grandson

nūmen, -inis (*n.*)	divine will
onus, -eris (*n.*)	burden, load
pavor, -ōris (*m.*)	trembling with fear
rōbur, -oris (*n.*)	oak, strength, force
speciēs, -ēī (*f.*)	sight, appearance, shape, semblance, sort
trabs, -bis (*f.*)	beam, ship
turris, -is (*f.*) (*acc.* -**im**; *abl.* -**ī**)	tower

4th

gemitus, -ūs	groaning
lūctus, -ūs	grief, moaning
nātus, -ūs	birth
ululātus, -ūs	howling

irregular

fās (*indec.*)	divine law, right

VERBA

-āre

(**conclāmō**) **conclāmāre**	shout, cry out
(**dominōr**) **dominārī**	be master, rule
(**explicō**) **explicāre, -uisse, -itum**	extricate, unfold, explain
(**fabricō**) **fabricāre**	forge, build, construct
(**flagrō**) **flagrāre**	burn
(**immolō**) **immolāre**	sacrifice, immolate
(**incitō**) **incitāre**	set in motion, stir up
(**īnstaurō**) **īnstaurāre**	renew
(**micō**) **micāre**	flicker, flash
(**obtruncō**) **obtruncāre**	slaughter, kill
(**penētrō**) **penētrāre**	penetrate
(**recūsō**) **recūsāre**	reject, refuse
(**resonō**) **resonāre**	resound
(**sonō**) **sonāre, -uisse, -itum**	sound
(**tonō**) **tonāre, -uisse**	thunder
(**trucīdō**) **trucīdāre**	slaughter

-ēre

(commoveō) commovēre (< movēre)	move, excite, cause
(egeō) egēre, eguisse	need
(fulgeō) fulgēre, -sisse	flash, gleam
(haereō) haerēre, -sisse, -sum	stick, cling

-ere

(alloquor) alloquī (< loquī)	speak to, address
(amplector) amplectī, -xum	embrace, cling to
(attingō) attingere, -tigisse, -tactum	touch, reach, arrive at, adjoin
(āvehō) āvehere (< vehere)	carry off, pass, go away
(comprehendō) comprehendere, -disse, -nsum	seize, include
(concēdō) concēdere (< cēdere)	go (away), yield, give up, concede, allow
(concīdō) concīdere, -disse, -sum	kill, beat
(cōnfugiō) cōnfugere (< fugere)	flee for refuge
(coniciō) conicere, -iēcisse, -iectum	throw, put
(contingō) contingere, -tigisse, -tactum	touch, be close to, be granted, to, happen
(corripiō) corripere (< rapere)	seize, rebuke
(dēcurrō) dēcurrere (< currere)	run down
(dēfīgō) dēfīgere (< fīgere)	fix, thrust, paralyze
(dēmittō) dēmittere (< mittere)	let fall, drop, lower
(discumbō) discumbere, -cubuisse, -cubitum	take one's place at table
(ēlābor) ēlābī (< labī)	slip out, escape
(ērigō) ērigere (< regere)	lift up, erect, cheer
(gemō) gemere, -isse, -itum	groan (for)
(īnspiciō) īnspicere, -spexisse, -spectum	examine, inspect
(pandō) pandere, -disse, -passum	spread out
(patefaciō) patefacere (< facere)	open, reveal

(perfundō) perfundere (**< fundere**)	wet, drench, imbue, fill
(praedīcō) praedīcere (< dīcere)	foretell, prophesy
(prōdūcō) prōdūcere (< dūcere)	extend
(repetō) repetere (< petere)	return to, repeat, claim back, recall
(respiciō) respicere, -exisse, -ectum	look back (at), heed, regard, have regard for
(restinguō) restinguere, -xisse, -ctum	put out, extinguish
(revīsō) revīsere (< vīsere)	revisit, visit
(ruō) ruere, -isse, -tum	rush, tumble down
(stringō) stringere, -nxisse, -ctum	draw, unsheathe
(tendō) tendere, tetendisse, tentum/tēnsum	stretch, spread, lay, make one's way, insist
(vādō) vādere	advance, go

irregular

(cōnferō) -ferre (< ferre)	bring (together), carry
(efferō) efferre (< ferre)	carry/bring out, lift, elate

ADIECTĪVA

1st/2nd

benignus, -a, -um	kind, benevolent
diūturnus, -a, -um	long, prolonged
fēstus, -a, -um	holiday, festal
īnfīrmus, -a, -um	weak
inultus, -a, -um	unavenged
laevus, -a, -um	left
occultus, -a, -um	hidden, secret
patrius, -a, -um	of the father, paternal
pavidus, -a, -um	terrified
profugus, -a, -um	fleeing, (*m.*) fugitive
rēgius, -a, -um	royal
saucius, -a, -um	wounded
scelerātus, -a, -um	accursed, criminal
suprēmus, -a, -um	highest, sovereign

suspectus, -a, -um	suspected, suspect
vāstus, -a, -um	desolate, vast, huge

3rd

āmēns (*gen.* **āmēntis**)	out of one's mind, mad
caelestis, -e	celestial, (*m. pl.*) gods
inēluctābilis, -e	inescapable, inevitable
inūtilis, -e	useless
tener, -era, -erum	tender, delicate
ūber, -eris	fertile

ADVERBIA

dūdum	a little while ago, formerly
nēquīquam	in vain, fruitlessly
pariter	equally, together
penitus	from within, deep, far
quā	which way, where
quondam	once, some day
undique	from all sides

XXXVIII: DVODEQVADRAGESIMVM: PIVS AENEAS (Vergil)[1]

[Ex Vergiliī Aenēidis librō III, solūtīs versibus]

I. Ørberg's Introduction

This chapter is a prose version of Book III of the *Aeneid*. Aeneas tells the story of his and his companions' dangerous voyage through the Aegean and Ionian Seas to Sicily. At the foot of Mount Etna (*Aetna*), they have a grim encounter with the Cyclops *Polyphēmus*, whom Odysseus (*Ulixēs*) shortly before had blinded. Aeneas ends his report with his father's death and burial during the Trojans' brief sojourn in Sicily as the guests of king *Acestēs*.

In antiquity, navigation was suspended in winter. Aeneas spends the winter building a fleet of twenty ships (*classem vīgintī nāvium*), and he is not ready to sail (*ventīs vēla dare*) until the early summer (*prīmā aestāte*).

On his long journey, Aeneas brought with him the Penates (*dī Penātēs*) of Troy—the name is used to refer to the tutelary gods not only of a household, but also of a city. In a dream, they tell Aeneas to depart from drought-stricken Crete and sail on to Italy, where a brilliant future awaits him and his descendants in a new city.

II. Auxilia Legendī

Penātēs: 1–47

2:          *classem vīgintī nāvium*: genitive of description.

3:          *prīmā aestāte*: "in the beginning of summer." Here *prīmus, -a, -um* is used in the sense of "the first part of…" (cf. *summus, medius, infimus*, Cap. XXXVI).

---

1. For an explanation of the line number references convention, see p. xxvi.

4:	*Anchīsēs nāvēs dēdūcere et ventīs vela dare iubēbat*: i.e., "*nāvēs dēdūcite et ventīs vela date!*"; *ventīs vela dare*: "give sails to the winds"—a regular Latin idiom for "start sailing."
16:	*ventus secundus*: a "following" wind fills the sails and is thus "favorable."
26–28:	*cum...coepit*: *cum inversum* (Cap. XXXVII); *adeō...ut*: result clause.
35:	*eōrum*: refers to *posterōs tuōs* (l.34): *nē recūsāveris!*: negative command with perfect subjunctive (Cap. XXXII).
39:	*Age, surge...*: *age* here is an exhortation ("act!" "get going," Cap. V).
45:	*paucīs* (sc. *hominibus*) *relictīs*: ablative absolute, i.e., "left behind."

Mare Īonium: 48–74

60:	*ad septentriōnēs*: the north stars, the north (Cap. XVI).
62:	*quō*: adverb of place to which.
66:	*nautīs metuendum*: dative of agent with gerundive.
69:	*clipeum, quem cuidam hostī adēmerat*: "took away from," dative of disadvantage with verbs of depriving, such as here, with *adimere* (Cap. XXXVIII).

Andromachē et Helenus: 75–129

76–77:	*rēgnō...potītum esse*: see grammar section above.
79:	*certior fierī*: see grammar section above.
83:	*ut Aenēam cōnspexit venientem*: *ut* + indicative meaning "when" (see Cap. XXXVII).
90:	*nē dubitāveris!*: negative command (see note to line 35 and Cap. XXXII).
92:	*parvā vōce*: ablative of manner (Cap. X).
102–103:	*quaesīvit "quae...vītanda essent?"*: indirect question (Cap. XIX); *ex mōre*: "according to custom."
108:	*tibi nāvigandum est*: passive periphrastic (Cap. XXXI) with a dative of agent.

118:            *praestat*: "It is better."

124:            *age, vāde*: see note to line 39.

Mōns Aetna: 130–213

134–135:   *cum...vidēret: cum* causal; *proficīscendī*: objective gentive with *signum*.

139:            *merō*: < *merum, -ī*: unmixed wine, ablative with *implēvit*.

141–142:   *dī potentēs*: vocative, *potentēs* + genitive: "with power over"; *secundī*: "favorable/favorably."

156:            *ignārī viae*: objective genitive (Cap. XXV).

176–177:   *quis esset?...unde venīret?*: indirect questions (Cap. XIX).

181:            *nōmine*: ablative of respect (Caps. XI, XIX).

182–185:   *vīdī eum...iacentem...frangere ac...dēvorāre.*

193–195:   *Vix haec dīxerat, cum ipsum Polyphēmum pāstōrem caecum inter pecudēs suās ambulantem vīdērunt et lītora nōta petentem*: this sentence illustrates the importance of "keep reading, note endings and word groupings." Except for *Vix haec dīxerat, cum...vīdērunt*, all words refer to Polyphemus, modified by an appositive (*pāstōrem caecum*) and two participles (*ambulantem, petentem*). Each participle is grouped with the words that apply to it: He is walking *inter pecudēs suās* and seeking familiar shores (*lītora nōta*).

III. VOCĀBULA

NŌMINA

1st

aurōra, -ae	dawn
patera, -ae	bowl
pestilentia, -ae	plague, pestilence
unda, -ae	wave
vidua, -ae	widow

2nd

antrum, -ī	cave, cavern
fūmus, -ī	smoke
iuvencus, -ī	young bull, bullock
lūcus, -ī	sacred grove
nimbus, -ī	rain cloud
posterī, -ōrum (*m. pl.*)	descendants, posterity
scopulus, -ī	rock
sepulcrum, -ī	tomb, grave

3rd

aequor, -ŏris (*n.*)	level surface, sea
genitor, -ōris (*m.*)	father
gurges, -itis (*m.*)	whirlpool, flood
lapis, -idis (*m.*)	stone, milestone
pondus, -eris (*n.*)	weight
terror, -ōris (*m.*)	fright, terror
vātēs, -is (*m./f.*)	prophet(ess), seer
volucris, -is (*f.*)	bird

4th

flētus, -ūs	weeping
occāsus, -ūs	setting
ortus, -ūs	rising, sunrise, origin

VERBA

-āre

(adstō) adstāre	stand by
(invitō) invitāre	invite, entertain
(moror) morārī	delay, stay, stop
(praestō) praestāre	furnish, fulfill, surpass
(sacrificō) sacrificāre	make a sacrifice

-ēre

(exterreō) exterrēre (< terrēre)	scare, terrify
(reor) rērī, ratum	reckon, think, believe
(torreō) torrēre, -uisse, -tōstum	scorch, parch

-ere

(agnōsco) agnōscere, -ōvisse	recognize
(circumvehō) circumvehere (< vehere)	go around, travel around
(concurrō) concurrere (< currere)	hurry together, clash
(condō) condere, -didisse, -ditum	put, hide, found, close
(contremēscō) contremēscere, -muisse	tremble, quake
(digredior) digredī, digressum	depart
(discernō) discernere	distinguish
(ēdō) ēdere, -didisse, -ditum	emit, bring forth, make
(ēmittō) ēmittere (< mittere)	send out, emit, utter
(excēdō) excēdere (< cēdere)	go away, depart
(incīdō) incīdere, -disse, -sum	cut into
(linquō) linquere, līquisse	leave
(pallēscō) pallēscere, -luisse	grow pale
(prōvehō) prōvehere (< vehere)	carry forward, convey
(subdūcō) subdūcere (< dūcere)	draw up, beach, lead off
(vescor) vescī	feed on, eat (+ *abl.*)

-īre

(experior) experīrī, -pertum	try, experience
(potior) potīrī, potītum	get possession of (+ *abl.*)
(sepeliō) -elīre, -elīvisse, -ultum	bury

irregular

(circumeō) circumīre (< īre)	go around/about, outflank
(dēferō) dēferre (< ferre)	carry, bring, report, confer, denounce

ADIECTĪVA

1st/2nd

cavus, -a, -um	hollow
curvus, -a, -um	curved, crooked, bent
extrēmus, -a, -um	outermost, utmost, last

infandus, -a, -um	horrible, unspeakable
longinquus, -a, -um	remote
repentīnus, -a, -um	sudden
stupefactus, -a, -um	amazed, stupefied
trepidus, -a, -um	alarmed, in panic
tumidus, -a, -um	swollen

3rd

horribilis, -e	horrible, terrifying
incrēdibilis, -e	incredible, unbelievable
īnfōrmis, -e	unshapely, ugly
potēns (*gen.* potēntis)	powerful, master(ing)
supplex (*gen.* supplicis)	suppliant

ADVERBIA

adeō	to such a degree, so, too
citō	quickly
interdiū	by day
nīmīrum	without doubt, evidently
noctū	by night, at night
quoad	until
totidem	as many

PRONŌMINA

egomet	I (myself)
quīcumque, -quae, -quod	whoever, whatever, any

ALIA

certiōrem facere	inform
sē cōnferre	go, betake oneself

XXXIX: VNDEQVADRAGESIMVM: KARTHAGO (Vergil)[1]

[Ex Vergiliī Aenēidis librō I, solūtīs versibus]

I. ØRBERG'S INTRODUCTION

It was the will of the gods that Aeneas should found a new kingdom in Italy, but not all the gods were favorably disposed. The goddess Juno hated all Trojans. The Trojan prince Paris, acting as judge in the beauty contest among the three goddesses Juno, Venus, and Minerva, had wounded her by giving the prize to Venus. Furthermore, she knew that the descendants of the Trojans were destined to destroy her favorite city, Carthage. Therefore, she did her utmost to prevent Aeneas and his companions from reaching their goal. It became a hard undertaking—a huge effort (*mōlis*) in Vergil's words—for Aeneas to lay the foundation of the Roman people:

> *Tantae mōlis erat Rōmānam condere gentem!*[2]

When the Trojans leave Sicily, Juno persuades Aeolus, ruler of the winds, to send a violent storm, which scatters the ships and drives them southward to the coast of Africa. Here Aeneas meets his mother, the goddess Venus, who shows him the way to Carthage. This city had just been founded by queen Dido, who had migrated from Tyre (*Tyrus*) in Phoenicia (*Phoenīcē*) after her brother, the king of Tyre, had murdered her husband. Queen Dido gives the exiled Trojans a heroes' welcome in her new city and, deeply infatuated with their gallant commander, she questions him about the fate of Troy and about his adventures. This concludes the first book of the *Aeneid*, which is retold in this chapter.

---

1. For an explanation of the line number references convention, see p. xxvi.
2. *Tantae mōlis* is *genetīvus quālitātis*, genitive of description (Caps. XIX, XXXVI).

II. Auxilia Legendī

Iūnō: 1–26

3:      *Iūnō…dīlēxisse dīcitur*: nominative and accusative with passive verb (Cap. XIII)

6:      *ōlim*: can refer to the present as well as the past: "at some time."

7–11:   Core of sentence: (Juno) *Trōiānōs ā Latiō arcēbat*. This core is introduced by a subordinate clause: (Juno) *nōndum oblīta erat causam* (*īrae ac dolōris*). Although there are no subordinating conjunctions, the two participles modifying the implied subject supply the subordination: (*id*) *metuēns* and *memor* (*veteris bellī*)—i.e., because she was afraid and mindful of the war (genitive with verbs of remembering and forgetting, Caps. XXV, XXXII). A relative clause (*quod ad Trōiam prō cārīs Argīs gesserat*) modifies *veteris bellī*; *causam īrae ac dolōris* (the direct object) is in apposition to *iūdicium Paridis* (the judgment of Paris).

16–18: *Mēne…posse? Nōnne…scelus?*: These reported questions are in the accusative and infinitive construction (like regular indirect statement) because they are rhetorical; that is, Juno isn't really asking a question. Rhetorical questions in indirect discourse use the accusative and infinitive construction; genuine questions in indirect discourse go into the subjunctive according to sequence of tense.

19:     *dignus* + ablative (Cap. XIX).

20–22: Although Latin word order is flexible, it is not random. Note how the words that go with the participle are grouped with it: *Tālia animō incēnsō sēcum cōgitāns*. Often in a Latin sentence, you have to be patient and keep reading to find the word that you might expect to come first in English.

26:     *formā pulcherrimam*: ablative of respect; so too at line 193.

Tempestās: 27–90

28:     *ubi haec audīvit*: "when…" (Cap. XXXVII).

35:     *quibus*: dative with *licuit*.

36–37: *Utinam…effūdissem*: past contrafactual wish (Cap. XXXIII).

41–43: *trēs…trēs…ūnam*: all with *nāvēs* understood; *in saxa latentia*: "onto hidden rocks."

44:         *in puppim*: pure *i*-stem (Cap. XVI).

56:         *dictō citius*: "faster than you could say it."

60:         *quibus*: ablative of means with *scopulōs* as antecedent; we might say every wave is broken *on* the rocks.

65:         *cibō*: ablative with *egentēs*.

77:         *ignārī…malōrum*: objective genitive (Cap. XXV).

78:         *graviōra*: object of the vocative *passī*.

82:         *mittite*: for *omittite*: "send away," "let go of."

83:         *forsan = fors (sit) an: fors* in this expression ("it might happen that" + subjunctive[3]) is used adverbially; *et = etiam*: "even," "also."

87:         *māximīs cūrīs*: ablative of cause with *aeger*; *vultū*: "with his (facial) expression."

90:         *dubiī utrum…crēdant*: indirect question (Cap. XIX).

Venus genetrīx: 91–156

94:         *quaerere quī hominēs incolerent*: indirect question (Cap. XIX).

96:         *cui*: dative with *obviam iit* ("whom she went to meet"); remember forms of *quī* at the beginning of a sentence = *et is*; therefore, *cui = et eī* (Cap. XXV).

101:        *quam tē appellem?*: deliberative subjunctive: "how should I address you"—Aeneas can see by her appearance that she is no ordinary mortal, perhaps not mortal at all (Cap. XIX).

103:        *forsitan ipsa Diāna sīs*: "perhaps you are Diana herself." For *forsitan*, see note on line 83.

104:        *sīs nōbīs fēlix et doceās…*: hortatory subjunctive (Cap. XXX); the hortatory subjunctive in the 2nd person ("please be… please teach us") is not common but is found in poetry and prohibitions (*nē* + perfect subjunctive).[4]

109–111:   *tālī honōre…dignam: dignus, -a, -um* + ablative of respect (Cap. XIX); *nōbīs mōs est…gestāre et…vēnārī: mōs est* can be followed by the infinitive, in addition to *ut* + subjunctive (Cap. XLIV; Cap. XXXVII, note to lines 6–7).

---

3. In poetry and in later Latin, *forsitan* and *forsan* can take the indicative.

4. 2nd person hortatory subjunctive is also found with indefinite subjects and in early Latin.

118:      *multa simulāns*: "feigning many things (to be true which aren't)" (*simulāre*: pretend something *is* which *is not*; *dissimulāre*: pretend that something *is not* which *is*).

122:      *suāsit ut...excēderet*: indirect command (Cap. XXVII).

128:      *opēs, -um* (f. pl.): resources, wealth (Cap. XXXIV).

133–135:   *Ō dea, sī ā prīmā orīgine repetēns labōrēs nostrōs nārrem, ante vesperam fīnem nōn faciam!*: ideal ("should-would") condition (Cap. XXXIII, XLI).

137–138:   *sum pius Aenēās*: *pius* means "dutiful," one distinguished by *pietās*, "dutiful conduct"; while it has religious overtones (dutiful conduct to the gods), it is also secular and includes conduct to others and to the state.

144:      *vidēris*: "you seem" + nominative and infinitive; *quī...advēneris*: perfect subjunctive in a relative causal clause ("because").

151:      *quid*: "why."

152:      *dextrās*: sc. *manūs*.

154:      *nē quis...posset*: negative purpose clause (Cap. XXVIII).

Dīdō rēgīna: 157–268

167:      *mīrābile dictū*: *dictū* is ablative (respect) of the supine (Cap. XXII).

171–172:   *rēbus suīs...cōnfīdere*: compound intransitive verb with the dative (Cap. XXXVII).

176:      *nostrī labōris*: genitive with *plēna*.

177:      *En*: interjection "look, there is Priam"; *laudī*: dative of possession; *sunt...sua praemia laudī*: "renown/glory has its own rewards."

186:      *aurō*: ablative of price (Cap. VIII).

189:      *manūs inermēs*: *inermis* = *sine armīs*.

195–196:   *Quālis...tālis*: a simile: "just like...so too."

199–200:   *quōsdam sociōs*: *quīdam*: certain companions (Cap. XXVIII).

204–205:   *tē ōrāmus nē*: indirect command; *nōn vēnimus ut*: purpose clause.

206:	*victīs*: dative of possession.
209:	*nostrum*: partitive genitive with *paucōs*.
210:	*quō*: ablative of comparison with *iūstior* (Cap. XXIV).
211–213:	mixed condition: the protasis (*quem sī dī vīvum servant*) is present subjunctive ideal ("should"), while the double apodosis (*referet, nec paenitēbit)* is future indicative ("more vivid").
219:	*Quis genus Aenĕadum, quis Trōiae nesciat urbem?* ("Who would not know the family of the sons of Aeneas, who would not know the city of Troy?"): rhetorical question (the answer to "who doesn't know" is "no one"), part of the potential subjunctive (Cap. XLI).
221:	*adeō*: modifies *obtūnsa*.
227–228:	*utinam…afforet*: see footnote 4 in this chapter and Cap. XLIII.
237:	*Aenēās…deō similis*: *similis* takes either the dative, as here, or the genitive (XLII.327–328).
240–244:	Reading help: vocative (*Ō rēgīna*) followed by two relative clauses, "you who" (*quae sola…miserāta es, quae…recipis*) and the main clause (*grātiās…nōn possumus*) and a wish (*dī… ferant*).
252:	*tēctīs nostrīs*: dative with intransitive *succēdite*.
253–254:	i.e., *similis fortūna voluit mē quoque iactātam cōnsistere hāc terrā.*
255:	*nōn ignāra malī*: objective genitive (Cap. XXV); *miserīs*: dative with intransitive *succurrere*.
256:	*haec memorāns*: *memorāre* sounds like our "remember," but it always involves speech: i.e., "mention," "remind of," "speak about."
263–264:	*praemittit…quī…nūntiet…dūcat*: relative clause of purpose.

Cupīdō: 269–316

270–272:	*cōnsilia…ut Cupīdō…veniat atque…incendat*: noun clause giving the content of Venus's plans (*cōnsilia*); *prō*: "in the place of"; *dictō…pāret*: dative with intransitive *pārēre*; the perfect passive participle *dictō* can be thought of as a condensed clause: "what she has said."

280–281:   *puerō tuendō incenditur*: ablative of means of the gerundive (Caps. XXXI, XXXVI).

304:     *conticuēre = conticuērunt* (Cap. XXXVI).

307–308:   *amor...cognōscere...et...audīre*: complementary infinitives (instead of the objective genitive of the gerund or gerundive) is poetical.

311–314:   *ut Graecī Trōiam īnsidiīs cēpissent atque incendissent, ut ipse cum patre et fīliō ex urbe flagrantī fūgisset et fātō pulsus per maria errāvisset*: *ut* = how; both *ut* clauses are indirect questions subordinate to *nārrāvit quae ipse vīderat* and are thus in the subjunctive according to sequence of tense.

III. Vocābula

Nōmina

1st

caterva, -ae	band, troop, crowd
hostia, -ae	sacrificial animal
industria, -ae	hard work, industry
īnsidiae, -ārum (*pl.*)	ambush, plot, wiles
ministra, -ae	female servant
nebula, -ae	mist, fog
praeda, -ae	booty, prey
procella, -ae	violent wind, gale
purpura, -ae	purple
rēgīna, -ae	queen
superbia, -ae	arrogance, pride

2nd

Āfricus, -ī	southwest wind
aper, aprī	wild boar
Auster, -trī	south wind
cervus, -ī	stag, deer
Eurus, -ī	southeast wind
fundāmentum, -ī	foundation
iūdicium, -ī	judgment, trial, court
pontus, -ī	sea

scēptrum, -ī	scepter
solium, -ī	throne
thēsaurus, -ī	treasure, treasury
torus, -ī	bed, couch
vadum, -ī	ford, shallows

3rd

Aquilō, -ōnis (*m.*)	north (northeast) wind
dapēs, -um (*f. pl.*)	feast, meal, food
dēcor, -ōris (*m.*)	beauty, grace
discrīmen, -inis (*n.*)	distinction, grave danger
error, -ōris (*m.*)	wandering, error
fax, facis (*f.*)	torch
fūnus, -eris (*n.*)	funeral, death
honōs/honor, -ōris (*m.*)	honor, high office
quiēs, -ētis (*f.*)	rest, repose, sleep
rūpēs, -is (*f.*)	crag, rock
sīdus, -eris (*n.*)	star, heavenly body
sūs, -suis (*m./f.*)	pig
tridēns, -entis (*m.*)	trident
vertex, -icis (*m.*)	whirlpool, peak, pole

5th

rabiēs, -ēī	rage, fury

VERBA

-āre

(apparō) apparāre	prepare, arrange
(bellō) bellāre	wage war, fight
(cēlō) cēlāre	conceal (from)
(dūrō) dūrāre	harden, hold out, last
(explōrō) explōrāre	reconnoiter, investigate
(gestō) gestāre	carry
(incūsō) incūsāre	reproach, accuse
(īnstō) īnstāre	press, urge, insist
(lībō) lībāre	make a libation, pour
(lūstrō) lūstrāre	irradiate, purify, survey

(miseror) miserārī	feel sorry for, pity
(nō) nāre	swim
(nūdō) nūdāre	bare, leave unprotected
(onerō) onerāre	load
(sēdō) sēdāre	allay, appease, calm
(simulō) simulāre	imitate, copy, pretend
(temptō) temptāre	try (to influence), attack
(vēnor) vēnārī	go hunting, hunt
(versō) versāre	turn over, ponder

-ēre

(aboleō) abolēre, -lēvisse, -litum	efface, obliterate
(arceō) arcēre, arcuisse, arctum	keep away
(immineō) imminēre (< minēre)	overhang, be imminent
(paeniteō) paenitēre, paenituisse	regret, repent
(pendeō) pendēre, pependisse	hang
(rigeō) rigēre	be stiff

-ere

(abripiō) abripere (< rapere)	drag away, carry off
(addūcō) addūcere (< dūcere)	lead, bring (to)
(appellō) appellere (< pellere)	drive, bring (to)
(circumagō) circumagere (< agere)	cause to turn around
(circumfundō) circumfundere (< fundere)	pour, spread around
(colligō) colligere (< legere)	gather, collect
(compellō) compellere (< pellere)	drive together, compel
(conticēscō) conticēscere, conticuisse	fall silent
(disiciō) disicere, disiēcisse, disiectum	scatter, break up
(dispellō) dispellere (< pellere)	drive apart
(ēlūdō) ēlūdere, ēlūsisse, ēlūsum	deceive, mock
(gignō) gignere, genuisse, genitum	beget, create, bear
(gradior) gradī, gressum	walk, proceed
(impellō) impellere (< pellere)	strike, drive, compel

(incēdō) incēdere (< cēdere)	walk, advance, occur
(obstupēscō) obstupēscere, obstupuisse	be stunned/astounded
(pingō) pingere, pinxisse, pictum	paint, embroider
(praemittō) praemittere (< mittere)	send in advance
(resurgō) resurgere (< surgere)	rise again, be restored
(scandō) scandere, scandisse, scansum	climb, mount
(succēdō) succēdere (< cēdere)	enter, succeed, follow
(succurō) succurrere (< currere)	(run to) help
(volvō) volvere, voluisse, volutum	roll, turn (over), ponder

-īre

(dēveniō) dēvenīre (< venīre)	come, arrive
(feriō) ferīre	strike, hit, kill
(ōrdior) ōrdīrī, orsum	begin (to speak)

ADIECTĪVA

1st/2nd

bellicōsus, -a, -um	warlike
fortūnātus, -a, -um	fortunate
impius, -a, -um	impious
īnscius, -a, -um	not knowing, unaware
intentus, -a, -um	intent, attentive
obtūnsus, -a, -um	blunt, dull

3rd

crēber, -ris, -re (-bra, -brum)	frequent, numerous
egēns (*gen.* egentis)	poor, needy
memor (*gen.* memoris)	mindful, reminding

PRONŌMINA

vōsmet	you, yourselves

ADVERBIA

clam	secretly
forsan	perhaps, maybe
obviam	(go to) meet, oppose, in the way
paulātim	little by little, gradually
saltem	at least, anyhow

XL: QVADRAGESIMVM:
INFELIX DIDO (Vergil)[1]

[Ex Vergiliī Aenēidis librō IV, solūtīs versibus]

I. ØRBERG'S INTRODUCTION

The main focus of Book IV of the *Aeneid* is the love story of Dido and Aeneas. After the death of her husband, Dido swore never to contract a new marriage (*coniugium*), but now she tells her sister Anna that she has fallen in love with her noble guest. Anna urges her to forget her dead husband and obey the dictates of love. During a hunting expedition, Dido and Aeneas seek shelter from the storm in a cave, where they are united by the design of Juno. The queen begins a relationship with Aeneas that she calls *coniugium*.

The rumor of this affair spreads rapidly among men and gods. When Jupiter hears that Aeneas is about to forget his divine mission, he sends Mercury to order him to sail: "*Nāviget!*"[2] Aeneas makes secret preparations for departure, but Dido suspects mischief and begs him not to leave her. When he tries to explain that he is destined by the gods to seek a new homeland in Italy, she flies into a rage, and after violent reproaches and threats, she retires without waiting for his reply. Aeneas makes his ships ready for sea, and when neither threats nor entreaties have any effect, Dido sees no alternative but to seek death. She tells her sister to build a pyre in the palace yard on the pretext of wanting to burn everything that reminds her of her faithless husband: his weapons, his clothes, his portrait, and their conjugal bed. By night, while Dido lies sleepless in her palace, Mercury orders Aeneas to put to sea at once, and at dawn the queen sees the Trojan fleet leaving the harbor. She heaps reproaches on herself and invokes the Furies to take revenge on Aeneas and his descendants. Then she mounts the pyre, draws Aeneas' sword, and throws herself on it. Her last words on the pyre, taken from the close of the fourth book (verses 651–660), can be read on p. 80.

---

1. For an explanation of the line number references convention, see p. xxvi.

2. Jussive subjunctive (Cap. XXXI).

Books V and VI of the *Aeneid* are here treated summarily. From Carthage the Trojans sail to Sicily, and Aeneas celebrates the anniversary of his father's death with sacrifices and games. Meanwhile the Trojan women set fire to the ships, but a rainstorm sent by Jupiter extinguishes the fire. Aeneas punishes the women by leaving most of them in Sicily when he sails on to Italy. In Campania he visits the Sibyl at Cumae. She takes him to the underworld, where he sees his dead father, who shows him the great Romans of the future from Romulus to Augustus. He ends with the famous words about the destiny of the Roman as ruler of the world:

> *Tū regere imperiō populōs, Rōmāne, mementō.*[3]
> *Hae tibi erunt artēs: pācisque impōnere mōrem,*
> *parcere subiectīs et dēbellāre superbōs.*

Livy's history of Rome, *ab Urbe Conditā*, picks up the narrative of Roman history in the next chapter with Aeneas' struggles in Italy, treated by Vergil in Books VII–XII of the *Aeneid*.

II. Auxilia Legendī

Flamma amōris: 1–45

4:          *fīxa*: with both *vultus* and *verba*.

8:          *nōn dubitō quīn*: see grammar section above.

10–12:   *mihi, nūllī virō*: datives (with *certum* and *iungere*, respectively); *coniugiō*: ablative; *esset…potuī*: present contrafactual condition with a modal verb in the apodosis (see on *posse* in grammar section above).

12:         *huius ūnīus*: genitive with *amōrī*, which is dative with the compound verb *succumbere*.

15–16:   *velim*: subjunctive in a wish, followed by the content of the wish (*dēvoret, percutiat*) without *ut* (see grammar section for Cap. LV).

19:         *habeat*: jussive subjunctive (Cap. XXXI).

25:         *quī hostēs nōs cingant*: indirect question (Cap. XXIX).

35–36:   *ante omnēs Iūnōnī, cui coniugia cūrae sunt*: "for whom marriages are an object of care" (double dative, Cap. XXXVI).

---

3. *Mementō* is the future imperative of *meminisse* (Cap. XXVI).

Fāma vēlōx: 46–69

47:	*vēnātum īre parat*: supine ("they prepare to go hunting").
58:	*malōrum atque mortis*: genitives with *causā*; *rēgīnae*: dative.
62:	*quā*: ablative of comparison with *vēlōcius* (Cap. XXIV).
66:	*variō sermōne*: ablative with *complēbat* (Cap. XXXVII).
68:	*rēgnī*: genitive with *oblītōs* (Caps. XXV, XXXII).

Nūntius deōrum: 70–164

73–74:	*Karthāgine*: locative (see summary above).
75:	*ideō*: "for that reason"; *nōn ideō…sed ut*: structure markers for the sentence.
79:	*quā spē*: ablative of cause.
80:	*Nāviget*: jussive subjunctive (Cap. XXXI).
84–85:	*Erat illī ēnsis*: dative of possession (Cap. XII).
87:	*uxōrius*: this adjective, meaning "of or belonging to a wife," suggests a man too fond of his wife, not a compliment in Latin.
88:	*rēgnī rērumque tuārum*: genitive with *oblītōs* (Caps. XXV, XXXII).
96–97:	*Heu, quid agat?…audeat?…ōrdiātur?*: deliberative questions (Cap. XXIX).
101:	*Quī = Et eī* (Cap. XXV).
106:	*dissimulāre*: see note 118 for Cap. XXXIX.
107:	*dextrā (manus) data*: i.e., as a pledge.
111:	*sī quid bene dē tē meruī*: "If I have deserved well from you in any way"; *bene/male merēre* (and *merērī*): "to earn favor/disfavor by one's behavior."
112:	*miserēre meī*: *miserērī* + genitive.
116–117:	*dum…dēstruat…abdūcat*: anticipatory subjunctives with *dum*.
117–119:	*Sī…habērem, sī quī…lūderet…vidērer*: present contrafactual condition (Cap. XXXIII).
125:	*animam dūcere*: "to draw breath."

132–133:   *deum…intrantem.*

134:     *dēsine*: with the ablative of separation *tuīs querēllīs* and the complementary infinitive *incendere.*

138:     *perfide*: vocative (as is *improbe*, l.146).

142–143:   *Itane vērō?*: sarcastic; *Putāsne eam rem dīs superīs cūrae esse?*: double dative (Cap. XXXVI).

159–160:   *ōrat* with a double construction: + accusative (*coniugium*) and two indirect commands (*neque ut…careat, sed ut…exspectet*).

162–163:   *dum…doceat*: anticipatory subjunctive.

Rogus Dīdōnis: 165–268

167:     *taedet eam vitae*: see above on impersonal verbs.

176–177:   *ratiōnem quae…reddat..aut…solvat*: descriptive relative clause (see grammar section above).

178:     *curīs exsolvere*: ablative of separation.

181:     *quō periī*: *quō* is the instrumental ablative of the relative pronoun referring to *lectum iugālem*: Dido blames her present state on her conjugal relationship with Aeneas.

188:     *crīnibus passīs*: ablative absolute, *passīs* from *pandere* ("spread out," "unkempt")—here as a part of her ritual as a priestess.

193:     *ovantēs*: the marginal note in your text explains this participle as "*superbē gaudēre*," and from Dido's perspective, that is a good interpretation. The participle of *ovāre*, however, means "exulting, joyful, triumphant" and does not in itself carry the sense of arrogance.

197:     *quīn morere*: *quīn* plus the imperative (see grammar section above).

202:     *deinde*: the mark (∩) over *ei* shows that these two vowels should be taken together (synizesis).

204:     *illa*: i.e., Dido.

206–208:   future condition.

209–210:   *Varium et mūtābile semper fēmina*: the qualifiers (*varium, mūtābile*) are neuter because he is speaking of women as a category. He does not mean Dido specifically, but all women— "Always changing and inconstant is woman."

210:	*noctī ātrae*: dative with the compound verb *immiscēre* (Cap. VIII).
214:	*ovantēs*: see note on l.193.
219:	*ex altā turrī*: pure *i*-stem (Cap. XVI).
221:	*advena, -ae*: one of the few masculine nouns of the first declension, like *agricola, poēta, nauta, incola, pīrāta*.
226:	*ēn*: interjection: "Behold! Look!"
229–230:	*Etiam sī pugnae fortūna dubia fuisset, quem metuī moritūra*: past contrafactual protasis (*sī...fuisset*) followed by an indicative rhetorical question, the answer to which is "no one" (see Cap. XLI).
230–233:	*Facēs in castra tulissem, carīnās flammīs dēlēvissem, filium et patrem cum genere exstīnxissem—et ipsa mēmet super eōs iēcissem*: pluperfect subjunctive in past potentials (Cap. XLI): "I could have brought...destroyed...annihilated...thrown."
238–240:	*implōret...videat...fruātur...cadat*: subjunctive of wish (see grammar section above).
243–244:	*sit...exoriātur*: jussive subjunctives (Cap. XXXI).
245–246:	*aliquis...quī...persequātur*: descriptive relative clause (Cap. XXXIX).
252:	*morāta < morārī* (Cap. XXXVIII).
256:	easier order: *vīxī et perēgī cursum quem fortūna dēderat*.
259:	*virum = marītum meum*.
260–261:	*sī...carīnae*: contrafactual condition (Cap. XXXIII).
264:	*ferrō collāpsam*: "having fallen on the sword."
266–268:	*nōn aliter quam sī...capta essent...volverentur*: conditional clause of comparison in secondary sequence.

Excerpta Aenēidis: 269–299

272–273:	*quae causa tantum ignem accenderit...*: indirect question.
281–282:	*cum...longī errōris taedēret*: see grammar section above on impersonal verbs.
284:	*quamquam...factī suī paenitēbat*: see grammar section above on impersonal verbs.

III. Vocābula

Nōmina

1st

advena, -ae	immigrant, foreigner
aula, -ae	palace
capra, -ae	goat
carīna, -ae	keel, ship
exuviae, -ārum (*pl.*)	clothing, armor
famula, -ae	servant girl, maid
plūma, -ae	feather
potentia, -ae	power
querēlla, -ae	complaint
spēlunca, -ae	cave, grotto
vāgīna, -ae	sheath
venia, -ae	favor, leave, pardon

2nd

astrum, -ī	star, constellation
coniugium, -ī	marriage
cōnūbium, -ī	marriage, intermarriage
dīvum, -ī	the open sky
iaculum, -ī	throwing-spear, javelin
iussum, -ī	command, order
mandātum, -ī	order
praedictum, -ī	prediction, prophecy
rogus, -ī	funeral pyre
thalamus, -ī	inner room, bedroom, marriage bed
vīsum, -ī	sight

3rd

aethēr, -eris (*m.*)	heaven, upper air, ether
altāria, -ium (*n. pl.*)	altar
ārdor, -ōris (*m.*)	burning, fire, ardor
cinis, -eris (*m.*)	ashes
cubīle, -is (*n.*)	bed, couch
cupīdō, -inis (*f.*)	desire, passion

fortitūdō, -inis (*f.*)	strength, bravery
fulmen, -inis (*n.*)	flash of lightning
grandō, -inis (*f.*)	hail
tigris, -is (*m./f.*)	tiger
ultrīx, -īcis (*f.*)	avenging

4th

amictus, -ūs	mantle, cloak
discessus, -ūs	departure
luxus, -ūs	extravagance, luxury
ūsus, -ūs	use, practice, usage

5th

effigiēs, -ēī	likeness, portrait

irregular

nefās	impious act, crime

VERBA

-āre

(advocō) advocāre	call, summon
(circumstō) circumstāre, circumstetisse	stand around, surround
(cūnctor) cūnctārī	hesitate
(dēbellō) dēbellāre	finish the war, subdue
(dissimulō) dissimulāre	conceal
(festīnō) festīnāre	hasten, hurry
(implōrō) implōrāre	beseech, implore
(īnflammō) īnflammāre	kindle, inflame
(mandō) mandāre	assign, order
(obstō) obstāre, obstitisse, obstitum	stand in the way
(ostentō) ostentāre	display ostentatiously
(ovō) ovāre	exult, rejoice
(reputō) reputāre	think over, reflect on
(sōlor) sōlārī, sōlātum	comfort

-ēre

(admoneō) admonēre (< monēre)	remind, advise, urge
(admoveō) admovēre (< movēre)	move near, put to
(immisceō) immiscēre, -scuisse, -xtum	mingle, merge (into)
(misereor) miserērī, miseritum	feel pity for
(taedet) taedēre, -duisse, -sum	be tired/sick of

-ere

(abrumpō) abrumpere (< rumpō)	break off
(concumbō) concumbere, -uisse, -itum	sleep (with)
(ēvānēscō) ēvānēscere, -uisse	vanish, disappear
(excipō) excipere (< capere)	receive, catch
(exsequor) exsequī (< sequī)	pursue, go on, execute
(exsolvō) exsolvere (< solvere)	set free, release
(fervō) fervere, feruisse	boil, seethe, swarm[4]
(furō) furere, furuisse	be mad, rage, rave
(illūdō) illūdere, -ūsisse, -ūsum	make a game of, fool
(incumbō) incumbere, -uisse, itum	lie down on
(īnsequor) īnsequī (< sequī)	follow, pursue
(nectō) nectere, nexuisse, nexum	attach
(obmūtēscō) obmūtēscere, -tuisse	become speechless
(peragō) peragere (< agere)	carry out, complete
(refellō) refellere, refellisse	refute
(sēcēdō) sēcēdere (< cēdere)	withdraw, rebel
(struō) struere, struxisse, structum	arrange, contrive, devise
(subiciō) subicere, -iēcisse, -iectum	put under, subject, add
(succumbō) succumbere, -uisse, -itum	yield, submit
(suscipiō) suscipere (< capere)	take up, receive, adopt

---

4. The more common form of this verb is *ferveō, fervēre, ferbuisse*; *fervĕre* (3rd declension) is less frequent. Here, it helps with the meter of the line.

-īre

    (praesentiō) praesentīre (< sentiō)   have a presentiment of

ADIECTĪVA

1st/2nd

ālātus, -a, -um	winged
attonitus, -a, -um	stunned, stupefied
dīlēctus, -a, -um	beloved, dear
hībernus, -a, -um	winter-, of winter
īnfēnsus, -a, -um	hostile
īnsepultus, -a, -um	unburied
invictus, -a, -um	unconquered, invincible
moribundus, -a, -um	dying
perfidus, -a, -um	faithless, treacherous
placidus, -a, -um	quiet, calm, gentle
placitus, -a, -um	pleasing, agreeable
sanguineus, -a, -um	bloodstained, bloodshot
uxōrius, -a, -um	attached to one's wife

3rd

dēmens (*gen.* **dēmēntis**)	out of one's mind, mad
iugālis, -e	marriage, conjugal
mūtābilis, -e	changeable
praeceps (*gen.* **praecipitis**)	headlong, precipitous
vigil (*gen.* **vigilis**)	wakeful, watchful

PRONŌMINA

    mēmet   me, myself

ADVERBIA

extemplō	at once
omnīnō	altogether
sponte	of my/his own accord

XLI: VNVM ET QVADRAGESIMVM: ORIGINES (Livy)[1]

[*Ex T. Līviī 'ab Urbe Conditā' librō I.1–7, nōnnūllīs mūtātīs et praetermissīs*]

I. ØRBERG'S INTRODUCTION

This and the following four chapters present the early history of Rome as recorded in the first "book" of the great Roman historian Livy (*Titus Līvius*), who lived in the time of Emperor Augustus (59 BC–AD 17). In 142 "books," Livy treated the history of Rome from the foundation of the city—hence the title of his work *ab Urbe Conditā*—down to his own time. Of this voluminous work, only 35 books have survived. These books cover the earliest period until 293 BC (books I–X), the Second Punic War, 218–201 BC (books XXI–XXX), and the subsequent period until 167 BC (books XXXI–XLV). We know the content of the lost books in broad outline through ancient summaries, called *periochae* (περιοχαί).

Livy's first book deals with the foundation of Rome and the seven Roman kings from *Rōmulus* to *Tarquinius Superbus*, who was expelled from Rome in 509 BC. In Cap. XLI, Livy's prose has been somewhat abridged and simplified, but even here many passages stand unaltered as Livy wrote them 2,000 years ago. In the following chapters, the text gets closer and closer to the original, and from XLV.22, the text is abridged, but otherwise unchanged.

Livy's account has been supplemented with excerpts from Ovid (*Ovidius*), especially from the didactic poem *Fāstī*, in which he goes through the Roman calendar and relates the legends connected with particular dates (e.g., the founding of Rome on April 21st).

What the Romans related about the origin of their city has little to do with reality. Livy is fully aware of this, but his delight in the old legends is unmistakable. In his preface, he says that if any people has the right to trace its origin to the war god Mars (the father of Romulus), it is the Roman people.

---

1. For an explanation of the line number references convention, see p. xxvi.

Livy begins his history with the arrival of Aeneas in Latium. He made peace with king *Latīnus*, who gave him his daughter *Lāvīnia* in marriage. This provoked war with the neighboring king Turnus, who was engaged to marry Lavinia. Turnus allied himself with the Etruscans (*Etrūscī*), but he was defeated by Aeneas. Ascanius, the son of Aeneas, founded the city of Alba Longa and became the first of a line of Alban kings. One of these kings, Numitor, was dethroned by his brother *Amūlius*. When Numitor's daughter Rea Silvia bore twins, Amulius ordered them to be exposed in the Tiber, but the boys, Romulus and Remus, drifted ashore. When they were found, a she-wolf was nursing them. Once grown, they killed Amulius and resolved to found a new city on the Tiber. An omen taken from the observation of the flight of birds (*auspicium*) seemed to favor Romulus, so he founded the city on the Palatine Hill. When Remus ridiculed his brother's work by leaping over the new walls, Romulus killed him. Finally, Livy tells the story of Hercules killing *Cācus* for robbing his cattle. This story explains the origin of the ancient *Āra Māxima* and the worship of the Greek god Hercules (Greek *Hēraklēs*) in Rome (see XXXVI.178–183).

As a supplement to Livy's account of Romulus and Remus, you read the passage in Ovid's *Fāstī* (383–418), in which the poet relates the story of the exposure of the twins and their miraculous rescue.

II. Auxilia Legendī

Trōiānī et Latīnī: 1–48

5–6:	*quibus*: dative with *superesse*; *nihil praeter arma et nāvēs superat*: *nihil* is subject of *superesse* (Cap. XVIII: "survive").
9:	*ad arcendam vim*: *ad* + accusative of gerund/gerundive to express purpose (Caps. XXXIII, XXXVI).
10:	*signum pugnandī*: objective genitive (Cap. XXV).
12–14:	the indirect questions ("*quī mortālēs essent, unde profectī quidve quaerentēs in agrum Laurentem exiissent?*") are introduced by the participle *interrogātus*.
24:	*brevī* = *brevī tempore* (cf. Cap. XXXVI.217).
28:	*molestē patiēns*: both here and at line 152 (*molestē ferret*), the expression approximates our "taking it badly."
28–29:	*advenam sibi praelātum esse*: the accusative and infinitive construction is used in implied indirect statement, which is very common. Turnus declared war because he took it badly (*molestē patiēns*) <u>that</u> a stranger had been preferred to him.

32–34:   *ut...conciliāret*: purpose clause with *utramque...appellāvit*, not result with *ita.*

38–39:   *minimē laetus...orīgine*: ablative of cause (Cap. XXXVI).

41–46:   *Aenēās, quamquam tanta...erat ut...implēvisset*: concessive clause (*quamquam*) introducing a result clause (*tanta...ut... implēvisset*); *opibus*: ablative of respect (Caps. XI, XXXIX).

47:          *quod*: antecedent is *proelium.*

Alba condita: 49–68

52:          *incolume < incolumis, -e*: "unharmed, safe" (Cap. XXXIII).

53–54:   *quis...affirmet*? Potential subjunctive in a rhetorical question; *hicine*: interrogative particle = *hicne.*

61:          *ferē*: adv. "approximately" (Cap. XXXIII).

62–66:   Reading practice: The core of this long sentence is: *opēs Latī-nōrum crēverant. Tantum* provokes the result clause (*ut...ausī sint*); further elaborating the thought is the ablative absolute (*māximē vīctīs Etrūscīs*) and the circumstances under which one might expect the Latins to be threatened—when Aeneas died and Lavinia ruled as regent for Ascanius (*nē morte quidem Aenēae nec deinde inter rēgnum muliebre et Ascaniī pueritiam*).

66–68:   *Pāx ita convēnerat ut Etrūscīs Latīnīsque fluvius Albula, quem nunc Tiberim vocant, fīnis esset*: result clause (Cap. XXXVII).

Rōmulus et Remus: 69–137

74–76:   Supply *ortus est* with all the noun/ablative of source combinations.

84:          *Plūs...vīs potuit: posse* alone means "have ability/power," so "force had more power."

86–88:   *fīliae Rēae Silviae*: dative of disadvantage with *adimit; cum virginem Vestālem eam lēgisset: virginem Vestālem* is predicative: "because he had chosen her *as* a Vestal virgin."

89:          *vī compressa*: i.e., "violated."

100–103:   *Ea adeō mītis fuisse dīcitur ut īnfantibus ūbera praebēret et pāstor rēgius eam linguā lambentem puerōs invēnerit—Faustulus eī nōmen fuit*: result clause.

104:                  For the gerundive (*ēducandōs dedit*), see Cap. XXXVI.

110:                  *impetūs faciēbant*: "to attack" (cf. l.115: *impetūs fierī*).

116–117:   *praedās agere*: *agere* is regularly used for carrying off booty (*praeda*) taken in war.

119–121:   *nam et iussū rēgis īnfantēs expositōs esse sciēbat et tempus quō ipse eōs sustulisset ad id tempus convenīre*: *sciēbat* introduces a double indirect statement; the second (*tempus…ad id tempus convenīre*) contains a subordinate clause (*quō ipse eōs sustulisset*) in which the main verb is subjunctive (see Cap. XXXVI: subordinate clauses in indirect statement have their verbs in the subjunctive according to sequence of tense).

124–127:   *Eōdem tempore Numitor…suspicābatur*: the main clause is actually just a subject, verb, and time marker; *suspicābatur* is completed by an accusative and infinitive in indirect statement (*nepōtēs suōs servātōs esse*); Numitor's reasoning is fleshed out by a *cum* clause (*cum…frātrēs*) and an ablative of means of the gerund with objects (*comparandō…*).

Rōma condita: 138–157

141–143:   *rēgnī*: objective genitive with *cupiditātem*; the indirect question begun by *uter* tells what was at stake in the competition between the brothers (*certāmen ortum est*).

149–150:   *Rōmulō*: dative with *favēre*.

152:                  *molestē ferret*: see note above for line 28.

156:                  *imperiō*: ablative with *potītus est*.

Sacra Herculis īnstitūta: 158–196

162–165:   *Herculēs…bovēs…ēgisse nārrātor ac…fessus…recubuisse*: nominative and infinitive in an indirect statement dependent on a passive verb (Cap. XXXVI); *mīrā speciē*: ablative of description; *nandō*: gerund of *nāre* ("to swim"), ablative of means.

166–167:   *ferōx vīribus*: ablative of respect.

174:                  *forās versa*: turned toward the outside; *forās*: adverb of place to which.

178:                  *Quem* = *Et eum* (Cap. XXV).

183–186:   The sentence is carried forward by the participles: *Evander...
                  arcessītus...intuēns rogitat*; *quī...esset*: indirect question.

189–190:   *dicātum īrī*: future infinitive passive (Cap. XXIII) in an indi-
                  rect statement.

190–191:   *ōlim* means "once, long ago, one day": i.e., refers to future as
                  well as past; *vocet*: subjunctive in a subordinate clause in *ōrātiō
                  oblīqua*.

Gemellī expositī: 197–231

203:              *recūsantēs*: "making an objection against," "being unwilling"
                  (here clearly it does not mean "refuse").

205–206:   i.e., the river Albula, after Tiberinus drowned in it, was called
                  the Tiber.

207:              *vidērēs*: indefinite potential subjunctive (see above).

208:              The apostrophe, or direct address, to the Circus Maximus is a
                  feature of poetry.

211:              *plūs vigōris*: partitive gentive with neuter pronoun; *iste*: i.e., the
                  one that you are carrying, Romulus.

214:              *in vōbīs*: i.e., Romulus and Remus (so too *vestrae orīginis*,
                  l.215).

215–216:   *At sī quis...esset...ferret*: present contrafactual conditions
                  (Cap. XXXIII).

217:              *Ferret..sī māter egēret*: present contrafactual conditions
                  (Cap. XXXIII); *māter* is subject of both clauses.

221:              *vāgiērunt = vāgīvērunt*; *putārēs*: indefinite potential subjunc-
                  tive (see above).

223:              *Sustinet impositōs summā cavus alveus undā = cavus alveus
                  puerōs impositōs summā undā sustinet*: "the hollowed bark
                  bore the boys on the top of the waves."

225:              *silvīs...opācīs*: dative with compound verb *appulsus* (*ad +
                  pellere*).

228:              *quis crēdat*: rhetorical question (see above); *puerīs*: dative with
                  intransitive *nocuisse*.

III. Vocābula

NŌMINA

1st

clāva, -ae	club, cudgel
cōpiae, -ārum (*pl.*)	resources, troops
cūstōdia, -ae	guard, custody, post
lupa, -ae	she-wolf
pueritia, -ae	boyhood, childhood

2nd

armentum, -ī	(herd of) cattle
auspicium, -ī	omen taken from birds
avus, -ī	grandfather
concilium, -ī	assembly, league
līmus, -ī	mud
mātrimōnium, -ī	matrimony, marriage
patruus, -ī	father's brother, uncle
stabulum, -ī	stable

3rd

auctor, -ōris (*m.*)	originator, founder, advocate, guarantor
conditor, -ōris (*m.*)	founder
crūdēlitās, -ātis (*f.*)	cruelty
discrīmen, -inis (*n.*)	distinction, grave danger
facinus, -ōris (*n.*)	deed, act, misdeed
latrō, -ōnis (*m.*)	brigand, robber
linter, -tris (*f./m.*)	small boat, skiff
necessitās, -ātis (*f.*)	need, necessity
nōbilitās, -ātis (*f.*)	renown, nobility, nobles
opēs, -um (*f. pl.*)	resources, wealth, power, influence
ops, -opis (*f.*)	power, aid, assistance
prīmōrēs, -um (*m.pl.*)	leading men, front ranks
societās, -ātis (*f.*)	partnership, alliance
sōlitūdō, -inis (*f.*)	loneliness, lonely place
stirps, -pis (*f.*)	origin, stock, offspring

vigor, -ōris (*m.*)	vigor
virginitās, -ātis (*f.*)	virginity
vultur, -is (*m.*)	vulture

4th

adventus, -ūs	arrival
partus, -ūs	(giving) birth
rītus, -ūs	rite, ceremony
saltus, -ūs	wooded hills; narrow pass
situs, -ūs	position, situation
vāgītus, -ūs	wail, squall

VERBA

-āre

(auspicor) auspicārī	take the auspices
(conciliō) conciliāre	win over
(dicō) dicāre	dedicate
(ēvocō) ēvocāre	call out, summon
(grātulor) grātulārī	congratulate
(lēgō) lēgāre	bequeath, send, delegate
(prōcreō) prōcreāre	engender, beget
(suspicor) suspicārī	guess, suspect
(trepidō) trepidāre	be in panic, tremble

-ēre

(praebeō) praebēre, -uisse, -itum	present, offer, show
(spondeō) spondēre, spondisse, spōnsum	pledge, promise, betroth
(tumeō) tumēre, -uisse, -itum	swell

-ere

(abdō) abdere, -didisse, -ditum	hide
(abigō) abigere, -ēgisse, -āctum (< agere)	drive away
(adipīscor) adipīscī, adeptum	obtain
(adolēscō) adolēscere, adolēvisse, adultum	grow up

(arguō) arguere, -uisse, -ūtum	reveal, affirm, accuse
(comprimō) comprimere (< premere)	compress, crush, suppress, rape
(cōnfundō) cōnfundere (< fundere)	mingle, upset, confuse
(cōnsulō) cōnsulere, -suluisse, -sultum	consult, take counsel
(dēdō) dēdere (< dare)	give up, devote
(dēficiō) dēficere (< facere)	fail, sink, wane, defect
(diffīdō) diffīdere, -īsum	distrust, despair of
(īcō) īcere, -īcisse, -ictum	strike, make, conclude
(īnstituō) īnstituere, -tuisse, -tūtum	set up, establish, start, appoint, train, instruct
(interimō) interimere (< emere)	kill
(lambō) lambere, -isse, -itum	lick, wash
(opprimō) opprimere (< premere)	press on, overwhelm

-īre

(intereō) interīre (< īre)	die, perish
(mūgiō) mūgīre, -īvisse, -ītum	low, bellow
(nūtriō) nūtrīre, -īvisse, -ītum	feed, suckle
(sitiō) sitīre, -īvisse, -ītum	be thirsty
(trānsiliō) trānsilīre, -iluisse, -ītum	jump over

irregular

(īnferō) īnferre (< ferre)	bring (in), cause, inflict

ADIECTĪVA

1st/2nd

ambō, -ae, -ō	both, the two
eximius, -a, -um	choice, outstanding
fētus, -a, -um	having young
fīnitimus, -a, -um	adjacent, neighboring
immātūrus, -a, -um	unripe, premature
immēnsus, -a, -um	immeasurable, endless
lacrimōsus, -a, -um	tearful, sad

opācus, -a, -um	shady
opulentus, -a, -um	wealthy, powerful
orbus, -a, -um	childless, orphaned
prosperus, -a, -um	successful, favorable
sacer, -ra, -rum	holy, sacred
siccus, -a, -um	dry
ūdus, -a, -um	wet
vetustus, -a, -um	ancient, old

3rd

duplex, -icis	double
hostīlis, -e	enemy, hostile
mītis, -e	gentle, mild, tame
muliebris, -e	of a woman
pūbēs, (*gen.* puberis)	mature, grown up (*m. pl.* adults)
puerīlis, -e	of children
sēgnis, -e	slothful, inactive
servīlis, -e	of a slave, servile
virīlis, -e	male, manly

ADVERBIA

falsō	false, deceived, wrong
nusquam	nowhere
ubicumque	wherever

ALIA

iussū[2]	by order of

---

2.   From *iussus, iussū* (m.) is a noun used only in the ablative singular.

XLII: ALTERVM ET QVADRAGESIMVM: BELLVM ET PAX (Livy)[1]

[Ex T. Līviī 'ab Urbe Conditā' librō I. 8–21, nōnnūllīs mūtātīs et praetermissīs]

I. ØRBERG'S INTRODUCTION

Once Romulus had secured his reign with laws and symbols of power, he increased the number of inhabitants by opening a place of refuge, called an *asȳlum* (from Greek ἄσυλον, sanctuary), for all kinds of immigrants. There was an influx of men of low rank, slaves as well as free men. The next problem for king Romulus was how to get wives for his new inhabitants. The neighboring peoples were contemptuous of the Romans and banned intermarriage (*cōnūbium*) with them. But Romulus devised a ploy: he invited Rome's neighbors with their families to games in Rome, and in the middle of the show, he gave a sign to the Roman men to carry off all the marriageable young women.

This outrage brought about Rome's first war with her neighbors. In the ensuing battle with the *Caenīnēnsēs*, Romulus distinguished himself by killing the enemy king and carrying his armor to the Capitol as an offering to *Iuppiter Feretrius*, to whom he vowed a temple. His most dangerous opponents, however, were the Sabines (*Sabīnī*). With the help of the treacherous *Tarpēia*, they managed to take the Capitol, the citadel of Rome, and from there they put the Roman army to flight; but Jupiter stayed the flight of the Romans when Romulus vowed him a temple at the foot of the Palatine Hill—the *templum Iovis Statōris* (XXXVI.172; *Stator* comes from *sistere* and can mean "Stayer").

During the renewed struggle, the Sabine women threw themselves between the opposing armies and persuaded their fathers and husbands to make peace. Romulus entered into an alliance with *Tatius*, the king of the Sabines. After a few years of joint rule, king Tatius was killed in a riot. This caused Romulus little regret. He also waged successful wars with *Fidēnae*, whose army he ambushed, and with the Etruscan city of *Vēiī*.

---

1. For an explanation of the line number references convention, see p. xxvi.

Legend has it that Romulus suddenly disappeared in a violent storm while he was mustering his troops in the *Campus Mārtius*. The senators told the suspicious soldiers that he had been carried off to heaven and deified.

After a short *interrēgnum*, the Sabine *Numa Pompilius* was chosen king of Rome, and his election was confirmed by *auspicia*. Unlike his warlike predecessor, Numa entered upon peaceful reforms. He built the shrine of Janus (*Iānus*) and had it closed as a sign that Rome was at peace (XXXVI.99–107). He rectified the calendar, giving the year twelve months instead of ten, and organized the worship of the gods.

In the first book of his poem *Ars amātōria*, Ovid tells the story of the Rape of the Sabine Women (as an illustration of what a dangerous place the theater is for young women). And in the *Fāstī* (III.215–228), Ovid tells us how the same women, clasping their babies, rush between the warring Romans and Sabines.

Livy makes use of the legendary history of Rome in his attempt to explain the origin of a great many political and religious institutions. He recounts that Romulus established a bodyguard of twelve *līctōrēs* as an explanation of the attendants who preceded the Roman consuls and other magistrates bearing the symbols of power, *fascēs* (rods) and *secūrēs* (axes). Romulus is also said to have instituted the offering of *spolia opīma* ("choice spoils"), i.e., the spoils taken by a Roman general from the enemy leader he had killed in battle, to *Iuppiter Feretrius* at his temple on the Capitoline. Several religious institutions are ascribed to the pious king Numa. An augur confirmed his election by *auspicia*, divination from the observation of birds; he founded new priesthoods, including the *virginēs Vestālēs*, priestesses of Vesta (XXXVI.111–115), the *Saliī*, priests of Mars, and the *pontificēs*, who were in control of religious matters in Rome. The term *interrēgnum* was still used in Republican times about a period when Rome had no consuls.

II. AUXILIA LEGENDĪ

Fascēs et secūrēs: insignia imperiī: 1–19

7–8:   *quī fascēs et secūrēs gerentēs rēgī anteīrent*: *rēgī* is dative with the compound verb *anteīrent* (Cap. XXXVII).

Sabīnae raptae: 20–55

21:      *cuilibet* < *quīlibet*: see indefinite pronouns (above).

27–28:   *tantam...mōlem*: a *mōles* is literally a huge, heavy mass, but it is used metaphorically (as here) for a huge power, great might.

29–30:   The indirect question (*num...aperuissent*) proceeds from the ablative absolute (*plērīsque rogitantibus*). Only women of ill repute would be in need of asylum, hence the Romans' anger (*aegrē passī sunt*).

30–31:   *Id Rōmānī iuvenēs aegrē passī sunt*: cf. *molestē patī* (Cap. XLI).

34–35:   *studiō etiam videndae novae urbis*: objective genitive of the gerundive with *studiō* (Cap. XXV).

39:              *brevī = brevī tempore* (Cap. XXV).

40:              *eō*: "to that place" (adv.).

50–51:   *quō* is ablative of comparison; the antecedent is *līberōrum* ("children, a thing than which nothing is dearer").

53–54:   *ad hoc*: adverbial: moreover, in addition.

Spolia opīma: 56–97

64:              *lentē agere*: "act indifferently, slowly."

68:              *sed iīs obviam it*: adverb *obviam* ("in the way"), with a verb of motion (Cap. XXXIX).

78:              *Iuppiter Feretrī*: vocative.

82:              *bīna*: distributive adjective (Cap. XXX) with *spolia opīma*; *tantum*: adverb.

83–84:   Note Latin's fondness for "sandwiching" modifying words: *fortūna id decus adipīscendī*: the gerund (*adipīscendī*) is genitive depending on the noun *fortūna*, and the object of *adipīscendī* lies between them (*adipīscī, adeptum esse*: "arrive at, get, gain").

91–92:   *ōrant* introduces an indirect command (*ut...accipiat*) followed by an indirect statement. What they said was "*dā veniam*" (becomes indirect command); *ita rēs Rōmānae coalēscere concordiā possunt* becomes accusative and infinitive construction.

94–95:   *minus certāminis fuit*: partitive genitive (Cap. XIX).

Bellum Sabīnum: 98–173

103:             *petītum*: supine (Cap. XXII).

105:             *aurō pollicendō*: gerundive construction, ablative of means (Cap. XXVI).

108:             *nē quis = nē aliquis* (Cap. XXII).

109–110:   Reading help: *Additur fābula* introduces an indirect statement (*Tarpēiam…postulāvisse*); the object of *postulāvisse* (*id*) leads in a subordinate clause in *ōrātiō oblīqua* (Cap. XXXVI): *quod in sinistrīs manibus habērent.*

111:      *armillās magnī ponderis*: genitive of description (Cap. XXXVI).

117–118:   *cupiditāte arcis reciperandae accēnsī*: objective genitive (Cap. XXV).

118:      *montem subiēre*: "they ascended the mountain."

128–129:   *arcē* < *arcēre* (Cap. XXXIX); *dēme* < *dēmere* (Cap. XXXV) = *dē emere*: "take away."

130–131:   *templum…quod monumentum sit…voveō*: "wish" (Cap. XXXIX).

132:      *velut sī sēnsisset audītās precēs*: *velut* ("as," "as if," Cap. XXVI); the pluperfect subjunctive underscores the contrafactual nature of the comparison.

132–134:   *"Hinc" inquit, "Rōmānī, Iuppiter Optimus Māximus resistere atque iterāre pugnam iubet!"*: i.e., *"resistite atque iterāte!"*

143–144:   *Ex equō tum Mettius pugnābat, eō facilius fuit eum pellere*: "it was all the easier to…" (literally: "by which the more easily").

152–153:   *crīnibus passīs*: ablative absolute, *passīs* from *pandere*: "spread out," "unkempt," a sign of distress; *victō malīs muliebrī pavōre*: ablative absolute with an ablative of means (*malīs*).

156:      *piget*: Cap. XL.

159:      *sine alterīs vestrum*: partitive genitive (Cap. XIX).

164:      *Rōmam*: accusative of place to which.

Fidēnātēs et Vēientēs victī: 174–220

175:      *Tatius*: for Tatius, king of the Sabines, see lines 63, 104, 171; *Lāvīniī*: locative.

177:      *aegrē…tulisse*: Cap. XXI (reading notes for line 28).

179–180:   *Itaque bellō quidem abstinuit*: *bellō* is ablative of separation with *abstinēre* (Cap. XXXVI).

185–186:   *priusquam…esset quam…vidēbatur*: first clause is an anticipatory subjunctive ("before it could be"); second is indicative ("than it [in fact] seemed it would be").

187:      *id agrī*: partitive genitive with a neuter pronoun (more examples in Cap. XLIV).

188:              *versī*: "turned themselves."

190:              *Rōmam*: accusative, not locative, because the messengers had to travel to Rome to make the announcement.

191–196:   Reading help: Remember that words are grouped together, so even long sentences such as this one can be read from beginning to end: *Ibi [modicō praesidiō relictō* (ablative absolute)]*, ēgressus (cum omnibus cōpiīs) partem mīlitum locīs occultīs sedēre (in īnsidiīs) iussit, ipse (cum parte māiōre atque omnī equitātū) profectus (ad ipsās prope portās Fidēnārum) accēdēns hostēs ad pugnam excīvit*: "having set out, he ordered, while he himself proceeded (*profectus*), approaching (*accēdēns*) Fidenae, he roused," etc.

193–194, 196:   *partem mīlitum; numerum Rōmānōrum modicum*: partitive genitives (Cap. XIX).

198:              *simulantēs*: see note XXIX.118.

202–203:   *prius paene quam…circumagerent*: see above note on lines 185–186.

206:              *Rōmānī velut ūnō agmine in oppidum irrūpērunt*: *velut* ("as," "as if," Cap. XXVI).

208:              *vastantēs*: "plundering, ravaging"; *iustī*: with *bellī*.

214:              *obviam ēgressī*: adverb *obviam* ("in the way"), with verb of motion (Cap. XXXIX).

217–218:   *urbe validā mūrīs ac sitū ipsō mūnītā abstinuit*: *urbe validā… mūnītā* is ablative of separation with *abstinēre* (Cap. XXXVI); *mūrīs ac sitū ipsō*: ablatives of means dependent on *mūnītā*.

219:              *ulcīscendī magis quam praedae studiō*: objective genitives with *studiō*; genitives can be combined (here we see a gerund and a noun).

220:              *pācem petītum…mittunt*: supine + object with verb of motion (Cap. XXXVI).

Rōmulus cōnsecrātus: 221–253

222:              *Haec Rōmulō rēgnante domī mīlitiaeque gesta sunt*: *gerere* is regularly used of official accomplishments, often called the *rēs gestae*; *domī mīlitiaeque* are both locative, frequently conjoined when referring to a leader's accomplishments: both domestic and military (at home and on the field).

223–224:   *in quadrāgintā deinde annōs*: "for" or "in the space of" forty years thereafter.

234:          *mīlitibus*: dative with the compound *abstulerit*: "took away from."

236:          *velut sī orbī factī essent*: *velut* ("as," "as if," Cap. XXVI); the subjunctive is used to underscore the contrafactual nature of the comparison.

241–242:   *aliquōs quī...arguerent*: relative clause of characteristic/description (Cap. XXXIX).

249:          *colant sciantque*: jussive subjunctives (Cap. XXXI).

Interrēgnum: 254–280

258–260:   *Timor incessit nē...adorīrētur*: fear clause (Cap. XXXII).

263–264:   *Dēnī simul quīnōs diēs*: distributive numbers (Cap. XXX) = ten sets of five days each (fifty days).

270:          *populō concedendum esse*: intransitive verb used impersonally in passive (Cap. XL) with the dative—the gerundive with *esse* to show obligation or necessity (passive periphrastic).

273:          *auctōrēs*: i.e., they would ratify the choice.

274–275:   *Quod...sit*: subjunctive of wish (Cap. XXXIX); the combination *bonum faustum felix* was a common prayer for the well-being of the republic.

276:          *vīsum est*: "it seemed" can often mean "it seemed good, it seemed proper, it was pleasing" + dative.

276–277:   *dignum quī*: descriptive relative clause (see above).

279–280:   *plēbī permissum est ut*: *permittere* is being used impersonally in passive, followed by a consecutive noun clause (Cap. XXXVII); *quis Rōmae rēgnārent*: indirect question.

Numa Pompilius rēx: 281–353

282–283:   *vir prūdentissimus iūris dīvīnī atque hūmānī*: *prūdēns* (Caps. XXV, XXVI, XXIX) takes an objective genitive.

290:          *arcessītus < arcessere* (Cap. XI): "summon"; *adeptus est*: see note above on lines 83–84 (*adipīscī*).

291–292:   *ad merīdiem versus*: *ad* + accusative *versus*: "toward" (Cap. XX).

296:          *fīnīvit*: In Cap. XXIX, you learned this verb as "finish," a mean-
              ing it gets from its base meaning of "put boundaries (*fīnēs*)
              around"; the augur does this mentally (*animō*) when he has
              prayed to the gods.

300:          *uti...dēclārēs*: wish; *uti* = *utinam.*

314–315:   *deōrum metum*: objective genitive (Cap. XXV); *Quī* = *metus.*

318–320:   *eius* = Egeria's; *sē* = Numa; *sacerdōtēs suōs cuique deōrum*:
              suum cuique: "to each his own" (Cap. XVIII).

323–324:   *quia...futūrum esset*: implied *ōrātiō oblīqua* (see grammar sec-
              tion above).

327–328   *plūrēs Rōmulī quam Numae similēs rēgēs fore putābat*: *similis*
              takes the dative or, as here, the genitive; *fore* = *futūrum esse*;
              the main clause (*sacerdōtem creāvit*) is introduced by a causal
              clause (*quia*) followed by a purpose (*nē*).

338–339:   *quibus...fierent*: implied *ōrātiō oblīqua* (see grammar section
              above).

341:          *ut esset quem*: descriptive relative clause (see grammar section
              above).

346:          *ad turbandam...pācem*: purpose.

350:          *alius aliā viā*: Cap. X.

Rapina Sabīnārum: 354–377

356–357:   *sibi quisque*: each for himself (XVIII); *quam velit*: indirect
              question.

359:          *signa...dēdit*: the missing word is *petīta* (with *signa*).

362–364:   *ut...utque...sīc*: simile.

365:          *nūllā*, i.e., *nūllā puellā*; *quī*: antecedent *color.*

370:          *geniālis praeda*: in apposition to *raptae puellae.*

377:          *scīstī* = *scīvistī.*

Mulierēs pācem faciunt: 378–393

380:          *ferrō mortīque*: datives with *parātae.*

383:          *pignora cara*: in apposition to *nātōs.*

384:        *passīs capillīs:* see above on lines 152–153.

386:        *quasi sentīrent:* "as if they could understand" (present contra-factual: "they are too young to understand").

388:        *tunc dēnique vīsum:* they've never seen their grandfathers before.

389:        *quī vix potest posse coāctus erat:* e.g., in their eagerness to end the conflict, their mothers are encouraging them to say "grandpa."

391:        *manūs* is the object of both *dant* and *accipiunt.*

393:        *scūtī:* genitive with *ūsus.*

III. Vocābula

NŌMINA

1st

agna, -ae	ewe lamb
armilla, -ae	bracelet
centuria, -ae	century (unit of 100)
columba, -ae	pigeon, dove
dīligentia, -ae	carefulness
mīlitia, -ae	military service

2nd

asȳlum, -ī	refuge, asylum
commodum, -ī	advantage, interest
fānum, -ī	shrine, consecrated spot
globus, -ī	globe, sphere, ball, band
interrēgnum, -ī	interval between reigns
lituus, -ī	augur's staff, trumpet
lūdicrum, -ī	sport, toy, show
mīrāculum, -ī	marvel
praesidium, -ī	protection, aid, garrison
quercus, -ī (*f.*)	oak
spectāculum, -ī	sight, spectacle
spolia, -orum (*n. pl.*)	spoils, booty

3rd

ancīle, -is (*n.*)	(sacred) shield
augur, -is (*m.*)	augur
cīvitās, -ātis (*f.*)	state, city, citizenship
clādēs, -is (*f.*)	disaster, defeat
cōntiō, -ōnis (*f.*)	meeting, assembly
decus, -oris (*n.*)	honor, ornament
fascēs, -ium (*m. pl.*)	bundle of rods, fasces
flāmen, -inis (*m.*)	flamen (priest)
foedus, -eris (*n.*)	treaty
gener, -erī (*m.*)	son-in-law
indignātiō, -ōnis (*f.*)	indignation, resentment
īnsigne, -is (*n.*)	mark, token, symbol
interrēx, -rēgis (*m.*)	intermediary regent
lēgātiō, -ōnis (*f.*)	embassy, deputation
līctor, -ōris (*m.*)	lictor
occāsiō, -ōnis (*f.*)	opportunity, chance
pignus, -oris (*n.*)	pledge
plēbs, -is (*f.*)	the (common) people
secūris, -is (*f.*) (*acc.* **-im**; *abl.* **-ī**)	axe
socer, -erī (*m.*)	father-in-law
tubicen, -inis (*m.*)	trumpeter

4th

concursus, -ūs	concourse, encounter
plausus, -ūs	applause

VERBA

-āre

(clāmitō) clāmitāre	shout loudly
(concitō) concitāre	stir up, incite
(cōnservō) cōnservāre	preserve, maintain
(cōnsociō) cōnsociāre	associate, share
(creō) creāre	create, appoint
(dēclārō) dēclārāre	show, declare, express
(dēsignō) dēsignāre	mark out

(dīmicō) dīmicāre	fight
(fugō) fugāre	put to flight, rout
(imperitō) imperitāre	govern, be in command
(impetrō) impetrāre	obtain (by request)
(indicō) indicāre	make known, declare
(iterō) iterāre	repeat, renew
(laniō) laniāre	tear
(migrō) migrāre	move, migrate
(mītigō) mītigāre	soothe
(notō) notāre	mark, note, censure
(populor) populārī	ravage, plunder
(prōvolō) prōvolāre	rush forth
(reciperō) reciperāre	recover, recapture
(saltō) saltāre	dance
(spoliō) spoliāre	strip (of arms), rob
(temperō) temperāre	moderate, temper, refrain
(vāstō) vāstāre	lay waste, ravage
(vēlō) vēlāre	cover
(violō) violāre	violate

-ēre

(piget) pigēre, piguit, pigitum	feel annoyance at, regret

-ere

(advertō) advertere (< vertere)	turn, direct (toward)
(coalēscō) coalēscere, -uisse, -itum	grow together, coalesce
(cōnscrībō) cōnscrībere (< scrībere)	enroll, compose, write
(convalēscō) convalēscere (< valēre)	grow strong, recover
(corrumpō) corrumpere (< rumpere)	spoil, corrupt, bribe
(dēcernō) dēcernere (< cernere)	decide, settle, fight
(dēlābor) dēlābī (< lābī)	slip down, descend
(discrībō) discrībere (< scībere)	divide up, distribute
(discurrō) discurrere (< currere)	run in several directions
(ēscendō) ēscendere (< scandere)	ascend, go up

(ēvādō) ēvādere (< vādere)	get out, escape, pass, turn out
(immittō) immittere (< mittere)	send in, send (into)
(inicō) inicere (< icere)	throw/lay on, instill
(invādō) invādere (< vādere)	enter, attack, invade
(irrumpō) irrumpere (< rumpere)	break, force one's way
(oppōnō) oppōnere (< pōnere)	put in the way, oppose
(percellō) percellere, -ulisse, -ulsum	strike (with fear)
(perfugiō) perfugere (< fugere)	take refuge
(prōcumbō) prōcumbere, prōcubuisse, prōcubitum	lean forward, bow down
(prōdō) prōdere (< dare)	hand down, betray
(profugiō) profugere (< fugere)	run away, flee
(respergō) respergere, respersisse, respersum	sprinkle, splatter
(sistō) sistere, stetisse, statum	halt, stop
(spernō) spernere, sprēvisse, sprētum	disdain, scorn

-īre

(adorior) adorīrī (< orīrī)	attack
(coorior) coorīrī (< orīrī)	break out, arise
(exciō) excīre, excīvisse, excitum	call out, summon
(exsiliō) exsilīre, -uisse	jump up

irregular

(anteeō) anteīre (< īre)	precede, surpass
(prōdeō) prōdīre (< īre)	come forward, go forth

ADIECTĪVA

1st/2nd

acceptus, -a, -um	well-liked, popular
aduncus, -a, -um	hooked, curved
amātōrius, -a, -um	of love
assiduus, -a, -um	constantly present
blandus, -a, -um	charming, ingratiating
dēnsus, -a, -um	thick, dense

externus, -a, -um	external, extraneous
fāstus, -a, -um	court-day, work day
faustus, -a, -um	fortunate, favorable
hodiernus, -a, -um	today's, of today
inīquus, -a, -um	uneven, unfair
īnspērātus, -a, -um	not hoped for, unexpected
lentus, -a, -um	slow
modicus, -a, -um	moderate
nefandus, -a, -um	heinous
nefāstus, -a, -um	public holiday
nocturnus, -a, -um	nocturnal, at night
novellus, -a, -um	new, young
obvius, -a, -um	coming to meet
opīmus, -a, -um	rich
peregrīnus, -a, -um	foreign, alien
sānctus, -a, -um	holy
vānus, -a, -um	empty, useless, vain
vīcīnus, -a, -um	neighboring

3rd

agrestis, -e	rustic, boorish, (*m.*) peasant
concors, (*gen.* -rdis)	harmonious, concordant
geniālis, -e	marriage-, conjugal
hospitālis, -e	hospitable, guest-
imbellis, -e	unwarlike, cowardly
sublīmis, -e	high (up), aloft
ūtilis, -e	useful

PRONŌMINA

quīlibet, quaelibet, quodlibet	any; no matter what/which

ADVERBIA

admodum	very much, quite
aegrē	with pain, unwillingly
aliquamdiū	for some time
cōnfestim	at once, immediately

deinceps	in succession, next
impūne	with impunity
proinde	accordingly

CONIUNCTIŌNĒS

cum…tum	not only…but also
uti	like, as, how

ALIA

auspicātō	after taking the auspices; with good omens
dē integrō	anew

XLIII: QVADRAGESIMVM TERTIVM: ROMA ET ALBA (Livy)[1]

[*Ex T. Līviī 'ab Urbe Conditā' librō I. 22–31, nōnnūllīs mūtātīs et praetermissīs*]

I. Ørberg's Introduction

The third Roman king, *Tullus Hostīlius*, was warlike, unlike his predecessor. He soon found a pretext for declaring war on Alba Longa, but before the decisive battle, his Alban opponent, *Mettius Fūfētius*—under the influence of the danger threatening them both from the Etruscans—proposed that they should settle their dispute with a minimum of bloodshed. There happened to be triplets in both armies, and it was agreed that the three Roman triplets, the *Horātiī*, should fight with the three Albans, the *Cūriātiī*. Livy gives a dramatic description of this triple combat. After the first violent clashes, only one Roman remained alive and unhurt facing three Albans who were more or less wounded. Horatius, the Roman soldier, seeing that he had no chance of holding his own against the other three, took to flight so as to separate his opponents, and with the wounded Albans following him at varying distances, he turned around and killed them one by one.

The triumphant Horatius then returned at the head of the jubilant Roman army, but in front of the Porta Capena, he met his sister, who was betrothed to one of the Curiatii. Seeing her fiancé's coat on her brother's shoulder she burst into tears, whereupon Horatius ran his sword through his unpatriotic sister.

According to the law, Horatius should have paid with his own life for this crime, but when the *duumvirī* appointed by the king had condemned him to the gallows for *perduelliō* (properly "high treason"—here in a wider sense), he at once appealed (*prōvocāvit*) to the people. In the subsequent trial (*iūdicium*), he was acquitted, not least because his father defended him. Horatius' father even declared that his daughter had been justly killed!

---

1. For an explanation of the line number references convention, see p. xxvi.

Mettius, who was now subject to Rome, planned treason against his new masters. During a joint battle against the towns of Fidenae and Veii, he moved his army away from the Romans, ready to join the enemy if they got the upper hand. But the Romans were victorious without Alban support, and Tullus took revenge. Mettius was put to death in a horrible way, and Alba Longa was destroyed and all its inhabitants moved to Rome. The population of Rome was doubled, and Mount Caelius was incorporated into the city. King Tullus Hostilius erected the first senate-house, which was named the *Cūria Hostīlia* (it was pulled down by Julius Caesar, see XXXVI.82–84 and 96–98).

Tullus also waged a successful war against the Sabines. Soon afterward Rome was afflicted with the plague. When the king himself fell ill, he at last began worshiping the gods, but did not perform the religious rites properly. Jupiter struck him with lightning.

The chapter ends with a short extract from the earliest work of M. Tullius Cicerō, written about 85 BC. It is the beginning of a textbook of rhetoric, *dē Inventiōne*, about the art of finding or devising the arguments and subject matter of a speech. Here he takes the trial of Horatius as an example of a difficult case, summarizing arguments on both sides.

II. Auxilia Legendī

Albānīs bellum indictum: 1–40

11–12:	*Forte ēvēnit ut…agerent*: noun clause of result (cf. *fit ut/accidit ut*, Cap. XXXII).
13:	*Albae*: locative.
14–15:	*Tullus imperāverat suīs ut sine morā <u>mandāta agerent</u>*: *mandāta agere* = "excecute his commands/commission."
17:	*sēgnius*: comparative adverb from *sēgnis, -e*: "more slowly."
19:	*rēs repetīverant*: see section on idioms above, cf. 24, 27.
24–25:	*nisi reddantur, bellum indīcere iussōs esse*: condition in *ōrātiō oblīqua* (see grammar section above).
26–27:	*uter…dīmīserit*: indirect question; *ut…vertant*: a wish ("may the gods," etc.).
29:	*domum*: accusative of place to which.
38:	*quoad = quō + ad*: "up to the point that, until."

Trigeminōrum pugna: 41–121

55:     *cupīdō imperiī*: objective genitive (Cap. XXV).

56–57:   *quō propior es, eō magis scīs*: see grammar section above on correlatives.

58–59:   *Memor estō*: future imperative (Cap. XXVI).

59–60:   *hās duās aciēs* <u>*spectāculō*</u> *fore* <u>*Etrūscīs*</u>: double dative (Cap. XXXVI).

65–66:   *cum* <u>*indole*</u>*, tum* <u>*spē*</u> *victōriae ferōcior erat*: "fiercer not only in character but also in hope of victory," ablatives of respect (Cap. XXXIX).

69:     *nec aetāte nec vīribus disparēs*: "unequal neither in age nor strength," ablatives of respect (Cap. XXXIX).

70–80:   *deōs patriōs...manūs*: see above on change of pronouns from direct to indirect statement.

80–81:   *cōnsēderant utrimque prō castrīs duo exercitūs*: "before," in this case "in front of" their respective camps.

84:     *ternī*: distributive number (Cap. XXX); *velut*: "as," "as if" in similes (Cap. XXVIII).

90–92:   *spectāculō essent*: dative of purpose (Cap. XL).

99:     *ut...sineret*: "as"; subordinate clause in indirect statement (dependent on *rātus*).

100–101:   *pugnātum est*: impersonal passive of intranstive verb (Cap. XL).

109:     *singulī*: distributive number (Cap. XXX).

106:     *dēfungī*: like *fungī* (Cap. XXXVIII), *dēfungī* is completed by an ablative of means.

109–110:   *nec spē nec vīribus parēs*: "equal neither in hope nor strength," ablatives of respect (Cap. XXXIX).

114:     *sustinentī*: dative with compound verb *dēfigere*, understand *Cūriātiō sustinentī*.

117:     <u>*eō*</u> <u>*māiōre*</u> *cum gaudiō quod*: "with <u>all</u> <u>the</u> <u>more</u> joy because."

Amor immātūrus: 122–181

124–125:   *sē...foret*: see section above on change of pronouns from direct to indirect statement.

131: *solvit crīnēs*: cf. *crīnibus passīs*, Caps. XL.188 and XLII.13.

136–137: *oblīta frātrum mortuōrum vīvīque, oblīta patriae*: *oblīvīscī* + the genitive (Cap. XXV).

137: *Sīc eat…*: subjunctive of wish (Cap. XXXIX).

140: *bene dē patriā meritus*: cf. Cap. XL, note to line 111.

141–144: <u>*secundum*</u> *iūdicium…,* <u>*secundum*</u> *lēgem: secundum* is here a preposition, meaning "according to, following."

145: *iudicent*: jussive subjunctive (Cap. XXXI).

146–147: *Sī vincent, caput obnūbitō! Īnfēlīcī arborī reste suspenditō!*: 3rd person imperative, the subject of which is the understood *lictor*, the person who will execute the punishment (named in line 157).

157: *perduelliō*: generally, "high treason," although scholars have worried about that application here. When convicted of *perduelliō*, a Roman citizen had the right to appeal his case to the people, for which the term is *ad populum prōvocāre*.

163–165: '*nē sē, quem paulō ante cum ēgregiā stirpe cōnspexissent, orbum līberīs facerent!*': *Cōnspexissent*: subjunctive in a relative clause in *ōrātiō oblīqua*; *orbum līberīs*: ablative of separation.

172–173: *pepererunt < pariō, parĕre, peperī, partum*: "bear, bring forth."

176–178: *Quō enim dūcere hunc iuvenem potestis ubi nōn sua decora eum ā tantā foeditāte suppliciī dēfendant?*: *dēfendant*: potential subjunctive (Cap. XLI); *potestis*: in indicative, Cap. XL; *sua decora*: sua, as often, refers to the logical, not actual subject.

Mettiī perfidia ac supplicium: 182–265

183–187: *Ira…ingenium dictātoris corrūpit*: i.e., Mettius was affected by the Albans' resentment; *coepit*: subject is Mettius.

188–189: *quia* <u>*suae cīvitātī*</u> *vīrēs* <u>*deesse*</u> *cernēbat: deesse* (= *dē* + *esse*) with the dative.

202: *Mettiō*: dative of possession(Cap. XII); *animī, fideī*: partitive genitives with *plūs.*

206–207: *Cōnsilium erat cum iīs sē iungere quibus fortūna victōriam daret: Cōnsilium erat* introduces an indirect statement (*cum iīs sē iungere*) followed by an indirect question (*quibus…daret*).

216:        *Latīnē scīre*: the regular idiom for knowing a language uses the adverb, just as with speaking (*Latīnē loquī*).

221:        *quō*: i.e., to the river.

231:        *parātīs omnibus*: ablative absolute.

236–238:   *Sī umquam...fuit quod...agerētis,...id proelium fuit*: past general condition (*fuit...fuit*, Cap. XLI), the protasis of which introduces a descriptive relative clause (Caps. XXXIX, XLII): "if it was ever the case that you should etc..."; *est quod* = "there is a reason why" + subjunctive is a common idiom; *deinde vestrae ipsōrum virtūtī*: with *gratiās agerētis* (*prīmum...deinde*); *vestrae ipsōrum* is emphatic: *vestrae*, meaning "yours" with *ipsōrum*, "of you yourselves"—this is a common use of *ipse* with the possessive adjectives (*meus, tuus, noster, vester*).

241:        like *iussū* (Cap. XLI), *iniussū* is found only in the ablative with a genitive or a possessive adjective.

243–244:   *ut et vōs, sī ego inde agmen abdūcere voluissem, fēcissētis*: past contrafactual condition (Cap. XLI).

244–246:   *Mettius...Mettius...Mettius*: the repetition of a word or phrase at the beginning of clauses adds emphasis and is called anaphora.

253:        *redeat*: jussive subjunctive (Cap. XLI).

255–256:   *Sī ipse discere possēs fidem ac foedera servāre, vīvum tē id docuissem*: "mixed condition": protasis (imperfect subjunctive) in a present contrafactual; apodosis (pluperfect subjunctive) in a past contrafactual: "if you were able...I would have taught."

258:        *ea sāncta crēdere* = *crēdere ea esse sancta*.

259–261:   *Ut igitur paulō ante animum (inter Fidēnātem Rōmānamque rem) ancipitem gessistī, ita iam corpus in duās partēs distrahendum dabis!*: *ut...ita*, "as...so too"; *animum gerere*: to have a mind/will that is (in this example) *ancipitem* (two-headed—or as we would say "two-faced").

Alba dīruta: 266–298

267–268:   *praemissī...erant...quī...trādūcerent*: relative clause of purpose (Cap. XXXIX).

271–272:   *effrāctīs portīs strātīsve mūrīs aut arce vī captā*: three ablative absolutes, the last one enclosing an ablative of means.

280:         *nātus...ēducātusque erat*: *erat* goes with both participles.

288:         *quibus* (sc. *annīs*): ablative of time; *funditus*: adv., "from the bottom, completely."

292–293:   *eam sēdem Tullus rēgiae capit*: *eam* refers to the Caelian hill; *sēdem* is predicative: Tullus chose it as the seat for the royal palace.

295:         *senātuī...auctō*: dative, indirect object.

Sabīnī dēvictī: 299–318

300–303:   *gentī...opulentissimae*, datives referring back to *Sabīnīs*; *virīs armīsque*: ablatives of respect.

306:         *silva Malitiōsa*: a forest in the Sabine territory.

307:         *plūrimum*: adverb with *valuit*.

311:         *dēvictīs Sabīnīs*: ablative absolute.

316–317:   *velut*: "as if," with the ablative absolute; *fortūnae*: dative with *īrātī*.

Tullus fulmine ictus: 319–335

320:         *Haud ita multō post pestilentia orta est*: ablative of degree of difference ("afterward by not much").

323:         *mīlitiae, domī*: both locatives.

325–328:   *Tunc adeō...ut quī anteā...ratus esset...repente...coleret religiōnibusque...implēret*: result clause containing, perhaps, a descriptive relative clause (*ratus esset*), or, as the marginalia take it, a concessive ("although") relative clause; *nihil minus rēgium*: "nothing less befitting a king."

Causa Horātiī: 336–358

345:         *indignē passus*: cf. *molestē fert/molestē patiens* (Cap. XLI).

353–354:   *necārī nōn oportuit*: "should not have been killed"; Latin keeps the present infinitive and puts *oportēre* in the past tense; here the indicative is used even though the sense is contrafactual ("should not have been killed, but he was") (cf. *posse* in the Rēs Grammaticae in Cap. XL and grammar section above).

III. VOCĀBULA

NŌMINA

1st

culpa, -ae	blame, fault, guilt
maestitia, -ae	sadness, sorrow
perfidia, -ae	faithlessness, treachery
quadrīgae, -ārum (*pl.*)	team of four horses
ruīna, -ae	collapse, ruin
turma, -ae	squadron

2nd

argūmentum, -ī	proof, argument
duumvirī, -ōrum (*pl.*)	board of two men
intervāllum, -ī	interval, space, distance
iugulum, -ī	throat
laqueus, -ī	loop, noose
palūdāmentum, -ī	military cloak
pōmērium, -ī	open space round town
servitium, -ī	slavery
spatium, -ī	space, distance, interval, walk, time, period
spōnsus, -ī	fiancé
statīva, -ōrum (*pl.*)	stationary camp (sc. *castra*)
vulgus, -ī	the (common) people

3rd

centuriō, -ōnis (*m.*)	centurion (officer)
complōrātiō, -ōnis (*f.*)	lamentation
cōnfluentēs, -ium (*m. pl.*)	confluence; place where two rivers unite
crīmen, -inis (*n.*)	charge, accusation
dēpulsiō, -ōnis (*f.*)	rebuttal
dictātor, -ōris (*m.*)	dictator
dīmicātiō, -ōnis (*f.*)	fight
ductor, -ōris (*m.*)	leader
foeditās, -ātis (*f.*)	ugliness, shame
indolēs, -is (*f.*)	character, nature

infīrmātiō, -ōnis (*f.*)	invalidation, rebuttal
intentiō, -ōnis (*f.*)	charge, accusation
inventiō, -ōnis (*f.*)	art of devising arguments
iūdex, -icis (*m.*)	judge
iūdicātiō, -ōnis (*f.*)	point at issue
lāmentātiō, -ōnis (*f.*)	wailing, lamentation
līberātor, -ōris (*m.*)	deliverer, liberator
perduelliō, -ōnis (*f.*)	treason
populāris, -is (*m.*)	fellow citizen
prōditiō, -ōnis (*f.*)	betrayal
prōvocātiō, -ōnis (*f.*)	appeal
pulvis, -eris (*m.*)	dust
quaestiō, -ōnis (*f.*)	inquiry, question
religiō, -ōnis (*f.*)	fear of the gods, religion
restis, -is (*f.*)	rope
ruptor, -ōris (*m.*)	one who breaks
strāgēs, -is (*f.*)	slaughter
trepidātiō, -ōnis (*f.*)	alarm, panic

4th

cruciātus, -ūs	torture
cultus, -ūs	cultivation, care, mode of life, worship
mōtus, ūs	movement, rising
status, -ūs	state, condition, order

VERBA

-āre

(adhortor) adhortārī	encourage, urge on
(colligō) colligāre	tie up, bind
(condemnō) condemnāre	condemn
(cōnflagrō) cōnflagrāre	be burnt
(cōntiōnor) cōntiōnārī	address a meeting
(decorō) decorāre	adorn, glorify
(duplicō) duplicāre	double
(exspīrō) exspīrāre	breathe one's last, die
(geminō) gemināre	double

(inclāmō) inclāmāre	shout (at)
(increpō) increpāre	rattle, clash, scold
(lacerō) lacerāre	tear
(ligō) ligāre	bind
(occupō) occupāre	occupy, take possession of
(prōclāmō) prōclāmāre	cry out
(prōvocō) prōvocāre	challenge, appeal
(pūrgō) pūrgāre	clean, purge, excuse
(reconciliō) reconciliāre	win back, reconcile
(renūntiō) renūntiāre	report, renounce
(stimulō) stimulāre	spur on, stimulate
(vagor) vagārī	wander, roam

-ēre

(dēspondeō) dēspondēre (< spondēre)	betroth, engage
(displiceō) displicēre, -uisse, -itum	displease, offend
(pertineō) pertinēre (< tenēre)	relate, pertain (to)
(suppleō) supplēre, -ēvisse, -ētum	fill up, reinforce

-ere

(abolēscō) abolēscere, abolēvisse, abolitum	decay, be forgotten
(absolvō) absolvere (< solvere)	free, acquit
(aggredior) aggredī, aggressum	attack, set about, try
(circumdūcō) circumdūcere (< dūcere)	lead around
(circumsistō) circumsistere, -stetisse	surround
(dēfungor) dēfungī, dēfunctum	complete
(dēvincō) dēvincere (< vincere)	defeat completely
(dīrigō) dīrigere (< regere)	arrange, direct
(dīruō) dīruere, dīruisse, dīrutum	demolish
(distrahō) distrahere (< trahere)	pull apart, break up
(ēdīcō) ēdīcere (< dīcere)	decree, fix
(effringō) effringere (< frangere)	break open

(illūcēscō) illūcēscere, -lūxisse, -lūctum	dawn, grow light
(indīcō) indīcere (< dīcere)	notify, declare
(interclūdō) interclūdere (< claudere)	shut out, cut off, block
(invehō) invehere (< vehere)	import, ride in
(obiciō) obicere (< iacere)	place before, expose
(obnūbō) obnūbere, -ūpsisse, -ūptum	veil, cover
(repetō) repetere (< petere)	return to, repeat, claim back, recall
(senēscō) senēscere, -uisse, -itum	grow old, weaken
(suspendō) suspendere, -disse, -sum	hang, suspend
(trādūcō) trādūcere (< dūcere)	move (across), pass
(trānsfīgō) trānsfīgere (< figere)	pierce

-īre

(saepiō) saepīre, -sisse, -tum	surround

ADIECTĪVA

1st/2nd

avītus, -a, -um	of a grandfather
citātus, -a, -um	speeded up, swift
cognātus, -a, -um	related
dīversus, -a, -um	opposite, different
hesternus, -a, -um	of yesterday
indemnātus, -a, -um	uncondemned
intāctus, -a, -um	untouched, uninjured
invītus, -a, -um	against one's will, unwilling
ōrātōrius, -a, -um	oratorical
trigeminus, -a, -um	triplet

3rd

anceps, -cipitis	double, undecided
atrōx, -ōcis	dreadful, atrocious
cīvīlis, -e	civic, civil
continēns, -entis	unbroken, adjacent

dēfōrmis, -e	ugly
dispār, -paris	unequal, different
dissimilis, -e	unlike, different
flēbilis, -e	plaintive
insānābilis, -e	incurable
miserābilis, -e	pitiable

ADVERBIA

identidem	repeatedly
nēquāquam	by no means, not at all
palam	openly, publicly
passim	far and wide, everywhere
postrēmum	for the last time
sēnsim	gradually, little by little
utrimque	on/from both sides

PRAEPOSITIŌNĒS

secundum (+ *acc.*)	along, after, according to

ALIA

iniussū[2]	without orders

---

2.   Cf. *iussū* (Cap. XLI)

XLIV: QVADRAGESIMVM QVARTVM: REGES ET REGINAE (Livy)[1]

[*Ex T. Līviī 'ab Urbe Conditā' librō I. 32–48, nōnnūllīs mūtātīs et praetermissīs*]

I. ØRBERG'S INTRODUCTION

This chapter deals with the three kings *Ancus Mārcius, Tarquinius Prīscus,* and *Servius Tullius.* Tarquinius' arrogant queen *Tanaquīl* and Servius' cruel daughter *Tullia,* who became the last queen in Rome, also play important roles in Livy's narrative of Rome's earliest years.

King Ancus Marcius, who was of a peaceful disposition like Numa, found himself compelled to declare war on the Latins (*Latīnī*) when they had made a raid on Roman territory and refused to return the spoils appropriated in the raid. This event gives Livy an occasion to quote the old rules of law (the *iūs fētiāle*) that were followed when restoration or compensation was demanded from the enemy (*rēs repetere*). If the demand was denied, war was declared. The Senate had to be consulted: each of the senators was asked his opinion, "*Quid cēnsēs?*" (this consultation was called *sententiam rogāre*). War was declared by an envoy, a *fētiālis*, who threw a bloody lance with an iron tip into the enemy's territory and recited the formula for war.

Ancus conquered a couple of neighboring towns, moved their inhabitants to Rome, and settled them on the Aventine Hill. He is said to have built the prison, the *Carcer*, north of the Forum (XXXVI.154), and the first bridge over the Tiber, the *pōns Sublicius* ("the pile bridge" from *sublica*, "stake" or "pile").

Meanwhile *Lucumō*, a rich and powerful man from the Etruscan city of *Tarquiniī*, had moved to Rome in search of fortune with his ambitious wife *Tanaquīl*. On their way, an extraordinary augury had confirmed their expectation of a glorious future: an eagle carried off Lucumo's cap and put it back on his head. In Rome, Lucumo, who called himself *Lūcius Tarquinius Prīscus,* won the favor of king Ancus. At the king's death, he became guardian of his two

---

1. For an explanation of the line number references convention, see p. xxvi.

189

minor sons. Before the election of the new king, he sent the sons away and so was chosen king of Rome.

King Tarquinius waged successful wars against the Latins and conquered several of their cities. After doubling his cavalry from 900 to 1,800 men, he defeated the Sabines and forced them to surrender the city of *Collātia*, where the king's nephew *Egerius* was made commander. In this connection, Livy quotes the old formula pronounced at the surrender of a defeated enemy.

After reigning for thirty-eight years, Tarquinius was murdered by order of Ancus's two slighted sons. At the instigation of Tarquinius's widow Tanaquil, the dead king's son-in-law *Servius Tullius* set himself up as king of Rome. This had been portended when, as a little boy, he was found asleep with a flame burning around his head.

King Servius Tullius has been credited with an important administrative reform: he divided the Roman people and the Roman army into five classes on the basis of a statement of each citizen's property (*cēnsus*). The classes were divided into centuries (*centuriae*), 193 in all. In the popular assembly, the *comitia centuriāta*, which enacted laws and elected magistrates, votes were taken by century, giving the wealthier citizens the majority.

Tarquinius Priscus's sons, *Lūcius* and *Arrūns*, refused to recognize their brother-in-law as lawful king. To appease them, Servius gave them his two daughters in marriage, but the couples were unevenly matched. Soon the more hot-tempered of the two, Tullia,[2] allied herself with the similarly disposed Lucius, and they had the other two put away. Tullia urged her new husband to seize power. He broke into the Senate-house and spoke out against the king. When king Servius appeared and protested against his son-in-law's usurpation, he was thrown out and soon after murdered.

Lucius's wife, the ferocious Tullia, was the first to salute her husband as the new king. When she was on her way home, her coachman suddenly stopped the carriage because he found the road blocked by the murdered king's body, but Tullia seized the reins and drove the carriage over her dead father.

The last reading, from book VI of Ovid's *Fāstī*, describes the crimes which began the reign of the last Roman king.

---

2.   Roman daughters were traditionally given the feminine form of the family's *gentīlicium* (family name), hence *Horātia* in Cap. XLIII and the two women named *Tullia* in this chapter.

II. Auxilia Legendī

Iūs fētiāle: 1–90

2:	*rēs*: i.e., the state; *omnium*: dependent on *prīmum*, "first of all."
7–8:	*et…et*: "both…and"; *avītae glōriae*: genitive with *memor* (cf. *oblivīscī*, Cap. XXV).
9:	*omnium prīmum*: "first of all"; *ut*: "as."
10–12:	*cīvibus…cupidīs, finitimīs cīvitātibus*: datives with *spēs facta est*; *in avī mōrēs atque īnsititūta rēgem abitūrum esse*: *abīre* + *in* = "be changed into."
15–17:	*repetentibus rēs Rōmānīs*: dative with *respōnsum reddunt*; *ratī* (from *rērī*) is the subject of *reddunt* (and introduces the indirect statement that precedes it).
18–19:	*Medium erat in Ancō ingenium, et Numae et Rōmulī memor*: *medium ingenium*, "a moderate disposition"; *rēgnō*: dative with *necessāriam*.
20:	*Cum…tum*: "both…and" (Cap. XLII).
23–24:	*iūs fētiāle*: The *Fētiālēs* were a college of priests who were consulted on matters of war and peace. Ancus is credited with writing the procedure through which war is declared (*bellum indīcitur*) and goods stolen in war demanded back (*rēs repetuntur*).
29:	*sit*: jussive subjunctive (Cap. XLI).
31:	*dēdī*: present passive infinitive of *dēdere*, "be surrendered."
32:	*sīveris*: perfect subjunctive of *sinere*, *sīvisse*, *situm*, synonym of *patī* and *ferre* (Cicero uses the three in a row: *nōn feram, nōn sinam, nōn patiar*); mixed condition: if I am (now), you should never allow.
39:	*māiōrēs nātū* = *patrēs*: *nātū* is a verbal noun from the verb *nāscī* ("to be born") and an ablative of respect (Cap. XXXIII); *adipīscāmur*: indirect question (Caps. XXIX, XXXIX).
43–48:	The king's speeches and the legal formula that follows (ll.53–60) preserve for us a flavor of the archaic and legal language of the Romans. Note the archaic *duellum* (l.47) instead of *bellum*. The king's initial question (ll.43–47) contains two strings of three verbs: *dedērunt, solvērunt, fēcērunt*, a list immediately repeated in *dari, solvī, fierī*. The Senate's response contains another triad, *cēnseō itaque cōnsentiō cōnscīscōque* (ll.47–48), all three of

which are repeated in the same order in the formula for declaring war (1.57). The present infinitive *fierī* is the subject of the verb *oportuit*; for the present infinitive with a verb of propriety or necessity, see Cap. XLIII, note to lines 353–354.

49–50:   *in sententiam īre*: Romans voted by separating themselves into two groups: the "yays" and the "nays." This method of expressing their opinion "with their feet" accounts for the verb of motion *īre*.

51–53:   *Fierī solēbat ut…dīceret*: noun clause of result (Cap. XXXVII).

64–65:   *dēmandātā cūrā*: ablative absolute; *sacrōrum*: objective genitive; *flāminibus sacerdōtibusque aliīs*: indirect object with *dēmandāre*.

72–73:   *Postrēmō omnī bellō Latīnō Medulliam compulsō*: i.e., the war is driven to Medullia. The accusative shows the movement of the troops to Medullia.

74:        *urbs tūta mūnītiōnibus praesidiōque validō fīrmāta*: a pair of ideas placed in exactly opposite order; *urbs* here is modified by two adjectives (*tūta, fīrmāta*), which are in turn qualified by two ablatives of means. The order is adjective (*tūta*), noun (*mūnītiōnibus*), noun/adjective (*praesidiōque validō*), adjective (*fīrmāta*); the chiasmus's order is ABBA.

76:        *ingentī praedā potēns*: ablative of respect (cf. ll.92–93: *dīvitiīs potēns*).

81:        *in Tiberī*: pure *i*-stem (Cap. XVI).

84–85:   *ad terrōrem crēscentis audāciae*: objective genitive (Cap. XXV).

Lucumō et Tanaquīl: 91–139

94–95:   *cupīdine…ac spē magnī honōris*: ablatives of cause with an objective genitive.

102:       *ventrem ferre*: as the margins state, this equals *gravida esse*, i.e., to be pregnant.

105–106:   *Cui cum dīvitiae iam animōs facerent, auxit uxor eius Tanaquīl*: understand *animōs* ("courage") also with *auxit*. When used in the plural, *animus* frequently means "spirit, courage," but can also mean, as here, "too much spirit," i.e., *superbia*.

108–109:   *exsule advenā ortum*: "an exile descended from a foreigner," in apposition to *Lucumōnem*, giving the words of the Etruscans' scorn (*spernentibus*).

109–111:   *Tanaquīl...oblītaque amōris patriae, <u>dummodo</u> virum honōrā-
            tum vidēret: dummodo* + the subjunctive, "as long as, provided
            that" (Cap. XL).

112–114:   "*in novō populō, <u>ubi</u> <u>omnis</u> <u>repentīna</u> <u>atque</u> <u>ex</u> <u>virtūte</u> <u>nōbilitās</u>
            <u>sit</u>, futūrum locum fortī ac strēnuō virō*": subordinate clause
            in *ōrātiō oblīqua* (Cap. XXXVI) = direct discourse: "*in novō
            populō, ubi omnis repentīna atque ex virtūte nōbilitās <u>est</u>, <u>erit</u>
            <u>locus</u> fortī ac strēnuō virō.*"

114–116:   *Facile persuādet Lucumōnī ut cupidō honōrum et cui Tarquiniī
            māterna tantum patria esset:* although this looks like an indi-
            rect command, it is not; it's a causal clause: "she easily per-
            suaded Lucumo because he was...and for him..."; *māterna
            tantum patria*: his fatherland only on his mother's side (his
            mother was from Tarquinia, his father from Corinth, l.97).

118–120:   *ventum erat* = *vēnērunt* (Cap. XL); *eī...sedentī...aufert*: "took
            away from," dative of reference with verbs of depriving, such
            as here, with *aufert* (cf. XXXVIII.69).

121:        *aptē*: "fitly," "rightly," "snugly."

122–123:   *perītus, -a, -um* + objective genitive (*caelestium prōdigiōrum*).

125:        *nūntiam* in apposition to *eam ālitem*: "came as a messenger."

127:        *dīvīnitus*: adverb, "by divine providence."

134–135:   *beneficiīsque quōs poterat sibi conciliandō* = *eōs quōs poterat
            beneficiīs sibi conciliat.*

136:        *brevī*: sc. *tempore.*

137–138:   *bellō domīque* = *domī mīlitiaeque* (l.154; cf. l.42).

L. Tarquinius Prīscus rēx: 140–223

142:        *glōriā*: ablative of respect with *pār* (Cap. XXXIII).

144:        *rēgī creandō*: dative of purpose (Cap. XXXVI) with the gerun-
            dive (= *ad rēgem creandum*).

145:        *vēnātum*: supine (Caps. XXII, XLV).

147–148:   "*Sē nōn rem novam petere, quia duo iam peregrīnī Rōmae rēgnā-
            vissent*": subordinate clause in *ōrātiō oblīqua* (Cap. XXXVI) =
            direct discourse: *nōn rem novam <u>petō</u>, quia duo iam peregrīnī
            Rōmae <u>rēgnāvērunt</u>.*

147–156:   Tarquinius Priscus's speech is reported, that is, in *ōrātiō obliqua.*

152–154:   *quā cīvīlibus officiīs fungantur hominēs*: subordinate clause in indirect discourse (Cap. XXXVI) = direct discourse: *quā*: ablative of time when (refers to *aetas*); *fungantur*: *fungī* + ablative of means (Cap. XXXVIII); *quam*: comparison with *māiōrem partem* (accusative of duration of time, Cap. XIII).

154–155:   *sub haud spernendō magistrō* = *sub magistrō quī haud spernendus est.*

160:        *centum in patrēs lēgit*: *patrēs* = *senātōrēs.*

164–165:   *praedāque inde māiōre quam spērāverat revectā*: ablative absolute containing a relative clause of comparison.

167–168:   *Loca dīvīsa patribus equitibusque*: "distributed to"; *ubi spectācula sibi facerent*: indirect question; *"forī" appellātī*: *forus* is the archaic form of *forum.*

171:        *coeptīs intervēnit*: dative with intransitive verb.

171–173:   *Adeōque ea subita rēs fuit ut prius Aniēnem trānsīrent hostēs quam obviam īre ac prohibēre exercitus Rōmānus posset* = *ea rēs fuit adeō subita ut hostēs trānsīrent Aniēnem prius quam Rōmānus exercitus obviam īre ac prohibēre posset.*

174–175:   *pugnātum est*: impersonal passive of an intransitive verb (Cap. XL).

178–179:   *numerō alterum tantum adiēcit*: "added a second (group) just as large to their number"; *prō*: "instead of," with *nōngentīs.*

181:        *sed praeterquam quod*: "beyond the fact that"; the *quod* clause is the object of *praeterquam.*

198–199:   *Sabīnīs*: dative with *adēmptum*, "taken from" (see note above on ll.118–120); *Collātiae*: locative.

204–205:   *esse in suā potestāte*: idiom: "to be one's own master, to be under one's own power."

210–212:   *dē ūniversā rē*: i.e., all the Latins taken as a whole; *omne nōmen Latīnum*: i.e., all the towns that comprised Latium.

Iuvenis indolis rēgiae: 224–246

225:      *vīsū mīrābile*: ablative of supine (Cap. XXII).

226–227: *puerō dormientī…caput ārsisse*: dative of reference (Cap. XXXVI); cf. the harmless fire that encircles the head of Ascanius (XXXVII.219ff). Servius Tullius was the child of a slave in the royal household.

231:      *donec* + anticipatory subjunctive (Cap. XXXVII).

236:      *omnī cūrā nostrā*: ablative of manner (Cap. XXV).

238:      *puerum filiī locō habēre*: "to consider the boy a son, in the status of a son." (We still say people are *in locō parentis* when they are assuming the responsibility of a parent.)

240–241: *quod…esset*: causal clause, "because he was"; *dīs cordī*: double dative ("dear to the gods," Cap. XXXVI); *iuvenis ēvāsit vērē indolis rēgiae*: genitive of description (Cap. XIX).

244–246: *quācumque dē causā*: "for whatever reason," i.e., whether or not his head really caught fire; *illī habitus*: "was held for him"; *crēdere prohibet*: "forbids (us) from believing that" + indirect statement; *servā nātum*: "born from a slave woman."

Servius Tullius rēx factus: 247–306

251:      *habēre*: "to consider"; *habēre prō* + ablative: "consider as."

261:      *ex compositō*: "by agreement, according to plan"; *ōrdītur*: "begins."

262:      *secūrim*: pure *i*-stem (Cap. XVI).

266–267: *quid reī esset*: partitive genitive with neuter pronoun (Cap. XLIV) in indirect question.

271–272: *eōrum quī*: Ancus's two sons; *aliēnīs manibus*: "with hands not their own," i.e., the shepherds who carried out the deed.

273–275: *sequere*: imperative of *sequī* (so too line 277); *fore = futūrum esse*; *dīvīnō quondam circumfūsō igne*: ablative of means; *excitet*: jussive subjunctive; *expergīscere*: imperative of *expergīscī*.

282:      *sōpītum esse*: "to be deprived of senses, be rendered unconscious."

283–284: *brevī ipsum eōs vīsūrōs esse*; *eōs*: pronoun shift in indirect statement; what she said was "*brevī ipsum vōs vidēbitis*."

284–285:	*dictō audientem esse* + dative (*Serviō Tulliō*): "obey."
285–286:	*aliīsque...mūneribus fūnctūrum*: *fungī* takes an ablative of means (Cap. XXXVIII).
295–296:	*ut*: when; *exsulātum*: supine.
297–299:	*nōn sōlum...sed etiam...quālis...tālis*: these syntax markers clarify the long sentence.
305–306:	*haud dubius rēx*: "without a doubt (now) the king" because he now has the approval of the people (*cum patribus tum plēbī probātus*).

Cēnsus īnstitūtus: 307–357

307:	*cēnsus* comes from *cēnsēre*, ("to assess, estimate"), whence the meaning "to judge, form a judgment" (cf. *quid cēnsēs*, ll.46–47).
310:	*prō habitū pecūniārum*: "in proportion to the state of their finances."
314–315:	*Ex iīs quī centum mīlium aeris aut māiōrem cēnsum habērent octōgintā cōnfēcit centuriās*: descriptive/generalizing relative clause (Caps. XXXIX, XLII).
317:	*forīs*: i.e., *mīlitiae*, "in the field."
317–318:	*fabrum* (= *fabrōrum*): *faber* means "craftsman"; these particular *fabrī* were assigned the care of war machines; *stipendia facere*: "earn wages."
319–326:	*septuāgintā mīlium, quīnquāgintā mīlium, quīnque et vīgintī mīlium, ūndecim mīlibus*: understand *aeris*, as in l.314; *ūndecim mīlibus* is ablative of price (Cap. VIII).
328–329:	*immūnis mīlitiā*: ablative of separation (Cap. XXXVI): the poor's freedom from military service also meant lack of political clout.
337:	*suovetaurīlia* (n. pl.) is a sacrifice of a swine, sheep, and bull offered at *lūstrātiōnēs*, purification ceremonies.
344:	*Vīminālem inde auget Ēsquiliniīs*: *Ēsquiliniīs* is ablative; the Esquiline is adjacent to the Viminal.
345–346:	*pōmērium prōfert*: Servius extended the pomerium, which, as you learned in XLIII.148–153, is the consecrated space on either side of the city wall which must be left free of buildings.

349: *iam tum erat inclutum*: *inclutum* is predicate adjective: the shrine was already famous at that time.

350–351: *id* = the temple; *factum (esse) fāma ferēbat*: i.e., "rumor had it"; *cōnsēnsum*: "concord" (cf.: *commūniter*); *deōs cōnsociātōs*: i.e., the various gods of the various *cīvitātēs* in Asia.

Tullia ferōx: 358–451

362: *vellent iubērentne sē rēgnāre*: the formula for asking the people to ratify anything is, in direct speech, *Velītis, iubeātis*, which is here reported indirectly.

366: *ipse iuvenis ārdentis animī*: genitive of description (Cap. XIX) as is *mītis ingeniī iuvenem* (1.369).

370: Latin expresses marriage differently for men, who lead women into matrimony (*in mātrimōnium dūcere*), and women, who are wed to their husbands (*nūbere*, intransitive with the dative).

371: *longē disparēs mōribus*: ablative of respect (Cap. XXXIII).

374–377: *admīrārī, dīcere, spernere, parcere*: historical infinitives.

384: *interdiū*: adv., "during the day."

385: *patī*: historical infinitive; *parricīdium*: parricide, as the name implies, is usually used of killing one's father but can be extended to the murder of a relative; *grātuīta*: "for nothing, with no profit."

388–389: take *regnum* with both infinitives, i.e., "*qui habēre rēgnum quam rēgnum spērāre mallet.*"

390: *quīn* = *quī nē*: "why don't you?"

392–394: *creat vocatque*: verbs are often singular in agreement with the last stated subject, even though there are multiple subjects (*Dī Penātēs, patris imāgō, domus rēgia, rēgāle solium, nōmen Tarquinium*).

395: *parum…animī*: "too little spirit," partitive genitive.

396: *ut*: "as"; *facesse*: imperative from the intensive *facessere*: "to do something eagerly," also "to retire, go away."

403–404: *Admonēre Tarquiniī Prīscī beneficiī ac prō eō grātiam repetere*: *admonēre* (historical infinitive) admits several constructions, among them, as here, the genitive ("remind of"); *beneficium*:

Roman society was bound together by *beneficia*, favors done that entailed gratitude (*grātia*) and loyalty.

405–406:   <u>*Cum*</u> *ingentia pollicendō,* <u>*tum*</u> *rēgis crīminibus, omnibus locīs crēscere: pollicendō, crīminibus*: ablatives of means (*crīmen* = "charge, accusation"); *ingentia*: "remarkable (things)"; *rēgis*: objective genitive; *crēscere*: historical infinitive.

412–413:   *āctum est dē* + ablative: "it's all over for x," "x is done for."

420:        *prīmōribus ēreptum*: dative of reference: "snatched from"; *sordidissimō cuique: quisque* + the superlative = "all the," so, here "all the most despicable people" (Cap. XXXI).

424–425:   *quā…audāciā*: ablative of manner (Cap. XXV).

432–433:   *multō et* <u>*aetāte*</u> *et* <u>*vīribus*</u> *validior*: ablative of degree of difference; *multō* (Cap. XVI), with the ablative of respect, *aetāte et vīribus* (Cap. XXXIII).

435:        *comitum < comes, comitis.*

439–441:   *(Tullia) nōn abhorret;…admonitū Tulliae id factum*: i.e.,*Tullia admonuit ut Servius interficerētur; satis cōnstat* (Cap. XLI).

Fīlia Impia (Ovidius: Fāstī. Ex librō VI): 452–473

454:        *perāctō*: "killed."

457:        *vīvere dēbuerant*: see Cap. XLIII grammar section on *dēbēre* and the infinitive.

459:        *sī ausūrī erāmus*: "if we were intending to venture."

460:        *rēgia rēs scelus est*: "crime is the prerogative of kings."

465:        *socerō*: dative of reference with verbs of depriving, such as here, *rapta* (Cap. XXXVIII).

466:        *sub*: not "under" but "at the foot of."

III. Vocābula

Nōmina

1st

contumēlia, -ae	insult, affront
fōrmula, -ae	terms, formula
licentia, -ae	wantonness, license

nūptiae, -ārum (*pl.*)	wedding
rīxa, -ae	quarrel, brawl
rota, -ae	wheel
salīnae, -ārum (*pl.*)	salt pans, salt works
serva, -ae	female slave

2nd

augurium, -ī	augury, omen
bonum, -ī	good, blessing (*pl.* goods)
captīvus, -ī	prisoner of war
carpentum, -ī	two-wheeled carriage
coepta, -ōrum (*pl.*)	beginnings, undertakings
comitia, -ōrum (*pl.*)	assembly of the people
dēlūbrum, -ī	temple, shrine
duellum, -ī	war
exōrdium, -ī	beginning
fīlum, -ī	thread, fillet
forum, -ī	public space, marketplace
hospitium, -ī	guest friendship/house
īnstitūtum, -ī	practice, custom, usage
iūmentum, -ī	beast of burden/draft
lūstrum, -ī	ceremony of purification
parricīdium, -ī	murder of near relation
pilleus, -ī	felt cap
postulātum, -ī	demand
sēcrētum, -ī	solitude, secrecy, seclusion, privacy
suffrāgium, -ī	vote
terminus, -ī	boundary(-stone)
testāmentum, -ī	will, testament
vehiculum, -ī	wagon, vehicle

3rd

agger, -eris (*m.*)	rampart
āles, -itis (*f.*)	large bird
arbiter, -trī (*m.*)	eyewitness, arbitrator
cōgitātiō, -ōnis (*f.*)	thought, reflection
cōnfessiō, -ōnis (*f.*)	admission, confession
cornicen, -inis (*m.*)	horn-blower, bugler

dēditiō, -ōnis (*f.*)	surrender, capitulation
diciō, -ōnis (*f.*)	dominion, power
dignitās, -ātis (*f.*)	worthiness, dignity, rank
exsul, -is (*m./f.*)	banished person, exile
fautor, -ōris (*m.*)	supporter
fraus, -audis (*f.*)	deceit, guile
furor, -ōris (*m.*)	madness
hērēs, -ēdis (*m.*)	heir
incursiō, -ōnis (*f.*)	incursion, inroad
indignitās, -ātis (*f.*)	indignity, humiliation
iūniōrēs, -um (*m. pl.*)	younger men
mūnītiō, -ōnis (*f.*)	fortification
novitās, -ātis (*f.*)	novelty, inexperience
pietās, -ātis (*f.*)	respect, devotion, piety
praecō, -ōnis (*m.*)	crier, announcer, herald
scrīptor, -ōris (*m.*)	writer
sēditiō, -ōnis (*f.*)	discord, insurrection
senectūs, -ūtis (*f.*)	old age
suovetaurīlia, -ium (*n. pl.*)	a sacrifice consisting of a swine, a sheep, and a bull
temeritās, -ātis (*f.*)	recklessness
tūtor, -ōris (*m.*)	guardian

4th

admonitus, -ūs	advice, prompting (only in *abl.*)
cēnsus, -ūs	assessment, registration
comitātus, -ūs	escort, retinue
cōnsēnsus, -ūs	concord, agreement
habitus, -ūs	state, condition
ictus, -ūs	stroke, blow
nurus, -ūs (*f.*)	daughter-in-law
tribus, -ūs (*f.*)	tribe (division of citizens)

VERBA

-āre

(affectō) affectāre	strive after, aspire to
(āmigrō) āmigrāre	go away, remove

(amplificō) amplificāre	enlarge
(commigrō) commigrāre	move, go and live
(dēmandō) dēmandāre	entrust, hand over
(domō) domāre, -uisse, -itum	tame, subdue
(exstimulō) exstimulāre	stir up, incite
(exsulō) exsulāre	live in exile
(fīrmō) fīrmāre	reinforce, strengthen
(frūstror) frūstrārī	deceive
(honōrō) honōrāre	honor
(īnstīgō) īnstīgāre	urge, incite
(praeparō) praeparāre	prepare
(testor) testārī	call to witness
(volitō) volitāre	fly about, flutter

-ēre

(abhorreō) abhorrēre, -uisse	be inconsistent with
(coerceō) coercēre, -cuisse, -citum	keep in control, restrain

-ere

(accingō) accingere (< cingere)	gird
(arripiō) arripere (< rapere)	grasp, take hold of
(compōnō) compōnere (< pōnere)	settle, arrange, compose
(cōnflīgō) cōnflīgere, -xisse, -ctum	clash, fight
(conquiēscō) conquiēscere	rest
(cōnscīscō) cōnscīscere, -īvisse, -ītum	decree, inflict (on)
(dēiciō) dēicere (< icere)	throw/bring down
(dēligō) dēligere (< legere)	pick out, choose
(dēlinquō) dēlinquere	misbehave, do wrong
(distribuō) distribuere, -buisse, -būtum	divide, distribute, share
(expergīscor) expergīscī, -perrēctum	wake up
(exposcō) exposcere (< poscere)	ask for, demand
(facessō) facessere	do eagerly, go away, be off
(fungor) fungī, fūnctum (+ *abl.*)	discharge, complete

(incurrō) incurrere (< currere)	rush in, make an inroad
(ingredior) ingredī, -gressum	enter, begin, walk
(maledīcō) maledīcere (< dīcere)	abuse, insult
(perpellō) perpellere (< pellere)	enforce
(persolvō) persolvere (< solvere)	pay in full, fulfill
(portendō) portendere (< tendere)	portend, presage
(profundo) profundere (< fundere)	pour out, shed
(revehō) revehere (< vehere)	bring back
(sīdō) sīdere, sēdisse, sessum	sit down, settle
(tingō) tingere, -xisse, -ctum	wet, soak

-īre

(acciō) accīre, -īvisse, -ītum	summon, send for
(cōnsentiō) cōnsentīre (< sentīre)	agree (on)
(ērudiō) ērudīre, -rudīvisse, -rudītum	instruct, educate
(impediō) impedīre, -pedīvisse, -pedītum	impede, obstruct
(interveniō) intervenīre (< venīre)	turn up, occur, disturb
(sōpiō) sōpīre, -īvisse, -ītum	put to sleep, stun

ADIECTĪVA

1st/2nd

amārus, -a, -um	bitter
aptus, -a, -um	fit, suitable, convenient
clandestīnus, -a, -um	secret, clandestine
conspicuus, -a, -um	conspicuous, spectacular
continuus, -a, -um	continuous, successive
ferrātus, -a, -um	tipped with iron
grātuītus, -a, -um	gratuitous, futile
inclutus, -a, -um	famous
īnfernus, -a, -um	of the underworld
lapideus, -a, -um	of stone, stone
lēgitimus, -a, -um	legal, lawful

māternus, -a, -um	maternal
paternus, -a, -um	paternal
perītus, -a, -um	practiced, expert
praecipuus, -a, -um	outstanding, exceptional
probātus, -a, -um	acceptable, pleasing
sanguinulentus, -a, -um	bloodstained
strenuous, -a, -um	active, vigorous

3rd

cōmis, -e	kind, affable
compos (*gen.* **compotis**)	in possession of (+ *gen.*)
exsanguis, -e	bloodless, lifeless
fētiālis, -e	fetial; diplomatic
immūnis, -e	exempt (from), tax-free (+ *abl.*)
pedester, -tris, -tre	pedestrian, infantry
rēgālis, -e	royal
senior (*gen.* **seniōris**)	older
terrestris, -e	earthly, terrestrial

ADVERBIA

dīvīnitus	by divine will
fermē	about, almost
prīvātim	privately, personally
properē	quickly
virītim	man by man

ALIA

ex compositō	according to agreement
nātū	older/younger (*abl.* māior/ minor [*n.*])
quō pactō	= *quō modō*: in what way, manner

XLV: QVADRAGESIMVM QVINTVM: ROMA LIBERATA (Livy)[1]

[Ex T. Līviī 'ab Urbe Conditā' librō I. 49–60, nōnnūllīs mūtātīs et omissīs]

I. Ørberg's Introduction

Rome's last king, *Lucius Tarquinius*, surnamed *Superbus* (*cui Superbō cognōmen datum est*), was a cruel tyrant who stopped at nothing to strengthen and expand his power. When the Latin *Turnus* dared to oppose him, the king had a large quantity of arms secretly hidden in Turnus' house; this was used as evidence in a false accusation of subversive activities, and he was condemned to death by his own countrymen. In this way, the Latins were pacified.

The city of *Gabiī* continued to defy Roman power. Unable to take the city by force, Tarquinius devised a plan to seize it by treachery. His youngest son Sextus came to Gabii pretending to have escaped from his cruel father and succeeded in winning the confidence of the inhabitants to such a degree that they chose him as their leader in the war with Rome. He now sent a messenger to his father asking how to make the most of his new power. Tarquinius gave no straightforward answer to the messenger, but while walking with him in his garden, he struck off the heads of the tallest poppies with his walking stick. When Sextus heard about this, he realized what his father wanted him to do: he killed or banished all the prominent Gabians and then delivered the defenseless city to the Roman king!

After telling the story of the oracle which promised *Brūtus* supremacy in Rome because he alone understood its hidden meaning, Livy proceeds to tell the dramatic events which led to the expulsion of the royal family from Rome.

During the siege of the city of *Ardea*, the king's three sons and *Collātīnus*, son of the king's cousin Egerius, started a quarrel about whose wife was the most virtuous. To decide the matter, they paid unannounced visits to their wives. Sextus Tarquinius became infatuated with the winner, Collatinus's beautiful

---

1. For an explanation of the line number references convention, see p. xxvi.

wife *Lucrētia*, whom they found spinning wool in her home in Collatia. A few days later Sextus went to Collatia, entered Lucretia's chamber sword in hand, woke the sleeping woman, and raped her. After his departure, Lucretia sent for her husband and her father, who arrived together with Brutus. She told them what she had suffered, demanded vengeance, and thrust a knife into her heart. Brutus grasped the bloody knife and swore that he would drive out the king and his family from Rome. The people and the army sided with Brutus, the king was banished with his wife and his three sons, and Brutus and Collatinus are elected the first Roman consuls by the popular assembly (the *comitia centuriāta*). This event is dated to the year 509 BC.

This chapter ends with Ovid's description of these events in the second book of his *Fāstī*. You have now finished an adapted narrative of Livy's first book. In the text that you have been reading, departures from the original have become less and less noticeable, and from line 222 in this chapter (*Muliebris certāminis laus…*), the text is unchanged. From now on, all the passages from Roman authors are presented unchanged—apart from omissions.

II. Auxilia Legendī

Tarquinius Superbus: 1–25

5:	*favisse < favēre*: "favor," intransitive + dative.
8–9:	*ut quī…regnāret*: causal clause.
10:	*per eam causam*: "under that pretext" (a frequent idiom).
12–13:	*…<u>unde</u> nihil aliud quam praedam spērāre <u>posset</u>*: adverbial final (purpose) clause.
15–19:	*<u>Hic</u> enim rēgum <u>prīmus</u> trāditum ā priōribus mōrem dē omnibus rēbus senātum cōnsulendī <u>solvit</u>, domesticīs cōnsiliīs rem pūblicam <u>administrāvit</u>*: *rēgum*: genitive with *prīmus*; *mōrem*: direct object of *solvit*, modified by *trāditum*; *cōnsulendī*: objective gentive dependent on *mōrem*; *senātum*: object of *cōnsulendī*; *domestica cōnsilia*: i.e., instead of resolutions by the senate.
23:	*Latinum nomen* = places that enjoyed Latin rights, *iūs Latīnum* (cf. ll.36, 81–82).
24:	*fīliam nūptum dat*: supine, see grammar section above.

Turnus Herdōnius: 26–89

27:            *diē certā*: although often masculine, *diēs* is sometimes femi-
               nine in the singular when refering to an established time, as
               here.

29–30:   *agere dē* + ablative: "negotiate about" (a frequent expression
               with several shades of meaning).

31:            *antequam sōl occideret*: subjunctive with anticipatory *ante-
               quam* (Cap. XLII).

33–34:   *invehere in* + accusative: "attack (with words)," "inveigh
               against."

35–36:   *Quicquam*: used only in negative clauses (Cap. XXVI).

37–38:   Note that the subjunctives (*indīxerit*, etc.) violate sequence of
               tense (Caps. XXXIII, XXXVI). Since the leading verb is plu-
               perfect (*erat invectus*). The primary sequence of the *ōrātiō
               oblīqua* represents the speech as more immediate and forceful.

40:            *exsulātum eant*: supine with verbs of motion (Cap. XXII,
               XXXVI, grammar section above).

41–42:   *portendī*: passive infinitive of *portendere*, in passive means
               "threaten" + dative; *sī sē audiant, domum omnēs inde abitūrōs*:
               future condition in *ōrātiō oblīqua* (Cap. XLIII): "*sī mē audiētis,
               domum omnēs hinc abībitis.*"

46:            *id temporis*: partitive genitive with a neuter pronoun: "at this
               point in time" (Caps. XVI, XXIX).

48:            *eōdem* = adverb of place to which: *eō* + suffix (*-dem*) meaning
               "to the same place."

52–53:   *...ut eundem terrōrem quō cīvium animōs domī oppresserat
               Latīnīs iniceret*: "so that he might keep the spirits of the citi-
               zens at home down *with the same terror (as the one) with
               which...*"

55:            *hospitium*: "inn, lodging place."

59:            *salūtī sibi atque illīs fuisse*: double dative: "had been (to) the
               salvation of..."; *salūs*, like *auxilium*, *bonum*, and *praesidium*,
               can be used in the dative to express purpose or tendency
               (Cap. XXXVI).

62–63:   *id verumne an falsum sit*: indirect question.

66–67:	*eō*: adverb "to that place" (cf. l.299); *ventum est*: impersonal passive of intransitive verb (Cap. XL).
69:	*cāritāte dominī*: ablative of cause (Cap. XXXVII) with an objective genitive (Cap. XXV).
70:	*enimverō = enim + verō*: "surely, truly" (when *enim* is combined with *verō*, it comes first in its clause, unlike *enim* alone, which comes second; see Cap. X).
76–78:	*Revocātīs deinde ad concilium Latīnīs, Tarquinius prīmum eōs collaudāvit 'quod Turnum prō manifēstō scelere meritā poenā affēcissent*': subjunctive in a clause of reported reason, reporting the reason why Tarquin praised the Latins. Were Livy giving his *own* reason, he would have used *affēcerant* (Cap. XLII).
78–79:	*ēgit dē renovandō foedere*: see on *agere dē* above (ll.29–30).
81–82:	*capita nōminis Latīnī*: just like our "heads of state," the heads (leaders) of the Latin league.
87–88:	*Tarquinius miscuit manipulōs ex Latīnīs Rōmānīsque, ut ex bīnīs singulōs faceret bīnōsque ex singulīs*: i.e., each maniple was made up half of Romans and half of Latins (*bīnōs ex singulīs*), and thus the two sides, the Romans and the Latins, were mixed into one (*singulōs ex bīnīs*).

Gabiī dolō captī: 90–167

92:	*quīn* (Cap. XL).
94–95:	*cum vēndendā praedā quadrāgintā talenta argentī fēcisset*: take *quadrāgintā* with *talenta*, not *praedā vēndendā*; *praedā vēndendā* is an ablative of means.
97:	*lentius spē*: ablative of comparison with a comparative adverb (Cap. XXIV).
98:	*vī adortus < adorior, adorīrī*: "attack (by force)."
99:	*arte Rōmānā*: in apposition to *fraude ac dolō*: ablative of means.
100:	*velut positō bellō*: *pōnere* standing for (as often) *dēpōnere*; *fundāmentīs templī iaciendīs*: you learned *iacere* as "throw, hurl" (Cap. XII), but it also means "set, establish, build."
102–103:	*ex compositō*: "according to plan"; *Gabiōs*: accusative of place to which; *patris in sē saevitiam nōn tolerandam*: a summary of

the complaint (*querēns*) that is detailed in the extended *ōrātiō oblīqua* that follows (ll.104–114).

106–108:   *sē…ēlāpsum*: accusative subject (with participial modifier) of *crēdidisse*; these two "sandwich" the further indirect statement: *nihil…hostēs L. Tarquiniī* (Cap. XXXVI).

108–114:   *quod sī apud eōs supplicibus locus nōn sit, pererrātūrum sē omne Latium, Volscōsque sē inde et Aequōs et Hernicōs petītūrum*: condition in *ōrātiō oblīqua*; *quod sī*: "but if," a common connective that always refers to what has just preceded; *dōnec*: "until," the original mood is obscured in *ōrātiō oblīqua*, but it would have been anticipatory subjunctive (Cap. XL); *quī… sciant et…parātī sint*: relative clause of characteristic.

115–117:   *quālis…, quālis…, tālis…esset*: subordinate clauses in *ōrātiō oblīqua* (Cap. XXXVI) secondary sequence with the historical present *mīrantur* (Cap. XXXVII).

118:        *futūrum ut*: see grammar section above.

123–126:   *quod…nōvisset scīretque*: see above: subjunctive of reported reason; *superbiam rēgiam*: royal arrogance, i.e., "the arrogance of the king."

126–129:   *ita cum sēnsim*: *cum* conjunction; *sēnsim*: "little by little"; *cum prōmptissimīs iuvenum*: *cum* preposition + ablative; *praedātum*: supine (so too *scīscitātum*, l.138); *dictīs…aptīs*: ablative absolute.

130:        *īnsciā multitūdine quid agerētur*: indirect question dependent on the *īnsciā* of the ablative absolute.

131:        *quibus*: antecedent: *proelia* (l.130); *esset*: subjunctive as part of the *cum* clause.

135–136:   *tantā cāritāte esse ut*: ablative of description (Cap. XXXII) followed by a result clause.

138–139:   *scīscitātum*: supine of purpose.

140:        *huic* nūntō: dative with *respōnsum est*; *dubiae fideī*: genitive of description (Cap. XXXVI).

142–144:   *papāver, -eris* (*n.*): the poppy flower; *interrogandō exspectandōque*: ablative of gerund (ablative of cause) dependent on *fessus*; *ut rē imperfectā*: "as his business remained unaccomplished."

145–146:   *quae dīxerit ipse quaeque vīderit*: perfect subjunctives in indirect questions.

148–149:   *ubi…vellet…praeciperet*: indirect questions.

149–151:   *multī palam* (*interfectī sunt*); *multī palam, quīdam*: asyndeton (lack of connectives).

157–159:   *negōtia*: antecedent of *quorum*; *ut…relinqueret*: substantive clause of result (Cap. XXXVII) dependent on *negōtia* (*quōrum*).

162–167:   Reading help: *mīlitiae*: "dative" (i.e., added to their military service); *sē…suīs*: indirect statement with *indignābātur*; sentence markers: *minus…quam*; *minōra* (with *opera*) *…māiōris* (genitive of description with *labōris*); *opera speciē minōra, sed labōris aliquantō māiōris*: tasks smaller in appearance (*speciē*, abl. of respect) but of much more (*aliquantō*, abl. of degree of difference); *ad*: take with both accusative gerundive phrases (*faciendōs…agendam*).

Respōnsum ōrāculī: 168–195

177:          *Tarquiniā…nātus*: ablative of source, "born from…."

178–179:   *nihil in animō suō rēgī timendum relinquere statuit* = *statuit relinquere* (complementary infinitive); *suō rēgī*: dative of agent with the gerundive *timendum*, i.e., *nihil in animō suō quod rēx timēret*.

183:          *lūdibrium*: "as a laughingstock," "as a a joke."

184:          *ventum est*: see note to lines 66–67.

185–186:   *cupīdō incessit animōs iuvenum scīscitandī 'ad quem eōrum rēgnum Rōmānum esset ventūrum'*: *cupīdō…scīscitandī* "sandwich" (Cap. XXXVII), followed by an indirect question dependent on *scīscitandī*.

187:          *ferunt*: i.e., *fāma est, trāditur*.

188:          *vestrum prīmus*: partitive gentive of *vōs* (Cap. XXIX).

189–193:   *ut…esset*: purpose clause; *Ignārus respōnsī, expers imperiī*: objective gentives (Cap. XXV).

192–193:   *ipsī* (nom.) *sortī* (dat.) *permittunt*: in line 173 *sors* means "oracle, oracular response"; here the sense is more "fortune, chance"; *Uter…daret*: indirect question in secondary sequence (*permittunt* is a historical present; see Cap. XXXVII); *rediissent* represents a future perfect indicative in secondary sequence (see Cap. XLIII); cf. direct discourse: *uter prior, cum Rōmam redierimus, mātrī ōsculum dabit.* Just as *redierimus* is a completed action in relation to *dabit*, so is *rediissent* a future completed action in relation to *daret*.

193–194:   *aliō*: adverb, "elsewhere, in a different direction," with *spectāre*; *velut sī prōlāpsus cecidisset, terram ōsculō tetigit*: as at XLII.134, the subjunctive underscores the contrafactual nature of the *velut sī*: Brutus had not slipped and fallen—he did so to conceal his understanding of the oracle.

195:   *scīlicet 'quod ea commūnis 'māter' omnium mortālium esset'*: subjunctive of reported reason (Cap. XLII).

Uxor castissima: 196–228

197:   *Reditum (est) inde Rōmam*: impersonal passive of intransitive (Cap. XL).

199–200:   *ut in eā regiōne et in eā aetāte*: "for," "considering"; *eaque...fuit*: "and this (its wealth) was the very reason for the war."

201–202:   *aerāriō*: Cf. Cap. XXXVI.133–134: *Aedēs Sāturnī est aerārium populī Rōmānī, id est locus ubi pecūnia pūblica dēpōnitur ac servātur*: sentence markers: *cum...tum.*

205:   *Temptāta rēs est sī...posset*: Indirect question with *sī* as "whether," "to see whether."

206:   *prōcēdere*: "to turn out, succeed"; *parum*: "too little, not well."

207:   *statīvīs (castrīs)*: a stationary camp (Cap. XLIII).

210:   *Egeriī fīlius*: for Egerius, see XLIV.104.

211:   *suam quisque*: "each praises his own (wife)" (Cap. XVIII).

213:   *quantum cēterīs praestet*: indirect question; *praestāre* + dative ("is superior to").

215–216:   *praesentēs (nōs) nostrārum (uxōrum) ingenia.*

217:   *age sānē*: colloquial: "come on then!" "so let's go!"(*age*: imperative, "come on"; *sānē*: adverb, "well, really, very").

219:   *nurus, -ūs* (f.): "daughter-in-law" (Cap. XLIV).

220:   *tempus terentēs*: *tempus terere*, "pass time," literally "wear away time."

222:          *muliebris certaminis laus*: objective genitive; *muliebris* is the adjective of *mulier penes* + accusative, "with, in the possession of" (only used with names of persons).

Lucrētia violāta: 229–273

232:          *ab ignārīs cōnsiliī*: *ab eis quī ignōrābant consilium Tarquiniī*; *cōnsiliī*: objective genitive (Cap. XXV).

234:          *strictō gladiō*: "with drawn sword" (ablative absolute).

237:          *moriēre = moriēris*.

241–242:   *in omnēs partēs*: in every respect; *versāre*: in the sense of "bend": "he tried to bend her feminine heart in every respect."

244:          *cum (tē) mortuā*.

247–249:   *expugnātō decore muliebrī*: ablative of cause with *ferōx*, as is *tantō malō* with *maesta*.

250–251:   *ut cum singulīs fidēlibus amīcīs veniant; ita factō mātūrātōque opus esse: rem atrōcem incidisse = cum singulīs fidēlibus amīcīs venīte! ita factō mātūrātōque opus est: rem atrōcem incidit; factō mātūrātōque opus est*: *opus* + ablative of perfect passive participles: "there is need of action (*factō*) and speed (*mātūrātō*)."

257–258:   *quaerentīque virō*: dative with *inquit*; *Satin' salvē?*: "are you OK?," "is everything all right?"; *quid salvī est…?* partitive genitive with a neuter pronoun (Caps. XVI, XXIX, XLIV); *mulierī āmissā pudīcitiā*: ablative absolute.

261–262:   *dexterās (mānūs)*; *haud impūne adulterō fore*: "this will not at all be without punishment for the adulterer" = *adulter puniētur*.

263–264:   *mihi sibique…pestiferum*: "destructive to me—and to him."

265–266:   *aegrum animī*: *animī* is locative, "sick at heart"; *āvertendō*: ablative of means; *ab coactā = a Lucretiā, quae coacta est*; *dēlictī*: objective genitive.

267:          *consilium*: "intention," compare the distinction "*mentem peccāre, nōn corpus*."

269:          "*Vōs*" *inquit* "*vīderitis quid illī dēbeātur*": "you will see to what is due to that man"; *vīderitis*: future perfect; *quid…dēbeātur*: indirect question.

270:          *peccātō, suppliciō*: ablatives of separation (Cap. XXXVI).

Rēgēs exāctī: 274–343

277–278:   *Per hunc…castissimum ante rēgiam iniūriam sanguinem*: prepositional phrase (*ante…iniūriam*) "sandwiched" inside another (*per…sanguinem*).

278–282:   *iūrō…mē…exsecūtūrum nec passūrum* (*esse*).

284–285:   *mīrāculō* (ablative of means) *reī* (genitive); *unde* (sc. *esset*) *ingenium*: indirect question (see ll.177–180: *Brūtus…stultitiam simulāvit*).

285:        *tōtī*: Latin often expresses with an adjective what in English we might convey with an adverb; so here, "completely."

289:        *concient mīrāculō…indignitāte*: *mīrāculō*: i.e., Brutus's ability to speak; *indigitāte*: i.e., Tarquin's rape of Lucretia.

291–294:   (*Brūtus*) *auctor…arma capiendī 'adversus hostīlia ausōs'*: implied indirect statement; '*quod virōs, quod Rōmānōs decēret!*': subordinate clause in implied indirect statement (Cap. XLII).

295–296:   *Ferōcissimus quisque iuvenum*: *quisque* with the superlative, "all the most spirited of the young men" (Cap. XXXI).

299:        *ventum est*: see note above on line 67.

302:        *curritur*: impersonal passive (Cap. XL).

303:        *Celerēs, -um* (m. pl.) = *equitēs, um* (and in this period = the bodyguard of the king, XLII.226–228).

306–307:   *ōrātiō nēquāquam eius pectoris ingeniīque*: genitive of description: "by no means in keeping with that (*eius*) state of mind and ability which…" (Cap. XXXVI); *ad eam diem*: "up to that day"; *dē vī ac libīdine* etc. refers to the subject of the *ōrātiō oblīqua, ōrātiō habita* (*dē* = ablative).

309–310:   *Tricipitīnus*: Sp. Lucrētius Tricipitīnus, pater Lucrētiae; '*cui morte fīliae causa mortis indignior ac miserābilior esset*' = '*cui causa mortis indignior ac miserābilior morte* (*quam mors*) *fīliae esset*': *esset*: subordinate clause in implied *ōrātiō oblīqua* (Cap. XLII).

311–312:   *plēbis…dēmersae*.

312–314:   *Rōmānōs…factōs*: accusative of exclamation (Cap. XV).

315:        *corporī*: dative with *invecta*; *nefandō vehiculō*: ablative of means.

318:        *imperium regī abrogāret*: "take the power away from (dative with compound verb) the king."

320–322:   *iūniōribus...lectīs armātīsque*: sandwich around the relative clause *quī...dabant nōmen dare*, "to enlist, enroll one's name"; *ad concitandum...exercitum* encloses (sandwiches) *inde adversus rēgem*.

323:      *praefectus urbis*: governor of the city of Rome.

325–326:   *exsecrantibus...mulieribusque*: ablative absolute.

327:      *rē novā*: political change.

334:      *Caere* (accusative): ancient Etruscan city, now Cervetri.

337:      *concīverat < conciēre*: "stir up, produce."

340:      *Rēgnātum* (*est*): impersonal passive of intransitive verb (Cap. XL); *ad līberātam* sc. *urbem*.

Hostis prō hospite (Ovidius: Fāstī. Ex librō II versūs 785–852): 345–413

347:      *sōle iam parante condere vultūs suōs* (*vultus* is usually singular).

350:      *errōris* with *quantum*; *animīs* with *inest*; *rērum*: objective genitive with *īnscia*.

351:      *fūnctus* + ablative of means.

355:      *nūpta pudīca*: vocative (i.e., Lucretia).

360–361:   *ut quondam stabulīs dēprēnsa relictīs/parva sub īnfēstō cum iacet agna lupō = ut quondam agna parva, stabulīs relictīs, iacet, dēprēnsa, sub īnfēstō lupō.*

362–364:   *quid faciat? Pugnet?...Clamet?...Effugiat?*: deliberative subjunctives (Cap. XLI).

368:      *nīl agis*: "you are accomplishing nothing."

370:      *ferēris*: "you will be said."

371:      *succubuit < succumbere* (Cap. XL).

373:      *quantō*: ablative of price (Cap. VIII).

378:      *habitus, -ūs*: appearance, condition (Cap. XLIV).

394–395:   *respicit nē nōn procumbat honestē = cūrat ut honestē procumbat; cūra* (Lucretiae) *cadentis*.

402–403:   *Per tibi ego hunc iūrō fortem castumque cruōrem/perque tuōs Mānēs, quī mihi nūmen erunt = ego tibi iūrō per hunc fortem castumque cruōrem perque tuōs Mānēs, quī mihi nūmen erunt.*

404:            *profugā* with *stirpe.*

408:            *animī mātrōna virīlis*: genitive of description (Cap. XXXVI):
                "a woman of manly courage."

III. Vocābula

NŌMINA

1st

epulae, -ārum (*pl.*)	meal, feast
exsequiae, -ārum (*pl.*)	funeral procession, rites
invidia, -ae	envy, ill will, dislike
iuventa, -ae	youth
magnificentia, -ae	magnificence
minae, -ārum (*pl.*)	threats
miseria, -ae	misfortune, misery
noxa, -ae	harm, guilt
nūpta, -ae	wife
palma, -ae	palm, hand
prūdentia, -ae	intelligence, proficiency
pudīcitia, -ae	chastity, virtue
saevitia, -ae	savageness, cruelty
stultitia, -ae	stupidity, folly

2nd

adulter, -erī	adulterer
adulterium, -ī	adultery
damnum, -ī	loss
dēlictum, -ī	misdeed, offense
exsilium, -ī	exile
lūdibrium, -ī	mockery, derision, sport
manipulus, -ī	maniple
operārius, -ī	laborer
ōrāculum, -ī	oracle
peccātum, -ī	error, offense
portentum, -ī	portent, prodigy
praefectus, -ī	prefect, commander

stuprum, -ī	rape, defilement
tribūnus, -ī	tribune

3rd

aequālis, -is (*m./f.*)	person of the same age
auctōritās, -ātis (*f.*)	authorization, authority
bellātor, -ōris (*m.*)	warrior
cāritās, -ātis (*f.*)	high price, love, esteem
castīgātor, -ōris (*m.*)	one who reproves, corrects
castitās, -ātis (*f.*)	chastity
crātis, -is (*f.*)	hurdle (of wickerwork)
dēdecus, -oris (*n.*)	disgrace, dishonor
libīdō, -inis (*f.*)	desire, lust
mentiō, -ōnis (*f.*)	mention, reference
opifex, -icis (*m.*)	workman, artisan
orbitās, -ātis (*f.*)	loss of children/parents
papāver, -eris (*n.*)	poppy
paucitās, -ātis (*f.*)	small number, paucity
penetrālia, -ium (*n. pl.*)	the interior
prōlēs, -is (*f.*)	offspring
simultās, -ātis (*f.*)	enmity, quarrel
sors, -rtis (*f.*)	lot, drawing lots, fortune
victrīx, -īcis (*f.*)	femal conqueror (she who is) victorious

4th

magistrātus, -ūs	office, magistrate

VERBA

-āre

(abrogō) abrogāre	repeal, cancel
(administrō) administrāre	conduct, administer
(aequō) aequāre	make equal, equal
(āvolō) āvolāre	fly off, rush off
(collaudō) collaudāre	commend, praise
(dēlīberō) dēlīberāre	deliberate
(dicitō) dicitāre	dictate
(dītō) dītāre	enrich

(exsecrōr) exsecrārī	curse
(inambulō) inambulāre	walk up and down
(inclīnō) inclīnāre	turn, bend, incline
(indignōr) indignārī	resent, be indignant
(iūrō) iūrāre	swear
(māchinōr) māchinārī	devise, plot
(mānō) mānāre	flow, be wet, drip
(mātūrō) mātūrāre	make haste, hurry
(peccō) peccāre	do wrong
(pererrō) pererrāre	wander through
(praedōr) praedārī	plunder, loot
(rebellō) rebellāre	reopen the war, revolt
(scīscitōr) scīscitārī	inquire, ask
(stīllō) stīllāre	drip
(stuprō) stuprāre	violate, rape
(tolerō) tolerāre	bear, endure

-ēre

(obsideō) obsidēre, -sidisse, -sessum	besiege
(paveō) pavēre, pavisse	be terrified
(reticeō) reticēre, -uisse	keep silent
(urgeō) urgēre, ursisse	press, oppress

-ere

(assūmō) assūmere (< sumere)	take, lay claim to
(coniciō) conicere (< icere)	throw, put together
(convehō) convehere (< vehere)	carry, gather
(dēcutiō) dēcutere, -ssisse, -ssum	knock off, shake off
(ēloquōr) ēloquī (< loquī)	express, tell
(exigō) exigere (< agere)	drive out, exact, require, pass
(extrahō) extrahere (< trahere)	pull out, extract
(imminuō) imminuere, -uisse, -ūtum	make smaller, reduce
(incalēscō) incalēscere, -uisse	become heated
(incidō) incidere, -cidisse, -cāsum	occur, present itself
(invīsō) invīsere (< vīsere)	go to see

(praecipiō) praecipere (< capere)	anticipate, advise, order
(prōlābor) prōlābī (< lābī)	slip, overbalance
(prōtegō) prōtegere (< tegere)	protect
(prōtrahō) prōtrahere (< trahere)	pull out, draw out
(terō) terere, trīvisse, trītum	wear out, use up, spend
(trānsfugiō) trānsfugere (< fugere)	go over, desert

-īre

(assentiō) assentīre (< sentīre)	agree with, assent
(lēniō) lēnīre, -īvisse, -ītum	placate, appease
(obeō) obīre (< īre)	meet, visit, go into, enter upon, set
(oborior) oborīrī (< orīrī)	spring up

ADIECTĪVA

1st/2nd

aerātus, -a, -um	fitted with bronze
ānxius, -a, -um	worried, worrying
brūtus, -a, -um	brutish, stupid
castus, -a, -um	chaste
centuriātus, -a, -um	voting in centuries
contēmptus, -a, -um	despicable
generōsus, -a, -um	noble
grandaevus, -a, -um	aged
honestus, -a, -um	honorable, respectable; (*n.*) virtue
impavidus, -a, -um	fearless
imperfectus, -a, -um	unfinished
impudīcus, -a, -um	unchaste, immoral
invīsus, -a, -um	odious, disliked
manifēstus, -a, -um	flagrant, plain
obstinātus, -a, -um	stubborn, obstinate
pestifer, -era, -erum	disastrous, pernicious
prōmptus, -a, -um	prompt, keen, ready
pudibundus, -a, -um	shamefaced
pudīcus, -a, -um	chaste, pure
sērus, -a, -um	late
voluntārius, -a, -um	voluntary

3rd

expers (*gen.* expertis)	having no share in
fidēlis, -e	faithful, loyal
inānis, -e	empty, gaping
iners (*gen.* inertis)	inactive, idle
īnsolēns (*gen.* īnsolentis)	haughty, arrogant
īnsōns (*gen.* īnsontis)	innocent
iuvenālis, -e	youthful
mātrōnālis, -e	of a married woman
perennis, -e	enduring, perpetual
praepotēns (*gen.* praepotentis)	very powerful
sēmianimis, -e	half alive

ADVERBIA

aliō	elsewhere
difficulter	with difficulty
enimvērō	truly, certainly
eōdem	to the same place
penes	in the possession of
quācumque	wherever
ultrō	spontaneously
usquam	anywhere

XLVI: QVADRAGESIMVM SEXTVM: POST REGES EXACTOS (Evtropivs)[1]

[*Ex Eutropiī Brevrāriō ab urbe conditā* I.9–III.6]

I. ØRBERG'S INTRODUCTION

The Roman historian Eutropius was commissioned by the Emperor *Valens* (AD 364–378) to write an abstract of Roman history, *Breviārium ab urbe conditā*. In his dedication to the Emperor Valens, Eutropius gives his goals for the *Breviārium*:

> *ab urbe conditā ad nostram memoriam, quae in negōtiīs vel bellicīs vel cīvīlibus ēminēbant, per ordinem temporum brevī narrātiōne collēgī*

Eutropius gives a brief outline (*brevī narrātiōne*), chronologically arranged (*per ordinem temporum*), of the outstanding (*ēminēbant*) events of Roman miltiary (*negōtiīs bellicīs*) and domestic (*negōtiīs cīvīlibus*) history from the founding of the city (*ab urbe conditā*) to his own time (*ad nostram memoriam*). He follows Livy for the early part of his work. Comparing the sentence structure of the two authors offers an exercise useful for your understanding of Latin.

Eutropius' style is extremely concise, lacking in literary merit, but nonetheless a model of clarity. The extract in this chapter covers the time from the expulsion of the Kings to the outbreak of the Second Punic War in 218 BC. Eutropius has based this part of his history on a summary of Livy, and his main interest is the feats of arms (*rēs gestae*) of the Romans. He mentions in passing the civil strife (*sēditiō*) between the patricians (the Senate) and the plebeians (*plēbēiī* or *plēbs*, "the common people"), which led to the election of tribunes of the people (*tribūnī plēbis*) charged with the protection of the people against the consuls and senators.

---

1. For an explanation of the line number references convention, see p. xxvi.

Roman Expansion

In this period of her history, Rome conquered all of Italy south of the Apennines and made war on the great naval power of Carthage. They first subdued various neighboring peoples, including the northern Etruscans. Camillus captured their southernmost city, Veii, in 396 BC. A few years later, Gauls from northern Italy descended on Rome. The Roman army was defeated on the banks of the *Allia*, a tributary of the Tiber, and the Gauls occupied the city except for the Capitoline (390 BC). After a long siege, Camillus, "the second founder of Rome," rescued the Romans.

In the following years, the Romans repulsed new Gallic attacks. After this, Rome's most dangerous enemies were the Samnites, who were defeated after long wars, and the Greeks in southern Italy. The Romans met with stubborn resistance from the city of Tarentum, whose Greek inhabitants appealed to king Pyrrhus of Epirus for help (280 BC). After some costly victories (hence the phrase "Pyrrhic victory"[2]), the king retired to Sicily. When he returned to the mainland, the Romans, who were now the undisputed masters of Italy south of the Apennines, defeated him.

First Punic War

The conquest of southern Italy led to war with Carthage, the great power of the Western Mediterranean. The First Punic War lasted from 264–241 (the Carthaginians, *Carthāginiēnsēs*, coming from Phoenicia, are also called *Poenī*, adjective *Pūnicus, -a, -um*). *Gāius Duīlius* led a large Roman fleet to victory over the Carthaginians in 260. The war continued with varying success on land and at sea. The Carthaginians took prisoner in Africa the Roman general Regulus. He was then sent to Rome with orders to persuade his countrymen to make peace with Carthage; instead he urged the Romans to fight on. He returned to Carthage, where he died under torture. In 241, a decisive sea battle was fought between the Roman and Carthaginian fleets of 300 and 400 ships respectively. The Romans were victorious, and the Carthaginians had to make peace and abandon Sicily.

Continued Expansion

In the following years, the Romans also conquered Sardinia and Corsica, and in northern Italy, they captured *Mediolānum* (Milan) from the Gauls. The victorious general *Mārcellus* killed the Gallic commander and carried his armor, the *spolia opīma*, in triumph to the Capitoline.

---

2.   Plutarch, *Life of Pyrrhus*, 21: "If we win one more battle against the Romans, we will be completely destroyed."

The chapter concludes with a quotation from book VI of the *Aeneid*: Anchises in the netherworld describing the triumphant Marcellus to Aeneas.

Roman Chronology

Roman chronology took the foundation of Rome as its point of departure. Dates are given in ordinal numbers (*annō, -ēsimō*) followed by *ab urbe conditā* (or *urbis conditae*, abbreviated *a.u.c.* or *u.c.*), e.g., *annō ducentēsimō quadrāgēsimō quīntō ab urbe conditā* (*annō CCXV a.u.c.*), "in the year 245 after the foundation of the city."

- *Annō trecentēsimō et quīntō decimō ab urbe conditā* (85)
- *Annō trecentēsimō sexāgēsimō quīntō ab urbe conditā* (95)
- *Annō trecentēsimō et alterō ab urbe conditā* (125)
- *Annō urbis conditā quadringentēsimō octōgēsimō prīmō* (288)
- *Annō quadringentēsimō septuāgēsimō septimō* (299)

The modem chronology "*annō Dominī*" (AD) dates only from the sixth century. The year 754 after the foundation of the city (*ab urbe conditā*) is the first year after the traditional birth of Christ (*post Christum nātum*).[3] After 509 BC (the year the kings were expelled from Rome), dates are sometimes given with the words *post rēgēs exāctōs* (or *ab expulsīs rēgibus*), "after the expulsion of the kings":

- *annō prīmō ab expulsīs rēgibus* (8)
- *tertiō annō post rēgēs exāctōs* (35, cf. 41, 48)
- *octāvō decimō annō postquam rēgēs ēiectī erant* (46: a variation on the phrase)

Another, very common way of marking the year is with the names of the two consuls in the ablative absolute, e.g.:

- *K. Fabiō et T. Vergīiō cōnsulibus* (67)
- *L. Genūciō et Q. Servīliō cōnsulibus* (145, cf. 194, etc.)
- *Ap. Claudiō (et) M. Fulviō cōnsulibus* (308, 264 BC)

---

3. Scholars dispute the date of Christ's birth.

To convert a Roman date to our system of dating:

- BC dates: subtract the Roman date from 753 (the year 245 *a.u.c.* is 509 BC)

- AD dates: subtract 753 from the Roman date

In the margin, dates are given a.C. = ante *Chrīstum*, BC (and p.C. = *post Chrīstum*, AD).

Roman Republican Government

In *Lingua Latina: Indices*, there is a list of Roman consuls with dates (*a.c.* and *u.c.*). After the list of consuls, there is a list of the triumphs of Roman generals beginning with Romulus' triumph over the *Caenīnēnsēs*. Such lists, called the *Fāstī cōnsulārēs* and *triumphālēs*, were set up on marble tablets in the Forum; several fragments of them have been found.

The consuls had no less authority than the kings, but the Romans tried to protect themselves against abuse of power by every year electing not one, but two new consuls. Only when the security of the State (*rēs pūblica*) was seriously endangered did they appoint a *dictātor*, who was given supreme power for a period of six months together with his subordinate, the *magister equitum* (see lines 43–47, 80, 100, 104, 185). Under the consuls, all important decisions were made in consultation with the Senate, whose members (called *senātōrēs* or *patrēs*) were the heads of the noble patrician families. The consuls and other magistrates were elected from their number.

II. Auxilia Legendī

Consuls et dictātōrēs: 1–123

2:              *hinc*: from this time.

3–4:   *hāc causā creātī ut* + a substantive causal clause introduced by a conditional protasis referring to the future; sequence is secondary: *coercēret* is incomplete action, as befits both the purpose clause and the condition; *voluisset* is pluperfect because the action of "wanting" is prior to that of "constraining."

4, 11–12:   *placuit nē*; *placuerat enim nē*: *placēre* in the past tenses means "it is (*placuit*) was (*placuerat*) decided, resolved" + a noun clause of the resolution.

11:             *Tarquiniō Collātīnō*: dative of disadvantage with *sublāta est* (< *tollere*); dignitās: "rank," "honorable place in society" (cf. l.43).

14:    *locō ipsīus*: "in his place."

21:    *dēfēnsōrem pudīcitiae suae*: because he avenged Tarquin's violation of Lucretia, thus becoming a symbolic defender of female chastity.

31:    *secundō quoque annō*: "also in the second year": i.e., *quŏque* (also) not *quōque* (from *quisque*), which would have meant "every second year" (Cap. XX).

45:    *dictātōr*: magistrate elected for a six-month (maximum) emergency term; the dictator was *magister populī* ("master of the infantry"); *Magister Equitum* ("master of the cavalry"), second in command to the dictator.

48:    *sēditiō*: "insurrection, sedition."

49–50:   *tamquam* (reported reason: see grammar section); *ipse*: i.e., *populus*.

51:    *per quōs*: relative clause of purpose (Cap. XXXIX).

54:    *Coriolī, Coriolōrum*: town in Latium.

57–58:   *Cn. Marcius*: usually referred to as *Coriolānus*, an honorific cognomen he earned fighting the city; *Volscōrum cīvitātem*: in apposition to *Coriolōs*.

60:    *mīliārium*: the emperor Augustus set up the *mīliārium aureum* ("golden milestone") in the forum to mark the end point of all military roads. Distances from this point to other places were given in terms of the milestones leading from this first one (but at the time referred to, *mīliārium* = *mille passūs*).

61–64:   *oppugnātūrus*: future participle for a pluperfect subjunctive in a past contracfactual condition = *oppugnāvisset*, protasis *vēnissent*: Coriolanus was intending to attack, if his mother and wife had not come; the future participle gives the sense that Corolianus was on the point of, he would have, had his mother and wife not come.

64–66:   *quī…esset*: descriptive (potential) relative clause with *secundus*; the descriptive relative clause is frequent with words such as *ūnus, sōlus* (*quī*) (Caps. XXXIX, XLIV).

71–72:   *quī…dēbērent*: descriptive relative clause (Caps. XXXIX, XLIV); *singulī*: "each of whom," "each individually."

82–83:   *in opere et arāns*: later Latin likes phrases that are not parallel (i.e., here we have a prepositional phrase linked with a present participle); *toga praetexta*: a toga fringed with a purple stripe was worn by higher magistrates; here the *toga praetexta* stands for the office of *dictātor* that Cincinnatus was about to assume. It was also worn by free-born children until they came of age for the toga of manhood (*toga virīlis*).

88:      *decemvirī*: this board of ten men codified the laws of Rome and had them inscribed on twelve bronze tablets, known as the "twelve tables" (*XII tabulae*).

90:      *stipendia*: both a year of military service (in the plural) and the pay or salary (in singular), whence we get "stipend."

98:      *urbī*: dative with *vīcīnae*; Rome is "<u>the</u> city."

108–109:   *eī*: *Camillō*; *quasi...dīvīsisset*: reported reason (see grammar section).

114:      *quicquam*: used only in negative clauses (Cap. XXVI); subject of *potuit*.

115–116:   *nē obsidērent*: purpose clause initiated by the ablative absolute *acceptō aurō*.

117–118:   *Gallīs superventum est*: impersonal passive; *supervenīre*: "overtake," "fall upon."

121:      *triumphāns*: the elaborate celebratory parade for victorious Roman generals, the Triumph, wound its way through the city, ending in the forum (see Cap. XXXVI: *Ad hoc templum imperātor victor post triumphum ascendit, ut Iovī Optimō Māximō sacrificium faciat, dum ducēs hostium, quī in triumphō ante currum imperātōris ductī sunt, ad supplicium trāduntur,* i.e., they were killed).

Post urbem captam: 124–180

126:      *prīmō* sc. *annō*.

140:      *post aliquantum* (sc: *tempus*); *nūllōs* (*tribūnōs*) *placuit fierī*: *placuit nūllōs* (*tribūnōs*) *fierī*.

151–152:   *sublātō torque aureō collōque suō impositō*: "doubled" ablative absolute: *torque aureō sublātō* (*et*) *impositō*; *collō suō*: dative with *impositō*; *Toquātī*: note that Titus Manlius had, before defeating the Gaul in single combat, only two names, the *prae-*

	nōmen (*Titus*) and *gentilīcium* (*Mānlius*); *Torquātus* becomes his *cognōmen* and is passed on to his descendants; so too with *Corvīnus* (l.171).
158:	*mīlitēs praestāre*: cities conquered by Rome had to furnish (*praestāre*) soldiers for the Roman army.
160:	*quī modus...efficiēbat*: "and this measure yielded 60,000 or more armed men."
161:	*parvīs adhūc Rōmānīs rēbus*: concessive = *cum rēs Rōmānae adhūc parvae essent*.
166:	*eī = Valeriō*.
164–171:	*Marcus Valerius* becomes *Marcus Valerius Corvīnus*: see note on lines 151–152.
178:	*in Rōstrīs*: see XXXVI.87–91: *Ante Comitium est locus superior ex quō ōrātōrēs verba faciunt ad populum. 'Rōstra' nōmen est huius locī, quia rōstrīs nāvium captārum ōrnātur 'rōstrum' enim vocantur eae hastae ferreae quae ē prōrā nāvis longae ēminent velut rōstrum avis.*

Samnītēs: 181–214

183–184:	*Samnītǎs*: Greek names in the 3rd declension plural often retain the *-ǎs* ending (instead of ēs); cf. ll.189, 205, 207.
188:	*nē sē absente pugnāret*: indirect command.
190–191:	*capitis damnātus*: the genitive is used with judicial expressions: accusations, condemnations (such as here), and acquitals; he was condemned with the loss of his head; *"quod sē vetante pugnāsset"*: subjunctive of reported reason (implied *ōrātiō oblīqua*) (Cap. XLII).
195–196:	*sub iugum*: the illustration in your text is a bit misleading. The "yoke" under which the Roman soldiers were forced to pass was made by making an arch of three spears, two uprights, and a third as a transverse bar.
196–197:	*pax solūta est*: the army had been coerced into making peace, which is legal only when ratified by the Senate; it was therefore revoked.
200:	*aquam Appiam indūxit*: Appius Claudius had built the first of the great Roman aquaducts (*aquaeductus*), known as the *Aqua*

Claudia, from his *gentīlicium*, while the road he had built is called the *Via Appia*.

204:        *lēgātus datus fuisset*: "had been given to him (*eī*) as a lieutenant."

Pyrrhus: 215–305

216:        *quia…fēcissent*: subjunctive of reported reason (Cap. XLII).

224:        *dūcī, ostendī…dīmittī*: all present passive infinitives with *iussit* (l.223).

225:        *quaecumque ā Rōmānīs agerentur*: subjunctive for a subordinate clause in implied indirect statement (Cap. XLII).

226:        *cum iam fugeret*: when he was beginning to flee; *iam* with the imperfect shows an action as just starting.

230:        *adversō vulnere*: the soldiers were killed while standing their ground and fighting, not running away; hence their wounds were in front, not in their backs.

232–233:   *sē tōtīus orbis dominum esse potuisse, sī tālēs sibi mīlitēs contigissent*: past contrafactual condition in *ōrātiō oblīqua*; *posse* is in the infinitive instead of the subjunctive (see Cap. XLIII, grammar section on *posse, oportēre, dēbēre*).

238:        *terrōre exercitūs*: ablative of cause (Cap. XXXVII) and objective genitive (Cap. XXV).

255:        *bīnōrum hostium*: distributive numbers (Cap. XXX): to regain their former status, each had to bring back the armor (*spolia*) stripped from two slain enemy soldiers.

266:        *Tarentum*: accusative of place to which (so too line 281).

267:        *interiectō annō*: "after the lapse of a year," "the second year later."

269:        *vīcīna castra*: i.e., two camps near each other.

273–274:   *quae…spopondisset*: subordinate clause in *ōrātiō oblīqua*: *iussit…(ea) dīcī quae…*

275:        *difficilius*: comparative of the adverb.

289:        *vēnēre = vēnērunt* (cf. l.292: *commōvēre*).

Bellum Pūnicum prīmum: 306–430

314:	*in fidem acceptae*: taken under the protection of Rome.
328:	*plūrimum possent*: "were extremely powerful."
334:	*in marī pugnātum (est)*: impersonal passive.
361–362:	*Et subācta Āfrica tunc fuisset, nisi quod tanta famēs erat ut diūtius exercitus exspectāre nōn posset*: *fuisset* marks the apodosis of a past contrafactual condition; the indicative protasis *nisi quod* ("except for the fact that") cuts off the possibility of the Romans conquering (they would have conquered except for the fact that there was a famine).
369:	*neque in aliquō animus hīs infrāctus fuit*: "nor in anyone was courage unboken by these events."
388:	*nihil quasi Rōmānus ēgit*: "did not act at all like a Roman," i.e., behaved as if he enjoyed none of the rights of being a Roman citizen.
392:	*tantī*: genitive of value (Cap. XXIX).
395:	*nūllus admīsit*: "no one granted an audience to."
414:	*Lilybaeum*: modern Marsala.
418:	*īnfīnītum*: "an endless supply."

Iānus iterum clausus: 431–473

439:	*modius trīticī*: the *modius* is the standard Roman measure for grain; *trīticum, -ī* is wheat.
445:	*Rōmānīs*: with *pārēre*, not *condiciōnibus*.
451:	*iīs*: dative with *contigerat*.
459:	*prō Rōmānīs cōnsēnsit*: "united on the side of the Romans."
462:	*per cōnsulem tantum*: adverb, not adjective: "by the consul alone."
472:	*stīpitī*: dative with compound *imposita*.

Spolia Opima Tertia (Aenēis VI.855–856): 475–477

477:	*super-ēminēre*: "be conspicious beyond all others."

III. Vocābula

Nōmina

1st

collēga, -ae (*m.*)	colleague
dictātūra, -ae	dictatorship
pompa, -ae	public procession
praetexta, -ae	toga with purple border

2nd

castellum, -ī	fort, stronghold
corvus, -ī	raven
elephantus, -ī	elephant
fiscus, -ī	public treasury
historicus, -ī	historian
iūgerum, -ī	area of about 2/3 of an acre
iugum, -ī	yoke, ridge
meritum, -ī	merit
mīliārium, -ī	milestone
modius, -ī	a Roman dry meausure, "peck"
naufragium, -ī	shipwreck
patrimōnium, -ī	patrimony, fortune
quadriennium, -ī	four years
tribūnus mīlitum	tribune of the military
tribūnus plēbis	tribune of the people
triennium, -ī	three years
trīticum, -ī	wheat
venēnum, -ī	poison

3rd

calamitās, -ātis (*f.*)	misfortune, calamity
cēnsor, -ōris (*m.*)	censor (magistrate)
dēprecātiō, -ōnis (*f.*)	entreaty, plea
diūrnitās, -ātis (*f.*)	long duration
explōrātor, -ōris (*m.*)	scout, spy
favor, -ōris (*m.*)	goodwill, favor
honestās, -ātis (*f.*)	honesty, virtue

permūtātiō, -ōnis (*f.*)	exchange
pugnātor, -ōris (*m.*)	fighter, combatant
stīpes, -itis (*m.*)	stake, stick
sūdor, -ōris (*m.*)	sweat
tīrō, -ōnis (*m.*)	recruit
unguis, -is (*m.*)	nail, claw

4th

complexus, -ūs	embrace
cōnsulātus, -ūs	consulate
flētus, -ūs	weeping

5th

perniciēs, -ēī	destruction

VERBA

-āre

(damnō) damnāre	condemn, sentence
(dēprecor) dēprecārī	beg, entreat
(perdomō) perdomāre	subjugate
(persevērō) persevērāre	persist, continue
(remandō) remandāre	send back word
(reparō) reparāre	repair, restore, renew
(repudiō) repudiāre	reject, refuse to accept
(sollicitō) sollicitāre	solicit, incite
(tractō) tractāre	handle, treat, manage
(vindicō) vindicāre	claim, avenge

-ēre

(obtineō) obtinēre (< tenēre)	hold, gain, obtain
(superēmineō) super-ēminēre	stand out above

-ere

(cōnsenēscō) cōnsenēscere, -uisse	grow old
(dēcipō) dēcipere (< capere)	deceive
(dēmergō) dēmergere, -merisse, -mersum	sink, plunge

(excīdō) excīdere, -disse, -sum	destroy
(expavēscō) expavēscere, -avisse, -atum	become frightened (at)
(impellō) impellere (< pellere)	strike, drive, compel
(īnfringō) īnfringere (< frangere)	break, crush
(obsequor) obsequī (< sequī)	comply with, obey
(perimō) perimere (< emere)	destroy, kill
(praesūmō) praesūmere (< sūmere)	take for oneself, assume
(redigō) redigere (< agere)	drive back, bring, reduce
(regredior) regredī, -gressum	go back, return
(restituō) restituere, -uisse, -utum	restore, rebuild, reinstate
(subigō) subigere (< agere)	subdue, drive, force
(trānsigō) trānsigere (< agere)	carry through, finish
(tribuō) tribuere, -uisse, -ūtum	grant, attribute

-īre

(comperio) comperīre, -erisse, -ertum	find out, learn, discover
(supervenio) supervenīre (< venīre)	appear, surpass

ADIECTĪVA

1st/2nd

honōrificus, -a, -um	honorable
incognitus, -a, -um	unknown
īnfinītus, -a, -um	unlimited, infinite
quadringentēsimus, -a, -um	four hundredth
rōstrātus, -a, -um	having a beaked prow
septuāgēsimus, -a, -um	seventieth
sexāgēsimus, -a, -um	sixtieth
torquātus, -a, -um	wearing a collar, necklace
trānsmarīnus, -a, -um	from beyond the seas
trecentēsimus, -a, -um	three hundredth

3rd

cōnsulāris, -e	consular
grandis, -e	big, large

īnfāmis, -e	disgraced
īnsignis, -e	noted, remarkable
nāvālis, -e	naval
singulāris, -e	single, singular, unique
trux (*gen.* **trucis**)	savage, grim

ADVERBIA

amplius	more
invicem	mutually, one another
retrō	back
secundō	for the second time
tertiō	for the third time

XLVII: QVADRAGESIMVM SEPTIMVM: GRAECI ET ROMANI (Avlvs Gellivs)[1]

I. Ørberg's Introduction

This chapter is taken from a collection of essays (*commentāriī*) written by *Aulus Gellius* about AD 150 and published in twenty books under the title *Noctēs Atticae*. The collection comprises his gleanings from years of reading and jotting down bits that intrigued him—a habit that was not peculiar to Gellius. The preface explains his decision to name his collection *Attic Nights*:

> *...quoniam longinquīs per hiemem noctibus in agrō, sīcuti dīxī, terrae Atticae commentātiōnēs hāsce lūdere ac facere exorsī sumus...*

Lūdere is important here: the *Attic Nights* represent the intellectual leisure time of a second-century AD member of the Roman elite. The essays cover a great variety of subjects (linguistic, philosophical, legal, literary, etc.) based on his extensive reading of Greek and Latin authors, whom he often quotes. Aulus Gellius has preserved many passages from lost works. The initial *commentārius* presents a chronological comparison of famous Greeks and Romans. Aulus Gellius observes that the illustrious Greek statesmen, philosophers, and poets lived long before Rome became a great power, and that Greek art and literature flourished long before the first Roman literary works appeared.

Most of the works of early Roman authors mentioned here are lost, except for some fragments, but twenty comedies by *Plautus* and six by *Terentius* (Terence) have been preserved. We also have a treatise *de Agrī Cultūrā* by *Catō*, which is the oldest surviving prose work in Latin.

Two short pieces from the same collection follow: one contains the story of the origin of the *Sibylline Books* (*librī Sibyllīnī*), the other some observations on

---

1. For an explanation of the line number references convention, see p. xxvi.

the different oaths uttered by men and women (observations which are confirmed by usage in the comedies of Plautus and Terence).

II. Auxilia Legendī

Graeci et Rōmānī (Ex Aulī Gelliī 'Noctium Atticārum' librō XVII capitulum XXI): 1–165

412: *ut…habērēmus, nē…dīcerēmus*: two purpose clauses introduce the sentence before we get to the main verb (*excerpēbamus*); *cōnspectum* < *cōnspectus, -ūs*: "a view, survey"; *incōnspectum* < *incōnspectus, -a, -um*: "indiscreet, imprudent," clearly a pun; *chronicī* = χρονικά: the Greek version of *annāle*: chronological records of important events; *quibus temporibus flōruissent… nōbilēs īnsignēsque…fuissent*: indirect questions. Gellius is making notes (*excerpēbamus*) from the *chronicī* so his readers know the answer to when illustrious Greeks and Romans were in their prime (*flōruissent*).

15: *dē pluribus (hominibus)…coniectūra fierī/coniectūram facere*: "make a conjecture, an inference about many others."

21: *Silviī*: see XLI.70–73.

22: *in prīmō* (sc. *librō*) *annālium*; cf. l.25: *in prīmō Chronicōrum*.

27–28: *ex illō nōbilī numerō sapientum*: Solon (638–558 BC) was one of a group of seven men famed for their wisdom.

32: *id* (the tyranny of Pisistratus) *eī* (i.e., *Solōnī*) *praedīcentī nōn crēditum est*: impersonal passive with dative (Cap. XL).

33: *Tarquinius*: XLV.1.

37: *Nepōs Cornēlius* = *Cornēlius Nepōs* (Cap. XLIX).

38: *Tullus Hostilius*: XLIII.2–3.

39: *poēmatīs*: ablative of respect with *clārum et nōbilem*.

47: *tribūnōs* (*plēbis*): XLVI.50.

48–49: *Coriolānus*: XLVI.56ff.

53: *plērāque Graeciā*: *plērique, -aeque, -aque*: "most (of)" (Cap. XXXIII).

60–61:   *per eās tempestātēs*: you learned (Cap. XVI) *tempestās* as "storm," but its primary meaning is "period of time." For the *decemvirī legibus scribundīs* (dative of purpose) and Twelve Tables, cf. XLVI.88.

73–74:   *quibus*: ablative of comparison, *nātū*, ablative of respect, both with *posterior*.

75:          *quibusdam temporibus iīsdem vixērunt*: there's no easy way around this clumsy phrase; "at certain times (i.e., not all of their lives) they lived at the same time," or, literally: "they lived at certain same times" = *iīsdem ferē temporibus*.

80:          *Athēniēnsibus*: dative with *praepositī sunt*.

83:          *Camillus*: XLVI.104, etc.

81–82:   *Sōcratēs Athēnīs capitis damnātus est*: genitive of the charge/penalty (Cap. XLVI, note on lines 190–191).

90–92:   *Mānlius...convictus est...damnātusque capitis*: genitive of the charge/penalty.

106:         *inque eō tempore*: *in* + a qualified ablative refers to the circumstances rather than the time.

118–119:   *cōnsulēs Tiberius Veturius et Spurius Postumius*: XLVI.194–195.

120:         *sub iugum*: XLVI.195–196.

125:         *Pyrrhus*: XLVI.215ff.

130:         *senātū mōvērunt*: removed from the Senate.

131:         *Nota = nota censōria*: the mark put by the names of those whom the censors condemn; *causam istī notae subscripsērunt*: accusative and dative with compound verb (Cap. XXXVII); *quod...comperissent...habēre*: subjunctive of reported reason (Cap. XLI); *grātiā*: with preceding genitive "for the sake of"; *argentum factum*: "wrought silver, silver plate"; there were sumptuary laws at Rome putting a limit on luxury.

136:         *bellum adversum Poenōs prīmum*: XL.306ff.

139:         *annīs posteā paulō plūribus quam vīgintī*: ablative of degree of difference with an ablative of comparison (Caps. XVI, XLIII): "afterward by a little more than twenty years."

145–150:   Reading help: [*quibus* (*cōnsulibus*) *nātum esse Q. Ennium poētam*] *M. Varrō…scrīpsit*; *eumque* (= *Ennium*)…*duodecimum Annālem scrīpsisse idque ipsum Ennium in eōdem librō dīcere.*

152–155:   *dē amīcōrum sententiā*: "on the advice of his friends"; *quod… esset iūrāssetque…habēre*: subjunctive of reported reason (Cap. XLII).

164–165:   *longius*: the comparative can mean "too," as here: "too long"; *bellum Poenōrum secundum*; cf. the beginning of the chapter; Gellius tells us his intention is to write about distinguished Greeks and Romans from the time of the founding of the city to the Second Punic War.

Librī Sibyllīnī (Ex Aulī Gelliī 'Noctium Atticārum' librō I capitulum XIX): 166–193

166:   For the Sibyl, see XL.288; the Sibylline books of oracles were consulted during times of crisis.

176:   *quasi dēsiperet*: subjunctive of reported reason (Cap. XLVI); for *quasi* with the subjunctive of reported reason, see Cap. XLVI.

178:   *eōdem pretiō*: ablative of price (so too ll.183–184) (Cap. VIII).

185:   *ōre iam sēriō atque attentiōre animō*: ablative of description (Cap. XXXII).

186:   *insuper* = "over"; *insuper habēre* = *contemnere*.

187:   *nihilō*: ablative of degree of difference with the comparative *minōre* (Caps. XVI, XLIII).

188–190:   *nusquam locī*: *locī* is a partitive genitive after the adverb *nusquam*; *constitit*: see above: "it has been agreed."

Dē iūre iūrandō (Ex Aulī Gelliī 'Noctium Atticārum' librō XI capitulum VI): 194–206

202:   *facile dictū*: ablative of the supine (Cap. XXII).

205:   *iūs iūrandum*: "a sworn oath."

III. Vocābula

NŌMINA

1st

adnotātiuncula, -ae	short note
cōnfīdentia, -ae	self-confidence
coniectūra, -ae	inferring, conjecture
cōnstantia, -ae	steadiness, persistence
historia, -ae	account, story, history
hospita, -ae	(female) guest, stranger
lībra, -ae	balance, pound (327 g)
philosophia, -ae	philosophy
tragoedia, -ae	tragedy

2nd

astrologus, -ī	astronomer
cognōmentum, -ī	surname
commentārius, -ī	notebook, record
dīvortium, -ī	divorce
dubium, -ī	point of separation
foculus, -ī	hearth
philosophus, -ī	philosopher
quīndecimvirī, -ōrum (*pl.*)	board of fifteen priests
sacrārium, -ī	sanctuary
scrīptum, -ī	writing, book
tyrannus, -ī	tyrant

3rd

iūs iūrandum (iūris iūrandī) (*n.*)	oath
obsidiō, -ōnis (*f.*)	siege
poēma, -atis (*n.*)	poem

VERBA

-āre

(celebrō) celebrāre	go to a place frequently or in great numbers, celebrate, extol
(circumvāllō) circumvāllāre	beset, surround

(cōnflīctō) cōnflīctāre	harass, distress
(dēiūrō) dēiūrāre	swear
(dēlīrō) dēlīrāre	be mad
(exagitō) exagitāre	stir, worry, harass
(mercōr) mercārī	buy, purchase
(nōbilitō) nōbilitāre	make famous
(obtrectō) obtrectāre	criticize, disparagement
(percontōr) percontārī	inquire (about), ask
(vēnumdō) vēnumdare (< dare)	put up for sale
(vexō) vexāre	harass, trouble, ravage

-ēre

(flōreō) flōrēre, flōruisse	bloom, flourish

-ere

(convincō) convincere (< vincere)	find guilty, convict
(dēpellō) dēpellere (< pellere)	drive down/off, avert
(dēscīscō) dēscīscere, -īvisse, -ītum	defect, withdraw
(dēsipiō) dēsipere, -uisse	be out of one's mind
(deūrō) deūrere (< ūrere)	burn
(excerpō) excerpere, -sisse, -tum	pick out
(exūrō) exūrere (< ūrere)	burn up
(obrēpō) obrēpere (< repere)	creep up, steal up
(prōpōnō) prōpōnere (< pōnere)	set up, propose
(subscrībō) subscrībere (< scrībere)	write underneath
(trānsgrediōr) trānsgredī, -gressum	cross

irregular

(obeō) obīre (< īre)	meet, visit, go into

ADIECTĪVA

1st/2nd

chronicus, -a, -um	written in the form of annals; annalistic
cōmicus, -a, -um	of comedy, comic

diūtinus, -a, -um	long, prolonged
ducentēsimus, -a, -um	two hundredth
factus, -a, -um	wrought
incōnspectus, -a, -um	unfounded
plērusque, plera-, plerum-	most (of), the greater part
quīngentēsimus, -a, -um	five hundredth
tragicus, -a, -um	tragic
ūndēvīcēsimus, -a, -um	nineteenth

3rd

annālis, -e	relating to a year
nātūrālis, -e	natural, of nature
orientālis, -e	eastern
sterilis, -e	barren, sterile

ADVERBIA

ecquid	…? if, whether
īnsuper	in addition
subinde	immediately afterward
temere	heedlessly

ALIA

edepol	by Pollux!
mecastor	by Castor!
mehercle	by Hercules!
nihilō	no, by no means
pondō	in weight, pounds

XLVIII: DVODEQVINQVAGESIMVM: BELLVM PVNICVM SECVNDVM (Livy)[1]

[*Ex T. Līviī 'ab Urbe Conditā' librīs XXI–XXX*]

I. ØRBERG'S INTRODUCTION

This long chapter contains extensive excerpts from Livy's description of the Second Punic War (218–201 BC), as well as selections from the *periochae*, or summaries, of Livy's history (as well as a selection from Eutropius). The outstanding Carthaginian leader in this war was *Hannibal*, who had sworn lifelong hostility to Rome.

The direct cause of the war was Hannibal's attack on the Spanish city of *Saguntum*, Rome's ally. On hearing that the city had fallen after a heroic defense, the Romans immediately declared war on Carthage (218 BC). Hannibal then led a large army from Spain across the Pyrenees and the Alps to northern Italy, where he defeated the Romans in two battles. The following year he marched south across the Apennines and ambushed a Roman army at Lake Trasimene (*lacus Trasumennus*). After these serious reverses the Romans appointed *Fabius Māximus* dictator. Fabius harassed Hannibal's army but avoided open battle. In 216, the consuls *Terentius Varrō* and *Aemilius Paulus* took the field against Hannibal at *Cannae*. Although numerically superior, the Romans suffered a shattering defeat: Aemilius Paulus was killed along with 50,000 Romans. After this, the greater part of southern Italy went over to Hannibal.

Meanwhile the Romans defeated Hannibal's brother *Hasdrubal* in Spain and in the following years, fought with some success in Italy. Hasdrubal crossed the Alps with a new army to join forces with his brother but was defeated and killed (207 BC). When the young Roman general *P. Cornēlius Scīpiō* succeeded in moving the war from Spain to Africa, the Carthaginians were forced to recall Hannibal. After his defeat at *Zama* in 202 Carthage was forced to make peace with Rome on severe terms.

---

1. For an explanation of the line number references convention, see p. xxvi.

In this chapter you read—with omissions, but no other changes—Livy's accounts of the siege of Saguntum and the declaration of war (from book 21), of the battle of Lake Trasimene and its repercussions in Rome (from book 22), of the battle of Cannae and the effect of the news in Carthage (from books 22 and 23), and finally of the recall of Hannibal and the conclusion of peace (from book 30). The summarizing passages in between are from the extant ancient abstracts (*Periochae*, περιοχαί) of Livy's history supplemented with a passage from Eutropius. *Periochae* of all except two of Livy's 142 books survive (written not by Livy, but sometime around the fourth century AD).

II. Auxilia Legendī

Iūs iūrandum Hannibalis [Ex librō XXI]: 1–90

4:	*Hannibale duce*: ablative absolute.
6:	*opibus*: ablative of respect (Cap. XXXIX).
7–8:	*hīs ipsīs...fuit*: dative of possession (Cap. XII); *tantum vīrium aut rōboris*: partitive genitives with neuter substantive (*tantum*, cf. Cap. XLIV).
9–11:	*Rōmānīs indignantibus*: ablative absolute; *quod...īnferrent... quod...crēderent*: subjunctive of reported reason (Cap. XLII); *imperitātum*: impersonal passive + dative (*victīs*); *victōribus*: dative with compound verb (*inferre*).
12–17:	*Fāma est* is followed by the accusative + infinitive; *Hanni-balem...iūre iūrandō adāctum* (*esse*); *adāctum esse*: infinitive from *adigere = ad + agere*; *adigere iūre iūrandō*: "cause to take an oath"; *fore = futūrum esse*.
15:	*eō = in Hispāniam*.
20–21:	*factio*: "a political group," "faction."
25–28:	*ut fīnis...esset amnis Hibērus...lībertās servārētur*: the terms of the treaty (*foedus*); *Saguntīnī*: the inhabitants of the town Saguntum; dative of reference with *lībertās servārētur*.
29–30:	*quīnam...esset*: indirect question; *quīnam*: interrogative pronoun (Cap. XXIII); *extemplō*: "immediately."
33:	*pūberem*: i.e., of military age.
39–40:	*nē quandō...exsuscitet*: *nē* (*ali*) *quandō*; negative purpose clause (Cap. XLII, Recēnsiō).

41:	*optimus quisque*: *quisque* with the superlative, "all the most spirited of the young men" (Cap. XXXI).
42:	*meliōrem* (sc. *partem*).
45–46:	*crēdere, intuērī*: historical infinitives (so too *mālle, cōnfīdere, audēre*, ll.50–52).
48:	*discernerēs*: see grammar section above on the generalizing potential subjunctive.
50:	*ubi (ali) quid*: *ubi*, "whenever," subjunctive with indefinite relative clasuse.
57:	*nihil vērī, nihil sānctī*: partitive genitives with neuter pronoun (Cap. XLIV).
58:	*religiō*: "scruples," "fear of the gods."
59:	*trienniō*: abative of time.
60–61:	*merēre (stipendia)*: "serve" (in the army); *nūllā rē praetremissā*: ablative absolute enclosing the descriptive relative clause *quae…esset*, especially common with indefinite or negative antecedents (Cap. XXXIX); *agenda magnō futūrō ducī*: dative of agent with the gerundive (Cap. XXXI).
62–64:	*velut…mandātum esset*: *velut* ("as," "as if," Cap. XXVI); the subjunctive is used to underscore the contrafactual nature of the comparison.
64–65:	*Quibus oppugnandīs quia*: the *quia* is postponed after the ablative of means: "Because by attacking these people (i.e., of Saguntum)."
66–68:	*ut non petiise…sed…tractus vidērī posset*: i.e., led to an inevitable war by attacking Saguntum's neighbors whose land lay outside Rome's stated border.
70:	*opulentusque praedā*: ablative of respect, cf. 77 (Cap. XXXIX).
87:	*fugam facere*: "to put to flight, cause to flee."

Saguntum exscissum: 91–218

95–99:	*retulissent…abstinēret*: see above on technical vocabulary; *placuisset*: see Cap. XLVI "Resolutions of the Senate"; cf. l.101: *relāta…rēs*.
100:	*omnium spē celerius*: "faster than everyone's anticipation" (not "hope").

101:            *dē integrō*: "anew" (Cap. XLII).

110:            *īnfestō exercitū*: in military language, the movement of troops
                usually does not have *cum*: "with a hostile army."

113:            *eum* (*mūrum*); *vīnea* means both "vine" and "vineyard"; in
                military language, it is a covering made like an arbor that pro-
                tects besieging soldiers.

115:            *in suspectō locō*: i.e., a place considered more likely to be
                attacked.

117:            *summovēre* = *summovērunt*: "drove away."

118–119:   *animus*: "courage"; *haud fermē*: "scarcely, hardly."

122–123:   *nōn multum abesset quīn…dēsererentur*: negative consecutive
                (result) clause, "not so far from, not so far but that" (Cap. XL);
                dēserere: abandon, desert.

129:            *mūrī*: genitive with *quantum*.

135:            *fūsum fugātumque* (*hostem*): "routed and put to flight."

138–139:   *missī obviam* + dative (*quibus*): "sent to meet"; *quī dīcerent*:
                relative clause of purpose (Cap. XXXIX) + *ōrātiō oblīqua*;
                Hannibalī: dative with *operae esse*, "to have the leisure to."

141:            *appārēbat*: impersonal, as frequently, "it was clear" (i.e., to
                Hannibal).

144:            *pars altera* = *factiō altera*.

147–149:   *viamque ūnam ad id…sī…vīvat*: the *sī* clause gives the content
                of *id*, which refers to *regnum*.

151–152:   *unde arcentur foedere*: by the conditions of the *foedus* (ll.25–28).

155:            *bonus*: sarcastic.

158–161:   *Dēdēmus*: future indicative (i.e., not a deliberative question);
                cēnseō…mittendōs: see section on technical vocabulary, above;
                quī…nūntient: relative clause of purpose (Cap. XXXIX); *ut…
                dēdant*: indirect command (Cap. XXIX).

163–164:   *adeō*: "indeed, for"; *prope*: adverb, "nearly"; *Hannibalis erat*:
                i.e., on Hannibal's side: partitive genitive.

166:            *tempus terere*: "wear away time, waste time" (see XLV.220 and
                cf. below l.550: *tempus teritur*).

167:            *mīlitem* = *mīlitēs*: collective noun.

173–174:   *eōs*: object of *adorta est*; *aliquantō*: ablative of degree of difference.

175–176:   *minōrem in diēs urbem Saguntīnī faciunt*: i.e., the defensible area of the city was growing daily smaller; *inopia omnium*: objective genitive (Cap. XXV).

177–179:   *omnia hostium*: "of the enemy, belonged to the enemy"; *expectātiō externae opis*: objective genitive (Cap. XXV).

180–181:   *Alcorus Hispānus*: Alcorus the Spaniard, also the subject of the next sentence—Alcorus was in Hannibal's army but was also known at Saguntum; *trāditō palam tēlō*: ablative absolute; *cūstōdibus*: dative with *trāditō*.

184:      *senātum dare* + dative: "give someone an opportunity to address the Senate."

185–186:   *vōbīs...est*: dative of possession.

192–193:   *bīnīs vestīmentīs*: distributive numerals because "two apiece, two each."

199:      *senātuī*: dative with *permixtum esset*, i.e., the people's council became mingled with the senate so they could hear.

202–203:   *eōdem*: adverb, "to the same place" (Cap. XLV); *sēmet*: *-met* is an intensive enclitic.

205–211:   *cum signum imperātōrī dedisset*: subject, *cohors*; *nōn... occāsiōne*: what Hanibal was thinking (*ratus*); *omnēs pūberēs*: all the young men of military age.

215:      *patrēs*: object of *cēpit. pudor nōn lātī auxiliī*: *pudor* with genitive of thing (Cap. XXIII): objective genitive.

216:      *dē summā rērum*: the good of the state, the common welfare (a frequent political expression); *velut si...esset*: present contrafactual.

Bellum Carthāginiēnsibus indictum: 219–253

220:      *nōminātae prōvinciae*: the conquered areas in which the consuls would operate in the coming year; *iūssī*: sc. *cōnsulēs*; *sortīrī*: i.e., a two-step process: first the provinces to which consuls will be assigned are named, then the consuls draw lots.

223:      *quanta parārī posset*: indirect question (Cap. XXIX).

228:      *iustō equitātū*: *iustus* used of military units means "at full strength."

233–237:   *mittunt ad percontandōs Carthāginiēnsēs...et...ut indīcerent*: both expressions of purpose (see Cap. XLII or summary of purpose clauses); *id quod factūrī vidēbantur*: indicative parenthetical statement within the reported (indirect) future protasis in the subjunctive.

238–239:   *senātus datus esset*: see above, note to line 184.

242:        *cēnseam*: "I should think" (see section on potential subjunctive above).

244:        *nisi...icta* (*est*); *foedus īcere*: "strike a treaty," "make a pact."

247–248:   *parturuit*: desiderative of *pariō, parere, peperī, partum* (Cap. X, "give birth"): desire to bring forth, produce, or to be in labor; *pariat*: jussive subjunctive; *sinū ex togā factō*: "creating a fold/ pocket in his toga."

250:        *sub hanc vocem*: "immediately after/as a response to this speech"; *daret*: reported imperative; *utrum vellet*: indirect question.

253:        *quibus acciperent*: subordinate clause in indirect speech (Cap. XXXVI).

Iter Hannibalis in Italiam: 254–271

255–256:   *in hīberna* (*castra*): winter quarters.

257–258:   *dē integrō*: "anew, afresh" (Cap. XLII).

262:        *ex periochā*: see introduction to this chapter (as well as Cap. XLI).

262–264:   *Pȳrēnaeum*: the Pyrenees; *Pȳrēnaeus saltus/Pȳrēnaeī montēs*: mountains between (modern) Spain and France.

267:        '*Āfricānī*'...*nōmen*: as a cognomen; cf. *Torquātus* and *Coriolānus*, Cap. XLVI, note to lines 57–58.

269:        *Āpennīnum*: the Apennine Mountains, which run like a spine down the Italian peninsula.

Lacus Trasumennus [Ex periochā librī XXII et ex librō XXII]: 272–388

These excerpts provide an opportunity of comparing Livy's original with the later summary.

275:        *cōs*: the regular abbreviation of *cōnsul*, in which the *n* was not pronounced.

280:        *quod agrī est*: partitive genitive with neuter pronoun (Cap. XLIV).

282–283:   *māximē montēs...subit*: "most closely goes up to the foot of the mountains."

284:    *via perangusta*: the prefix *per-* before adjectives and adverbs has intensive force ("very...").

284–285:   *ubi...cōnsīderet*: adverbial final clause in secondary sequence with historical present; *modo*: i.e., only those troops.

288:    *ad ipsās faucēs saltūs*: "close to the very entrance of the mountain pass/defile"; *faucēs* = "throat," used for a narrow entrance.

289–290:   *ut, ubi intrāssent...essent*: both a purpose (final) clause and a condition in implied *ōrātiō oblīqua* (reporting Hannibal's reasons for placing the troops); the pluperfect subjunctive represents a future perfect: "So that, when the Romans have entered...everything would be..."

292:    *inexplōrātō*: adverb, i.e., without first making a reconnaissance.

294:    *id tantum hostium*: partitive genitive with neuter pronoun (Cap. XLIV).

297–299:   *clausum...et circumfūsum*: both with *hostem*; *signum... invādendī*.

300:    *eō magis...quod*: "all the more because."

301:    *nebula*: i.e., the fog/mist off the lake; *campō quam montibus*: ablatives: "thicker on the plain than on the mountains."

302:    *Rōmānus = Rōmānī*: collective noun.

303–305:   *ante...quam satis īnstruerētur...aut...possent*: anticipatory subjunctives (Cap. XLII); *stringī gladiī*: cf. *gladiīs strictīs* (XXXVII.352), *strictō gladiō* (XLIII.134); *stringī* is present passive infinitive.

306:    *perculsīs < percellere* (Cap. XLII): ablative absolute.

307:    *ut...patitur*: i.e., to the degree that time and the terrain allowed.

312:    *in dexterā*, sc. *manū*.

313–314:   *salūtis spem*: objective genitive (Cap. XXV); *dux adhortātorque* are predicative with *factus* (*fierī*): "each man became his own leader and exhorter."

315–318:   *Tantus fuit...ut...sēnserit*: result (consecutive) clauses express the consequence that follows a cause and generally take a subjunctive of incomplete action (present or imperfect). When, however, the author wants to move the focus from the impetus (leading verb) to the outcome (subordinate verb), the perfect subjunctive is used, an exception to the rule for sequence of tense (Cap. XLII, Recēnsiō); *cursū*: ablative, "from their course."

321: *rōbora virōrum*: *rōbus, -oris* (n.) is an exceptionally hard oak, thence "hardness, strength" (see l.8); when used of soldiers it means "the best troops," subject of *sequēbantur*.

324: *Īnsuber*: *Īnsubria* was in northern Italy, near Milan; *faciē quoque*: i.e., in addition to his distinguishing armor, ablative of means with *nōscitans*.

325–328: *populāribus...dēpopulātus*: *populārēs* are fellow members of your *populus*; *dēpopulārī*: ravage, pillage (also from *populus*, with debated etymology); *perēmptōrum...civium* < *perimere*, *-emisse, -emptum = perdere, dēlēre*) with *Mānibus*: the spirits of the dead.

332: *pavōrī*: dative with intransitive verb *obstāre*.

337–338: *inter paucās (clādēs)...clādēs*: a disaster "among few (disasters)"; i.e., one of the worst (*clādēs, -is*, Cap. XLII).

341–342: *petiēre = peti(v)ērunt*; *periēre = periērunt* (Cap. XLII).

347: *frequentis cōntiōnis modō turba*: "like a crowded assembly of the people"; *versa*: with *turba*.

351: *alius ab aliō implētī*: *alius* is in apposition to *implētī*.

354–355: *exercitūs victī*: genitive with *cāsūs*; *quot...tot*: "as many as."

356–357: *merēre (stipendia)*: see note to lines 60–61; *ignōrantium*: with *eōrum...quorum*; *quae fortūna...esset*: indirect question.

358–359: *quid spēret aut timeat*: indirect deliberative question (Cap. XXIX); direct would be "*Quid spērēmus aut timeāmus?*"

360: *posterō*: sc. *diē*: "on the next day and for several days following."

363–364: *circumfundēbantur*: "kept crowding around" + dative *obviīs*; *priusquam...inquīsiissent*: although *priusquam*, when it refers to something anticipated or expected, is generally followed by the imperfect subjunctive (Cap. XLII), there are a few isolated examples (four of them in Livy) where *priusquam* is followed by the pluperfect subjunctive. Here, the pluperfect subjunctive stands for a future perfect: "they could not be torn away before they (will have) asked."

365:	*cernerēs*: see grammar section above on the 2nd person singular generalizing potential subjunctive.
375–377:	*quōnam...possent*: indirect question; *resistī*: present passive infinitive representing the impersonal passive.
379–381:	*quattuor...circumventa* (*esse*): *ōrātiō oblīqua*.
382–383:	*dictātōrem...magistrum equitum*: Cap. XLVI, introduction and note on line 45.
386:	*vidērētur*: impersonal 3rd person + dative, "seems right, good" to someone.
387:	*Penātibus*: Cap. XXXVIII, introduction.

Q. Fabius Māximus Cūnctātor [Ex periochā librī XXII]: 389–406

394–395:	*tamquam*: on the grounds that, accusing him of being; *Efficere ut* + subjunctive: noun clause of result (Cap. XXVIII, Recēnsiō; Cap. XXXVII).
398:	*discrīmine*: ablative of separation with *līberātus*.
401–405:	core of sentence: *Hannibal...praesidium...fugāvit et...transgressus est saltum.*
406:	*Ūnus homō nōbīs cunctandō restituit rem*: this famous line comes not from Livy but Ennius's *Annālēs* (XXXVI.164–165); it is written in dactylic hexameter (Cap. XXXIV): *ūnŭs hŏ | mō nō | bīs cūnc | tān dō | rēstĭtŭ | īt rēm.*

Cannae [Ex Eutropiī Breviāriī librō III et ex Līviō librō XXII]: 407–592

These excerpts provide another opportunity of comparing Livy's original, this time with Eutropius's *Breviārium*.

411:	*Fabiō*: i.e., Quintus Fabius Maximus.
413:	*nōn aliter...quam*: "in no other way...than"; *differendō*: gerund ablative of means.
414:	*cum*: with *pugnātum esset*, not *impatientiā*, which is an ablative of cause (Cap. XXXVII).
419–420:	*Poenum = Poenos*: collective noun.
421:	*bīna castra*: distributive numerals are used with *pluralia tantum* (Cap. XXX, XXXIII).

422:          *utrīsque castrīs affluēns* < *adfluere* + dative; *aditus, -ūs*: "an access"; *aquātor*: "a water carrier."

428:          *inconditam turbam*: i.e., the *aquātōrēs*; *in...portās*: all one prepositional phrase; *ēgressī*: the Numidians; *ēvectī sunt*: "they advanced" (cf. l.6: *Cornēlius equō vehitur*); *statiōnem...prō vallō*: a guard post built in front of the camp fortifications.

430–435:   structure: *adeō...ut*: result clause; *ea ūna causa...quod*: causal clause; *ea ūna causa...tenuerit Rōmānōs nē extemplō trānsīrent*: clause of hindering (see grammar section above); *ab tumultuāriō auxiliō*: *tumultuārius*, in military language, means "hastily raised, put together quickly or suddenly"; *auxilium*: collective for *auxilia, -ōrum*: auxiliary troops, usually formed from allies, here: the Numidians; *ea modo ūna causa*: the reason (*causa*) is contained in the clause *quod...fuit*: when the consuls were in the field together, the high command alternated on a daily basis; Varro is, Livy tells us, the impatient one (l.414).

436:          *nihil cōnsultō Paulō*: ablative absolute, i.e., without asking Paulus's opinion.

439:          *eās quās*: with *cōpiās*.

443:          *intrā peditēs...iūnctī*: the infantry was stationed toward the inside (i.e., from the allied cavalry at the furthest end, *extrēmī*) and joined (*iūnctī*) to the Roman infantry at the center (*in medium*).

448:          *Baliārēs, -ium*: inhabitants of the Balearic Islands (Maiorca and Minorca, now called Menorca) off the coast of Spain— they were famous as slingers.

449–450:   *ut...ita*: "as...in the same way" (Cap. XIX).

455:          *stetēre* = *stetērunt*.

462–463:   *frontibus...adversīs*: ablative of attendant circumstances: i.e., the cavalries charged each other head on, because there was no room for maneuvering.

469:          *sub...finem*: "toward the end of."

471–472:   *impulēre* = *impulērunt*; *cuneus*: a wedge, so troops that form a protruding wedge (see marginal illustration).

474–475:   *Āfrī circā iam cornua fēcerant*: "The Africans on the sides [i.e., of the Romans who have flattened the projecting wedge (*cuneus*) and are proceeding into the apparently retreating hollow (*sinus*) in the battleline (*aciēs*)] had now made the wings of the battle line (ends of a horn, surrounding the Romans)."

476:      *extendendō*: ablative of means (Cap. XXV) of gerund; object: *cornua*; *et* = *etiam*: "even."

477–479:   *dēfūnctī nēquīquam proeliō ūnō*: i.e., the battle against the wedge (*cuneus*) of Gauls and Spaniards was won, but to no good purpose since the Romans are now surrounded.

479–480:   *nōn tantum...sed etiam* = *nōn sōlum...sed etiam* (Cap. XX); *eō...quod*: "for this reason, that..."

484:      *proelium restituit*: "revived, restored the battle."

485–486:   *omissīs...equīs*: i.e., the cavalry dismounted to fight; *et* = *etiam* with *ad regendum equum*; *dēficiēbant*: "were failing" + accusative (*cōnsulem*); *dēficere*, usually intransitive, can also be used transitively.

489:      *pellere*: i.e., *fugāre*; so too *pepulērunt*, l.490.

496:      *vīrium aliquid*: partitive genitive with neuter pronoun (Cap. XLIV).

497–498:   *nē...fēceris*: prohibition (Cap. XXXII).

500:      *macte virtūte estō*: a phrase that is found sixteen times in Latin literature, almost half of them in Livy: "honored in your manliness/virtue" or "well done, bravo"; *cavē...absūmās*: *cavē*, with or without *nē*, plus the subjunctive: "beware, avoid, guard against" (Cap. XXVII).

501:      *exiguum tempus...ēvādendī*.

503:      *patere*: imperative of *patior, patī*.

505:      *Haec eōs agentēs*: *haec* is the object of *eōs agentēs* (which is, in turn, the object of *oppressēre* (= *oppressērunt*); *agentēs* = *dīcentēs*.

506–507:   *ignōrantēs quis esset*: indirect question.

522–523:   *nōbilitāte...strāge*: ablatives of respect (Cap. XXXIX) with *pār...gravior foediorque*, respectively; *patere* < *patior, patī, passum*: imperative.

524:    *ad Alliam...ad Cannās: ad* does not always imply motion but can signify "at" or "in regard to"; cf. below, line 551: *ad* + numbers, "about"; *Allia*: see margins.

528–529:   *suādērentque ut...sūmeret et daret*: indirect command (Cap. XXVII).

530–533:   *ratus* (< *reor, rērī*) *cessandum*(*esse*); *minimē*: in replies, means not "very little" but "not at all" and is emphatic; *ut...scias*: purpose clause enclosing indirect question (*quid...āctum*); *ut...sciant*: purpose clause with indirect statement: i.e., *ut sciant me venisse prius quam sciant me venturum esse.*

532:    *equite = equitibus*: collective noun.

534–535:   *Hannibalī* <u>nimis</u> *laeta rēs est vīsa* <u>māiorque</u> <u>quam</u> <u>ut</u> *eam statim capere animō posset*: comparative clause (see grammar section above); *capere animō*: grasp mentally, take in; *voluntātem*: "inclination, desire."

537:    *pēnsāre*: "weigh"; *temporis opus esse*: usually with ablative or infinitive (Cap. XIX), very rarely with genitive.

538:    *dī dedēre* (= *dedērunt*): *dedere* is stronger than *dare*, and *nīmīrum* is here, as frequently, ironic or sarcastic.

540:    *salūtī fuisse urbī atque imperiō*: double datives (Cap. XXXVI).

544:    *ad multum diēī*: "till late in the day": partitive genitive with neuter pronoun (Cap. XLIV); *dūcere*: here used intransitively of a general: lead, march.

547:    *mātūrior ipsīus spē*: ablative of comparison with a comparative adverb (Cap. XXIV); cf. *lentius spē* (XLV.97).

551:    *ad* + numerals: "about," see also line 565.

555–556:   *genere clāra ac dīvitiīs*: ablatives of respect (Cap. XXXIX); some of the narrative has been omitted here and *cēterum* ("moreover") *cum*, etc., begins a new subject, the choice of leader.

560:    *proximē*: temporal, "very recently."

565:    *ad quattuor mīlia*: "about, approximately."

569:    *Rōmam*: accusative of place to which with *allātum fuerat*, which introduces the indirect statements *nē...sociōrumque.*

577–578:   *Hannibalis...factam*: i.e., has become his; *tantā mōle*: "by such a heap (of disaster)"; see XLII.28; *nūlla alia gēns...nōn obruta esset*: *nūlla...nōn*, "every"; past potential subjunctive.

589:      *classī…stantī*: datives with *praeesset*.

590:      *cōnsulī ut…venīret*: implied indirect command with *scrībendum*.

Māgō nūntius victōriae [Ex librō XXIII]: 593–681

597:      *dēficientēs*: "defecting" (Cap. XLI).

598:      *mare Īnferum*: the Tyrrhenian (Tuscan) sea off the western coast of Italy, as opposed to the *Adriāticum/Superum Mare* off the eastern coast, separating Italy and the Balkan Penninsula.

603–604:   '*ut suae lēgēs, suī magistrātūs Capuae essent*': *suae, suī*: both refer to Capua; *Capuae* is dative; *ut…essent*: noun clause with *condiciō*, "stipulations to the effect that."

605:      *urbem*: i.e., Capua.

606–608:   *precantibus…nē…utque*: indirect commands; *nē (ali)quid sēriae reī*: partitive genitive with neuter pronoun (Cap. XLIV).

610:      *ōrātiō perblanda*: see note above on line 284.

612:      *praepōnere* + accusative and dative: "put *x* (acc.) ahead of *y* (dat.)."

617:      *nōn ex ipsā aciē*: i.e., not immediately after the battle.

619:      *dēficiēbant*: see note above to line 597.

630:      *anulōs aureōs*: these are the gold rings worn by Roman knights.

631–632:   *mētientibus*: dative of reference, "according to those who measured them"; *sint quīdam auctōrēs*: + the indirect report of what those *auctōrēs* have written (*dīmidium suprā trēs modiōs explēvisse*).

633:      *īnsigne*: "distinctive mark of rank," referring to the gold rings.

636–637:   *et tot aciēs victōris etiam cōpiās parte aliquā minuisse*: *aciēs* = *pugnae*; *etiam victōris*: i.e., in addition to the losses of the Romans, with *cōpiās*; *parte aliquā*: "in some degree."

639:      *bene meritīs dē*: *bene merērī dē* + ablative: "deserve well from"; *meritīs* is dative with *mīlitibus*.

642:      *Hannō*: leader of the opposite faction, see l.36.

644:      *paenitet*: see Cap. XL on impersonal verbs.

648:      *Respondeam Himilcōni*: "I might answer…" (see section on potential subjunctive).

649:        *dēsiise...dēsitūrum*: from *dēsinere*, "stop, desist"; + comple-
           mentary infinitives (*paenitēre, incūsāre*).

652–653:   *Himilcōnī cēterīsque Hannibalis satellitibus*: dative with *laeta*;
           iam: "already."

656–657:   *quō magis dare quam accipere possumus vidērī pācem=* (*tem-
           pore*) *quō possumus vidērī magis dare quam accipere pācem*;
           vereor nē...ēvādat: fear clause (see above, Recēnsiō).

659–663:   *Quid aliud rogārēs, sī essēs victus?...Quid aliud, sī spoliātus,
           sī exūtus castrīs essēs, peterēs?*: mixed contrafactual condi-
           tions: protases present tense, apodoses past; *exuere*: "deprive,
           strip of."

660:        *bīna castra*: see above, note to line 421.

665:        *velim seu Himilcō seu Māgō respondeat...*: "I would like H. or
           M. to answer..." (see section on potential subjunctive above).

666:        *Latīnī nōminis*: allied to Rome with certain rights.

670–671:   *quid animōrum quidve speī*: partitive genitive with neuter pro-
           noun (Cap. XLIV); *scīre velim*: "I would like to know" (see sec-
           tion on potential subjunctive above).

675:        *allātum est*: impersonal.

677:        *quā diē*: the usually masculine *diēs* can be feminine, especially
           when it refers to a fixed time (Cap. XIII).

679:        *senātūs cōnsultum*: see above on technical vocabulary; here
           about the Carthaginian "Senate."

Mārcellus et Scīpiō [Ex Periochā librōrum XXIII–XXX]: 682–777

696–697:   *servōrum māximē operā*: *operā* in the ablative means "through
           the agency of."

704:        *ante annōs*: before he turned thirty-six, the legal age for an
           aedile.

708:        *et ingentem virum gessit*: "he conducted himself as a great man."

711–713:   *annō octāvō quam in Hispāniam iērunt*: there is an implicit
           comparison after designations of time (and expressions of
           number or quantity) that sparks the *quam* which here can be
           treated like *postquam*.

720–721:   *sibi mortem cōnscīre*: "to commit suicide."

722:        *secūrī ferīri*: i.e., "to behead."

723–724:	*antequam legeret*: *priusquam* + *subjunctive* (Cap. XLII); *in sinū*: in a fold of his clothing (to read later); *lēge agī*: "proceed according to law, execute the sentence."
726:	*comitiīs* (dative) *apud populum quaererētur*: the question was put to the vote of the people in the comitia.
727:	*volente* with complementary infinitive *suscipere*, the object of which is *id*.
734:	*speculandī causā*: purpose (Cap. XXVI).
741:	*ductū*: Cap. XLVIII, verbal nouns: "under the leadership of."
742:	*nōn minōre operā*: "no less through the agency of…"; cf. lines 696–697.
743:	*ita*: with *relictīs castrīs*.
751:	*si in Āfricam trāiēcisset*: pluperfect subjunctive represents a future perfect indicative in the protasis of a condition in *ōrātiō oblīqua* in secondary sequence; the protasis must be supplied from *auxilium pollicēbātur* (see summary of conditions).
755:	*Syphāx*: king of a Numidian tribe neighboring that of Masinissa.
760:	*Utica*: in Africa. Scipio had been beseiging Utica for forty days.
761:	*Lūstrum*: every five years the censors made a census after which there was a lustration, a purifiying sacrifice consisting of a swine, sheep, and bull, called a *suovetaurīlia* (XLIV.377).
766:	*bīna castra*: see above, line 421.
768–769:	*per*: "through the agency of"; *cēpit*: subject is Scipio.
770–772:	Sophonisba chose to drink the poison (*venēnum*) rather than to be taken to Rome with Scipio as part of the spoils of war; the *periochae*, being summaries, do not give the full story.
772–773:	*Effectum est…ut…*: noun clause of effecting (*verba curandī*: Caps. XXVII, XXXVII).

Reditus Hannibalis atque clādēs [Ex librō et Periochā librī XXX]: 778–865

779:	*nihil ultrā reī*: partitive genitive with neuter pronoun (Cap. XLIV) separated by adverb.
788:	*exsultāre*: "to revel, boast"; *efferet sēsē*: *sē efferre* = "elevate oneself, be haughty."

787–790:   *hāc dēfōrmitāte*: ablative of cause (Cap. XXXVII) with the genitive *reditūs meī*; *tam P. Scīpiō...quam Hannō* both are subjects of *exsultābit atque efferent sēsē*; *domum nostram*: i.e., the Barca lineage (see ll.20–21).

791–800:   *ōrātiō oblīqua* dependent on *ferunt*; *in sē quoque*: with *exsecrātum*; *quod...dūxisset*: subjunctive of reported reason (Cap. XLII); *mīlitem = mīlitēs*: collective noun; *cruentum*: with *mīlitem*: i.e., immediately when they were still covered in (Roman) blood after the battle of Cannae; *cōnsenuisse*: "had grown old."

813:     *Hadrūmētum*: Hannibal's military base during the battle at Zama.

814:     *priusquam excēderet* (Cap. XLII); *expertus < experīrī* (Cap. XLII), the object of which is *omnia*.

820–823:   *omnēs*: object of *stimulābat*; *ad Carthāginem dēlendam*: see summary of expressions of purpose (Cap. XLII); *tam mūnītae et tam validae urbis*: objective genitives with *obsidiō*; take *esset* both with *quanta rēs* and with *obsidiō*: *reputārent* is subjunctive with *cum*; *esset* in indirect question dependent on *reputārent*.

824–825:   *condiciōnēs...ut*: see above, note to lines 603–604.

826–834:   *tenērent...redderent...domārent...gererent...redderent...facerent...solverent...darent*: reported imperatives; *pēnsiōnibus aequiīs*: "in payments of equal amounts."

835–836:   *Hās condiciōnēs*: object of both *referre* and *ēderent*; *domum*: i.e., Carthage.

837:     *quam...esset*: subordinate clause in *ōrātiō oblīqua* (Cap. XXXVI); subject of *esset* is *pāx*; *quam*: "how."

839–840:   *nē...mitterent lēgātōs*: negative command in *ōrātiō oblīqua = nōlīte mittere*.

845:     *vidērētur*: cf. note to line 386 above.

850:     *iūssit*: sc. Scipio.

851:     *quīdam tradunt = quīdam narrant, scrībunt*.

852–853:   *tam lūgubre fuisse Poenīs quam sī ipsa Carthāgō ārdēret*: *quam sī* introduces a conditional comparative clause, which follows sequence of tense (here secondary).

854–858:   *Annīs ante quadrāgintā pāx cum Carthāginiēnsibus postrēmō factā est, Q. Lutātiō A. Mānliō cōnsulibus*: Livy is referring to the First Punic War (264–241 BC); *Bellum initum annīs post tribus et vīgintī, P. Cornēliō Ti. Semprōniō cōnsulibus, fīnitum est septimō decimō annō, Cn. Cornēliō P. Aeliō cōnsulibus*: Second Punic War (218–201 BC).

863:    *pondō*: see section on Libra/Pondus in Cap. XLVII.

III. VOCĀBULA

NŌMINA

1st

angustiae, -ārum (*pl.*)	narrowness, pass, defile
armātūra, -ae	armament, armed troops
funda, -ae	sling
impatientia, -ae	impatience, lack of endurance
indūtiae, -ārum (*pl.*)	armistice, truce
lancea, -ae	lance, spear
perfuga, -ae	deserter
reliquiae, -ārum (*pl.*)	remnants, remains
summa, -ae	total, sum, main part
trāgula, -ae	spear, javelin
victima, -ae	victim (sacrificial)
vigilia, -ae	night watch

2nd

acervus, -ī	heap, pile
angulus, -ī	angle, corner
cōnsultum, -ī	resolution
cuneus, -ī	wedge
dīmidium, -ī	half
excidium, -ī	destruction
hīberna, -ōrum (*n. pl.*)	winter quarters
mōmentum, -ī	movement, motion; moment
mūnīmentum, -ī	fortification
oppidānī, -ōrum (*m. pl.*)	townspeople
pālus, -ī	stake

praetōrium, -ī	general's tent
sarmentum, -ī	brushwood, branch
supplēmentum, -ī	reinforcement, supplement
viāticum, -ī	provision for a journey
vitium, -ī	defect, fault, vice

3rd

adhortātor, -ōris (*m.*)	one who encourages
aedīlis, -is (*m.*)	aedile (magistrate)
aquātor, -ōris (*m.*)	one who fetches water
ariēs, -ētis, (*m.*)	ram, battering ram
calcar, -cāris (*n.*)	spur; stimulus
dēfōrmitās, -tātis (*f.*)	deformity
dēspērātiō, -tiōnis (*f.*)	desperation
expectātiō, -tiōnis (*f.*)	awaiting, expectation
faucēs, -ium (*f. pl.*)	upper part of the throat; opening; pass
grātēs (nom. and acc. *f. pl.*)	thanks
maeror, -ōris (*m.*)	grief
missile, -is (*n.*)	missle
obses, -idis (*m.*)	hostage
obtrectātiō, -tiōnis (*f.*)	criticism, disparagement
oppugnātiō, -tiōnis (*f.*)	attack, assault
pēnsiō, -ōnis (*f.*)	payment, installment
possessiō, -ōnis (*f.*)	possession, occupation
praetor, -ōris (*m.*)	praetor (magistrate)
prōpraetor, -ōris (*m.*)	propraetor
quaestor, -ōris (*m.*)	quaestor (magistrate)
satelles, -itis (*m.*)	attendant, henchman
statiō, -tiōnis (*f.*)	station, post

4th

aditus, -ūs	approach, access
apparātus, -ūs	preparation, equipment
assēnsus, -ūs	approval, assent
commeātus, -ūs	supplies, provisions
reditus, -ūs	return
trānsitus, -ūs	crossing, passage

VERBA

-āre

(adamō) adamāre	fall in love with
(alligō) alligāre	tie, fasten to
(aquor) aquārī	fetch water
(assignō) assignāre	assign, allocate
(castīgō) castīgāre	correct, reprove
(comparō) comparāre	prepare, provide; compare
(cōnsultō) cōnsultāre	deliberate, debate
(crīminor) crīminārī	accuse
(dēnuntiō) dēnuntiāre	denounce
(dēpopulor) dēpopulārī	sack
(ēnervō) ēnervāre	weaken, enervate
(epulor) epulārī	dine, feast
(exanimō) exanimāre	kill; die
(exsultō) exsultāre	jump up; rejoice
(exsuscitō) exsuscitāre	rouse, kindle
(grātificor) grātificārī	oblige, gratify (+ *dat.*)
(irrītō) irrītāre	excite, stimulate
(luxurior) luxuriārī	revel, live in luxury
(nōscitō) nōscitāre	recognize
(obligō) obligāre	bind
(pālor) pālārī	stray, be dispersed
(pēnsō) pēnsāre	weigh, ponder, consider
(perōrō) perōrāre	conclude (a speech)
(pervāstō) pervāstāre	completely devastate
(quassō) quassāre	shake, damage, batter
(speculor) speculārī	spy, reconnoiter
(succlāmō) succlāmāre	shout in response

-ēre

(absterreō) absterrēre (< terrēre)	scare away
(circumsedeō) circumsedēre (< sedēre)	besiege
(expleō) explēre (< plēre)	fill, complete, satisfy
(īnsideō) īnsidēre (< sedēre)	hold, occupy, be seated
(oppleō) opplēre (< plēre)	fill up, cover

(permisceō) permiscēre (< miscēre)	mix thoroughly
(profiteor) profitērī (< fatērī)	declare, offer
(prōmineō) prōminēre (< minēre)	project, stick out
(prōmoveō) prōmovēre (< movēre)	push forward, advance
(submoveō) submovēre (< movēre)	remove, drive off

-ere

(adigō) adigere (< agere)	drive, compel (to)
(adsuēscō) adsuēscere, adsuētum	get accustomed
(affluō) affluere (< fluere)	flow near
(assurgō) assurgere (< surgere)	rise
(āvellō) āvellere, āvelisse	tear away
(circumfundō) circumfundere (< fundere)	pour/spread around
(contrādīcō) contrādīcere (< dīcere)	speak against, oppose
(dēposcō) dēposcere (< poscere)	demand
(dēscrībō) dēscrībere (< scrībere)	draw, describe
(dētrahō) dētrahere (< trahere)	pull off, remove
(dīripio) dīripere (< rapere)	plunder, loot, rob
(dispōnō) dispōnere (< pōnere)	arrange, station
(disserō) disserere (< serere)	discuss, argue
(ēvehō) ēvehere (< vehere)	carry out, *pass.* ride out
(exclūdō) exclūdere (< claudere)	shut out, cut off
(exscindō) exscindere (< scindere)	demolish, destroy
(exuō) exuere, exūtum	take off, deprive of
(frendō) frendere, frenduisse, frēsum	gnash one's teeth
(inquīrō) inquīrere (< quaero)	inquire, make inquiries
(interpōnō) interpōnere (< pōnere)	place between
(intrōdūcō) intrōdūcere (< dūcere)	lead/bring in, introduce
(irruō) irruere (< ruere)	rush in, charge

(nītor) nītī, nīsusm	exert oneself, strive
(obruō) obruere (< ruere)	cover up, bury, crush
(obsistō) obsistere, -stitisse, -stitum	resist
(ommittō) ommittere (< mittere)	abandon, leave off/out
(patēscō) patēscere, patuisse	be laid open, extend
(perfungor) perfungī (< fungī)	carry through, finish (+ *abl.*)
(pervādō) pervādere (< vādere)	go through, spread, pervade
(praecēdō) praecēdere (< cēdere)	go on ahead, precede
(praetervehor) praetervehī (< vehere)	ride/drive/sail past
(prōcidō) prōcidere, prōcidisse (< cadere)	fall forward, collapse
(prōsternō) prōsternere (< sternere)	knock down, overthrow
(rescindō) rescindere (< scindere)	demolish, cancel, annul
(subdō) subdere (< dare)	lay under, subdue, substitue
(succingō) succingere (< cingere)	surround
(trāicio) trāicere (< icere)	take across, cross, pierce
(trānscendō) trānscendere (< scendere)	climb across, cross
(trānsvehō) trānsvehere (< vehere)	carry (*pass.* sail) across
(vergō) vergere	slope, point, turn

-īre

(blandior) blandīrī	coax, urge
(circumveniō) circumvenīre	surround
(commūniō) commūnīre	fortify
(ēmūniō) ēmūnīre	fortify
(expediō) expedīre	make ready, extricate, explain
(mētior) mētīrī	measure
(nequiō) nequīre	be unable
(parturiō) parturīre	be ready to give birth to
(sortior) sortīrī	draw lots

irregular

(differo) differre (< ferre)	postpone, defer, differ

ADIECTĪVA

1st/2nd

callidus, -a, -um	clever, cunning
cōnfertus, -a, -um	dense, compact
fūnestus, -a, -um	deadly, grievous, sinister
impedītus, -a, -um	obstructed, encumbered
imprōvīsus, -a, -um	unforeseen, unexpected
incautus, -a, -um	incautious, unsuspecting
labōriōsus, -a, -um	hard, laborious
praetōrius, -a, -um	of the commander; (*m.*) an expraetor
perangustus, -a, -um	very narrow
solitus, -a, -um	ususal
tumultuārius, -a, -um	hurried, disorderly
ūnicus, -a, -um	one and only, sole
vagus, -a, -um	wandering

3rd

cōnsulāris, -e	consular; (*m.*) an exconsul
equestris, -e	equestrian
habilis, -e	fit, appropriate
libēns (*gen.* **libentis**)	willing, glad
lūgubris, -e	sad, grievous
memorābilis, -e	memorable
quīnquerēmis, -e	having five banks of oars; (*f.*) ship with five banks of oars
recēns (*gen.* **recentis**)	fresh
repēns (*gen.* **repentis**)	sudden, unexpected
sōspes (*gen.* **sōspitis**)	safe and sound
tolerābilis, -e	tolerable
trirēmis, -e	having three banks of oars; (*f.*) ship with three banks of oars

PRONŌMIA

ecquis ecquid	anyone/thing who? anyone, anything
sēmet	intensive of sē

ADVERBIA

alibī	elsewhere
haudquāquam	by no means
inexplōrātō	without reconnoitering
macte (virtūte estō)	well done!
tūtō	safely
vidēlicet	evidently, of course
vixdum	scarcely yet, only just

CONIŪGĀTIŌNĒS

necdum	and (/but) not yet

XLIX: VNDEQVINQVAGESIMVM: HANNIBAL (Nepos)[1]

[Ex Cornēliī Nepōtis librō 'dē Excellentibus Ducibus Exterārum Gentium']

I. ØRBERG'S INTRODUCTION

Cornēlius Nepōs (ca. 100–ca. 25 BC) wrote a chronicle of world history, of which only fragments survive quoted by Aulus Gellius (see Cap. XLVII, ll.25 and 37) as well as a collection of biographies, *dē virīs illūstribus*. From this collection, we still have the book dealing with foreign generals. The last biography in the book is that of *Hannibal*, which is reproduced in this chapter.

Cornelius Nepos is not a very reliable historian. With your knowledge of events, you can detect some inaccuracies in his report: he has Hannibal march on Rome immediately after the battle of Cannae and then tells of events that took place the previous year.

Nepos, however, is not writing history, but biography, and his narrative is very different from that of Livy.

From Nepos we learn what Hannibal did after his defeat at Zama. Under his competent leadership, Carthage soon recovered, but when the Romans demanded his surrender, he took refuge with king *Antiochus III* of Syria. Hannibal encouraged the king to invade Italy, but Antiochus only sent an army to Greece, where he was beaten by the Romans (see next chapter). Hannibal fled to Crete and from there to king *Prūsiās* of *Bīthynia*. A delegation was sent from Rome to demand his surrender, but Hannibal escaped this humiliation by taking poison (183 or 182 BC).

The concluding text is Livy's account of a conversation, which Scipio is said to have had with Hannibal at Ephesus. The conversation presents an interesting, albeit fanciful, portrait of the two great generals.

---

1. For an explanation of the line number references convention, see p. xxvi.

262

II. Auxilia Legendī

Hannibal, Hanilaris fīlius, Karthāginiēnis: 1–255

3:        *superārit* = *superāverit*: syncopated form (see grammar section above); perfect subjunctive in a consecutive noun clause with *vērum est* (Cap. XXXVII).

5–6:   *antecēdat*: subjunctive in subordinate clause in *ōrātiō oblīqua* (Cap. XXXVI); *quotienscumque*: *cumque* makes *quotiens* indefinite (cf. l.38, and below, l.55: *quācumque*).

7:        *congressus…discessit*: subject is Hannibal; *eō*: *populus Rōmānus*.

13:       *patriā pulsus*: 195 BC, see lines 147ff.

15–18:   *nam*: introduces the reason for the preceding statement (as in line 6), but the explanation of *animō bellāre cum Rōmānīs* is here postponed until after the introduction of Antiochus; *ut omittam*: "Leaving out Philip," "Passing by Philip"; *absēns*: sc. Hannibal was in Italy when Philip V, king of Macedon, became an enemy of the Romans.

19–25:   *Ad quem cum* (l.19)…*commemorāsset* (l.25) is all part of the *cum* clause; *quem/eius*: Antiochus; *commemorāsset* = *commemorāvisset*, syncopated form (see grammar section above); … *lēgātī…Rōmānī, quī…explōrārent darentque operam cōnsiliīs clandestīnīs*: relative claue of purpose (Cap. XXXIX); *operam dare…ut*: "to endeavor that" + subjunctive (see above section on idioms); *ut Hannibalem in suspīciōnem rēgī addūcerent*: purpose clause (Caps. XXVIII, XLII); *tempore datō*: "when the opportunity presented itself."

28:       *Karthāgine*: ablative of place from which.

31–32:   *ab eō petere coepissem nē dubitāret dūcere*: indirect command (Cap. XXVII, *verba postulandī*).

34–35:   *cēterīs* (*hominibus*) *remōtīs*: ablative absolute; *tenentem*: sc. *mē*.

36:       *fore* = *futūrum esse* (Cap. XLV).

37–38:   *nēminī dubium esse dēbeat quīn*: Cf. Cap. XL (*nōn dubitō quīn*, l.8); *eādem mente*: ablative of description (Cap. XXXII).

40–42:   *cēlāris* = *cēlāveris*: usually with two accusatives ("hide something from someone"); future condition, as is *frūstrāberis sī nōn…posueris*.

43:         *Hāc...quā dīximus*: *quam dīximus*: an accusative relative pro-
            noun can be attracted into the case (ablative) of its antecedent.

44–45:   *Hasdrubal*: Hannibal's brother-in-law (XLVIII.20); *suffectus*:
            "chosen or elected in place of someone else" (here because the
            elder Hasdrubal had died).

47:         *Karthāginem*: accusative of motion: the announcement had to
            "travel" to Carthage.

48:         *quīnque et vīgintī annīs*: ablative of comparison with *minor*.

50:         *Saguntum foederātam*: i.e., allied to the Romans by a *foedus*
            ("treaty").

52:         *cum Hasdrubale frātre*: his actual brother, not the brother-in-
            law of lines 44–45.

55:         *quācumque*: adv.; see above on *quotienscumque* (l.6).

57:         *Alpēs, -ium*: feminine plural.

62:         *itinera mūnīvit*: "he opened up travel routes"; *elephantus
            ornātus īre*: as opposed to *homo inermis vix poterat rēpere*
            ("crawl," l.63); war elephants were equipped (*ornātus*) with
            towers.

68:         *tertiō*: adverb, "for a third time."

69–70:   *manum cōnserere*: "engage in close combat."

71:         *Ligurēs*: inhabitants of Liguria, the Ligurians.

74:         *etiamnunc*: "even yet, even under these circumstances."

76:         *occīdit*: with both clauses (*C. Flāminium...circumventum* and
            C. Centēnium...occupantem).

85–86:   *urbī*: dative with *propinquīs...montibus*; *morārī*: delay, stay;
            cum...habuisset...reverterētur: subject is Hannibal.

88–90:   *Hic*: Hannibal; *exercitūs*: objective genitive with *ūllō dētrī-
            mentō*; *dedit verba*: "tricked" (see section on idioms, above).

91:         *sarmenta...dēligāta*: Cf. XLVIII.402–403.

92:         *eiusque generis*: genitive of description.

96–97:   *magistrum equitum*: Cap. XLVI; *parī ac dictātōrem imperiō*:
            ablative of description or quality; adjectives which mark
            equality or similarity often take *atque* or its shortened form *ac*;
            parī ac: "equal to."

99:	*in Lūcānīs*: the Lucani lived in southern Italy; *absēns*: Hannibal's brother Mago was in charge (XLVIII.58).
102:	*longum est*: "it is tedious, too long," cf. XLVII.164: *sed prōgressī longius sumus*.
103–104:	*quantus ille fuerit*: "How great he was" indirect question.
110:	*fugārat = fugāverat*: syncopated form (see grammar section above).
107:	*dēfēnsum*: supine (Caps. XXII, XLV).
111–112:	*impraesentiārum*: perhaps from *"in praesentiā rērum"*: "for the present"; *componere bellum*: "put an end to the war"; *quō valentior posteā congrederētur*: relative clause of purpose with a comparative; *quō valenior = ut eō valentior* (see grammar section above).
113:	*convēnit...convēnerunt*: *convēnit* is impersonal (Cap. XLI), *convēnerunt* is personal; both signify reaching an agreement.
115:	*incrēdibile dictū*: ablative of respect of supine (Cap. XXXIX).
117:	*Numidae, -ārum* (m. pl.): Numidians, fighting for the Romans.
122:	*ācerrimē*: "very/most vigorously, vehemently."
124:	*nihilō sētius*: "nonetheless."
125:	*ūsque ad...cōnsulēs*: temporal, "up to the time when Sulpicius and Aurelius were consuls."
125–130:	*lēgātī...vēnērunt, quī...agerent...[et] corōnā aureā eōs dōnarent simulque peterent*: relative clause of purpose (Cap. XXXIX); (for *corōnā aureā...dōnarent*, see grammar section above); *peterent ut...essent...redderentur*: indirect command (Cap. XXVII, *verba postulandī*); *obsidēs*: "hostages."
131:	*ex senātūs cōnsultō*: "by decree of the senate," cf. XLVIII.679.
132:	*quō locō*: i.e., at Fregellae.
133–136:	*quod Hannibalem, cuius...foret,...habērent*: subordinate clauses in *ōrātiō oblīqua* (Cap. XXXVI); *cuius operā*: "through whose agency," Cf. Cap. XLVIII.696–697; *foret = esset* (Cap. XLIII).
141:	*parī...ac*: see above, note to lines 96–97.
147–148:	*Hōs Hannibal ratus suī exposcendī grātiā missōs*: *ratus...missōs*: compressed indirect statement dependent on the participle ratus (from *reor, rērī*: "think"); *grātiā*: just like *causā* (Cap. XXVI);

grātiā in the ablative can take a preceding genitive to mean "for the sake of, in order to"; *suī* is the genitive of the reflexive pronoun *sē* (cf. *meī* and *tuī* as genitives of *ego* and *tū*) (Cap. XXIX) = *ratus hōs...missōs esse ut sē exposcerent*.

148–149:   *senātus darētur*: *senātum dare* + dative: "give someone an opportunity to address the Senate."

149–150:   *clam <-> palam*.

151–152:   *nāvēs...quae eum comprehenderent sī possent cōnsequī, mīsērunt*: both a relative clause of purpose (Cap. XXXIX), "sent ships to," and conditional (future condition in secondary sequence), "to seize him if they could catch him"; *pūblicārunt = pūblicāvērunt*: "confiscate."

153:    *iūdicārunt = iūdicāvērunt*.

154–156:   *sī...voluisset...dīmicāsset* (= *dīmicāvisset*): past contrafactual condition.

158:    *vidēbat...nūllā dēseruit in rē*: subject is Hannibal (i.e., Hannibal continued to support Antiochus even though the latter was a disappointment); *praefuit*: subject is Antiochus.

159:    *iīsque*: ablative of means referring to the ships (and their military crew).

162:    *suī*: sc. *mīlitēs*, his own soldiers.

163–164:   *verēns nē*: fear clause (Caps. XXXII, XLVIII); *accidisset...sī suī fēcisset potestātem*: past contrafactual condition; "*potestātem suī facere*": to create an opportunity (for others) to have access to oneself; *suī* is the genitive of the reflexive pronoun *sē* (cf. l.148; Cap. XXIX).

165:    *ut...cōnsīderāret*: purpose; *quō sē cōnferret*: indirect question.

166–167:   *in magnō sē fore...nisi quid prōvidisset*: future condition in *ōrātiō oblīqua*, secondary sequence; in direct speech: *in magnō perīculō erō, nisi quid prōvīderō*.

170:    *plumbum, -ī*: "lead"; *summās*: sc. *amphorās*.

172–173:   *simulāns sē suās fortūnās illōrum fideī crēdere*: the change in pronouns reflects a shift in locution. What Hannibal said (direct statement) was "*meās fortūnās vestrae fideī crēdo*"; in *ōrātiō oblīqua*, the pronouns shift (see Cap. XLIII on pronoun changes): "I entrust my fortunes to your honesty," becomes in reported speech, "he entrusted his fortunes to the honesty of those men." But in Nepos's narrative, "those men" (*illōrum*) are represented as "these men, the ones I was just writing about" (*hīs...inductīs*).

177:        *īnscientibus iīs*: ablative absolute; *tolleret...dūceret*: sc. as object *amphorās*.

181–182:   *eōdem animō*: ablative of description; *neque aliud quicquam... quam*: "nothing other than."

183:        *quem*: i.e., *Prūsiam*.

188:        *quō magis cupiēbat*: *quō = et eō*: "and therefore, for this reason."

189–190:   *quem sī <u>remōvisset</u>, faciliōra sibi cētera <u>fore</u> arbitrābātur*: condition in *ōrātiō oblīqua* in secondary sequence (Cap. XLIII); the direct statement would have been: *"sī eum remōverō, faciliōra mhi cētera erunt"*; *fore = futūrum esse*, the future infinitive of *esse*; *remōvisset* represents a future perfect indicative in secondary sequence (see summary of conditions).

191:        *tālem iniit ratiōnem*: *inīre ratiōnem*: "to reckon, calculate"; "hit on the following plan."

193:        *classe...erant dēcrētūrī*: "they were intending to contend by naval battle"; *erat pugnandum*: impersonal passive of the passive periphrastic with an intransitive verb (Cap. XL).

199–200:   *praecipit...quem sī aut cēpissent aut interfēcissent, magnō iīs... praemiō fore*: condition in *ōrātiō oblīqua* (Cap. XLIII), dependent on a historical present (Cap. XXXVII), hence the secondary sequence; the direct statement would have been: *eum sī aut cēperitis aut interfēceritis, magnō vobis praemiō erit*.

202:        *Bithȳniī*: Prusias (as the marginal note to l.180 in your text points out) was king of Bithynia.

208:        *concitārunt = concitāvērunt*.

210:        *quid potissimum*: "what most of all," i.e., the snakes or the enemy ships.

215:        *accidit...ut...cēnārent*: noun clause of result (Cap. XXXVII).

219–221:   *quī Hannibale vīvō numquam sē sine īnsidiīs futūrōs exīstimārent*: relative causal clause, "because they thought" (Cap. XXXIX); *mīsērunt...quī ab rēge peterent*: relative clause of purpose (Cap. XXXIX).

222–223:   '*nē inimīcissimum suum sēcum habēret, sibique dēderet*': indi-
           rect command with *petere* (Cap. XXVII, *verba postulandī*); the
           reflexive pronouns do not all refer to the subject of the main
           verb (*peterent*, l.221); *sēcum habēre* means "to keep to oneself,"
           that is, for Prusias to keep the Romans' greatest enemy (*inimī-
           cissimum suum*, Hannibal) to himself (*sēcum*, Prusias) but
           turn him over to them (*sibi*, the Romans). The switch of refer-
           ents for reflexives in indirect speech is not uncommon, but it
           rarely impedes understanding.

224–226:   *illud recūsāvit nē id ā sē fierī postulārent*: *recūsāre* ("object to")
           here takes an object clause (*nē* + the subjunctive); *illud*: i.e.,
           the latter request; *quod adversus iūs hospitiī esset*: descriptive
           (potential) clause (Cap. XLII); "*ipsī, sī possent, comprehen-
           derent*": condition in *ōrātiō oblīqua* (Cap. XLIII): direct state-
           ment would have been "*ipsī, sī potestis, comprehendite eum!*"
           The sequence is secondary; the protasis is subjunctive as a
           subordinate clause in *ōrātiō oblīqua* (Cap. XXXVI) and the
           protasis is subjunctive as a reported imperative, virtually an
           indirect command.

228:       *datum erat mūnerī*: *mūnerī* is dative of purpose: "to give for
           the purpose of a gift/to give as a gift" (Caps. XXXVI, XL);
           aedificārat = aedificāverat.

230:       *nē ūsū venīret*: "lest it should happen" (see section on idioms,
           above).

239:       *aliēnō arbitriō*: "on someone else's decision."

241:       *cōnsuērat = cōnsuēverat*: syncopated form (see grammar sec-
           tion above); *cōnsuēscere = cōnsuēvisse*: "get accustomed," like
           nōscere "get to know" (Cap. XXIV) have a present sense in
           the perfect tense and an imperfect sense in the pluperfect;
           cōnsuēverat = solēbat: "was accustomed."

243–244:   *Quibus cōnsulibus interierit, nōn convenit*: for *nōn convenit*, see
           note above on line 113; *quibus…interierit*: indirect question.

Scīpiō et Hannibal [Ex T. Līviī librī XXXV Periochā]: 256–275

259:       *Ephesī*: locative; Ephesus is near the coast of Asia Minor (see
           map in Cap. LIII of your text).

260–261:   *sī fierī posset*: if it were possible (Cap. XXXVI); *eī…eximeret*:
           dative: "remove <u>from him</u>."

266:    *vīsere*: "to go to see," "to visit" (Cap. XXX).

267:    *Quaerentī*: sc. *Scīpiōnī* = *cum Scīpiō quaereret*.

269:    *loca capere*: "set up a position, select a place for camp"; *praesidia disponere*: "set up guard posts" (military terms).

III. Vocābula

Nōmina

1st

amphora, -ae	amphora (jar)
avāritia, -ae	greed, avarice
corōna, -ae	wreath

2nd

adversārius, -ī	opponent, adversary
arbitrium, -ī	decision, wish
bīduum, -ī	two days
classiāriī, -ōrum (*pl.*)	marines
dētrīmentum, -ī	harm, loss
plumbum, -ī	lead
praeceptum, -ī	instruction, order
prōpatulum, -ī	forecourt
puerulus, -ī	small boy

3rd

cohortātiō, -ōnis (*f.*)	exhortation
cōnsuētūdō, -inis (*f.*)	custom, habit
doctor, -ōris (*m.*)	teacher, learned man
facultās, -ātis (*f.*)	capability, possibility, (*pl.*) resources
hērēditās, -ātis (*f.*)	inheritance
nātiō, -ōnis (*f.*)	people, nation
patrēs cōnscrīptī	senators
serpēns, -entis (*m.*)	snake, serpent
suspīciō, -ōnis (*f.*)	suspicion
vectīgal, -ālis (*n.*)	tax

4th

dīlēctus, -ūs	recruitment; choice
obitus, -ūs	death
vīsus, -ūs	sight, vision

VERBA

-āre

(comprobō) comprobāre	approve, confirm
(cōnsīderō) cōnsīderāre	observe, reflect
(dēbilitō) dēbilitāre	weaken
(dēligō) dēligāre	tie up, fasten
(dispālōr) dispālārī	wander about
(ēnumerō) ēnumerāre	count up, enumerate
(īnfitior) īnfitiārī	deny
(īnsidior) īnsidiārī	lie in wait, lie in ambush
(mētor) mētārī	measure off, lay out
(peragrō) peragrāre	travel over
(prōflīgō) prōflīgāre	defeat decisively, crush
(pūblicō) pūblicāre	make public property, confiscate
(verba dō) verba dare	deceive, cheat

-ēre

(dissideō) dissidēre (< sedēre)	disagree, differ
(indigeō) indigēre, -uisse, -itum	need, desire
(prōvideō) prōvidēre (< vidēre)	see to it, take care

-ere

(acquiēscō) acquiēscere, -ēvisse, -ētum	go to rest; die
(antecēdō) antecēdere (< cēdere)	precede, surpass
(concīdō) concīdere, -īdisse, -īsum	fall (down), collapse
(concipiō) concipere (< capere)	receive, catch, conceive
(congredīor) congredī, -gressum	meet, join battle, fight
(cōnserō) cōnserere, -uisse, -tum	join, connect

(cōnsuēscō) cōnsuēscere, -ēvisse, -ētum	get used/accustomed to
(excidō) excidere, -idisse, -isum	fall out, be dropped
(eximō) eximere (< emere)	take away, remove
(obdūcō) obdūcere (< dūcere)	draw over (to cover)
(pendō) pendere, pependisse, pensum	weigh, pay
(rēpō) rēpere, rēpsisse, rēptum	crawl
(sēiungō) sēiungere (< iungere)	separate
(sufficiō) sufficere (< facere)	appoint, substitute

ADIECTĪVA

1st/2nd

aēneus, -a, -um	of bronze/copper
districtus, -a, -um	busy
foederātus, -a, -um	federated, allied
nauticus, -a, -um	nautical, naval
prīstinus, -a, -um	former, original, pristine
rōbustus, -a, -um	strong, robust
venēnātus, -a, -um	poisoned, poisonous

3rd

excellēns (*gen.* **excellentis**)	outstanding
exter, -era, -erum	external, foreign
fictilis, -e	earthen, earthenware
imprūdēns (*gen.* **imprūdentis**)	ignorant, imprudent
innumerābilis, -e	countless, innumerable
īnsciēns (*gen.* **īnscientis**)	not knowing, unaware

ADVERBIA

aliās	at another time, at another place
eā	that way, there
fortuītō	by chance, fortuitously
hāc	this way
impresentiārum	at the present moment

posteāquam	afterward, since
nōnnihil	not a little, something
potissimum	preferably, especially
quotiēnscumque	every time that
setīus	nonetheless
utpote	namely
ūtrobīque	in both places

L: QVINQVAGESIMVM:
GRAECIA LIBERATA (Livy)[1]

[*Ex T. Līviī 'ab Urbe Conditā' librīs XXXI–XLV*]

I. ØRBERG'S INTRODUCTION

The victory over Carthage gave the Romans control of the Western Mediterranean. They now directed their attention to the East. In this chapter, you read extracts from Livy's account, supplemented by the *periochae*, of the conflict between Rome and the two great powers of the Eastern Mediterranean, *Macedonia* and *Syria*.

The Romans feared that king Philip (*Philippus*) V of Macedonia (221–179 BC), who had supported Hannibal in the Second Punic War, would conquer all the free states of Greece and the kingdom of *Pergamum* in Asia Minor. To prevent this, they declared war and sent an army to "liberate" Greece. After a few years' fighting, the Romans, under *Flāminīnus*, won a decisive victory over Philip (197 BC), and during the Isthmian Games at Corinth, the liberation of Greece was solemnly proclaimed. Only in 194, after conquering the insubordinate tyrant *Nabis* of Sparta, could Flamininus leave Greece with his army, and in Rome he celebrated a triumph lasting three days.

The next war was with king *Antiochus* III of Syria (223–187 BC), who ruled a large kingdom in the Eastern Mediterranean including most of Asia Minor. Antiochus invaded Greece, where he was supported by the Aetolians, but was defeated by the Romans at *Thermopylae* in 191. The Roman consul *Acilius* put an end to the war in Greece by capturing the heavily fortified city of *Hēraclēa* from the Aetolians. The Romans, commanded by *L. Cornēlius Scīpiō*, the brother of Scipio Africanus, carried the war over to Asia Minor. With the support of king *Eumenēs* of Pergamum, they defeated Antiochus in 190 and compelled him to give up Asia Minor west of Mount Taurus.

---

1. For an explanation of the line number references convention, see p. xxvi.

After the death of king Philip, his son *Perseus* succeeded to the throne of Macedonia. The new king's aggressive policy brought about a new war with Rome, which lasted four years and ended with the final defeat of Perseus by *L. Aemilius Paulus* at the battle of Pydna in 168. Macedonia was now made a Roman province.

At the end of book 45 of his Roman history, the last that has been preserved, Livy tells of the events after the battle of Pydna: the arrival of the news in Rome, the capture of Perseus, and Aemilius Paulus's splendid triumph. A few days before and after this triumph, the victorious general lost his two youngest sons, but he bore this terrible blow with Roman virtue and gravity. In a public speech to the people, he expressed his gratitude that the gods had seen fit to let the change of fortune that must follow upon such a great success overtake his family and not Rome. Chapter 51 will take up the narrative of Roman history with Paulus' son who was adopted by Scipio Africanus (Publius Cornelius Scipio Aemelianus). The summary (*periocha*) of Book 46 shows Paulus as a man of great integrity:

> *L. Aemilius Paulus, quī Persen vīcerat, mortuus. Cuius tanta abstinentia fuit ut cum ex Hispāniā et ex Macedoniā immensās opēs rettulisset, vix ex auctiōne eius redactum sit, unde uxōrī eius dōs solverētur* (*abstinentia*: self-restraint; *auctio, ōnis*: an auction to sell his goods after his death; *redactum < redigere*: brought back; *dōs, dōtis*: dowry: this marriage portion would have been returned to his wife after Paulus' death).

Notā bene: This chaper covers about eighty years of Roman history, with excerpts from books 31 through 45 of Livy's *ab Urbe Conditā*. That's about 740 pages of Latin text in the Teubner Edition, here represented in 676 lines of Latin. Such a condensation of material gives a rather sweeping view of Roman history, highlighting a few events and eclipsing, by necessity, others.

II. Auxilia Legendī

Philippus [Ex librīs et periochā librōrum XXXI–XXXIV]: 1–97

13–14:   *in faucibus: fauces, -ium*: "narrow opening" or "mountain pass" (Cap. XLVIII.288); *fugātumque coēgit in rēgnum revertī*: i.e., *coēgit Philippum fugātum in rēgnum revertī* or *coēgit Philippum postquam ille fugātus est in rēgnum revertī*.

15:    *sociīs Aetōlīs*: in military terms, troops are used as an ablative of means instead of agent (*ab* + ablative).

18–19:   *cum Philippō…aciē victō dēbellāvit*: "he finished the war with Philip by defeating his army in battle at Cynoscephalae"; *aciēs, -eī* (f.): the front line of battle; here: "an army arranged for battle"; it can also mean the battle itself (cf. XLVIII.636).

22:       *signīs collātīs*: the *signa* ("banners" or "standards") of a Roman army symbolized the army itself and, as well as being of paramount importance, are part of many military idioms; *signa conferre* means "to engage in close battle."

25:       *in cōntiōne*: i.e., in front of the people.

27:       *brevī*: sc. *tempore*.

28–29:   *in vīllam pūblicam*: the *Vīlla Pūblica*, located in the *Campus Mārtius* (XXXVI.8–9); Livy 4.22 cites its construction for the use of the censors in 434 BC (*Eō annō C. Fūrius Paculus et M. Geganius Macerīnus cēnsōrēs vīllam pūblicam in campō Mārtiō probāvērunt, ibique prīmum cēnsus populī est āctus*).

32–34:   *mōre māiōrum*: the *mōs māiōrum* ("the way our ancestors did things") was the touchstone of Roman cultural practice: "in the traditional practice," "in the traditional manner"; *dēcrētī*: sc. *sunt*; *daret*: subjunctive in a jussive subjunctive in indirect speech implied by *cōnsiliō*.

36–46:   *ut omnēs…habērent…dēdūceret…trāderet…habēret…gereret… daret…populō Rōmānō*: noun clause giving the content of the conditions of peace (*lēgēs*); were they in direct speech, they would have been jussives subjunctives.

39–43:   *quae = quae Graecōrum cīvitātēs*; so too *vacuās* (*cīvitātēs*); *Isthmiōrum tempus*: the Isthmian Games (*lūdicrum*, l.49 = *lūdus*) at the Isthmus of Corinth, celebrated every five years; *nāvēs tēctās*: i.e., ships with decks.

45:       *iniussū senātūs*: like *iussū* (Cap. XLI), *iniussū* is found only in the ablative with a genitive or a possessive adjective.

50–52:   *cum…tum = et…et* (Cap. XLII); *ad solitōs modo ūsūs*: "not only for the usual enjoyments" (i.e., going to the games and the market).

53–54:   *qui…status…esset?*: indirect question.

55–56:   *praecō, -ōnis* (Cap. XLIV); *tubicen, tubicinis* (Cap. XLII).

59:       *immūnēs*, i.e., *vectīgālibus*: *immūnis, -e* (Cap. XLIV); *vectīgal, -ālis* (Cap. XLIX).

61:          *Magnētas*: Greek names in the 3rd declension plural often retain the *-ăs* ending (instead of *-ēs*).

64–65:   *māius gaudium fuit quam quod...acciperent*: relative comparative clause (Cap. XLVIII); *crēdere*: historical infinitive, subject: *quisque*.

71–72:   *nihil omnium bonōrum*: partitive genitive with neuter pronoun (Cap. XLIV); *multitūdinī*: dative with the comparative *grātius*, "more pleasing to..."

78–80:   *in ūnum*: "into one place, together"; *cupientium, iacientium*: genitives with the ablative absolute *ruente turbā*; *adīre contingere*: two separate actions without a conjunction (called asyndeton) = *adire et contingere*; *perīculō*: ablative of separation with *procul* (Cap. XXXVI).

81–88:   *quae...bella gerat prō lībertāte aliōrum! nec hoc...praestet, sed...trāiciat...ubīque...sint*: the relative clause, which extends over the punctuation (i.e., all the verbs have [*gens*] *quae* as subject), can be interpreted as simply a subordinate clause in *ōrātiō oblīqua* (Cap. XXXVI) or a relative descriptive (generic) clause (Cap. XLI).[2]

83:          *suā impensā*: "at its own expense."

84–86:   *hoc*: subject of *praestet*; *finitimīs*: "neighbors, people on its borders"; *propinquae vīcīnitātis*: genitive of description; *vīcīnitas*: "proximity, vicinity."

86–88:   *maria trāicere*: "cross the seas"; *trāiciat nē...sit, ubique...sint*: a compound purpose clause, the first element marked negative by *nē*, the second unmarked but positive (i.e., *ut ubīque*).

88–89:   *līberātās*: sc. *esse* (still part of the reported speech of the people—but it's also the accusative of exclamation; see Cap. XXXIX).

Triumphus Flāminīnī [Ex librō XXXIV]: 98–128

100:       *Vēris initiō*: "at the beginning of spring," cf. l.140; *vēnit*: sc. *T. Quīnctius Flāminīnus*.

101:       *in contiōnis modum*: "in the manner of an assembly."

102:       *ōrsus < ordīrī*: i.e., *coepit loquī*; *Rōmānīs*: dative; Livy switches construction midsentence (leaving *imperātōrum* not strictly

---

2. As you will learn the more you read Latin, a simple and exact classification of a clause is not always possible—or necessary.

dependent on anything); this construction is called *anaco-luton* and is best interpreted as indicated by the marginalia in the text (*et ab rēbus gestīs imperātōrum*).

106:    *in animō esse*: "to have in mind," "to have an intention" (cf. margin of XLIII.250–251).

107–108:   *respiciunt*: i.e., the assembled Greeks; *praesidium*: i.e., *Rōmānum*.

110–111:   *prōsequentibus cūnctīs...acclāmantibus*: ablative absolute; *Elatēa*: see line 35.

112:    *unde erat trāiectūrus*: here, as often, the future particple signals intention: "whence he planned to cross over" (to Italy).

114:    *prope trimphantēs*: the adverb qualifies that the atmosphere was one of a triumph, but an actual triumph has to be declared by the senate.

115–117:   *senātus...Quīnctiō...datus est*: *senatus dare* + dative: "give someone an opportunity to address the Senate"; *ad rēs gestās ēdisserendās*: purpose.

119–120:   *aurum argentumque factum īnfectumque et signātum*: gold and silver both "wrought" (*factum*), "unwrought" (*īnfectum*), and "embossed" (*signātum*); *aurī*: genitive with *milia*; *pondō*: "in weight."

122:    *dōna cīvitātum*: in apposition to *corōnae*.

123:    *hostia = victima*: animal for sacrifice (Cap. XXXIX).

127:    *ut exercitū...dēportātō*: *ut = prō ut* (*prout*); causal, "as."

Antiochus [Ex librīs et periochā librōrum XXXV–XXXVIII]: 129–275

138–139:   *in convīviīs et vīnum sequentibus voluptātibus*: "in dinner parties and in the pleasures that follow upon (drinking) wine."

143:    *dūcere*: used of a general in an absolute sense, "march, move": historical infinitive.

146:    *omnī contractā iuventūte*: ablative absolute; *contractā*: "collected, gathered together."

148:    *quō = et eō* (adverb); *aliquantō*: ablative of degree of difference with *pauciōrēs*.

153:    *in septentriōnem versa*: *versa* refers to Epirus grammatically, by extension to the whole list of cities, *septentriōnem* (Cap. XVI);

this whole section is best read with an eye on the map on p. 262 of your text.

154:          *Phthīōtae Achaeī*: the Achaeans of Phthiotis.

158:          *prōmunturium* (Cap. XXXIX).

161:          *in cuius valle ad Māliacum sinum vergente*: i.e., the valley verges on the Malian bay.

162–163:   *Haec ūna mīlitāris via est quā trādūcī exercitūs, sī nōn prohibeantur, possint*: a main clause with *ūnus* (or *sōlus*) is often followed by a descriptive relative clause (Caps. XXXIX, XLII), while the *sī nōn prohibeantur* is equivalent to a negative proviso clause (*dummodo nē…*): see Cap. XL.

165–167:   *locus appellātur, nōbilis Lacedaemoniōrum adversus Persās morte magis memorābilī quam pugnā*: *morte* and *pugnā* are both ablatives of respect with *nōbilis* (the Greek historian Herodotus narrates the famous battle of Thermopylae in Book VII of his Persian Wars).

168:          *haudquāquam parī…animō*: i.e., unequal to the courage of Leonidas (the Spartan leader) at the time (*tum*) of the Persian War (see margin note).

169:          *cum duplicī vāllō fossāque et mūrō etiam permūniisset omnia*: for the parts of a Roman army camp, see Cap. XII.

171:          *eā*: "on that side" (sc. *parte*).

172:          *praesidiō*: dative of purpose (Cap. XXXVI).

176–177:   *timor…nē…invenīret*: fear clause (Caps. XXXII, XLVIII); *ad trānsitum*: "as a means of passage."

187:          *priusquam* + subjunctive (Cap. XLII).

188–189:   *artā fronte, ad nātūram et angustiās locī*: the *frons* of a battle-line is the vanguard (front); *ad*: "in accordance with."

192:          *ab omnī parte*: "on every side," cf. ll.215–216; *aditūs*: object of *temptantēs*.

194:          *locō*: ablative of separation with *pulsī*.

195: *prope alterum vāllum, hastīs prae sē obiectīs*: the ablative absolute tells us how the "Macedonians"[3] created a second, virtual
(*prope*) rampart with their long spears held out in front.

195–200: *Multī* (sc. *Rōmānī*) *aut recessissent aut plūrēs cecidissent, nī M.
Porcius ab iugō Callidromī,…appāruisset*: past contrafactual
condition.

200–201: *Macedonēs quīque aliī = Macedonēs et aliī quī*; *prīmō*: adverb,
"at first."

203: *subsidiō*: dative of purpose (Cap. XXXVI); *ut prīmum*:
Cap. XXXVII.

204: *aperuērunt < aperīre*: open, reveal.

205: *tantus repente pavor omnēs cēpit ut abiectīs armīs fugerent*: result clause.

206: *perexiguā*: the prefix *per-* before adjectives and adverbs has intensive force ("very…").

207: *sub adventum*: "around the time of his arrival."

211–213: *Inde cōnsul M. Catōnem, per quem scīret…Rōmam mīsit*: relative clause of purpose with verb of motion (Cap. XXXIX); *quae
gesta esset*: indirect question (Cap. XXIX and *Notā Bene* in
Cap. XXXIX); *haud dubiō auctōre*: i.e., so that the senate
would hear the news from a reliable source.

216: *equō moenia est circumventus*: "rode his horse around the
walls" (cf. l.6, *Cornēlius equō vehitur*).

217: *Hēraclēa sita est in rādīcibus Oetae montis, ipsa in campō, ar-
cem imminentem locō altō et undique praecipitī habet*: i.e., the
city itself lies at the foot of the mountain in a plain but also has
a citidel high up on the mountain.

221: *operibus magis quam armīs*: *opus, -eris* (n.) as a military term
is either "fortification" or "a siege-engine."

225: *segnius*: comparative adverb from *sēgnis, -e*, "more slowly."

226–227: *dīmicātiōne*: ablative of separation with *vacuum*.

228: *diurnō*: dative with *continuātus…est*.

---

3. As the marginalia tells you, these are Antiochus's soldiers drawn up in Macedonian
fashion.

231:        *quartā vigiliā*: ablative of time; the night was divided into four watches (*vigiliae*) of three hours each.

232:        *ab unā* (sc. *parte*); *tenēre intentōs mīlitēs*: *intentōs* is predicative: "keep the soldiers alert."

235:        *quī oppugnārent intentī signum exspectābant*: *exspectāre*, a verb that signals an expectation for the future, is often followed by an anticipatory subjunctive with the verb conforming to sequence of tense (compare the conjunction *dum* + the anticipatory subjunctive in Cap. XL); here, the relative clause reveals what the alert troops are ready to do when they get the sign.

240:        *ab urbe*: i.e., the Romans who were approaching the citadel from the city below.

241–242:   *nūllā ibi praeparātā rē ad...tolerandum*: ablative absolute with a gerundive purpose clause explaining *rē*.

245:        *pācis petendae ōrātōrēs*: gerundive phrase; genitive of description that is equivalent to a purpose clause.

260–261:   *omnibus prōvinciīs...cēderet*: ablative of separation, "withdraw from" (Cap. XXXVIII).

262:        *cognōmine frātrī exaequātus*: i.e., 'Āfricānus,' cf. l.271; *frātrī*: dative with *exaequāre*; *cognōmine*: ablative of respect (Cap. XXXIX).

263:        *Eumenis*: genitive (*Eumenēs, -is*); *quō iuvante*: ablative absolute.

266:        *praefectōs classis*: the *praefectus* is the person in charge, and *praefectus classis* is an admiral.

271:        *peculātus, -ūs*: "embezzlement of public money"; here, genitive of the charge with *accūsātus damnātuque* (Cap. XLVI).

Perseus victus [Ex librīs et periochā librōrum XL–XLV]: 276–383

281–283:   *Eumenēs,...questus est*: *queror, querī, questum* means "to complain"; here, Eumenes is making a formal complaint to the Senate; *in populum Rōmānum referuntur*: *referuntur*: see Cap. XLVIII on *referre*; an official announcement made to the Roman people; *ob quās* (*iniūriās*); *eī*: i.e., Perseus.

287:        *parum*: "too little, not enough."

288: *dē agrō*: about respective territories (Carthage claimed the Numidians under Masinissa had illegally appropriated a considerable amount of land).

290: *continet*: the unstated subject is Book XLIII (see margins).

299: *rebellāsset*: syncopated pluperfect subjunctive (Cap. XLIX); for *rebellāre*, see Cap. XLV.

302: *Tertiō diē Perseum quam pugnātum erat*: there is an implicit comparison after designations of time (and expressions of number or quantity) that sparks the *quam* which here can be treated like *postquam* (cf. XLVIII.711–713).

308: *diē alterō*: "on the second day."

311: *Persea*: Greek accusative singular of Perseus.

316–317: *praeceptam…laetitiam*: i.e., the people were already celebrating.

324–325: *ēvānuit*: *ēvānescere, ēvānuisse*: "vanish, disappear"; *certae reī gaudium*: objective genitive (Cap. XXV); *gaudium* is a more inward joy than *laetitia*, which refers to a more outward expression of joy (ll.317 and 330); *tamquam* qualifies *certae*; *insidēre*: "settle, occupy" (+ dat.).

326: *vērīs nūntiīs*: ablative of means with *firmātum est*.

329–330: *Et altera…laetitia*: subject: "another outbreak of joy," i.e., a second story about the crowd's joy; *circēnsis turbae*: genitive with *laetitia*; *similis vērī*: *similis* takes the dative or, as here, the genitive.

330–334: *C. Liciniō cōnsulī…ēscendentī…trādidisse dīcitur*: flexible word order allows the important person in this sentence (the consul) to be put in a position of prominence, as frequently; the consul was "going up" to a position whence he could give the signal for the race to start.

333: *quī…dīceret*: subjunctive in a subordinate clause in *ōrātiō oblīqua* (Cap. XLII); *laureātās litterās*: dispatches announcing victory were adorned with laurel leaves.

335–336: *ad forōs pūblicōs*: from *forus, -ī* (not *forum, -ī*): the rows of seats in the Circus reserved for senators and knights (Livy I.35: *loca dīvīsa patribus equitibusque*); cf. l.339, *prō forīs pūblicīs*.

340: *signīs collātīs*: "in a pitched battle," see line 22.

351–352:   *dē…referrētur*: see Cap. XLVIII, section on technical vocabu-
               lary, still with *ut* (l.350); *vēnissent* is equivalent to a future per-
               fect indicative (in secondary sequence).

355–357:   *ingentem…*: with *turbam*, object of the participle *trahentēs*, sc.
               lēgātī.

358:           *tantum temporis retentī dum exponerent*: i.e., they were retained
               (by the Senate) as much time as needed to relate; *tantum* is not
               correlative here with *quantae*; *tantum* is neuter singular with
               partitive genitive; *quantae* is interrogative adjective with *rēgiae
               cōpiae*; *dum*: anticipatory subjunctive (Cap. XL).

361:           *iactūra*: "loss": an idiom from seafaring, it comes from *iacere*
               and means "a throwing overboard" (see Cap. XXIX).

365:           *eadem haec*: neuter plural (i.e., the same news they had re-
               ported to the Senate).

367:           *prō sē quisque*: "each on his own behalf."

368–369:   *īre…complērī*: historical infinitives (Cap. XLIV).

371–372:   *in quīnque diēs*: "for five days"; *circā omnia pulvīnāria*: "around
               all the couches of the gods," standard phrasing for the giving
               of a *supplicātiō* at all the temples.

378:           *In cōnsulis verba iūrāverant*: "took the military oath"; *in verba
               iūrāre* is to swear according to a defined formula.

379:           *nūntiā(vē)runt*: syncopated perfect.

380:           *Gentius*: cf. ll.291, 298.

381–382:   L. Anicius was the praetor and general in charge; *ductū auspi-
               ciōque L. Aniciī praetōris* refers to *rēs gestae*.

Perseus captus [Ex librō XLV]: 384–506

386:           *ignōbilēs*: men of no rank or distinction.

388:           *sortī hūmānae*: dative with the compound *illacrimāre*.

388–392:   *quod quī…oppugnāsset…esset*: subjunctive of reported reason
               (Cap. XLII); *rēgnō*: ablative with *contentus*; *fānī religiōne*: "by
               of the sacredness of the shrine," parallel with *nōn vīribus suīs*;
               Reading help: *quod quī paulō ante nōn contentus rēgnō
               Macedoniae Dardanōs Illyriōsque oppugnāsset, is tum āmissō
               exercitū, extorris rēgnō, in parvam īnsulam compulsus, supplex,
               fānī religiōne, nōn vīribus suīs tūtus esset.*

394:       *fortūnam suam*: object of *ignōrantis.*

397:       *cuius nōminis oblīvīscendum victō esset*: indirect question; *oblīvīscendum esset*: impersonal passive of intransitive verb (Cap. XL and Recēnsiō, Cap. XLIV); *victō*: dative of agent with gerundive (Cap. XXXI).

403–405:   *Perseō...amplectente, Paulō...tendente*: ablative absolutes; '*ut sē suaque omnia in fidem et clēmentiam populī Rōmānī permitteret*': indirect command (Cap. XXIX).

406–407:   *Dum haec aguntur, classis Cn. Octāviī Samothrācam est appulsa...*: in the omitted text, Octavius also tries to convince Perseus to surrender at Samothrace (cf. ll.311–312).

409–410:   *trānsīre*: historical infinitive (Cap. XLIV); *fugae*: objective genitive with *cōnsilium*, which is the object of *capere.*

413:       *sublātum < tollere*: "to take on board (ship)."

418:       *fugae*: objective genitive with *cōnsciīs*; *postīcum*: back door.

421:       *dum...dēferrētur*: anticipatory subjunctive (Cap. XL).

423:       *vagārī, vagātum*: Cap. XLIII; *petēbat!*: bear in mind that all punctuation in your text is modern, not ancient.

428–429:   *Macedonas*: Greek names in the 3rd declension plural often retain the -*ăs* ending (instead of -*ēs*), cf. l.535; *ēlēctī*: with *līberī*; *rēgis*: with *ministerium.*

430:       *nē tum quidem*: "not even then" (Cap. XVII).

433–435:   *sī trānsīrent...servātūrōs* (*esse*): future condition in *ōrātiō oblīqua* (Cap. XLIII); *essent...habērent...relīquissent*: verbs in subordinate clauses in *ōrātiō oblīqua* go into the subjunctive according to sequence of tense (Cap. XXXVI).

441:       *trādidit*: subject = Perseus.

443:       *eōdem*: adverb, "to the same place" (Cap. XLV), i.e., the praetorian ship.

446–447:   *in* (*suā*) *potestāte eum esse et addūcī*: "Perseus was under his (Octavius's) control and being conducted to him (Paulus)"; *esse in potestāte* is a legal phrase meaning "to be under someone's control."

448:       *Secundam eam Paulus* (*sīcut erat*) *victōriam ratus = Paulus ratus eam esse secundam victōriam*: Pydna being the first victory and the surrender of Perseus the second; *sīcut erat*: "as in fact it was."

451:    *manēre frequentēs*: i.e., "to remain continuously or regularly."

453:    *aliās*: adverb, "at any other time" (Cap. XLIX); *Syphāx*: a Numidian king during the Second Punic War.

454:    *patrum aetāte*: "in their fathers' time."

455–457:   *praeterquam quod*: "beyond that" (i.e., that Syphax was brought into a Roman camp as a captive king); *comparandus*: i.e., Syphax with Perseus; *nec suā (fāmā) nec gentis fāmā*: ablatives of respect with *comparandus*; *accessiō*: "an addition," here used to mean that Syphax was not the main enemy, the *caput bellī* (Hannibal was); for Gentius, see lines 290–300.

458–462:   *nec ipsīus tantum patris avīque cēterōrumque quōs sanguine et genere contigēbat fāma cōnspectum eum efficiēbat* = *nec tantum fāma ipsīus patris avīque cēterōrumque (quōs sanguine et genere contigēbat) efficiēbat eum cōnspectum; contingere aliquem aliquā rē*: to be connected to someone in some way, so "the reputation of those to whom he was related by blood and family"; the *nec tantum* (= *et non tantum*) is picked up by *sed* in the next clause: *sed effulgēbant*: Perseus gets to "shine" through his association, as the king of Macedon, with Philip II and Alexander the Great.

464–465:   *nūllō...quī...faceret*: descriptive relative clause (Caps. XXXIX, XLII).

467:    *submōtō*: *submovēre* when used of lictors is a technical term that means "clear away (people standing in the way)"; it can be used impersonally, both as a finite verb and, as here, in the ablative.

469–472:   [*Cōnsul*] *submittentemque sē* [= *rēgem*] *ad pedēs sustulit*: *attingere genua*: to lower himself to the ground and touch (the consul's) knees would have been a sign of submission; much of the action in this compressed sentence takes place in participles—pay attention to the cases to make interpretation easier.

473–476:   *quā iniūriā subactus*: "incited by what injustice"; *quō... addūceret*: the adverb *quō* ("to the end that," "with the result that") here completes the consecutive clause (result clause, Cap. XXVIII; RECĒNSIŌ, Cap. XLII): Perseus's intention was so reckless and dangerous that it led to his own destruction.

477–480:　　*Sī…accēpissēs, minus…mīrārer*: contracfactual condition (Cap. XXXIII; Cap. XLI): this condition is "mixed": the protasis is past ("if you had received") while the apodosis is present ("I would be less amazed"); the apodosis of the condition introduces an indirect statement (*ignōrāsse tē*), which in turn introduces an indirect question (*quam gravis aut amīcus aut inimīcus esset populus Rōmānus*).

481–484:　　*pācis…meminissēs*: verbs of remembering and forgetting (Cap. XXXII) take the genitive; *quōrum*: antecedent is the *iīs* in *cum iīs* (i.e., the Romans); *quōrum…expertus essēs*: subordinate clause in indirect statement (Cap. XXXVI).

486:　　*nec…nec…respondēret*: take the negatives closely with the verb: Perseus didn't respond either when questioned or blamed.

489–491:　　*cāsibus cognita populī Rōmānī clēmentia nōn modo spem tibi, sed prope certam fīdūciam salūtis praebet = clēmentia populī Rōmānī cognita cāsibus* (ablative of the source of the information: "known in") *multōrum rēgum populōrumque* (genitives with *cāsibus*) *praebet tibi nōn modo spem* (*salūtis*) *sed prope certam fīdūciam salūtis.*

492:　　*Graecō sermōne…Latīnē*: Paulus, like many elite Romans, spoke Greek in addition to Latin.

496:　　*decet*: with both *cōnsulere* and *crēdere*; *cum*: causal; *quid… ferat*: indirect question.

499:　　*infringet < in + frangere.*

501:　　*invītātus*: entertained.

Macedonia prōvincia [Ex librō XLV]: 507–601

510–511:　　*inclutī* with *regnī*, genitive with *fīnis*; *numerābant*: the implied subject is the Macedonians.

514:　　*obscūrā…famā*: ablative of description (Cap. XXXII).

515–517:　　*inde ac per eum*: *ac* (*atque*) = *et*: both from the time of Philip (*inde*) and through his efforts (*per eum*); *sē…continuit… amplexa*: subject is *gēns Macedonum* (also the subject of *superfūdit* in line 518).

519–520:　　*prīmum*: the list is continued by *hinc* (l.521), *tum* (l.522), and *inde* (l.523); *quā*: adverb, "where" (Cap. XXXVII); *prope*: modi-

fies *immēnsō*; *immēnsō spatiō*: ablative of description; *omnia...*
suae diciōnis fēcit: (Alexander) "put all under his authority."

521:      *Arabas*: Greek names in the 3rd declension plural often retain
the *-ăs* ending (instead of *-ēs*).

524:      *distractum* < *distrahere*: "pull apart, break up" (Cap. XLIII).

527:      *stetit*: subject is *Macedonum rēgnum*.

528–529:   *dē prōvinciīs referentibus*: the idiom *referre* (*ad senātum*) is
used about submitting an issue for the deliberation of the Senate (Cap. XLVIII).

530–531:   *dē sententiā lēgātōrum*: "in accordance with the judgment of the
legates"; *rēs compōnere*: "restore to their proper condition";
dōnec...composuissent: represents a future perfect indicative in
a subordinate clause in *ōrātiō oblīqua* in secondary sequence.

533–534:   *decem...quīnque* (*lēgātōs*); *in*: i.e., to be sent into.

536:      *ut...appārēret*: impersonal, as frequently, "to make it clear" +
dative.

540:      *ad Aeginium et Agassās dīripiendās*: *dīripere* is a military term
meaning "plunder, lay waste."

542:      *ūtī*: + ablative *initiō* (Cap. XXVII).

544–545:   Your text leaves out Paulus's command that statue bases in
front of the Temple of Apollo, begun by Perseus to support
statues of himself, be used to support statues of Paulus. A base
from one of these statues survives in the museum at Delphi.

545–546:   *ad spectāculum*: i.e., sightseeing; the *Eurīpus* is a strait between
the Greek mainland and the island of Euboea; *tantae īnsulae...*
iūnctae: in apposition to Euboea; *ponte*: ablative of means;
continentī: dative of the participle, sc. *terrae*: the mainland.

548–549:   *statiōne*: ablative of respect with *inclutum*; *quondam*: "formerly"; *mīlle navium*: genitive with *statiōne*.

551:      Agamemnon is *rēx ille rēgum*, "that famous king of kings," because he was head of the Greek expedition against the Trojans;
he used his daughter Iphigenia as a human sacrifice to propiti-
ate Artemis (Diana).

555:      *praeses, praesidis*: guardian, the one who presides over, with
arcis: the acropolis.

556:	*alterō diē*: "the next day."
557–558:	*praebuēre*: *praebuērunt*.
559:	*opibus*: ablative of respect with *haud parem*.
562:	*aegrī...sacrāverant*; *mercēdem*: in apposition to *quae* (= *dōna*); *remediōrum salūtārium*: objective genitive with *mercēdem*.
567–568:	*haud secus quam sī...immolātūrus esset*: "hardly otherwise than if " = "just as if "; the sense of futurity is achieved through the use of a future participle; imperfect subjunctive in a conditional clause of comparison in secondary sequence.
572–573:	*dēnōs prīncipēs*: a group of ten leaders from each of the city-states (*cīvitātēs*); distributive number (Cap. XXX).
577–579:	*sermōne Graecō referēbat*: Octavius translated everything Paulus had said into Greek.
584–587:	*Nōmina deinde sunt recitāta...mors dēnūntiāta*: in a section omitted from your text, Livy explains that the people deported to Italy were all cronies of Perseus and thus represented a danger to Greek freedom; with this in mind, the next sentence (that Paulus gave laws as if to allies) does not seem so odd; *placēret*: see Cap. XLVI for the language of official decrees and resolutions.
591–594:	*artificum...multitūdō et āthlētārum et nōbilium equōrum*: *multitūdō* with all three genitives; *convēnit*: singular to agree with *multitūdō* but applies to both *multitūdō* and *lēgātiōnēs*; *omnis generis*: gentive of description (Cap. XIX).
594–595:	*quidquid...solet*: subject of *factum est*; *deōrum hominumque causā*: *causa* with preceding genitive (Cap. XXVI).
597:	*ad quae*: i.e., *ad spectācula danda*; *prūdentia*: "skill"; Paulus wanted the Greeks to see how sophisticated he was at giving games (a skill at which Romans at that point had little practice: *rudēs*).
599:	*epulae, -ārum*: "a feast"; *et opulentiā et cūrā eādem*: ablatives of manner; *dictum*: "saying."
600:	*eiusdem esse*: "characteristic of the same person": see grammar section above.

Fortūna pūblica et prīvāta [Ex librīs et periochā librōrum XLV]: 602–676

608: *Secūtī...filiī duo Q. Māximus et P. Scīpiō*: Paulus originally had four sons; the two that followed their birth father's chariot had been given up in adoption to Quintus Fabius Maximus and P. Cornelius Scipio. They took the names of their adoptive families and added a form of the birth name as a further *cognōmen* (thus the *Aemiliānus* in both their names); see lines 670–671.

613: *hostium*: i.e., the Romans, Perseus's enemies.

615–616: *duōbus datīs in adoptiōnem* (the two in line 608); *quōs...sōlōs nōminis, sacrōrum familiaeque hērēdēs*: *hērēdēs* is predicative (whom he had as the sole heirs); the genitives give the content of the legacy (*nōminis, sacrōrum familiaeque*).

619–621: *dēstinantēs*: "intending, fixing their minds on" with *similēs... triumphōs*; *vehī...oportuerat*: "should have been carried" (but weren't): see Cap. XLIII, note to lines 353–354.

623: *mōre cēterōrum imperātōrum*: for *mōre* ("in the manner of") and the genitive, see note above to lines 32–34.

626–627: *et quā felīctāte...et quae duo fulmina*: indirect questions; *perculerint < percellere* (Cap. XLII).

629: *spectāculō vōbīs*: double dative (Cap. XXXVI).

630: *paucīs*: sc. *verbīs*.

631–632: *eō quō dēbeō animō* (see marginalia = *eō animō quō dēbeō*): ablative of manner (Cap. XXV).

633–634: *classem...solvere*: "launch the fleet."

641: *saltus, -ūs*: "a narrow pass" (Cap. XLI); *ad*: "near."

642: *redēgī < redigere*: "drive back" (Cap. XLVI).

645: *gravius*: adjective with *bellum* (not the comparative adverb).

646: *secundārum*: here, "favorable"; *velut prōventus, -ūs*: like a "crop," "harvest" (i.e., successful result).

648: *gaza*: a Persian word that passed into Greek and then Latin, meaning "treasure."

651: *eōque*: "and for that reason" (i.e., *nimia*).

653: *trāiciendā < trāicere < trans iacere*: "throw across": here, "transport" (contrast meaning in note on lines 81–88 above).

655: *quod ultrā precārer*: descriptive relative clause with indefinite antecedent (as often).

660: *meā tam īnsignī calamitāte*: ablative of cost; *dēfūnctam*: finished (its cycle of rolling downward) (*ex summō retrō volvī*) from being too much (*nimia*, l.651).

661–662: *lūdibrium*: "mockery of" + genitive; *interpositus* (< *interponere*) + dative: *triumphus interpositus est duōbus fūneribus*: "set in between."

Graecia Capta [Q. Horātius Flaccus: Epistulae II.1.156–157]: 677–680

Grāecĭă cāptă fĕrŭm vīctōrēm cēpĭt, ĕt ārtēs

īntŭlĭt āgrēstī Lătĭō.

III. Vocābula

NŌMINA

1st

ārea, -ae	open space, site
āthlēta, -ae (*m.*)	athlete, prizefighter
clēmentia, -ae	clemency, mercy
disciplīna, -ae	instruction, discipline
fīdūcia, -ae	trust, confidence
gaza, -ae	treasure
impēnsa, -ae	cost, expenditure
māceria, -ae	brick or stone wall, garden wall
mercātūra, -ae	trade, commerce
opulentia, -ae	sumptuosness
scālae, -ārum (*pl.*)	ladder
trānsfuga, -ae (*m.*)	deserter

2nd

coniūrātī, -ōrum (*pl.*)	conspirators
documentum, -ī	example, proof
impedīmentum, -ī	obstacle
lembus, -ī	small boat

ministerium, -ī	office of a minister, ministry, service
postīcum, -ī	backdoor
subsidium, -ī	support, help, resource
tabernāculum, -ī	tent
tribūtum, -ī	tax
trīduum, -ī	three days

3rd

accessiō, -ōnis (*f.*)	addition, accessory
adoptiō, -ōnis (*f.*)	adoption
artifex, -icis (*m.*)	craftsman, master, artist
callis, -is (*f.*)	track, path
expedītiō, -ōnis (*f.*)	foray, raid, expedition
fōns, fontis (*m.*)	spring, source
incolumitās, -ātis (*f.*)	soundness, safety
līs, litis (*f.*)	dispute, lawsuit
māiōrēs, -um (*m. pl.*)	ancestors
miserātiō, -ōnis (*f.*)	compassion, pity
murmur, -uris (*n.*)	mutter, murmur
mūtātiō, -ōnis (*f.*)	change, alteration
nāvālia, -ium (*n. pl.*)	dockyard
ōmen, -inis (*n.*)	sign, token, omen
percontātiō, -ōnis (*f.*)	interrogation, question
praeses, -idis (*m./f.*)	guardian
pulvīnar, -āris (*n.*)	couch for the gods
rādīx, -īcis (*f.*)	root, foot, base
servātor, -ōris (*m.*)	savior
successor, -ōris (*m.*)	successor
supplicātiō, -ōnis (*f.*)	thanksgiving
trānsitiō, -ōnis (*f.*) (< **trānsīre**)	crossing over, defection
tribūnal, -ālis (*n.*)	dais, platform
vertex, -icis (*m.*)	whirlpool, peak, pole
vīcīnitās, -ātis (*f.*)	neighborhood, vicinity
voluptās, -ātis (*f.*)	pleasure, delight

4th

conventus, -ūs	assembly
ēventus, -ūs	outcome, result
flātus, -ūs	blowing, breeze
fremitus, -ūs	rumble, growl
mercātus, -ūs	market, fair
peculātus, -ūs	embezzlement
prōventus, -ūs	growth, crop, harvest
sēnsus, -ūs	power of perception, sensation

5th

prōgeniēs, -ēī	offspring, descent

VERBA

-āre

(abaliēnō) abaliēnāre	separate, alienate
(acclāmō) acclāmāre	shout, proclaim
(amplō) amplāre	extend, enlarge
(contemplor) contemplārī	look at, observe
(continuō) continuāre	continue, prolong
(dēportō) dēportāre	convey, bring back
(dēstinō) dēstināre	designate, establish
(distō) distāre	be distant
(exaequō) exaequāre	make equal
(hībernō) hībernāre	spend the winter
(illacrimō) illacrimāre	weep over
(pācō) pācāre	subdue
(praeoccupō) praeoccupāre	preoccupy
(prōnūntiō) prōnūntiāre	proclaim, announce
(trānsportō) trānsportāre	carry across, transport

-ēre

(aveō) avēre	be eager, desire, long
(dēfleō) dēflēre (< flēre)	weep for
(effulgeō) effulgēre, -fulsisse, -fulsum	shine forth
(percēnseō) percēnsēre, -cēnsuisse	enumerate, survey

-ere

(abscēdō) abscēdere (< cēdere)	go away, withdraw
(cōnsurgō) cōnsurgere (<surgere)	stand up, rise
(dēlitēscō) dēlitēscere, -uisse	hide oneself
(dēvehō) dēvehere (< vehere)	carry, convey
(dīlūcēscō) dīlūcēscere, -lūxisse	dawn, become light
(dirimō) dirimere (< emere)	divide, interrupt
(ēdisserō) ēdisserere, -seruisse, -serutum	set forth, expound
(incrēscō) incrēscere (< crēscere)	grow, increase
(īnsīdō) īnsīdere (< sīdere)	occupy, settle, be fixed
(intercēdō) intercēdere (< cēdere)	intervene, intercede
(intermittō) intermittere (< mittere)	interupt, discontinue
(porrigō) porrigere (< regere)	stretch out
(prōsequor) prōsequī (< sequī)	accompany, honor
(submittō) submittere (< mittere)	lower
(superfundō) superfundere (< fundere)	pour over
(trānsmittō) trānsmittere (< mittere)	send over, cross

-īre

(permūniō) permūnīre	fortify

irregular

(circumeō) circumīre (< īre)	go around, outflank
(introeō) introīre (< īre)	enter

ADIECTĪVA

1st/2nd

artus, -a, -um	close, tight, deep
cōnscius, -a, -um	privy (to), accomplice (+ *gen.*)
cōnspectus, -a, -um	conspicuous, remarkable
contentus, -a, -um	stretched, content, satisfied
diurnus, -a, -um	of the day, daily
īnfectus, -a, -um	unwrought, not effected
invius, -a, -um (< via)	trackless, impassable

laureātus, -a, -um	adorned with laurel
mīrābundus, -a, -um	wondering, full of wonder
perexiguus, -a, -um	very small
praetextātus, -a, -um	wearing a toga praetexta
praetōrius, -a, -um	of the praetor; of the general
pullus, -a, -um	somber, grey
quīnquāgēsimus, -a, -um	fiftieth
signātus, -a, -um	marked, sealed
violentus, -a, -um	violent, impetuous

3rd

extorris, -e (< **terra**)	exiled, banished
ignōbilis, -e	unknown, of low birth
immemor, (*gen.* -oris)	unmindful, forgetful (of) (+ *gen.*)
inexpugnābilis, -e	impregnable
sēmiermis, -e (< **arma**)	half-armed

ADVERBIA

plērumque	mostly
porrō	forward, ahead
raptim	hurriedly
tantummodo	only, merely
utcumque	no matter how, however
violenter	violently, impetuously
vulgō	commonly

PRAEPOSITIŌNĒS

secus	otherwise

CONIUNCTIŌNĒS

nī	= nisi: unless, if not

ALIA

quaesō	I ask you, please

LI: VNVM ET QVINQVAGESIMVM: SCIPIO AEMILIANVS (Livy/Sallust)[1]

[*Ex T. Līviī 'ab Urbe Conditā' librōrum XLVIII–LXI Periochīs*]

I. Ørberg's Introduction

Book 45 of Livy's *ab Urbe Conditā* is the last to have survived. The hope of finding at least some of the remaining books has never been fulfilled. But instead of the full text, we have brief summaries, called the *Periochae*, of the content of the 142 books. In this chapter, we reproduce extracts from the *Periochae* of books 48–61, which deal with the period from the Third Punic War (149–146 BC) to the death of *Gāius Gracchus* (121).

Under the terms of the peace following the Second Punic War, Carthage was not allowed to build ships nor conduct wars (XLVIII.825–834). The Numidians were an inveterate problem for Carthage (XL.25–28). In a shrewd political move, Masinissa had befriended Rome during the Second Punic Wars (XLVIII.750–752). Following the Second Punic War, the Numidians made incursions into Carthaginian territory. Reports of Carthage mobilizing to defend itself and of supplies of timber (for the building of ships) angered the Romans.

The son of Aemilius Paulus, *P. Cornēlius Scīpiō Aemiliānus*, figures largely in this period of Roman history. He had been adopted by P. Cornelius Scipio, the son of Scipio Africanus, and in accordance with Roman custom, he was given the name of his adoptive father with the second cognomen *Aemiliānus* after his birth father. He was an outstanding general and statesman. When the Third Punic War broke out in 149, he served with distinction in Africa. In the following year, he was elected consul although under the normal age, and in 146 he conquered and destroyed Carthage. In the same year, the Romans destroyed the rich Greek city of Corinth, the center of the Achaean League (*Concilium Achāicum*) which had rebelled against Rome. Scipio's last exploit was the con-

---

1. For an explanation of the line number references convention, see p. xxvi.

quest of *Numantia*, the capital of the *Celtibērī* in Spain, in 133. This put an end to organized resistance to the Romans in Spain.

During the following years, internal conflicts emerged in Rome. There was popular discontent with the ruling class, the *nōbilitās* or *ōrdō senātōrius*, who had a monopoly of all public offices. This discontent was fostered by social problems resulting from the wars, which had dispossessed many Italian peasants of their land. *Tiberius* and *Gāius Gracchus* proposed agrarian reforms intended to provide land for the thousands of landless peasants who had come to Rome.

The Gracchi paid with their lives for their reform policy, but their work had a lasting effect on Roman politics. From then on the conservative senators, who called themselves *optimātēs*, "the best," struggled with a strong reformist party, known as *populārēs*.[2] At the end of the chapter you read an extract from the *Bellum Iugurthīnum* (see Cap. LII) by Sallust (*Sallustius*); the historian gives his opinion of the political conflicts in Rome and the reasons for them. While the summaries represent Livy taking a censorious tone about the activities of the Gracchi, the excerpt from Sallust clearly shows his sympathy for the reformers. The waning of Roman values is a recurrent theme in Latin literature. Sallust dates the onset of this decline to the removal of Rome's greatest enemies (especially Carthage):[3]

> *luxuriae enim peregrīnae orīgō ab exercitū Asiāticō invecta in urbem est. iī prīmum lēctōs aerātōs, uestem strāgulam pretiōsam, plagulās et alia textilia, et quae tum magnificae supellēctilis habēbantur, monopodia et abacōs Rōmam advēxērunt. tunc psaltriae sambūcistriaeque et convīvālia alia lūdōrum oblectāmenta addita epulīs; epulae quoque ipsae et cūrā et sūmptū maiōre apparārī coeptae. tum coquus, vīlissimum antīquīs mancipium et aestimātiōne et ūsū, in pretiō esse, et quod ministerium fuerat, ars habērī coepta. vix tamen illa quae tum cōnspiciēbantur, sēmina erant futūrae luxuriae.*

Tiberius and Gaius Gracchus were closely connected with the family of the Scipios. Their mother, *Cornēlia*, was a daughter of Scipio Africanus, and their sister, *Semprōnia*, married Scipio Aemilianus. These family relations are shown in the genealogical table of the Scipio family on p. 294 of Rōma Aeterna. The first ancestor is *Scīpiō Barbātus*, whose sarcophagus with a legible inscription is pictured at the beginning of the chapter.

---

2.   Although *populārēs* had been in use since Plautus, the word *optimātēs* was coined by Cicero, so makes its first recorded appearance at least fifty years after the Gracchi.

3.   Livy puts it earlier, when Gaius Manlius Vulso triumphed over the Asiatic Gauls (*ab Urbe Conditā* 39).

II. Auxilia Legendī

Bellum Pūnicum tertium: 1–118

1:             *Gulussa, Masinissae fīlius*: for Masinissa, king of Numidia and friend of Rome during the Second Punic War, see XLVIII.750–751: *Et amīcitiā factā cum Masinissā, rēge Numidārum.* Gulussa continued the tradition of being *amīcus Rōmānus*.

4:             *bellum indīcere*: "declare war" (Cap. XLIII).

5–6:   *temere*: adv.: "heedlessly, rashly" (Cap. XLVII); *explōrātum*: supine (Cap. XXII).

9:             *dēprehendere*: "observe" or "detect" (especially to catch someone doing wrong); the subject of *dēprendisse* is *sē*.

11:            *cōnfestim* (Cap. XLII) = *statim*.

13:            *placuit*: "it was decided" (by the Senate); so too line 25 below (Cap. XLVI: resolutions of the senate).

14:            *exussissent* < *exūrere* (Cap. XLVII): "burn up."

15–16:   *referrent* (*ad senātum*): see XLVIII, section on technical vocabulary.

20–23:   *Inter C. & S...dīversīs certātum sententiīs est*: impersonal (*certātum est*): Cato and Scipio exchange arguments (*dīversae sententiae*) in the Senate; *alter sapientissimus*: Cato; *alter optimus*: Scipio.

26–27:   *sociō, amīcō*: datives with compound *intulissent*.

30–31:   *Uticēnsēs*: citizen of Utica (XLVIII.760): "*cīvitās Āfricae maritima*" (marginalia).

36:            *perstārētur*: impersonal passive.

38–39:   *acceptīs...īnstrumentīs bellī* (*sī qua Carthāgine erant*): all part of one ablative absolute, with the clause *quōs imperāverant* referring to *obsidibus* and *sī qua Carthāgine erant* to the weapons and instruments of war; *sī qua = sī aliqua*.

44–45:   *Obsidērī oppugnārīque coepta est Carthāgō ā L. Mārcio M'. Mānīlio cōnsulibus*: with passive infinitives the perfect passive of *incipere*, here *coepta est*, is used in preference to the active *coepit, -ērunt* (i.e., *L. Mārcius M'. Mānīlius cōnsulēs Carthāginem obsidēre et oppugnāre* <u>coepērunt</u>).

46–49:   *cum...caderentur*: all one clause; *irrūpissent < irrumpere*: "burst into, force one's way in" (Cap. XLII); *oppidānus, -ī*: "a townsman" (< *oppidum*).

48–53:   Reading help (a good sentence for comparing the style of Livy with the much more careless prose of the *periochae*): *et... castrōrumque* connect the two main clauses (reworded): *per Scīpiōnem castellum Rōmānum līberātum est* and *Scīpiō praecipuam glōriam castrōrum līberātōrum tulit; castrōrum līberātōrum*: objective genitive with *glōriam*.

53–54:   *irritus*: "invalid, ineffectual"; *Carthāginis*: objective genitive with *oppugnātiōne*.

56:       *saltum inīquum*: "a steep, disadvantageous mountain pass"; *prīmō*: adverb (cf. *deinde*, l.57).

58–59:   *complūrium*: genitive plural with *sententiīs*, which in turn is an ablative of means with *victus*: Scipio was overruled.

62–63:   *turma, -ae*: troop, division of the Roman cavalry (XLIII.297); *incolumēs < incolumis, -e*: "safe, unharmed" (Caps. XXXIII, XLI); *et = etiam*, "even."

64:       *prōmptus, -a, -um*: "prompt, keen, ready" (Cap. XLV); *prōmptiōris linguae*: genitive of description (Caps. XIX, XXXVI).

66:       *umbrās volitāre*: "flit about like shadows."

69:       *fābulam*: i.e., that he is the son of Perseus (for whom, see Cap. L): he apparently physically favored the former king.

72:       *ēducandum*: gerundive of purpose with *traditum* (Cap. XXXVI).

80–81:   *ēdidit < ēdere*: produce, perform; *adeō...ut...genuerit*: result clause.

86:       *item*: Scipio; *Phamae*: Phameas Hamilco.

94–95:   *suffragantis plēbis* is genitive with *certāmine*, while *repugnantibus eī* (*plēbī*) *aliquamdiū patribus* is an ablative absolute; *lēgibus solūtus*: "exempted from the laws."

97:       *Pseudo-Philippus*: i.e., Andriscus (l.67); *caesō...praetōre.*

101:      *per partēs*: "part by part, bit by bit."

103:      *extrā sortem*: "without drawing lots"; see the note at XLVIII.220 (*Nōminātae iam anteā cōnsulibus prōvinciae erant; tum sortīrī iussī*).

106–108: *castra...sita...dēlēta sunt.*

110:          *quam = postquam.*

116:          *patris suī*: Aemilius Paulus.

117–118:   *lūdōs fēcit trānsfugāsque ac fugitīvōs bēstiīs obiēcit*: deserters
              and runaways were thrown to the beasts as a part of the *lūdī* in
              thanksgiving to the gods and celebration of the Roman victory.

Bellum Achāicum: 119–138

120:          *Achaeīs*: the inhabitants of Achaea, the Achaean league
              (*Achāicum concilium*, l.122), an organization of the city-states
              of Achaea (territory to the west of Corinth) which may date
              back to the fifth century BC. By this period, membership in-
              cluded all of the Peloponnese, including Corinth; *Corinthī*:
              locative.

121:          *sub diciōne Philippī*: see Cap. L *Graecia Līberāta*.

125–126:   *mortem sibi cōnsciscere*: "commit suicide"; cf. XLVIII.720
              (*Prīncipēs Campānōrum venēnō sibi mortem cōnscīvērunt*).

131:          *auxiliō*: dative of purpose (Cap. XXXVI).

132:          *abstinetissimum virum ēgit*: "behaved/acted as a most temper-
              ate man" (cf. XLVI.388: *nihil quasi Rōmānus ēgit*).

135:          *Andriscō*: see l.67.

137–138:   *signa aerea marmoreaque*: bronze and marble statues removed
              from Greece and brought to Rome.

Hispānia pācāta: 139–215

142:          *Lūsītānia*: territory on the west-central and southern coast of
              Hispānia.

144–146:   *nihilō*: ablative of comparison with comparative adverb *fēlīcius*:
              Tantumque terrōris...ut...exercitū: fear clause (Cap. XXXII);
              cōnsulārī with both *duce, exercitū*.

147:          *Celtibērōs*: the Celtiberians lived in central Spain.

150:          *Termestīnōs*: the inhabitants of Termes, a town in Celtiberia.

151–152:   *Numantīnī*: the inhabitants of Numantia, a city in Celtiberia;
              pācem īnfirmātam: *īnfirmāre*: "nullify, make void."

153–154:   *rēbus in Hispāniā prosperē gestīs*: not an ablative absolute,
              but a dative with *lābem* ("stigma, blot") *imposuit*; *aequīs*

condiciōnibus: "on equal terms," as opposed to ones that favored Rome.

162:    *salūbris, -e*: conducive to health; here, conducive to better behavior, "improving"; genitive of description.

165:    *caesus*: i.e., flogged, but not killed, as *sēstertiō nummō vēniit* (from *vēnīre*, not *venīre*) shows.

172:    *accidit*: you have learned *accidere* (Cap. XXVI) as "happen," but it can also be used (as here, with *vōx*) to mean "strike the senses" + dative (*cōnscendentī*).

174:    *exūtus*: deprived of + ablative of separation.

180:    *Gallaecōs*: inhabitants of Gallaecia, also called Callaecia, territory in northwest Hispānia.

181:    *Vaccaeōs*: the Vaccaeī lived in central *Hispānia*.

182–183:   *Ad exsolvendum foederis Numantīnī religiōne populum (Rōmānum)*: *religiōne*: ablative of separation with *exsolvendum*; *religiōne foederis*: the sacred oath contained within a treaty.

188–190:   *cōnsulātus*: "the office of consul"; *illī*: dative with *nōn licēret*.

196:    *in opere*: "at work."

197–198:   *septēnōs*: distributive, "seven each" (Cap. XXX); *incēdentī*: dative with *dīcēbat*; *vāllāre*: to use *vāllī* ("stakes") to build a *vāllum* ("rampart"), here used metaphorically to mean "protect."

199–201:   *dēsinitō*: future imperative (Cap. XXXIII); Scipio will give the order to stop carrying the stakes after...; *Quem mīlitem... dēprehendit, sī Rōmānus esset...cedīdit*: general condition with an iterative subjunctive in the protasis for repeated action.

200:    *vītis*: grapevine; *cecīdit*: see note above to line 165 on *caesus*.

205:    *mōs esset*: often followed by a noun clause of result (Caps. XXXVII), also, as here, with dative (*aliīs imperātōribus*) and infinitive.

206:    *in pūblicās tabulās*: "into the public accounts."

205:    *ex hīs* (*mūneribus*).

208ff: *pābulātum*: supine of purpose (Cap. XXIII); *quia dīceret*: *quia* almost always takes the indicative, unless it is followed by a subjunctive of reported reason (Cap. XLV); rarely, as here, the verb of saying can get drawn into the subjunctive as reported reason; "*velōcius eōs absūmptūrōs frūmentī quod habērent, sī*

plūrēs fuissent": future condition in *ōrātiō oblīqua* in secondary sequence. In direct speech, the condition would have been:
"*velōcius iī absūment frūmentī quod habent, sī plūrēs fuerint*";
frūmentī quod: partitive genitive; the antecedent of *quod* (i.e.,
id) is, as often, to be supplied by the reader.

Gracchī et lēgēs agrāriae: 216–279

220–222:   *exardescere*: to be inflamed into (such a state of rage); *in eum
                furōrem exārsit ut*: result clause; *abrogāret*: deprive + accusa-
                tive of thing and dative of person (i.e., *M. Octāviō…dēfendentī*);
                lēge lātā: ablative absolute, "by passing a law."

224:            *creāret*: second part of the result clause.

225:            *quā sibi lātius agrum patefeceret*: "by which law a greater ex-
                panse of land would lie open to them"; i.e., the triumvirs ex-
                panded the amount of land that could be judged private or
                part of the *ager pūblicus*.

226:            *quā…quā*: adverbs, "where."

228–229:   *spērandī*: with *cupiditātem*; *amplum modum*: object of *spērandī*.

230–232:   "*ut…dīviderētur*": i.e., the terms of the law he revealed.

235–236:   *in Gracchum*: "against Gracchus"; *perōrāsset*: the *perōrātiō* is
                the end of the speech, but the verb means, in addition to
                "bring a speech to its close," to "argue from beginning to end."

236–237:   *ad populum*: i.e., compelled to go (*raptus*) from the Senate to
                the Rostra in the forum; *plēbī*: dative with *dēlātus*; *cōntiōnārī*:
                "to deliver a speech before the assembly."

239:            *ab optimātibus*: see the introduction to this chapter.

243:            *rogātio*: a proposed law; + *ferre* = *lēgem ferre* (marginalia).

244:            *licēret*: impersonal; *vellet*: subject is the candidate for *tribūnus
                plēbis*.

251:            *adversārētur*: i.e., opposed the commission of the triumvirs.

253:            *tamquam*: "as if, on the grounds that" + subjunctive of re-
                ported reason (Cap. XLVI).

255:            *simultās*: quarrel (Cap. XLV).

263:            *frūmentāriam* (sc. *lēgem*); *sēnīs* (*assibus*): distributive number
                (Cap. XXX); *triens, -entis*: one third (as an *as*), both are abla-
                tives of price.

267:    *consentientem...corrumperet*: i.e., seduce (by offer of more power) the knights, destroying the current agreeable balance of power; *in Cūriam*: i.e., be enrolled in the Senate; the Equestrians were a separate order, although they shared the same interests as the Senators.

269–270:   *bis tantum vīrium*: "twice as much power" (i.e., six hundred of the nine hundred members of the Senate would be Equestrians).

272:    *colōniae dēducerentur*: *colōniam dēducere*: "to lead out (and establish) a colony"; *ūna*: sc. *colōnia*.

277–278:   *vocātō...populō*: ablative absolute.

Cīvitas Dīlacerāta [Ex C. Sallustiī Crispī 'Bellō Iugurthīnō']: 280–326

284–285:   *ortus est* (< *orīrī*) + ablative of source; *dūcere*, like *habēre*, can mean "consider"; *ante Carthāginem dēlētam*: same construction as *ab urbe conditā*: "before the destruction of Carthage."

288:    *bonae artēs*: "good moral practices."

290–292:   *incessēre* = *incessērunt*; *quod*: antecedent is *ōtium*; *asperius acerbiusque*: comparative adjectives with *ōtium*.

293:    *nōbilitās*: collective noun with plural verb: *coepēre* = *coepērunt*.

299:    *agitābātur*: *agitāre*, frequentative of *agere*, is a favorite word of Sallust; *bellī domīque*: like *domī mīlitiaeque* (Caps. XLI, XLIV): locatives; *paucōrum*: i.e., the nobles.

302:    *cum paucīs*: i.e., they share the plunder with few; *dīripere*: "plunder, ravage."

303–304:   *Intereā parentēs aut parvī līberī mīlitum, uti quisque potentiōrī cōnfīnis erat, sēdibus pellēbantur*: poor farmers called off to war left behind parents and children unable to keep up small farms, which were taken over by their wealthy neighbors to create huge farms, called *lātifundia*.

306:    *ipsa* = *avāritia cum potentiā*.

308:    *quī...antepōnerent*: descriptive relative clause (Cap. XXXIX); *antepōnere*: "to put *x* (accusative) in front of *y* (dative)."

309:    *permixtiō*: "disturbance created by mixing together."

313:    *in lībertātem vindicāre*: "set free, emancipate"; *paucōrum*: again, the nobles.

314:            *eō*: "for that reason" (with *perculsa*).

316:            *eadem*: neuter plural object of *ingredientem*.

317–318:   *alterum...alterum*: "the one...the other"; *colōnīs dēdūcendīs*:
                dative of purpose (Cap. XLVII).

319:            *Gracchīs*: dative.

320–321:   *bonō*: dative, sc. *hominī*; *satius*: "better"; *iniūriam*: object of
                vincere; *malō mōre*: ablative of manner.

322:            *eā victōriā*: ablative with *ūsa* (< *ūtor*).

323–324:   *plūs...timōris quam potentiae*.

325:            *pessum*: adverb: "to the ground"; *pessum dare*: "put an end to,
                ruin, destroy."

III. Vocābula

Nōmina

1st

abundantia, -ae	overflow, abundance
cavea, -ae	cage, coop
colōnia, -ae	settlement, colony
furca, -ae	fork, forked frame
lascīvia, -ae	wantonness
luxuria, -ae	extravagance, luxury
modestia, -ae	restraint
offēnsa, -ae	offense, resentment
senecta, -ae	old age

2nd

dēcrētum, -ī (< cernere)	resolution, decree
fragmentum, -ī (< frangere)	fragment, piece
nervus, -ī	sinew, muscle; vigor
praeverbium, -ī	prefix
scortum, -ī	prostitute, harlot
subsellium, -ī	bench
vāllus, -ī	stake (for a palisade)

3rd

aedīlitās, -ātis (*f.*)	aedileship
āctiō, -ōnis (*f.*) (< agere)	action, delivery
dissēnsiō, -ōnis (*f.*) (< sentīre)	disagreement
dominātiō, -ōnis (*f.*)	dominion, power
ēruptiō, -ōnis (*f.*) (<rumpere)	a breaking out, sally, eruption
formīdō, -inis (*f.*)	dread, terror
lābēs, -is (*f.*)	stain, disgrace
optimātēs, -ium (*m. pl.*)	the nobility
paelex, -icis (*f.*)	concubine
permixtiō, -ōnis (*f.*)	mixture, disturbance, chaos
prōditor, -ōris (*m.*)	traitor
quaestiō, -ōnis (*f.*)	inquiry, subject of inquiry
rogātiō, -ōnis (*f.*)	proposed law, bill
triēns, -entis (*m.*)	third of an *as*
vēnātor, -ōris (*m.*)	hunter

4th

circuitus, -ūs	rotation, circumference
tribūnātus, -ūs	office of tribune

VERBA

-āre

(adversor) adversārī	oppose, resist (+ *dat.*)
(agitō) agitāre	move, stir, plan
(complōrō) complōrāre	lament, bewail
(dīlacerō) dīlacerāre	tear to pieces
(exonerō) exonerāre	unburden
(īnfirmō) īnfirmāre	weaken, refute, annul
(pābulor) pābulārī	forage
(perrogō) perrogāre	ask in turn
(perstō) perstāre	stand firm, persist
(prōmulgō) prōmulgāre	announce, publish
(suffrāgor) suffrāgārī	vote for, support
(vāllō) vāllāre	fortify, defend
(vindicō) vindicāre	claim, avenge
(vituperō) vituperāre	criticize, blame

-ēre

(admisceō) admiscēre -miscuisse	mix (in), add
(polleō) pollēre	be strong
(vigeō) vigēre, -uisse	be vigorous

-ere

(abstrahō) abstrahere (< trahere)	remove, separate
(antepōnō) antepōnere (< pōnere)	place before, prefer
(dētegō) dētegere (< tegō)	uncover, disclose
(dispergō) dispergere, -sisse, -sum	scatter, disperse
(ēvincō) ēvincere (< vincere)	conquer; persuade
(exārdēscō) exārdēscere, -ārsisse	flare up
(fingō) fingere, finxisse, fictum	form, make up, invent
(obstruō) obstruere, -struxisse, -structum	bar, block
(polluō) polluere, -uisse, -ūtum	soil, violate, degrate
(recīdō) recīdere, -cidisse, -āsum (< caedere)	cut away, cut down
(revincō) revincere (< vincere)	conquer
(sēcernō) sēcernere (< cernere)	separate, detach
(sublegō) sublegere (< legere)	gather

irregular

(coeō) coīre (< īre)	come together, gather

ADIECTĪVA

1st/2nd

agrārius, -a, -um	agrarian
bellicus, -a, -um	of war, military
ērudītus, -a, -um	well instructed, learned
extrāneus, -a, -um	foreign, stranger
frūmentārius, -a, -um	of or belonging to wheat, grain
ignōminiōsus, -a, -um	disgraceful
irritus, -a, -um	invalid, ineffectual
moderātus, -a, -um	restrained, moderate

modestus, -a, -um	restrained, modest, calm
noxius, -a, -um	guilty
perniciōsus, -a, -um	destructive, disasterous
prōgnātus, -a, -um	born, son (of) (+ *abl.*)
ratus, -a, -um	valid, fixed, certain
remōtus, -a, -um	remote, distant
sēditiōsus, -a, -um	seditious

3rd

abstinēns, (*gen.* **-entis**)	self-restrained
asper, -era, -erum	rough, harsh, grievous
cōnfīnis, -e	adjacent, neighboring
ēloquēns, (*gen.* **-entis**) (< **loquī**)	eloquent
praedīves, (*gen.* **-itis**)	very rich
salūber, -bris, -bre	healthy, salutary
triumvirālis, -e	of the triumvirs

PRONŌMINA

quīvīs, quaevīs, quodvīs	no matter what, any

ADVERBIA

satius	better, preferable

NUMERĪ

octōgēsimus, -a, -um	eightieth
septēnī, -ae, -a	seven (each)

ALIA

per vicem	by turns, one after another
pessum dāre	destroy, ruin

LII: ALTERVM ET QVINQVAGESIMVM: IVGVRTHA (Sallust)[1]

[*Ex C. Sallustiī Crispī 'Bellō Iugurthīnō'*]

I. Ørberg's Introduction

The Roman historian Sallust, *C. Sallustius Crispus* (86–ca. 34 BC), was on Caesar's side during the civil war between Caesar and Pompey. Caesar rewarded him by making him governor of *Numidia*. His knowledge of this province was useful to him in writing his *Bellum Iugurthīnum*, a description of the war that the Romans had to wage for six years (112–106) against the Numidian king Jugurtha (*Iugurtha*), the grandson of *Masinissa*. Cap. LII contains excerpts from this work.

If Jugurtha was able to become a dangerous adversary of Rome, it was largely due to the incompetence and corruption of Roman politicians. Time after time Jugurtha succeeded in bribing influential Romans to comply with his demands. In this way he became absolute ruler of Numidia; when finally the Romans declared war, he bribed the consul *Calpurnius Bēstia* to cease hostilities. The disclosure of such corruption within the Senate aroused a storm of indignation in the Roman people. Jugurtha was summoned to Rome under safe conduct to give evidence, but he bribed one of the tribunes to forbid him to speak.

The first Roman commander to oppose Jugurtha effectively was *Q. Metellus*; but before winning a final victory, he was succeeded by *C. Marius*. Marius was a *novus homō* in Roman politics, i.e., the first man in his family to obtain high public office. Marius put an end to the war in Numidia and with the help of his young staff officer *Lucius Cornēlius Sulla*, caught Jugurtha in a trap. The king was taken to Rome to adorn Marius's triumph.

An opponent of the aristocratic senatorial government, Sallust emphasizes the inefficiency of the ruling class and the achievements of Marius during the Jugurthine war.

---

1. For an explanation of the line number references convention, see p. xxvi.

II. Auxilia Legendī

4:          *obviam itum est*: impersonal passive + dative (for the idiom, see Cap. XXXIX).

5:          *huiusce modī*: *-ce* is a demonstrative particle adding further "pointing" to the demonstrative *huius*, genitive of description dependent on *reī*, itself dependent on *initium*.

10:         *Scīpiō Āfricānus*: Cf. XLVIII.266–267.

12:         *facinora*: *facinus* is often used in Latin to denote a crime, but it comes from *facere* and can just mean, as here, "deed, act."

13:         *Syphax*: XLVIII.764–774; L.453–457.

15:         *rēgī dōnō dedit*: double dative (Cap. XXXVI); object is *quāscumque...cēperat*.

21:         *ortus*: i.e., *nātus*.

24–26:   *Quī = et is* (Cap. XXXIX); *vīribus, faciē, ingeniō*: ablatives of respect (Cap. XXXIX); *multō māximē*: *multō* intensifies the adverb *māximē*; *nōn sē luxuī neque inertiae corrumpendum dedit*: Cap. XXXVI. Note the switch after l.26 from indicative to historical infinitives.

28:         *cum...anteīret...tamen...esse*: *cum* concessive (Cap. XXXVII) in a subordinate clause in indirect statement; *glōriā*: ablative of respect (Cap. XXXIX).

33:         *rēgnō suō glōriae fore*: double dative (Cap. XXXVI).

34–35:   *exāctā suā aetāte et parvīs līberīs*: ablative absolutes; *crescere*: increase in power and esteem.

36–37:   *multa cum animō suō volvēbat*: *volvere* here, "reflect upon," as often: *mortālium*, i.e., *hominum*.

39:         *ad hoc*: adverbial "moreover, in additon."

40–41:   *ex quibus, sī tālem virum dolīs interfēcisset, nē qua sēditiō aut bellum orīrētur, ānxius erat*: *interfēcisset* represents a future perfect indicative in the protasis reported condition in secondary sequence; the apodosis is a fear clause (*nē...orīrētur*) from *ānxius erat*.

42–43:   *neque per vim neque insidiīs*: Sallust likes such unparalled juxapostions (instead of *neque vī neque insidiīs* or *neque per vim neque per insidiās*).

44:      *manū prōmptus*: "ready in respect to his hand," i.e., a man of action, quick to take action.

45:      *obiectāre*: "expose him to" + dative ("toss him in front of").

47:      *bellō Numantīnō*: see Cap. LI, *Hispānia pācāta*.

49–50:   *ostentandō, saevitiā*: ablatives of means, again, note lack of strict parallelism; *occāsūrum*: future particple of *occĭdere* ("die," related to *cadere*) not *occīdere* ("strike down," related to *caedere*).

52:      *aliter ac = aliter quam.*

53:      *ubi = ubi prīmum* (Cap. XXXVII).

56–57:   *pārendō/eundō*: ablatives of means of the gerund (Cap. XXVI).

57–59:   *tantam...ut*: result clause (Cap. XLII); *Numantīnīs māximō terrōrī esset*: double dative.

61–62:   *novī*: for the *novus homo*, see the introduction to this chapter; *quibus*: dative; *bonō honestōque*: neuter substantives, ablatives of comparison with *potiōrēs*; *potior* ("more preferable") comes from same root as *posse* and has a positive form *potis* ("possible, able"); *factiōsī*: i.e., given to allying themselves with factions supporting political interests; *apud sociōs*: i.e., in the provinces among the allies.

64–66:   *accendēbant*: imperfect of repeated action; *sī...occidisset fore uti...potīrētur...esse*: indirect statement dependent on the gerund (abl.) of the frequentative *pollicitandō*; *potīrī*: usually with the ablative, here with the genitive; *occidisset*: represents future perfect indicative in protasis of a reported future condition, with the apodosis *fore uti*.

69:      *prō cōntiōne*: i.e., in a speech given before the assembled soldiers.

70–72:   *prīvātim*: i.e., he should not solicit the friendship of individuals but the state; *neu quibus: neu = nēve (nē-ve)* and thus *quibus = aliquibus; quibus* is dative with *largīrī*, which you learned in Cap. XVII means "give generously," but which often carries the pejorative meaning "to bribe."

74:      *multōrum*: genitive of possesssion; *suīs artibus*: see Cap. LI, note on line 288.

75–76:   *quās...redderet*: relative clause of purpose; *eārum (litterārum).*

78:      *certō sciō*: "I know for a fact"; *tibi...gaudiō*: double dative.

79:	*ut…sit…nītēmur*: final (purpose) clause of the end strived after (*verba curandī*); cf. l.120: *ēnītiminī nē*.
81:	*Ēn*: exclamatory particle, like *ecce*; *tē atque avō suō Masinissā*: ablatives of respect with *dignum*.
84:	*grātiā*: not only the favor and esteem (both given and received) but also the influence standing and influence one attains through this esteem.
91:	*huiusce modī*: see note above on line 5.
93–94:	*quam sī genuissem*: comparative clauses follow sequence of tense; *exīstimāns nōn minus mē tibi quam sī genuissem ob beneficia cārum fore*: i.e., *exīstimāns mē, ob beneficia, tibi fore nōn minus cārum quam sī genuissem*.
95–96:	*ut omittam*: "Leaving out the other (*alia*)…"
103–105:	*moneō obtestorque tē utī hōs, quī tibi genere propinquī, beneficiō meō frātrēs sunt, cārōs habeās*: i.e., *moneō obtestorque tē utī habeās hōs cārōs, quī tibi genere propinquī, beneficiō meō frātrēs sunt*; *utī…mālīs*: present subjunctive of *mālle* (Caps. XXVIII, XXXIII).
108:	*queas*: *quīre* (see marginalia) is not found in all forms; *queas* is 2nd person singular present subjunctive "one is not able" (Cap. XLI).
109–110:	*fīdum* is predicate: "what person outside the family (*aliēnum*) will you find loyal."
114–115:	*aetāte…prior*: i.e., *māior nātū*; *nē aliter quid ēveniat*: like line 79, final (purpose) clause of the end strived after (*verba curandī*); *aliter*: other than the good situation they now enjoy.
117:	*facere*: sc. *iniūriam* (as opposed to *accipere iniūriam*).
121:	*ficta*: i.e., insincere.
122:	*animō agitabat*: cf. ll.36–37.
125:	*iūsta, -ōrum*: fitting ceremonies, esp. for funerals; *rēgulī*: diminuitive of *rēgēs*: princes.
129:	*cōnsulta*: i.e., *cōnsulta rēgis*: all of Micipsa's decrees.
132:	*ipsum illum*: Jugurtha himself (emphatic).
135–137:	*ea…quibus*; *cum animō habēre = in animō habēre*: "intend, have in mind"; *ea…quibus…caperētur*: indirect question.

140–141:   *finēs…cōnstituī*: i.e., they divided the kingdom among them (*singulīs*); *ad utramque rem*: i.e., *thēsaurōs* and *finēs imperiī*.

144:       *thesaurīs*: with *propinqua*; *proximus līctor*: for the lictors see the introduction to Cap. XLII; the *prīmus līctor* walked first in the procession and the *proximus līctor* was last in line and therefore closest to the magistrate and the one most likely to receive the magistrate's orders. Either the idea of attendants like lictors had been adopted in Numidia, or Sallust is describing the relationship in the cultural terms of his audience.

145–146:   *quem…cāsū ministrum oblātum*: "whom by chance was offered to him as an accomplice."

146–147:   *ille*: Jugurtha; *impellitque uti…eat*: indirect command; *tamquam* with *vīsēns*: "as if/as though going to look it over."

148:       *vērae (clāvēs)*.

149:       *postulāret*: subordinate clause in *ōrātiō oblīqua*.

155:       *clausa*: "locked rooms."

156:       *tugurium*: "hut," like *casa* (in margins), a very simple dwelling, as opposed to *domus* or *villa*.

157:       *quō*: adverb of place to which; *initiō*: ablative of time when.

164:       *illum alterum*: Jugurtha.

165–166:   *partim…aliās*: another example of Sallust's fondness for *variātiō* in the same phrase; *imperiō suō*: dative.

167–168:   *quī…docērent*: relative clause of purpose (Cap. XXXIX).

169:       *frētus, -a, -um*: "relying upon" + ablative.

172:       *patrātīs*: *patrāre*, cf. *impetrāre = in + patrāre* (Cap. XLII).

173:       *omnis Numidiae potiēbatur*: *potīrī* with genitive instead of ablative.

177–178:   *praecipit…uti*: indirect command.

179–180:   *postrēmō quaecumque possint largiundō parāre nē cūnctentur = postrēmō nē cūnctentur largiundō parāre quaecumque possint*.

181–182:   *aliīs*: indirect object of *misēre*.

187–209:   This is an abridged version of Adherbal's speech as found in Sallust.

190:       *nepōtem*: "grandson."

195–196:   *vōs in meā iniūriā dēspectī estis*: "in the wrongdoing done to me, you are being scorned."

199–201:   *quod in familiā nostrā fuit*: "as much as was in our family's power"; *quod in familiā nostrā fuit praestitit uti in omnibus bellīs adesset vōbīs* = (*nostra familia*) *praestitit* (*id*) *quod in familiā nostrā fuit*: *uti in omnibus bellīs adesset vōbīs*.

201–202:   *per ōtium*: as opposed to *in omnibus bellīs*; *uti...sīmus*: consecutive noun clause with *in vestrā manū est*.

205–206:   *Quid agam? Aut quō...accēdam?*: deliberative questions (Caps. XXIX, XLI).

211:    *frētī*: see note to line 69; *paucīs*: sc. *verbīs*.

216:    *Numantiae*: locative.

218–219:   *Senātus...consulitur*: the consul or presiding member of the Senate put the matter formally before the Senate to get their opinion.

221–223:   *grātiā, vōce...omnibus modīs*: ablatives of means with *nitēbantur*: *nitēbantur* = *contendēbant*; *prō*: "on behalf of."

229:    *verō*: dative with *anteferēbat* (*ferre/ponere x* [accusative] to *y* [dative]).

230:    *dēcrētum...uti*: subjunctive noun clause with the words of the decree.

232–235:   *Opīmius*: as with Scaurus (ll.226–228), Sallust first praises the man he is about to vituperate; *C. Gracchō et M. Fulviō Flaccō interfectīs*: see LI.275–279.

238:    *perfēcit ut*: consecutive noun clause of result (Cap. XXXVII); *anteferre* + accusative and dative: see note to line 229.

240:    *paucīs* (*hominibus*): dative with *cārior*.

247–252:   Reading help: *Postquam...Iugurtha...videt,...animum intendit*; clauses in *ōrātiō oblīqua* follow *videt* [*sēsē adeptum* [*esse*] *praemia sceleris*], *ratus* [*certum esse* [*id*] *quod ex amīcīs apud Numantiam accēperat*] and *accēperat* [*omnia Rōmae vēnālia esse*]; *accēperat*: sometimes subordinate clauses in *ōrātiō oblīqua* are left in the indicative; *simul et*: "and at the same time"; *animum intendere*: "direct one's thoughts."

263:    *questum*: supine.

265:            *dēcrēvit*: i.e., Adherbal *dēcrēvit*.

265–266:   *eō magis*: "all the more because he" but with the negative *neque* it becomes "not at all" or "no less"; *quippe quī*: *quippe* introduces an explanation; it can be used, as here, with indicative ("inasmuch as") or with a descriptive relative clause.

268:            *manū*: "band."

270:            *cēterum*: "moreover"; *quā*: adverb "wherever."

271–272:   *vāstāre…augēre*: historical infinitives (Cap. XLIV).

272:            *eō…utī…esset*: result.

278:            *plērumque noctis*: neuter pronoun with partitive genitive (Cap. XLIV): "the greater part of the night."

280–281:   *partim, aliōs*: see note above on lines 165–166; *sumentēs*: with *aliōs*.

282–285:   *multitūdō togātōrum*: a great number of Roman civilians (not soldiers); *moenibus*: ablative of separation; *nī…fuisset…coeptum atque patrātum bellum foret*: past contrafactual condition.

286:            *vīneīs*: see note on XLVIII.113.

287–288:   *tempus lēgātōrum…antecapere*: "take (the town) before the time of the legates' return."

291:            *adulēscentēs*: perhaps underscores the Senate's disparagment of the Numidian problem; *lēgantur, quī ambōs rēgēs adeant… nūntient*: relative clause of purpose (Cap. XXXIX).

292:            *verbīs*: "on behalf of," "in the name of."

297:            *rūmor clēmēns*: i.e., milder than the truth of the situation.

298:            *quōrum*: with *ōrātiō*.

300–301:   *ab optimō quōque*: for *quisque* with the superlative, see Cap. XXXI = "all the best men."

304–305:   *quō plūra…eō minus*: *quō* and *eō* are used with comparatives as correlatives: "the more…the less"; *fēcisset*: subordinate clause in *ōrātiō oblīqua*.

305–306:   *dolīs*: ablative of means; *vītae suae*: dative with *īnsidiātum* (*esse*).

308:            *iūs gentium*: i.e., the law of nations, to act in self-defense; *factūrum…sī…prohibuerit*: future condition in *ōrātiō oblīqua*.

311:	*cōpia*: + genitive "opportunity of." Adherbal was in the besieged town of Cirta.
317:	*temptāre*: historical infinitive (Cap. XLIV).
320:	*trahī*: "extended, prolonged."
321–323:	*eōs...cōnfirmat uti...pergerent*: indirect command, "encouraged, inspired."
325:	*fuēre quī* + descriptive relative clause with an indefinite antecedent (Caps. XXXIX, XLII).
327–328:	*illīs rēgis fautōribus*: dative of agent with *ēnīsum est*, a *verbum curandī* that takes the clause *nē tāle dēcrētum fieret* (see note to line 79 above).
330:	*grātiā*: as often, "influence."
336–337:	*accēdat*: jussive: a reported command; *ubi*: "when"; *accēpit*: "heard"; *audīverat*: indicative even though it is in *ōrātiō oblīqua* because it represents a fact outside of the indirect speech.
341–342:	*quod ab oppugnātiōne nōn dēsisteret*: subjunctive of reported reason (Cap. XLII).
344:	*Cirtae*: locative; *Ītalicī*: i.e., the *togātī* mentioned above, Italians living in Cirta.
345–347:	*cōnfīsī*: "trusting": begins the indirect statement (*propter magnitūdinem populī Rōmānī*) *inviolātōs sēsē fore*; *dēditiōne factā*: ablative absolute; *dēfensābantur*: Sallust likes frequentative verbs (*dēfensārī < defendere*); see also *adventāre* (below, l.363).
348:	*vītam pacīscatur*: i.e., surrender on the condition that his life be spared.
349:	*fidē*: ablative of comparison with *potiōra*; see note to lines 61–62.
350:	*sī adversārētur*: imperfect subjunctive representing a future indicative in virtual *ōrātiō oblīqua* (Cap. XLII); Adherbal was thinking "if I go against them" (*sī adversar*); *adversārī*: "to resist or oppose in what one says or thinks," as opposed to what one does (*resistere, obsistere*).
359:	*quī...portārētur*: relative clause of purpose.
362:	*iīsque praecipit...aggrediantur*: indirect command without *ut*.

365–366:   *dēditum*: supine; *nisi...vēnissent* = *nisi vēnistis*; *dēcrēvēre...
             uti...dēcēderent*: jussive noun clause.

376:         *bellum trahere*: see note above on line 320.

381:         *potentiae*: dative with *infestus*.

383:         *datā fidē pūblicā*: i.e., a guarantee of safe conduct; *indicium*:
             "evidence, testimony."

384–385:   *pecūniae acceptae*: genitive of the charge (Cap. LXVI).

390–391:   *tametsī...erat...C. Baebium...parat*: Sallust leaves out the *ta-
             men* that one might expect after *tametsī*; although (*tametsī*)
             Jugurtha was very confident, bolstered (*cōnfirmātus*)...he
             (still) acquired (*parat*) Baebius; *cuius impudentiā...mūnītus
             foret*: consecutive clause (result) stemming from the *magnā
             mercēde* (but this is one of many Latin clauses about whose
             syntactical classification one could argue at length—other can-
             didates are purpose and virtual *ōrātiō oblīqua*).

397–401:   *quamquam...intellegat*: subordinate clause in *ōrātiō oblīqua*
             introducing an indirect question (*quibus...ēgerit*); *sī aperiat...
             sitam*: reported condition: "if he tells the truth, there is hope
             for him."

404–405:   *Baebius*, as *tribūnus plēbis*, has the right of veto, against which
             the Senate can do nothing.

407:         *quae īra fierī amat*: "the things which anger loves to give rise
             to."

408:         *lūdibriō*: dative of purpose "held as an object of derision."

410:         *exagitābat*: i.e., made them anxious; *animī augēscunt*: i.e., at
             again besting the Senate and the people.

413:         *Iugurthae*: dative with *adversus* = *contrā Iugurtham*.

416–417:   *Huic...persuādet...petat*: indirect command with *ut* omitted;
             quoniam ex stirpe Masinissae sit: subjunctive of reported rea-
             son (Cap. XLII).

419:         *Quae postquam* = *et postquam ea* (*quae* = *et ea*).

420–422:   *Bomilcarī...imperat...paret ac...interficiat*: indirect command
             with *ut* omitted; *Iugurtha* is subject of *imperat*.

426–427:   *īnsidiās tendit*: *tendere* on analogy with stretching out nets for
             prey; *ex eō numerō quī ad caedam parātī erant* = *ex eō numerō*

eōrum quī ad caedam parātī erant; paulō incōnsultius: comparative adverb with ablative of degree of difference.

433:   *eō*: adverb, i.e., toward Rome.

434–435:   *urbem vēnālem et mātūrē peritūram, sī ēmptōrem invēnerit!*: future condition in *ōrātiō oblīqua*.

445:   *armōrum aliquantum*: "a considerable amount of weaponry"; neuter with partitive genitive.

452:   *homō novus*: see introduction to this chapter and lines 61–62.

455:   *aegrē ferēns*: *fere* with adverb: to "take" in a certain way (Cap. XXI)—also *aegerrimē tulit* in line 458; Metellus is angry because he wants sole credit for the victory; *bellum trahere*: see note on line 320 above.

457:   *Quirītēs*: a Sabine name that the Romans used of themselves as citizens in their civic as opposed to military capacity.

459–463:   *num...sit*: indirect question; *sī quem...mittātis*: fills out the thought of *num id mutāre melius sit*—to send another member of the nobility instead of Marius; *Hominem multārum imāginum et nūllīus stipendiī*: genitives of description; *imāginēs* were the ancestral portraits of noble ancestors on which the nobility prided themselves; these were carried in funeral processions; a man of *nūllīus stipendiī* is one who has never served in the army and thus has no military experience; *ēvenit ut... quaerat*: noun clause of result (consecutive noun clause) (Cap. XXXII).

463–466:   *sciō...quī...coeperint*: descriptive relative clause (Caps. XXXIX, XLII); i.e., they don't begin to study military science until they are already in an office that will require military leadership; Marius's speech has been abridged.

471:   *faciant idem māioribus*: "let them do the same thing (i.e., *contemnere*) to their ancestors."

475–476:   *quantō...tantō*: ablatives of degree of difference of the correlatives (Cap. XLIII); *illōrum*: their ancestors.

477:   *Huiusce reī inopiam*: objective genitive; *huiusce reī* refers to illustrious ancestors; *meamet*: *mea* + *met* (intensive particle), i.e., as opposed to those of his ancestors.

481:   *nova nōbilitās*: as soon as he became consul, Marius became *nōbilis*.

484:     *fideī causā*: "in order to obtain your trust."

487:     *adversō corpore*: because he was facing the battle, not running away.

491:     *composita*: polished and rhetorical; *parvī*: genitive of value (Cap. XXIX); *facere* + genitive of value and accusative of thing is a common idiom.

492:     *illīs*: dative; *artificiō*: ablative with *opus est* (Cap. XXXII).

494–496:   *quippe quae*: see note above on lines 265–266; *doctōribus*: dative with intransitive *prōfuerant*; *nihil* is adverbial; *doctus sum* + accusative of thing learned.

505–507:   *tūtārī* < *tuērī*: "guard, protect": another example of Sallust's fondness for frequentatives; *avāritiam, imperītiam atque superbiam*: i.e., not Jugurtha's but the Roman generals' who fought him; *locōrum sciēns*: objective genitive; the army (and leaders—*ducum*, l.508) referred to are Roman, not Numidian: Marius is recruiting soldiers.

514–515:   *Quae sī dubia aut procul essent, tamen omnēs bonōs reī pūblicae subvenīre decēbat*: mixed condition with present contrafactual as protasis and imperfect indicative in apodosis: even were the protasis true (which it isn't), it would still be fitting; verbs of obligation and duty, already have a potential sense and occur in the indicative in contrafactual apodoses.

519–520:   *commeātū*: "supplies."

522–523:   *scrībere = conscrībere*: "enlist, enroll"; *ex classibus*: for the division of the Roman people into five classes based on wealth, see introduction to Cap. XLIV; *uti cuiusque libīdō erat*: "according to each one's eagerness" (i.e., he signed up anyone who wanted to go); *capite cēnsōs*: described at XLIV.327–329.

533–534:   *effūsōs hostēs*: i.e., the Romans will have to split up to pursue the dispersed kings.

539:     *antevenīre*: "anticipate."

542:     *armīs*: ablative of separation with *exuere*: "strip of, deprive of"; they had to divest themselves of their weapons and flee.

545:     *levī imperiō*: ablative of description: "ruled with a light hand"; *habēbantur*: "considered" (Cap. XXVIII).

548:        *praeter oppidō propinqua* = *praeter <u>loca</u> oppidō propinqua*: *alia omnia* (*sunt*)…

549–550:   *eius* (*oppidī*) *potiundī…cupīdō*: objective genitive of gerundive (*potīrī* often takes the genitive in Sallust, but it can also take the ablative and the accusative, the easiest explanation here).

550–551:   *cum…tum* = *et…et.*

556–557:   *uti…ēgrederentur parātōs esse iubet*: noun clause giving the content of *parātōs.*

560–561:   *intervallō*: ablative of degree of difference with *nōn amplius*; *quam occultissimimē potest*: *quam* + superlative (Cap. XXVII).

568–569:   *ad hoc…potestāte*: last item in the list of subjects of *coēgēre.*

572–573:   The abridgment of the narrative causes a slightly jarring transition here. In the full narrative Sallust explains that the treatment of Capsa, although it was *contrā iūs bellī*, was a military necessity because of its strategic location and the inhabitants' character.

579:        *tantī virī rēs admonuit*: *admonēre* can mean "recalls to mind" + accusative, or, as here, genitive; *nōs*: Sallust inserts himself into the narrative.

585:        *altitūdō*: "height" or, as here, "depth, extent"; *ad simulanda negōtia*: "for feigning things are other than they are."

591–592:   *simul et*: "and at the same time" (above 249); *Bocchum*: see lines 449–451.

593:        *addūceret*: imperative in indirect statement.

596–597:   *sī…compositum foret* = *compositum esset*: pluperfect subjunctive representing a future perfect indicative in a conditional protasis in *ōrātiō oblīqua* in secondary sequence (apodosis to be understood from *pollicētur Numidiae partem tertiam*); *bellum compōnere*: "bring a war to an end."

600–601:   *vix decimā parte diēī relictā*: the day was divided into twelve parts, the length of which varied with the time of year (and thus position of the sun).

604:        *capientēs*: subject of *dēfensābant*; *aliōs*: object.

606:        *tegere*, sc. *mīlitēs.*

613:　　　　*locī difficulitātis*: in a section that has been omitted, Marius has led the army up a steep slope.

620:　　　　*dē imprōvīsō*: adverbial, "unexpectedly."

629–630:　　*hībernācula, -ōrum*: "tents for winter quarters," "winter quarters"; *expedītus, -ī < expedīre*: i.e., a lightly armed (unimpeded) soldier who can therefore move quickly; *loca sōla*: "deserted places."

631:　　　　*obsessum*: supine; *turrim < turris, -is* (f.) (Cap. XXXVII) one of the few pure *i*-stem nouns (Cap. XVI).

635:　　　　*sī placeat*: i.e., Mariō.

638:　　　　*cognōscit*: "makes himself familiar with."

639:　　　　*indūtiae, -ārum*: "truce, cessation of hostilities."

640–641:　　*lēgātīs*: with *petentibus*.

644:　　　　*memor* + genitive (Cap. XXXVIII).

645:　　　　*facere grātiam*: "grant dispensation," "overlook an offense."

646:　　　　*meruerit*: future perfect.

649:　　　　*funditor*: a soldier who fights with a sling, "a slinger."

650:　　　　*in campīs patentibus*: "on the open plains."

653:　　　　*praesidiō*: dative of purpose.

654:　　　　*eum* (*diem*).

658–659:　　*totiēs fūsum*: with *Numidam*.

661:　　　　*castra mētābatur*: "was pitching camp"; *cum…nūntiant*: *cum inversum* (Cap. XXVII).

662–663:　　*duum mīlium intervāllō*: see note on lines 560–561.

671:　　　　*dēligeret*: reported command.

675:　　　　*id omittō*: *id = bellum facere*; *omittere*: "stop, cease."

681–682:　　*in grātiā habēre*: "to feel grateful."

685:　　　　*rētulisse*: see grammar section above on *rēferre*.

686–688:　　*cōpiam Iugurthae*: access to Jugurtha; *Quem sī…trādidisset… adventūram*: future condition in *ōrātiō oblīqua*.

691–692:　　*cuius*: objective genitive with *avidissimus*.

695–697: *posse…pōnī*: indirect statement within an indirect statement, dependent on *cognitum* (*esse*); *pōnī* = *compōnī*; for *bellum compōnere*, see note on lines 596–597 above; *exquīreret*: indirect imperative (so too *daret* at line 701).

700–702: *parum*: "too little"; *operam dare*: see Cap. XLIX, idioms; *ūnā*: adverb, "together"; *venīrētur*: impersonal passive, with *ab omnibus*.

707: *ex illīus sententiā*: "in accordance with Sulla's demand."

712: *prōcēdit*: subject is Bocchus; *facillimum vīsū*: supine in ablative of respect (Cap. XXXIX); *īnsidiantibus* (*Rōmānīs*).

723: *magnā glōriā*: ablative of manner (Cap. XXV).

III. Vocābula

NŌMINA

1st

adulēscentia, -ae	youth
concubīna, -ae	concubine
ignāvia, -ae	idleness, cowardice
imperītia, -ae	inexperience, ignorance
impudentia, -ae	shamelessness
inertia, -ae	idleness, sloth
pēnūria, -ae	scarcity, want
phalerae, -ārum (*pl.*)	military decoration
sapientia, -ae	wisdom
sarcina, -ae	pack, kit
socordia, -ae	sluggishness, indolence

2nd

ācta, -ōrum (*n. pl.*)	deeds, actions
administer, -trī	assistant, helper
artificium, -ī	skill, art, cunning
flāgitium, -ī	disgrace
hībernācula, -ōrum (*n. pl.*)	winter camp/quarters
inceptum, -ī	undertaking, enterprise
indicium, -ī	information, disclosure

iūsta, -ōrum (*n. pl.*)	due ceremonies, funeral rites
latrōcinium, -ī	robbery
necessārius, -ī	relative, friend
quīnquennium, -ī	five years
rēgulus, -ī	petty king, prince
reus, -ī	defendant, accused
suffīxum, -ī	suffix
vexillum, -ī	standard, ensign

3rd

adoptātiō, -ōnis (*f.*)	adoption
altitūdo, -inis (*f.*)	height, depth
asperitās, -ātis (*f.*)	roughness, ruggedness
cicātrīx, -īcis (*f.*)	scar
clāritūdo, -inis (*f.*)	fame, renown
commūtātiō, -ōnis (*f.*)	change
cōnsultor, -ōris (*m.*)	adviser, counselor
difficultās, -ātis (*f.*)	difficulty
dīvīsiō, -ōnis (*f.*)	division
ēmptor, -ōris (*m.*)	buyer
funditor, -ōris (*m.*)	slinger
īnsidiātor, -ōris (*m.*)	waylayer, one who lies in ambush
largītiō, -ōnis (*f.*)	largesse, bribery
largītor, -ōris (*m.*)	one who gives generously
negōtiātor, -ōris (*m.*)	trader, agent
pollicitātiō, -ōnis (*f.*)	promise
speculātor, -ōris (*m.*)	scout, spy

4th

ēgressus, -ūs	going out
sonitus, -ūs	noise, sound

VERBA

-āre

(adoptō) adoptāre	adopt
(adventō) adventāre	approach
(arrogō) arrogāre	claim as one's own; claim for someone else

(cōnfīrmō) cōnfīrmāre	assure, encourage
(dēprāvō) dēprāvāre	pervert, distort
(disceptō) disceptāre	decide, debate, discuss
(dīvulgō) dīvulgāre	make public, divulge
(equitō) equitāre	ride on horseback
(haesitō) haesitāre	hesitate, be uncertain
(iaculor) iaculārī	throw (the javelin)
(impugnō) impugnāre	attack, oppose
(negitō) negitāre	deny repeatedly
(obiectō) obiectāre	throw before or against; expose, abandon
(observō) observāre	observe, respect
(obtestor) obtestārī	beseech, implore
(occursō) occursāre	run to meet
(patrō) patrāre	achieve, carry through
(pollicitor) pollicitārī	promise
(scrūtor) scrūtārī	examine, search
(sustentō) sustentāre	sustain, maintain, endure
(tūtor) tūtārī	protect

-ēre

(permaneō) permanēre (< manēre)	remain, continue

-ere

(accersō) accersere, -īvisse, -ītum	send for, fetch
(acquīrō) acquīrere, -īvisse, -ītum	acquire, procure
(adnītor) adnītī, -īsum	exert oneself, strive
(antecapiō) antecapere (< capere)	anticipate
(anteferō) anteferre (< ferre)	prefer
(appetō) appetere (< petere)	try to reach, seek, desire
(atterō) atterere (< terere)	wear (down), weaken
(augēscō) augēscere	begin to grow, increase
(dēfēndō) dēfendere, -isse, -ēnsum	defend, maintain

(dērelinquō) dērelinquere (< relinquere)	leave behind
(dīlābor) dīlābī (< lābī)	fall apart, perish
(ēnītor) ēnītī, ēnīsum	strive, exert oneself
(extollō) extollere (< tollere)	raise, praise, extol
(exuō) exuere, -uisse, -ūtum	take off, deprive of
(illicō) illicere, -ēxisse, -ectum	entice, attract
(īnsuēscō) īnsuēscere, -ēvisse, -ētum	become accustomed
(intendō) intendere, -disse, -tum	strain, direct, strive
(pacīscor) pacīscī, pactum	contract/stipulate for
(pertimēscō) pertimēscere, -muisse (< timēre)	be frightened (of)
rēfert (meā) rēferre	it is important (for me)
(strepō) strepere, -uisse	make a noise
(tābēscō) tābēscere, -uisse	waste away, decay

-īre

(anteveniō) antevenīre (< venīre)	forestall, anticipate
(mōlīor) mōlīrī, mōlītum	labor, strive
(obveniō) obvenīre (< venīre)	meet, fall to the lot of
(subveniō) subvenīre (< venīre)	come to help (+ *dat.*)

irregular

(queō) quīre, quīvisse, quitum	be able to

ADIECTĪVA

1st/2nd

abditus, -a, -um	hidden, remote
adulterīnus, -a, -um	forged, false
avidus, -a, -um	greedy, eager (+ *gen.*)
contumēliōsus, -a, -um	insulting, outrageous
decōrus, -a, -um	becoming, fitting
dēfessus, -a, -um	worn out, tired
factiōsus, -a, -um	factious, scheming
fācundus, -a, -um	eloquent
flāgitiōsus, -a, -um	disgraceful
frētus, -a, -um	relying on, confident of (+ *abl.*)

imbēcillus, -a, -um	weak
incōnsultus, -a, -um	thoughtless, rash
incultus, -a, -um	uncultivated, untilled
opportūnus, -a, -um	convenient, exposed (to)
permagnus, -a, -um	very large
portuōsus, -a, -um	having many harbors
praedātōrius, -a, -um	plundering
sēmisomnus, -a, -um	half-asleep
tumulōsus, -a, -um	hilly

3rd

familiāris, -e	intimate (as noun: close friend)
mediocris, -e	moderate, ordinary
pollēns (*gen.* pollentis)	strong, powerful
sciēns (*gen.* scientis)	having knowledge of (+ *gen.*)
vehemēns (*gen.* vehementis)	violent, vigorous
vēnālis, -e	for sale

ADVERBIA

abundē	amply, more than needed
accūrātē	carefully
dē/ex imprōvīsō	unexpectedly, suddenly
dehinc	next, then
īlicō	at once
in prōmptū	visible, manifest, easy
mātūrē	quickly, early
necessāriō	necessarily, unavoidably
ōcissimē	most quickly
partim	in part, partly
quippe	inasmuch as, for
sēcrētō	in private

CONIUNCTIŌNĒS

tametsī	although, notwithstanding

LIII: CAPITVLVM QVINQVAGESIMVM TERTIVM: MARIVS ET SVLLA[1]

[*Ex Eutropiī Breviāriō ab urbe conditā, V et VI*]

I. ØRBERG'S INTRODUCTION

This chapter contains the part of Eutropius's history which deals with the years 105–67 BC. In this period Rome continued to expand its power in the East, while at home it was weakened by internal dissension that finally ended in a bloody civil war. The great generals Marius, Sulla, and Pompey *(Pompēius)* saved Rome from external enemies. In the years 102 and 101 Marius checked and defeated the advancing Germanic tribes of the *Cimbrī* and *Teutonēs*. In 90 a number of Italic peoples, who had been allies of Rome, started a revolt in order to obtain Roman citizenship; in this "Social War" (*bellum sociāle,* from *socius,* "ally") Sulla distinguished himself. He was therefore chosen by the senate to command the Roman army that was sent to fight Rome's new enemy, king *Mithridātēs* of *Pontus,* who had subjugated most of Asia Minor and Greece. However, the Roman people wanted Marius to be sent against Mithradates, so Sulla had first to march on Rome to oust Marius and his supporters. Then he crossed to Greece, where he defeated Mithridates in several battles; but before he had won the final victory, he made peace with Mithridates and returned with his army to Rome. The popular party had seized power during his absence, but Sulla crushed his opponents and took cruel revenge on them.

In this civil war young Pompey fought on Sulla's side and won such spectacular victories in Sicily and Africa that Sulla granted him a triumph in spite of his young age. In 76 BC Pompey went to Spain, where he helped to crush the rebellion of *Sertōrius,* a supporter of Marius who had offered strong resistance for several years. Returning from Spain in 71 BC Pompey conducted mopping-up operations after the Servile War (*Bellum servīle*) against *Spartacus,* the glad-

---

1. For an explanation of the line number references convention, see p. xxvi.

iator who had incited a large number of slaves to open warfare against their Roman masters.

In the meantime Mithridates had started a new war against Rome by occupying Bithynia, whose late king had bequeathed his kingdom to the Romans. The Roman general *Lūcullus* drove Mithridates out of Bithynia and even invaded his own kingdom of Pontus, so that he had to seek refuge with king *Tigrānēs* of *Armenia,* his son-in-law. Lucullus marched into Armenia and defeated Tigranes, but a mutiny among the troops he had left in Pontus prevented him from following up his victories. Mithridates launched a new offensive and regained Pontus. Lucullus was then recalled and superseded by *M'. Acīlius Glabriō* in 67 BC.

In the same year Pompey was given the command of the war against the well-organized pirates who, in collusion with king Mithridates, made the whole Mediterranean unsafe and even threatened Rome's supply lines. Within a few months Pompey succeeded in ridding the seas of pirates.

In 66 BC, while Pompey was in *Cilicia* on the south coast of Asia Minor with his army, the tribune of the people, C. *Mānīlius,* proposed a law (*Lēx Mānīlia*) giving Pompey supreme command of the war against Mithridates. Among the speakers who pleaded for the law in the popular assembly were C. *Iūlius Caesar* and M. *Tullius Cicerō.*

This is the time when Cicero began to assert himself in Roman politics. The chapter ends with an extract from Cicero's work *Brūtus* or *dē clārīs ōrātōribus,* in which he tells us about his training as an orator, his relations with other famous orators of the time, and his election as praetor for 66 BC—the year he made his great speech for Pompey—and as consul for the year 63 BC.

II. Auxilia Legendī

Bellum Cimbricum: 1–28

7–9:   *Timor…nē…venīret*: fear clause (Cap. XLVIII).

11:           *eī…dēcrētum*: allotted to him by decree.

13:           *prōtrahēbatur*: imperfect of repeated action.

26:           *ex hīs*: sc. *signīs*.

Bellum sociāle: 29–48

32:           *cessārent*: syncopated perfect.

37:           *occīsus est*: repeat with all three subjects.

43:           *Sulla*: Cap. LII.

Bellum Mithridāticum prīmum: 49–104

52:          *bellō cīvīlī*: dative.

53–59:   Structure: *cum Sulla...mitterētur...isque...tenēret, ut...tollerentur, Marius affectāvit ut...mitterētur*; *affectāre*: "aim at," "strive to."

69:          *eī*: *populō Rōmānō*.

70–71:   *sī...faceret...et ipse paterētur*: condition in indirect discourse but apodosis attracted into the subjunctive; see marginal note in text.

96:          *dē pāce agī*: passive of *agere dē* + ablative: "negotiate about."

Bellum cīvīle: 105–152

110:          *prōscrīpsērunt*: people who were proscribed were not only exiled (*exsulem*, margins) but also forfeited their property.

115:          *trāiēcit* < *trāicere* (Cap. XLVIII); *gestūrus*: future participle of purpose or intention (Cap. XLII).

127:          *Praeneste*: accusative of place to which (Cap. XL).

132:          *īnsatiābilī īrā*: ablative of cause (Cap. XXXVII).

143:          *ingentī glōriā*: ablative of manner (Cap. XXV).

144:          *quod*: "a thing which."

150:          [*bella*] *cōnsūmpsērunt*.

Sertōrius: 153–187

161:          *quī Iugurtham rēgem vīcit*: Cap. LII.

164:          *impār pugnae*: "unequal to the fight."

181:          *in diciōnem redēgit*: "he brought (the Isauri) back (*redigere*) under (Roman) dominion (*diciō*)."

Bellum Mithridāticum tertium: 188–275

195:          *ab eō aciē*: "by him (Mithradates) in a battle."

204:          *mīlia*: sc. *mīlitum*.

216:          *Italiae*: dative with *calamitātēs*; *bellō*: dative with compound verb.

223:          *nāvālem*: sc. *pugnam*; *eius*: i.e., Mithradates's.

226:    *invāsit* (sc. *et*) *cēpit*: asyndeton (lack of connectives) adds to the sense of Lucullus's rapidity.

232:    *eīdem*: dative of separation or disadvantage (Cap. XXXVIII); *susceptus*: "received," "given shelter to."

233–235:   *quī...imperābat, vīcerat,...occupāverat*: another list in asyndeton.

238–240:   *rēgem...venientem.*

246–247:   *occāsiōnem...irrumpendī.*

248:    *Lūcullō parantī*: dative with *successor est missus.*

251:    *Bessīs*: dative with *intulit.*

258–259:   *māiōre glōriā*: ablative of manner; *tantōrum rēgnōrum*: objective genitive; *cum...redīsset: cum* causal.

273:    *ēgregius*: predicate.

M. Tullius Cicerō [Ex M. Tulliī Cicerōnis 'Brūtō' sīve 'Dē clārīs ōrātōribus']: 276–412

286:    *iūre cīvīlī īnstituerētur: īnstituere* ("form the mind," "instruct") + ablative; *iūs cīvīle*: "civil law."

288:    *audiēbat*: often used of listening to the lectures (or as here, speeches) as a student.

295–296:   *genere ferventī ac vehementī*: ablative with *ūterētur*; a vigorous (*vehmens*) and passionate (*fervens*)—and physically taxing—oratorical style (*genus*).

297:    *aliquamdiū*: "for some time" (Cap. XLVII).

309:    *meditātiō*: a synonym for *cōgitātiō*, as the marginal note says, but also, and more to the point here: "practice," "exercise"; cf. *exercitātiōnibus* in l.309.

312–315:   *vel quod...vel quod: quod* causal, *vel* gives not mutually exclusive alternatives and is almost *et...et; cōnsuētūdinem*: + objective genitive *dīcendī; nisi...docērī*: contrafactual condition.

318–319:   *quantum nōs efficere potuissēmus*: "to the (greatest) extent that we (i.e., "I") had been able to accomplish"; subjunctive by attraction because it is an integral part of the thought in the purpose clause to which it is subordinated.

322–323:   *tantum...ut...esset*: result clause; *commendātiōnis* is partitive genitive with neuter pronoun *tantum* (Cap. XLIV); *ūlla...*

quae...vidērētur: generic relative clause after negative antecedent (Cap. XXXIX).

333–334:   *laterum magna contentiō*: great straining of the lungs; *latera* are the flanks of the upper body, also used to refer to the power of the lungs in oratory; *eō magis...quod*: "all the more because."

337–338:   *potius...quam*: rather than; *quodvīs*: Cap. LI; *addeundum...discēdendum*: sc. *esse* with both.

341–342:   *ut*: substantive noun clause with *ea causa*, i.e., *ea causa ut* (Cap. XXXVII); *proficīscendī*: gerund with *causa*.

348:        *veteris Acadēmīae*: the "old" Academy refers to Plato's philosophical school in the grove of Academus; in Cicero's time there was a school of Platonic philosophy called the "new" Academy.

349–351:   *fuī*: Cicero's use of the perfect here shows he is thinking of this time as an episode in his past rather than the extent of time (six months) that he spent with Antiochus. *studium...renovāvī*: the thought between the object (*studium*) and the verb (*renovāvī*) is expanded by *cultum, auctum*, both of which refer to *studium*; *hōc...doctōre*: ablative absolute.

355–356:   *post = posteā*; *studeō* + dative: devote (oneself) to; *ipsīs libentibus*: a nod both to their graciousness and his own talent.

358–359:   *assiduissimē*: constantly.

361:        *prīncipēs*: predicate ("were counted as the most distinguished").

363–364:   *cum...tum: et...et; in vērīs causīs*: i.e., ones that he actually delivered; *scrīptōrem*: implies not just for his own cases but as a writer for others.

366–367:   *sī modo*: "if only" limits the statement; Molon applied himself to subdue, "if he could," Cicero's overly exuberant style.

368:        *iuvenīlī quādam*: take with both nouns *impūnitāte et licentiā*; *dīcendī*: also with both nouns.

372:        *dēferverat*: "had stopped boiling," "had calmed down," cf. l.295 (*genere ferventī*).

372–373:   *vīrēs*: take also with *acccesserat; mediocris habitus*: a normal appearance (i.e., Cicero's body was no longer too thin but in the middle between extremes).

374–375:   *mē*: object of *incitārent*.

377–378:	*rēs est mihi cum aliquō*: "I am concerned with": i.e., Cicero saw Hortensius as his principal rival.
380:	*ūnum…annum*: accusative of extent of time: "during that one year."
383:	*Siciliēnsis annus*: "a year in Sicily."
384:	*prīnceps*: i.e., *prīnceps ōrātōr*.
386–387:	*quidquid esset*: with *illud*, a gesture of modesty in regard to his talent; subordinate clause in indirect discourse.
389:	*nimis multa videor dē mē* (sc. *loquī* or *dīcere*): "I seem to be talking much too much about myself"; *ipse praesertim* (sc. *cum loquar*): "especially (since) I myself (am doing the talking)."
394:	*patrōciniō*: acting as a legal advocate; *Siciliēnsī*: just as the *annus Siciliēnsis* (the Sicilian year) means "a year in Sicily," *in patrōciniō Siciliēnsī*: in legal advocacy for the Sicilians.
398:	*nostrum illud quod erat*: sc. *ingenium ōrātōrium* as at l.385 (*illud, quidquid esset*); *quod erat* and *quantumcumque erat*: both to soften what could be construed as Cicero vaunting his talent when his point is to underscore the work necessary to succeed at oratory (ll.91–92).
399–400:	*ut…omittam*: "leaving a lot unsaid" (Cap. LXIX notes 15–18).
402:	*nam*: explains the *incrēdibilī populī voluntāte* in l.401; *exquīsītius*: "extremely attentive to detail," with *genus*; *novitāte*: ablative of means.

III. VOCĀBULA

NŌMINA

1st

cēnsūra, -ae (*f.*)	censorship
doctrīna, -ae (*f.*)	teaching instruction
ēloquentia, -ae (*f.*)	eloquence
figūra, -ae (*f.*)	form, appearance
praetūra, -ae (*f.*)	praetorship
quaestūra, -ae (*f.*)	quaestorship

2nd

aedīlicius, -ī (*m.*)	exaedile
biennium, ī (*n.*)	two years
clībanārius, -ī (*m.*)	cuirassier; heavily armored soldier
patrōcinium, -ī (*n.*)	protection, defense
patrōnus, -ī (*m.*)	patron, leader, advocate
prōpositum, -ī (*n.*)	objective, point
sagittārius, -ī (*m.*)	archer, bowman

3rd

āctor, -ōris (*m.*)	pleader, advocate
assiduitās, -ātis (*f.*)	perseverance
celeritās, -ātis (*f.*)	speed, swiftness
commendātiō, -ōnis (*f.*)	recommendation, praise
contentiō, -ōnis (*f.*)	tension, exertion
exercitātiō, -ōnis (*f.*)	exercise, practice
gracilitās, -ātis (*f.*)	slenderness, thinness
impūnitās, -ātis (*f.*)	impunity, license
īnfirmitās, -ātis (*f.*)	weakness
interniciō, -ōnis (*f.*)	annihilation, massacre
mātūritās, -ātis (*f.*)	ripeness, maturity
meditātiō, -ōnis (*f.*)	reflection, practicing
moderātiō, -ōnis (*f.*)	moderation, restraint
remissiō, -ōnis (*f.*)	relaxation
rhētor, -oris (*m.*)	teacher of rhetoric
varietās, -ātis (*f.*)	variety, diversity

4th

successus, -ūs	success

VERBA

-āre

(abundō) abundāre	overflow, be rich (in) (+ *abl.*)
(applicō) applicāre	attach
(commentor) commentārī	think about, practice
(commoror) commorārī	stay, linger
(commūtō) commūtāre	change (completely)

(congregō) congregāre	bring together, gather
(dēclāmitō) dēclāmitāre	make practice speeches
(ēlabōrō) ēlabōrāre	work out, prepare
(ēlūcubrō) ēlūcubrāre	prepare by lamplight
(exercitō) exercitāre	train, exercise
(moderor) moderārī	temper, moderate
(redundō) redundāre	overflow, be exuberant
(reportō) reportāre	carry back, bring home
(suppeditō) suppeditāre	supply

-ēre

(asserō) asserere, -uisse, -rtum	claim
(dēfervēscō) dēfervēscere	calm down
(diffluō) diffluere	overflow
(ēvertō) ēvertere	overturn, overthrow
(excellō) excellere	be outstanding, excel
(perspiciō) perspicere	survey, recognize
(prōscrībō) prōscrībere	proscribe, outlaw
(reprimō) reprimere, repressisse, -essum	check, repress, restrain
(resīdō) resīdere, -sēdisse	sink back, subside

-īre

(oboediō) oboedīre	obey (+ *dat.*)

ADIECTĪVA

1st/2nd

celebrātus, -a, -um	crowded, celebrated, famous
commōtus, -a, -um	nervous, unsettled, emotionally moved
disertus, -a, -um	eloquent
exercitātus, -a, -um	practiced, proficient
exquīsītus, -a, -um	attentive to every detail, meticulous
īnfinītus, -a, -um	unlimited, infinite
numerōsus, -a, -um	numerous, many
ōrnātus, -a, -um	embellished, distinguished
perfectus, -a, -um	perfect
pīrāticus, -a, -um	of pirates

prōcērus, -a, -um	tall, long
quantuscumque, -a, -um	however great/much
sescentēsimus, -a, -um	six hundreth

3rd

fervēns (*gen.* **-entis**)	hot, boiling, ardent
īnsatiābilis, -e	insatiable
iuvenīlis, -e	youthful
lēnis, -e	gentle, mild
locuplēs (*gen.* **-ētis**)	rich, wealth
sociālis, -e	of allies, social
vulgāris, -e	common, everyday

ADVERBIA

praesertim	especially

NUMERĪ

quīntō	for the fifth time

LIV: QVINQVAGESIMVM QVARTVM: CN. POMPEIVS MAGNVS (Cicero)[1]

[*Ex M. Tuliī Cicerōnis ōrātiōne dē imperiō Cn. Pompēiī*]

I. Ørberg's Introduction

This chapter contains the main part of Cicero's speech *dē imperiō Cn. Pompēiī* (or *prō lēge Mānīliā*), the speech that Cicero delivered in support of the law that gave Pompey the command of the Roman army in the war against king Mithridates.

Cicero's short introduction, here omitted, aims to win over his audience, thus making them more receptive to what he has to say. Cicero proceeds to his argument, telling his audience exactly how he will proceed: the character of the war, the magnitude, and the appropriate general (*dē genere bellī...de magnitūdine...dē imperātōre dēligendō*, 17–19). The first section gives a survey of the military situation in the East after the recall of Lucullus. His argument points to the following ways that Rome's vital interests are at stake in the war:

1. The honor of the Roman people is involved, for Mithridates' murderous assault on Roman citizens must not remain unavenged.

2. Rome's Eastern allies, who are overrun or threatened to be overrun by the enemy, are eagerly hoping for Roman help.

3. The war has had serious consequences for the revenues of the Roman State, since it makes it impossibe to levy taxes (*vectīgālia*) in the richest of all the provinces of the Empire.

4. A large number of Roman citizens are threatened with economic ruin. Especially threatened are members of the equestrian order (*ōrdō equester*) including the *pūblicānī*, the provincial tax collectors.

In the following section (*dē magnitūdine bellī*), Cicero deals with the war situation in greater detail. He describes Lucullus' successful campaign and Mithridates'

---

1. For an explanation of the line number references convention, see p. xxvi.

headlong flight. In carefully chosen words, he alludes to the soldiers' failing discipline, which has provoked the new enemy offensive, and the defeat of the Roman army.

After evoking the seriousness of the situation, Cicero turns to the real issue: the appointment of a new commander in the war against Mithridates. He mentions the necessary qualifications of a great general and shows that Pompey possesses them all. This leads to an unreserved eulogy of Pompey's brilliant achievements in all the wars he has fought, especially in the recent war against the pirates. Cicero concludes that Pompey is the only one who can win the war, especially since he happens to be stationed with a strong army near the theater of war.

There is no doubt that Cicero's admiration for Pompey's military ability was genuine. And indeed Pompey proved to be the right man for the task. The Lex Manilia was passed, giving Pompey supreme command in the East; he defeated both Mithridates and Tigranes and extended Roman rule over vast new territories.

The Cicero text is followed by extracts from the extant summaries of books 100–102 of Livy. The subject is Pompey's great victories in the East, ending with the conquest of Jerusalem (*Hierosolyma*) in 63 BC. In the same year, Cicero, as consul, disclosed the conspiracy that Catiline (*Catilīna*) had organized in order to seize power in Rome. Catiline was forced to leave Rome, the leaders of the conspiracy were caught and executed, and the next year Catiline himself was killed in battle.

Finally, there is an extract from Eutropius about Caesar's wars of conquest in Gaul (which he has described himself in his *Commentāriī dē bellō Gallicō*) about Crassus's unsuccessful campaign against the Parthians (*Parthī*) and about the civil war between Caesar and Pompey. This civil war ended with Pompey's defeat in the battle of *Pharsālus* (48 BC) and his flight to Egypt, where he was killed.

II. Auxilia Legendī

Quirītēs! 1–19

3:          *Quirītēs*: Cicero's speech is not to the senate but to the people of Rome from the rostra in the forum.

4:          *alter relictus, alter lacessītus*: the rest of the sentence applies to each subject (i.e., *alter relictus...arbitrātur, alter lacessītus arbitrātur*).

6:          *Equitibus Rōmānīs*: dative; the knights were heavily invested in the collection of taxes in the East and thus in danger of personal financial losses (in addition to the losses to the Roman treasury); *honestissimīs*: from the meaning of "morally probative" acquires the additional sense of "respectable."

7–15:   all in *ōrātiō oblīqua*, giving the reported contents of the letter; *vestrīs vectīgālibus*: dative with *finitimum*: i.e., "your revenues," meaning "the places from which you collect revenues"; *successerit*: perfect subjunctive in a subordinate clause in *ōrātiō oblīqua*; *parātum esse*: refers to Glabrio, accusative in indirect statement.

16:    *Causa quae sit vidētis*: you might expect *causam* (the object of *vidētis*) but here, as very commonly, the antecedent (*causa*) is attracted into the case of the pronoun (*quae*) that introduces the indirect question (*Quae sit causa?*).

Dē genere bellī: 20–178

21–23:   *eius bellī quod…dēbeat*: descriptive relative clause (Cap. XXXIX).

23–31:   *agere*, as you have already seen, has a wide range of meanings. *Agere* in the passive marks what is "at stake" or "in question": *in quō <u>agitur</u> populī Rōmānī glōria…<u>agitur</u> salūs sociōrum… <u>aguntur</u> certissima populī Rōmānī vectīgālia…<u>aguntur</u> bona multōrum cīvium…* The repetition of the same word at the beginning of a series of clauses is called *anaphora*, a frequent and effective rhetorical device; *cōnsulere* + dative: meaning, "consult the interests of," "take care of."

32:    *glōriae, laudis*: objective genitives with *appetentēs, avidī*.

36–38:   *quī…cūrāvit*: In 88 BC over 80,000 civilians (Roman citizens and Italian settlers) were killed at Mithradates's behest.

40–41:   *sed ab illō tempore annum iam tertium et vīcēsimum rēgnat*: *iam* is used with the accusative of duration of time (Cap. XIII) to show how long something has been going on (present, as here) or had been going on (imperfect).

45–46:   *ita…ut*: result (so too in lines 49–50).

46:    *insignia victōriae* (*insigne, -is*, n.): i.e., Sulla and Murena brought back the trappings of victory, but Mithrades was still in power, as the next sentence makes clear.

50–52:   *laus est tribuenda [ob id] quod ēgērunt, venia [est] danda [ob id] quod relīquērunt.*

56–64:   See "Reading Long Sentences" in the introduction to this book in which this complex period is made easier by separating out the subordinate clauses. Here is a rewritten simplification of the sentence:

             Mithradātēs māximās classēs aedificāvit ōrnāvitque; exercitūsque permagnōs quibuscumque ex gentibus poterat comparāvit; simulavit sē Bosporānīs finitimīs suīs bellum īnferre. Deinde (i.e., posteā) usque in Hispāniam lēgātōs ac litterās mīsit ad eōs ducēs quibuscum tum bellum gerēbāmus. [Hoc fēcit] ut, cum duōbus in locīs disiūnctissimīs māximēque dīversīs ūnō cōnsiliō ā bīnīs hostium cōpiīs bellum terrā marīque gererētur, vōs ancipitī contentiōne districtī dē imperiō dīmicārētis.

56–58:   *rem cōnferre ad/in aliquid = rē ūtī; quibuscumque...potuisset:* "from whatever peoples he had been able."

60:          *quibuscum = cum quibus.*

65–66:   *Sertōriānae atque Hispāniēnsis:* genitives referring to *partis*.

69:          *rēs gestae:* "accomplishments."

70–72:   *fēlīcitātī, virtūtī, culpae, fortūnae:* datives with *tribuenda esse*.

74:          *eī:* dative of disadvantage; *falsa:* also with *laus*.

76–77:   *vidēte quem vōbīs animum suscipiendum putētis:* literally: "consider (*vidēre*) what disposition (*animum*) you think must be adopted by you"; *quem...putētis:* indirect question.

81:          *quō...animō:* ablative of description.

82–83:   *Corinthum patrēs vestrī, tōtīus Graeciae lūmen, exstīnctum esse voluērunt = patrēs vestrī voluērunt Corinthum, tōtīus Graeciae lūmen, exstīnctum esse.*

86:          *Illī = patrēs vestrī* (also line 88).

90–93:   *Vidēte nē = cavēte nē:* Cf. line 27; *pulcherrimum fuit:* subject is the clause *tantam...trādere;* so too *id...posse* is the subject of *turpissimum sit.*

94:          *Quid?:* Cicero is very fond of an emphatic *quid* beginning a sentence. Here *quid quod* might be translated as "what about the fact that," but sometimes the emphatic *quid* means something like "how" or "why," and sometimes it is almost untranslatable.

97:       *tōtī Asiae*: dative with *imminent*.

101–104:   *dēposcere*: with *audent*; *id*: refers to *dēposcere*; *cum praesertim vōs alium* [i.e., *M. Acīlium Glabriōnem*] *mīseritis*: *cum* causal.

105:      *in quō summa sint omnia*: "on whom depends everything of critical importance" (lit., "all the most important things").

107:      *tametsī*: "although"; *vēnerit*: subordinate clause in indirect statement.

111–112:   *dignōs...quōrum...commendētis*: descriptive relative clause (Cap. XLII).

113–115:   *hōc* = "for this reason"; *eius modī hominēs...mittimus ut*: result clause from *eius modī* ("men of the sort that the result is...").

117:      *hunc*: i.e., Pompey (the *talis vir* of line 112); *audiēbant*: "kept hearing about."

124:      *ūnā cum*: "along with."

126–128:   *cum dē māximīs vestrīs vectīgālibus agātur*: impersonal *agī* + *dē*; cf. LIII.96, *iussit cum Sullā dē pāce agī*; *tanta*: i.e., so small (in comparison with Asia); *iīs...contentī*: satisfied with + ablative, i.e., the revenues are so small it's almost not worth keeping the other provinces safe from incursion.

132:      *omnibus terrīs*: dative with *antecellat*.

133:      *bellī ūtilitātem*: "what is useful for war."

136:      *dētrīmentum accipitur*: "a loss is suffered."

139:      *pecua* < *pecū*; one of several words for "farm animals."

141–142:   *decuma* = *decima*, from *decimus, -a, -um* (i.e., a tenth part of the profits); as the marginalia in the text tell you, it equals *decima pars frūgum*, a tithe which forms the landowners' tax in the provinces; *scrīptūra, -ae*: a tax paid on public pastures (see marginalia: *mercēs prō pāstiōne in agrō pūblicō*).

145:      *vectīgālia pēnsitant*: "pay taxes."

149:      *salīnae, -ārum* (f. pl.): "salt-works."

149–150:   *sē habēre*: "be in a certain condition or state" (e.g., *magnō perīculō*).

152:     *quī vōbīs frūctuī sunt*: double dative: dative of tendency (*frūctuī*) and dative of reference (*vōbīs*); see Cap. XXXVI.

153-154:   *eōs...calamitāte...formīdine līberātōs*: ablative of separation with *līberāre*.

155-159:   Reading help: main clause: *Ac nē illud quidem vōbīs neglegendum est* followed by explanatory relative clause (*quod... dictūrus*) and a relative clause explaining the content of *illud* (*quod...pertinet*: *bona* here means "goods" in the material sense); *quōrum...habenda est ratiō*, as explained in the margins, "make an account, calculation for"; antecedent of *quōrum* is *cīvium Rōmānōrum*.

160:     *honestissimī*: see above on line 6 for *honestus*; *ōrnātssimī*: "adorned with all the good qualities."

161-162:   *quōrum ipsōrum* = the *pūblicānī*; *vōbīs cūrae esse*: another double dative (see line 152).

166-168:   *hominēs..., quibus vōs absentibus cōnsulere dēbētis*: cf. ll.29-31 above: *cōnsulere* + dative meaning "consult the interests of."

169:     *Est...hūmānitātis vestrae...sapientiae* (*vestrae*): genitives of characteristic (a form of partitive genitive): "it is part/characteristic of your sense of human dignity...wisdom."

171-172:   *multōrum...nōn posse*: indirect statement with *vidēre*.

175-178:   *num dubitandum vōbīs sit*: indirect question; *ad id bellum incumbere in quō...dēfendantur*: subordinate clause in the indirect statement, but the relative pronoun (*id* refers to bellum) can also lead to a descriptive subjunctive clause: "the kind of war in which..."

Dē magnitūdine bellī: 179-272

184:     *vōbīs*: dative of agent with gerundives.

185-206:   a very long period: Cicero begins with a purpose clause (*ut omnēs intellegant*) with a dependent indirect statement (*mē L. Lūcullō...impertīre laudis*) that itself contains a correlative clause of comparison (*tantum...quantum*); the main verb (*dīcō*) then ushers in a long list, in indirect statement, of what Lucullus has accomplished. The best way to approach such a long period is to read it several times: the first time, just get the structure, as outlined in the introduction ("Reading Long Sentences"). In order to do this, it's best to look for signals:

- *atque ut...intellegant*: tells you we have a *ut* +subjunctive clause (you'll have to wait for a bit to figure out what kind); *intellegant* leads you to expect *ōrātiō oblīqua*).

- *tantum...quantum*: comparative correlative clause ("as much as") in the subjunctive because the *quantum* clause is a subordinate clause in *ōrātiō oblīqua*.

- *dīcō*: now you know *atque ut* is a purpose clause ("I am telling you so that"), and you can expect another indirect statement giving the content of what Cicero wants to tell his audience.

192:        *quam* (i.e., *urbem*)...*līberāvit*: indicative in a subordinate clause in *ōrātiō oblīqua* emphasizes the fact of Lucullus's accomplishment; the indicative in l.200 (*erant*) comes in a parenthetical, explanatory clause.

206–207:   *laudis*: partitive genitive with *satis*; *atque ita*: also with *laudis*: "such praise that."

216–219:   i.e., *praedicant eam* (*Medeam*) *dissipāvisse membra frātris suī in iīs locīs quā parēns persequerētur sē* (*Medeam*).

227:        *diffīdentem rēbus suīs*: dative, "in despair about his circumstances."

231–233:   *numquam...putāvit*: i.e., with whom the Romans had no intention of interferring.

235–236:   *causā* + a preceding genitive of the gerund or gerundive (Cap. XXVI).

238:        *tametsī...tamen*: "although...nevertheless."

239:        *ūsus erat*: "had experienced" + ablative.

242:        *fuit enim illud extrēmum ut*: the upshot was that... (see note above on lines 175–178).

245:        *cōnfirmārat* = *cōnfirmāverat*.

247–249:   *fierī solēre...ut*: consecutive noun clause; *ferē*: "for the most part; *fortūnae alliciant opēs*; *eōrum*: *multōrum*.

251–252:   *tantum*: object of *efficere*; *tantum...quantum*.

254:        *eō*: ablative with *contentus* and refers to the *ut...attingeret*.

259:        *praeterīre*: the *praeterītiō*, or "passing over," is a common rhetorical feature in which a speaker calls attention to something by saying he will not talk about it. Here Cicero spares the listeners a rehearsal of the defeat while still reminding them of the danger of the enemy; cf. *praetereō* (l.268).

263:          *aliquā ex parte*: "in some degree."

264–266:   *modum statuendum* (*esse*) + dative (*diūturnitātī*); *vetere exemplō*: "in accordance with long-standing precedent."

269:          *quantum...putētis*: subjunctive in an indirect question dependent on *coniectūrā perspicite*.

Dē imperātōre dēligendō: 273–536

274:          *quārē esset*: indirect question.

276:          *restat ut*: "it remains that" + consecutive noun clause.

278–280:   *utinam...habērētis*: unfulfilled wish in present time (Cap. XXXIX); *cōpiam tantam...ut*: result clause; *quemnam...praeficiendum* (*esse*) *putārētis*: indirect question.

282–285:   *ūnus*: alone; *quī...glōriam, memoriam virtūte superārit*: perfect subjunctive (*superāverit*) in a descriptive relative clause (*ūnus quī*) with an ablative of specification (*virtūte*), with the second object (*memoriam*) needing to be understood in terms of the first (*glōriam*): Pompey's military prowess (*virtūs*) has surpassed the glory not only of his contemporaries but also (that recorded in) the historical accounts of men of the past (*memoria antīquitātis*).

286–288:   Cicero takes up each of the four qualities in order; the section on the virtues of Pompey is by far the longest, divided itself into military valor (to line 373) and then a transition (ll.374–379) to a more encompassing definition of virtue.

- *scientia reī mīlitāris*: ll.289–307.

- *virtūs*: ll.308–455.

- *auctōritās*: ll.456–492.

- *fēlīcitās*: ll.493–519.

289–290:   *Quis igitur hōc homine scientior umquam aut fuit aut esse dēbuit?*: One of the several examples in this speech of a rhetorical question, a formal question asked to produce an effect and not to be answered. The obvious answer to the question is: *Nēmō!* But no answer is expected; the rhetorical question is

Cicero's way of saying that there never was a more knowledgeable man than Pompey.

291:    *bellō...hostibus*: ablatives of attendant circumstances.

292–293:   *extrēma pueritia miles...fuit*: *extrēmus, -a, -um* can mean "end of "; *medius* (Cap. XXX), "middle of" and *prīmus* (e.g., *prīmā aestāte*, XXXVIII.3), "beginning of."

294–295:   *cum hoste...cum inimīcō*: Cicero is drawing a distinction between an enemy of the state (*hostis*) and a personal enemy (*inimīcus*).

301–302:   *quod...genus...in quō...exercuerit*: descriptive relative clause (Cap. XXXIX).

305:    *gesta...confecta*: "waged...brought to an end."

306:    *in ūsū mīlitārī*: "in military skill" (acquired by practice).

309–310:   *quid est quod quisquam...possit*: this rhetorical question (see 289–290) expects the negative "*nihil est quod...*" The verb of the relative clause (*quod...possit*) is in the subjunctive because it is a relative clause of tendency (see Cap. XXXIX), also sometimes called a descriptive relative clause or a relative clause of characteristic.

312:    *vulgō*: the ablative of *vulgus* is equivalent to an adverb, "commonly."

316ff: *testis*: anaphora of the same word "witness" seven times in rapid succession at the beginning of a series of clauses (ll.316, 318, 320, 321, 323, 325, 329), the seventh an encompassing plural (*testēs*).

319–320:   *multīs perīculīs*: ablative of separation with *explicāvit*; *terrōre, celeritāte*: ablatives of means.

321:    *eōrum ipsōrum*: i.e., *hostium*.

330–332:   *omnia dēnique maria, cum ūniversa, tum in singulīs ōrīs omnēs sinūs atque portūs*: i.e., both the seas taken as a whole and in each of the bays and ports individually.

336:    *hieme*: ablative of time when; *refertō...marī*: ablative of attendant circumstances.

338–340:   *quis umquam arbitrārētur...*: *arbitrārētur* is imperfect potential subjunctive; the question is rhetorical: "who ever would have thought?" Answer: no one. The questions that follow are indicative to emphasize their historical fact.

343:          *cuī praesidiō*: double dative.

346–350:   *Tantam…tam…ut…audiātis*: result clause.

353–354:   *obeundī negōtiī…cōnsequendī quaestūs*: gerundive genitives with *studiō*.

361–362:   *duābus Hispāniīs et Galliā Trānsalpīnā praesidiīs ac nāvibus cōnfirmātā*: an adjective can modify the closer noun (*Galliā Trānsalpīnā*) but refer to both (*duābus Hispāniīs et Galliā Trānsalpīnā*).

368–369:   *partim ūnīus huius sē imperiō ac potestātī dēdidērunt*: the genitive depends on the datives *imperiō ac potestātī* but is thrown to the front of the clause to put the emphasis on Pompey. The skillful movement of words to an emphatic place in the sentence (often the very beginning or the end) is called *hyperbaton*.

372–373:   *Pompēius extrēmā hieme apparāvit, ineunte vēre suscēpit, mediā aestāte cōnfēcit*: see note on lines 292–293 above. Here *extrēmā* and *mediā* mean "end of" and "middle of." Cicero could have written "*prīmō vēre*" as a parallel to *extēmā hieme* and *mediā aestāte*. Instead, he varies the expression by using *ineunte vēre* using the ablative absolute with the present participle of *in-īre*.

380:          *quantā innocentiā*: ablative of description; so too the following ablatives.

384:          *cōnsīderēmus*: hortatory subjunctive (Cap. XXX); *summa enim sunt omnia*: i.e., in Pompey can be found the highest quality of all the virtues.

385:          *ex aliōrum contentiōne*: "in comparison with other generals": Cicero goes on to denigrate the behavior of other, unnamed *imperātōrēs*.

386–387:   *ūllō in numerō putāre*: to consider of any account/value; *ūllō*, used only in negative contexts, demonstrates that the question is rhetorical and expects a negative response (Cap. XIX); *vēneant atque vēnierint*, from *vēnīre* (Cap. XXXVI), not *venīre*.

393:          *pecūniam in quaestū relinquere*: "to loan money at interest."

396:          *ante*: adverb.

398:      *quōcumque ventum sit*: for the impersonal *ventum esse*, see Cap. XL.

401:      *recordāminī*: imperative.

402–405:   *plūrēs*: with *urbēs…an…cīvitātēs*: *armīs, hībernīs*: ablatives of means, both with genitives.

408–409:   *cēterīs*: dative with *excellere*.

408–411:   *tantum…ut nōn modo…sed nē…quidem…dīcātur*: result clause; *nocuisse* + dative (*cuiquam pācātō*).

413–415:   *sumptum facere in aliquem*: spend money on someone; *vīs*: force, violence; *nē cupientī…cuiquam*: i.e., even those who want to incur expense on the military's behalf are not allowed.

424:      *retardārunt* = *retardāverunt* (cf. below, *obtemperārint*, l.512 and *obsecundārint*, l.513).

430–432:   *omnēs…intuentur*.

433–434:   *hāc quondam continentiā*: ablative of description; *fuisse* and *quondam* both refer the listener to the past and liken Pompey to the great men of Roman history; *quod*: antecedent is 'crēdere fuisse hominēs Rōmānōs hāc quondam continentiā'.

435:      *falsō*: adverb; *memoriae proditum*: "handed down as a record/ memorial"(< *prodere*).

440:      *dē aliōrum iniūriīs*: i.e., about the wrongs done to others.

442:      *dignitāte, facilitāte*: ablatives of respect; *principibus, īnfimīs*: datives with *excellit* and *par*, respectively.

443–444:   *dīcendī gravitāte et cōpiā*: Pompey spoke with fluency (*cōpia*) serious authority (*gravitās*); ablatives of respect (as is *cōnsiliō*); *in quō ipsō*: i.e., in the oratorical art.

445:      *hōc ipsō ex locō*: addressing the people from the rostra in the forum.

446–448:   *fidem*: with *sānctissimam*; *hūmānitāte tantā est*: ablative of description; *difficile dīctū* (Caps. XXII, XXXIX).

451:      *quisquam dubitābit quīn*: for *quīn* clauses with *dubitāre*, see Caps. XXIX, XLII; the rhetorical question supplies the necessary negative; cf. l.457: *nēminī dubium est quīn*.

452:      *nostrae memoriae*: partitive gentive with *bella*.

457–458:	*plūrimum posse*: "to have the greatest ability."
461–462:	*ut* depends on *tantīs rēbus* (result clause).
458–463:	The subject of *pertinēre* is *quid hostēs, quid sociī dē imperātōribus nostrīs exīstiment* (subjunctive in an indirect question with *quis ignōrat*); the result clause (*in tantīs rēbus*) *ut aut metuant aut contemnant, aut ōderint aut ament* separates the subject (*hominēs*) of the indirect statement dependent on *sciāmus* from its predicate (*commovērī*).
467:	*quō*: adverb.
470:	*sibi*: i.e., *populō Rōmānō*; *omnium gentium*: genitive with *commūne*.
472–475:	*ut...cōnfīrmem*: suggests that Cicero has much more he could say; *quantum...in bellō*: indirect question; *sūmantur*: hortatory subjunctive.
478–479:	*spē ac nōmine*: ablatives of cause; *quantam...potuisset*: comparative clause.
479–486:	Reading help: ablative absolute followed by relative clause (*acceptā...admonuī*), followed by *cum* circumstantial (*cum... habēret*) and a past contrafactual condition (*āmīsissētis...nisi fortūna...attulisset*); *dīvīnitus*: "by divine providence."
489–492:	*quī...perfēcerit, quī...dēfenderit*: relative causal clauses (Cap. XXXIX).
493–494:	*praestāre dē sē ipsō*: offer surety for on one's own behalf.
499–500:	as in lines 361–362, *commissōs* refers to both *imperia mandāta* and *exercitūs* but agrees only with the closer noun, *exercitūs*.
500–503:	*quibusdam summīs virīs*: dative with *adiūncta*.
505–507:	*hāc...moderātiōne...ut...ut*: result clauses; *nē...videātur*: purpose clause.
509:	*domī mīlitiae = domī mīlitiaeque*: "at home and abroad."
517:	*ut...sit*: with *velle et optāre* (l.519).
518–519:	for *causā* with preceding genitives, see note above on lines 235–236.
525:	*bonī*: partitive gentive with *tantum*.

528–530:   *sī…esset…erat dēligendus atque mittendus*: like modal verbs
             (e.g., *posse, dēbēre*, etc., Cap. XLVI) in contrafactual condi-
             tions future participles and gerundives with a past tense of *esse*
             are regularly in the indicative, not subjunctive.

532:         *ab iīs quī habent*: i.e., other generals who have armies under
             their control.

Finis Mithridatis [Ex T. Liviī librōrum C–CIII Periochīs]: 537–569

The juxtaposition of the summaries (*periochae*) of Livy's work with the Cicero
you've just read underscore Cicero's rhetorical periods. The summaries are just
that: synopses of information, while Cicero's points are meant to be listened to,
not read, and he conveys his message as much by the construction of his sentences as by the content.

552:         *parum*: "too little, not sufficiently."

554–555:   *Hierosolyma*: Jerusalem.

558–559:   *dē caede…incendiīs…rē pūblicā*.

556–564:   *Catilīna*: You can learn more about Lucius Sergius Catilina
             and his conspiracy against Rome from both Sallust (who wrote
             a history of the event and an excerpt of whose history of the
             war against Jugurtha you read in Cap. LI) and Cicero, who
             published four speeches against Catiline (*In Catilīnam* I–IV).

Finis Pompēiī [Ex Eutropiī Breviāriī librō VI]: 570–617

575:         *vicendō*: ablative of means with *prōcessit*: see Cap. XXVI.

582–583:   *contrā ōmen et auspicia*: the pre-battle signs showing the gods'
             approval or disapproval of a proposed action; *duce*: in apposi-
             tion to *Surēnā*.

601–602:   *prīmō proeliō*: see note above on lines 372–373.

608:         *subāctūrae si…dūcerentur*: as the margin note tells you,
             subāctūrae (agreeing with *Rōmānae cōpiae*) here is equivalent
             to *quae subigere potuissent*, that is, equivalent to the apodosis
             of a contrafactual condition: the troops would have been able
             to conquer the whole world were they being led against bar-
             barians. For the imperfect (*dūcerentur*) and a future participle
             (*subāctūrae*) see above note on lines 528–530 and Cap. XLVI.

III. Vocābula

NŌMINA

1st

administra, -ae	assistant, helper
continentia, -ae	restraint, self-control
cultūra, -ae	cultivation, care
decuma, -ae	tithe, tenth part
innocentia, -ae	innocence, integrity
latebrae, -ārum	hiding place
macula, -ae	stain, blemish
misericordia, -ae	pity
repulsa, -ae	defeat (in an election)
querimōnia, -ae	complaint, protest
scientia, -ae	knowledge
scrīptūra, -ae	tax on grazing rights
temperantia, -ae	self-control, moderation

2nd

dēsīderium, -ī	desire, longing
domicilium, -ī	dwelling, residence
firmāmentum, -ī	support, strength
incommodum, -ī	disadvantage, misfortune
nāviculārius, -ī	ship-owner
perfugium, -ī	place of refuge, shelter
pūblicānus, -ī	tax-gatherer, publican

3rd

admurmurātiō, -ōnis (*f.*)	murmur
amoenitās, -ātis (*f.*)	pleasantness, beauty
amplitūdō, -inis (*f.*)	size, extent, greatness
antīquitās, -ātis (*f.*)	antiquity, ancient times
cognitiō, -ōnis (*f.*)	getting to know, study
collēctiō, -ōnis (*f.*)	collecting, gathering
comparātiō, -ōnis (*f.*)	preparation, provision, comparison
coniūrātiō, -ōnis (*f.*)	conspiracy, plot
cōnspīrātiō, -ōnis (*f.*)	agreement, conspiracy
dēlectātiō, -ōnis (*m.*)	delight, pleasure

dēlīberātiō, -ōnis (*f.*)	deliberation
excursiō, -ōnis (*f.*)	sortie, sally
facilitās, -atis (*f.*)	ease, facility
gravitās, -ātis (*f.*)	weight, gravity, dignity
hūmānitās, -atis (*f.*)	human feeling, culture
irruptiō, -ōnis (*f.*)	violent entry, assault
longinquitās, -ātis (*f.*)	remoteness
mānsuētūdō, -inis (*f.*)	mildness, clemency
oblīviō, -ōnis (*f.*)	a forgetting; oblivion
offēnsiō, -ōnis (*f.*)	setback, misfortune
opīniō, -ōnis (*f.*)	opinion, belief
opportūnitās, -ātis (*f.*)	convenience, advantage
pāstiō, -ōnis (*f.*)	pasturage
petītiō, -ōnis (*f.*)	pursuit, candidature
prōgressiō, -ōnis (*f.*)	advance
rēmex, -igis (*m.*)	oarsman, rower
splendor, -ōris (*m.*)	brightness, splendor
ūbertās, -ātis (*f.*)	fruitfulness
ūtilitās, -ātis (*f.*)	interest, advantage
vīlitās, -ātis (*f.*)	cheapness, low price

4th

centuriātus, -ūs	office of century
exōrsus, -ūs	beginning
frūctus, -ūs	produce, fruit
quaestus, -ūs	income, profit
sūmptus, -ūs	expenditure, expense

Heteroclitic

pecua, -um (*n. pl.*)[2]	farm animals

VERBA

-āre

(adōrnō) adōrnāre	equip
(attenuō) attenuāre	make thin, reduce
(commendō) commendāre	entrust, commit

---

2. For *pecus* see grammar section for this chapter.

(concertō) concertāre	fight
(coniūrō) coniūrāre	swear together, conspire
(cōnsalūtō) cōnsalūtāre	greet, hail
(dēvocō) dēvocāre	call away, divert
(exportō) exportāre	export
(dissipō) dissipāre	scatter, spread
(īnflō) īnflāre	inflate, puff up, elate
(minitor) minitārī	threaten
(negōtior) negōtiārī	do business, trade
(obsecundō) obsecundāre	comply with, obey (*intr. + dat.*)
(obtemperō) obtemperāre	obey (*intr. + dat.*)
(opīnor) opīnārī	think, believe
(pēnsitō) pēnsitāre	pay
(praedicō) praedicāre	declare
(recordor) recordārī	call to mind, recollect
(recreō) recreāre	restore, revive
(retardō) retardāre	delay, hold up
(remoror) remorārī	delay, linger
(tardō) tardāre	make slow, delay

-ēre

(medeor) medērī (+ *dat.*)	heal, cure, remedy

-ere

(affingō) affingere (< fingere)	add, fabricate
(afflīgō) afflīgere, -ixisse, -ictum	cast down, deject, afflict
(antecellō) antecellere	surpass, excel
(concupīscō) concupīscere, -īvisse (< cupere)	desire, covet
(congerō) congerere (< gerere)	bring together, collect
(dēprimō) dēprimere (< premere)	press down, sink
(dēprōmō) dēprōmere (< prōmere)	take out
(ēmergō) ēmergere (< mergere)	come out, emerge
(ēruō) ēruere, -uisse, -utum	unearth, clear up
(expetō) expetere (< petere)	request, demand, desire

(inveterāscō) inveterāscere, -āvisse (< vetus)	grow old, become fixed
(īrāscor) īrāscī, īrātum (< īra)	be angry
(lacessō) lacessere, -īvisse, -ītum	challenge, provoke
(prōficiō) prōficere (< facere)	progress, be successful

-īre

(impertiō) impertīre, -īsse, -ītum (< pars)	give a share of, impart

ADIECTĪVA

1st/2nd

adventīcius, -a, -um	from without, foreign
coniūrātus, -a, -um	sworn, joined by an oath
disiūnctus, -a, -um	distant
exsecrandus, -a, -um	accursed
gnāvus, -a, -um	diligent, active
imperātōrius, -a, -um	of a general
inaudītus, -a, -um	unheard (of)
ingrātus, -a, -um	unpleasant, ungrateful
iniūriōsus, -a, -um	unjust, wrongful
īnsolitus, -a, -um	unusual, unwonted
opīmus, -a, -um	rich
ōrnātus, -a, -um	adorned, distinguished
permultī, -ae, -a	a great many
religiōsus, -a, -um	devout, holy
taeter, -tra, -trum	foul, horrible
tempestīvus, -a, -um	timely, suitable
ūndēquīnquāgēsimus, -a, -um	forty-ninth

3rd

impudēns (*gen.* **impudentis**)	shameless, impudent
innocēns (*gen.* **innocentis**)	innocent, blameless
lacrimābilis, -e	mournful, pitiful
perbrevis, -e	very short
vectīgālis, -e	tax-paying, tributary

ADVERBIA

cōnsultō	deliverately
quōcumque	(to) wherever

ALIA

propter esse	to be nearby

LV: QVINQVAGESIMVM QVINTVM: DE RE PVBLICA (Cicero)[1]

[Ex M. Tullii Cicerōnis dē rē pūblicā librīs]

I. Ørberg's Introduction

After suppressing the Catilinarian conspiracy, Cicero regarded himself as the savior of the Roman people. Nevertheless, his expectation of a brilliant political career as the leader who was to unite all good forces in defense of the established order was deeply disappointed. The optimates, fearing Catiline, had ensured Cicero's election as consul. But in the following years, Cicero was pushed into the background, as Pompey came to an understanding with the leaders of the democratic party, Caesar and Crassus (the First Triumvirate, 60 BC, LIV.555–556). When the tribune *P. Clōdius*, Cicero's bitter opponent, had him exiled in the spring of 58, Pompey and Caesar acquiesced. When, after eighteen months in exile, he returned to Rome (in 57), Cicero largely retired from public life and devoted himself to literary work. During the years 54–52, he wrote the *dē Rē Pūblicā*, a treatise on political science. The last two chapters of *RŌMA AETERNA* contain extracts from this work.

Dē Rē Pūblicā is a dialogue in six books modeled on the *Republic* of Plato (who is mentioned by the participants more frequently than appears in our excerpt). Apart from the conclusion, *Somnium Scīpiōnis*, the work was lost until December 1819, when Angelo Mai, the head of the Vatican Library, discovered a manuscript from ca. AD 400 containing most of books I and II and fragments of books III–V. The manuscript was discovered in a palimpsest (*palimpsestus*, from Greek, meaning 're-scraped'): often the costly pages of a book were reused by painting over an older text (in this case, Cicero's *dē Rē Pūblicā*) to make room for a new one. *Dē Rē Pūblicā* was discovered underneath Augustine's commentary on the Psalms. Page 386 shows the text (with

---

1. For an explanation of the line number references convention, see p. xxvi.

Augustine's text removed); as you can see, the scribes wrote in narrow columns in captial letters without word breaks or punctuation.

In Cap. LV, you read extracts from books I and II of *dē Rē Pūblicā*. It is a dialogue between *Scīpiō Aemiliānus* and some of his friends who arrive at his country house in 129 BC during the *fēriae Latīnae*, a three-day religious holiday (that commemorated the alliance of the Latins with the Romans: Varro, *de linguā Latīnā*, 6.25). Immediately after this holiday, Scipio was found dead in his bed (see Cap. LI.251–253). It was widely held that he had been murdered at the instigation of his brother-in-law *C. Gracchus*, whose reform efforts he had opposed. This turbulent political situation is the background for Cicero's dialogue.

After a preliminary discussion about astronomy, Scipio's learned friend *C. Laelius* raises the question of how to unite the conflicting parties in Rome. He asks Scipio to set out his ideas about the best form of government. Government, according to Cicero, is the exercise and application of virtue; knowledge of virtue is not enough. This exercise and application is government: *Nec vērō habēre virtūtem satis est, quasi artem aliquam, nisi ūtāre* (= *ūtāris*). *Etsi ars quidem, cum eā nōn ūtāre, scientia tamen ipsa tenērī potest, virtūs in ūsū suī tota posita est. Ūsus autem eius est maximus cīvitātis gubernātiō* (*dē Rē Pūblicā* I.2).

Our text begins with Scipio's definition of '*rēs pūblica*' and goes on to discuss the three forms of government: *rēgnum, cīvitās optimātium,* and *cīvitās populāris* (Cicero's translation of the Greek terms *monarchía, aristocratía,* and *dēmocratía*). As serious objections can be raised to each of the forms, he advocates a combination of the three. The essence of the Roman republic derives from this combination.

In book II, Scipio describes the development of Rome from earliest times. This selection includes his account of the first two kings, Romulus and Numa, and his presentation of Tarquinius Superbus as an illustration of the degeneration of monarchy into tyranny.

The discussion continues for two days (books III–VI). Recovered fragments and references in later authors show that they discussed the qualities of the ideal statesman (*rēctor reī pūblicae*) and the honors and rewards that await him. Scipio then relates a strange dream he had twenty years before. The dialogue ends with this dream, the *Somnium Scīpiōnis* (see Cap. LVI).

II. Auxilia Legendī

Persōnae: 1–10

> P. Scīpiō Aemilānus Āfricānus, *senex*
> Q. Aelius Tūberō, *iuvenis*
> L. Fūrius Philus, *senior*

P. Rutilius Rūfus, adulēscēns
C. Laelius, senex
Sp. Mummius, senex
C. Fannius, iuvenis
Q. Mūcius Scaevola, iuvenis
M'. Mānīlius, senex

Fēriae Latīnae (from Book I): 11–156

11–15:	Sentence structure: double *cum* clause: *cum P. Āfricānus... cōnstituisset* and (*cum*) *familiārissimīque...dīxissent*; each of the *cum* clauses has an accusative + infinitive: *cōnstituisset in hortīs esse* and *dīxissent ventitātūrōs sē esse* (= *ad tē ventitābimus*); main subject/verb: *Q. Tūberō, sorōris fīlius, prīmus vēnit*; *hic Paulī fīlius*: for Scipio Aemilianus Africanus as the son of Aemilius Paulus, see L.670–672; *ventitāre*: frequentative verb of *venīre*; *māne* (Cap. XIII): "in the morning."
15–16:	*cōmiter*: adverb from *cōmis, -e* (Cap. XLIV), "kindly, affably"; *tam māne*: idiomatic, "so early."
22:	*permagnum est*: "a very great thing"; *ōtiōsum*: with *tē*; *mōtū*: "disturbance," "upheaval."
24:	*mehercule*: see Cap. XLVII; *operā*: Cap. XXXIV: "exertions, labor"; ablative of respect (Cap. XXXIX; so too *animō*).
26:	*relaxēs oportet*: see grammar section above.
28:	*abūtī*: here in a good sense (not "abuse"): fully enjoy + ablative of means (*ūtī*, Cap. XXVII); *fierī potest*: Cap. XXXVI.
29–30:	*aliquid*: accusative as adverb, "somewhat, in some degree"; *ut...admoneāmur*: purpose.
31:	*vīsne...videāmus*: see grammar section above.
32–33:	*dē istō "alterō sōle"*: Cicero talks about this (among others) prodigy also at *dē Dīvīnātiōne* (Book I.97).
35:	*Quam vellem...habērēmus*: see grammar section; Panaetius: Stoic philopher from Rhodes, to whom Cicero refers frequently and whose Middle Stoicism was the basis for Cicero's *dē Officiīs*.
36:	*cum...tum*: Cap. XXXVI.
38:	*loquar*: future indicative.

39:        *nostrō illī familiārī*: dative with *assentior*; *quō*: ablative of comparison, i.e., *Panaetiō*.

40:        *eius modī*: genitive of description (Cap. XLII).

41–43:   *quī...dēposuerit...dīxerit*: causal clause (Caps. XXXIX, XLII); *dīxerit ea (quae...quaererentur) aut māiōra...aut nihil...attinēre*; *quam...possit*: comparative clause.

54:        *Numantiae*: for Scipio at Numantia, see LI.186ff.

59:        *puer*: Romans often referred to male slaves as "*puer*."

61:        *ē cubiculō*: Tubero had come to him *māne*, before Scipio had a chance to dress; it was not unusual for Romans to entertain close friends *in cubiculō*.

62:        *inambulāre*: "walk up and down."

65:        *generōs < gener, -erī*: "son-in-law."

67–68:   *convertit sē in porticū et coniēcit in medium Laelium*: i.e., he had been facing them, turned around, and arranged the group around Laelius.

69:        *mīlitiae*: locative (XLII.222), as is *domī* (l.70).

72–73:   *ūnō aut alterō spatiō*: spatium, "space," can be used to refer to the act of walking through a space: "one or two rounds of the portico"; *essent*: with *collocūtī*.

74–75:   *placitum est ut*: "it seemed a good idea to."

81–82:   *agendum accūrātius*: i.e., speak and behave more formally (lit.: "with more care") as a reflection of respect in which the assembled company is held.

86–87:   *quidnam* (Cap. XXIII: "what in the world?") *sentīrem*: indirect question; *dē hōc quod...cōnstāret*: "about this thing about which there is agreement" (*cōnstāre*: Cap. XLVII).

88:        *ain' vērō = aisne vērō*: other than here, this expression occurs only in the Roman comedians Plautus and Terence; Cicero usually uses "*ain' tu*" and "*ain' tandem*." The expressions are very colloquial (humorously so, coming so soon after *agendum accūrātius*).

92:        *quae*: i.e., *domus*.

94:        *quamque = et quam*; *domicilium, patriam*: both predicate, "as a home," "as a fatherland."

98:     *avidōs sapientiae*: objective genitive (Cap. XXV).

102:    *aliquid*: i.e., about the two suns; *sērius*: "too late."

104:    *integrum*: "fresh, new" (they haven't started a discussion yet).

105:    *concesserō*: using an independent future perfect where we might expect the future is a feature of colloquial speech.

106:    *immō vērō*: *immō* means "on the contrary," and *vērō* strengthens it.

107:    *parumper*: "for a little while."

109:    *quōs*: antecedent *astrōrum*: *Archimēdēs*, cf. XLVIII.708–710; the *spaera aēnea* of which they speak is one of two models of the heavens that Marcellus (see Cap. XLVIII) took after the siege of Syracuse; one he had in his home, and the other was deposited in the Temple of Virtue; *arte mīrābilī*: ablative of manner with *effectā*.

111:    *eius modī*: "of that sort,"(Cap. XLII) genitive of description.

117:    *cum tū...quaesieris, ego...putem*: both verbs go with *cum*.

118–120: *quid enim mihi*: quid "why"; *mihi*: ethical dative (see grammar section above); *hōc avunculō*: "with this man (i.e., Scipio) as an uncle": ablative of attendant circumstances with *nātus*.

122–123: *Tiberius Gracchus*: LI.57ff.

125:    *nē metueritis*: perfect subjunctive in a negative command (Cap. XXXII).

126:    *nūllus*: i.e., *sōl alter*; *sit sānē*: jussive: "by all means (*sānē*) let there be (a second sun)"; *modo nē*: "provided it is not."

127:    *scīre*: with *possumus* (l.129).

129–130: *fierī potest ut* (Cap. XXXVI).

131–132: *secus*: adverb "other than it should be"; *sī id effectum sit*: i.e., an undivided Senate and people.

134:    *nōbīs*: dative of agent.

136:    *ūsuī cīvitātī*: double dative (Cap. XXXVI).

140–141: *potissimum*: superlative adverb; *rogēmus*: hortatory subjunctive followed by an indirect command.

148–149:   *prīncipem reī pūblicae*: you have seen *prīnceps* meaning "em-
              peror" (Cap. XXXVI) and "leading men"; Laelius is calling
              Scipio the "most distinguished citizen of the republic"; *dē...*
              dīcere: the content of *id...fierī voluī*; *aequum*: fair and right that
              the leading man should speak first.

150:          *solitum*: modifies *tē*; the historian Polybius (ca. 200–118 BC,
              cf. XLIX.246) was deported to Italy after the battle of Pydna
              (L.302ff) against Perseus, where he met and became close to
              Scipio. He was with Scipio at the destruction of Carthage (*Bel-*
              lum Pūnicum Tertium, LI.1ff) and the destruction of Corinth
              (*Bellum Achāicum*, LI.119ff).

152:          *multa colligere*: i.e., bring together many points, arguments.

154–156:   *fēceris...grātum*: "you will have done all of us (*nōbīs omnibus*)
              a favor."

Dē tribus rērum pūblicārum generibus: 157–242

158:          *ut poterō*: "as much as I am able."

159–161:   *eā lēge...ut*: "on the grounds that": noun clause of result (Caps.
              XXXII, XXXVII); *omnibus*: ablative with *ūtendum esse*; *velīs*:
              2nd person singular indefinite in a condition in *ōrātiō oblīqua*
              dependent on *crēdō*; *eius reī* depends on *nōmen*; *quod sit*
              nōmen eius reī: indirect question with *conveniat*; *quid dēclā-*
              rētur: indirect question with *explicētur*; Scipio wants to begin
              by defining terms, specifically, *rēs pūblica*.

170:          *quōquō modō congregātus*: *quōquō modō* ("in any way at all")
              is disparaging.

175:          *domiciliōrum causā*: "for the sake of" + preceding genitive.

177–178:   *distīnctam*: agrees with the closer noun (*urbem*) but applies
              also to *oppidum*.

189:          *rēgī*: from *rĕgĕre*, not *rēx, rēgis*.

191:          *sī teneat*: protasis of ideal condition (Caps. XXXIII, XLI).

199:          *aliquō...nōn incertō statū*: ablative of description.

200–202:   *expertēs...coummūnis iūris et cōnsiliī*: genitive with adjective
              expers (< *ex* + *pars*, Cap. XLV); *particeps* < *partem capere*: "take
              a share in" + genitive.

203:          *careat*: *carēre* + ablative of separation (Cap. XX).

215–216:	In the sections ommitted, Scipio says each of the three un-mixed constitutions contain the seeds of their own destruc-tion and on their own do not make for a stable state.
218–220:	*praestat...praestābit*: on *praestāre*, "stand out, be superior," see Cap. XXXVIII; *rēgiō...ipsī*: dative with *praestābit*; *ex tribus prīmīs...modīs*: Scipio recommends a mixed constitution.
222–223:	*auctōritātī*: dative with *impartītum ac tribūtum*; *prīncipum*: genitive; *iūdiciō voluntātī*: dative with *servātās*.
225:	*quā* (*auctōritāte*); *carēre*: see note above on line 203; *diūtius*: comparative adverb: "for too long a time"; *līberī*: "free people."
226–229:	*prīma*: neuter plural: the three unmixed constitutions (ll.182–185); the rest of the sentence gives a summary of the flaws discussed in the omitted passage (see ll.215–216).
233–236:	*nōta sunt omnibus quaesīta autem ā nōbīs iam diū*: i.e., they have subjected the general opinion to detailed inquiry: *nūllam* (*rem pūblicam*) *omnium rērum pūblicārum...conferendam esse.*
240:	*ad exemplum*: "as a model, example."

Dē vetere rē pūblicā Rōmānā (from Book II): 243–471

250–251:	*fuissent*: causal clause in *ōrātiō oblīqua*; *cōnstituissent*: sub-junctive in descriptive relative clause in indirect statement; *singulī...quī suam quisque...cōnstituissent*: for *suam quisque*, see Cap. XVIII: "individuals who each established his own..."; *rem pūblicam*: the list of prominent political leaders which fol-lows shows Scipio is not talking about a *rēs pūblica* in the Roman sense.
253:	*quae* (*rēs pūblica*); *esset*: subordinate clause in indirect state-ment.
255–257:	*nōn ūnīus...ingeniō sed multōrum*: the ablative of means goes with both genitives; *vīta...saeculīs et aetātibus*: ablatives of time within which ("during the lifetime...").
257–259:	*neque ūllum ingenium tantum...ut*: result clause; *quem*: the antecedent is *quisquam*.
259–261:	*ūnō tempore*: take closely with *cūncta ingenia collāta*: i.e., the intelligence of those living at one time if gathered into one could not...; *tantum...ut*: result.
267:	*aliquam*: sc. *rem pūblicam*.

269–272:   Easier word order: *Quod exōrdium īnstitūtae reī pūblicae habēmus* tam *clārum ac* tam *omnibus nōtum* quam *huius urbis condendae prīncipium profectum ā Rōmulō?* (*Quod* is an interrogative adjective.)

272–275:   *Quī nātus...dīcitur...iussus esse*: *dīcitur* with nominative and accusative, Caps. XIII and XXXVI; *ob labefactandī rēgnī timōrem*: objective genitive (Cap. XXV).

275–276:   *silvestris bēluae*: with *ūberibus*; *esset...sustentātus*: although the myth applies to both brothers, only Romulus is the focus.

277–280:   *ut adolēverit*: "when": subjunctive in a subordinate clause in *ōrātiō oblīqua*; *vīribus, ferōcitāte*: ablatives of respect; *omnibus*: dative with *praestitisse*; *tantum...ut*: result; *quī...agrōs ubi hodiē est haec urbs incolēbant*: the indicative shows that, in the mind of the speaker, these clauses are extraneous to the indirect statement.

285:         *auspicātō*: one word ablative absolute < *auspicārī*, "after taking the auspices," part of Romulus's thinking (i.e., if the auspices were good); easier word order: *prīmum cōgitāvisse urbem condere et firmāre rem pūblicam dīcitur.*

287–290:   *novum quoddam et subagreste cōnsilium*: object of *persecūtus est*; *perceleriter...subagreste*: *per* as a prefix "very"; *sub*: "somewhat."

291:         *magnī hominis et iam tum longē prōvidentis*: genitive of characteristic with *cōnsilium*.

292:         *honestō...locō*: ablative of source with *ortās*; when they went to neighboring villages asking for wives, the early Romans were mocked with a questioning suggestion that they open the city to the asylum of women as well (Cap. XLII.28–31). The only woman, the assumption is, who would need an asylum is one of damaged virtue, thus the stress on women of virtuous character in *honestō locō*.

293:         *lūdōrum grātiā*: *grātiā* with a preceding genitive, like *causā* (l.175); *quōs* (*ludōs*).

295:         *amplissimārum*: here, "esteemed."

298:         *īcit*: perfect tense (present: *ĭcit*).

299:         *mātrōnīs ipsīs quae raptae erant ōrantibus*: ablative absolute surrounding a relative clause.

300:	*ascīvit*: *ascīscere* involves a measure of decision-making: "to approvingly receive (information) as true or (a person/state) in some capacity."
303–312:	Reading help: *cum* clause, followed by concessive clauses (*quamquam dēlēgerat...populumque...discrīpserat...sed quamquam*) that contain two subordinate clauses, followed by the main (*tamen*) clause; *nōmine*: with agreeing *suō* and both genitives (*Tatiī, Lucumōnis*); *quās cūriās eārum nōmine...quae*: antecedent of *quae* is *eārum*; *pācis et foederis*: objective genitives with *ōrātrīcēs*; *quae ex Sabīnīs virginēs raptae posteā fuerant ōrātrīcēs pācis et foederis*: see Cap. XLII.151–159; *ea = tribūs et cūriās*; *multō*: with *magis*.
314:	*Lycūrgus*: cf. l.252; *Spartae*: locative.
316:	Easier word order: *cīvitātēs (singulārī imperiō et potestāte rēgiā) tum melius gubernārī et rēgī sī auctōritās optimī cuiusque ad illam vim dominātiōnis adiuncta esset*; *singulārī...rēgiā*: ablatives of means; *optimī cuiusque...auctōritās*: *quisque* with superlative: "all the best men" (Cap. XXXI).
317–318:	*quasi senātū fultus*: Cicero uses *quasi* when employing metaphorical speech; *fulcīre* ("prop up"): applicable only metaphorically to the Senate.
319:	*cum* concessive: "although."
322:	*auspiciīs...obsecūtus est*: "yielded to."
325–326:	*auspiciīs...augurēs*: the *augurēs* were a group of priests whose responsibility it was to observe natural signs (including the flights of birds: *auspicium < avēs, spicio*) as signs from the gods meant to guide future actions (XLII.289–302); *cooptāvit*: Romulus chose augurs.
327–330:	Death of Romulus: XLII.221ff.
329:	*tantum est cōnsecūtus ut*: "he was so successful that"; *cōnsequī*: "succeed."
330–331:	*opīniōnem*: i.e., even if not true, the rumor proves his greatness; *nēmō...mortālis*.
332:	*potuit*: past potential: "one one could have" (Cap. XL).
334–336:	with sense markers: *ut id* (*dē Rōmulō*) (*Proculō Iūliō, hominī agrestī*), *crēderētur quod multīs iam ante saeculīs* (*nūllō aliō dē mortālē*) *homines credidissent*; *id*: an adverbial accusative with

	the impersonal passive *crēderētur*; *Proculō Iūliō, hominī agrestī*: dative with *crēderētur*: i.e., he was believed.
337:	*quō* (= *ut*) *illī* (*patrēs*) *ā sē invidiam interitūs* (objective genitive with *invidiam*) *Rōmulī pellerent*.
343:	*ut*: "as."
345–347:	*vidēmus...tē ingressum* (*esse*); *ratiōne ad disputandum novā quae nusquam est in Graecōrum librīs*: Scipio has broken away from the Greek precedent and is taking a new approach to analyzing the best form of state; the Romans were in constant competition with the Greeks, and this is a reminder that they were innovators on their own terms; *prīnceps ille*: Plato (cf. ll.267–268); Laelius's comparison of Scipio's process versus Plato's seems a bit tendentious.
348:	*āream*: Plato's building ground was his *Republic*.
350–351:	*ā vītā hominum abhorrentem et mōribus*: i.e., because it was an ideal state, not one based on actual lived experience; *exemplārī*: cf. *exemplum* (l.240).
354–355:	*ut...tribuere...mālīs quam...fingere et disputēs...*
358:	*tē reliquōs rēgēs persquente*: ablative absolute.
360:	*quibus*: dative with *tribuisset*; *eōrum līberōs*: the descendants of the original *pātrēs* were called *patriciī*.
365:	*dēsīderiō*: ablative of cause.
366–367:	*novam et inaudītam...ratiōnem*; *interrēgnī ineundī*: objective genitive with *ratiō*; *cēterīs gentibus*: dative of reference: "by other peoples."
368:	*quoad*: "as long as; up to the point that"; like *dum* (Cap. XL), *quoad* takes the subjunctive when it looks forward to what is anticipated; *ut...esset*: purpose clause.
371–373:	*fūgit*: i.e., escaped his mind; *nōn dēligendum...sed habendum*: "not chosen but held" (Sparta's kingship was hereditary); *sī modo*: "if only"; *potuit*: indicative for subjunctive with a modal verb (see line 332).
374:	*quī modo* = *dummodo* + subjunctive: "provided that" (Cap. XL); *Herculis stirpe generātus*: ablative of source (Caps. XXX-VII): the two royal families of Sparta were thought to be descendants of Hercules.

| 375–376: | *etiam*: modifies *tum*; *vīdērunt virtūtem et sapientiam rēgālem* (*quaerī oportēre*), *nōn prōgeniem quaerī oportēre*. |

375–376: *etiam*: modifies *tum*; *vīdērunt virtūtem et sapientiam rēgālem* (*quaerī oportēre*), *nōn prōgeniem quaerī oportēre*.

379–380: *Numa*: XLII.281ff; *ascīvit*: see note above on line 300; *accīvit*: XLIV.150 (marginalia): *accīre*: "summons" (rare); *Sabīnum* = Numa; *Curibus*: Cures, a Sabine town, ablative of place from which.

381–383: *incēnsōs*: with *hominēs Rōmānōs*; *īnstitūtō Rōmulī*: because of Romulus's practice; *bellicīs studiīs*: ablatives of means with *incēnsōs*; *exīstimāvit eōs paulum ab illā cōnsuētūdine esse revocandōs*: Cf. XLII.303–305.

385: *virītim*: adverb < *vir*.

386: *colendīs agrīs*: ablative of means; *commodīs omnibus*: ablative with *abundāre*.

388: *convalēscere*: "gain strength"; *quōrum*: i.e., *iūstitia et fidēs*; *patrōciniō*: "defense," "protection" Cf. LIII.293.

390–391: *auspiciīs māiōribus inventīs*: i.e., auspices marked as especially significant.

390–400: Numa and the priesthoods: cf. XLIII.325ff.

392–393: *sacrīs...pontificēs quīnque praefēcit*: *praeficere* + accusative and dative ("put 'acc.' in charge of 'dat.'"); *cōnsuētūdine et cupiditāte*: ablatives of cause (Cap. XXXVII).

403: *Polybius*: see note above to line 150.

405: for the importance of *diūrnitas*, see lines 179–183.

407–411: Cf. Cap. XLV.

412: *rēx ille*: Tarquinius Superbus; *prīmum*: picked up by *deinde* (l.415).

413: *integrā mente*: ablative of description.

418ff: Cap. XLV.230ff.

421: *ingeniō et virtūte*: ablatives of respect with *praestāns* (Cap. XXXIX).

423: *prīvātus*: i.e., did not hold public office.

425–430: *Quō auctōre et prīncipe*: ablative absolute.

concitāta: with ablatives of means *querēllā* and *recordātiōne*; *exsulem...esse iussit*: XLV.317–320.

431–432:	*dē rēge dominus*: i.e., from being a king he turned into a master; *ūnīus-que vitiō*: because of the fault of one man; *reī pūblicae*: with *genus*; cf. ll.179–286.
435:	*consulere* + dative: "take care of, look to the interests of"; *ut parēns* < *parēns, -entis* (*părĕre*), not *pārēre*.
436:	*quam* + superlative (Cap. XXVII): "the best possible condition."
439:	*simulatque* = *simul atque* (Cap. XXXVII).
442–443:	*figūrā, immanitāte*: ablatives of respect (Cap. XXXIX); *immānitas*: "monstrousness."
448–449:	*sit*: jussive; *perītus, tūtor, prōcūrātor* + objective genitives (Cap. XXV).
451:	*facite ut agnōscātis*: noun clause of result (Cap. XXXVII).
455:	*decemvirōs*: XLV.85–88.
462:	*virīs bene dē rē pūblicā meritīs*: "for men who have deserved good from the republic."
466–468:	*bonīs…rēctōribus*: dative of agent with *servāta*, which refers to *stabiliōra…genera*.

III. VOCĀBULA

NŌMINA

1st

aliēnigena, -ae (*m.*)	foreigner, stranger
bēlua, -ae	beast, wild animal
caerimōnia, -ae	rite, ceremony
fēriae, -ārum (*pl.*)	festival days, holidays
īnsolentia, -ae	unusualness; arrogance
sphaera, -ae	globe, sphere

2nd

prātulum, -ī	meadow, lawn
cūnābula, -ōrum (*n. pl.*)	cradle

3rd

aequābilitās, -tātis (*f.*)	equality
celebritās, -tātis (*f.*)	large assembly; renown
commūniō, -ōnis (*f.*)	partnership, sharing
cōnfūsiō, -ōnis (*f.*)	mixture; disorder, confusion
coniūnctiō, -ōnis (*f.*)	union, conjunction
cōnsīderātiō, -ōnis (*f.*)	consideration, reflection
cōnstitūtiō, -ōnis (*f.*)	constitution; order, arrangement
dēpopulātiō, -ōnis (*f.*)	plundering
discrīptiō, -ōnis (*f.*)	distribution
disputātiō, -ōnis (*f.*)	an arguing, discussion
exemplar, -āris (*n.*)	pattern, model
ferōcitās, -ātis (*f.*)	fierceness; ferocity
firmitūdo, -dinis (*f.*)	stability, firmness
immānitās, -tātis (*f.*)	monstrousness, brutality
inīquitās, -tātis (*f.*)	unfairness
ōrātrīx, -trīcis (*f.*)	female suppliant
pariēs, -etis (*m.*)	wall (of a house)
perceptiō, -ōnis (*f.*)	a gathering; perception
prōcūrātor, -ōris (*m.*)	manager, superintendent
rēctor, -ōris (*m.*)	ruler, governor

4th

arbitrātus, -ūs (< **arbitrārī** Cap. XXII)	choice, decision
coetus, -ūs (< **coīre** Cap. LI)	gathering, society
dominātus, -ūs (< **dominārī** Cap. XXXVII)	dominion, power
excessus, -ūs (< **excēdere** Cap. XXXVIII)	departure, death
impulsus, -ūs (< **impellere** Cap. XXXIX)	impact, impulse
interitus, -ūs (< **interīre** Cap. XLI)	death
interventus, -ūs (< **intervenīre** (Cap. XLIV)	arrival

VERBA

-āre

(accomodō) accommodāre	fit, adapt
(approbō) approbāre	approve
(commūnicō) commūnicāre	share
(cooptō) cooptāre	choose (as colleague)
(disputō) disputāre	argue, discuss
(flāgitō) flāgitāre	demand insistently
(generō) generāre	beget, produce
(investīgō) investīgāre	inquire into, investigate
(labefactō) labefactāre	shake, undermime
(locuplētō) locuplētāre	enrich
(maculō) maculāre	stain, defile
(multō) multāre	punish
(nūncupō) nūncupāre	designate, call
(obscūrō) obscūrāre	obscure, darken
(relāxō) relaxāre	relax, relieve
(sociō) sociāre	join, unite
(ventitō) ventitāre	come frequently

-ēre

(attineō) attinēre (< tenēre)	concern, relate to
(compāreō) compārēre, -uisse	appear
(perhibeō) perhibēre (< habēre)	report, say

-ere

(abūtor) abūtī, -ūsum (+ abl.)	use up, take advantage of
(ascīscō) ascīscere, -scīvisse, -scītum	admit, adopt
(assequor) assequī (< sequī)	attain to, achieve
(assīdō) assīdere (< sidere)	sit down
(conquīrō) conquīrere (< quaerere)	search out, investigate
(distinguō) distinguere, -xisse, -ctum	distinguish, mark, characterize
(existō) exsistere, -itisse, -itum	appear, arise

(nancīscor) nancīscī, nactum/ nanctum	get, obtain, find, meet
(recidō) recidere (< cadere)	fall back

-īre

(dēvinciō) dēvincīre (< vincīre)	bind
(dissentiō) dissentīre (< sentīre)	disagree
(fulciō) fulcīre, -sisse, -tum	hold up, support
(impartīo) impartīre = impertīre (Cap. LIV)	give a share of, impart

ADIECTĪVA

1st/2nd

adultus, -a, -um (< adolēscere Cap. XLI)	fullgrown, adult
aprīcus, -a, -um	sunny
fēriātus, -a, -um	keeping holiday
inveterātus, -a, -um	hardened by age, of long-standing
pergrātus, -a, -um	very pleasing
periūcundus, -a, -um	very agreeable
permolestus, -a, -um	very troublesome
perpaucī, -ae, -a	very few
prōnus, -a, -um	leaning forward, inclined
quaestōrius, -a, -um	of, belonging to a quaestor
ratus (reor)	valid, fixed, certain in proportion
sempiternus, -a, -um	everlasting, eternal
subnīxus, -a, -um	resting on, relying on

3rd

aequābilis, -e	equal
dēterior, -ius	worse
particeps (*gen.* participis) (+ *gen.*)	having a share in
populāris, -e	of the people, popular
pudēns (*gen.* pudentis)	modest, behaving properly
silvestris, -e	of the woods, wild
stabilis, -e	firm, stable
subagrestis, -e	somewhat rustic

PRONŌMINA

quāliscumque, quālecumque   of whatever sort

ADVERBIA

parumper   for a short while
paululum   a little
perceleriter   very quickly
postrīdiē   on the following day
sērius (*comp. of* sērō)   rather late, too late
sērō   late, too late
vicissim   in turn

CONIUNCTIŌNĒS

atquī   but, and yet
quamvīs   however, although

ALIA

hercule   by Hercules! really!

LVI: QVINQVAGESIMVM SEXTVM: SOMNIVM SCIPIONIS (Cicero/Horace)[1]

[*Ex M. Tullii Cicerōnis dē rē pūblicā librō VI*
et
Ex Q. Horātiī Flaccī 'Carminum' librō I, carmen XXII ad Fuscum]

I. ØRBERG'S INTRODUCTION

The *Somnium Scīpiōnis* has been preserved in full because it was separately transcribed and annotated by the Neo-Platonist Macrobius in the fifth century AD. Even in antiquity, it was considered a free-standing narrative in addition to being a part of *dē Rē Pūblicā*.

Scipio tells about his visit to king Masinissa of Numidia during the Third Punic War. The ninety-year-old king entertained his Roman visitor with stories about his famous grandfather, Scipio Africanus the Elder (*Māior*), whom he remembered from the Second Punic War. After this conversation, Scipio dreamed that his grandfather appeared before him among the heavenly stars and spoke to him about the great deeds he was to perform for his country and about the reward awaiting him in heaven. Scipio's dead father, Aemilius Paulus (Cap. L.608ff.), also stepped forward and spoke admonitory words to his son. The grandfather went on to describe the structure of the universe—the immovable earth surrounded by eight revolving spheres—and the music of the spheres, which the human ear cannot perceive. He pointed out the five zones of the globe, only two of which are habitable. He put forward evidence for the immortality of the soul (taken from Plato's *Phaedrus*) and concluded with an exhortation to use one's immortal soul in the service of one's country.

The *Somnium Scipiōnis* should not be taken as "the ancient view" but *one* ancient view. It is heavily influenced by Stoicism.

As an appendix, the Cicero text is followed by an Ode, i.e., a lyric poem, by Horace (*Q. Horātius Flaccus*, 65–8 BC). The poem begins with a Stoic sentiment

---

1. For an explanation of the line number references convention, see p. xxvi.

367

that coordinates well with Cicero's text. It also demonstrates the kind of rhetorical argument often found in Horace's poetry: the first two stanzas make a claim, the middle two give an illustrative example, and the final two the poet's broad application of the lesson to be learned. Guiltlessness is a safeguard against all dangers, the poet solemnly declares. He illustrates (not very solemnly) this maxim with an incident that happened while he was strolling in the woods and singing about his beloved *Lalagē*: a formidable wolf turned away and fled! The poem concludes that he will always love and sing about Lalage wherever he may travel.

The addressee, Aristius Fuscus, was Horace's close friend. As the addressee, he appears here and in Epistles 1, letter 10. He also plays a role in Satire 1.9 (as the man who refuses to help Horace get away from the unwanted attentions of a man in the forum) and in Satire 1.10 (as a respected reader of Horace's poetry). If Horace's poetry is any guide, the two friends shared a sense of humor and, although this ode was set to music as a hymn in the early nineteenth century and solemnly sung, there is little solemn about it.

Horace's models are the Greek lyric poets Alcaeus (*Alkaios*) and Pindar (*Pindaros*). The meter in the present poem is called *Sapphic* after the Greek poetess *Sapphō*. In the GRAMMATICA LATINA section, there is an explanation of the meter and the division of the poem into four-line stanzas (*strophae*).

II. AUXILIA LEGENDĪ

Masinissa senex: 1-19

4:          *nihil...potius, quam ut Masinissam convenīrem*: comparative clause + subjunctive (Cap. XLVIII).

6:          *ut* = when + indicative.

7:          *grātēs*: archaic form of *grātiam*, used especially in prayers.

10-11:   *nōmine ipsō*: as it recalls his good friend Africanus; ablative of means with *recreor*: "invigorated."

16:          *apparātū rēgiō*: "with royal magnificence," a different sense from XLVIII.126.

Fātōrum via: 20-60

21:          *cubitum*: accusative supine of purpose.

22-23:   *quī...vigilāssem*: causal clause; *artior...somnus*: "a deeper sleep" or, taken closely with *complexus*: "sleep embraced me more close(ly)."

24:        *fit…ut*: noun clause of result (Cap. XXXVII).

26:        *Ennius*: see Cap. XXXVI note on line 162.

28:        *imāgine*: a wax image of distinguished ancestors kept in the home: see Cap. LII, note on lines 459–463.

30:        *cohorruī < cohorrescere*: "shudder"; *ades*: imperative + *animō*: "pull yourself together"; although the phrase can also mean "pay attention."

34–35:   *dē excelsō et plēnō stēllārum illūstrī et clārō quōdam locō*: four adjectives in two pairs describe *quōdam locō: excelsō et plēnō stēllārum* and *illūstrī et clārō*.

37–38:   *id cognōmen…partum quod*.

40:        *obieris < ob-eō, īre* (cf. *obviam*).

41–42:   *dēligēre*: future passive (*dēligēris*); *absēns*: i.e., even though not in Rome for the elections.

43:        *currū in Capitōlium invectus*: i.e., in a triumph.

44:        *nepōtīs*: for land reform of Tiberius Gracchus, see LI.216ff.

46:        *ostendās oportēbit*: see grammar section above; *patriae*: dative with *ostendās*.

47–48:   *ancipitem*: "two-headed"; i.e., unfixed, undecided.

49–52:   *septēnōs octiēs*: distributive adjective + distributive adverb: 8 x a group of 7 years; mystical numbers (*plēnus*, "complete"); *alter alterā* (Cap. XXXVII, Rᴇᴄᴇ̄ɴsɪō), matched by mystical language (*summam fātālem*).

55–56:   *nē multa* (*dīcam*): idiomatic: "lest I go on too long" (of getting to the point); *cōnstituās oportet*: see grammar section above; *sī…effūgeris*: on the rumors surrounding Scipio's death, see LI.251–256.

Mors et vīta: 61–113

62:        *quō = ut* when used with a comparative (*alacrior*): Cap. XLIX.

66:        *fruor* + ablative (Cap. XXXVIII).

67–68:   *quod quidem in terrīs fiat*: descriptive relative clause expressing a limit or restriction ("nothing more acceptable (*acceptius*) of what (at least) happens on earth"); *sociātī*: agrees with closer noun (*coetūs*), refers also to *concilia*.

73:             *Paulus*: Aemelius Paulus, father of Scipio (L.668–671).

84:             *nōn est ita*: "no" (just as *est ita* can mean "yes").

87:             *hāc lēge*: according to this law; *hāc lēge...quī* = *hāc lēge ut*: rela-
                tive noun clause (*verba postulandī*, Caps. XXVII, XXXVII);
                these clauses are partly result explaining the content of the *lēx*,
                and partly purpose, looking to the inherent demand.

90:             *sīdera*: constellations, while *stella* is an individual star.

92–93:   *et tibi...et piīs omnibus*: datives of agent with gerundive *reti-
                nendus*.

94:             *iniŭssū*: "without the order"; *ille* refers to *animus*.

98:             *cole*: imperative (*colere*); *in parentibus, propinquīs, patriā*: "in
                the case of/in respect of."

107:            *eae magnitūdinēs*: "those vastnesses."

112–113:   *me imperiī nostrī...paenitēret*: for *paenitēre* with accusative of
                person and genitive of thing, see Cap. XL; subjunctive in a re-
                sult clause (*ita...parva...ut*).

Cursūs stēllārum: 114–139

117:            *tibi*: ethical dative (Cap. LV).

120:            *arcēns*: "enclosing" (*arcēre*, Cap. XXXIX).

121:            *īnfixī illī cursūs sempiternī*: the "fixed stars" of the outermost
                rim that seems not to move relative to the other stars.

122–123:   *septem*: sc. *cursūs*; *contrāriō mōtū...atque*: a movement differ-
                ent than (the movement of) the sky.

126:            *horribilis terrīs*: because Mars is the god of war.

138:            *nūtū*: *nūtus* is a downward movement, usually of the head, a
                nod, but also, as here, the force of gravity.

Cantus sphaerārum: 140–170

The description of the music of the spheres is difficult and has inspired much
scholarly argument. The notes below aim at elucidating the Latin not the
dynamics of the vision.

144–148:   *Hic*: sc. *sonus*; *prō ratā parte*: "proportionally"; *coniūnctus*:
                "composed"; *intervāllīs*: understand (from the next clause)
                the pushing onward (*impulsū*) and movement (*mōtū*) of the

heavenly bodies (*orbium*)—these cause the irregular but harmonized pauses (musical intervals) that occur in the constant motion of the heavens; *acūta*: "sharp or high-pitched"; *gravibus*: "heavy or low-pitched"; *concentus, -ūs*: "harmony."

149:     *nātūra fert ut*: *verba postulandī*: "nature requires that" (Cap. XXVII); *extrēma*: as the context makes clear, this refers to the outer edges as judged from the middle, not just the outer rim.

156–158:   *eadem vīs est duōrum*: the rotation of the moon and the *caelum* move at different speeds but with the same power or energy; *septem…quī numerus rērum omnium ferē nōdus est*: for seven as one of the perfect numbers, see lines 49–52.

159:     *nervīs*: strings on a musical instrument; *cantibus*: *cantus, -ūs* is properly the music made by voice or instrument.

162:     *obsurduērunt*: "have grown deaf."

164:     *Catadūpa, -ōrum*: a famous waterfall (cataract) on the Nile.

166–168:   *hic*: the sound of the music of the spheres; *tōtīus mundī*: genitive with *conversiōne*; *sonitus*: "the sound (made by)" + ablative, *incitātissimā conversiōne*.

169–170:   *nequītis*: < *nequeō, nequīre,* plural because although he is talking to Scipio, he refers to all living people; *aciēs* is often used of acuity of vision.

Angustiae terrārum: 171–231

178–181:   *quam celebritātem…quam…glōriam*: interrogative adjectives; *expetendam*: "that ought to be sought," i.e., worthwhile; *habitārī, habitātur*: impersonal; *ubi habitātur* with *in ipsīs quasi maculīs*; *vāstās sōlitūdinēs interiectās* (*esse*) with *vidēs*.

187–188:   *quibusdam…cingulīs*: ablative of means dependent on and enclosing *redimītam* (< *redimīre*: "encircle") and *circumdatam* ("wrapped around"), which refer to *terram*.

189–190:   *verticibus ipsīs*: ablative with *subnīxōs* ("propped up by, supported by"); *ex utrāque parte*: "on both sides" (i.e., poles of the earth); *pruīnā*: "frost."

193:     *nihil ad vestrum genus*: a common idiom sc. (as in margins), *pertinet*.

194:            *aquilō, -ōnis* (m.): "the north wind"; *cerne*: imperative of *cer-nere*, "perceive"; *quam*: interrogative adverb introducing indirect question (so too in line 199: *quam sit parvus vidēs*).

197–198:   *marī quod 'Atlanticum', quod 'Magnum', quem 'Ōceanum'*: Atlanticum and Magnum are both adjectives, while Oceanus is a proper name (masculine gender), and the gender of the relative (*antecedent marī*) has been attracted into the gender of Oceanus.

200–201:   *cuiusquam nostrum nōmen*: "the name of any of us": *cuiusquam* (< *quisquam*, used in negative contexts) is genitive with *nōmen* and *nostrum* is partitive genitive with *cuiusquam* (Caps. XXIX, XL).

203–204:   *in reliquīs (orientis aut obeuntis sōlis) ultimīs aut (aquilōnis austrīve) partibus*: *reliquīs, ultimīs* refer to all *partibus*, while the partitive gentives, east (*orientis...sōlis*) or west (*obeuntis sōlis*), north or south (*aquilōnis austrīve*) enumerate them; *Quibus*: i.e., the furthest regions of the world.

208–210:   *sī cupiat...prodere*; *prōlēs*: "offspring" (XLVI.851); *nostrum*: see note above on lines 200–201.

211:            *tempore certō*: "at fixed times."

214:            *quid...interest* + accusative and infinitive: "what difference does it make that..."

215–216:   *nūllus*: sc. *sermo*; *certē meliōrēs*: according to the persistent Roman belief that their ancestors were more virtuous than their contemporaries.

217–218:   *nōmen nostrum*: adjective, not genitive of pronoun; *memoriam cōnsequī*, "achieve the memory (of)"; *ūnīus annī*: i.e., of a year measured by the completion of all stellar rotations.

225:            *dēficere sōl*: an eclipse of the sun; a second eclipse (l.228) will signal the end of a complete year.

230:            *habētō*: future imperative, "consider the year complete."

Dē glōriā aeternā et animō immortālī: 232–298

233–234:   *dēspērāveris*: perfect subjunctive in the protasis of a future-less-vivid condition; the sense of the condition: if you should lose hope of eternal life here, what value is the tiny bit of glory that you attain on earth? (i.e., "none"); *magnīs et praestantibus*

	virīs: dative of possession with *omnia sunt*; *quantī*: genitive of value (Cap. XXIX).
236:	*partem exiguam*: i.e., *vīcēsimam partem* (ll.230–231).
237–239:	*sī volēs…dēderis…posueris*: indicatives in a future-more-vivid condition.
241:	*quid…loquantur*: indirect question; *ipsī videant*: jussive, "let them see to it" (i.e., that's their concern, not yours).
247:	*bene meritīs dē patriā*: *meritīs* is dative with *aditum patet*; the expression is idiomatic: to those who have "earned well" (proved deserving) from the point of view of someone else (*dē* + the ablative).
248–249:	*vestīgiīs*: dative with *ingressus* (cf. our "followed in your footsteps"); *decorī vestrō*: dative with intransitive *dēfuī*.
251:	*ēnītere*: imperative.
253:	*mēns cuiusque is est quisque*: "the mind (heart, soul) of each person is that person"; *mēns* is that hegemonic principle of life (in the *Tusculan Disputations* 3.5, Cicero says *mēns cui regnum totīus animī ā nātūrā tribūtum est*).
254–258:	*tam…quam*.
258–260:	*ut…sic*: "as…so": POINTS OF STYLE, Cap. XIX; *mundum…mortālem*: object of *movet*.
261:	*movētur*: "is in motion, moves itself," not "is moved" (which implies an external propulsion); see line 265: *quod sē ipsum movet*.
266:	*cēterīs*: dative with *hic fōns, hoc prīncipium*.
269–270:	*nec enim esset id prīncipium quod gignerētur aliunde*: contrafactual (*quod* "whatever" instead of *sī*): "whatever arises/comes into being from another source (other than itself) could not be this beginnning/first principle/originator."
271–272:	*prīncipium exstīnctum*: the participle (as often) implies a condition: "if the beginning has been deprived of life."
275–277:	*vel concidat…cōnsistat necesse est nec…nancīscātur*: see grammar section above on *necesse est* + the subjunctive; both subjects go with all verbs: *omne caelum omnisque nātūra concidat et cōnsistat nec vim ūllam nancīscātur*; *quā moveātur*: generic/ descriptive consecutive clause (see below l.280).

279–280:   *quod...moveātur*: subordinate clause in indirect statement; *quis est qui...neget*: descriptive relative clause (Caps. XXXIX, XLII).

292–293:   *dēdidērunt*: < *dēdere* + accusative and dative, "surrender" (Cap. XLI); *eārum* = *voluptātibus*.

294:          *libīdinum*: genitive with *impulsū*; *oboedientium* agrees with *libīdinum*; *voluptātibus* is dative with *oboedientium*.

295:          *corporibus*: ablative of separation with *ēlāpsī*.

296–297:   *multīs...saeculīs*: ablative of time within which.

Integer Vītae: 299–325

300–301:   *carminum*: genitive plural of *carmen*, "lyric poem"; *Fuscum*: see introduction to this chapter above.

302:          *integer vītae scelerisque pūrus*: epexegetical genitives (see grammar section).

303–304:   *eget*: *egēre* (Cap. XXXVII), like *carēre*, with ablatives of separation *iaculīs, arcū, gravidā phaeretrā*; *Maurus, -a, -um*: the *Maurī* live in *Maurētānia*; cf. Cap. LII.

306:          *Syrtēs*: Syrtis (Greek Σύρτις) means "sandbank"; Syrtis Māior and Syrtis Minor are gulfs in the area of the Mediterranean Sea around Africa (see margins).

307:          *facturus*: with *integer, pūrus*; *iter facere*: "journey."

308:          *Caucasus*: mountain range between Black Sea and Caspian Sea in Asia; cf. above, line 201 and margin; *quae loca* = *loca quae*; *fābulōsus*: "storied"; i.e., about which people tell a lot of stories.

309:          *lambit*: like the *lupa* of XLI.230–231: *Quōs lupa nūtrit...,/et lambit linguā corpora bīna suā.*

310:          *namque*: introduces the exemplum that "proves" Horace's assertion in lines 1–8 of the poem; *silvā...in Sabīnā*: Horace owned a farm and villa in the Sabine hills.

311:          *Lalagēn*: A girl's name, Lalagē, from the Greek Λαλαγή, related to the Greek verb "lalein" (λαλεῖν), which means "chatter, prattle."

312:          *cūrīs...expedītīs*: *expedīre* means "to unshackle the feet, to free"; it is used of light-armed soldiers who are free of heavy burdens (in this case, anxieties, *cūrae*) and thus able to travel quickly.

313:     *inermem*: *sine armīs,* modifies *mē* (l.9).

314:     *portentum* (Cap. XLVI): "monster."

315:     *Dauniās*: only here in Latin; Daunus a legendary king of Apu-
         lia (in the *Aeneid*, Turnus's father); subject of *alit.*

316–317: *Iuba*: king of Numidia and part of Mauretania (contemporary
         with Horace); *leōnum*: objective genitive with *nūtrix*; *ārida
         nūtrix*: in apposition to *tellūs.*

318:     *piger, -ra, -rum* (Cap. XXI): "lazy" (see margins); *pigrīs*: abla-
         tive of place where.

320:     *latus*: i.e., the furthest edge.

320–321: *urget*: agrees with *malus Iuppiter* but refers to *nebulae* as well.

323:     *domibus*: dative with *negātā.*

III. Vocābula

NŌMINA

1st
illecebra, -ae	enticement, allurement
pharētra, -ae	quiver
pruīna, -ae	hoarfrost, rime
zōna, -ae	belt, zone

2nd
aesculētum, -ī	oak forest
aevum, -ī	lifetime, life
cingulus, -ī (also: cingulum, -ī)	belt
nōdus, -ī	knot, bond
pūnctum, -ī	dot, point, speck
radius, -ī	ray

3rd
caelitēs, -um (*m. pl.*)	gods
candor, -ōris (*m.*)	whiteness, brightness
cōnservātor, -ōris (*m.*)	savior, guardian
conversiō, -ōnis (*f.*)	rotation, revolution
ēluviō, -ōnis (*f.*)	flood, inundation

exustiō, -ōnis (*f.*)	conflagration
fulgor, -ōris (*m.*)	flash; flash of lightning
līmes, -ītis (*m.*)	path, track
moderātor, -ōris (*m.*)	ruler, director
pietās, -tātis (*f.*)	respect, devotion, dutiful conduct
posteritās, -tātis (*f.*)	future, posterity
tellūs, -ūris (*f.*)	earth
temperātiō, -ōnis (*f.*)	fit proportion, organizing principle

4th

ānfrāctus, -ūs	orbit (of the sun); lit. bending, recurving
concentus, -ūs	harmony
nūtus, -ūs	nod, gravitation
pulsus, -ūs	thrust, impulse

VERBA

-āre

(amputō) amputāre	cut off
(animō) animāre	give life to
(collācrimō) collācrimāre	burst into tears
(dīlātō) dīlātāre	spread, expand
(laxō) laxāre	loose, untie, release
(lūstrō) lūstrāre	irradiate, purify, survey
(pervolō) pervolāre	move rapidly, rush, fly
(trānatō) trānatāre	swim across
(volūtō) volūtāre	roll, pass, whirl

-ēre

(arrīdeō) arrīdēre (< **rīdēre**)	smile at
(cieō) ciēre, cīvisse, citum	set in motion, move
(contueor) contuērī (< **tuērī**)	look at, contemplate
(ēlūceō) ēlūcēre (< **lūcēre**)	shine forth

-ere

(accolō) accolere (< **colere**)	live near
(cohorrēscō) cohorrēscere	shudder
(cōnectō) cōnectere, -uisse, -xum	join together

(dēfugiō) dēfugere (< fugere)	escape, avoid
(īnfīgō) īnfīgere (< fīgere)	fix, fasten
(ingemēscō) ingemēscere	groan, moan
(īnsistō) īnsistere, -itisse	stand (on), pursue
(interrumpō) interrumpere (< rumpere)	break up, cut, interrupt
(obrigēscō) obrigēscere, -uisse	become stiff
(obsurdēscō) obsurdēscere, -uisse	become deaf
(offendō) offendere, -disse, -sum	hit upon, come upon, find
(renāscor) renāscī, -ātum	be reborn, be recreated

-īre

(dēfīniō) dēfīnīre (< finīre)	delimit
(redimiō) redimīre, -isse, -ītum	encircle, surround

ADIECTĪVA

1st/2nd

aestīvus, -a, -um	of summer
aestuōsus, -a, -um	sweltering, seething
āridus, -a, -um	dry, barren
cadūcus, -a, -um	ready to fall, perishable
citimus, -a, -um (sup. of citer)	nearest
concitātus, -a, -um	fast, rapid
excelsus, -a, -um	lofty, high
excitātus, -a, -um (< excitāre Caps. XIV, XIX)	lively, vigorous, loud
extimus, -a, -um (sup. of exter)	outermost, farthest
fābulōsus, -a, -um	fabulous, celebrated in fable
globōsus, -a, -um	spherical, round
hērēditārius, -a, -um	inherited, hereditary
inanimus, -a, -um	lifeless, inanimate
incitātus, -a, -um (< incitāre Caps. XXXVII, XXXVIII)	fast-moving, rapid
lacteus, -a, -um	milky
rutilus, -a, -um	red
stēllifer, -era, -erum	star-bearing
subiectus, -a, -um (+ dat.)	situated under

torridus, -a, -um	scorched, parched
trānsversus, -a, -um	placed crosswise

3rd

alacer, -cris, -cre	lively, eager, keen
austrālis, -e	southern
fātālis, -e (cf. fātum, -ī Caps. XXXIV, XXXIX)	fateful, destined
fragilis, -e (< frangere Caps. XXIV, XLIII, XLVI)	fragile, frail
habitābilis, -e (< habitāre Caps. V, XLIII)	habitable
hebes (*gen.* hebetis)	dull, blunt
immōbilis, -e (< movēre)	immovable, motionless
inhospitālis, -e (< hospes, l.30, hospitālis, ll.42, 45)	inhospitable
lūnāris, -e (< luna, l.13)	of the moon, lunar
septentrionālis, -e (< septentriōnēs, ll.16, 50)	northern

ADVERBIA

aliunde	from another place, person, thing
citrō: ultrō citrōque	to and fro, on both sides
quōcircā	hence, therefore
quoūsque	how long? till when?
ōcius (comp. without positive)	quicker, sooner
octiēs (Cap. XXX: distributive numbers)	eight times
subter	below, underneath

Latin–English Vocabulary

A

ā/ab/abs *prp + abl* from, of, since, by

ab-aliēnāre turn away, alienate

ab-dere -didisse -ditum hide

ab-ditus -a -um hidden, remote

ab-dūcere take away, carry off

ab-errāre wander away, stray

ab-esse ā-fuisse be absent/away/distant, fall short, be wanting

ab-horrēre ab be inconsistent with

ab-icere throw away

ab-igere -ēgisse -āctum drive away

ab-īre -eō -iisse go away

ab-olēre efface, obliterate

ab-olēscere -ēvisse be effaced/forgotten

ab-ripere drag away, carry off

ab-rogāre repeal, cancel

ab-rumpere break off

abs *v.* ā/ab/abs

abs-cēdere go away, withdraw

absēns -entis *adi* absent

ab-solvere free, acquit

abs-terrēre frighten away, deter

abs-tinēns -entis self-restrained

abs-tinēre -uisse -tentum keep off

abs-trahere remove, separate

ab-sūmere consume, waste, destroy

abundāns -antis overflowing, abundant

abundantia -ae *f* overflow, abundance

abundāre (+ *abl*) overflow, be rich (in)

abundē amply, more than needed

ab-ūtī + *abl* use up, take advantage of

ac *v.* atque/ac

ac-cēdere approach, come near

ac-cendere -disse -ēnsum light, inflame

acceptus -a -um + *dat* well-liked, popular

accersere -īvisse -ītum send for, fetch

accessiō -ōnis *f* addition, accessory

ac-cidere -disse happen, occur, be heard

ac-cingere gird, *pass* gird oneself

ac-cipere receive, get, hear

ac-cīre summon, send for

ac-clāmāre shout, proclaim

ac-colere live near

ac-commodāre fit, adapt

ac-cubāre recline at table

ac-cumbere -cubuisse lie down at table

accūrātē carefully

ac-currere -rrisse -rsum come running

ac-cūsāre accuse

ācer -cris -cre keen, active, fierce

acerbus -a -um sour, bitter

acervus -ī *m* heap, pile

aciēs -ēī *f* line of battle, battle, sight

ac-quiēscere go to rest, die

ac-quīrere -sīvisse -sītum acquire, procure

ācta -ōrum *n pl* deeds, actions

āctiō -ōnis *f* action, delivery

āctor -ōris *m* pleader, advocate

acūtus -a -um sharp

ad *prp + acc* to, toward, by, at, till

ad-amāre fall in love with

ad-dere -didisse -ditum add

ad-dūcere lead, bring (to)

ad-eō *adv* to such a degree, so, too

ad-esse af-fuisse (+ *dat*) be present, stand by

ad-hortārī encourage, urge on

ad-hortātor -ōris *m* one who encourages

ad-hūc so far, till now, still

ad-icere add

ad-igere -ēgisse -āctum drive, compel (to)

ad-imere -ēmisse -ēmptum take away (from), steal

ad-ipīscī -eptum obtain

ad-īre -eō -iisse -itum go to, approach

aditus -ūs *m* approach, access

ad-iungere join to, add, attach

ad-iuvāre help

ad-minister -trī *m* assistant, helper

ad-ministra -ae *f* assistant, helper

ad-ministrāre conduct, administer

ad-mīrārī admire, wonder at

admīrātiō -ōnis *f* wonder, admiration

ad-miscēre mix (in), add

ad-mittere let in, admit

ad-modum *adv* very much, quite

ad-monēre remind, advise, urge

ad-monitus -ūs *m* advice, prompting

ad-movēre move near, put to

admurmurātiō -ōnis *f* murmur

ad-nectere -xuisse -xum attach, connect

ad-nītī exert oneself, strive

adnotātiuncula -ae *f* short note

adolēscere -ēvisse grow up

ad-optāre adopt

adopt(āt)iō -ōnis *f* adoption

ad-ōrāre worship, adore

ad-orīrī attack

ad-ōrnāre equip

ad-stāre stand by

ad-suēscere get accustomed

adulēscēns -entis *m* young man

adulēscentia -ae *f* youth

adulter -erī *m* adulterer

adulterīnus -a -um forged, false

adulterium -ī *n* adultery

adultus -a -um full-grown, adult

aduncus -a -um hooked, curved

ad-vehere carry, convey (to)

advena -ae *m/f* immigrant, foreigner

ad-venīre arrive

adventāre approach

adventicius -a -um from without, foreign

adventus -ūs *m* arrival

adversārī oppose, resist

adversārius -ī *m* opponent, adversary

adversus/-um *prp* + *acc* toward, against

adversus -a -um facing, opposed, front, contrary, unfavorable

ad-vertere turn, direct (toward)

ad-vocāre call, summon

aedēs -is *f* temple, *pl* house

aedificāre build

aedificium -ī *n* building

aedīlicius -ī *m* ex-aedile

aedīlis -is *m* aedile (magistrate)

aedīlitās -ātis *f* aedileship

aeger -gra -grum sick, ill

aegrē with pain, unwillingly

aegrōtāre be ill

aegrōtus -a -um sick

aēneus -a -um of bronze/copper

aequābilis -e equal

aequābilitās -ātis *f* equality

aequālis -is *m/f* person of the same age

aequāre make equal, equal

aequē equally

aequinoctium -ī *n* equinox

aequor -is *n* surface, sea

aequus -a -um level, equal, fair, calm

āēr -eris *m* air

aerārium -ī *n* public treasury

aerātus -a -um fitted with bronze

aereus -a -um of bronze/copper

aes aeris *n* copper, bronze, money

aesculētum -ī *n* oak forest

aestās -ātis *f* summer

aestimāre value, estimate

aestīvus -a -um of summer

aestuōsus -a -um sweltering, seething

aetās -ātis *f* age, lifetime, life

aeternus -a -um eternal, everlasting

aethēr -eris *m* heaven, upper air, ether

aevum -ī *n* time space, lifetime, life

affectāre strive after, aspire to

affectus -a -um affected by illness, ill

affectus -ūs *m* mood, feeling

af-ferre at-tulisse al-lātum bring, report, announce, bring about, cause

af-ficere affect, stir, visit with

af-fingere add, fabricate

af-firmāre assert, affirm, prove

af-flīgere -xisse -ctum cast down, deject, afflict

af-fluere flow near

Āfricus -ī *m* south-west wind

age -ite + *imp* come (on)! well, now

ager -grī *m* field

agere ēgisse āctum drive, do, perform, act, spend, live, *pass* go on

agere (cum) discuss, plead

agitur (rēs/dē rē) is at stake

āctum est (dē) it is all up (with)

agger -eris *m* rampart

ag-gredī -ior -gressum attack, set about, try

agitāre move, stir, plan (vītam) agitāre live animō/sēcum agitāre think about, consider

agitātiō -ōnis *f* brandishing

agmen -inis *n* army on the march, file

agna -a *f* ewe lamb

agnōscere -ōvisse   recognize
agnus -ī *m*   lamb
agrārius -a -um   agrarian
agrestis -e   rustic, boorish, *m* peasant
agricola -ae *m*   farmer, peasant
ain'   you don't say? really?
āiō ais ait āiunt   say
āla -ae *f*   wing
alacer -cris -cre   lively, eager, keen
ālātus -a -um   winged
albus -a -um   white
alere -uisse altum   nurse, feed, nourish
āles -itis *f*   large bird
aliās *adv*   at another time
al-ibī *adv*   in another place, elsewhere
alinēnigena -ae *m*   foreigner, stranger
aliēnus -a -um   someone else's
aliō *adv*   elsewhere
ali-quamdiū   for some time
ali-quandō   once, at last
ali-quantum   a good deal
ali-quī -qua -quod   some
ali-quis -quid   someone, something
ali-quot *indēcl*   some, several
aliter   otherwise
ali-unde   from elsewhere, from others
alius -a -ud   another, other
   aliī…aliī   some…others
   alius aliā viā   each in his own way
al-licere -iō -lēxisse -lectum   attract
al-ligāre   tie, fasten (to)
al-loquī   speak to, address
altāria -ium *n pl*   altar
altē   deep, deeply
alter -era -erum   one, the other (of two), second
altitūdō -inis *f*   height, depth
altum -ī *n*   the open sea
altus -a -um   high, tall, deep
alveus -ī *m*   trough
amāns -antis *m*   lover

amāre   love
amārus -a -um   bitter
amātōrius -a -um   of love
ambō -ae -ō   both, the two
ambulāre   walk
ā-mēns -entis   out of one's mind, mad
amīca -ae *f*   girlfriend
amīcitia -ae *f*   friendship
amictus -ūs *m*   mantle, cloak
amīcus -ī *m*   friend
amīcus -a -um   friendly
ā-migrāre   go away, remove
ā-mittere   lose
amnis -is *m*   river
amoenitās -ātis *f*   pleasant-ness, beauty
amoenus -a -um   lovely, pleasant
amor -ōris *m*   love
amphitheātrum -ī *n*   amphitheater
amphora -ae *f*   amphora (jar)
am-plectī -xum   embrace, cling to
ampliāre   enlarge
amplificāre   enlarge
amplitūdō -inis *f*   size, extent, greatness
amplius *adv comp*   more
amplus -a -um   large, big
amputāre   cut off
an   or,…(really)? if
anceps -cipitis   double, undecided
ancīle -is *n*   sacred shield
ancilla -ae *f*   female slave, servant
ānfrāctus -ūs *m*   orbit (of the sun)
anguis -is *m*   snake, serpent
angulus -ī *m*   angle, corner
angustiae -ārum *f pl*   narrowness, pass, defile
angustus -a -um   narrow
anima -ae *f*   breath, life, soul, ghost
anim-ad-vertere   notice
animal -ālis *n*   animal, living being
animāre   give life to
animus -ī *m*   mind, soul, courage

in animō est (mihi)   I have in mind, intend
annālēs -ium *m pl*   annals
anniversārius -a -um   annual
annus -ī *m*   year
annuus -a -um   for one year, annual
ante *prp + acc, adv*   in front of, before
anteā   before, formerly
ante-capere   anticipate
ante-cēdere   precede, surpass
ante-cellere   surpass, excel
ante-ferre   prefer
ante-hāc   formerly
ante-īre   precede, surpass
ante-pōnere   place before, prefer
ante-quam   before
ante-venīre   forestall, anticipate
antīquitās -ātis *f*   antiquity, ancient times
antīquus -a -um   old, ancient, former
antrum -ī *n*   cave, cavern
ānulus -ī *m*   ring
anus -ūs *f*   old woman
ānxius -a -um   worried, worrying
aper aprī *m*   wild boar
aperīre -uisse -rtum   open, disclose
apertus -a -um   open
apis -is *f*   bee
ap-parāre   prepare, arrange
apparātus -ūs *m*   prepara-tion, equipment
ap-pārēre   appear
appellāre   call, address
ap-pellere   drive, bring (to)
ap-petere   try to reach, seek, desire
ap-plicāre   attach
ap-pōnere   place (on), serve
ap-portāre   bring
ap-prehendere   seize
ap-probāre   approve
ap-propinquāre (+ *dat*)   approach, come near
aprīcus -a -um   sunny
Aprīlis -is (mēnsis)   April

aptē   neatly, aptly
aptus -a -um   suitable, convenient
apud *prp* + *acc*   beside, near, by
aqua -ae *f*   water
aquārī   fetch water
aquātor -ōris *m*   one who fetches water
aquila -ae *f*   eagle
Aquilō -ōnis *m*   north (north-east) wind
āra -ae *f*   altar
arānea -ae *f*   spider, cobweb
arāre   plow
arātor -ōris *m*   plowman
arātrum -ī *n*   plow
arbiter -trī *m*   eyewitness, arbitrator
arbitrārī   think, believe
arbitrātus -ūs *m*   choice, decision
arbitrium -ī *n*   decision, wish
arbor -oris *f*   tree
arcēre   keep away
arcessere -īvisse -ītum   send for, fetch
arcuātus -a -um   arched
arcus -ūs *m*   bow, (triumphal) arch
ārdēns -entis   burning, ardent
ārdēre -sisse -sum   burn
ārdor -ōris *m*   burning, fire, ardor
arduus -a -um   steep
ārea -ae *f*   open space, site
argenteus -a -um   silver-, of silver
argentum -ī *n*   silver
arguere -uisse -ūtum   reveal, affirm, accuse
argūmentum -ī *n*   proof, argument
āridus -a -um   dry, barren
ariēs -etis *m*   ram, battering ram
arma -ōrum *n pl*   arms
armāre   arm, equip
armātūra -ae *f*   armament, armed troops
armātus -a -um   armed
armentum -ī *n*   (herd of) cattle

armilla -ae *f*   bracelet
ar-rīdēre   smile at
ar-ripere   grasp, take hold of
ar-rogāre   claim
ars artis *f*   art, skill
artifex -icis *m*   craftsman, master, artist
articifium -ī *n*   skill, art, cunning
artus -a -um   close, tight, deep
arvum -ī *n*   (plowed) field
arx arcis *f*   hill-top, citadel
as assis *m*   as (copper coin)
a-scendere -disse   climb, go up, mount
a-scīscere -īvisse -ītum   admit, adopt
asinīnus -a -um   ass's
asinus -ī *m*   ass, donkey
asper -era -erum   rough, harsh, grievous
a-spergere -sisse -sum   sprinkle, scatter (on)
asperitās -ātis *f*   roughness, ruggedness
a-spicere   look at, look
assēnsus -ūs *m*   approval, assent
as-sentīre/-rī + *dat*   agree with, assent
as-sequī   attain to, achieve
as-serere -uisse -rtum   claim
as-sīdere   sit down
assiduitās -ātis *f*   perseverance
assiduus -a -um   constantly present
as-signāre   assign, allocate
as-sūmere   take, lay claim to
as-surgere   rise
astrologus -ī *m*   astronomer
astrum -ī *n*   star, constellation
asȳlum -ī *n*   refuge, asylum
at   but, yet, at least
āter -tra -trum   black, dark
āthlēta -ae *m*   athlete, prizefighter
atque/ac   and, as, than
atquī   but, and yet
ātrium -ī *n*   main room, hall, house

atrōx -ōcis *adi*   dreadful, atrocious
attat!   ah!
attentus -a -um   attentive
at-tenuāre   make thin, reduce
at-terere   wear (down), weaken
at-tinēre ad   concern, relate to
at-tingere -tigisse -tāctum   touch, reach, arrive at, adjoin
attonitus -a -um   stunned, stupefied
auctor -ōris *m*   originator, founder, advocate, guarantor
auctor esse   advise, advocate, relate
auctōritās -ātis *f*   authorization, authority
audācia -ae *f*   boldness, audacity
audāx -ācis *adi*   bold, audacious
audēre ausum esse   dare, venture
audīre   hear, listen
   dictō audiēns esse   obey
au-ferre abs-tulisse ab-lātum   carry off, take away
au-fugere   run away, escape
augēre -xisse -ctum   increase
augēscere   grow, increase
augur -is *m*   augur
augurium -ī *n*   augury, omen
augustus -a -um   venerable, majestic
Augustus -ī (mēnsis)   August
aula -ae *f*   palace
aura -ae *f*   breeze, wind
aurātus -a -um   gilded
aureus -a -um   gold-, *m* gold piece
aurīga -ae *m*   charioteer, driver
auris -is *f*   ear
aurōra -ae *f*   dawn
aurum -ī *n*   gold
auspicārī   take the auspices

auspicium -ī *n*   omen taken from birds
Auster -trī *m*   south wind
austrālis -e   southern
aut or
   aut…aut   either…or
autem but, however
autumnus -ī *m*   autumn
auxilium -ī *n*   help, assistance
auxilia -ōrum *n pl*   auxiliary forces
avāritia -ae *f*   greed, avarice
avārus -a -um   greedy, avaricious
ā-vehere   carry off; *pass* go away
ā-vellere -lisse -vulsum   tear away
avēre   be eager, desire, long
āversus -a -um   having the back turned
ā-vertere   turn aside, divert, avert
avidus -a -um (+ *gen*)   greedy, eager
avis -is *f*   bird
avītus -a -um   of his grandfather
ā-volāre   fly off, rush off
avunculus -ī *m*   (maternal) uncle
avus -ī *m*   grandfather

B

baculum -ī *n*   stick
bālāre   bleat
balneae -ārum *f pl*   public baths
balneum -ī *n*   bath, bathroom
barba -ae *f*   beard
barbarus -a -um   foreign, barbarian
basilica -ae *f*   basilica
bāsium -ī *n*   kiss
beātus -a -um   happy
bellāre   wage war, fight
bellātor -ōris *m*   warrior
bellicōsus -a -um   warlike
bellicus -a -um   of war, military
bellum -ī *n*   war
bellus -a -um   lovely, pretty

bēlua -ae *f*   beast, wild animal
bene well
beneficium -ī *n*   benefit, favor
benignus -a -um   kind, benevolent
bēstia -ae *f*   beast, animal
bēstiola -ae *f*   small animal, insect
bibere -bisse   drink
bibliothēca -ae *f*   library
bīduum -ī *n*   two days
biennium -ī *n*   two years
bīnī -ae -a   two (each)
bis twice
blandīrī   coax, urge
blandus -a -um   charming, ingratiating
boārius -a -um   cattle-
bonum -ī *n*   good, blessing
bonus -a -um   good
bōs bovis *m/f*   ox
bracchium -ī *n*   arm
brevī *adv*   soon
breviārium -ī *n*   summary
brevis -e   short
brūtus -a -um   brutish

C

cachinnus -ī *m*   laugh, guffaw
cadere cecidisse   fall
cadūcus -a -um   ready to fall, perishable
caecus -a -um   blind
caedere cecīdisse caesum   beat, fell, kill
caedēs -is *f*   killing, slaughter, blood
caelestis -e   celestial, *m pl* gods
caelitēs -um *m pl*   gods
caelum -ī *n*   sky, heaven
caerimōnia -ae *f*   rite, ceremony
calamitās -ātis *f*   misfortune, calamity
calamus -ī *m*   reed, pen
calcar -āris *m*   spur
calceus -ī *m*   shoe
calida -ae *f*   hot water
calidus -a -um   warm, hot
callidus -a -um   clever, cunning

callis -is *f*   track, path
calor -ōris *m*   warmth, heat
campus -ī *m*   plain
cancer -crī *m*   crab, Cancer
candēlābrum -ī *n*   candelabrum
candidus -a -um   white, bright
candor -ōris *m*   whiteness, brightness
canere cecinisse   sing, crow, play, sound, sing of, prophesy
canis -is *m/f*   dog
cantāre   sing, sing of
cantus -ūs *m*   singing, music
capere -iō cēpisse captum   take, catch, capture, get, hold
capillus -ī *m*   hair
capitulum -ī *n*   chapter
capra -ae *f*   goat
captīvus -ī *m*   prisoner-of-war
caput -itis *n*   head, chief, capital, person, life, death penalty
carcer -eris *m*   prison
cardō -inis *m*   door pivot, hinge
carēre + *abl*   be without, lack
carīna -ae *f*   keel, ship
cāritās -ātis *f*   high price, love, esteem
carmen -inis *n*   song, poem
carō carnis *f*   flesh, meat
carpentum -ī *n*   two-wheeled carriage
carpere -psisse -ptum   gather, pick, crop
cārus -a -um   dear
casa -ae *f*   cottage, hut
castellum -ī *n*   fort, stronghold
castīgāre   correct, reprove
castīgātor -ōris *m*   one who reproves
castitās -ātis *f*   chastity
castra -ōrum *n pl*   camp
castus -a -um   chaste
cāsus -ūs *m*   fall, chance, accident
catēna -ae *f*   chain

caterva -ae *f* band, troop, crowd
cauda -ae *f* tail
caudex -icis *m* trunk, blockhead
causa -ae *f* cause, reason, case
  gen (/meā) + causā for the sake of
causālis -e causal
cautus -a -um cautious
cavea -ae *f* cage, coop
cavēre cāvisse cautum beware (of)
cavus -a -um hollow
cēdere cessisse go, withdraw
cēlāre conceal (from)
celeber -bris -bre crowded, well-known
celebrāre celebrate, extol
celebrātus -a -um celebrated
celebritās -ātis *f* crowding, reputation
celer -eris -ere swift, quick
celeritās -ātis *f* speed, swiftness
cella -ae *f* temple chamber, chapel
celsus -a -um tall
cēna -ae *f* dinner
cēnāre dine, have dinner
cēnsēre -uisse -sum think, decide, assess
cēnsor -ōris *m* censor (magistrate)
cēnsūra -ae *f* censorship
cēnsus -ūs *m* assessment, registration
centēsimus -a -um hundredth
centum a hundred
centuria -ae *f* century (unit of 100)
centuriātus -a -um voting in centuries
centuriātus -ūs *m* office of centurion
centuriō -ōnis *m* centurion (officer)
cēra -ae *f* wax
cerebrum -ī *n* brain
cernere crēvisse crētum discern, perceive

certāmen -inis *n* contest, fight
certāre contend, fight
certē certainly, at any rate
certō *adv* for certain
certus -a -um certain, sure
  certiōrem facere inform
  certum mihi est my mind is made up
cervus -ī *m* stag, deer
cessāre leave off, cease
cēterī -ae -a the other(s), the rest
cēterum *adv* besides, however
cēterus -a -um remaining
charta -ae *f* paper
chronicī -ōrum (librī) annals
cibus -ī *m* food
cicātrīx -īcis *f* scar
ciēre cīvisse citum set in motion, move
cingere -nxisse -nctum surround
cingulus -ī *m* belt
cinis -eris *m* ashes
-cipere -iō-cēpisse -ceptum
circā *prp* + *acc, adv* round, round about
circēnsēs -ium *m pl* games in the circus
circēnsis -e of the circus
circiter about
circu-īre -eō -iisse -itum go round, outflank
circuitus -ūs *m* rotation, circumference
circum *prp* + *acc, adv* round, round about
circum-agere cause to turn round
circum-dare surround, put round
circum-dūcere lead round
circum-fundere pour/spread round
circum-īre -eō -iisse -itum go round/about, outflank
circum-sedēre besiege
circum-silīre -uisse hop about
circum-sistere -stitisse surround
circum-stāre stand round, surround

circum-vāllāre beset, surround
circum-vehī go round, travel round
circum-venīre surround
circus -ī *m* circle, orbit, circus
cis *prp* + *acc* on this side of
citātus -a -um speeded up, swift
citerior -ius *comp* nearer
citimus -a -um *sup* nearest
citō *adv, comp* citius quickly
citrā *prp* + *acc* on this side of
citrō: ultrō citrōque to and fro, on both sides
cīvīlis -e civic, civil
cīvis -is *m/f* citizen, countryman
cīvitās -ātis *f* state, city, citizenship
clādēs -is *f* disaster, defeat
clam secretly
clāmāre shout
clāmitāre shout loudly
clāmor -ōris *m* shout, shouting
clandestīnus -a -um secret, clandestine
clāritūdō -inis *f* fame, renown
clārus -a -um bright, clear, loud, famous
classiāriī -ōrum *m pl* marines
classis -is *f* fleet, class (of citizens)
claudere -sisse -sum shut, close, enclose
claudus -a -um lame
clāva -ae *f* club, cudgel
clāvis -is *f* key
clēmēns -entis *adi* mild, lenient
clēmentia -ae *f* clemency, mercy
clībanārius -ī *m* cuirassier
clipeus -ī *m* round shield
clīvus -ī *m* slope, sloping street
cloāca -ae *f* sewer
co-alēscere -aluisse grow together, coalesce

cocus -ī *m* cook
coep- coept- *v.* incipere
coepta -ōrum *n pl* undertaking, enterprise
co-ercēre keep in control, restrain
coetus -ūs *m* gathering, society
cōgere co-ēgisse -āctum compel, force, summon
cōgitāre think
cōgitātiō -ōnis *f* thought, reflection
cognātus -a -um related
cognitiō -ōnis *f* getting to know, study
cognōmen -inis *n* surname
cognōmentum -ī *n* surname
cognōscere -ōvisse -itum get to know, recognize
co-horrēscere -ruisse shudder
cohors -rtis *f* cohort, bodyguard
cohortārī exhort
cohortātiō -ōnis *f* exhortation
co-īre -eō -iisse -itum come together, gather
colere -uisse cultum cultivate, foster, devote oneself to, worship
col-lābī fall down, collapse
col-lacrimāre burst into tears
col-laudāre commend, praise
collēctiō -ōnis *f* collecting, gathering
collēga -ae *m* colleague
col-ligāre tie up, bind
col-ligere -lēgisse -lēctum gather, collect
collis -is *m* hill
col-locāre place
col-loquī talk, converse
colloquium -ī *n* conversation, parley
col-lūcēre shine
collum -ī *n* neck
colōnia -ae *f* settlement, colony
colōnus -ī *m* (tenant-) farmer, settler
color -ōris *m* color

colossus -ī *m* large statue, colossus
columba -ae *f* pigeon, dove
columna -ae *f* column
coma -ae *f* hair
comes -itis *m* companion
cōmicus -a -um of comedy, comic
cōmis -e kind
comitārī accompany
comitātus -ūs *m* escort, retinue
comitia -ōrum *n pl* assembly of the people
commeātus -ūs *m* supplies, provisions
com-memorāre mention
com-mendāre entrust, commit
commendātiō -ōnis *f* recommendation, praise
commentārī think about, practice
commentārius -ī *m* notebook, record
com-migrāre move, go and live
com-mittere engage (in battle), entrust, expose (to)
commodum -ī *n* advantage, interest
com-morārī stay, linger
commōtus -a -um excited, passionate
com-movēre move, excite, cause
commūnicāre share
commūniō -ōnis *f* partnership, sharing
com-mūnīre fortify
commūnis -e common
com-mūtāre change (completely)
commūtātiō -ōnis *f* change
cōmoedia -ae *f* comedy
com-parāre (1) prepare, provide
com-parāre (2) compare
comparātiō -ōnis *f* (1) preparation, provision
comparātiō -ōnis *f* (2) comparison
com-pārēre appear
com-pellere drive, force

com-perīre -risse -rtum find out, learn, discover
com-plectī -plexum hug, embrace, surround, include
com-plēre -ēvisse -ētum fill, complete
complexus -ūs *m* embrace
com-plōrāre lament, bewail
complōrātiō -ōnis *f* lamentation
com-plūrēs -a several
com-pōnere settle, arrange, compose
compos -otis + *gen* in possession of
compositum: ex c.ō by prearrangement
compositus -a -um wellordered, compound
com-prehendere seize, include
com-primere -pressisse -pressum compress, crush, suppress, rape
com-probāre approve, confirm
com-putāre calculate, reckon
cōnārī attempt, try
con-cēdere go (away), yield, give up, concede, allow
concentus -ūs *m* harmony
con-certāre fight
con-cidere -disse fall (down), collapse
con-cīdere -disse -sum kill, beat
con-ciēre -cīvisse -citum stir up, excite
conciliāre win over
concilium -ī *n* assembly, league
con-cipere receive, catch, conceive
con-citāre stir up, incite
concitātus -a -um fast, rapid
con-clāmāre shout, cry out
concordia -a *f* concord
concors -rdis *adi* harmonious, concordant
concubīna -ae *f* concubine

con-cumbere -cubuisse sleep (with)

con-cupīscere -īvisse desire, covet

con-currere -rrisse -rsum hurry together, clash

concursus -ūs *m* concourse, encounter

con-cutere -iō-ssisse -ssum shake

con-demnāre condemn

con-dere -didisse -ditum put, hide, found, close

condiciō -ōnis *f* condition

conditor -ōris *m* founder

cō-nectere join together

cōn-ferre con-tulisse col-lātum bring (together), carry, confer, compare, apply
sē cōnferre betake oneself, go
arma/signa cōnferre join battle, fight

cōnfertus -a -um dense, compact

cōnfessiō -ōnis *f* admission, confession

cōnfestim at once, immediately

cōn-ficere make, accomplish, exhaust, subdue, kill

cōn-fīdentia ae *f* self-confidence

cōn-fīdere (+ *dat*) trust, be sure

cōnfīnis -e adjacent, neighboring

cōn-firmāre assure, encourage

cōn-fitērī -fessum confess

cōn-flagrāre be burnt

cōnflīctāre harass, distress

cōn-flīgere -xisse -ctum clash, fight

cōn-fluentēs -ium *m pl* confluence

cōn-fluere flow together, meet

cōn-fugere flee for refuge

cōn-fundere mingle, upset, confuse

cōnfūsiō -ōnis *f* disorder, confusion

con-gerere bring together, collect

con-gredī -ior -gressum meet, join battle, fight

con-gregāre bring together, gather

con-icere throw, put

coniectūra -ae *f* inferring, conjecture

con-iugium -ī *n* marriage

con-iūnctiō -ōnis *f* union, conjunction

coniūnctus -a -um connected, associated

con-iungere join, connect

coniūnx -iugis *m/f* consort, wife

con-iūrāre swear together, conspire
coniūrātus -a -um sworn, joined by an oath

con-iūrātī -ōrum *m pl* the conspirators

con-iūrātiō -ōnis *f* conspiracy, plot

con-quiēscere rest

con-quīrere -sīvisse -sītum search out, investigate

cōn-salūtāre greet, hail

cōn-scendere -disse mount, board

cōn-scīscere -īvisse -ītum decree, inflict (on)

cōnscius -a -um (+ *gen*) privy (to), accomplice

cōn-scrībere enrol, compose, write

cōnscrīptī: patrēs c. senators

cōn-secrāre consecrate, deify

cōn-senēscere -nuisse grow old

cōnsēnsus -ūs *m* concord, agreement

cōn-sentīre agree (on)

cōn-sequī follow, overtake, achieve

cōn-serere -uisse -rtum join
manum cōnserere join battle

cōn-servāre preserve, maintain

cōnservātor -ōris *m* savior, guardian

cōn-sīderāre observe, reflect

cōnsīderātiō -ōnis *f* observation, reflection

cōn-sīdere -sēdisse sit down, settle

cōnsilium -ī *n* advice, decision, council, intention, plan, sense

cōn-sistere -stitisse stop, halt

cōn-sociāre associate, share

cōn-sōlārī comfort, console

cōnsonāns -antis *f* consonant

cōnspectus -a -um conspicuous, remarkable

cōnspectus -ūs *m* sight, view, survey

cōn-spicere catch sight of, see

cōnspicuus -a -um conspicuous, spectacular

cōnspīrātiō -ōnis *f* agreement, conspiracy

cōnstāns -antis *adi* steady, firm

cōnstantia -ae *f* steadyness, persistence

cōn-stāre -stitisse stand firm, remain, cost
cōnstāre ex consist of
cōnstat it is a fact, is is known

cōn-stituere -uisse -ūtum establish, erect, set up, fix, decide

cōnstitūtiō -ōnis *f* organization

cōn-suētūdō -inis *f* custom, habit

cōn-suēscere - ēvisse get used/accustomed to

cōn-suēvisse *perf* be accustomed

cōnsul -is *m* (cōs.) consul

cōnsulāris -e consular, *m* ex-consul

cōnsulātus -ūs *m* consulate

cōn-sulere -uisse -ltum consult, take counsel
cōnsulere + *dat* look after, take care of

cōnsultāre deliberate, debate

cōnsultō *adv* deliberately

cōnsultor -ōris *m* adviser, counselor

cōnsultum -ī *n* resolution

cōn-sūmere use up, spend, exhaust

cōn-surgere stand up, rise

con-temnere -mpsisse -mptum despise, scorn

con-templārī look at, observe

contemptus -a -um despicable

con-tendere -disse -tum strain, exert (oneself), hasten, contend

contentiō -ōnis *f* tension, exertion, contest, comparison

contentus -a -um content

con-ticēscere -ticuisse fall silent

continēns -entis *adi* unbroken, adjacent

continēns -entis *f* (terra) continent

continentia -ae *f* restraint, self-control

con-tinēre -uisse -tentum keep, retain, contain

con-tingere -tigisse touch, be close to, (+ *dat*) -tāctum be granted to, happen

continuāre continue, prolong

continuō *adv* immediately

continuus -a -um continuous, successive

cōntiō -ōnis *f* meeting, assembly

cōntiōnārī address a meeting

contrā *prp* + *acc, adv* against, facing, on the other side, in return

contrā-dīcere speak against, oppose

con-trahere contract, wrinkle

contrārius -a -um opposite, contrary

con-tremēscere -muisse tremble, quake

con-tuērī look at, contemplate

contumēlia -ae *f* insult, affront

contumēliōsus -a -um insulting, outrageous

con-turbāre mix up, confound

cōnūbium -ī *n* marriage, intermarriage

con-valēscere -luisse grow strong, recover

convallis -is *f* valley

con-vehere carry, gather

con-venīre come together, meet, be agreed, be settled convenīre (ad/+ *dat*) fit, be fitting

conventus -ūs *m* meeting

conversiō -ōnis *f* rotation, revolution

con-vertere turn, change

con-vincere find guilty, convict

convīva -ae *m/f* guest

convīvium -ī *n* dinner-party

con-vocāre call together

co-optāre choose (as colleague)

co-orīrī break out, arise

cōpia -ae *f* abundance, means, control, *pl* resources, troops

cōpulāre join, connect

cōpulātīvus -a -um copulative

coquere -xisse -ctum cook

cor cordis *n* heart cordī esse + *dat* be dear/pleasing

cōram *prp* + *abl, adv* before, in person

cornicen -inis *m* horn-blower, bugler

cornū -ūs *n* horn, wing (of army)

corōna -ae *f* wreath

corpus -oris *n* body

cor-rigere -rēxisse -rēctum correct

cor-ripere seize, rebuke

sē corripere start up, hurry off

cor-rumpere spoil, corrupt, bribe

corvus -ī *m* raven

cotīdiē every day

crās tomorrow

crassus -a -um thick, fat

crātis -is *f* hurdle (of wickerwork)

creāre create, appoint

crēber -bra -brum frequent, numerous

crēdere -didisse -ditum believe, trust, entrust

cremāre burn, cremate

crēscere -ēvisse grow, increase

crīmen -inis *n* charge, accusation

crīminārī accuse

crīnis -is *m* hair

cruciāre torture, torment

cruciātus -ūs *m* torture

crūdēlis -e cruel

crūdēlitās -ātis *f* cruelty

cruentus -a -um blood-stained, bloody

cruor -ōris *m* blood

crūs -ūris *n* leg

crux -ucis *f* cross

cubāre -uisse -itum lie (in bed)

cubiculum -ī *n* bedroom

cubīle -is *n* bed, couch

culīna -ae *f* kitchen

culmen -inis *n* summit, top, peak, roof

culpa -ae *f* blame, fault, guilt

culter -trī *m* knife

cultūra -a *f* cultivation

cultus -ūs *m* cultivation, care, mode of life, worship

cum *prp* + *abl* with

cum *coniūnctiō* when, as cum prīmum + *perf* as soon as cum…tum… not only… but also

cūnābula -ōrum *n pl* cradle

cūnae -ārum *f pl* cradle

cūnctārī hesitate

cūnctātor -ōris *m*   one who hesitates
cūnctus -a -um   whole, *pl* all
cuneus -ī *m*   wedge
cupere -iō -īvisse   desire
cupiditās -ātis *f*   desire
cupīdō -inis *f*   desire, passion
cupidus -a -um (+ *gen*)   desirous (of), eager (for)
cūr   why
cūra -ae *f*   care, anxiety, concern
    cūrae esse + *dat*   be of concern
cūrāre   care for, look after, take care, undertake
    cūrāre + *acc., ger.* undertake
cūria -ae *f*   curia (division of the people, Senate-house)
currere cucurrisse   run
currus -ūs *m*   chariot
cursus -ūs *m*   running, race, journey, course, orbit, career
curvus -a -um   curved, crooked, bent
cūstōdia -ae *f*   guard, custody, post
cūstōdīre   guard
cūstōs -ōdis *m*   guardian, guard

D

dactylus -ī *m*   dactyl (—∪∪)
damnāre   condemn, sentence
damnum -ī *n*   loss
dapēs -um *f pl*   feast, meal, food
dare dedisse datum   give
    sē dare   give oneself up (to)
dē *prp* + *abl*   (down) from, of, about, for, after
dea -ae *f, pl dat/abl* -ābus   goddess
dē-bellāre   finish the war, subdue
dēbēre   owe, be obliged
dēbilis -e   weak

dēbilitāre   weaken
dē-cēdere   go away, depart, die
decem   ten
December -bris (mēnsis)   December
decem-virī -ōrum *m pl*   commission of ten
decēre   be fitting, become
dē-cernere   decide, settle, fight
deciēs   ten times
decimus -a -um   tenth
dē-cipere   deceive
dē-clām(it)āre   make practice speeches
dē-clārāre   show, declare, express
dēclīnāre   decline, inflect
decor -ōris *m*   beauty, grace
decorāre   adorn, glorify
decōrus -a -um   handsome
dēcrētum -ī *n*   resolution, decree
decuma -ae *f*   tithe
dē-currere -rrisse -rsum   run down
decus -oris *n*   honor, ornament
dē-cutere -iō -cussisse -cussum   knock off
dē-decus -oris *n*   disgrace, dishonor
dē-dere -didisse -ditum   give up, devote
dē-dicāre   dedicate
dēditiō -ōnis *f*   surrender, capitulation
dē-dūcere   lead/bring down, launch
de-esse dē-fuisse (+ *dat*)   be missing, fail
dē-fendere -disse -ēnsum   defend, maintain
dēfēnsāre   defend
dēfēnsor -ōris *m*   defender
dē-ferre   carry, bring, report, confer, denounce
dē-fervēscere   calm down
dēfessus -a -um   worn out, tired
dē-ficere   fail, sink, wane, defect
dē-fīgere   fix, thrust, paralyse

dē-fīnīre   delimit
dē-flēre   weep for
dē-fōrmis -e   ugly
dēfōrmitās -ātis *f*   ugliness
dē-fugere   escape, avoid
dē-fungī   finish, have done, die
de-hinc   next, then
dē-icere   throw/bring down
dein   afterward, then
deinceps   in succession, next
de-inde/dein   afterward, then
dē-iūrāre   swear
dē-lābī   slip down, descend
dēlectāre   delight, please
dēlectātiō -ōnis *m*   delight, pleasure
dēlēre -ēvisse -ētum   delete, efface, destroy
dē-līberāre   deliberate
dē-līberātiō -ōnis *f*   deliberation
dēliciae -ārum *f pl*   delight, pet
dēlictum -ī *n*   misdeed, offense
dē-ligāre   tie up, fasten
dē-ligere -lēgisse -lēctum   pick out, choose
dē-linquere   misbehave, do wrong
dēlīrāre   be mad
dē-litēscere -tuisse   hide oneself
delphīnus -ī *m*   dolphin
dēlūbrum -ī *n*   temple, shrine
dē-mandāre   entrust, hand over
dē-mēns -entis   out of one's mind, mad
dēmere -mpsisse -mptum   remove
dē-mergere   sink, plunge
dē-mittere   let fall, drop, lower
dē-mōnstrāre   point out, show
dēmum *adv*   at last, only
dēnārius -ī *m*   denarius (silver coin)
dēnī -ae -a   ten (each)
dēnique   finally, at last

dēns dentis *m* tooth
dēnsus -a -um thick, dense
dē-nūntiāre announce, order
dē-nuō anew, again
deorsum *adv* down
dē-pellere drive down/off, avert
dē-pōnere put/lay down, deposit
dē-populārī sack, plunder
dē-populātiō -ōnis *f* plundering
dē-portāre convey, bring back
dē-poscere demand
dē-prāvāre pervert
dē-precārī beg, entreat
dē-precātiō -ōnis *f* entreaty, plea
dē-prehendere/-prēndere seize, come on, surprise
dē-primere -essisse -essum press down, sink
dē-prōmere take out
dēpulsiō -ōnis *f* rebuttal
dē-relinquere leave behind
dē-rīdēre laugh at, make fun of
dē-scendere -disse go down, descend
dē-scīscere -īvisse -ītum defect
dē-scrībere draw, describe
dē-serere -uisse -rtum leave, desert
dēsertus -a -um deserted
dēsīderāre long for, miss
dēsīderium -ī *n* desire, longing
dē-signāre mark out
dēsignātus -a -um appointed, designate
dē-silīre -uisse jump down
dē-sinere -siisse -situm finish, stop, end
dē-sipere -iō be out of one's mind
dē-sistere -stitisse leave off, cease
dē-spērāre lose hope, despair (of)
dēspērātiō -ōnis *f* despair
dē-spicere look down (on), despise

dē-spondēre -disse -sum betroth, engage
dēstināre designate, destine
dē-struere demolish
dē-tegere disclose
dē-tergēre wipe off
dēterior -ius *comp* worse
dē-terrēre deter
dēterrimus -a -um *sup* worst
dē-trahere pull off
dētrīmentum -ī *n* harm, loss
de-ūrere burn
deus -ī *m, pl* deī/diī/dī god
dē-vehere carry, convey
dē-venīre come, arrive
dē-vincere defeat completely
dē-vincīre bind
dē-vocāre call away, divert
dē-vorāre swallow up, devour
dexter -t(e)ra -t(e)rum right; *f* right hand, the right
dicāre dedicate
dīcere -xisse dictum say, call, speak
diciō -ōnis *f* dominion, power
dictāre dictate
dictātor -ōris *m* dictator
dictātūra -ae *f* dictatorship
dictitāre keep saying
dictum -ī *n* saying, words
dictō audiēns esse obey
diēs -ēī *m (f)* day, date
in diēs daily
dif-ferre dis-tulisse dīlātum postpone, defer, differ
dif-ficilis -e, *sup* -illimus difficult, hard
difficultās -ātis *f* difficulty
difficulter *adv* with difficulty
dif-fidere + *dat* distrust, despair of
dif-fluere overflow
digitus -ī *m* finger
dignitās -ātis *f* worthiness, dignity, rank
dignus -a -um worthy
dī-gredī -ior -gressum go away, depart

dī-lābī fall apart, perish
dī-lacerāre tear to pieces
dī-lātāre spread, expand
dīlēctus -a -um beloved, dear
dīlēctus -ūs *m* recruitment
dīligēns -entis *adi* careful, diligent
dīligentia -ae *f* carefulness
dīligere -ēxisse -ēctum love, be fond of
dī-lūcēscere -lūxisse dawn, become light
dī-micāre fight
dīmicātiō -ōnis *f* fight
dīmidium -ī *n* half
dīmidius -a -um half
dī-mittere send away, dismiss
diphthongus -ī *f* diphthong
dī-rigere -rēxisse -rēctum arrange, direct
dir-imere -ēmisse -ēmptum divide, interrupt
dī-ripere plunder, loot, rob
dī-ruere demolish
dīrus -a -um dreadful
dis-cēdere go away, depart
dis-ceptāre debate, discuss
discere didicisse learn
dis-cernere distinguish
discessus -ūs *m* departure
disciplīna -ae *f* instruction, discipline
discipulus -ī *m* pupil, disciple
discordia -ae *f* disagreement, discord
di-scrībere divide up, distribute
discrīmen -inis *n* distinction, grave danger
discrīptiō -ōnis *f* distribution
dis-cumbere -cubuisse take one's place at table
dis-currere -rrisse -rsum run in several directions
disertus -a -um eloquent
dis-icere scatter, break up
disiūnctīvus -a -um separative, disjunctive
dis-iūnctus -a -um distant
dis-iungere separate

dis-pālārī wander about
dis-pār -paris *adi* unequal, different
dis-pellere drive apart
di-spergere -sisse -sum scatter, disperse
dis-plicēre + *dat* displease, offend
dis-pōnere arrange, station
dis-putāre argue, discuss
disputātiō -ōnis *f* argument, discussion
dissēnsiō -ōnis *f* disagreement
dis-sentīre disagree
dis-serere -uisse -rtum discuss
dis-sidēre -sēdisse disagree, differ
dis-similis -e unlike, different
dis-simulāre conceal
dis-sipāre scatter, spread
dis-suādēre advise not to
di-stāre be distant
di-stinguere -stīnxisse -stīnctum distinguish, mark, characterize
dis-trahere pull apart, break up
dis-tribuere divide, distribute, share
districtus -a -um busy
dītāre enrich
diū, *comp* diūtius, *sup* diūtissimē long
diurnus -a -um of the day, daily
diūtinus -a -um long, prolonged
diūturnitās -ātis *f* long duration
diūturnus -a -um long, prolonged
dīversus -a -um opposite, different
dīves -itis/dīs dītis *adi* rich, wealthy
dīvidere -īsisse -īsum separate, divide, share
dīvīnitus *adv* by divine will
dīvīnus -a -um divine
dīvīsiō -ōnis *f* division
dīvitiae -ārum *f pl* riches
dīvortium -ī *n* divorce

dī-vulgāre make public, divulge
dīvum -ī *n* the open sky
dīvus -a -um divine, *m* god
docēre -uisse doctum teach, instruct, produce
doctor -ōris *m* teacher
doctrīna -ae *f* teaching, instruction
doctus -a -um learned, skilled
documentum -ī *n* example, proof
dolēre hurt, feel pain, grieve
dolor -ōris *m* pain, grief
dolus -ī *m* guile, deceit, cunning
domāre -uisse -itum tame, subdue
domesticus -a -um domestic, household-
domī *loc* at home
domicilium -ī *n* dwelling, residence
domina -ae *f* mistress
dominārī be master, rule
dominātiō -ōnis *f* dominion, power
dominātus -ūs *m* dominion, power
dominus -ī *m* master
domum *adv* home
domus -ūs *f, abl* -ō house, home
dōnāre give, present with
dōnec as long as, until
dōnum -ī *n* gift, present, reward
dormīre sleep
dorsum -ī *n* back, ridge
dubitāre doubt, be in doubt
  dubitāre + *īnf* hesitate
dubius -a -um undecided, doubtful
  n: sine/procul dubiō without doubt, certainly
du-centēsimus -a -um two hundredth
du-centī -ae -a two hundred
dūcere -xisse ductum lead, guide, draw, trace, construct, consider
  uxōrem dūcere marry

ductor -ōris *m* leader
ductus -ūs *m* leadership, command
  aquae ductus aqueduct
dūdum *adv* a little while ago
duellum -ī *n* war
dulcis -e sweet
dum while, as long as, till, provided that, if only
dum-modo provided that, if only
dumtaxat only, just
duo -ae -o two
duo-decim twelve
duo-decimus -a -um twelfth
duo-dē-trīgintā twenty-eight
duo-dē-vīgintī eighteen
duplex -icis *adi* double
duplicāre double
dūrāre harden, hold out, last
dūrus -a -um hard
duum-virī -ōrum *m pl* board of two men
dux ducis *m* leader, chief, general

E

ē *v.* ex/ē
eā *adv* that way, there
ēbrius -a -um drunk
ecce see, look, here is
ecquid …? if, whether
ec-quis/quī (if) any(one)?
edepol by Pollux!
ē-dere -didisse -ditum emit, bring forth, make known, publish, do
ē-dīcere decree, fix
ē-disserere set forth, expound
ēducāre bring up
ē-dūcere lead out, draw out
ef-ferre ex-tulisse ē-lātum carry/bring out, lift, elate
  sē efferre exult
ef-ficere make, effect, cause
effigiēs -ēī *f* likeness, portrait
ef-fringere -ēgisse -āctum break open

ef-fugere   escape, run away, avoid
ef-fulgēre   shine forth
ef-fundere   shed, overflow, loosen
effūsus -a -um   disorderly, headlong
egēns -entis   poor, needy
egēre + *abl*   need
ego mē mihi/mī (*gen* meī) I, me, myself
ego-met   I (myself)
ē-gredī -ior -gressum   go out, go beyond
ēgregius -a -um   outstanding, excellent
ēgressus -ūs *m*   going out
eia   ah! hey!
ē-icere   throw out
    sē ēicere   rush out
ē-lābī   slip out, escape
ē-labōrāre   work out, prepare
ēlēctus -a -um   selected, picked
ēlegāns -antis *adi*   refined, skilful
elephantus -ī *m*   elephant
ē-līdere -sisse -sum   omit, elide
ē-ligere -lēgisse -lēctum   choose, select
ēloquēns -entis *adi*   eloquent
ēloquentia -ae *f*   eloquence
ē-loquī   express, tell
ē-lūcēre   shine forth
ē-lūcubrāre   prepare by lamplight
ē-lūdere   deceive, mock
ēluviō -ōnis *f*   flood, inundation
emere ēmisse ēmptum   buy
ē-mergere   come out, emerge
ē-minēre   stick out, project
ē-mittere   send out, emit, utter
ēmptor -ōris *m*   buyer
ē-mūnīre   fortify
ēn   look, here is
ē-nervāre   weaken, enervate
enim   for
enim-vērō   truly, certainly

ē-nītī -nīsum   strive, exert oneself
ēnsis -is *m*   sword
ē-numerāre   count up, enumerate
eō *adv*   to that place, there
eō *abl* + *comp*   so much
eōdem *adv*   to the same place
epigramma -atis *n*   epigram
epistula -ae *f*   letter
epulae -ārum *f*   meal, feast
epulārī   dine, feast
eques -itis *m*   horseman, knight
equester -tris -tre   cavalry-, equestrian
equidem   indeed, for my part
equitāre   ride on horseback
equitātus -ūs *m*   cavalry
equus -ī *m*   horse
ergā *prp* + *acc*   toward
ergō   therefore, so
ē-rigere -rēxisse -rēctum   lift, erect, cheer
ē-ripere -iō -uisse -reptum   snatch away, deprive of
errāre   wander, stray
error -ōris *m*   wandering, error
ē-rubēscere -buisse   blush
ē-rudīre   instruct, educate
ērudītus -a -um   well-instructed, learned
ē-ruere -ruisse -rutum   unearth, clear up
ē-rumpere   break out
ēruptiō -ōnis *f*   sally, sortie
erus -ī *m*   master
ē-scendere -disse   ascend, go up
esse sum fuisse futūrum esse/fore   be
ēsse edō ēdisse ēsum   eat
et   and, also
    et...et   both...and
et-enim   and indeed, for
etiam   also, even, yet
    etiam atque etiam   again and again
etiam-nunc   still
et-sī   even if, although
euax!   bravo!
Eurus -ī *m*   south-east wind

ē-vādere -sisse -sum   get out, escape, pass, turn out
ē-vānēscere -nuisse   vanish, disappear
ē-vehere   carry out, *pass* ride out
ē-venīre   happen, fall by lot
ēventus -ūs *m*   outcome, result
ē-vertere   overturn, overthrow
ē-vincere   persuade, bring about
ē-vocāre   call out, summon
ē-volāre   fly out
ē-volvere   unroll
ex/ē *prp* + *abl*   out of, from, of, since, after, according to
ex-aequāre   make equal
ex-agitāre   stir, worry, harass
ex-animāre   kill, *pass* die
ex-ārdēscere -ārsisse   flare up
ex-audīre   hear
ex-cēdere   go away, depart
excellēns -entis *adi*   outstanding
ex-cellere   be outstanding, excel
excelsus -a -um   lofty, high
ex-cerpere -psisse -ptum   pick out
excessus -ūs *m*   departure, death
ex-cidere -disse   fall out, be dropped
ex-cīdere -disse -sum   destroy
excidium -ī *n*   destruction
ex-cipere   receive, catch
ex-cīre -cīvisse   call out, summon
ex-citāre   wake up, arouse
excitātus -a -um   loud, shrill
ex-clāmāre   cry out, exclaim
ex-clūdere -sisse -sum   shut out, cut off
ex-cōgitāre   think out, devise
ex-cruciāre   torture, torment

ex-currere -rrisse -rsum run out, rush out

excursiō -ōnis *f* sortie, sally

ex-cūsāre excuse

exemplar -āris *n* pattern, model

exemplum -ī *n* example, model

ex-ercēre exercise, practice, worry

exercitāre train, exercise

exercitātiō -ōnis *f* exercise, practice

exercitātus -a -um practiced, proficient

exercitus -ūs *m* army

ex-haurīre drain, empty, exhaust, endure

ex-igere -ēgisse -āctum drive out, exact, require, pass

exiguus -a -um small, scanty

ex-imere -ēmisse -ēmptum take away, remove

eximius -a -um choice, outstanding

ex-īre -eō -iisse -itum go out

ex-īstimāre consider, think

exitus -ūs *m* exit, way out, end

ex-onerāre unburden

exōrdium -ī *n* beginning

ex-orīrī rise, arise

ex-ōrnāre adorn, decorate

exōrsus -ūs *m* beginning

ex-pavēscere -pāvisse become frightened (at)

ex-pedīre make ready, extricate, explain

expedītiō -ōnis *f* foray, raid, expedition

expedītus -a -um ready for action

ex-pellere dive out, expel

ex-pergīscī -perrēctum wake up

ex-perīrī -pertum try, experience

ex-pers -rtis *adi + gen* having no share in

ex-petere request, demand, desire

ex-plānāre explain

ex-plēre -ēvisse -ētum fill, complete, satisfy

explētīvus -a -um expletive

ex-plicāre -uisse -itum extricate, unfold, explain

ex-plōrāre reconnoitre, investigate

explōrātor -ōris *m* scout, spy

ex-pōnere put out, put ashore, expose

ex-portāre export

ex-poscere ask for, demand

ex-pugnāre conquer

ex-pugnātiō -ōnis *f* conquest

ex-quīrere -sīvisse -sītum ask about, examine

exquīsītus -a -um studied, meticulous

ex-sanguis -e bloodless, lifeless

ex-scindere demolish, destroy

exsecrandus -a -um accursed

ex-secrārī curse

ex-sequī pursue, go on, execute

exsequiae -ae *f pl* funeral

ex-silīre -uisse jump up

exsilium -ī *n* exile

ex-sistere -stitisse appear, arise

ex-solvere set free, release

ex-spectāre wait (for), expect

exspectātiō -ōnis *f* exspectation

ex-spīrāre breathe one's last, die

ex-stimulāre stir up, incite

ex-stinguere -stīnxisse -stīnctum extinguish, put out, kill, annihilate

ex-struere erect, build

exsul -is *m/f* banished person, exile

exsulāre live in exile

ex-sultāre rejoice greatly, exult

ex-suscitāre rouse, kindle

extemplō at once

ex-tendere -disse -tum stretch out, extend

exter -era -erum external, foreign

externus -a -um external, extraneous

ex-terrēre scare, terrify

extimus -a -um *sup* outermost, farthest

ex-tollere raise, praise, extol

ex-torris -e exiled, banished

extrā *prp + acc, adv* outside

ex-trahere pull out, extract

extrāneus -a -um foreign, stranger

extrēmus -a -um *sup* outermost, utmost, last; *n* end, utmost danger

ex-uere -uisse -ūtum take off, deprive of

ex-ūrere burn up

exustiō -ōnis *f* conflagration

exuviae -ārum *f pl* clothing, armor

F

faber -brī *m* artisan, smith

fabricāre forge, build, construct

fābula -ae *f* story, fable, play

fābulārī talk, chat

fābulōsus -a -um fabulous, celebrated

facere -iō fēcisse factum make, do, cause esteem, facere + *gen* value

facessere go away, be off

faciēs -ēī *f* appearance, form, face

facile *adv, sup* -illimē easily, readily

facilis -e, *sup* -illimus easy, complaisant

facilitās -ātis *f* ease, complaisance

facinus -oris *n* deed, act, misdeed

factiō -ōnis *f* party, faction

factiōsus -a -um factious, scheming

factum -ī *n* deed, act

factus -a -um wrought

facultās -ātis *f* possibility; *pl* resources

fācundus -a -um   eloquent
fallāx -ācis *adi*   deceitful
fallere fefellisse falsum
   deceive, fail to keep
falsus -a -um, *adv* -ō   false,
   deceived, wrong
falx -cis *f*   sickle
fāma -ae *f*   rumor,
   reputation
famēs -is *f*   hunger, famine
familia -ae *f*   household,
   family, slaves
familiāris -e   intimate; *m*
   close friend
famula -ae *f*   servant-girl,
   maid
famulus -ī *m*   servant, slave
fānum -ī *n*   shrine, conse-
   crated spot
fārī   speak
fās *n indēcl*   divine law,
   right
   fās est   it is right, it is
   allowed
fascēs -ium *m pl*   bundle of
   rods, fasces
fāstī -ōrum *m pl*   list of
   festivals, calendar
fāstus -a -um: **diēs fāstus**
   court-day, workday
fātālis -e   fateful, destined
fatērī fassum   admit,
   confess, profess
fatīgāre   tire out, weary,
   worry
fātum -ī *n*   fate, destiny,
   death
faucēs -ium *f pl*   pass, defile
faustus -a -um   fortunate,
   favorable
fautor -ōris *m*   supporter
favēre fāvisse + *dat*   favor,
   support
favor -ōris *m*   goodwill,
   favor
fax facis *f*   torch
Februārius -ī (mēnsis)
   February
fēlīcitās -ātis *f*   good
   fortune, luck
fēlīx -īcis *adi*   fortunate,
   propitious
fēmina -ae *f*   woman
fenestra -ae *f*   window
fera -ae *f*   wild animal

ferē   about, almost, usually
fēriae -ae *f pl*   festival days,
   holidays
fēriātus -a -um   keeping
   holiday
ferīre   strike, hit, kill
fermē   about, almost
ferōcitās -ātis *f*   fierceness,
   ferocity
ferōx -ōcis *adi*   fierce,
   ferocious
ferrātus -a -um   tipped
   with iron
ferre tulisse lātum   carry,
   bring, bear, endure, report,
   propose
ferreus -a -um   of iron,
   iron-
ferrum -ī *n*   iron, steel,
   sword
fertilis -e   fertile
ferus -a -um   wild
fervēns -entis   hot, boiling,
   ardent
fervere/-ēre ferbuisse   boil,
   seethe, swarm
fessus -a -um   tired, weary
festīnāre   hasten, hurry
fēstus -a -um: **diēs fēstus**
   holiday, festival
fētiālis -e   fetial
fētus -a -um   having young
-ficere -iō -fēcisse -fectum
fictilis -e   earthen,
   earthenware-
fictus -a -um   untrue, made
   up
fidēlis -e   faithful, loyal
fīdere fīsum esse + *dat*
   trust, rely on
fidēs -eī *f*   trust, faith,
   loyalty, promise
fidēs -ium *f pl*   lyre
fidicen -inis *m*   lyre-player
fīdūcia -ae *f*   trust,
   confidence
fīdus -a -um   faithful,
   reliable
fierī factum esse   be made,
   be done, become, happen,
   result
figere -xisse -xum   fix,
   fasten, pierce
figūra -ae *f*   form,
   appearance

filia -ae *f, pl dat/abl* -ābus
   daughter
filiola -ae *f*   little daughter
filiolus -ī *m*   little son
filius -ī *m*   son
filum -ī *n*   thread, fillet
fingere finxisse fictum
   form, make up, invent
finīre   limit, finish, delimit
finis -is *m*   boundary, end;
   pl territory
finitimus -a -um   adjacent,
   neighboring
firmāmentum -ī *n*   support,
   strength
firmāre   reinforce,
   strengthen
firmitūdō -inis *f*   stability,
   firmness
firmus -a -um   strong,
   stable, firm
fiscus -ī *m*   public treasury
flāgitāre   demand
   insistently
flāgitiōsus -a -um
   disgraceful
flāgitium -ī *n*   disgrace
flagrāre   burn
flāmen -inis *m*   flamen
   (priest)
flamma -ae *f*   flame
flāre   blow
flātus -ūs *m*   blowing,
   breeze
flēbilis -e   plaintive
flectere -xisse -xum   bend,
   turn
flēre -ēvisse   cry, weep (for)
flētus -ūs *m*   weeping
flōrēre   bloom, flourish
flōs -ōris *m*   flower
flūctus -ūs *m*   wave
fluere -ūxisse   flow
flūmen -inis *n*   river
fluvius -ī *m*   river
foculus -ī *m*   brazier
focus -ī *m*   hearth
foederātus -a -um   feder-
   ated, allied
foeditās -ātis *f*   ugliness,
   shame
foedus -a -um   ugly,
   hideous, shameful
foedus -eris *n*   treaty
folium -ī *n*   leaf

fōns fontis *m*   spring, source
forās *adv*   out
fore īnf fut < esse
forī -ōrum *m pl*   seats (in the circus)
foris -is *f*   leaf of a door, door
forīs *adv*   outside, out of doors
fōrma -ae *f*   form, shape, beauty
formīdō -inis *f*   dread, terror
fōrmōsus -a -um   beautiful
fōrmula -ae *f*   terms, formula
forsitan/forsan   perhaps, maybe
fortasse   perhaps, maybe
forte *adv*   by chance
fortis -e   strong, brave
fortitūdō -inis *f*   strength, bravery
fortuītō *adv*   by chance, fortuitously
fortūna -ae *f*   fortune
fortūnātus -a -um   fortunate
forum -ī *n*   square
fossa -ae *f*   ditch, trench
fragilis -e   fragile, frail
fragmentum -ī *n*   fragment, piece
fragor -ōris *m*   crash
frangere frēgisse frāctum   break, shatter
frāter -tris *m*   brother
fraus -audis *f*   deceit, guile
fremere -uisse   growl
fremitus -ūs *m*   rumble, growl
frendere   gnash one's teeth
frequēns -entis *adi*   numerous, frequent
fretum -ī *n*   strait
frētus -e -am + *abl*   relying on, confident of
frīgēre   be cold
frīgidus -a -um   cold, chilly, cool
frīgus -oris *n*   cold
frōns -ondis *f*   foliage, leaves
frōns -ontis *f*   forehead, brow, front

frūctus -ūs *m*   produce, fruit
frūgēs -um *f pl*   fruit, crops
fruī + *abl*   enjoy
frūmentārius -a -um   corn-
frūmentum -ī *n*   corn, grain
frūstrā   in vain
frūstrārī   deceive
fuga -ae *f*   flight
fugāre   put to flight, rout
fugere -iō fūgisse   run away, flee
fugitīvus -a -um   runaway
fulcīre -sisse -tum   hold up, support
fulgēre -sisse   flash, gleam
fulgor -ōris *m*   flash
fulgur -uris *n*   flash of lightning
fulmen -inis *n*   flash of lightning
fūmus -ī *m*   smoke
funda -ae *f*   sling
fundāmentum -ī *n*   foundation
fundere fūdisse fūsum   pour, shed, rout
funditor -ōris *m*   slinger
funditus *adv*   to the bottom, utterly
fundus -ī *m*   bottom
fūnestus -a -um   grievous, sinister
fungī fūnctum + *abl*   discharge, complete
vītā fungī   die
fūnis -is *m*   rope
fūnus -eris *n*   funeral, death
fūr -is *m*   thief
furca -ae *f*   fork, forked frame
furere   be mad, rage, rave
furor -ōris *m*   madness
fūrtum -ī *n*   theft
futūrus -a -um (*v.* esse)   future
(tempus) futūrum   future

G

gallus -ī *m*   cock, rooster
gaudēre gavīsum esse   be glad, be pleased
gaudium -ī *n*   joy, delight
gaza -ae *f*   treasure

gemellus -ī *m*   twin
gemere -uisse -itum   groan (for)
gemināre   double
geminus -a -um   twin
gemitus -ūs *m*   groaning
gemma -ae *f*   precious stone, jewel
gemmātus -a -um   set with a jewel
gena -ae *f*   cheek
gener -erī *m*   son-in-law
generāre   beget, produce
generōsus -a -um   noble
genetrīx -īcis *f*   mother
geniālis -e   marriage-, conjugal
genitor -ōris *m*   father
gēns gentis *f*   people, race, family
genū -ūs *n*   knee
genus -eris *n*   kind, sort, race, gender
genus hominum   human race, mankind
gerere gessisse gestum   carry, bear, carry on, do, act as; *pass* go on
gestāre   carry
gignere genuisse genitum   beget, create, bear
glaciēs -ēī *f*   ice
gladiātor -ōris *m*   gladiator
gladiātōrius -a -um   gladiatorial
gladius -ī *m*   sword
globōsus -a -um   spherical, round
globus -ī *m*   globe, sphere, ball, band
glōria -ae *f*   glory
glōriārī   boast
glōriōsus -a -um   glorious, boastful
gnāvus -a -um   diligent, active
gracilis -e, *sup* gracillimus   slender, slim
gracilitās -ātis *f*   slenderness, thinness
gradī -ior gressum   walk, proceed
gradus -ūs *m*   step, degree
Graecus -a -um   Greek
grammatica -ae *f*   grammar

grammaticus -a -um grammatical
grandaevus -a -um aged
grandis -e big, large
grandō -inis *f* hail
grātēs *f pl* thanks
grātia -ae *f* favor, goodwill, popularity, gratitude
  grātiā (/meā) + *gen* for the sake of
  grātiam habēre + *dat* be grateful
  grātiās agere + *dat* thank
grātificārī + *dat* oblige, gratify
grātuitus -a -um gratuitous, futile
grātulārī + *dat* congratulate
grātus -a -um pleasing, grateful
gravidus -a -um pregnant, laden
gravis -e heavy, grave, low
gravitās -ātis *f* weight, gravity, dignity
gremium -ī *n* lap
grex -egis *m* flock, herd, band
gubernāre steer, govern
gubernātor -ōris *m* steersman
gurges -itis *m* whirlpool, flood
gustāre taste

H

habēre have, hold, make, regard
  sē habēre + *adv* get on, be
habilis -e fit, appropriate
habitābilis -e inhabitable
habitāre dwell, live, inhabit
habitus -ūs *m* state, condition
hāc *adv* this way
haerēre -sisse -sum stick, cling
haesitāre hesitate, be uncertain
hasta -ae *f* lance
haud not
haud-quāquam by no means

haurīre -sisse -stum draw, bail, drink, engulf
hebes -etis dull, blunt
heia ah! come on!
hendeca-syllabus -a -um of eleven syllables
herba -ae *f* grass, herb
hercule by Hercules! really
hērēditārius -a -um inherited, hereditary
hērēditās -ātis *f* inheritance
hērēs -ēdis *m* heir
herī yesterday
hesternus -a -um of yesterday
heu o! alas!
heus hey! hello!
hexa-meter -trī *m* hexameter
hībern(ācul)a -ōrum *n pl* winter camp/quarters
hībernāre spend the winter
hībernus -a -um winter-, of winter
hic haec hoc this
hīc here
hiems -mis *f* winter
hinc from here, hence
historia -ae *f* account, story, history
historicus -ī *m* historian
hodiē today
hodiernus -a -um today's, of today
holus -eris *n* vegetable
homō -inis *m* human being, person
honestās -ātis *f* honesty, virtue
honestus -a -um honorable; *n* virtue
honor v. honōs
honōrāre honor
honōrificus -a -um honorable
honōs/honor -ōris *m* honor, high office
hōra -ae *f* hour
horrendus -a -um dreadful
horrēre bristle, stand on end, shudder (at)
horribilis -e horrible, terrifying

horror -ōris *m* dread, horror
hortārī encourage, urge
hortus -ī *m* garden
hospes -itis *m* guest, guest-friend
hospita -ae *f* (female) guest, stranger
hospitālis -e hospitable, guest-
hospitium -ī *n* guest friendship/house
hostia -ae *f* sacrificial animal
hostīlis -e enemy-, hostile
hostis -is *m* enemy
hūc here, to this place
hūmānitās -ātis *f* human feeling, culture
hūmānus -a -um human
humī *loc* on the ground
humilis -e, *sup* -illimus low, humble, lowly
humus -ī *f* ground, earth

I

iacere -iō iēcisse iactum throw, hurl, utter, lay
iacēre lie
iactāre throw, toss, hurl, utter
iactūra -ae *f* throwing away, loss
iaculārī throw (the javelin)
iaculum -ī *n* throwing-spear, javelin
iam now, already
iambus -ī *m* iamb (∪—)
iānitor -ōris *m* doorkeeper
iānua -ae *f* door
Iānuārius -ī (mēnsis) January
ibi there
ibī-dem in the same place
īcere īcisse ictum strike, make, conclude
-icere -iō -iēcisse -iectum
ictus -ūs *m* stroke, blow
īdem eadem idem the same
identidem repeatedly
id-eō for that reason
idōneus -a -um fit, suitable, capable

īdūs -uum *f pl* the 13th/15th (of the month)
iecur -oris *n* liver
igitur therefore, then, so
ignārus -a -um ignorant, unaware
ignāvia -ae *f* idleness, cowardice
ignis -is *m* fire
ignōbilis -e unknown, of low birth
ignōminiōsus -a -um disgraceful
ignōrāre not know
ignōscere -ōvisse + *dat* forgive
ignōtus -a -um unknown
īlicō at once
il-lacrimāre + *dat* weep over
ille -a -ud that, the one, he
illecebra -ae *f* attraction, allurement
illīc there
il-licere -iō -ēxisse -ectum entice, attract
illinc from there
illūc there, thither
il-lūcēscere -lūxisse dawn, grow light
il-lūdere make game of, fool
illūstrāre illuminate, make clear
illūstris -e brilliant, illustrious
imāgō -inis *f* picture, portrait, vision
imbēcillus -a -um weak
im-bellis -e unwarlike, cowardly
imber -bris *m* rain, shower
imitārī imitate
im-mānis -e savage, fierce
immānitās -ātis *f* brutality, fierceness
im-mātūrus -a -um unripe, premature
im-memor -oris *adi* (+ *gen*) unmindful, forgetful (of)
im-mēnsus -a -um immeasurable, endless
im-minēre + *dat* overhang, be imminent

im-minuere make smaller, reduce
im-miscēre: sē i. (+ *dat*) mingle, merge (into)
im-mittere send in, send (into)
immō no, on the contrary
im-mōbilis -e immovable, motionless
im-molāre sacrifice, immolate
im-mortālis -e immortal
im-mūnis -e (+ *abl*) exempt (from), tax-free
im-pār -aris *adi* unequal
im-partīre give a share of, impart
im-patiēns -entis *adi* not enduring, impatient
impatientia -ae *f* impatience
im-pavidus -a -um fearless
impedīmentum -ī *n* obstacle
impedīre impede, obstruct
impedītus -a -um obstructed, encumbered
im-pellere strike, drive, compel
im-pendēre + *dat* impend, threaten
impēnsa -ae *f* cost, expenditure
imperāre (+ *dat*) command, order, levy, requisition, rule
imperātor -ōris *m* general, emperor
imperātōrius -a -um of a general
im-perfectus -a -um unfinished
imperitāre (+ *dat*) govern, be in command
imperītia -ae *f* inexperience, ignorance
im-perītus -a -um unskilled, ignorant
imperium -ī *n* command, empire
im-pertīre give a share of, impart
impetrāre obtain (by request)
impetus -ūs *m* onset, attack, charge

im-piger -gra -grum active, industrious
im-pius -a -um impious
im-plēre -ēvisse -ētum fill, fulfill, achieve
im-plicāre -uisse -itum enfold
im-plōrāre beseech, implore
impluvium -ī *n* water basin
im-pōnere place (in/on), put
impraesentiārum at the present moment
im-primere -pressisse-pressum press (into), stamp, impress
im-probus -a -um bad, wicked
im-prōvīsus -a -um unforeseen, unexpected ex/dē imprōvīsō unexpectedly, suddenly
im-prūdēns -entis *adi* unwise, incautious
im-pudēns -entis *adi* shameless, impudent
impudentia -ae *f* shamelessness
im-pudīcus -a -um unchaste, immoral
im-pugnāre attack, oppose
impulsus -ūs *m* impact, impulse
impūne with impunity
impūnitās -ātis *f* impunity, licence
īmus -a -um *sup* lowest
in *prp* + *abl* in, on, at *prp* + *acc* into, on (to), against
in-ambulāre walk up and down
in-animus -a -um lifeless, inanimate
inānis -e empty, gaping
in-audītus -a -um unheard (of)
in-calēscere -luisse become heated
in-cautus -a -um incautious, unsuspecting
in-cēdere walk, advance, occur

in-cendere -disse -ēnsum set on fire, inflame

incendium -ī *n* fire, conflagration

inceptum -ī *n* undertaking, enterprise

in-certus -a -um uncertain

in-cidere -disse occur, present itself

in-cīdere -disse -sum cut

in-cipere -iō coepisse coeptum begin

in-citāre set in motion, stir up

incitātus -a -um fast-moving, rapid

in-clāmāre shout (at)

in-clīnāre turn, bend, incline

in-clūdere -sisse -sum shut up

inclutus -a -um famous

in-cognitus -a -um unknown

incohāre start work on, begin

incola -ae *m/f* inhabitant

in-colere inhabit

incolumis -e unharmed, safe, intact

incolumitās -ātis *f* safety

in-commodum -ī *n* disadvantage, misfortune

inconditus -a -um unpolished, rough

in-cōnspectus -a -um unfounded

in-cōnsultus -a -um thoughtless, rash

in-crēdibilis -e incredible, unbelievable

in-crepāre -uisse -itum rattle, clash, scold

in-crēscere grow, increase

in-cultus -a -um uncultivated, untilled

in-cumbere -cubuisse lie down on incumbere ad/in apply/ devote oneself to

in-currere -rrisse -rsum rush in, make an inroad

in-cursiō -ōnis *f* incursion, inroad

in-cūsāre reproach, accuse

inde from there, thence (forth)

in-demnātus -a -um uncondemned

index -icis *m* list, catalog

in-dicāre make known, declare

in-dīcere notify, declare

indicium -ī *n* information, disclosure

indigēre be without, lack

indignārī resent, be indignant

indignātiō -ōnis *f* indignation, resentment

indignitās -ātis *f* indignity, humiliation

in-dignus -a -um unworthy, shameful

in-doctus -a -um ignorant

indolēs -is *f* character, nature

in-dūcere lead, bring (in), introduce

induere -uisse -ūtum put on (clothes) indūtus (+ *abl*) dressed (in)

industria -ae *f* hard work, industry

industrius -a -um diligent, industrious

indūtiae -ae *f pl* armistice, truce

in-ēluctābilis -e inescapable, inevitable

in-ermis -e unarmed, defenceless

in-ers -ertis inactive, idle

inertia -ae *f* idleness, sloth

in-esse be (in)

in-explōrātō *adv* without reconnoitering

in-expugnābilis -e impregnable

in-exspectātus -a -um unexpected

īn-fāmis -e disgraced

īn-fandus -a -um horrible

īnfāns -antis *m/f* little child, baby

īn-fectus -a -um unwrought, not effected

īn-fēlīx -īcis *adi* unlucky, unfortunate

īnfēnsus -a -um hostile

īnferior -ius *comp* lower, inferior

īnfernus -a -um of the underworld

īn-ferre in-tulisse il-lātum bring (in), cause, inflict

īnferus -a -um lower

Īnferī -ōrum *m pl* the underworld

īnfēstāre make unsafe, infest

īnfēstus -a -um unsafe, infested, hostile

īn-fīdus -a -um faithless

īn-fīgere fix, fasten

īnfimus -a -um *sup* lowest, the bottom of

īnfīnītus -a -um unlimited, infinite

īnfīrmāre weaken, refute, annul

īnfīrmātiō -ōnis *f* invalidation, rebuttal

īnfīrmitās -ātis *f* weakness

īn-fīrmus -a -um weak

īnfitiārī deny

īn-flammāre kindle, inflame

īn-flāre inflate, puff up, elate

īn-flectere bend, turn, inflect

īn-fluere flow into

īn-fōrmis -e unshapely, ugly

īnfrā *prp + acc, adv* below

īn-fringere -frēgisse -frāctum break, crush

in-gemēscere -muisse groan, moan

ingenium -ī *n* nature, character

ingēns -entis *adi* huge, vast

in-grātus -a -um ungrateful

in-gredī -ior -gressum enter, begin, walk

in-hospitālis -e inhospitable

in-hūmānus -a -um inhuman

in-icere throw/lay on, instil

in-imīcus -ī *m* (personal) enemy

in-inimīcus -a -um
unfriendly
inīquitās -ātis *f* unfairness
in-īquus -a -um uneven,
unfair
in-īre -eō -iisse -itum enter
(upon), begin
initium -ī *n* beginning
iniūria -ae *f* injustice,
wrong
iniūriōsus -a -um unjust,
wrongful
in-iussū + *gen* without
orders
in-iūstus -a -um unjust,
unfair
in-nocēns -entis *adi* innocent, blameless
innocentia -ae *f* innocence,
integrity
in-numerābilis -e count-
less, innumerable
inopia -ae *f* lack, scarcity
inquit -iunt (he/she) says/
said
inquam I say
in-quīrere -sīvisse -sītum
inquire, make inquiries
īn-sānābilis -e incurable
īnsānia -ae *f* madness
īn-sānus -a -um mad,
insane
īn-satiābilis -e insatiable
īn-sciēns -entis *adi* not
knowing, unaware
īn-scius -a -um not
knowing, unaware
īn-scrībere write on,
inscribe, entitle
īnscrīptiō -ōnis *f* inscription, title
īn-sepultus -a -um unburied
īn-sequī follow, pursue
īn-sīdere -sēdisse -sessum
occupy, settle, be fixed
īn-sidēre -sēdisse hold,
occupy, be seated
īnsidiae -ārum *f pl*
ambush, plot, wiles
īnsidiārī (+ *dat*) lie in wait,
lie in ambush
īnsidiātor -ōris *m* way-
layer, bandit
īnsigne -is *n* mark, token,
symbol

īnsignis -e noted,
remarkable
īn-sistere -stitisse stand (on)
īn-solēns -entis *adi* haughty,
arrogant
īnsolentia -ae *f* arrogance
īn-solitus -a -um unusual,
unwonted
īn-sōns -ontis *adi* innocent
īn-spērātus -a -um
unhoped for, unexpected
īn-spicere examine,
inspect
īn-stāre press, urge, insist
īn-staurāre renew
īnstigāre incite, urge
īnstīnctus -a -um roused
īn-stituere -uisse -ūtum set
up, establish, start,
appoint, train, instruct
īnstitūtum -ī *n* practice,
custom, usage
īn-struere draw up,
arrange, equip
īnstrūmentum -ī *n* tool(s),
instrument
īn-suēscere -ēvisse -ētum
become accustomed
īnsula -ae *f* island
īn-super in addition
īnsuper habēre overlook,
neglect
in-tāctus -a -um
untouched, uninjured
integer -gra -grum intact,
unhurt, blameless
intel-legere -lēxisse -lēctum
understand, realize
in-tendere -disse -tum
strain, direct, strive
intentiō -ōnis *f* charge,
accusation
intentus -a -um intent,
attentive
inter *prp* + *acc* between,
among, during
inter sē (with) one
another
inter-cēdere intervene,
intercede
inter-clūdere -sisse -sum
cut off, block
inter-diū by day
inter-dum now and then
inter-eā meanwhile

inter-esse be between
interesse + *dat* attend,
take part in
interest it matters
inter-ficere kill
inter-icere place between,
insert, add
interiectus situated
between
interiectīs...
(*abl*) after..., at the end
of...
interim meanwhile
inter-imere -ēmisse
-ēmptum kill
interior -ius *comp* interior,
inner (part of)
inter-īre -eō -iisse die,
perish
interitus -ūs *m* death
inter-mittere interrupt,
discontinue
interniciō -ōnis *f* annihila-
tion, massacre
internus -a -um inner,
internal
inter-pellāre interrupt
inter-pōnere place
between
inter-rēgnum -ī *n* interval
between reigns
inter-rēx -rēgis *m* interme-
diary regent
inter-rogāre ask, question
inter-rumpere break up,
cut, interrupt
inter-vāllum -ī *n* interval,
space, distance
inter-venīre (+ *dat*) turn
up, occur, disturb
interventus -ūs *m* arrival
intrā *prp* + *acc* inside,
within
intrāre enter
intrō-dūcere lead/bring in,
introduce
intro-īre -eō -iisse
-itum go inside, enter
intuērī look at, watch
intus *adv* inside
in-ultus -a -um unavenged
in-ūtilis -e useless
in-vādere -sisse
-sum enter, attack,
invade

in-validus -a -um   infirm, weak
in-vehere   import; *pass* ride in
   invehī in   attack in words, inveigh
in-venīre   find, meet, devise, invent
inventiō -ōnis *f*   art of devising arguments
in-vestīgāre   inquire into, investigate
in-veterāscere -rāvisse   grow old, become fixed
in-vicem   mutually, one another
in-victus -a -um   unconquered, invincible
in-vidēre + *dat*   envy, grudge
invidia -ae *f*   envy, ill will, dislike
in-violātus -a -um   unhurt
in-vīsere   go to see
invīsus -a -um   odious, disliked
invītāre   invite, entertain
invītus -a -um   unwilling, against…'s will
in-vius -a -um   trackless, impassable
in-vocāre   call upon, invoke
iocōsus -a -um   humorous, funny
ipse -a -um   himself, that very
īra -ae *f*   anger
īrāscī   be angry
īrātus -a -um   angry
īre eō iisse itum   go
irrītāre   excite, stimulate
ir-ritus -a -um   invalid, ineffectual
ir-ruere   rush in, charge
ir-rumpere   break, force one's way
irruptiō -ōnis *f*   violent entry, assault
is ea id   he, she, it, that
iste -a -ud   this, that (of yours)
ita   so, in such a way
ita-que   therefore
item   likewise, also

iter itineris *n*   journey, march, way
iterāre   repeat, renew
iterum   again, a second time
iubēre iussisse iussum   order, tell
iūcundus -a -um   pleasant, delightful
iūdex -icis *m*   judge
iūdicāre   judge, try, decide
iūdicātiō -ōnis *f*   point at issue
iūdicium -ī *n*   judgement, trial, court
iugālis -e   marriage-, conjugal
iūgerum -ī *n*   area of ±2500 m²
iugulāre   kill, slaughter
iugulum -ī *n*   throat
iugum -ī *n*   yoke, ridge
Iūlius -ī (mēnsis)   July
iūmentum -ī *n*   beast of burden/draft
iungere iūnxisse iūnctum   join, combine, form
iūniōrēs -um *m pl*   younger men (17–45)
Iūnius -ī (mēnsis)   June
iūrāre   swear
iūs iūris *n*   law, right, justice, court
   iūre   justly, rightly
iūs iūrandum iūris -ī *n*   oath
iussū *abl* + *gen*   by order of
iussum -ī *n*   command, order
iūsta -ōrum *n pl*   the last honors
iūstitia -ae *f*   justice
iūstus -a -um   just, fair, due, proper
iuvāre iūvisse iūtum   help, delight
iuvenālis -e   youthful
iuvencus -ī *m*   young bull
iuvenīlis -e   youthful
iuvenis -is *m*   young man
iuventa -ae *f*   youth
iuventūs -ūtis *f*   youth, young men
iūxtā *prp* + *acc, adv*   by, next to, after, alike

K

kalendae -ārum *f pl*   the 1st (of the month)
kalendārium -ī *n*   calendar

L

labefactāre   shake, undermine
lābēs -is *f*   stain, disgrace
lābī lāpsum   slip, drop, fall
labor -ōris *m*   work, toil
labōrāre   work, take trouble, suffer
labōriōsus -a -um   hard, laborious
labrum -ī *n*   lip
labyrinthus -ī *m*   labyrinth
lac lactis *n*   milk
lacerāre   tear
lacertus -ī *m*   (upper) arm
lacessere -īvisse -ītum   challenge, provoke
lacrima -ae *f*   tear
lacrimābilis -e   mournful, pitiful
lacrimāre   shed tears, weep
lacrimōsus -a -um   tearful, sad
lacteus -a -um   milky
lacus -ūs *m*   lake
laedere -sisse -sum   injure, hurt
laetārī   rejoice, be glad
laetitia -ae *f*   joy
laetus -a -um   glad, happy
laevus -a -um   left, *f* the left (hand)
lambere -bisse   lick, wash
lāmentātiō -ōnis *f*   wailing, lamentation
lāna -ae *f*   wool, wool spinning
lancea -ae *f*   lance, spear
laniāre   tear
lapideus -a -um   of stone, stone-
lapis -idis *m*   stone, milestone
laqueus -ī *m*   loop, noose
largīrī   give generously
largītiō -ōnis *f*   largesse, bribery
largītor -ōris *m*   who gives generously

largus -a -um generous
lascīvia -ae *f* wantonness
latebra -ae *f* hiding-place
later -eris *m* brick
latēre be hidden, hide
latericius -a -um of brick
Latīnus -a -um Latin
lātrāre bark
latrō -ōnis *m* brigand, robber
latrōcinium -ī *n* robbery
latus -eris *n* side, flank
lātus -a -um broad, wide
laudāre praise
laureātus -a -um adorned with laurel
laurus -ī *f* laurel
laus laudis *f* praise, merit
lavāre lāvisse lautum wash, bathe
laxāre loose, untie, release
lectīca -ae *f* litter, sedan
lectulus -ī *m* (little) bed
lectus -ī *m* bed, couch
lēctus -a -um select, picked
lēgāre bequeath, send, delegate
lēgatiō -ōnis *f* embassy, deputation
lēgātus -ī *m* envoy, lieutenant, legate
legere lēgisse lēctum read, choose, gather
legiō -ōnis *f* legion
legiōnārius -a -um legionary
lēgitimus -a -um legal, lawful
lembus -ī *m* small boat
lēnīre placate, appease
lēnis -e gentle, mild
lentus -a -um slow
leō -ōnis *m* lion
levāre lift, raise
levis -e light, slight
lēx lēgis *f* law, condition, term
lībāre make a libation, pour
libellus -ī *m* little book
libēns -entis *adi* willing, glad
libenter with pleasure, gladly

liber -brī *m* book
līber -era -erum free
līberāre free, set free, deliver
līberātor -ōris *m* deliverer, liberator
libēre: libet (+ *dat*) it pleases
līberī -ōrum *m pl* children
lībertās -ātis *f* freedom, liberty
lībertīnus -ī *m* freedman
libīdō -inis *f* desire, lust
lībra -ae *f* balance, pound (327 g)
licentia -ae *f* wantonness, licence
licēre: licet + *dat* it is allowed, one may
līctor -ōris *m* lictor
ligāre bind
ligneus -a -um wooden
lignum -ī *n* wood
līlium -ī *n* lily
līmen -inis *n* threshold
līmes -itis *m* path, track
līmus -ī *m* mud
līnea -ae *f* string, line
lingua -ae *f* tongue, language
linquere līquisse lictum leave
linter -tris *m* small boat
līs lītis *f* dispute, lawsuit
littera -ae *f* letter
lītus -oris *n* beach, shore
lituus -ī *m* augur's staff, trumpet
loca -ōrum *n pl* regions, parts
locāre place
locuplēs -ētis *adi* rich, wealthy
locuplētāre enrich
locus -ī *m* (*pl* -a -ōrum *n*: *v. suprā*) place, position, rank, room, opportunity
longē far, by far
longinquitās -ātis *f* remoteness
longinquus -a -um remote
longitūdō -inis *f* length
longus -a -um long
loquī locūtum speak, talk

lūcēre lūxisse shine
lucerna -ae *f* lamp
lucrum -ī *n* profit, gain
luctārī wrestle
lūctus -ūs *m* grief, mourning
lūcus -ī *m* sacred grove
lūdere -sisse -sum play
lūdibrium -ī *n* toy, laughing-stock
lūdic(er) -cra -crum of sport, of games
lūdicrum -ī *n* show
lūdus -ī *m* play, game, school
lūgēre -xisse mourn, grieve (over)
lūgubris -e sad, grievous
lūmen -inis *n* light
lūna -ae *f* moon
lūnāris -e of the moon, lunar
lupa -ae *f* she-wolf
lupus -ī *m* wolf
lūstrāre irradiate, purify, survey
lūstrum -ī *n* ceremony of purification
lūx lūcis *f* light, daylight
luxuria -ae *f* extravagance, luxury
luxuriārī revel, live in luxury
luxus -ūs *m* extravagance, luxury

M

māceria -ae *f* stone wall, garden wall
māchina -ae *f* machine
māchinārī devise, plot
macte virtūte (estō) well done! bravo!
macula -ae *f* stain, blemish
maculāre stain, defile
maerēre grieve
maeror -ōris *m* grief
maestitia -ae *f* sadness, sorrow
maestus -a -um sad, sorrowful
magis more
magister -trī *m* schoolmaster, teacher

magister equitum   master of the horse

magistrātus -ūs *m*   office, magistrate

magnificentia -ae *f*   magnificence

magnificus -a -um   magnificent, splendid

magnitūdō -inis *f*   size, greatness

magnus -a -um   big, large, great

māior -ius *comp*   bigger, greater, older

māiōrēs -um *m pl*   ancestors

Māius -ī (mēnsis)   May

male *adv*   badly, ill

male-dīcere + *dat*   abuse, insult

maleficium -ī *n*   evil deed, crime

malitia -ae *f*   wickedness

mālle māluisse   prefer

malum -ī *n*   evil, trouble, harm

mālum -ī *n*   apple

malus -a -um   bad, wicked, evil

mamma -ae *f*   mummy

mānāre   flow, be wet, drip

mandāre   assign, order

mandātum -ī *n*   order

māne *indēcl n, adv*   morning, in the morning

manēre mānsisse   remain, stay

Mānēs -ium *m pl*   Manes, spirits of the dead

manifēstus -a -um   flagrant, plain

manipulus -ī *m*   maniple

mānsuētūdō -inis *f*   mildness, clemency

manus -ūs *f*   hand, power, force, troop

mare -is *n*   sea

margarīta -ae *f*   pearl

maritimus -a -um   sea-, coastal

marītus -ī *m*   husband

marmor -oris *n*   marble

marmoreus -a -um   made of marble, marble-

Mārtius -ī (mēnsis)   March

māter -tris *f*   mother

māteria -ae *f*   material, occasion

māternus -a -um   maternal

mātrimōnium -ī *n*   matrimony, marriage

mātrōna -ae *f*   married woman

mātrōnālis -e   of a married woman

mātūrāre   make haste, hurry

mātūrē   quickly, early

mātūritās -ātis *f*   ripeness, maturity

mātūrus -a -um   ripe, mature, timely, early

mausōlēum -ī *n*   mausoleum

māximē   most, especially

māximus -a -um *sup*   biggest, greatest, oldest

mecastor   by Castor!

medērī + *dat*   heal, cure, remedy

medicus -ī *m*   physician, doctor

mediocris -e   moderate, ordinary

meditārī   think about, contemplate

meditātiō -ōnis *f*   reflection, practicing

medium -ī *n*   middle, centre

medius -a -um   mid, middle

meherc(u)le   by Hercules!

mel mellis *n*   honey

melior -ius *comp*   better

melius *adv*   better, rather

mellītus -a -um   sweet

membrum -ī *n*   limb

mementō -tōte *imp*   remember! don't forget!

mē-met   me, myself

meminisse + *gen/acc*   remember, recollect

memor -oris *adi* (+ *gen*)   mindful, reminding

memorābilis -e   memorable

memorāre   mention, speak (of)

memoria -ae *f*   memory, record   m.ae trādere/mandāre   put on record   post hominum m.am   in human memory

mendum -ī *n*   mistake, error

mēns mentis *f*   mind

mēnsa -ae *f*   table   mēnsa secunda   dessert

mēnsis -is *m*   month

mentiō -ōnis *f*   mention, reference

mentīrī   lie

mercārī   buy, purchase

mercātor -ōris *m*   merchant

mercātōrius -a -um   merchant-

mercātūra -ae *f*   trade, commerce

mercātus -ūs *m*   market, fair

mercēs -ēdis *f*   wage, fee, rent

merēre/-rī   earn, deserve   bene m. dē   behave well toward

mergere -sisse -sum   dip, plunge, sink

merīdiēs -ēī *m*   midday, noon, south

meritum -ī *n*   merit

meritus -a -um   well-deserved

merum -ī *n*   neat wine

merus -a -um   pure, neat, undiluted

merx -rcis *f*   commodity; *pl* goods

metallum -ī *n*   metal

mētārī   measure off, lay out

metere -messum   reap, harvest

mētīrī mēnsum   measure

metuere -uisse   fear

metus -ūs *m*   fear

meus -a -um, *voc* mī   my, mine

micāre   flicker, flash

migrāre   move, migrate

mīles -itis *m*   soldier

mīliārium -ī *n*   milestone

mīlitāre   serve as a soldier

mīlitāris -e   military
mīlitia -ae *f*   military service
  mīlitiae (*loc*)   in the field,
  in war
mīlle, *pl* mīlia -ium *n*
  thousand
minae -ārum *f pl*   threats
minārī   threaten
minimē   by no means, not
  at all
minimum *adv*   very little
minimus -a -um *sup*   small-
  est, youngest
minister -trī *m*   servant
ministerium -ī *n*   atten-
  dance
ministra -ae *f*   female
  servant
minitārī   threaten
minor -us *comp*   smaller,
  younger
minuere -uisse -ūtum
  diminish, reduce
minus -ōris *n, adv*   less
  sī minus   if not
mīrābilis -e   marvelous,
  wonderful
mīrābundus -a -um
  wondering
mīrāculum -ī *n*   marvel
mīrārī   wonder (at), be
  surprised
mīrus -a -um   surprising,
  strange
miscēre -uisse mixtum
  mix, mix up, stir up
misellus -a -um   poor,
  wretched
miser -era -erum   unhappy,
  miserable
miserābilis -e   pitiable
miserārī   feel sorry for, pity
miserātiō -ōnis *f*   compas-
  sion, pity
miserērī + *gen*   feel pity for
miseria -ae *f*   misfortune,
  misery
misericordia -ae *f*   compas-
  sion, pity
missile -is *n*   missile
mītigāre   soothe
mītis -e   gentle, mild, tame
mittere mīsisse missum
  send, throw
moderārī   temper, moderate

moderātiō -ōnis *f*   moderation, restraint
moderātor -ōris *m*   ruler
moderātus -a -um
  restrained, moderate
modestia -ae *f*   restraint
modestus -a -um
  restrained, modest
modicus -a -um   moderate
modius -ī *m*   peck (8.75 1)
modo   only, just
  modo…modo   now…
  now
modus -ī *m*   manner, way,
  measure, size, amount,
  limit
  nūllō modō   by no means
huius/eius modī   of this/
  that kind
moenia -ium *n pl*   walls
mōlēs -is *f*   mass, bulk,
  effort
molestus -a -um   troublesome
  molestē patī/ferre   be
  annoyed (at)
mōlīrī   labor, strive
mollīre   make soft, soften
mollis -e   soft
mōmentum -ī *n*   moment
monēre   remind, advise,
  warn
monitus -ūs *m*   advice,
  prompting
mōns montis *m*   mountain
mōnstrāre   point out, show
mōnstrum -ī *n*   monster
monumentum -ī *n*   memorial, monument
mora -ae *f*   delay
morārī   delay, stay, stop
morbus -ī *m*   disease,
  illness
mordēre momordisse -sum
  bite
morī mortuum   die
moribundus -a -um   dying
mors mortis *f*   death
mortālis -e   mortal, human
mortuus -a -um (< morī)
  dead
mōs mōris *m*   custom,
  usage, manner
mōtus -ūs *m*   movement,
  rising

movēre mōvisse -tum
  move, stir, ponder
mox   soon
mūgīre   low, bellow
muliebris -e   of a woman
mulier -eris *f*   woman
multāre   punish
multī -ae -a   many, a great
  many
multitūdō -inis *f*   large
  number, multitude
multō + *comp/sup*   much,
  by far
multum -ī *n, adv*   much, a
  good deal
  multum diēī   late in the
  day
multus -a -um   much, a
  good deal of
  in/ad multam noctem
  till late in the night
mundus -ī *m*   world,
  universe
mundus -a -um   clean, neat
mūnīmentum -ī *n*
  fortification
mūnīre   fortify, guard,
  construct
mūnītiō -ōnis *f*
  fortification
mūnītus -a -um   well
  fortified, secure
mūnus -eris *n*   gift, task,
  duty
murmur -uris *n*   mutter,
  murmur
mūrus -ī *m*   wall
mūs mūris *m*   mouse
Mūsa -ae *f*   Muse
mūtābilis -e   changeable
mūtāre   change, exchange
mūtātiō -ōnis *f*   change
mūtus -a -um   dumb
mūtuus -a -um   on loan
  mūtuum dare/
  sūmere   lend/borrow

N

nam   for
-nam   …ever?
namque   for
nancīscī nactum   get,
  obtain, find, meet
nāre   swim
nārrāre   relate, tell

nārrātiō -ōnis *f* narrative
nāscī nātum be born
nāsus -ī *m* nose
nāta -ae *f* daughter
natāre swim
nātiō -ōnis *f* people, nation
nātū *abl*: māior/minor n. older/younger
nātūra -ae *f* nature
nātūrālis -e natural, of nature
nātus -a -um (< nāscī) born
    XX annōs nātus 20 years old
nātus -ī *m* son
naufragium -ī *n* shipwreck
nauta -ae *m* sailor
nauticus -a -um nautical, naval
nāvālia -ium *n pl* dockyard
nāvālis -e naval
nāvicula -ae *f* boat
nāviculārius -ī *m* shipowner
nāvigāre sail
nāvigātiō -ōnis *f* sailing, voyage
nāvis -is *f* ship
-ne …? if, whether
nē that not, lest, that
    nē…quidem not even
    nē multa to be brief, in short
nebula -ae *f* mist, fog
nec v. ne-que/nec
necāre kill
nec-/neque-dum and (/but) not yet
necessārius -a -um, *adv* -ō necessary
necessārius -ī *m* relative, friend
necesse est it is necessary, one must
necessitās -ātis *f* need, necessity
nectere -x(u)isse -xum attach
ne-fandus -a -um heinous
ne-fās *indēcl n* impious act, crime
ne-fāstus -a -um: diēs n. public holiday
negāre deny, say that…not
negitāre deny repeatedly

neglegēns -entis *adi* careless
neglegere -ēxisse -ctum neglect, disregard
negōtiārī do business, trade
negōtiātor -ōris *m* trader
negōtium -ī *n* business, activity, affair
nēmō, *acc* -inem, *dat* -inī no one, nobody
nepōs -ōtis *m* grandson
nēquam *adi indēcl sup* nēquissimus worthless, bad
nē-quāquam by no means, not at all
ne-que/nec and/but not, nor, not
    n. …n. neither…nor
nē-quiquam to no effect, in vain
ne-quīre -eō -īvisse be unable to
nervus -ī *m* sinew, muscle
nescio-quis someone or other, some
ne-scīre not know
neu *v.* nē-ve/neu
neuter -tra -trum neither
nē-ve/neu and (that) not, nor
    n. …n. (that) neither… nor
nex necis *f* killing, murder
nī *v.* nisi
nīdus -ī *m* nest
niger -gra -grum black
nihil/nīl nothing; *adv* not at all
nihilō + *comp* no, by no means
    nihilō minus/sētius nonetheless
nimbus -ī *m* rain-cloud
nī-mīrum *adv* without doubt, evidently
nimis too, too much
nimium -ī *n, adv* too much, too
nimius -a -um too big
nisi/nī if not, except, but
nītī nīsum exert oneself, strive
    nītī in depend on

niveus -a -um snow-white
nix nivis *f* snow
nōbilis -e well known, famous
nōbilitāre make famous
nōbilitās -ātis *f* renown, nobility, nobles
nocēre + *dat* harm, hurt
noctū by night, at night
nocturnus -a -um nocturnal, at night
nōdus -ī *m* knot
nōlī -īte *imp* (< nōlle) + *inf* don't…!
nōlle nōluisse be unwilling, not want
nōmen -inis *n* name, fame, nation
    nōmen dare offer oneself, enroll
nōmināre name, call
nōn not
nōnae -ārum *f pl* 5th/7th (of the month)
nōnāgēsimus -a -um ninetieth
nōnāgintā ninety
nōn-dum not yet
nōn-gentī -ae -a nine hundred
nōn-ne not?
nōn-nihil not a little, something
nōn-nūllī -ae -a some, several
nōn-numquam sometimes
nōnus -a -um ninth
nōs nōbīs we, us, ourselves
nōscere nōvisse get to know; *perf* know
nōscitāre recognize
noster -tra -trum our, ours
nostrum *gen* of us
nota -ae *f* mark, sign, slur
notāre mark, note, censure
Notus -ī *m* south wind
nōtus -a -um known
novellus -a -um new, young
novem nine
November -bris (mēnsis) November
nōvisse (<nōscere) know
novissimē quite recently
novissimus -a -um last

novitās -ātis *f* novelty, inexperience
novus -a -um new, inexperienced
nox noctis *f* night
noxa -ae *f* harm, guilt
noxius -a -um guilty
nūbere -psisse + *dat* marry nuptum dare give in marriage
nūbēs -is *f* cloud
nūbilus -a -um cloudy
nūdāre bare, leave unprotected
nūdus -a -um naked, bare, unarmed
nūgae -ārum *f pl* idle talk, rubbish
nūllus -a -um no
num ...? if, whether
nūmen -inis *n* divine will
numerāre count
numerōsus -a -um numerous, many
numerus -ī *m* number, class
nummus -ī *m* coin, sesterce
numquam never
nunc now
nūncupāre designate, call
nūntia -ae *f* messenger
nūntiāre announce, report
nūntius -ī *m* messenger, message
nūper recently
nupta -ae *f* wife
nuptiae -ārum *f pl* wedding
nurus -ūs *f* daughter-in-law
nusquam nowhere
nūtrīre feed, suckle
nūtrīx -īcis *f* nurse
nūtus -ūs *m* nod, gravitation
nux nucis *f* nut
Nympha -ae *f* nymph

O

ō o!
ob *prp* + *acc* on account of, before
ob-dūcere draw over (to cover)
ob-equitāre ride up to
ob-icere place before, expose

ob-iectāre expose
ob-īre -eō -iisse -itum meet, visit, go into, enter upon, set
obitus -ūs *m* death
ob-ligāre bind
oblīquus -a -um slanting, indirect
oblīviō -ōnis *f* oblivion
oblīvīscī -lītum + *gen/acc* forget
ob-mūtēscere -tuisse become speechless
ob-nūbere veil, cover
ob-oedīre + *dat* obey
ob-orīrī spring up
ob-rēpere creep up, steal up
ob-rigēscere -guisse become stiff
ob-ruere -ruisse -rutum cover up, bury, crush
obscūrāre obscure, darken
obscūrus -a -um dark, obscure, uncertain
ob-secundāre + *dat* comply with, obey
ob-sequī + *dat* comply with, obey
ob-servāre observe, respect
obses -idis *m* hostage
ob-sidēre -sēdisse -sessum besiege
obsidiō -ōnis *f* siege
ob-sistere -stitisse resist
ob-stāre stand in the way
obstinātus -a -um stubborn, obstinate
ob-struere bar, block
ob-stupēscere -puisse be stunned/astounded
ob-surdēscere -duisse become deaf
ob-temperāre + *dat* obey
ob-testārī beseech, implore
ob-tinēre -uisse -tentum hold, gain, obtain
ob-trectāre criticize, disparage
obtrectātiō -ōnis *f* criticism, disparagement
ob-truncāre slaughter, kill
obtūnsus -a -um blunt, dull

ob-venīre fall to the lot of
ob-viam ire (+ *dat*) (go to) meet, oppose
obvius -a -um coming to meet
obvius esse/fierī + *dat* meet
occāsiō -ōnis *f* opportunity, chance
occāsus -ūs *m* setting
occidēns -entis *m* west
oc-cidere -disse fall, sink, set, die, end
oc-cīdere -disse -sum kill
occultāre hide
occultus -a -um hidden, secret
occupāre occupy, take possession of
oc-currere -rrisse + *dat* meet
oc-cursāre run to meet
ōceanus -ī *m* ocean
ocellus -ī *m* (little) eye
ōcissimē *sup* most quickly
ōcius *comp* more quickly
octāvus -a -um eighth
octiēs eight times
octingentī -ae -a eight hundred
octō eight
Octōber -bris (mēnsis) October
octōgēsimus -a -um eightieth
octōgintā eighty
oculus -ī *m* eye
ōdisse hate
odium -ī *n* hatred
odor -ōris *m* smell
of-fendere -disse -ēnsum come upon, find
offēnsa -ae *f* offense, resentment
offēnsiō -ōnis *f* setback, misfortune
of-ferre ob-tulisse -lātum offer, present
officium -ī *n* duty, task
ōlim once, long ago, one day
ōmen -inis *n* omen, augury
o-mittere abandon, leave off/out
omnīnō altogether

omnis -e all, every
onerāre load
onus -eris *n* burden, load
opācus -a -um shady
opem -is -e *acc gen abl*
  power, aid, assistance
opera -ae *f* effort, pains,
  service
  operam dare (ut + *dat*)
    apply oneself
  operae nōn est (mihi) (I)
    can't spare the time
operārius -ī *m* labourer
operīre -uisse -rtum cover
opēs -um *f pl* resources,
  wealth, power, influence
opifex -icis *m* workman,
  artisan
opīmus -a -um rich
opīnārī think, believe
opīniō -ōnis *f* opinion,
  belief
oportēre: oportet it is
  right, you should
opperīrī -ertum wait (for),
  await
oppidānī -ōrum *m pl*
  townspeople
oppidum -ī *n* town
op-plēre -ēvisse -ētum fill
  up, cover
op-pōnere put in the way,
  oppose
opportūnitās -ātis *f* conve-
  nience, advantage
opportūnus -a -um convenient, exposed
op-primere -pressisse
  -pressum press on,
  overwhelm
op-pugnāre attack
oppugnātiō -ōnis *f* attack,
  assault
optāre wish
optimātēs -ium *m pl* the
  nobles/conservatives
optimus -a -um *sup* best,
  very good
opulentia -ae *f*
  sumptuousness
opulentus -a -um wealthy,
  powerful
opus -eris *n* work, task
opus est it is needed
ōra -ae *f* border, coast

ōrāculum -ī *n* oracle
ōrāre pray, beg
ōrātiō -ōnis *f* speech
ōrātor -ōris *m* speaker,
  orator, envoy
ōrātōrius -a -um oratorical
ōrātrīx -īcis *f* female
  suppliant
orbis -is *m* circle, orbit,
  sphere
  orbis (terrārum) the
    world
orbitās -ātis *f* loss of
  children/parents
orbus -a -um childless,
  orphaned
ōrdināre arrange,
  regulate
ōrdīrī ōrsum begin (to
  speak)
ōrdō -inis *m* row, rank,
  order, class
  (ex) ōrdine in order, in
    sequence
oriēns -entis *m* east
orientālis -e eastern
orīgō -inis *f* beginnings,
  origin
orīrī ortum rise, appear,
  spring
ōrnāmentum -ī *n* ornament, jewel
ōrnāre equip, adorn
ōrnātus -a -um ornate,
  distinguished
ortus -ūs *m* rising, sunrise,
  origin
os ossis *n* bone
ōs ōris *n* mouth, face
ōscitāre gape, yawn
ōsculārī kiss
ōsculum -ī *n* kiss
ostendere -disse show,
  demonstrate
ostentāre display ostenta-
  tiously
ōstiārius -ī *m* door-keeper,
  porter
ōstium -ī *n* door, entrance
ōtiōsus -a -um leisured,
  idle
ōtium -ī *n* leisure, peace
ovāre exult, rejoice
ovis -is *f* sheep
ōvum -ī *n* egg

P

pābulārī forage
pābulum -ī *n* fodder
pācāre subdue
pacīscī pactum contract/
  stipulate for
pactō: quō pactō how
paelex -icis *f* concubine
paene nearly, almost
paen-īnsula -ae *f* peninsula
paenitēre: p.et mē (+ *gen*) I
  regret/repent
pāgina -ae *f* page
palam openly, publicly
  palam facere make
    generally known
pālārī stray, be dispersed
pallēre be pale
pallēscere -luisse grow
  pale
pallidus -a -um pale
pallium -ī *n* cloak, mantle
palma -ae *f* palm, hand
palpitāre beat, throb
palūdāmentum -ī *n* military cloak
palūs -ūdis *f* fen, swamp
pālus -ī *m* stake
pandere -disse passum
  spread out
pānis -is *m* bread, loaf
papae! hey!
papāver -eris *n* poppy
papȳrus -ī *f* papyrus
pār paris *adi* equal,
  adequate
parāre prepare, provide, get
parātus -a -um ready
parcere pepercisse + *dat*
  spare
parēns -entis *m/f* father,
  mother
  parentēs -um *m pl*
    parents
parere -iō peperisse -rtum
  give birth to, lay, produce
pārēre (+ *dat*) obey
pariēs -etis *m* wall (of a
  house)
pariter equally, together
parricīda -ae *m* parricide
parricīdium -ī *n* murder of
  near relation
pars -rtis *f* part, direction,
  party

particeps -ipis *adi* + *gen*
having a share in
partim in part, partly
partim…partim/aliī
some…others
partīrī share, divide,
distribute
parturīre be ready to give
birth to
partus -ūs *m* (giving) birth
parum too little, not quite
parum-per for a short
while
parvulus -a -um little, tiny
parvus -a -um little, small
pāscere pāvisse pāstum
pasture, feed, feast
passer -eris *m* sparrow
passim far and wide,
everywhere
passus -ūs *m* pace (1.48 m)
pāstiō -ōnis *f* pasturage
pāstor -ōris *m* shepherd
pate-facere open, reveal
pate-fierī be revealed
patēns -entis *adi* open
pater -tris *m* father; *pl*
senators
patera -ae *f* bowl
patēre be open, spread
paternus -a -um of the
father, paternal
patēscere -tuisse open
patī passum suffer, bear,
allow
aegrē/molestē patī
resent, be indignant
patiēns -entis *adi* patient
patientia -ae *f* forbearance,
patience
patrāre carry through
patria -ae *f* native country/
town
patricius -a -um patrician
patrimōnium -ī *n* patri-
mony, fortune
patrius -a -um of the
father, paternal
patrōcinium -ī *n* protection, defence
patrōnus -ī *m* patron,
pleader, advocate
patruus -ī *m* father's
brother, uncle
paucī -ae -a few, a few

paucitās -ātis *f* small
number, paucity
paulātim little by little,
gradually
paulisper for a short time
paulō + *comp*, ante/post a
little
paululum a little
paulum a little, little
pauper -eris *adi* poor
pavēre be terrified
pavidus -a -um terrified
pavor -ōris *m* terror, fright
pāx pācis *f* peace
peccāre do wrong
peccātum -ī *n* error,
offense
pectus -oris *n* breast
pecua -um *n pl* farm
animals
peculātus -ūs *m* embezzlement
pecūlium -ī *n* money given
to slaves
pecūnia -ae *f* money
pecūniōsus -a -um wealthy
pecus -udis *f* farm animal,
sheep
pecus -oris *n* livestock,
sheep, cattle
pedes -itis *m* foot-soldier
pedester -tris -tre pedes-
trian, infantry
pēior -ius *comp* worse
pellere pepulisse pulsum
push, drive (off)
-pellere -pulisse -pulsum
Penātēs -ium *m* Penates,
tutelary gods
pendere pependisse pēnsum
weigh, pay
pendēre pependisse hang
penes *prp* + *acc* in the
possession of
penetrālia -ium *n pl* the
interior
penetrāre penetrate
penitus *adv* from within,
deep, far
penna -ae *f* feather
pēnsāre weigh, ponder,
consider
pēnsiō -ōnis *f* payment,
installment
pēnsitāre pay

pēnsum -ī *n* task
penta-meter -trī *m*
pentameter
pēnūria -ae *f* scarcity,
want
per *prp* + *acc* through,
by, during
per sē by oneself,
single-handed
per-agere carry out,
complete
per-agrāre travel over
per-angustus -a -um very
narrow
per-blandus -a -um very
charming
per-brevis -e very short
per-celer -is -e very fast
per-cellere -ulisse -ulsum
strike (with fear)
per-cēnsēre enumerate
perceptiō -ōnis *f* gathering
per-contārī inquire
(about), ask
percontātiō -ōnis *f* inter-
rogation, question
per-currere -rrisse -rsum
run over, pass over
per-cutere -iō -cussisse
-cussum strike, hit
per-dere -didisse -ditum
destroy, ruin, waste, lose
per-domāre subjugate
perduelliō -ōnis *f* treason
peregrīnus -a -um foreign,
alien
perennis -e enduring,
perpetual
per-errāre wander through
per-exiguus -a -um very
small
perfectus -a -um perfect
per-ferre carry, endure
per-ficere complete,
accomplish
perfidia -ae *f* faithlessness,
treachery
perfidus -a -um faithless,
treacherous
perfuga -ae *m* deserter
per-fugere take refuge
per-fugium -ī *n* place of
refuge, shelter
per-fundere wet, drench,
imbue, fill

per-fungī + *abl*   carry through, finish

pergere per-rēxisse   proceed, go on

per-grātus -a -um   very pleasing

per-hibēre   report, say

perīculōsus -a -um   dangerous, perilous

perīculum -ī *n*   danger, peril

per-imere -ēmisse -ēmptum   destroy, kill

periocha -ae *f*   summary

per-īre -eō -iisse   perish, be lost

peristȳlum -ī *n*   peristyle

perītus -a -um + *gen*   practiced, expert

per-iūcundus -a -um   very agreeable

per-magnus -a -um   very large

per-manēre   remain, continue

per-miscēre   mix, blend

per-mittere   allow, permit, leave

permixtiō -ōnis *f*   disturbance, chaos

per-molestus -a -um   very troublesome

per-movēre   move deeply

per-multī -ae -a   a great many

per-mūnīre   fortify thoroughly

per-mūtāre   exchange

permūtātiō -ōnis *f*   exchange

perniciēs -ēī *f*   destruction

perniciōsus -a -um   destructive, disastrous

per-ōrāre   conclude

per-paucī -ae -a   very few

per-pellere   enforce

perpetuus -a -um   continuous, permanent

per-rogāre   ask in turn

per-saepe   very often

per-sequī   follow, pursue

per-sevērāre   persist, continue

per-solvere   pay in full, fulfill

persōna -ae *f*   character, person

per-spicere   survey, recognize

per-stāre   stand firm, persist

per-suādēre -sisse + *dat*   persuade, convince

per-territus -a -um   terrified

per-timēscere -muisse   be frightened (of)

per-tinēre (ad)   relate, pertain (to)

per-turbāre   upset

per-vādere -sisse -sum   spread, pervade

per-vāstāre   devastate completely

per-venīre   get to, reach

per-volāre   move rapidly, rush, fly

pēs pedis *m*   foot

pessimus -a -um *sup*   worst

pessum dare   destroy, ruin

pesti-fer -era -erum   disastrous, pernicious

pestilentia -ae *f*   plague, pestilence

pestis -is *f*   plague, disaster

petasus -ī *m*   hat

petere -īvisse -ītum   make for, aim at, attack, seek, ask for, request

petītiō -ōnis *f*   pursuit, candidature

phalerae -ārum *f pl*   military decoration

phantasma -atis *n*   ghost, apparition

pharetra -ae *f*   quiver

philosophia -ae *f*   philosophy

philosophus -ī *m*   philosopher

pietās -ātis *f*   respect, devotion, piety

piger -gra -grum   lazy, torpid

pigēre: piget mē (+ *gen*)   I am displeased, I regret

pignus -oris *n*   pledge

pila -ae *f*   ball

pilleus -ī *m*   felt cap

pīlum -ī *n*   spear, javelin

pingere pīnxisse pictum   paint, embroider   tabula picta   painting

pīpiāre   chirp

pīrāta -ae *m*   pirate

pīrāticus -a -um   of pirates

pirum -ī *n*   pear

piscātor -ōris *m*   fisherman

piscis -is *m*   fish

pius -a -um   dutiful, devoted, pious

placēre + *dat*   please

placidus -a -um   quiet, calm, gentle

placitus -a -um   pleasing, agreeable

plānē   plainly, clearly

plānus -a -um   plain, clear

plaudere -sisse (+ *dat*)   clap, applaud

plausus -ūs *m*   applause

plēbēiī -ōrum *m pl*   plebeians

plēb(ē)s -is *f*   the (common) people

plēnus -a -um (+ *gen/abl*)   full (of)

plērī-que plērae- plēra-   most, most people

plērumque *adv*   mostly

plērus-que plēra- plērum-   most (of), the greater part

plōrāre   cry

plūma -ae *f*   feather

plumbum -ī *n*   lead

plūrēs -a *comp*   more

plūrimī -ae -a *sup*   most, a great many

plūrimum -ī *n, adv*   most, very much

plūrimus -a -um   very much, a lot of

plūs plūris *n, adv*   more

pōculum -ī *n*   cup, glass

poēma -atis *n*   poem

poena -ae *f*   punishment, penalty   poenās dare   suffer punishment

poēta -ae *m/f*   poet

poēticus -a -um   poetical

pollēns -entis *adi*   strong

pollēre   be strong

pollicērī   promise

pollicitārī   promise

pollicitātiō -ōnis *f*　promise
polluere -uisse -ūtum　soil, violate, degrade
pōmērium -ī *n*　open space round town
pompa -ae *f*　ceremonial procession
pondō *indēcl*　in weight, pounds
pondus -eris *n*　weight
pōnere posuisse positum place, put, pitch, lay down, take off, give up
　positum esse (in)　be situated, lie, depend
pōns pontis *m*　bridge
pontifex -icis *m*　high priest
pontus -ī *m*　sea
populārī　ravage, plunder
populāris -e　of the people, popular
populāris -is *m*　fellow citizen
populus -ī *m*　people, nation
porcus -ī *m*　pig
por-rigere　stretch out
porrō　forward, ahead
porta -ae *f*　gate
portāre　carry
por-tendere -disse -tum portend, presage
portentum -ī *n*　portent, prodigy
porticus -ūs *f*　portico, colonnade
portuōsus -a -um　having many harbors
portus -ūs *m*　harbor
poscere popōscisse demand, call for
posse potuisse　be able
possessiō -ōnis *f*　possession, occupation
possidēre -sēdisse　possess, own
post *prp + acc, adv*　behind, after, later
post-eā　afterward, later
posteā-quam　after, since
posterī -ōrum *m pl*　descendants, posterity
posterior -ius *comp*　back-, hind-, later

posteritās -ātis *f*　future, posterity
posterus -a -um　next, following
posthāc　from now on, hereafter
postīcum -ī *n*　backdoor
post-quam　after, since
postrēmō *adv*　finally
postrēmum *adv*　for the last time
postrēmus -a -um *sup*　last
postrī-diē　on the following day
postulāre　demand, require
postulātum -ī *n*　demand
pōtāre　drink
potēns -entis *adi*　powerful, master(ing)
potentia -ae *f*　power
potestās -ātis *f*　power
pōtiō -ōnis *f*　drinking, drink
potior -ius *comp*　preferable, better
potīrī + *abl/gen*　take possession of, hold
potissimum *adv sup*　preferably, especially
potius *adv comp*　rather
prae *prp + abl*　before, for
praebēre　present, offer, show
prae-cēdere　go on ahead, precede
praeceps -ipitis *adi*　headlong, precipitous
praeceptum -ī *n*　instruction, order
prae-cipere　anticipate, advise, order
praecipitāre　throw/fall/ rush headlong
praecipuē　especially, above all
praecipuus -a -um　outstanding, exceptional
prae-clārus -a -um　splendid, excellent
praecō -ōnis *m*　crier, announcer, herald
praeda -ae *f*　booty, prey
praedārī　plunder, loot
praedātōrius -a -um plundering

prae-dicāre　declare
prae-dīcere　foretell, prophesy
praedictum -ī *n*　prediction, prophecy
praedium -ī *n*　estate
prae-dīves -itis *adi*　very rich
praedō -ōnis *m*　robber, pirate
prae-esse (+ *dat*)　be in charge (of)
praefectus -ī *m*　prefect, commander
prae-ferre　prefer
prae-ficere　put in charge of
prae-mittere　send in advance
praemium -ī *n*　reward, prize
prae-nōmen -inis *n*　first name
prae-occupāre　preoccupy
prae-parāre　prepare
prae-pōnere (+ *dat*)　put in charge of
prae-potēns -entis *adi*　very powerful
praesēns -entis *adi*　present, instant
　(tempus) praesēns　present
prae-sentīre　have a presentiment of
praesertim　especially
praeses -idis *m/f*　guardian
praesidium -ī *n*　protection, aid, garrison
praestāns -antis *adi* outstanding
prae-stāre -stitisse　furnish, fulfill, surpass
　praestat　it is better
prae-sūmere　take for oneself, assume
praeter *prp + acc*　past, besides, except
　praeter spem　contrary to expectation
praeter-eā　besides
praeter-īre　pass by, pass, pass over
praeteritus -a -um　past
　(tempus) praeteritum the past

praeter-mittere omit, neglect, let pass

praeter-quam quod apart from the fact that

praeter-vehī ride/drive/sail past

prae-texta: toga p. toga with purple border

praetextātus -a -um wearing a toga praetexta

praetor -ōris *m* praetor, commander

praetōrium -ī *n* general's tent

praetōrius -a -um of the commander

praetōrius -ī *m* ex-praetor

praetūra -ae *f* praetorship

praeverbium -ī *n* prefix

prāt(ul)um -ī *n* meadow, lawn

prāvus -a -um faulty, wrong

precārī pray

precēs -um *f pl* prayers

prehendere -disse -ēnsum grasp, seize

premere pressisse press, harass, press hard pressum on, repress

pretiōsus -a -um precious

pretium -ī *n* price, value, reward

prīdem long ago

prī-diē the day before

prīmō *adv* at first, first

prīmōrēs -um *m pl* leading men, front ranks

prīmum *adv* first quam prīmum as soon as possible

prīmus -a -um first

prīnceps -ipis *adi, m* first, chief, emperor

prīncipium -ī *n* beginning, origin, basis

prior -ius first, former, front-

prīstinus -a -um former, previous

prius *adv* before

prius-quam before

prīvātim *adv* privately, personally

prīvātum -ī *n* private property

prīvātus -a -um private, holding no office

prō *prp + abl* before, on, for, instead of, as, according to

prō! o!

probāre approve of, prove

probātus -a -um acceptable, pleasing

probus -a -um good, honest, proper

prō-cēdere advance, go on, succeed

procella -ae *f* violent wind, gale

procērus -a -um tall, long

prō-cidere -disse fall forward, collapse

prō-clāmāre cry out

prō-cōnsul -is *m* (prōcōs.) proconsul, governor

prō-creāre engender, beget

procul far away, far (from) procul dubiō without doubt

prō-cumbere -cubuisse lean forward, bow down

prō-cūrāre attend to, administer

prōcūrātor -ōris *m* manager, superintendent

prō-currere -rrisse -rsum run forward, charge

prō-dere -didisse -ditum hand down, betray

prōd-esse prō-fuisse + *dat* be useful, do good

prōdigium -ī *n* prodigy

prōd-īre -eō -iisse -itum come forward, go forth

prōditiō -ōnis *f* betrayal

prōditor -ōris *m* traitor

prō-dūcere bring forth, extend

proelium -ī *n* battle

profectō indeed, certainly

prō-ferre fetch, produce, extend

prō-ficere progress, be successful

proficīscī -fectum set out, depart

pro-fitērī -fessum declare, offer

prō-flīgāre defeat decisively, crush

pro-fugere run away, flee

profugus -a -um fleeing; *m* fugitive

pro-fundere pour out, shed

prōgeniēs -ēī *f* offspring, descent

prō-gnātus -a -um (+ *abl*) born, son (of)

prō-gredī -ior -gressum go forward, advance

prōgressiō -ōnis *f* advance

pro-hibēre keep off, prevent, forbid

prō-icere throw (forward)

pro-inde (+ *imp*) accordingly

prō-lābī slip, overbalance

prōlēs -is *f* offspring

prōlētāriī -ōrum *m pl* lowest class of citizens

prōmere -mpsisse -mptum take out

prō-minēre project, stick out

prōmissum -ī *n* promise

prō-mittere promise

prō-movēre push forward, advance

prōmptū: in p. within reach, easy

prōmptus -a -um prompt, keen, ready

prō-mulgāre announce, publish

prōmunturium -ī *n* headland, promontory

prō-nūntiāre proclaim, announce

prōnus -a -um leaning forward, inclined

prōpatulum -ī *n* forecourt

prope *prp + acc, adv* near, nearly

properāre hurry

properē quickly

propinquus -a -um near, close, *m* relative

propior -ius *comp* nearer, closer

propius *adv comp*   nearer
prō-pōnere   set up, propose
prōpositum -ī *n*   objective, point
prō-praetor -ōris *m*   propraetor
proprius -a -um   own, proper
propter *prp* + *acc, adv*   because of, near
propter-eā   therefore
prōra -ae *f*   prow
prō-scrībere   proscribe, outlaw
prō-sequī   accompany, honor
prō-silīre -uisse   spring forth
prosperus -a -um   successful, favorable
prō-spicere   look out, look ahead
prō-sternere   knock down, overthrow
prō-tegere   protect
prōtinus   at once
prō-trahere   pull out, draw out
prō-vehī -vectum   sail out
prōventus -ūs *m*   growth, crop, harvest
prō-vidēre   see to it, take care
prōvincia -ae *f*   province, charge
prō-vocāre   challenge, appeal
prōvocātiō -ōnis *f*   appeal
prō-volāre   rush forth
proximus -a -um *sup*   nearest, next
proximus -ī *m*   close relative
prūdēns -entis *adi*   prudent, clever
prūdentia -ae *f*   intelligence, proficiency
pruīna -ae *f*   hoarfrost, rime
pūbēs -eris *adi*   mature, grown-up
pūblicānus -ī *m*   tax-gatherer, publican
pūblicāre   confiscate
pūblicum -ī *n*   public funds

pūblicus -a -um   public, state-
   rēs pūblica   affairs of state, the state
pudēns -entis *adi*   modest, virtuous
pudēre pudet mē (+ *gen*)   I am ashamed (of)
pudibundus -a -um   shamefaced
pudīcitia -ae *f*   chastity, virtue
pudīcus -a -um   chaste
pudor -ōris *m*   shame, decency
puella -ae *f*   girl
puer -erī *m*   boy, slave; *pl* children
puerīlis -e   of children
pueritia -ae *f*   boyhood
puerulus -ī *m*   small boy
pugna -ae *f*   fight
pugnāre   fight
pugnātor -ōris *m*   fighter, combatant
pugnus -ī *m*   fist
pulcher -chra -chrum   beautiful, fine
pulchritūdō -inis *f*   beauty
pullus -ī *m*   young one, chicken
pullus -a -um   somber, grey
pulmō -ōnis *m*   lung
pulsāre   strike, hit, knock (at)
pulsus -ūs *m*   thrust, impulse
pulvīnar -āris *n*   couch for the gods
pulvis -eris *m*   dust
pūnctum -ī *n*   dot, point, speck
pūnīre   punish
puppis -is *f*, *acc* -im, *abl* -ī   stern, poop
pūrgāre   clean, purge, excuse
purpura -ae *f*   purple
pūrus -a -um   clean, pure
putāre   think, suppose

Q

quā   which way, where (sī/nē/num) quā   by any road, anywhere

quā-cumque   wherever
quadrāgēsimus -a -um   fortieth
quadrāgintā   forty
quadrātus -a -um   square
quadriennium -ī *n*   four years
quadrīgae -ārum *f pl*   team of four horses
quadringentēsimus -a -um   four hundredth
quadringentī -ae -a   four hundred
quaerere -sīvisse -sītum   look for, seek, ask (for)
quaesō   I ask you, please
quaestiō -ōnis *f*   inquiry, question
quaestor -ōris *m*   quaestor
quaestōrius -a -um   fit to be a quaestor
quaestūra -ae *f*   quaestorship
quaestus -ūs *m*   income, profit
quālis -e   what sort of, (such) as
quālis-cumque   of whatever sort
quālitās -ātis *f*   quality
quam   how, as, than
   quam + *sup*   as...as possible
quam-diū   how long, (as long) as
quam-ob-rem   why
quamquam   although
quam-vīs   however, although
quandō   when, seeing that (sī/nē/num) quandō   at any time, ever
quantitās -ātis *f*   quantity, size
quantō + *comp* (tantō...)   how much, the...(the...)
quantum -ī *n, adv*   how much, (as much) as
   quantī *gen pretiī*   of what worth
quantus -a -um   how large, (as large) as
quantus-cumque -a- -um-   however great/much
quā-propter   why

quā-rē why, therefore, hence
quārtum/quārtō *adv* for the fourth time
quārtus -a -um fourth
  quārta pars fourth, quarter
quasi as, like, as if
quassāre shake, damage, batter
quater four times
quatere -iō shake
quaternī -ae -a four (each)
quattuor four
quattuor-decim fourteen
-que and
quercus -ī f oak
querēlla -ae f complaint
querī questum complain, grumble
querimōnia -ae f complaint, protest
quī quae quod who, which, he who
quī quae quod (...?) what, which
quī qua quod (sī/nē...) any
quia because
quic-quam -quid v. quid-
quī-cumque quae- quod- whoever, whatever, any
quid (v. quis) what, anything
quid *adv* why
quī-dam quae- quod-/quid- a certain, some(one)
quidem indeed, certainly
  nē quidem not even
quidnī why not
quid-quam/quic-quam anything
quid-quid/quic-quid whatever, anything that
quiēs -ētis f rest, repose, sleep
quiēscere -ēvisse rest
quiētus -a -um quiet
quī-libet quae- quod- no matter what/which
quīn why not, do...! come!
  quīn (etiam) indeed, even
  (nōn...) quīn + *coni* (but) that
quī-nam v. quis-nam
quīn-decim fifteen

quīndecim-virī -ōrum *m pl* board of fifteen priests
quīngentēsimus -a -um five hundredth
quīn-gentī -ae -a five hundred
quīnī -ae -a five (each)
quīnquāgēsimus -a -um fiftieth
quīnquāgintā fifty
quīnque five
quīnquennium -ī n five years
quīnque-rēmis (nāvis) having five banks of oars
quīnquiēs five times
Quīntīlis -is (mēnsis) July
quīntum/quīntō *adv* for the fifth time
quīntus -a -um fifth
quippe (quī/quae) inasmuch as, for
quīre -eō -īvisse be able to
Quirītēs -ium *m pl* Roman citizens
quis quae quid who, what
quis quid (sī/num/nē...) anyone, anything
quis-nam (quī-) quid-nam who/what ever?
quis-quam anyone
quis-que quae- quod- each
quis-quis anyone who, whoever
quī-vīs quae- quod- no matter what, any
quō *adv* where (to)
quō + *comp* (eō...) the... (the...)
  quō + *coni* in order that (thereby)
quo-ad until
quō-circā hence, therefore
quō-cumque *adv* wherever
quod (= quia) because, that
  quod sī if however, but if
quod n what, which, that which
quō-modo how
quondam once, some day
quoniam since, seeing that, as
quoque also, too
quot *indēcl* how many, (as many) as

quot-annīs every year
quotiēs how often, as often as
quotiēs-cumque every time that
quo-ūsque how long? till when?

R

rabiēs -ēī f rage, fury
radius -ī m ray
rādīx -īcis f root, foot, base
rāmus -ī m branch, bough
rapere -iō -uisse -ptum carry off, *pass* rush off
rapidus -a -um rushing, rapid
rapīna -ae f carrying off, plunder
raptim hurriedly
rārō *adv* rarely, seldom
rārus -a -um rare
ratiō -ōnis f account, consideration, reason, method, affair
  ratiōnem habēre + *gen* take into account
ratiōnālis -e of reasoning
ratis -is f raft
ratus -a -um valid, fixed, certain
  prō ratā parte in proportion
re-bellāre reopen the war, revolt
re-cēdere go back, retire
recēns -entis *adi* fresh
re-cidere reccidisse fall back
re-cīdere -disse -sum cut off, remove
reciperāre recover, recapture
re-cipere receive, admit, accept
  sē recipere retire, return, recover
recitāre read aloud
re-cognōscere recognize
re-conciliāre win back, reconcile
re-cordārī call to mind, recollect
recordātiō -ōnis f recollection

re-creāre restore, revive

rēctor -ōris *m* ruler, governor

rēctus -a -um straight, direct, straightforward, right, correct
    rēctā (viā) straight

re-cumbere -cubuisse lie down

re-cūsāre reject, refuse

red-dere -didisse -ditum give back, render

red-igere -ēgisse -āctum drive back, bring, reduce

red-imere -ēmisse -ēmptum ransom

redimīre encircle, surround

red-īre -eō -iisse -itum go back, return
    ad sē redīre return to one's senses

reditus -ūs *m* return

re-dūcere lead back, bring back

red-undāre overflow, be exuberant

re-fellere -lisse refute

re-ferre rettulisse relātum bring back, return, report, enter, refer
    referre (dē) make a proposal

rē-ferre rē-fert (meā) it is important (for me)

re-ficere restore, repair

re-fugere flee back, escape, recoil

rēgālis -e royal

regere rēxisse rēctum direct, guide, govern

rēgia -ae *f* royal palace

rēgīna -ae *f* queen

regiō -ōnis *f* region, district

rēgius -a -um royal

rēgnāre reign, rule

rēgnum -ī *n* kingship, kingdom, reign

re-gredī -ior -gressum go back, return

rēgula -ae *f* ruler

rēgulus -ī *m* petty king, prince

re-laxāre relax, relieve

religiō -ōnis *f* fear of the gods, religion

religiōsus -a -um sacred

re-linquere leave

reliquiae -ārum *f pl* remnants, remains

reliquum -ī *n* remainder, future

reliquus -a -um remaining, left

re-mandāre send back word

re-manēre remain, stay behind

remedium -ī *n* remedy

rēmex -igis *m* oarsman, rower

rēmigāre row

re-minīscī + *gen/acc* recollect

remissiō -ōnis *f* relaxation

remissus -a -um gentle, relaxed

re-mittere send back, relax

re-morārī delay

remōtus -a -um remote, distant

re-movēre remove

rēmus -ī *m* oar

re-nāscī be reborn, be re-created

re-novāre renew, resume

re-nūntiāre report, renounce

re-parāre repair, restore, renew

re-pellere reppulisse -pulsum drive back, repel, rebuff

repēns -entis *adi* sudden, unexpected

repente *adv* suddenly

repentīnus -a -um sudden

rēpere -psisse -ptum crawl

reperīre repperisse repertum find, discover, devise, invent

re-petere return to, repeat, claim back, recall
    rēs repetere claim return of property

re-pōnere put back

re-portāre carry back, bring home

re-prehendere blame, censure

re-primere -essisse -essum check, repress, restrain

repudiāre reject, refuse to accept

re-pugnāre fight back, resist

repulsa -ae *f* defeat (in an election)

re-putāre think over, reflect on

re-quiēscere rest

re-quīrere -sīvisse -sītum seek, ask

rērī ratum reckon, think, believe

rēs reī *f* thing, matter, affair
    rēs (pūblica) affairs of state, the state

re-scindere demolish, cancel, annul

re-sīdere -sēdisse sink back, subside

re-sistere -stitisse + *dat* halt, resist

re-sonāre resound

re-spergere -sisse -sum sprinkle, splatter

re-spicere look back (at), heed, regard, have regard for

re-spondēre -disse -sum answer

respōnsum -ī *n* answer

re-stāre -stitisse remain, be left
    restat (ut) it remains

re-stinguere -stīnxisse -stīnctum put out, extinguish

restis -is *f* rope

re-stituere -uisse -ūtum rebuild, restore, reinstate

re-surgere rise again, be restored

re-tardāre delay, hold up

rēte -is *n* net

re-ticēre keep silent

re-tinēre -uisse -tentum hold back

re-trahere pull back, bring back

retrō back

reus -ī *m* defendant, accused

re-vehere bring back

re-venīre come back

revertī -tisse -sum return, come back

re-vincere conquer

re-vīsere   revisit, visit

re-vocāre   call back, recall, revoke

rēx rēgis *m*   king

rhētor -oris *m*   teacher of rhetoric

rīdēre -sisse -sum   laugh, make fun of

rīdiculus -a -um   ridiculous

rigāre   irrigate

rigēre   be stiff

rīpa -ae *f*   bank

-ripere -iō -uisse -reptum

rīsus -ūs *m*   laughter, laugh

rīte *adv*   with due rites, properly

rītus -ūs *m*   rites, ceremonies

rīvus -ī *m*   brook, channel

rixa -ae *f*   quarrel, brawl

rōbur -oris *n*   oak, strength, force

rōbustus -a -um   strong, robust

rogāre   ask, ask for

rogātiō -ōnis *f*   proposed law, bill

rogitāre   ask (repeatedly)

rogus -ī *m*   funeral pyre

Rōmānus -a -um   Roman

rosa -ae *f*   rose

rōstra -ōrum *n pl*   speakers' platform

rōstrātus -a -um   having a beaked prow

rōstrum -ī *n*   beak, beaked prow

rota -ae *f*   wheel

rotundus -a -um   round

ruber -bra -brum   red

rubēre   be red, blush

rudis -e   crude, rude

ruere ruisse   rush, tumble down

ruīna -ae *f*   collapse, ruin

rūmor -ōris *m*   rumor

rumpere rūpisse ruptum   burst, break, break off

rūpēs -is *f*   crag, rock

ruptor -ōris *m*   one who breaks

rūrī *loc*   in the country

rūrsus *adv*   again

rūs rūris *n*   the country

rūsticus -a -um   rural, rustic, farm-

rutilus -a -um   red

S

sacculus -ī *m*   purse

saccus -ī *m*   sack

sacer -cra -crum   holy, sacred

sacerdōs -ōtis *m/f*   priest, priestess

sacrāre   consecrate

sacrārium -ī *n*   sanctuary

sacrificāre   make a sacrifice

sacrificium -ī *n*   sacrifice

sacrum -ī *n*   sacred object, sacrifice

saeculum -ī *n*   generation, age, century

saepe -ius -issimē   often

saepīre   surround

saevitia -ae *f*   savageness, cruelty

saevus -a -um   fierce, cruel

sagitta -ae *f*   arrow

sagittārius -ī *m*   archer, bowman

sāl salis *m*   salt, wit

salīnae -ārum *f pl*   salt-pans

salīre -uisse   jump

saltāre   dance

saltem   at least, anyhow

saltus -ūs *m*   wooded hills

salūber -bris -bre   healthy, salutary

salūs -ūtis *f*   health, salvation, safety
salūtem dīcere + *dat* greet

salūtāre   greet

salūtāris -e   wholesome, salutary

salvāre   save

salvē -ēte   hallo, good morning

salvēre iubēre   greet

salvus -a -um   safe, unharmed

sānāre   heal, cure

sānctus -a -um   holy

sānē   certainly, quite

sanguineus -a -um   blood-stained, bloodshot

sanguinulentus -a -um   blood-stained

sanguis -inis *m*   blood, race, relationship

sānus -a -um   healthy, well

sapere -iō -iisse   be wise, have sense

sapiēns -entis *adi*   wise

sapientia -ae *f*   wisdom

sarcina -ae *f*   pack, kit

sarmentum -ī *n*   brush-wood, branch

satelles -itis *m*   henchman, attendant

satis   enough, rather

satius *comp* < satis   better, preferable

saucius -a -um   wounded

saxum -ī *n*   rock

scaena -ae *f*   scene, stage

scaenicus -a -um   theatrical

scālae -ārum *f pl*   ladder

scalpellum -ī *n*   scalpel, surgical knife

scamnum -ī *n*   stool

scandere -disse -ānsum   climb, mount

scelerātus -a -um   accursed, criminal

scelestus -a -um   criminal, wicked

scelus -eris *n*   crime

scēptrum -ī *n*   sceptre

sciēns -entis *adi* + *gen*   having knowledge of

scientia -ae *f*   knowledge

scīlicet   of course

scindere -idisse -issum   tear, tear up

scīre   know

scīscitārī   inquire, ask

scopulus -ī *m*   rock

scortum -ī *n*   prostitute, whore

scrībere -psisse -ptum   write, describe, enroll

scrīptor -ōris *m*   writer

scrīptum -ī *n*   writing, book

scrīptūra -ae *f*   tax on grazing rights

scrūtārī   examine, search

scūtum -ī *n*   shield

sē/sēsē *acc/abl, dat* sibi   himself, each other

secāre -uisse -ctum   cut

sē-cernere   separate, detach

sēcrētō *adv*   in private

sēcrētum -ī *n*   seclusion, privacy
secundō *adv*   for the second time
secundum *prp + acc*   along, after, according to
secundus -a -um   second, favorable
secūris -is *f, acc* -im, *abl* -ī   axe
secus *adv*   otherwise
sed   but
sēdāre   allay, appease, calm
sē-decim   sixteen
sedēre sēdisse   sit
sēdēs -is *f*   seat, abode, dwelling
sēditiō -ōnis *f*   discord, insurrection
sēditiōsus -a -um   seditious
sēgnis -e   slothful, inactive
sē-iungere   separate
sella -ae *f*   stool, chair
semel   once
sēmen -inis *n*   seed, offspring
sē-met   himself, themselves
sēmi-animis -e   half-alive
sēmi-ermis -e   half-armed
sēmi-somnus -a -um   half-asleep
semper   always
sempiternus -a -um   everlasting, eternal
senātor -ōris *m*   senator
senātus -ūs *m*   senate, assembly, sitting
senecta -ae *f*   old age
senectūs -ūtis *f*   old age
senēscere -nuisse   grow old, weaken
senex senis *m*   old man
sēnī -ae -a   six (each)
senior -ōris *comp*   older
sēnsim   gradually, little by little
sēnsus -ūs *m*   sense, sensation
sententia -ae *f*   opinion, sentence
sentīre sēnsisse -sum   feel, sense, think
sepelīre -īvisse -ultum   bury
septem   seven

September -bris (mēnsis)   September
septen-decim   seventeen
septēnī -ae -a   seven (each)
septentriōnālis -e   northern
septentriōnēs -um *m pl*   north
septimus -a -um   seventh
septingentēsimus -a -um   seven hundredth
septin-gentī -ae -a   seven hundred
septuāgēsimus -a -um   seventieth
septuāgintā   seventy
sepulcrum -ī *n*   tomb, grave
sequī secūtum   follow
serēnus -a -um   clear, cloudless, calm
serere sēvisse satum   sow, plant
sērius *comp adv* < sērō   later, too late
sērius -a -um   serious
sermō -ōnis *m*   talk, language
sērō *adv, comp* sērius   late
serpēns -entis *m*   snake, serpent
sērus -a -um   late
serva -ae *f*   female slave
servāre   preserve, save
servātor -ōris *m*   savior
servīlis -e   of a slave, servile
servīre + *dat*   be a slave, serve
servitium -ī *n*   slavery
servitūs -ūtis *f*   slavery
servus -ī *m*   slave, servant
sescentēsimus -a -um   six hundredth
ses-centī -ae -a   six hundred
sēsē *v.* sē
sēstertius -ī *m*   sesterce (coin)
sētius nihilō sētius   none the less
seu *v.* sī-ve/seu
sevērus -a -um   stern, severe
sex   six
sexāgēsimus -a -um   sixtieth
sexāgintā   sixty

sexiēs   six times
Sextīlis -is (mēnsis)   August
sextus -a -um   sixth
sī   if
sīc   in this way, so, thus
siccāre   dry, drain
siccus -a -um   dry
sīc-ut/-utī   just as, as
sīdere sēdisse sessum   sit down, settle
sīdus -eris *n*   star, heavenly body
signāre   mark, seal, stamp
significāre   indicate, mean
significātiō -ōnis *f*   intimation, meaning
signum -ī *n*   sign, seal, signal, statue, ensign
silentium -ī *n*   silence
silēre   be silent
silva -ae *f*   wood, forest
silvestris -e   of the woods, wild
similis -e (+ *gen/dat*), *sup* -illimus   similar, like
   vērī similis   probable, convincing
simplex -icis *adi*   simple, single, plain
simul   together, at the same time
   simul (atque) + *perf*   as soon as
simulācrum -ī *n*   image, statue
simulāre   pretend
simultās -ātis *f*   enmity, quarrel
sīn   but if
sine *prp + abl*   without
sinere sīvisse situm   let, allow
singulāris -e   single, singular, unique
singulī -ae -a   one (each), each
sinister -tra -trum   left, *f* the left (hand)
sinus -ūs *m*   bay, fold (of toga), breast
sī-quidem   seeing that, since
sistere   halt, stop
sitīre   be thirsty
sitis -is *f*   thirst

situs -a -um   situated, based, dependent

situs -ūs *m*   position, situation

sī-ve/seu   or, or if   s. ...s.   whether...or

socer -erī *m*   father-in-law

sociālis -e   of allies, social

sociāre   join, unite

societās -ātis *f*   partnership, alliance

socius -ī *m*   companion, partner, ally

socordia -ae *f*   sluggishness, indolence

sōl -is *m*   sun

sōlārī   comfort

solēre -itum esse   be accustomed

sōlitūdō -inis *f*   loneliness, lonely place

solitus -a -um   usual

solium -ī *n*   throne

sollicitāre   solicit, incite

solum -ī *n*   soil, ground, floor

sōlum *adv*   only

sōlus -a -um   alone, lonely

solūtus -a -um ōrātiō s.a   prose

solvere -visse solūtum   untie, loosen, dissolve, abolish, discharge, pay   nāvem solvere   cast off, set sail

somnium -ī *n*   dream

somnus -ī *m*   sleep

sonāre -uisse   sound

sonitus -ūs *m*   noise, sound

sonus -ī *m*   sound

sōpīre   cause to sleep, stun   sōpītus   sleeping, asleep

sordēs -ium *f pl*   dirt

sordidus -a -um   dirty, mean, base

soror -ōris *f*   sister

sors -rtis *f*   lot, drawing lots, fortune

sortīrī   draw lots

sōspes -itis *adi*   safe and sound

spargere -sisse -sum   scatter

spatium -ī *n*   space, distance, interval, walk, time, period

speciēs -ēī *f*   sight, appearance, shape, semblance, sort, species

spectāculum -ī *n*   sight, spectacle, *pl* seats

spectāre   watch, look at   spectāre ad   face, tend to, aim at

spectātor -ōris *m*   spectator

spectātus -a -um   manifest, undisputed

speculārī   spy, reconnoiter

speculātor -ōris *m*   scout, spy

speculum -ī *n*   mirror

specus -ūs *m*   cave, grotto

spēlunca -ae *f*   cave, grotto

spērāre   hope (for)

spernere sprēvisse -ētum   disdain, scorn

spēs -ēī *f*   hope

sphaera -ae *f*   globe, sphere

-spicere -iō -spexisse -spectum

spīrāre   breathe, blow

splendēre   shine

splendidus -a -um   shining, splendid

splendor -ōris *m*   brightness, splendor

spolia -ōrum *n pl*   spoils, booty

spoliāre   strip (of arms), rob

spondēre spopondisse spōnsum   pledge, promise, betroth

spondēus -ī *m*   spondee (——)

spōnsus -ī *m*   fiancé

sponte (meā/suā)   of my/his own accord

stabilis -e   firm, stable

stabulum -ī *n*   stable

stadium -ī *n*   running-track

stāgnum -ī *n*   pool, pond

stāre stetisse   stand, endure, cost

statim   at once

statiō -ōnis *f*   post, guard, anchorage

statīva -ōrum *n pl*   permanent camp

statua -ae *f*   statue

statuere -uisse -ūtum   fix, determine, decide

status -ūs *m*   state, condition, order

stēlla -ae *f*   star

stēllifer -era -erum   star-bearing

sterilis -e   barren, sterile

sternere strāvisse strātum   spread, knock down   viam sternere   pave a road

stīllāre   drip

stilus -ī *m*   stylus, writing

stimulāre   spur on, stimulate

stipendium -ī *n*   soldier's pay, service

stīpes -itis *m*   stake, stick

stirps -pis *f*   origin, stock, offspring

strāgēs -is *f*   slaughter

strāmentum -ī *n*   straw

strēnuus -a -um   active, vigorous

strepere -uisse   make a noise

strepitus -ūs *m*   noise, din

stringere -īnxisse -ictum   draw, unsheathe

strophē -ae *f*   verse, stanza

struere -ūxisse -ūctum   arrange, contrive, devise

studēre + *dat*   devote oneself to

studiōsus -a -um (+ *gen*)   interested (in)

studium -ī *n*   interest, study

stultitia -ae *f*   stupidity, folly

stultus -a -um   stupid, foolish

stupe-factus -a -um   amazed, stupefied

stupēre   be aghast

stuprāre   violate, rape

stuprum -ī *n*   rape

suādēre -sisse -sum + *dat*   advise

sub *prp* + *abl/acc*   under, near

sub-agrestis -e   somewhat boorish

sub-dere -didisse -ditum   set (spurs to)

sub-dūcere　draw up, beach, lead off

sub-icere　put under, subject, add

sub-iectus -a -um + *dat*　situated under

sub-igere -ēgisse -āctum　subdue, drive, force

sub-inde　immediately afterward

sub-īre -eō -iisse -itum　go under, undergo

subitō *adv*　suddenly

subitus -a -um　sudden

sub-legere　appoint

sublīmis -e　high (up), aloft

sub-mergere　sink

sub-mittere　lower

sub-movēre　remove, drive off

sub-nīxus -a -um + *abl*　resting on, relying on

sub-scrībere　write underneath

subsellium -ī *n*　bench

subsidium -ī *n*　support, help, resource

subter *adv*　below, underneath

sub-terrāneus -a -um　underground

sub-urbānus -a -um　near the city

sub-venīre + *dat*　come to help

suc-cēdere (+ *dat*)　enter, succeed, follow

successor -ōris *m*　successor

successus -ūs *m*　success

suc-cingere　surround

suc-clāmāre　shout in response

suc-cumbere -cubuisse + *dat*　yield, submit

suc-currere -rrisse + *dat*　(run to) help

sūdor -ōris *m*　sweat

suf-ficere　appoint, substitute

suffixum -ī *n*　suffix

suf-frāgārī　vote for, support

suffrāgium -ī *n*　vote

sūmere -mpsisse -mptum　take, take up, adopt, assume

summa -ae *f*　total, sum, main part

summus -a -um *sup*　highest, greatest, top of

sūmptus -ūs *m*　expenditure, expense

su-ove-taurīlia -ium *n pl*　purificatory sacrifice

super *prp + acc, adv*　on, on top (of), above
　prp + abl　on, about

superāre　cross, surpass, overcome, defeat, remain

superbia -ae *f*　arrogance, pride

superbus -a -um　haughty, proud

super-ēminēre　stand out above

super-esse　be left, be over, survive

super-fundere　pour over, spread

superior -ius *comp*　higher, superior, former

superus -a -um　upper

super-venīre (+ *dat*)　appear, surprise

suppeditāre　supply

supplēmentum -ī *n*　reinforcement

sup-plēre -ēvisse -ētum　fill up, reinforce

supplex -icis *adi*　suppliant

supplicātiō -ōnis *f*　thanksgiving

supplicium -ī *n*　(capital) punishment

suprā *prp + acc*　above, on, over
　adv　above, further back

suprēmus -a -um *sup*　highest, sovereign

surdus -a -um　deaf

surgere sur-rēxisse　rise, get up

sur-ripere　steal

sūrsum *adv*　up, upward

sūs suis *f*　pig

sus-cipere　take up, receive, adopt

suscitāre　wake up, rouse

suspectus -a -um　suspected, suspect

sus-pendere -disse -ēnsum　hang, suspend

suspicārī　guess, suspect

su-spicere　look up (at)

suspiciō -ōnis *f*　suspicion

sustentāre　sustain, maintain, endure

sus-tinēre -uisse -tentum　support, sustain, maintain, endure

suus -a -um　his/her/their (own)

syllaba -ae *f*　syllable

synōnymum -ī *n*　synonym

T

tabella -ae *f*　(writing-) tablet

tabellārius -ī *m*　letter-carrier

taberna -ae *f*　shop, stall

tabernāculum -ī *n*　tent

tabernārius -ī *m*　shop-keeper

tābēscere -buisse　waste away, decay

tabula -ae *f*　(writing-) tablet, painting

tabulārium -ī *n*　record-office

tacēre　be silent (about)

tacitus -a -um　silent

taedēre taedet mē (+ *gen*)　I am tired/sick of

taeter -tra -trum　foul, horrible

talentum -ī *n*　talent

tālis -e　such

tam　so, as

tam-diū　so long, as long

tamen　nevertheless, yet

tam-etsī　although

tam-quam　as, like, as though

tandem　at last, do...! then (...?)

tangere tetigisse tāctum　touch

tantum -ī *n*　so much
　tantī *gen pretiī*　of such worth
　alterum tantum　twice as much

tantum *adv*　so much, only

tantum-modo　only, merely

tantun-dem just as much
tantus -a -um so big, so great
tardāre delay
tardus -a -um slow, late
tata -ae *m* daddy
taurus -ī *m* bull
tēctum -ī *n* roof, house
tēctus -a -um covered, decked
tegere tēxisse tēctum cover, conceal
tellūs -ūris *f* earth
tēlum -ī *n* spear, weapon
temerārius -a -um reckless
temere *adv* heedlessly
temeritās -ātis *f* recklessness
temperantia -ae *f* self-control, moderation
temperāre moderate, temper, refrain
temperātiō -ōnis *f* organizing power
temperātus -a -um moderate, restrained
tempestās -ātis *f* storm, period
tempestīvus -a -um timely, suitable
templum -ī *n* temple, (sacred) space
temptāre try (to influence), attack
tempus -oris *n* time, opportunity
tendere tetendisse stretch, spread, lay, make tentum/tēnsum one's way, insist
tenebrae -ārum *f pl* darkness
tenebricōsus -a -um dark
tener -era -erum tender, delicate
tenēre -uisse -ntum hold, keep (back), reach, hold one's course, sail
tenuis -e thin
ter three times
terere trīvisse trītum wear out, use up, spend
tergēre -sisse -sum wipe
tergum -ī *n* back
terminus -ī *m* boundary (-stone)

ternī -ae -a three (each)
terra -ae *f* earth, ground, country
terrēre frighten
terrestris -e earthly, terrestrial
terribilis -e terrible
terror -ōris *m* fright, terror
tertium/tertiō *adv* for the third time
tertius -a -um third
testāmentum -ī *n* will, testament
testārī call to witness
testis -is *m/f* witness
thalamus -ī *m* bedroom
theātrum -ī *n* theater
thema -atis *n* stem, theme
thermae -ārum *f pl* public baths
thēsaurus -ī *m* treasure
tībiae -ārum *f pl* flute
tībīcen -inis *m* flute-player
tigris -is *f* tiger
timēre fear, be afraid (of)
timidus -a -um fearful, timid
timor -ōris *m* fear
tingere tīnxisse tīnctum wet, soak
tīrō -ōnis *m* recruit
titulus -ī *m* title
toga -ae *f* toga
togātus -a -um wearing the toga
tolerābilis -e tolerable
tolerāre bear, endure
tollere sus-tulisse sublātum raise, pick up, remove, abolish, put an end to
tonāre -uisse thunder
tonitrus -ūs *m* thunder
torquātus -a -um wearing a collar
torquis -is *m* collar
torrēre -uisse tōstum scorch, parch
torridus -a -um scorched, parched
torus -ī *m* bed
tot *indēcl* so many
tot-idem *indēcl* as many
totiēs so many times
tōtus -a -um the whole of, all

trabs -bis *f* beam, ship
tractāre handle, treat, manage
trā-dere -didisse -ditum hand over, deliver, tell
trā-dūcere move (across), pass
tragicus -a -um tragic
tragoedia -ae *f* tragedy
trāgula -ae *f* spear, javelin
trahere -āxisse -actum drag, pull, draw, derive, draw out, protract
trā-icere take across, cross, pierce
trā-natāre swim across
tranquillitās -ātis *f* calmness
tranquillus -a -um calm, still
trāns *prp + acc* across, over, beyond
trān-scendere -disse climb across, cross
trāns-ferre transfer, convey, carry
trāns-fīgere pierce
trāns-fuga -ae *m* deserter
trāns-fugere go over, desert
trāns-gredī -ior -gressum cross
trāns-igere -ēgisse -āctum carry through, finish
trān-silīre -uisse jump over
trāns-īre -eō -iisse -itum cross, pass, go over
trānsitiō -ōnis *f* crossing over, defection
trānsitus -ūs *m* crossing, passage
trāns-marīnus -a -um from beyond the seas
trāns-mittere send over, cross
trāns-portāre carry across, transport
trāns-vehere carry (*pass* sail) across
trāns-versus -a -um placed crosswise
trecentēsimus -a -um three hundredth

tre-centī -ae -a   three hundred
trē-decim   thirteen
tremere -uisse   tremble
trepidāre   be in panic, tremble
trepidātiō -ōnis *f*   alarm, panic
trepidus -a -um   alarmed, in panic
trēs tria   three
tribuere -uisse -ūtum   grant, attribute
tribūnal -ālis *n*   dais, platform
tribūnātus -ūs *m*   office of tribune
tribūnus -ī *m*   tribune
tribus -ūs *f*   tribe (division of citizens)
tribūtum -ī *n*   tax
trīcēsimus -a -um   thirtieth
trīclīnium -ī *n*   dining-room
tridēns -entis *m*   trident
trīduum -ī *n*   three days
triennium -ī *n*   three years
triēns -entis *m*   third of an as
trigeminus -a -um   triplet
trīgintā   thirty
trīnī -ae -a   three
trirēmis -e   trireme
trīstis -e   sad
trīstitia -ae *f*   sadness
trīticum -ī *n*   wheat
triumphālis -e   triumphal
triumphāre   celebrate a triumph
triumphus -ī *m*   triumph
trium-virī -ōrum *m pl*   commission of three
trium-virālis -e   of the triumvirs
trochaeus -ī *m*   trochee (—∪)
trucīdāre   slaughter
trux -ucis *adi*   savage, grim
tū tē tibi (*gen* tuī)   you, yourself
tuba -ae *f*   trumpet
tubicen -inis *m*   trumpeter
tuērī tūtum   guard, protect, look at
tugurium -ī *n*   hut

tum   then
    cum...tum...   not only... but also...
tumēre   swell
tumidus -a -um   swollen
tumulōsus -a -um   hilly
tumultuārī   make an uproar
tumultuārius -a -um   casual, unplanned
tumultus -ūs *m*   uproar
tumulus -ī *m*   hillock, burial-mound
tunc   then
tunica -ae *f*   tunic
turba -ae *f*   disorder, throng, crowd
turbāre   stir up, disturb, upset
turbidus -a -um   agitated, stormy
turgid(ul)us -a -um   swollen
turma -ae *f*   squadron
turmātim   in squadrons
turpis -e   ugly, foul, shameful
turris -is, *acc* -im, *abl* -ī   tower
tūtārī   protect
tūtō *adv*   safely
tūtor -ōris *m*   guardian
tūtus -a -um   safe
tuus -a -um   your, yours
tyrannis -idis *f*   tyranny
tyrannus -ī *m*   tyrant

U

ūber -eris *n*   udder
ūber -eris *adi*   fertile
ūbertās -ātis *f*   fruitfulness
ubi   where
    ubi (prīmum) + *perf*   as soon as
ubi-cumque   wherever
ubī-que   everywhere
ūdus -a -um   wet
ulcīscī ultum   revenge, avenge
ūllus -a -um   any
ulterior -ius *comp*   farther, more distant
ultimus -a -um *sup*   most distant, last
    ad ultimum   finally

ultor -ōris *m*   avenger
ultrā *prp* + *acc, adv*   beyond, further
ultrīx -īcis *adi f*   avenging
ultrō   spontaneously
    ultrō citrō(que)   back and forth
ululāre   howl
ululātus -ūs *m*   howling
umbra -a *f*   shade, shadow
umerus -ī *m*   shoulder
ūmidus -a -um   wet, moist
umquam   ever
ūnā *adv*   together
unda -ae *f*   wave
unde   from where
ūn-dē-centum   ninety-nine
ūn-decim   eleven
ūndecimus -a -um   eleventh
ūn-dē-trīgintā   twenty-nine
ūn-dē-vīcēsimus -a -um   nineteenth
ūn-dē-vīgintī   nineteen
undique   from all sides
unguis -is *m*   nail, claw
ūnī -ae -a   one
ūnicē   particularly
ūnicus -a -um   one and only, sole
ūniversus -a -um   the whole of, entire
ūnus -a -um   one, only
    ad ūnum   without exception
ūnus-quisque   each one
urbānus -a -um   of the city, urban
urbs -bis *f*   city
ūrere ussisse ustum   burn
urgēre -sisse   press, oppress
usquam   anywhere
ūsque   up (to), all the time
ūsus -ūs *m*   use, practice, usage
    ūsū venīre   occur
    ūsuī/ex ūsū esse   be of use
ut/utī   like, as, how
    ut + *coni*   that, in order that, to
    ut (prīmum) + *perf*   as soon as

ut-cumque no matter how, however

uter utra utrum which (of the two)

uter-que utra- utrum- each of the two, both

utī *v.* ut

ūtī ūsum + *abl* use, enjoy

ūtilis -e useful

ūtilitās -ātis *f* interest, advantage

utinam I wish that, if only…!

utpote namely

utrimque on/from both sides

utrobīque in both places

utrum… an … or…? whether… or

ūva -ae *f* grape

uxor -ōris *f* wife

uxōrius -a -um attached to one's wife

V

vacuus -a -um empty

vādere advance, go

vadum -ī *n* ford; *pl* shallows

vagārī wander, roam

vāgīna -ae *f* sheath

vāgīre wail, squall

vāgītus -ūs *f* wail, squall

vagus -a -um wandering, roaming

valdē strongly, very (much)

valē -ēte farewell, goodbye

valēns -entis *adi* strong

valēre be strong, be well

valētūdō -inis *f* health, illness

validus -a -um strong

vāllāre fortify, defend

vallis -is *f* valley

vāllum -ī *n* rampart

vāllus -ī *m* stake (for a palisade)

vānus -a -um empty, useless, vain

varietās -ātis *f* variety, diversity

varius -a -um varied, different

vās vāsis *n*, *pl* -a -ōrum vessel, bowl

vāstāre lay waste, ravage

vāstus -a -um desolate, vast, huge

vātēs -is *m/f* prophet(ess), seer

-ve or

vectīgal -ālis *n* (indirect) tax

vectīgālis -e tax-paying, tributary

vehemēns -entis *adi* violent

vehere vēxisse vectum carry, convey; *pass* ride, sail, travel

vehiculum -ī *n* waggon, vehicle

vel or, even

vēlāre cover

velle volō voluisse want, be willing

vēlōx -ōcis *adi* swift, rapid

vēlum -ī *n* sail

vel-ut like, as

vēna -ae *f* vein

vēnālis -e for sale

vēnārī go hunting, hunt

vēnātor -ōris *m* hunter

vēn-dere -didisse sell

venēnātus -a -um poisoned, poisonous

venēnum -ī *n* poison

venia -ae *f* favor, leave, pardon

venīre vēnisse ventum come

vēn-īre -eō -iisse be sold

venter -tris *m* belly, stomach

ventitāre come frequently

ventus -ī *m* wind

vēnun-dare put up for sale

venustus -a -um charming

vēr vēris *n* spring

verbera -um *n pl* lashes, flogging

verberāre beat, flog

verbum -ī *n* word, verb

verērī fear

vergere slope, point, turn

vērō really, however, but neque/nec vērō but not

versāre turn over, ponder

versārī turn, move about, be

versiculus -ī *m* short verse

versus -ūs *m* line, verse

versus ad…v. toward

vertere -tisse -sum turn, change

vertex -icis *m* whirlpool, peak, pole

vērum but

vērum -ī *n* truth vērī similis probable, convincing

vērus -a -um true, real, proper

vescī + *abl* feed on, eat

vesper -erī *m* evening

vesperī *adv* in the evening

vester -tra -trum your, yours

vestibulum -ī *n* forecourt

vestīgium -ī *n* footprint, trace

vestīmentum -ī *n* garment, clothing

vestīre dress

vestis -is *f* clothes, cloth

vestrum *gen* of you

vetāre forbid

vetus -eris, *sup* -errimus old

vetustās -ātis *f* age

vetustus -a -um ancient, old

vexāre harass, trouble, ravage

vexillum -ī *n* standard, ensign

via -ae *f* road, way, street

viāticum -ī *n* provision for a journey

vicem in/per vicem in turn, mutually

vīcēsimus -a -um twentieth

vīcīnitās -ātis *f* neighborhood, vicinity

vīcīnus -a -um neighboring

vicissim in turn

victima -ae *f* victim

victor -ōris *m*, *adi* conqueror, victorious

victōria -ae *f* victory

victrīx -īcis *adi f* victorious

vīcus -ī *m* street, village

vidēlicet evidently, of course

vidēre vīdisse vīsum see; *pass* seem
vidua -ae *f* widow
vigēre be vigorous
vigil -is *adi* wakeful, watchful
vigilāns -antis *adi* waking, wakeful
vigilāre be awake
vigilia -ae *f* night watch, vigil
vīgintī twenty
vigor -ōris *m* vigor
vīlis -e cheap
vīlitās -ātis *f* cheapness, low price
vīlla -ae *f* country house, villa
vincere vīcisse victum defeat, overcome, win
vincīre -nxisse -nctum tie
vinc(u)lum -ī *n* bond, chain
vindicāre claim, avenge
vīnea -ae *f* vineyard, mantlet
vīnum -ī *n* wine
violāre violate
violentus -a -um, *adv* -nter violent, impetuous
vir -ī *m* man, husband
vīrēs -ium *f pl* strength
virga -ae *f* rod
virginitās -ātis *f* virginity

virgō -inis *f* maiden, young girl
virīlis -e male
virītim man by man, evenly
virtūs -ūtis *f* valor, courage
vīs, *acc* vim, *abl* vī force, violence, power, value, quantity, number
viscera -um *n pl* internal organs
vīsere -sisse go and see, visit
vīsum -ī *n* sight
vīsus -ūs *m* sight
vīta -ae *f* life
vītāre avoid
vītis -is *f* vine, centurion's staff
vitium -ī *n* defect, fault, vice
vituperāre criticize, blame
vīvere vīxisse live, be alive
vīvus -a -um living, alive, live
vix hardly
vix-dum scarcely yet, only just
vocābulum -ī *n* word
vōcālis -is *f* vowel
vocāre call, summon, invite
vocāre in + *acc* bring into, expose to
volāre fly

volitāre fly about, flutter
volucris -is *f* bird
voluntārius -a -um voluntary
voluntās -ātis *f* will
voluptās -ātis *f* pleasure, delight
volūtāre roll, *pass* whirl
volvere -visse volūtum roll, turn (over), ponder; *pass* turn, revolve
vorāgō -inis *f* abyss, whirlpool
vorāre swallow, devour
vōs vōbīs you, yourselves
vōs-met you, yourselves
vovēre vōvisse vōtum promise, vow
vōx vōcis *f* voice
vulgāris -e common, everyday
vulgō adv commonly
vulgus -ī *n* the (common) people
vulnerāre wound
vulnus -eris *n* wound
vultur -is *m* vulture
vultus -ūs *m* countenance, face

Z

zephyrus -ī *m* west wind
zōna -ae *f* girdle, zone

Grammatica Latina

THE PARTS OF SPEECH

The **parts of speech**, or word classes, are:

- **Noun** (or **substantive**), e.g. *Mārcus, Rōma, puer, oppidum leō, aqua, color, pugna, mors,* etc.
- **Adjective**, e.g. *Rōmānus, bonus, pulcher, brevis,* etc.
- **Pronoun**, e.g. *tū, nōs, is, hic, ille, quis, quī, nēmō,* etc.
- **Verb**, e.g. *amāre, habēre, venīre, emere, īre, esse,* etc.
- **Adverb**, e.g. *bene, rēctē, fortiter, ita, nōn, hīc,* etc.
- **Conjunction**, e.g. *et, neque, sed, aut, quia, dum, sī, ut,* etc.
- **Preposition**, e.g. *in, ab, ad, post, inter, sine, dē,* etc.
- **Interjection**, e.g. *ō, ei, heu, heus, ecce,* etc.
- **Numerals** are nouns and adjectives which denote numbers, e.g. *trēs, tertius, ternī.*
- Adverbs, conjunctions, prepositions and interjections are **indeclinable** words, so-called **particles**.

parts of speech:
nouns (substantives)
adjectives
pronouns
verbs
adverbs
conjunctions
prepositions
interjections

numerals

particles

NOUNS

Gender, number, case

There are three **genders: masculine**, e.g. *servus,* **feminine**, e.g. *ancilla,* and **neuter**, e.g. *oppidum.*

There are two **numbers: singular**, e.g. *servus,* and **plural**, e.g. *servī.* Nouns which have no singular are called **plūrālia tantum.**

There are six **cases: nominative**, e.g. *servus,* **accusative**, e.g. *servum,* **genitive**, e.g. *servī,* **dative**, e.g. *servō,* **ablative**, e.g. *(ā) servō,* and **vocative**, e.g. *serve.*

genders: masc., m.
            fem., f.
            neut., n.

numbers: sing. pl.
cases: nom.
            acc.
            gen.
            dat.
            abl.
            voc.

Stem and ending

The **stem** is the main part of a word, e.g. *serv-, ancill-, oppid-, magn-, brev-,* to which various inflectional **endings** are added, e.g. *-um, -ī, -am, -ae, -ō, -ēs, -ibus.*

In the examples in this book the stem is separated from the ending with a thin vertical stroke [|], e.g. *serv|us, serv|ī.*

stems: *serv-, ancill-, oppid-,* etc.

endings: *-ī, -am, -ae,* etc.

Declensions

There are five **declensions**:

1st declension: gen. sing. *-ae*, e.g. *īnsul|a -ae.*

2nd declension: gen. sing. *-ī*, e.g. *serv|us -ī, oppid|um -ī.*

3rd declension: gen. sing. *-is*, e.g. *sōl sōl|is, urb|s -is.*

4th declension: gen. sing. *-ūs*, e.g. *man|us -ūs.*

5th declension: gen. sing. *-ēī/-eī*, e.g. *di|ēs -ēī, r|ēs -eī.*

First Declension

Genitive: sing. *-ae*, pl. *-ārum*.

Example: *īnsul|a -ae* f.

	sing.	pl.
-a	-ae	
-am	-ās	
-ae	-ārum	
-ae	-īs	
-ā	-īs	

	sing.	pl.
nom.	*īnsul|a*	*īnsul|ae*
acc.	*īnsul|am*	*īnsul|ās*
gen.	*īnsul|ae*	*īnsul|ārum*
dat.	*īnsul|ae*	*īnsul|īs*
abl.	*īnsul|ā*	*īnsul|īs*

Masculine (male persons): *nauta, agricola, aurīga, pīrāta, poēta*, etc.

Second Declension

Genitive: sing. *-ī*, pl. *-ōrum*.

1. Masculine.

Examples: ***equ|us -ī, liber libr|ī, puer puer|ī.***

	sing.	pl.	sing.	pl.	sing.	pl.
-us/-	-ī					
-um	-ōs					
-ī	-ōrum					
-ō	-īs					
-ō	-īs					
-e						

	sing.	pl.	sing.	pl.	sing.	pl.
nom.	*equ|us*	*equ|ī*	*liber*	*libr|ī*	*puer*	*puer|ī*
acc.	*equ|um*	*equ|ōs*	*libr|um*	*libr|ōs*	*puer|um*	*puer|ōs*
gen.	*equ|ī*	*equ|ōrum*	*libr|ī*	*libr|ōrum*	*puer|ī*	*puer|ōrum*
dat.	*equ|ō*	*equ|īs*	*libr|ō*	*libr|īs*	*puer|ō*	*puer|īs*
abl.	*equ|ō*	*equ|īs*	*libr|ō*	*libr|īs*	*puer|ō*	*puer|īs*
voc.	*equ|e*					

A few are feminine, e.g. *hum|us -ī, papyr|us -ī, Aegypt|us -ī, Rhod|us -ī.*

Nom. sing. *-ius*, voc. *-ī: Iūlius, Iūlī! fīlius, fīlī!*

2. Neuter.

Example: ***verb|um -ī.***

	sing.	pl.
-um	-a	
-um	-a	
-ī	-ōrum	
-ō	-īs	
-ō	-īs	

	sing.	pl.
nom.	*verb|um*	*verb|a*
acc.	*verb|um*	*verb|a*
gen.	*verb|ī*	*verb|ōrum*
dat.	*verb|ō*	*verb|īs*
abl.	*verb|ō*	*verb|īs*

Third Declension

Genitive: sing. *-is*, pl. *-um/-ium*.

[A] Genitive plural: *-um*.

1. Masculine and feminine.

Examples: *sōl sōl|is* m., **leō** *leōn|is* m., **vōx** *vōc|is* f.

	sing.	pl.	sing.	pl.	sing.	pl.		
nom.	*sōl*	*sōl|ēs*	*leō*	*leōn|ēs*	*vōx*	*vōc|ēs*	*-/-s*	*-ēs*
acc.	*sōl|em*	*sōl|ēs*	*leōn|em*	*leōn|ēs*	*vōc|em*	*vōc|ēs*	*-em*	*-ēs*
gen.	*sōl|is*	*sōl|um*	*leōn|is*	*leōn|um*	*vōc|is*	*vōc|um*	*-is*	*-um*
dat.	*sōl|ī*	*sōl|ibus*	*leōn|ī*	*leōn|ibus*	*vōc|ī*	*vōc|ibus*	*-ī*	*-ibus*
abl.	*sōl|e*	*sōl|ibus*	*leōn|e*	*leōn|ibus*	*vōc|e*	*vōc|ibus*	*-e*	*-ibus*

[1] Nom. *-er*, gen. *-r|is*: *pater patr|is* m., *māter mātr|is* f. *-er -r|is*

[2] Nom. *-or*, gen. *-ōr|is*: *pāstor -ōr|is* m. *-or -ōr|is*

[3] Nom. *-ōs*, gen. *-ōr|is*: *flōs flōr|is* m. *-ōs -ōr|is*

[4] Nom. *-ō*, gen. *-in|is*: *virgō -in|is* f., *homō -in|is* m. *-ō -in|is*

[5] Nom. *-x*, gen. *-g|is*: *lēx lēg|is* f., *rēx rēg|is* m. *-x -g|is*

[6] Nom. *-ex*, gen. *-ic|is*: *index -ic|is* m. *-ex -ic|is-s -t|is*

[7] Nom. *-s*, gen. *-t|is*: *aetās -āt|is* f., *mīles -it|is* m. *-s -d|is*

[8] Nom. *-s*, gen. *-d|is*: *laus laud|is* f., *pēs ped|is* m.

[9] Irregular nouns: *sanguis -in|is* m.; *coniūnx -iug|is* m./f.; *senex sen|is* m.; *bōs bov|is* m./f., pl. *bov|ēs boum*, dat./abl. *bōbus/būbus*.

2. Neuter

Examples: *ōs ōr|is*, **corpus** *corpor|is*, **opus** *-er|is*, **nōmen** *nōmin|is*.

	sing.	pl.	sing.	pl.		
nom.	*ōs*	*ōr|a*	*corpus*	*corpor|a*	*-*	*-a*
acc.	*ōs*	*ōr|a*	*corpus*	*corpor|a*	*-*	*-a*
gen.	*ōr|is*	*ōr|um*	*corpor|is*	*corpor|um*	*-is*	*-um*
dat.	*ōr|ī*	*ōr|ibus*	*corpor|ī*	*corpor|ibus*	*-ī*	*-ibus*
abl.	*ōr|e*	*ōr|ibus*	*corpor|e*	*corpor|ibus*	*-e*	*-ibus*
nom.	*opus*	*oper|a*	*nōmen*	*nōmin|a*		
acc.	*opus*	*oper|a*	*nōmen*	*nōmin|a*		
gen.	*oper|is*	*oper|um*	*nōmin|is*	*nōmin|um*		
dat.	*oper|ī*	*oper|ibus*	*nōmin|ī*	*nōmin|ibus*		
abl.	*oper|e*	*oper|ibus*	*nōmin|e*	*nōmin|ibus*		

Irregular nouns: *cor cord|is*; *caput capit|is*; *lac lact|is*; *os oss|is* (gen. pl. *-ium*); *mel mell|is*; *iter itiner|is*; *vās vās|is*, pl. *vās|a -ōrum* (2nd decl.); *thema -at|is*. *-ma -mat|is*

[B] Genitive plural: *-ium*.

1. Masculine and feminine.

Examples: ***nāv|is*** *-is* f., ***urb|s*** *-is* f., ***mōns*** *mont|is* m.

	sing.	pl.	sing.	pl.	sing.	pl.
nom.	*nāv|is*	*nāv|ēs*	*urb|s*	*urb|ēs*	*mōns*	*mont|ēs*
acc.	*nāv|em*	*nāv|ēs*	*urb|em*	*urb|ēs*	*mont|em*	*mont|ēs*
gen.	*nāv|is*	*nāv|ium*	*urb|is*	*urb|ium*	*mont|is*	*mont|ium*
dat.	*nāv|ī*	*nāv|ibus*	*urb|ī*	*urb|ibus*	*mont|ī*	*mont|ibus*
abl.	*nāv|e*	*nāv|ibus*	*urb|e*	*urb|ibus*	*mont|e*	*mont|ibus*

Left margin:
-(i)s   -ēs
-em   -ēs
-is   -ium
-ī   -ibus
-e   -ibus

-is, acc. -im, abl. -ī

[1] Nom. *-is*, acc. *-im* (pl. *-īs*), abl. *-ī*: *pupp|is -is* f., *Tiber|is -is* m.

-ēs -is

[2] Nom. *-ēs*, gen. *-is*: *nūb|ēs -is* f.

-x -c|is

[3] Nom. *-x*, gen. *-c|is*: *falx falc|is* f.

[4] Irregular nouns: *nox noct|is* f.; *nix niv|is* f.; *carō carn|is* f.; *as ass|is* m.; *vīs*, acc. *vim*, abl. *vī*, pl. *vīr|ēs -ium* f.

2. Neuter

Examples: ***mar|e*** *-is*, ***animal*** *-āl|is*.

	sing.	pl.	sing.	pl.
nom.	*mar|e*	*mar|ia*	*animal*	*animāl|ia*
acc.	*mar|e*	*mar|ia*	*animal*	*animāl|ia*
gen.	*mar|is*	*mar|ium*	*animāl|is*	*animāl|ium*
dat.	*mar|ī*	*mar|ibus*	*animāl|ī*	*animāl|ibus*
abl.	*mar|ī*	*mar|ibus*	*animāl|ī*	*animāl|ibus*

Left margin:
-e/-   -ia
-e/-   -ia
-is   -ium
-ī   -ibus
-ī   -ibus

Fourth Declension

Genitive: sing. *-ūs*, pl. *-uum*.

Examples: ***port|us*** *-ūs* m., ***corn|ū*** *-ūs* n.

	sing.	pl.	sing.	pl.
nom.	*port|us*	*port|ūs*	*corn|ū*	*corn|ua*
acc.	*port|um*	*port|ūs*	*corn|ū*	*corn|ua*
gen.	*port|ūs*	*port|uum*	*corn|ūs*	*corn|uum*
dat.	*port|uī*	*port|ibus*	*corn|ū*	*corn|ibus*
abl.	*port|ū*	*port|ibus*	*corn|ū*	*corn|ibus*

Left margin:
-us -ūs   -ū -ua
-um -ūs   -ū -ua
-ūs -uum   -ūs -uum
-uī -ibus   -ū -ibus
-ū -ibus   -ū -ibus

dom|us -ūs f., abl. *-ō*, pl. *dom|ūs -ōrum (-uum)*, acc. *-ōs*.

Fifth Declension

Genitive: sing. *-ēī/-eī*, pl. *-ērum*.

Examples: ***di|ēs*** *-ēī* m. (f.), ***rēs*** *reī* f.

nom.	*di|ēs*	*di|ēs*	*rēs*	*rēs*
acc.	*di|em*	*di|ēs*	*rem*	*rēs*
gen.	*di|ēī*	*di|ērum*	*reī*	*rērum*
dat.	*di|ēī*	*di|ēbus*	*reī*	*rēbus*
abl.	*di|ē*	*di|ēbus*	*rē*	*rēbus*

Left margin:
-ēs   -ēs
-em   -ēs
-ēī/-eī   -ērum
-ēī/-eī   -ēbus
-ē   -ēbus

ADJECTIVES

First and Second Declensions

[A] Genitive singular -ī -ae -ī.

Example: *bon|us -a -um.*

	sing. masc.	fem.	neut.	pl. masc.	fem.	neut.			
nom.	bon|us	bon|a	bon|um	bon|ī	bon|ae	bon|a	-us	-a	-um
acc.	bon|um	bon|am	bon|um	bon|ōs	bon|ās	bon|a	-um	-am	-um
gen.	bon|ī	bon|ae	bon|ī	bon|ōrum	bon|ārum	bon|ōrum	-ī	-ae	-ī
dat.	bon|ō	bon|ae	bon|ō	bon|īs	bon|īs	bon|īs	-ō	-ae	-ō
abl.	bon|ō	bon|ā	bon|ō	bon|īs	bon|īs	bon|īs	-ō	-ā	-ō
voc.	bon|e						-ī	-ae	-ī

Examples: *niger -gr|a -gr|um, līber -er|a -er|um.*

	sing. masc.	fem.	neut.	masc.	fem.	neut.			
nom.	niger	nigr|a	nigr|um	līber	līber|a	līber|um	-ōs	-ās	-a
acc.	nigr|um	nigr|am	nigr|um	līber|um	līber|am	līber|um	-ōrum	-ārum	-ōrum

Additional endings column:

-īs	-īs	-īs
-īs	-īs	-īs
-er	-(e)r|a	-(e)r|um

etc. (as above, but voc. = nom. *-er*)

[B] Genitive singular *-īus.*

Example: *sōl|us -a -um,* gen. *-īus,* dat. *-ī.*

	sing.	masc.	fem.	neut.				
sing.	nom.	sōl|us	sōl|a	sōl|um	pl. (as *bon|ī -ae -a*)	-us	-a	-um
	acc.	sōl|um	sōl|am	sōl|um		-um	-am	-um
	gen.	sōl|īus	sōl|īus	sōl|īus		-īus	-īus	-īus
	dat.	sōl|ī	sōl|ī	sōl|ī		-ī	-ī	-ī
	abl.	sōl|ō	sōl|ā	sōl|ō		-ō	-ā	-ō

Third Declension

[A] Genitive plural *-ium* (abl. sing. *-ī*).
Example: *brev|is -e.*

	sing. masc./fem.	neut.	pl. masc./fem.	neut.				
nom.	brev|is	brev|e	brev|ēs	brev|ia	-is	-e	-ēs	-ia
acc.	brev|em	brev|e	brev|ēs	brev|ia	-em	-e	-ēs	-ia
gen.	brev|is	brev|is	brev|ium	brev|ium	-is	-is	-ium	-ium
dat.	brev|ī	brev|ī	brev|ibus	brev|ibus	-ī	-ī	-ibus	-ibus
abl.	brev|ī	brev|ī	brev|ibus	brev|ibus	-ī	-ī	-ibus	-ibus

Examples: *ācer ācr|is ācr|e, celer -er|is -er|e.*

	sing. masc. fem.	neut.	masc. fem.	neut.			
nom.	ācer ācr|is	ācr|e	celer celer|is	celer|e	-er -(e)r|is	-(e)r|e	
acc.	ācr|em	ācr|e	celer|em	celer|e	-(e)r|em	-(e)r|e	

etc. (as above) etc. (as above)

Examples: *fēlīx,* gen. *-īc|is; ingēns,* gen. *-ent|is (-x < -c|s, -ns < -nt|s)*

	sing. masc./fem.	neut.	masc./fem.	neut.		
nom.	fēlīx	fēlīx	ingēns	ingēns	-s	-s
acc.	fēlīc|em	fēlīx	ingent|em	ingēns	-em	-s
gen.	fēlīc|is	fēlīc|is	ingent|is	ingent|is	-is	-is

etc. (as above) etc. (as above)

[B] Genitive plural *-um* (abl. sing. *-e*).

Examples: **prior** *prius*, gen. *priōr|is*; **vetus**, gen. *veter|is*.

		masc./fem.	neut.	masc./fem.	neut.
sing.	nom.	*prior*	*prius*	*vetus*	*vetus*
	acc.	*priōr|em*	*prius*	*veter|em*	*vetus*
	gen.	*priōr|is*	*priōr|is*	*veter|is*	*veter|is*
	dat.	*priōr|ī*	*priōr|ī*	*veter|ī*	*veter|ī*
	abl.	*priōr|e*	*priōr|e*	*veter|e*	*veter|e*
pl.	nom.	*priōr|ēs*	*priōr|a*	*veter|ēs*	*veter|a*
	acc.	*priōr|ēs*	*priōr|a*	*veter|ēs*	*veter|a*
	gen.	*priōr|um*	*priōr|um*	*veter|um*	*veter|um*
	dat.	*priōr|ibus*	*priōr|ibus*	*veter|ibus*	*veter|ibus*
	abl.	*priōr|ibus*	*priōr|ibus*	*veter|ibus*	*veter|ibus*

So *pauper* (m./f.), gen. *-er|is*; *dīves*, gen. *dīvit|is*.

Comparison

There are three **degrees: positive**, e.g. *longus*, **comparative**, e.g. *longior*, and **superlative**, e.g. *longissimus*.

The comparative ends in *-ior* and is declined like *prior*. The superlative ends in *-issim|us* (*-im|us*) and is declined like *bon|us*.

[A] Superlative *-issim|us*.

pos. *long|us -a -um* *brev|is -e* *fēlīx -īc|is*
comp. *long|ior -ius -iōr|is* *brev|ior -ius -iōr|is* *fēlīc|ior -ius -iōr|is*
sup. *long|issim|us -a -um* *brev|issim|us -a -um* *fēlīc|issim|us -a -um*

[B] Superlative *-rim|us, -lim|us*.

pos. *piger -gr|a -gr|um* *celer -er|is -er|e* *facil|is -e*
comp. *pigr|ior -ius -iōr|is* *celer|ior -ius -iōr|is* *facil|ior -ius -iōr|is*
sup. *piger|rim|us -a -um* *celer|rim|us -a -um* *facil|lim|us -a -um*

[C] Irregular comparison

positive	comparative	superlative
bon|us -a -um	*melior -ius -iōr|is*	*optim|us -a -um*
mal|us -a -um	*pēior -ius -iōr|is*	*pessim|us -a -um*
magn|us -a -um	*māior -ius -iōr|is*	*māxim|us -a -um*
parv|us -a -um	*minor minus -ōr|is*	*minim|us -a -um*
mult|um -ī	*plūs plūr|is*	*plūrim|um -ī*
mult|ī -ae -a	*plūr|ēs -a -ium*	*plūrim|ī -ae -a*
(*īnfrā*) *īnfer|us*	*īnferior -ius -iōr|is*	*īnfim|us/īm|us -a -um*
(*suprā*) *super|us*	*superior -ius -iōr|is*	*suprēm|us/summ|us -a -um*
(*intrā*)	*interior -ius -iōr|is*	*intim|us -a -um*
(*extrā*)	*exterior -ius -iōr|is*	*extrēm|us -a -um*
(*citrā*)	*citerior -ius -iōr|is*	*citim|us -a -um*
(*ultrā*)	*ulterior -ius -iōr|is*	*ultim|us -a -um*
(*prae*)	*prior -ius -iōr|is*	*prīm|us -a -um*
(*post*)	*posterior -ius -iōr|is*	*postrēm|us -a -um*
(*prope*)	*propior -ius -iōr|is*	*proxim|us -a -um*
vetus -er|is	*vetustior -ius -iōr|is*	*veterrim|us -a -um*

(margin notes)
- -
-em -
-is -is
-ī -ī
-e -e
-ēs -a
-ēs -a
-ium -ium
-ibus -ibus
-ibus -ibus

degrees:
positive (pos.)
comparative (comp.)
superlative (sup.)

-us -a -um / -(i)s (-e)
-ior -ius -iōr|is
-issim|us -a -um

-er -il|is
-(e)rior -ilior
-errim|us -illim|us

ADJECTIVES AND ADVERBS

Adjectīves of the 1st/2nd declension form adverbs in *-ē*, e.g. *rēct|us* > *rēct|ē*.

Adjectives of the 3rd declension form adverbs in *-iter*, e.g. *fort|is* > *fort|iter*.

The comparative of the adverbs ends in *-ius* (= neuter of the adjective), e.g. *rēct|ius*, the superlative ends in *-issimē* (*-imē*), e.g. *rēct|issimē*.

Adjective declension	Adverb positive	comparative	superlative
1st/2nd *rēct|us -a -um*	*rēctē*	*rēctius*	*rēctissimē*
pulcher -chr|a -um	*pulchrē*	*pulchrius*	*pulcherrimē*
miser -er|a -er|um	*miserē*	*miserius*	*miserrimē*
3rd *fort|is -e*	*fortiter*	*fortius*	*fortissimē*
ācer ācr|is ācr|e	*ācriter*	*ācrius*	*ācerrimē*
celer -er|is -er|e	*celeriter*	*celerius*	*celerrimē*
fēlīx	*fēlīciter*	*fēlīcius*	*fēlīcissimē*

Nom. sing. *-ns*, adverb *-nter*: *prūdēns -ent|is*, adv. *prūde<u>nter</u>*.

Some adjectives of the 1st/2nd declension form adverbs in *-ō*, e.g. *certō, falsō, necessāriō, rārō, subitō, tūtō, prīmō, postrēmō* (adjectives: *cert|us, fals|us, necessāri|us*, etc.).

Irregular adverbs: *bene* < *bon|us*, *male* < *mal|us*, *valdē* < *valid|us*, *facile* < *facil|is*, *difficulter* < *difficil|is*, *audācter* < *audāx*.

-ē

-iter

-ius
-issimē

-nter (< *-ntiter*)

-ō

NUMERALS

Roman	Arabic	Cardinal numbers	Ordinal numbers	Distributive numbers
I	1	*ūn|us -a -um*	*prīm|us -a -um*	*singul|ī -ae -a (ūn|ī)*
II	2	*du|o -ae -o*	*secund|us*	*bīn|ī*
III	3	*tr|ēs -ia*	*terti|us*	*tern|ī (trīn|ī)*
IV	4	*quattuor*	*quārt|us*	*quatern|ī*
V	5	*quīnque*	*quīnt|us*	*quīn|ī*
VI	6	*sex*	*sext|us*	*sēn|ī*
VII	7	*septem*	*septim|us*	*septēn|ī*
VIII	8	*octō*	*octāv|us*	*octōn|ī*
IX	9	*novem*	*nōn|us*	*novēn|ī*
X	10	*decem*	*decim|us*	*dēn|ī*
XI	11	*ūn-decim*	*ūn-decim|us*	*ūn-dēn|ī*
XII	12	*duo-decim*	*duo-decim|us*	*duo-dēn|ī*
XIII	13	*trē-decim*	*terti|us decim|us*	*tern|ī dēn|ī*
XIV	14	*quattuor-decim*	*quārt|us decim|us*	*quatern|ī dēn|ī*
XV	15	*quīn-decim*	*quīnt|us decim|us*	*quīn|ī dēn|ī*
XVI	16	*sē-decim*	*sext|us decim|us*	*sēn|ī dēn|ī*
XVII	17	*septen-decim*	*septim|us decim|us*	*septēn|ī dēn|ī*
XVIII	18	*duo-dē-vīgintī*	*duo-dē-vīcēsim|us*	*duo-dē-vīcēn|ī*
XIX	19	*ūn-dē-vīgintī*	*ūn-dē-vīcēsim|us*	*ūn-dē-vīcēn|ī*
XX	20	*vīgintī*	*vīcēsim|us*	*vīcēn|ī*
XXI	21	*vīgintī ūn|us /ūn|us et vīgintī*	*vīcēsim|us prīm|us /ūn|us et vīcēsim|us*	*vīcēn|ī singul|ī /singul|ī et vīcēn|ī*
XXX	30	*trīgintā*	*trīcēsim|us*	*trīcēn|ī*
XL	40	*quadrāgintā*	*quadrāgēsim|us*	*quadrāgēn|ī*
L	50	*quīnquāgintā*	*quīnquāgēsim|us*	*quīnquāgēn|ī*
LX	60	*sexāgintā*	*sexāgēsim|us*	*sexāgēn|ī*
LXX	70	*septuāgintā*	*septuāgēsim|us*	*septuāgēn|ī*
LXXX	80	*octōgintā*	*octōgēsim|us*	*octōgēn|ī*
XC	90	*nōnāgintā*	*nōnāgēsim|us*	*nōnāgēn|ī*
C	100	*centum*	*centēsim|us*	*centēn|ī*
CC	200	*ducent|ī -ae -a*	*ducentēsim|us*	*ducēn|ī*
CCC	300	*trecent|ī*	*trecentēsim|us*	*trecēn|ī*
CCCC	400	*quadringent|ī*	*quadringentēsim|us*	*quadringēn|ī*
D	500	*quīngent|ī*	*quīngentēsim|us*	*quīngēn|ī*
DC	600	*sescent|ī*	*sescentēsim|us*	*sescēn|ī*
DCC	700	*septingent|ī*	*septingentēsim|us*	*septingēn|ī*
DCCC	800	*octingent|ī*	*octingentēsim|us*	*octingēn|ī*
DCCCC	900	*nōngent|ī*	*nōngentēsim|us*	*nōngēn|ī*
M	1000	*mīlle*	*mīllēsim|us*	*singula mīlia*
MM	2000	*duo mīlia*	*bis mīllēsim|us*	*bīna mīlia*

[1] *ūn\|us -a -um* is declined like *sōl\|us*: gen. *-īus*, dat. *-ī*.

[2] *du\|o -ae -o* and *tr\|ēs -ia*:

	masc.	fem.	neut.	masc./fem.	neut.
nom.	*du|o*	*du|ae*	*du|o*	*tr|ēs*	*tr|ia*
acc.	*du|ōs/o*	*du|ās*	*du|o*	*tr|ēs*	*tr|ia*
gen.	*du|ōrum*	*du|ārum*	*du|ōrum*	*tr|ium*	*tr|ium*
dat.	*du|ōbus*	*du|ābus*	*du|ōbus*	*tr|ibus*	*tr|ibus*
abl.	*du|ōbus*	*du|ābus*	*du|ōbus*	*tr|ibus*	*tr|ibus*

[3] *mīl\|ia -ium* (n. pl.) is declined like *mar\|ia* (3rd decl.).

Numeral adverbs

1× semel	6× sexiēs	11× ūndeciēs	40× quadrāgiēs	90× nōnāgiēs
2× bis	7× septiēs	12× duodeciēs	50× quīnquāgiēs	100× centiēs
3× ter	8× octiēs	13× ter deciēs	60× sexāgiēs	200× ducentiēs
4× quater	9× noviēs	20× vīciēs	70× septuāgiēs	300× trecentiēs
5× quīnquiēs	10× deciēs	30× trīciēs	80× octōgiēs	1000× mīliēs

PRONOUNS

Personal Pronouns

	1st person		2nd person	
	sing.	pl.	sing.	pl.
nom.	*ego*	*nōs*	*tū*	*vōs*
acc.	*mē*	*nōs*	*tē*	*vōs*
gen.	*meī*	*nostrī/nostrum*	*tuī*	*vestrī/vestrum*
dat.	*mihi*	*nōbīs*	*tibi*	*vōbīs*
abl.	*mē*	*nōbīs*	*tē*	*vōbīs*

objective gen.:
nostrī, vestrī

partitive gen.:
nostrum, vestrum
mī = mihi

3rd person and demonstrative pronoun

	sing.			pl.			reflexive
	masc.	fem.	neut.	masc.	fem.	neut.	pronoun
nom.	*i|s*	*e|a*	*i|d*	*i|ī*	*e|ae*	*e|a*	
acc.	*e|um*	*e|am*	*i|d*	*e|ōs*	*e|ās*	*e|a*	*sē*
gen.	*e|ius*	*e|ius*	*e|ius*	*e|ōrum*	*e|ārum*	*e|ōrum*	
dat.	*e|ī*	*e|ī*	*e|ī*	*i|īs*	*i|īs*	*i|īs*	*sibi*
abl.	*e|ō*	*e|ā*	*e|ō*	*i|īs*	*i|īs*	*i|īs*	*sē*

nom. pl. e|ī = i|ī
sēsē = sē

e|īs = i|īs

Possessive Pronouns

	sing.	pl.
1st pers.	*me|us -a -um*	*noster -tr|a -tr|um*
2nd pers.	*tu|us -a -um*	*vester -tr|a -tr|um*
3rd pers.	*su|us -a -um* (reflexive)	

me|us, voc. sing. *mī.*

eius, eōrum, eārum (gen. of is ea id)

Demonstrative Pronouns

		sing.			pl.		
		masc.	fem.	neut.	masc.	fem.	neut.
[1]	nom.	*hic*	*haec*	*hoc*	*hī*	*hae*	*haec*
	acc.	*hunc*	*hanc*	*hoc*	*hōs*	*hās*	*haec*
	gen.	*huius*	*huius*	*huius*	*hōrum*	*hārum*	*hōrum*
	dat.	*huic*	*huic*	*huic*	*hīs*	*hīs*	*hīs*
	abl.	*hōc*	*hāc*	*hōc*	*hīs*	*hīs*	*hīs*
[2]	nom.	*ill|e*	*ill|a*	*ill|ud*	*ill|ī*	*ill|ae*	*ill|a*
	acc.	*ill|um*	*ill|am*	*ill|ud*	*ill|ōs*	*ill|ās*	*ill|a*
	gen.	*ill|īus*	*ill|īus*	*ill|īus*	*ill|ōrum*	*ill|ārum*	*ill|ōrum*
	dat.	*ill|ī*	*ill|ī*	*ill|ī*	*ill|īs*	*ill|īs*	*ill|īs*
	abl.	*ill|ō*	*ill|ā*	*ill|ō*	*ill|īs*	*ill|īs*	*ill|īs*

[3] *ist|e -a -ud* is declined like *ill|e -a -ud.*

[4] *ips|e -a -um* is declined like *ill|e* except neut. sing. *ips|um.*

[5] *is ea id,* demonstrative and personal: see above.

[6] *ī-dem ea-dem idem* (< *is ea id* + *-dem*):

	sing.			pl.		
	masc.	fem.	neut.	masc.	fem.	neut.
nom.	*īdem*	*eadem*	*idem*	*iīdem*	*eaedem*	*eadem*
acc.	*eundem*	*eandem*	*idem*	*eōsdem*	*eāsdem*	*eadem*
gen.	*eiusdem*	*eiusdem*	*eiusdem*	*eōrundem*	*eārundem*	*eōrundem*
dat.	*eīdem*	*eīdem*	*eīdem*	*iīsdem*	*iīsdem*	*iīsdem*
abl.	*eōdem*	*eādem*	*eōdem*	*iīsdem*	*iīsdem*	*iīsdem*

īdem < is-dem
-n-dem < -m-dem
nom. pl. eīdem = iīdem
eīsdem = iīsdem

Interrogative Pronouns

[1] *quis quae quid* (subst.); *quī/quis... quae... quod...* (adj.).

	sing.			pl.		
	masc.	fem.	neut.	masc.	fem.	neut.
nom.	quis/quī	quae	quid/quod	quī	quae	quae
acc.	quem	quam	quid/quod	quōs	quās	quae
gen.	cuius	cuius	cuius	quōrum	quārum	quōrum
dat.	cui	cui	cui	quibus	quibus	quibus
abl.	quō	quā	quō	quibus	quibus	quibus

[2] *uter utr|a utr|um*, gen. *utr|īus*, dat. *utr|ī* (like *sōl|us*, but nom. m. sing. *uter*).

Relative Pronoun

[1] *quī quae quod*

	sing.			pl.		
	masc.	fem.	neut.	masc.	fem.	neut.
nom.	quī	quae	quod	quī	quae	quae
acc.	quem	quam	quod	quōs	quās	quae
gen.	cuius	cuius	cuius	quōrum	quārum	quōrum
dat.	cui	cui	cui	quibus	quibus	quibus
abl.	quō	quā	quō	quibus	quibus	quibus

[2] *quī- quae- quod-cumque* (indefinite relative) = *quis-quis quid-quid/quic-quid* (indecl. subst.).

Indefinite Pronouns

nēmō < ne- + homō

[1] *nēmō*, acc. *nēmin|em*, dat. *nēmin|ī*.

nīl = nihil

[2] *nihil*, neuter (indecl.).

[3] *ūll|us -a -um* and *nūll|us -a -um* are declined like *sōl|us*.

neuter < ne- + uter

[4] *neuter -tr|a -tr|um* and *uter-que utr|a-que utr|um-que* are declined like *uter*: gen. *neutr|īus, utr|īus-que*.

[5] *alter -er|a -er|um*, gen. *-er|īus*, dat. *-er|ī*.

[6] *ali|us -a -ud*, dat. *ali|ī* (gen. *alter|īus*).

The following pronouns are declined like *quis/quī*:

n. pl. (ali-)qua

[7] *ali-quis/-quī -qua -quid/-quod* and (*sī, nisi, nē, num*) *quis/ quī qua quid/quod*.

[8] *quis-quam quid-quam/quic-quam*.

-n-dam < -m-dam

[9] *quī-dam quae-dam quid-dam/quod-dam*, acc. sing. m. *quen-dam*, f. *quan-dam*, gen. pl. m./n. *quōrun-dam*, f. *quārun-dam*.

[10] *quis-que quae-que quid-que/quod-que*.

[11] *quī- quae- quid-/quod-vīs* = *quī- quae- quid-/quod-libet*.

VERBS

Voice and Mood

The **voice** of the verb is either **active**, e.g. *amat,* or **passive**, e.g. *amātur.* Verbs which have no active voice (except participles and gerund), e.g. *cōnārī, loquī,* are called **deponent** verbs.

The **moods** of the verb are: **infinitive**, e.g. *amāre,* **imperative**, e.g. *amā,* **indicative**, e.g. *amat,* and **subjunctive**, e.g. *amet.*

voice:	act.
	pass.

mood:	inf.	ind.
	imp.	subj.

Tense, Number, Person

The **tenses** of the verb are: **present**, e.g. *amat,* **future**, e.g. *amābit,* **imperfect**, e.g. *amābat,* **perfect**, e.g. *amāvit,* **pluperfect**, e.g. *amāverat,* and **future perfect**, e.g. *amāverit.*

The **numbers** of the verb are: **singular**, e.g. *amat,* and **plural**, e.g. *amant.*

The **persons** of the verb are: **1st person**, e.g. *amō,* **2nd person**, e.g. *amās,* and **3rd person**, e.g. *amat.* Verbs which have no 1st and 2nd persons, e.g. *licēre* and *pudēre,* are called **impersonal**.

tense:	pres.	perf.
	imperf.	
pluperf.		
	fut.	fut. perf.
number:	sing.	
	pl.	

person:	1
	2
	3

Conjugations

There are four **conjugations**:

[1] **1st conjugation**: inf. *-āre, -ārī* e.g. *amāre, cōnārī.*

[2] **2nd conjugation**: inf. *-ēre, -ērī* e.g. *monēre, verērī.*

[3] **3rd conjugation**: inf. *-ere, -ī* e.g. *legere, ūtī.*

[4] **4th conjugation**: inf. *-īre, -īrī* e.g. *audīre, partīrī.*

conjugations:

[1] *-āre/-ārī*

[2] *-ēre/-ērī*

[3] *-ere/-ī*

[4] *-īre/-īrī*

Stem

Verbal stems:

The **present stem**, e.g. *amā-, monē-, leg-, audī-.*

The **perfect stem**, e.g. *amāv-, monu-, lēg-, audīv-.*

The **supine stem**, e.g. *amāt-, monit-, lēct-, audīt-.*

verbal stems:

present stem [–]

perfect stem [~]

supine stem [≈]

Personal endings

[1]	Active		Passive	
	sing.	pl.	sing.	pl.
pers. 1	*-m/-ō*	*-mus*	*-r/-or*	*-mur*
pers. 2	*-s*	*-tis*	*-ris*	*-minī*
pers. 3	*-t*	*-nt*	*-tur*	*-ntur*

[2] Endings of the perfect indicative active:

	sing.	pl.
pers. 1	*~ī*	*~imus*
pers. 2	*~istī*	*~istis*
pers. 3	*~it*	*~ērunt (~ēre)*

after a consonant:

-ō	*-imus*	*-or*	*-imur*
-is	*-itis*	*-eris*	*-iminī*
-it	*-unt*	*-itur*	*-untur*

Conjugation

[A] Active

Infinitive

present			
[1] *amā|re*	[2] *monē|re*	[3] *leg|ere*	[4] *audī|re*
perfect			
amāv|isse	*monu|isse*	*lēg|isse*	*audīv|isse*
future			
amāt|ūr|um esse	*monit|ūr|um esse*	*lēct|ūr|um esse*	*audīt|ūr|um esse*

Left margin:
[1, 2, 4] [3]
−*re* −*ere*
~*isse*
≈*ūr\|us -a -um esse*

Indicative

[1, 2, 4] [3]
−*ō* −*ō*
−*s* −*is*
−*t* −*it*
−*mus* −*imus*
−*tis* −*itis*
−(*u*)*nt* −*unt*

present

sing. 1	*am|ō*	*mone|ō*	*leg|ō*	*audi|ō*
2	*amā|s*	*monē|s*	*leg|is*	*audī|s*
3	*ama|t*	*mone|t*	*leg|it*	*audi|t*
pl. 1	*amā|mus*	*monē|mus*	*leg|imus*	*audī|mus*
2	*amā|tis*	*monē|tis*	*leg|itis*	*audī|itis*
3	*ama|nt*	*mone|nt*	*leg|unt*	*audi|unt*

[1, 2] [3, 4]
−*ba\|m* −*ēba\|m*
−*bā\|s* −*ēbā\|s*
−*ba\|t* −*ēba\|t*
−*bā\|mus* −*ēbā\|mus*
−*bā\|tis* −*ēbā\|tis*
−*ba\|nt* −*ēba\|nt*

imperfect

sing. 1	*amā|ba|m*	*monē|ba|m*	*leg|ēba|m*	*audi|ēba|m*
2	*amā|bā|s*	*monē|bā|s*	*leg|ēbā|s*	*audi|ēbā|s*
3	*amā|ba|t*	*monē|ba|t*	*leg|ēba|t*	*audi|ēba|t*
pl. 1	*amā|bā|mus*	*monē|bā|mus*	*leg|ēbā|mus*	*audi|ēbā|mus*
2	*amā|bā|tis*	*monē|bā|tis*	*leg|ēbā|tis*	*audi|ēbā|tis*
3	*amā|ba|nt*	*monē|ba|nt*	*leg|ēba|nt*	*audi|ēba|nt*

[1, 2] [3, 4]
−*b\|ō* −*a\|m*
−*b\|is* −*ē\|s*
−*b\|it* −*e\|t*
−*b\|imus* −*ē\|mus*
−*b\|itis* −*ē\|tis*
−*b\|unt* −*e\|nt*

future

sing. 1	*amā|b|ō*	*monē|b|ō*	*leg|a|m*	*audi|a|m*
2	*amā|b|is*	*monē|b|is*	*leg|ē|s*	*audi|ē|s*
3	*amā|b|it*	*monē|b|it*	*leg|e|t*	*audi|e|t*
pl. 1	*amā|b|imus*	*monē|b|imus*	*leg|ē|mus*	*audi|ē|mus*
2	*amā|b|itis*	*monē|b|itis*	*leg|ē|tis*	*audi|ē|tis*
3	*amā|b|unt*	*monē|b|unt*	*leg|e|nt*	*audi|e|nt*

~*ī*
~*istī*
~*it*
~*imus*
~*istis*
~*ērunt*

perfect

sing. 1	*amāv|ī*	*monu|ī*	*lēg|ī*	*audīv|ī*
2	*amāv|istī*	*monu|istī*	*lēg|istī*	*audīv|istī*
3	*amāv|it*	*monu|it*	*lēg|it*	*audīv|it*
pl. 1	*amāv|imus*	*monu|imus*	*lēg|imus*	*audīv|imus*
2	*amāv|istis*	*monu|istis*	*lēg|istis*	*audīv|istis*
3	*amāv|ērunt*	*monu|ērunt*	*lēg|ērunt*	*audīv|ērunt*

~*era\|m*
~*erā\|s*
~*era\|t*
~*erā\|mus*
~*erā\|tis*
~*era\|nt*

pluperfect

sing. 1	*amāv|era|m*	*monu|era|m*	*lēg|era|m*	*audīv|era|m*
2	*amāv|erā|s*	*monu|erā|s*	*lēg|erā|s*	*audīv|erā|s*
3	*amāv|era|t*	*monu|era|t*	*lēg|era|t*	*audīv|era|t*
pl. 1	*amāv|erā|mus*	*monu|erā|mus*	*lēg|erā|mus*	*audīv|erā|mus*
2	*amāv|erā|tis*	*monu|erā|tis*	*lēg|erā|tis*	*audīv|erā|tis*
3	*amāv|era|nt*	*monu|era|nt*	*lēg|era|nt*	*audīv|era|nt*

~*er\|ō*
~*eri\|s*
~*eri\|t*
~*eri\|mus*
~*eri\|tis*
~*eri\|nt*

future perfect

sing. 1	*amāv|er|ō*	*monu|er|ō*	*lēg|er|ō*	*audīv|er|ō*
2	*amāv|eri|s*	*monu|eri|s*	*lēg|eri|s*	*audīv|eri|s*
3	*amāv|eri|t*	*monu|eri|t*	*lēg|eri|t*	*audīv|eri|t*
pl. 1	*amāv|eri|mus*	*monu|eri|mus*	*lēg|eri|mus*	*audīv|eri|mus*
2	*amāv|eri|tis*	*monu|eri|tis*	*lēg|eri|tis*	*audīv|eri|tis*
3	*amāv|eri|nt*	*monu|eri|nt*	*lēg|eri|nt*	*audīv|eri|nt*

Subjunctive

present

						[1]	[2, 3, 4]
sing.1	am|e|m	mone|a|m	leg|a|m	audi|a|m	(-)e|m	-a|m
2	am|ē|s	mone|ā|s	leg|ā|s	audi|ā|s	(-)ē|s	-ā|s
3	am|e|t	mone|a|t	leg|a|t	audi|a|t	(-)e|t	-a|t
pl.1	am|ē|mus	mone|ā|mus	leg|ā|mus	audi|ā|mus	(-)ē|mus	-ā|mus
2	am|ē|tis	mone|ā|tis	leg|ā|tis	audi|ā|tis	(-)ē|tis	-ā|tis
3	am|e|nt	mone|a|nt	leg|a|nt	audi|a|nt	(-)e|nt	-a|nt

imperfect

						[1, 2, 4]	[3]
sing.1	amā|re|m	monē|re|m	leg|ere|m	audī|re|m	-re|m	-ere|m
2	amā|rē|s	monē|rē|s	leg|erē|s	audī|rē|s	-rē|s	-erē|s
3	amā|re|t	monē|re|t	leg|ere|t	audī|re|t	-re|t	-ere|t
pl.1	amā|rē|mus	monē|rē|mus	leg|erē|mus	audī|rē|mus	-rē|mus	-erē|mus
2	amā|rē|tis	monē|rē|tis	leg|erē|tis	audī|rē|tis	-rē|tis	-erē|tis
3	amā|re|nt	monē|re|nt	leg|ere|nt	audī|re|nt	-re|nt	-ere|nt

perfect

sing.1	amāv|eri|m	monu|eri|m	lēg|eri|m	audīv|eri|m	≈eri|m
2	amāv|eri|s	monu|eri|s	lēg|eri|s	audīv|eri|s	≈eri|s
3	amāv|eri|t	monu|eri|t	lēg|eri|t	audīv|eri|t	≈eri|t
pl.1	amāv|eri|mus	monu|eri|mus	lēg|eri|mus	audīv|eri|mus	≈eri|mus
2	amāv|eri|tis	monu|eri|tis	lēg|eri|tis	audīv|eri|tis	≈eri|tis
3	amāv|eri|nt	monu|eri|nt	lēg|eri|nt	audīv|eri|nt	≈eri|nt

pluperfect

sing.1	amāv|isse|m	monu|isse|m	lēg|isse|m	audīv|isse|m	≈isse|m
2	amāv|issē|s	monu|issē|s	lēg|issē|s	audīv|issē|s	≈issē|s
3	amāv|isse|t	monu|isse|t	lēg|isse|t	audīv|isse|t	≈isse|t
pl.1	amāv|issē|mus	monu|issē|mus	lēg|issē|mus	audīv|issē|mus	≈issē|mus
2	amāv|issē|tis	monu|issē|tis	lēg|issē|tis	audīv|issē|tis	≈issē|tis
3	amāv|isse|nt	monu|isse|nt	lēg|isse|nt	audīv|isse|nt	≈isse|nt

Imperative

present

					[1, 2, 4]	[3]
sing.	amā	monē	leg|e	audī	–	-e
pl.	amā|te	monē|te	leg|ite	audī|te	-te	-ite

future

sing.	amā|tō	monē|tō	leg|itō	audī|tō	-tō	-itō
pl.	amā|tōte	monē|tōte	leg|itōte	audī|tōte	-tōte	-itōte

Participle

present

					[1, 2]	[3, 4]
	amā|ns -ant|is	monē|ns -ent|is	leg|ēns -ent|is	audi|ēns -ent|is	-ns	-ēns
					-nt|is	-ent|is

future

	amāt|ūr|us -a -um	monit|ūr|us -a -um	lēct|ūr|us -a -um	audīt|ūr|us -a -um	≈ūr|us -a -um

Supine

I	amāt|um	monit|um	lēct|um	audīt|um	≈um
II	amāt|ū	monit|ū	lēct|ū	audīt|ū	≈ū

Gerund

					[1, 2]	[3, 4]
acc.	ama|nd|um	mone|nd|um	leg|end|um	audi|end|um	-nd|um	-end|um
gen.	ama|nd|ī	mone|nd|ī	leg|end|ī	audi|end|ī	-nd|ī	-end|ī
abl.	ama|nd|ō	mone|nd|ō	leg|end|ō	audi|end|ō	-nd|ō	-end|ō

[B] Passive

Infinitive

	[1]	[2]	[3]	[4]
present	*amā*|*rī*	*monē*|*rī*	*leg*|*ī*	*audī*|*rī*
perfect	*amāt*|*um esse*	*monit*|*um esse*	*lēct*|*um esse*	*audīt*|*um esse*
future	*amāt*|*um īrī*	*monit*|*um īrī*	*lēct*|*um īrī*	*audīt*|*um īrī*

[1, 2, 4] -rī   [3] -ī

≈us -a -um esse

≈um īrī

Indicative

present

		[1]	[2]	[3]	[4]
sing.	1	*am*|*or*	*mone*|*or*	*leg*|*or*	*audi*|*or*
	2	*amā*|*ris*	*monē*|*ris*	*leg*|*eris*	*audī*|*ris*
	3	*amā*|*tur*	*monē*|*tur*	*leg*|*itur*	*audī*|*tur*
pl.	1	*amā*|*mur*	*monē*|*mur*	*leg*|*imur*	*audī*|*mur*
	2	*amā*|*minī*	*monē*|*minī*	*leg*|*iminī*	*audī*|*minī*
	3	*ama*|*ntur*	*mone*|*ntur*	*leg*|*untur*	*audi*|*untur*

[1, 2, 4] -or -ris -tur -mur -minī -(u)ntur   [3] -or -eris -itur -imur -iminī -untur

imperfect

		[1]	[2]	[3]	[4]
sing.	1	*amā*|*ba*|*r*	*monē*|*ba*|*r*	*leg*|*ēba*|*r*	*audi*|*ēba*|*r*
	2	*amā*|*bā*|*ris*	*monē*|*bā*|*ris*	*leg*|*ēbā*|*ris*	*audi*|*ēbā*|*ris*
	3	*amā*|*bā*|*tur*	*monē*|*bā*|*tur*	*leg*|*ēbā*|*tur*	*audi*|*ēbā*|*tur*
pl.	1	*amā*|*bā*|*mur*	*monē*|*bā*|*mur*	*leg*|*ēbā*|*mur*	*audi*|*ēbā*|*mur*
	2	*amā*|*bā*|*minī*	*monē*|*bā*|*minī*	*leg*|*ēbā*|*minī*	*audi*|*ēbā*|*minī*
	3	*amā*|*ba*|*ntur*	*monē*|*ba*|*ntur*	*leg*|*ēba*|*ntur*	*audi*|*ēba*|*ntur*

[1, 2] -ba\|r -bā\|ris -bā\|tur -bā\|mur -bā\|minī -ba\|ntur   [3, 4] -ēba\|r -ēbā\|ris -ēbā\|tur -ēbā\|mur -ēbā\|minī -ēba\|ntur

future

		[1]	[2]	[3]	[4]
sing.	1	*amā*|*b*|*or*	*monē*|*b*|*or*	*leg*|*a*|*r*	*audi*|*a*|*r*
	2	*amā*|*b*|*eris*	*monē*|*b*|*eris*	*leg*|*ē*|*ris*	*audi*|*ē*|*ris*
	3	*amā*|*b*|*itur*	*monē*|*b*|*itur*	*leg*|*ē*|*tur*	*audi*|*ē*|*tur*
pl.	1	*amā*|*b*|*imur*	*monē*|*b*|*imur*	*leg*|*ē*|*mur*	*audi*|*ē*|*mur*
	2	*amā*|*b*|*iminī*	*monē*|*b*|*iminī*	*leg*|*ē*|*minī*	*audi*|*ē*|*minī*
	3	*amā*|*b*|*untur*	*monē*|*b*|*untur*	*leg*|*e*|*ntur*	*audi*|*e*|*ntur*

[1, 2] -b\|or -b\|eris -b\|itur -b\|imur -b\|iminī -b\|untur   [3, 4] -a\|r -ē\|ris -ē\|tur -ē\|mur -ē\|minī -e\|ntur

perfect

		[1]	[2]	[3]	[4]
sing.	1	*amāt*|*us* *sum*	*monit*|*us* *sum*	*lēct*|*us* *sum*	*audīt*|*us* *sum*
	2	*es*	*es*	*es*	*es*
	3	*est*	*est*	*est*	*est*
pl.	1	*amāt*|*ī* *umus*	*monit*|*ī* *sumus*	*lēct*|*ī* *sumus*	*audīt*|*ī* *sumus*
	2	*estis*	*estis*	*estis*	*estis*
	3	*sunt*	*sunt*	*sunt*	*sunt*

≈us -a (-um) sum es est ≈ī -ae (-a) sumus estis sunt

pluperfect

		[1]	[2]	[3]	[4]
sing.	1	*amāt*|*us* *eram*	*monit*|*us* *eram*	*lēct*|*us* *eram*	*audīt*|*us* *eram*
	2	*erās*	*erās*	*erās*	*erās*
	3	*erat*	*erat*	*erat*	*erat*
pl.	1	*amāt*|*ī* *erāmus*	*monit*|*ī* *erāmus*	*lēct*|*ī* *erāmus*	*audīt*|*ī* *erāmus*
	2	*erātis*	*erātis*	*erātis*	*erātis*
	3	*erant*	*erant*	*erant*	*erant*

≈us -a (-um) eram erās erat ≈ī -ae (-a) erāmus erātis erant future perfect

	amāt|us	monit|us	lēct|us	audīt|us	≈us -a (-um)
sing.1	erō	erō	erō	erō	erō
2	eris	eris	eris	eris	eris
3	erit	erit	erit	erit	erit
	amāt|ī	monit|ī	lēct|ī	audīt|ī	≈ī -ae (-a)
pl.1	erimus	erimus	erimus	erimus	erimus
2	eritis	eritis	eritis	eritis	eritis
3	erunt	erunt	erunt	erunt	erunt

Subjunctive
Present

					[1]	[2, 3, 4]
sing.1	am|e|r	mone|a|r	leg|a|r	audi|a|r	(–)e|r	–a|r
2	am|ē|ris	mone|ā|ris	leg|ā|ris	audi|ā|ris	(–)ē|ris	–ā|ris
3	am|ē|tur	mone|ā|tur	leg|ā|tur	audi|ā|tur	(–)ē|tur	–ā|tur
pl.1	am|ē|mur	mone|ā|mur	leg|ā|mur	audi|ā|mur	(–)ē|mur	–ā|mur
2	am|ē|minī	mone|ā|minī	leg|ā|minī	audi|ā|minī	(–)ē|minī	–ā|minī
3	am|e|ntur	mone|a|ntur	leg|a|ntur	audi|a|ntur	(–)e|ntur	–a|ntur

Imperfect

					[1, 2, 4]	[3]
sing.1	amā|re|r	monē|re|r	leg|ere|r	audī|re|r	–re|r	–ere|r
2	amā|rē|ris	monē|rē|ris	leg|erē|ris	audī|rē|ris	–rē|ris	–erē|ris
3	amā|rē|tur	monē|rē|tur	leg|erē|tur	audī|rē|tur	–rē|tur	–erē|tur
pl.1	amā|rē|mur	monē|rē|mur	leg|erē|mur	audī|rē|mur	–rē|mur	–erē|mur
2	amā|rē|minī	monē|rē|minī	leg|erē|minī	audī|rē|minī	–rē|minī	–erē|minī
3	amā|re|ntur	monē|re|ntur	leg|ere|ntur	audī|re|ntur	–re|ntur	–ere|ntur

Perfect

	amāt|us	monit|us	lēct|us	audīt|us	≈us -a (-um)
sing.1	sim	sim	sim	sim	sim
2	sīs	sīs	sīs	sīs	sīs
3	sit	sit	sit	sit	sit
	amāt|ī	monit|ī	lēct|ī	audīt|ī	≈ī -ae (-a)
pl.1	sīmus	sīmus	sīmus	sīmus	sīmus
2	sītis	sītis	sītis	sītis	sītis
3	sint	sint	sint	sint	sint

Pluperfect

	amāt|us	monit|us	lēct|us	audīt|us	≈us -a (-um)
sing.1	essem	essem	essem	essem	essem
2	essēs	essēs	essēs	essēs	essēs
3	esset	esset	esset	esset	esset
	amāt|ī	monit|ī	lēct|ī	audīt|ī	≈ī -ae (-a)
pl.1	essēmus	essēmus	essēmus	essēmus	essēmus
2	essētis	essētis	essētis	essētis	essētis
3	essent	essent	essent	essent	essent

Participle
Perfect

	amāt|us	monit|us	lēct|us	audīt|us	≈us -a -um
	-a -um	-a -um	-a -um	-a -um	

Gerundive

					[1, 2]	[3, 4]
	ama|nd|us	mone|nd|us	leg|end|us	audi|end|us	–nd|us -a	–end|us -a
	-a -um	-a -um	-a -um	-a -um	-um	-um

Deponent verbs

Left margin notes:

[1, 2, 4]   [3]
-rī   -ī
≈us -a -um esse
≈ūr|us -a -um esse

3rd pers. sing.
≈(i)tur
≈(ē)bā|tur
-b|itur   -ē|tur
≈us -a -um est
≈us -a -um erat
≈us -a -um erit

(-)ē|tur   -ā|tur
≈(e)rē|tur
≈us -a -um sit
≈us -a -um esset

[1, 2, 4]   [3]
-re   -ere
-minī   -iminī

[1, 2]   [3, 4]
-ns   -ēns
≈us -a -um
≈ūr|us -a -um
-um -ū

[1, 2]   [3, 4]
-nd|um   -end|um

-nd|us -a   -end|us -a
  -um   -um

Infinitive

pres.	cōnā|rī	verē|rī	ūt|ī	partī|rī
perf.	cōnāt|um esse	verit|um esse	ūs|um esse	partīt|um esse
fut.	cōnāt|ūr|um esse	verit|ūr|um esse	ūs|ūr|um esse	partīt|ūr|um esse

Indicative

pres.	cōnā|tur	verē|tur	ūt|itur	partī|tur
imperf.	cōnā|bā|tur	verē|bā|tur	ūt|ēbā|tur	parti|ēbā|tur
fut.	cōnā|b|itur	verē|b|itur	ūt|ē|tur	parti|ē|tur
perf.	cōnāt|us est	verit|us est	ūs|us est	partīt|us est
pluperf.	cōnāt|us erat	verit|us erat	ūs|us erat	partīt|us erat
fut. perf.	cōnāt|us erit	verit|us erit	ūs|us erit	partīt|us erit

Subjunctive

pres.	cōn|ē|tur	vere|ā|tur	ūt|ā|tur	parti|ā|tur
imperf.	cōnā|rē|tur	verē|rē|tur	ūt|erē|tur	partī|rē|tur
perf.	cōnāt|us sit	verit|us sit	ūs|us sit	partīt|us sit
pluperf.	cōnāt|us esset	verit|us esset	ūs|us esset	partīt|us esset

Imperative

sing.	cōnā|re	verē|re	ūt|ere	partī|re
pl.	cōnā|minī	verē|minī	ūt|iminī	partī|minī

Participle

pres.	cōnā|ns	verē|ns	ūt|ēns	parti|ēns
perf.	cōnāt|us	verit|us	ūs|us	partīt|us
fut.	cōnāt|ūr|us	verit|ūr|us	ūs|ūr|us	partīt|ūr|us

Supine cōnāt|um -ū   verit|um -ū   ūs|um -ū   partīt|um -ū

Gerund

	cōna|nd|um	vere|nd|um	ūt|end|um	parti|end|um

Gerundive

	cōna|nd|us	vere|nd|us	ūt|end|us	parti|end|us

Third conjugation: present stem -i

Examples: **capere, patī** (present stem: capi-, pati-)

Left margin notes:

i > e before r

cape|re < *capi|re
capī < *capi|ī
patī < *pati|ī

cape|ris < *capi|ris
pate|ris < *pati|ris

Infinitive

	act.	pass.	dep.
present	cape|re	cap|ī	pat|ī

Indicative

present		act.	pass.	dep.
sing.	1	capi|ō	capi|or	pati|or
	2	capi|s	cape|ris	pate|ris
	3	capi|t	capi|tur	pati|tur
pl.	1	capi|mus	capi|mur	pati|mur
	2	capi|tis	capi|minī	pati|minī
	3	capi|unt	capi|untur	pati|untur

imperfect				
sing.	1	capi|ēba|m	capi|ēba|r	pati|ēba|r
	2	capi|ēbā|s	capi|ēbā|ris	pati|ēbā|ris
	3	capi|ēba|t	capi|ēbā|tur	pati|ēbā|tur
pl.	1	capi|ēbā|mus	capi|ēbā|mur	pati|ēbā|mur
	2	capi|ēbā|tis	capi|ēbā|minī	pati|ēbā|minī
	3	capi|ēba|nt	capi|ēba|ntur	pati|ēba|ntur

future

sing.	1	capi|a|m	capi|a|r	pati|a|r
	2	capi|ē|s	capi|ē|ris	pati|ē|ris
	3	capi|e|t	capi|ē|tur	pati|ē|tur
pl.	1	capi|ē|mus	capi|ē|mur	pati|ē|mur
	2	capi|ē|tis	capi|ē|minī	pati|ē|minī
	3	capi|e|nt	capi|e|ntur	pati|e|ntur

Subjunctive
present

sing.	1	capi|a|m	capi|a|r	pati|a|r
	2	capi|ā|s	capi|ā|ris	pati|ā|ris
	3	capi|a|t	capi|ā|tur	pati|ā|tur
pl.	1	capi|ā|mus	capi|ā|mur	pati|ā|mur
	2	capi|ā|tis	capi|ā|minī	pati|ā|minī
	3	capi|a|nt	capi|a|ntur	pati|a|ntur

imperfect

sing.	1	cape|re|m	cape|re|r	pate|re|r
	2	cape|rē|s	cape|rē|ris	pate|rē|ris
	3	cape|re|t	cape|rē|tur	pate|rē|tur
pl.	1	cape|rē|mus	cape|rē|mur	pate|rē|mur
	2	cape|rē|tis	cape|rē|minī	pate|rē|minī
	3	cape|re|nt	cape|re|ntur	pate|re|ntur

cape\|rem < *capi\|rem

Imperative

sing.	cape		pate|re
pl.	capi|te		pati|minī

cape < *capi

Participle

present	capi|ēns -ent|is	pati|ēns -ent|is

Gerund capi\|end\|um pati\|end\|um

Gerundive capi\|end\|us pati\|end\|us

Irregular verbs I: present stem

1. Infinitive *es\|se* (stem *es-, er-, s-*)

Indicative			Subjunctive		Imperative	
pres.	imperf.	fut.	pres.	imperf.	pres.	fut.
s|um	er|a|m	er|ō	s|i|m	es|se|m		
es	er|ā|s	er|is	s|ī|s	es|sē|s	es	es|tō
es|t	er|a|t	er|it	s|i|t	es|se|t	es|te	es|tōte
s|umus	er|ā|mus	er|imus	s|ī|mus	es|sē|mus		
es|tis	er|ā|tis	er|itis	s|ī|tis	es|sē|tis		
s|unt	er|a|nt	er|unt	s|i|nt	es|se|nt		

er- ante vōcālem

in composite verbs:
ab- ad- de- in- inter- prae-
prōd- super-esse
prōd-est prō-sunt
 prōd-e... prō-s...
de-est dē-sunt
in-est īn-sunt

2. Infinitive *posse*

Indicative			Subjunctive	
pres.	imperf.	fut.	pres.	imperf.
pos-sum	pot-eram	pot-erō	pos-sim	possem
pot-es	pot-erās	pot-eris	pos-sīs	possēs
pot-est	pot-erat	pot-erit	pos-sit	posset
pos-sumus	pot-erāmus	pot-erimus	pos-sīmus	possēmus
pot-estis	pot-erātis	pot-eritis	pos-sītis	possētis
pos-sunt	pot-erant	pot-erunt	pos-sint	possent

pot-e...
pos-s...

nōlle < ne- + velle
mālle < magis + velle

3. Infinitive *velle, nōlle, mālle*

Indicative

pres.			
	vol|ō	nōl|ō	māll|ō
	vīs	nōn vīs	māvīs
	vul|t	nōn vult	māvult
	vol|umus	nōl|umus	māl|umus
	vul|tis	nōn vultis	māvultis
	vol|unt	nōl|unt	māl|unt
imperf.	vol|ēba|m	nōl|ēba|m	māl|ēba|m
	vol|ēbā|s	nōl|ēbā|s	māl|ēbā|s
fut.	vol|a|m	nōl|a|m	māl|a|m
	vol|ē|s	nōl|ē|s	māl|ē|s

Subjunctive

pres.			
	vel|i|m	nōl|i|m	māl|i|m
	vel|ī|s	nōl|ī|s	māl|ī|s
	vel|i|t	nōl|i|t	māl|i|t
	vel|ī|mus	nōl|ī|mus	māl|ī|mus
	vel|ī|tis	nōl|ī|tis	māl|ī|tis
	vel|i|nt	nōl|i|nt	māl|i|nt
imperf.	velle|m	nōlle|m	mālle|m
	vellē|s	nōllē|s	māllē|s
	velle|t	nōlle|t	mālle|t
	vellē|mus	nōllē|mus	māllē|mus
	vellē|tis	nōllē|tis	māllē|tis
	velle|nt	nōlle|nt	mālle|nt

Participle

pres.	vol|ēns	nōl|ēns	

Imperative

nōl\|ī -īte + inf.

sing.		nōl|ī	
pl.		nōl|īte	

4. Infinitive *ī\|re*

Indicative			Subjunctive		Imperative	
pres.	imperf.	fut.	pres.	imperf.	pres.	fut.
e|ō	ī|ba|m	ī|b|ō	e|a|m	ī|re|m	ī	ī|tō
ī|s	ī|bā|s	ī|b|is	e|ā|s	ī|rē|s	ī|te	ī|tōte
i|t	ī|ba|t	ī|b|it	e|a|t	ī|re|t	Participium	
ī|mus	ī|bā|mus	ī|b|imus	e|ā|mus	ī|rē|mus	i|ēns e|unt|is	
ī|tis	ī|bā|tis	ī|b|itis	e|ā|tis	ī|rē|tis	Gerundium	
e|unt	ī|ba|nt	ī|b|unt	e|a|nt	ī|re|nt	e|und|um	

passive (impersonal)
ī\|rī
ī\|tur ī\|bā\|tur ī\|b\|itur
e\|ā\|tur ī\|rē\|tur
gerundive:
e\|und\|um (est)

5. Infinitive *fi\|erī*

Indicative				Subjunctive
pres.	imperf.	fut.	pres.	imperf.
fī|ō	fī|ēba|m	fī|a|m	fī|a|m	fī|ere|m
fī|s	fī|ēbā|s	fī|ē|s	fī|ā|s	fī|erē|s
fī|t	fī|ēba|t	fī|e|t	fī|a|t	fī|ere|t
fī|mus	fī|ēbā|mus	fī|ē|mus	fī|ā|mus	fī|erē|mus
fī|tis	fī|ēbā|tis	fī|ē|tis	fī|ā|tis	fī|erē|tis
fī|unt	fī|ēba|nt	fī|e|nt	fī|a|nt	fī|ere|nt

6. Infinitive: active *fer|re*, passive *fer|rī*

Indicative

	act.	pass.		act.	pass.
pres.	*fer|ō*	*fer|or*	imperf.	*fer|ēba|m*	*fer|ēba|r*
	fer|s	*fer|ris*		*fer|ēbā|s*	*fer|ēbā|ris*
	fer|t	*fer|tur*			
	fer|imus	*fer|imur*	fut.	*fer|a|m*	*fer|a|r*
	fer|tis	*fer|iminī*		*fer|ē|s*	*fer|ē|ris*
	fer|unt	*fer|untur*		*fer|e|t*	*fer|ē|tur*

Subjunctive

	act.	pass.		act.	pass.
pres.	*fer|a|m*	*fer|a|r*	imperf.	*fer|re|m*	*fer|re|r*
	fer|ā|s	*fer|ā|ris*		*fer|rē|s*	*fer|rē|ris*
	fer|a|t	*fer|ā|tur*		*fer|re|t*	*fer|rē|tur*
	fer|ā|mus	*fer|ā|mur*		*fer|rē|mus*	*fer|rē|mur*
	fer|ā|tis	*fer|ā|minī*		*fer|rē|tis*	*fer|rē|minī*
	fer|a|nt	*fer|a|ntur*		*fer|re|nt*	*fer|re|ntur*

	Imperative	Participle	Gerund	Gerundive
pres.	*fer fer|te*	*fer|ēns*	*fer|end|um*	*fer|end|us*
fut.	*fer|tō -tōte*			

7. Infinitive: act. *ēs|se*, pass. *ed|ī*

Indicative			Subjunctive	
pres.	imperf.	fut.	pres.	imperf.
ed|ō	*ed|ēba|m*	*ed|a|m*	*ed|i|m (-a|m)*	*ēs|se|m*
ēs	*ed|ēbā|s*	*ed|ē|s*	*ed|ī|s (-ā|s)*	*ēs|sē|s*
ēs|t	*ed|ēba|t*	*ed|e|t*	*ed|i|t (-a|t)*	*ēs|se|t*
ed|imus	*ed|ēbā|mus*	*ed|ē|mus*	*ed|ī|mus (-ā|mus)*	*ēs|sē|mus*
ēs|tis	*ed|ēbā|tis*	*ed|ē|tis*	*ed|ī|tis (-ā|tis)*	*ēs|sē|tis*
ed|unt	*ed|ēba|nt*	*ed|e|nt*	*ed|i|nt (-a|nt)*	*ēs|se|nt*

pass. ind. pres. 3rd pers.
ēs|tur ed|untur

	Imperative	Participle	Gerund	Gerundive
pres.	*ēs ēs|te*	*ed|ēns*	*ed|end|um*	*ed|end|us*
fut.	*ēs|tō -tōte*			

8. Infinitive *da|re*

Present stem *da-* (short *a*): *da|re, da|mus, da|ba|m, da|b|ō, da|re|m*, etc., except *dā* (imp.), *dā|s* (ind. pres. 2 sing.), *dā|ns* (pres. part.).

Defective verbs

9. *ait*

Indicative

pres.	*āi|ō*	--	imperf.	*āi|ēba|m*	*āi|ēbā|mus*
	ai|s	--		*āi|ēbā|s*	*āi|ēbā|tis*
	ai|t	*āi|unt*		*āi|ēba|t*	*āi|ēba|nt*

ain'? = ais-ne?

10. *inquit*

Indicative

pres.	*inquam*	--	fut.	--
	inquis	--		*inquiēs*
	inquit	*inquiunt*		*inquiet*

11. Verbs without present stem:

memin|isse (imperative: *memen|tō -tōte*)

ōd|isse

Irregular verbs II: perfect and supine stems

First conjugation

	pres. inf.	perf. inf.	perf. part./sup.
ac-cubāre	1. *cubā|re*	*cubu|isse*	*cubit|um*
	2. *vetā|re*	*vetu|isse*	*vetit|um*
ex-plicāre	3. *im-plicā|re*	*-plicu|isse*	*-plicit|um*
	4. *secā|re*	*secu|isse*	*sect|um*
ad-iuvāre	5. *iuvā|re*	*iūv|isse*	*iūt|um*
	6. *lavā|re*	*lāv|isse*	*laut|um/lavāt|um*
	7. *stā|re*	*stet|isse*	
prae-stāre	8. *cōn-stā|re*	*-stit|isse*	
circum-dare	9. *da|re*	*ded|isse*	*dat|um*

Second conjugation

	pres. inf.	perf. inf.	perf. part./sup.
	10. *docē|re*	*docu|isse*	*doct|um*
	11. *miscē|re*	*miscu|isse*	*mixt|um*
	12. *tenē|re*	*tenu|isse*	*tent|um*
abs- re- sus-tinēre	13. *con-tinē|re*	*-tinu|isse*	*-tent|um*
	14. *cēnsē|re*	*cēnsu|isse*	*cēns|um*
	15. *dēlē|re*	*dēlēv|isse*	*dēlēt|um*
	16. *flē|re*	*flēv|isse*	*flēt|um*
com- ex-plēre	17. *im-plē|re*	*-plēv|isse*	*-plēt|um*
	18. *cavē|re*	*cāv|isse*	*caut|um*
	19. *favē|re*	*fāv|isse*	*faut|um*
per- re-movēre	20. *movē|re*	*mōv|isse*	*mōt|um*
	21. *sedē|re*	*sēd|isse*	*sess|um*
	22. *possidē|re*	*possēd|isse*	*possess|um*
in-vidēre	23. *vidē|re*	*vīd|isse*	*vīs|um*
	24. *augē|re*	*aux|isse*	*auct|um*
	25. *lūcē|re*	*lūx|isse*	
	26. *lūgē|re*	*lūx|isse*	
	27. *iubē|re*	*iuss|isse*	*iuss|um*
dē-rīdēre	28. *rīdē|re*	*rīs|isse*	*rīs|um*
dis- per-suādēre	29. *suādē|re*	*suās|isse*	*suās|um*
dē-tergēre	30. *tergē|re*	*ters|isse*	*ters|um*
re-manēre	31. *manē|re*	*māns|isse*	*māns|um*
	32. *re-spondē|re*	*-spond|isse*	*-spōns|um*
	33. *mordē|re*	*momord|isse*	*mors|um*
	34. *fatē|rī*	*fass|um esse*	
	35. *cōn-fitē|rī*	*-fess|um esse*	
	36. *solē|re*	*solit|um esse*	
	37. *audē|re*	*aus|um esse*	
	38. *gaudē|re*	*gavīs|um esse*	

Third conjugation

39.	*leg|ere*	*lēg|isse*	*lēct|um*
40.	*ē-lig|ere*	*-lēg|isse*	*-lēct|um*
41.	*em|ere*	*ēm|isse*	*ēmpt|um*
42.	*red-im|ere*	*-ēm|isse*	*-ēmpt|um*
43.	*cōn-sīd|ere*	*-sēd|isse*	
44.	*ēs|se ed|ō*	*ēd|isse*	*ēs|um*
45.	*ag|ere*	*ēg|isse*	*āct|um*
46.	*cōg|ere*	*co-ēg|isse*	*co-āct|um*
47.	*cap|ere -iō*	*cēp|isse*	*capt|um*
48.	*ac-cip|ere -iō*	*-cēp|isse*	*-cept|um*	re-cipere
49.	*fac|ere -iō*	*fēc|isse*	*fact|um*	imp. fac!
50.	*af-fic|ere -iō*	*-fēc|isse*	*-fect|um*	cōn- ef- inter- per- ficere
51.	*iac|ere -iō*	*iēc|isse*	*iact|um*	
52.	*ab-ic|ere -iō*	*-iēc|isse*	*-iect|um*	ad- ē- prō-icere
53.	*fug|ere -iō*	*fūg|isse*		au- ef-fugere
54.	*vinc|ere*	*vīc|isse*	*vict|um*	
55.	*fund|ere*	*fūd|isse*	*fūs|um*	ef-fundere
56.	*re-linqu|ere*	*-līqu|isse*	*-lict|um*	
57.	*rump|ere*	*rūp|isse*	*rupt|um*	ē-rumpere
58.	*frang|ere*	*frēg|isse*	*frāct|um*	
59.	*carp|ere*	*carps|isse*	*carpt|um*	
60.	*dīc|ere*	*dīx|isse*	*dict|um*	imp. dīc! dūc!
61.	*dūc|ere*	*dūx|isse*	*duct|um*	ab- ē- re-dūcere
62.	*scrīb|ere*	*scrīps|isse*	*scrīpt|um*	in-scrībere
63.	*nūb|ere*	*nūps|isse*	*nupt|um*	
64.	*a-spic|ere -iō*	*-spex|isse*	*-spect|um*	cōn- dē- prō- re- su-spicere
65.	*al-lic|ere -iō*	*-lēx|isse*	*-lect|um*	
66.	*reg|ere*	*rēx|isse*	*rēct|um*	
67.	*cor-rig|ere*	*-rēx|isse*	*-rēct|um*	
68.	*perg|ere*	*per-rēx|isse*		
69.	*surg|ere*	*sur-rēx|isse*		
70.	*dīlig|ere*	*dīlēx|isse*	*dīlēct|um*	
71.	*intelleg|ere*	*intellēx|isse*	*intellēct|um*	
72.	*negleg|ere*	*neglēx|isse*	*neglēct|um*	
73.	*cing|ere*	*cīnx|isse*	*cīnct|um*	
74.	*iung|ere*	*iūnx|isse*	*iūnct|um*	ad- con- dis-iungere
75.	*coqu|ere*	*cox|isse*	*coct|um*	
76.	*trah|ere*	*trāx|isse*	*tract|um*	con- dē- re-trahere
77.	*veh|ere*	*vēx|isse*	*vect|um*	ad- in-vehere
78.	*in-stru|ere*	*-strūx|isse*	*-strūct|um*	
79.	*flu|ere*	*flūx|isse*		in-fluere
80.	*vīv|ere*	*vīx|isse*		part. fut. vīct|ūr|us
81.	*sūm|ere*	*sūmps|isse*	*sūmpt|um*	cōn-sūmere
82.	*prōm|ere*	*prōmps|isse*	*prōmpt|um*	
83.	*dēm|ere*	*dēmps|isse*	*dēmpt|um*	

	84.	ger|ere	gess|isse	gest|um
	85.	ūr|ere	uss|isse	ust|um
	86.	fīg|ere	fīx|isse	fīx|um
īn-flectere	87.	flect|ere	flex|isse	flex|um
ac- dis- prō- re- cēdere	88.	cēd|ere	cess|isse	cess|um
	89.	claud|ere	claus|isse	claus|um
	90.	in-clūd|ere	-clūs|isse	-clūs|um
	91.	dīvid|ere	dīvīs|isse	dīvīs|um
	92.	lūd|ere	lūs|isse	lūs|um
	93.	laed|ere	laes|isse	laes|um
	94.	ē-līd|ere	-līs|isse	-līs|um
	95.	plaud|ere	plaus|isse	plaus|um
ā- ad- dī- per- prō- re-mittere	96.	mitt|ere	mīs|isse	miss|um
	97.	quat|ere -iō	--	quass|um
	98.	per-cut|ere -iō	-cuss|isse	-cuss|um
sub-mergere	99.	merg|ere	mers|isse	mers|um
	100.	sparg|ere	spars|isse	spars|um
	101.	a-sperg|ere	-spers|isse	-spers|um
	102.	prem|ere	press|isse	press|um
	103.	im-prim|ere	-press|isse	-press|um
	104.	contemn|ere	contēmps|isse	contēmpt|um
	105.	stern|ere	strāv|isse	strāt|um
	106.	cern|ere	crēv|isse	crēt|um
	107.	ser|ere	sēv|isse	sat|um
	108.	arcess|ere	arcessīv|isse	arcessīt|um
	109.	cup|ere -iō	cupīv|isse	cupīt|um
	110.	sap|ere -iō	sapi|isse	
	111.	pet|ere	petīv|isse	petīt|um
	112.	quaer|ere	quaesīv|isse	quaesīt|um
	113.	re-quīr|ere	-quīsīv|isse	-quīsīt|um
	114.	sin|ere	sīv|isse	sit|um
	115.	dēsin|ere	dēsi|isse	dēsit|um
ap- dē- ex- im- prae- re-pōnere	116.	pōn|ere	posu|isse	posit|um
	117.	al|ere	alu|isse	alt|um
in-colere	118.	col|ere	colu|isse	cult|um
	119.	dēser|ere	dēseru|isse	dēsert|um
	120.	rap|ere -iō	rapu|isse	rapt|um
sur-ripere	121.	ē-rip|ere -iō	-ripu|isse	-rept|um
	122.	trem|ere	tremu|isse	
	123.	frem|ere	fremu|isse	
re-cumbere	124.	ac-cumb|ere	-cubu|isse	
	125.	tang|ere	tetig|isse	tāct|um
	126.	cad|ere	cecid|isse	
oc-cidere	127.	ac-cid|ere	-cid|isse	
	128.	caed|ere	cecīd|isse	caes|um
	129.	oc-cīd|ere	-cīd|isse	-cīs|um

130. *curr|ere*	*cucurr|isse*	*curs|um*	
131. *ac-curr|ere*	*-curr|isse*	*-curs|um*	*ex- oc- per- prō-currere*
132. *par|ere -iō*	*peper|isse*	*part|um*	
133. *pell|ere*	*pepul|isse*	*puls|um*	
134. *parc|ere*	*peperc|isse*		
135. *can|ere*	*cecin|isse*		
136. *fall|ere*	*fefell|isse*		*per- red- trā-dere*
137. *ad-d|ere*	*-did|isse*	*-dit|um*	
138. *crēd|ere*	*crēdid|isse*	*crēdit|um*	
139. *vēnd|ere*	*vēndid|isse*		*dē- re-sistere*
140. *cōn-sist|ere*	*-stit|isse*		
141. *scind|ere*	*scid|isse*	*sciss|um*	
142. *bib|ere*	*bib|isse*		
143. *dēfend|ere*	*dēfend|isse*	*dēfēns|um*	*ap- re-prehendere*
144. *prehend|ere*	*prehend|isse*	*prehēns|um*	*cōn- dē-scendere*
145. *a-scend|ere*	*-scend|isse*	*-scēns|um*	
146. *ac-cend|ere*	*-cend|isse*	*-cēns|um*	
147. *ostend|ere*	*ostend|isse*	*ostent|um*	*ā- con-vertere*
148. *vert|ere*	*vert|isse*	*vers|um*	
149. *minu|ere*	*minu|isse*	*minūt|um*	
150. *statu|ere*	*statu|isse*	*statūt|um*	
151. *cōn-stitu|ere*	*-stitu|isse*	*-stitūt|um*	
152. *indu|ere*	*indu|isse*	*indūt|um*	
153. *metu|ere*	*metu|isse*		
154. *solv|ere*	*solv|isse*	*solūt|um*	*ē-volvere*
155. *volv|ere*	*volv|isse*	*volūt|um*	*re-quiēscere*
156. *quiēsc|ere*	*quiēv|isse*		
157. *crēsc|ere*	*crēv|isse*		
158. *ērubēsc|ere*	*ērubu|isse*		
159. *nōsc|ere*	*nōv|isse*		
160. *ignōsc|ere*	*ignōv|isse*	*ignōt|um*	
161. *cognōsc|ere*	*cognōv|isse*	*cognitum*	
162. *pāsc|ere*	*pāv|isse*	*pāstum*	
163. *posc|ere*	*poposc|isse*		
164. *disc|ere*	*didic|isse*		
165. *fer|re*	*tul|isse*	*lāt|um*	
166. *af-fer|re*	*at-tul|isse*	*ad|lātum*	
167. *au-fer|re*	*abs-tul|isse*	*ab|lātum*	
168. *ef-fer|re*	*ex-tul|isse*	*ē-lāt|um*	
169. *of-fer|re*	*ob-tul|isse*	*ob-lāt|um*	
170. *re-fer|re*	*rettul|isse*	*re-lāt|um*	*per- prae- prō- trāns- ferre*
171. *toll|ere*	*sustul|isse*	*sublāt|um*	
172. *in-cip|ere -iō*	*coep|isse*	*coept|um*	
173. *fīd|ere*	*fīs|um esse*		*cōn-fīdere*
174. *revert|ī*	*revert|isse*	*revers|um*	
175. *loqu|ī*	*locūt|um esse*		*col-loquī*

côn- per-sequī	176.	*sequ|ī*	*secūt|um esse*	
	177.	*quer|ī*	*quest|um esse*	
	178.	*mor|ī -ior*	*mortu|um esse*	
	179.	*pat|ī -ior*	*pass|um esse*	
prō-gredī	180.	*ē-gred|ī -ior*	*-gress|um esse*	
	181.	*ūt|ī*	*ūs|um esse*	
	182.	*complect|ī*	*complex|um esse*	
	183.	*lāb|ī*	*lāps|um esse*	
	184.	*nāsc|ī*	*nāt|um esse*	
	185.	*proficīsc|ī*	*profect|um esse*	
	186.	*oblīvīsc|ī*	*oblīt|um esse*	

Fourth conjugation

	187.	*aperī|re*	*aperu|isse*	*apert|um*
	188.	*operī|re*	*operu|isse*	*opert|um*
	189.	*salī|re*	*salu|isse*	
circum- prō-silīre	190.	*dē-silī|re*	*-silu|isse*	
ex-haurīre	191.	*haurī|re*	*haus|isse*	*haust|um*
	192.	*vincī|re*	*vīnx|isse*	*vīnct|um*
	193.	*sentī|re*	*sēns|isse*	*sēns|um*
ad- con- in- per- re- venīre	194.	*venī|re*	*vēn|isse*	*vent|um*
	195.	*reperī|re*	*repper|isse*	*repert|um*
ab- ad- ex- per- red- sub- trāns-īre	196.	*ī|re e|ō*	*i|isse*	*it|um*
	197.	*opperī|rī*	*oppert|um esse*	
pres. stem orī-/ori-	198.	*orī|rī ori|tur*	*ort|um esse*	

Irregular verbs III

		pres. inf.	perf. inf.
	199.	*vel|le vol|ō*	*volu|isse*
	200.	*nōl|le*	*nōlu|isse*
inter- prae- super- esse	201.	*māl|le*	*mālu|isse*
	202.	*es|se sum*	*fu|isse*
fut. part. futūr|us	203.	*posse pos-sum*	*potu|isse*
fut. inf. futūr|um esse, fore	204.	*ab-esse*	*ā-fu|isse*
	205.	*ad-esse ad-/as-sum*	*af-fu|isse*
	206.	*de-esse dē-sum*	*dē-fu|isse*
	207.	*prŏd-esse prŏ-sum prŏ-fu|isse*	
	208.	*fi|erī fī|ō*	*fact|um esse*

ALPHABETICAL LIST OF IRREGULAR VERBS

(Numbers refer to the lists of irregular verbs by conjugation that begin on page 349.)

A

abdūcere 61
abesse 204
abicere 52
abīre 196
abstinēre 13
accēdere 88
accendere 146
accidere 127
accipere 48
accubāre 1
accumbere 124
accurrere 131
addere 137
adesse 205
adicere 52
adīre 196
adiungere 74
adiuvāre 5
admittere 96
advehere 77
advenīre 194
afferre 166
afficere 50
agere 45
alere 117
allicere 65
āmittere 96
aperīre 187
appōnere 116
apprehendere 144
arcessere 108
ascendere 145
aspergere 101
aspicere 64
audēre 37
auferre 167
aufugere 53
augēre 24
āvertere 148

B

bibere 142

C

cadere 126
caedere 128
canere 135

capere 47
carpere 59
cavēre 18
cēdere 88
cēnsēre 14
cernere 106
cingere 73
circumdare 9
circumsilīre 190
claudere 89
cōgere 46
cognōscere 161
colere 118
colloquī 175
complectī 182
complēre 17
cōnficere 50
cōnfīdere 173
cōnfitērī 35
coniungere 74
cōnscendere 145
cōnsequī 176
cōnsīdere 43
cōnsistere 140
cōnspicere 64
cōnstāre 8
cōnstituere 151
cōnsūmere 81
contemnere 104
continēre 13
contrahere 76
convenīre 194
convertere 148
coquere 75
corrigere 67
crēdere 138
crēscere 157
cubāre 1
cupere 109
currere 130

D

dare 9
dēesse 206
dēfendere 143
dēlēre 15
dēmere 83

dēpōnere 116
dērīdēre 28
dēscendere 145
dēserere 119
dēsilīre 190
dēsinere 115
dēsistere 140
dēspicere 64
dētergēre 30
dētrahere 76
dīcere 60
dīligere 70
dīmittere 96
discēdere 88
discere 164
disiungere 74
dissuādēre 29
dīvidere 91
docēre 10
dūcere 61

E

ēdūcere 61
efferre 168
efficere 50
effugere 53
effundere 55
ēgredī 180
ēicere 52
ēlīdere 94
ēligere 40
emere 41
ēripere 121
ērubēscere 158
ērumpere 57
esse 202
ēsse 44
ēvolvere 155
excurrere 131
exhaurīre 191
exīre 196
explēre 17
expōnere 116

F

facere 49
fallere 136
fatērī 34

favēre 19
ferre 165
fīdere 173
fierī 208
fīgere 86
flectere 87
flēre 16
fluere 79
frangere 58
fremere 123
fugere 53
fundere 55

G

gaudēre 38
gerere 84

H

haurīre 191

I

iacere 51
ignōscere 160
implēre 17
implicāre 3
impōnere 116
imprimere 103
incipere 172
inclūdere 90
incolere 118
induere 152
īnflectere 87
īnfluere 79
īnscrībere 62
īnstruere 78
intellegere 71
interesse 202
interficere 50
invehere 77
invenīre 194
invidēre 23
īre 196
iubēre 27
iungere 74
iuvāre 5

L

lābī 183
laedere 93

lavāre 6
legere 39
loquī 175
lūcēre 25
lūdere 92
lūgēre 26

M

mālle 201
manēre 31
mergere 99
metuere 153
minuere 149
miscēre 11
mittere 96
mordēre 33
morī 178
movēre 20

N

nāscī 184
neglegere 72
nōlle 200
nōscere 159
nūbere 63

O

oblīvīscī 186
occidere 127
occīdere 129
occurrere 131
offerre 169
operīre 188
opperīrī 197
orīrī 198
ostendere 147

P

parcere 134
parere 132
pascere 162
patī 179
pellere 133

percurrere 131
percutere 98
perdere 137
perferre 165
perficere 50
pergere 68
perīre 196
permittere 96
permovēre 20
persequī 176
persuādēre 29
pervenīre 194
petere 111
plaudere 95
pōnere 116
poscere 163
posse 203
possidēre 22
praeesse 202
praeferre 165
praepōnere 116
praestāre 8
prehendere 144
premere 102
prōcēdere 88
prōcurrere 131
prōdesse 207
prōferre 165
proficīscī 185
prōgredī 180
prōicere 52
prōmere 82
prōmittere 96
prōsilīre 190
prōspicere 64

Q

quaerere 112
quatere 97
querī 177
quiēscere 156

R

rapere 120
recēdere 88
recipere 48
recumbere 124
reddere 137
redimere 42
redīre 196
redūcere 61
referre 170
regere 66
relinquere 56
remanēre 31
remittere 96
removēre 20
reperīre 195
repōnere 116
reprehendere 144
requiēscere 156
requīrere 113
resistere 140
respondēre 32
retinēre 13
retrahere 76
revenīre 194
revertī 174
rīdēre 28
rumpere 57

S

salīre 189
sapere 110
scindere 141
scrībere 62
secāre 4
sedēre 21
sentīre 193
sequī 176
serere 107
sinere 114
solēre 36

solvere 154
spargere 100
stāre 7
statuere 150
sternere 105
suādēre 29
subīre 196
submergere 99
sūmere 81
superesse 202
surgere 69
surripere 121
suspicere 64
sustinēre 13

T

tangere 125
tenēre 12
tergēre 30
tollere 171
trādere 137
trahere 76
trānsferre 165
trānsīre 196
tremere 122

U

ūrere 85
ūtī 181

V

vehere 77
velle 199
vēndere 139
venīre 194
vertere 148
vetāre 2
vidēre 23
vincere 54
vincīre 192
vīvere 80
volvere 155

INDEX OF NOUNS, ADJECTIVES AND VERBS

Nouns

1st Declension

Gen. sing. *-ae*, pl. *-ārum*

Feminine

āla	*fenestra*	*littera*	*puella*
amīca	*fera*	*lucerna*	*pugna*
amīcitia	*fīlia*	*lūna*	*rēgula*
ancilla	*fōrma*	*mamma*	*rīpa*
anima	*fortūna*	*margarīta*	*rosa*
aqua	*fossa*	*māteria*	*sagitta*
aquila	*fuga*	*mātrōna*	*scaena*
arānea	*gemma*	*memoria*	*sella*
audācia	*gena*	*mēnsa*	*sententia*
bēstia	*glōria*	*mora*	*silva*
catēna	*grammatica*	*Mūsa*	*stēlla*
cauda	*grātia*	*nātūra*	*syllaba*
causa	*hasta*	*nāvicula*	*tabella*
cēna	*herba*	*nota*	*tabula*
cēra	*hōra*	*opera*	*terra*
charta	*iactūra*	*ōra*	*toga*
columna	*iānua*	*paenīnsula*	*tunica*
cōmoedia	*iniūria*	*pāgina*	*turba*
cōpia	*inopia*	*palma*	*umbra*
culīna	*īnsula*	*patientia*	*ūva*
cūra	*invidia*	*patria*	*vēna*
dea	*īra*	*pecūnia*	*via*
domina	*lacrima*	*penna*	*victōria*
epistula	*laetitia*	*persōna*	*vigilia*
fābula	*lāna*	*pila*	*vīlla*
fāma	*lectīca*	*poena*	*vīnea*
familia	*līnea*	*porta*	*virga*
fēmina	*lingua*	*prōvincia*	*vīta*

(pl.)

cūnae	*dīvitiae*	*nōnae*	*tenebrae*
dēliciae	*kalendae*	*nūgae*	*tībiae*

Masculine (/feminine)

agricola	*convīva*	*nauta*	*poēta*
aurīga	*incola*	*parricīda*	*pīrāta*

2nd Declension

Gen. sing. *-ī*, pl. *-ōrum*
1. Nom. sing. *-us* (*-r*)
Masculine

agnus	deus	locus	pugnus
amīcus	digitus	lūdus	pullus
animus	discipulus	lupus	rāmus
annus	dominus	marītus	rēmus
ānulus	equus	medicus	rīvus
asinus	erus	modus	sacculus
avunculus	fīlius	mundus	saccus
barbarus	fluvius	mūrus	servus
cachinnus	fundus	nāsus	sēstertius
calamus	gallus	nīdus	somnus
calceus	gladius	numerus	sonus
campus	hortus	nummus	stilus
capillus	inimīcus	nūntius	tabernārius
cibus	labyrinthus	ōceanus	taurus
circus	lacertus	ocellus	titulus
cocus	lectus	oculus	tyrannus
colōnus	lēgātus	ōstiārius	umerus
delphīnus	libellus	petasus	ventus
dēnārius	lībertīnus	populus	zephyrus

(nom. sing. *-er*)

ager agrī	faber -brī	magister -trī	puer -erī
culter -trī	liber -brī	minister -trī	vesper -erī

(pl.)
līberī

Feminine

humus	papyrus	Aegyptus	Rhodus

2. Nom. sing. *-um*, plur *-a*
Neuter

aedificium	exemplum	mōnstrum	scamnum
aequinoctium	factum	negōtium	scūtum
arātrum	fātum	odium	saeculum
argentum	ferrum	officium	saxum
ātrium	fīlum	oppidum	scalpellum
aurum	folium	ōrnāmentum	signum
auxilium	forum	ōsculum	silentium
baculum	fretum	ōstium	solum
balneum	frūmentum	ōtium	speculum
bāsium	fūrtum	ōvum	stipendium
bellum	gaudium	pābulum	studium
beneficium	gremium	pullium	supplicium
bonum	imperium	pecūlium	talentum
bracchium	impluvium	pēnsum	tēctum
caelum	ingenium	perīculum	templum
capitulum	initium	peristylum	tergum
cerebrum	īnstrūmentum	pīlum	theātrum
colloquium	labrum	pirum	triclīnium
collum	lignum	pōculum	vāllum
cōnsilium	līlium	praedium	vēlum
convīvium	lucrum	praemium	verbum
cubiculum	maleficium	pretium	vestīgium
dictum	malum	prīncipium	vestīmentum
dōnum	mālum	prōmissum	vīnum
dorsum	mendum	respōnsum	vocābulum

(pl.)

arma -ōrum	castra -ōrum	loca -ōrum	vāsa -ōrum

3rd Declension

Gen. sing. *-is*
1. Gen. pl. *-um*
Masculine

āēr āeris	*gladiātor -ōris*	*piscātor -ōris*
amor -ōris	*grex -egis*	*praedō -ōnis*
arātor -ōris	*gubernātor -ōris*	*prīnceps -ipis*
bōs bovis	*homō -inis*	*pudor -ōris*
calor -ōris	*hospes -itis*	*pulmō -ōnis*
carcer -eris	*iānitor -ōris*	*rēx rēgis*
cardō -inis	*imperātor -ōris*	*rūmor -ōris*
clāmor -ōris	*iuvenis -is*	*sacerdōs -ōtis*
color -ōris	*labor -ōris*	*sāl salis*
comes -itis	*leō -ōnis*	*sanguis -inis*
coniūnx -iugis	*mercātor -ōris*	*senex senis*
cruor -ōris	*mīles -itis*	*sermō -ōnis*
dolor -ōris	*mōs mōris*	*sōl sōlis*
dux ducis	*ōrdō -inis*	*spectātor -ōris*
eques -itis	*passer -eris*	*tībīcen -inis*
fidicen -inis	*pāstor -ōris*	*timor -ōris*
flōs -ōris	*pater -tris*	*victor -ōris*
frāter -tris	*pedes -itis*	
fūr fūris	*pēs pedis*	

(pl.)

parentēs -um	*septentriōnēs -um*

Feminine

aestās -ātis	*māter -tris*	*quālitās -ātis*
aetās -ātis	*mentiō -ōnis*	*ratiō -ōnis*
arbor -oris	*mercēs -ēdis*	*salūs -ūtis*
condiciō -ōnis	*mulier -eris*	*servitūs -ūtis*
crux -ucis	*multitūdō -inis*	*significātiō -ōnis*
cupiditās -ātis	*nārrātiō -ōnis*	*soror -ōris*
expugnātiō -ōnis	*nāvigātiō -ōnis*	*tempestās -ātis*
fēlīcitās -ātis	*nex necis*	*tranquillitās -ātis*
hiems -mis	*nūtrīx -īcis*	*uxor -ōris*
imāgō -inis	*nux nucis*	*valētūdō -inis*
laus laudis	*ōrātiō -ōnis*	*virgō -inis*
legiō -ōnis	*pāx pācis*	*virtūs -ūtis*
lēx lēgis	*potestās -ātis*	*voluntās -ātis*
lībertās -ātis	*pōtiō -ōnis*	*vorāgō -inis*
lūx lūcis	*pulchritūdō -inis*	*vōx vōcis*

(pl.)

frūgēs -um	*opēs -um*	*precēs -um*

Neuter (pl. nom. /acc. *-a*)

agmen -inis	*holus -eris*	*pectus -oris*
caput -itis	*iecur -oris*	*pecus -oris*
carmen -inis	*iter itineris*	*phantasma -atis*
certāmen -inis	*iūs iūris*	*praenōmen -inis*
cognōmen -inis	*lac lactis*	*rūs rūris*
cor cordis	*latus -eris*	*scelus -eris*
corpus -oris	*līmen -inis*	*sēmen -inis*
crūs -ūris	*lītus -oris*	*tempus -oris*
epigramma -atis	*mel mellis*	*thema -atis*
flūmen -inis	*mūnus -eris*	*vās vāsis*
frīgus -oris	*nōmen -inis*	*vēr vēris*
fulgur -uris	*opus -eris*	*vulnus -eris*
genus -eris	*ōs ōris*	

(pl.)

verbera -um	*viscera -um*

2. Gen. pl. *-ium*
Masculine

amnis	*hostis*	*oriēns -entis*
as assis	*ignis*	*orbis*
cīvis	*imber -bris*	*pānis*
collis	*īnfāns -antis*	*piscis*
dēns dentis	*mēnsis*	*pōns pontis*
ēnsis	*mōns montis*	*testis*
fīnis	*occidēns -entis*	*venter -tris*

Feminine

apis	*famēs -is*	*ovis*
ars artis	*foris*	*pars partis*
auris	*frōns -ontis*	*puppis*
avis	*gēns gentis*	*ratis*
caedēs -is	*mēns mentis*	*sitis*
carō carnis	*merx -rcis*	*urbs -bis*
classis	*mors -rtis*	*vallis*
clāvis	*nāvis*	*vestis*
cohors -rtis	*nix nivis*	*vītis*
cōnsonāns -antis	*nox noctis*	*vōcālis*
falx -cis	*nūbēs -is*	

(pl.)

fidēs -ium	*sordēs -ium*	*vīrēs -ium*

Neuter

animal -ālis	*mare -is*	*rēte -is*

(pl.)

mīlia -ium	*moenia -ium*

4th Declension
Gen. sing. *-ūs*, pl. *-uum*
Masculine

affectus	*cursus*	*impetus*	*sinus*
arcus	*equitātus*	*lacus*	*strepitus*
cantus	*exercitus*	*metus*	*tonitrus*
cāsus	*exitus*	*passus*	*tumultus*
cōnspectus	*flūctus*	*portus*	*versus*
currus	*gradus*	*rīsus*	*vultus*

Feminine

anus	*domus*	*manus*

(pl.)
īdūs -uum

Neuter

cornū	*genū*

5th Declension
Gen. sing. *-ēī/-eī* (pl. *-ērum*)
Feminine

aciēs -ēī	*glaciēs -ēī*	*fidēs -eī*	*spēs -eī*
faciēs -ēī	*speciēs -ēī*	*rēs reī*	

Masculine

diēs -ēī	*merīdiēs -ēī*

ADJECTIVES

1st/2nd Declension
Nom. sing. m. *-us*, f. *-a*, n. *-um*

acerbus	ferus	mellītus	rēctus
acūtus	fessus	mercātōrius	reliquus
adversus	fīdus	merus	rīdiculus
aegrōtus	foedus	meus	Rōmānus
aequus	fōrmōsus	minimus	rūsticus
albus	frīgidus	mīrus	saevus
aliēnus	fugitīvus	misellus	salvus
altus	futūrus	molestus	sānus
amīcus	gemmātus	mortuus	scaenicus
amoenus	gladiātōrius	mundus	scelestus
angustus	glōriōsus	mūtus	secundus
antīquus	grātus	mūtuus	septimus
apertus	gravidus	necessārius	serēnus
arduus	horrendus	nimius	sērius
argenteus	ignārus	niveus	sevērus
armātus	ignōtus	nōnus	sextus
asinīnus	immātūrus	nōtus	siccus
attentus	improbus	novus	situs
aureus	īmus	nūbilus	sordidus
avārus	incertus	nūdus	studiōsus
barbarus	inconditus	obscūrus	stultus
beātus	indignus	octāvus	summus
bellus	indoctus	optimus	superbus
bonus	industrius	ōtiōsus	superus
caecus	īnferus	pallidus	surdus
calidus	īnfēstus	parātus	suus
candidus	īnfidus	parvulus	tacitus
cārus	īnfimus	parvus	tantus
cautus	inhūmānus	pecūniōsus	tardus
celsus	inimīcus	perīculōsus	temerārius
centēsimus	iniūstus	perpetuus	tenebricōsus
certus	internus	perterritus	timidus
cēterus	invalidus	pessimus	tertius
clārus	iocōsus	plānus	togātus
claudus	īrātus	plēnus	tranquillus
clausus	iūcundus	poēticus	turbidus
contrārius	iūstus	postrēmus	turgidus
crassus	laetus	praeteritus	tūtus
cruentus	laevus	prāvus	tuus
cūnctus	largus	pretiōsus	ultimus
cupidus	Latīnus	prīmus	ūmidus
decimus	lātus	prīvātus	ūniversus
dignus	legiōnārius	propinquus	urbānus
dīmidius	ligneus	proprius	vacuus
dīrus	longus	proximus	validus
doctus	maestus	pūblicus	varius
dubius	magnificus	pūrus	venustus
dūrus	magnus	quantus	vērus
ēbrius	malus	quārtus	vīvus
ēgregius	maritimus	quiētus	-issimus
exiguus	mātūrus	quīntus	sup.
falsus	māximus	rapidus	-ēsimus
ferreus	medius	rārus	num.

(pl.)

cēterī	paucī	singulī	ducentī
multī	plērī-que	bīnī	trecentī
nōnnūllī	plūrimī	cēt.	cēt.

Nom. sing. -er -(e)ra -(e)rum

aeger -gra -grum	niger -gra -grum	ruber -bra -brum
āter -tra -trum	noster -tra -trum	sinister -tra -trum
dexter -tra -trum	piger -gra -grum	vester -tra -trum
impiger -gra -grum	pulcher -chra	līber -era -erum
integer -gra -grum	-chrum	miser -era -erum

3rd Declension

Nom. sing. m./f. -is, n. -e

brevis	fertilis	levis	rudis
circēnsis	fortis	mīlitāris	similis
commūnis	gracilis	mīrābilis	tālis
crūdēlis	gravis	mollis	tenuis
dēbilis	humilis	mortālis	terribilis
difficilis	immortālis	nōbilis	trīstis
dulcis	incolumis	omnis	turpis
facilis	inermis	quālis	vīlis

Nom. sing. m./f./n. -ns, gen. -ntis

absēns	dēpōnēns	ingēns	prūdēns
amāns	dīligēns	neglegēns	sapiēns
clēmēns	frequēns	patiēns	-ns part.
cōnstāns	impatiēns	praesēns	pres.

Nom. sing. m./f./n. -x, gen. -cis

audāx	fēlīx	īnfēlīx
fallāx	ferōx	vēlōx

Nom. sing. m. -er, f. -(e)ris, n. -(e)re

ācer ācris	celer -eris	September -bris
Octōber -bris	November -bris	December -bris

VERBS

1st Conjugation

Inf. pres. act. *-āre*, pass. *-ārī*

aberrāre	*dare*	*iuvāre*	*properāre*
accubāre	*dēlectāre*	*labōrāre*	*pugnāre*
accūsāre	*dēmōnstrāre*	*lacrimāre*	*pulsāre*
adiuvāre	*dēsīderāre*	*lātrāre*	*putāre*
adōrāre	*dēspērāre*	*laudāre*	*recitāre*
aedificāre	*dēvorāre*	*lavāre*	*rēgnāre*
aegrōtāre	*dictāre*	*levāre*	*rēmigāre*
aestimāre	*dōnāre*	*līberāre*	*repugnāre*
affirmāre	*dubitāre*	*memorāre*	*revocāre*
amāre	*ēducāre*	*mīlitāre*	*rigāre*
ambulāre	*errāre*	*mōnstrāre*	*rogāre*
appellāre	*ēvolāre*	*mūtāre*	*rogitāre*
apportāre	*excitāre*	*nārrāre*	*salūtāre*
appropin-	*exclāmāre*	*natāre*	*salvāre*
quāre	*excōgitāre*	*nāvigāre*	*sānāre*
arāre	*excruciāre*	*necāre*	*secāre*
armāre	*excūsāre*	*negāre*	*servāre*
bālāre	*exīstimāre*	*nōmināre*	*signāre*
cantāre	*exōrnāre*	*numerāre*	*significāre*
cēnāre	*explānāre*	*nūntiāre*	*spectāre*
certāre	*expugnāre*	*occultāre*	*spērāre*
cessāre	*exspectāre*	*oppugnāre*	*spīrāre*
circumdare	*fatīgāre*	*optāre*	*stāre*
clāmāre	*flāre*	*ōrāre*	*suscitāre*
cōgitāre	*gubernāre*	*ōrdināre*	*turbāre*
commemo-	*gustāre*	*ōrnāre*	*ululāre*
rāre	*habitāre*	*ōscitāre*	*verberāre*
comparāre	*iactāre*	*palpitāre*	*vetāre*
computāre	*ignōrāre*	*parāre*	*vigilāre*
cōnstāre	*illūstrāre*	*perturbāre*	*vītāre*
conturbāre	*imperāre*	*pīpiāre*	*vocāre*
convocāre	*implicāre*	*plōrāre*	*volāre*
cōpulāre	*interpellāre*	*portāre*	*vorāre*
cruciāre	*interrogāre*	*postulāre*	*vulnerāre*
cubāre	*intrāre*	*pōtāre*	
cūrāre	*invocāre*	*praestāre*	

Deponent verbs

admīrārī	*fārī*	*luctārī*	*tumultuārī*
arbitrārī	*hortārī*	*minārī*	*versārī*
comitārī	*fābulārī*	*mīrārī*	
cōnārī	*imitārī*	*ōsculārī*	
cōnsōlārī	*laetārī*	*precārī*	

2nd Conjugation
Inf. pres. act. *-ēre*, pass. *-ērī*

abstinēre	favēre	merēre	retinēre
appārēre	flēre	miscēre	rīdēre
audēre	frīgēre	monēre	rubēre
augēre	gaudēre	mordēre	salvēre
carēre	habēre	movēre	sedēre
cavēre	horrēre	nocēre	silēre
cēnsēre	iacēre	oportēre	solēre
complēre	impendēre	pallēre	studēre
continēre	implēre	pārēre	stupēre
dēbēre	invidēre	patēre	suādēre
decēre	iubēre	permovēre	sustinēre
dēlēre	latēre	persuādēre	tacēre
dērīdēre	libēre	placēre	tenēre
dētergēre	licēre	possidēre	tergēre
dēterrēre	lūcēre	pudēre	terrēre
dissuādēre	lūgēre	remanēre	timēre
docēre	maerēre	removēre	valēre
dolēre	manēre	respondēre	vidēre

Deponent verbs

cōnfitērī	intuērī	verērī
fatērī	tuērī	

3rd Conjugation
Inf. pres. act. *-ere*, pass. *-ī*
1. Ind. pres. pers. 1 sing. *-ō, -or*

abdūcere	*coquere*	*inclūdere*	*quaerere*
accēdere	*corrigere*	*incolere*	*quiēscere*
accendere	*crēdere*	*induere*	*recēdere*
accidere	*crēscere*	*īnflectere*	*recognōscere*
accumbere	*currere*	*īnfluere*	*recumbere*
accurrere	*dēfendere*	*īnscrībere*	*reddere*
addere	*dēmere*	*īnstruere*	*redimere*
adiungere	*dēscendere*	*intellegere*	*redūcere*
admittere	*dēserere*	*invehere*	*regere*
adnectere	*dēsinere*	*iungere*	*relinquere*
advehere	*dēsistere*	*laedere*	*remittere*
agere	*dētrahere*	*legere*	*repōnere*
alere	*dīcere*	*lūdere*	*reprehendere*
animadvertere	*dīligere*	*mergere*	*requiēscere*
āmittere	*dīmittere*	*metere*	*requīrere*
appōnere	*discēdere*	*metuere*	*resistere*
apprehendere	*discere*	*minuere*	*retrahere*
arcessere	*disiungere*	*mittere*	*rumpere*
ascendere	*dīvidere*	*neglegere*	*scindere*
aspergere	*dūcere*	*nōscere*	*scrībere*
āvertere	*ēdūcere*	*nūbere*	*serere*
bibere	*effundere*	*occidere*	*sinere*
cadere	*ēlīdere*	*occīdere*	*solvere*
caedere	*ēligere*	*occurrere*	*spargere*
canere	*emere*	*ostendere*	*statuere*
carpere	*ērubēscere*	*parcere*	*sternere*
cēdere	*ērumpere*	*pāscere*	*submergere*
cernere	*ēvolvere*	*pellere*	*sūmere*
cingere	*excurrere*	*percurrere*	*surgere*
claudere	*expōnere*	*perdere*	*tangere*
cōgere	*extendere*	*pergere*	*tollere*
cognōscere	*fallere*	*permittere*	*trādere*
colere	*fīdere*	*petere*	*trahere*
cōnfidere	*fīgere*	*plaudere*	*tremere*
coniungere	*flectere*	*pōnere*	*ūrere*
cōnscendere	*fluere*	*poscere*	*vehere*
cōnsīdere	*frangere*	*praepōnere*	*vēndere*
cōnsistere	*fremere*	*prehendere*	*vertere*
cōnstituere	*fundere*	*premere*	*vincere*
cōnsūmere	*gerere*	*prōcēdere*	*vīsere*
contemnere	*ignōscere*	*prōcurrere*	*vīvere*
contrahere	*impōnere*	*prōmere*	
convertere	*imprimere*	*prōmittere*	

Deponent verbs

colloquī	*lābī*	*persequī*	*revertī*
complectī	*loquī*	*proficīscī*	*sequī*
cōnsequī	*nāscī*	*querī*	*ūtī*
fruī	*oblīvīscī*	*reminīscī*	

2. Ind. pres. pers. 1 sing. *-iō, -ior*

abicere	*cōnspicere*	*iacere*	*rapere*
accipere	*cupere*	*incipere*	*recipere*
adicere	*dēspicere*	*interficere*	*sapere*
afficere	*efficere*	*parere*	*surripere*
allicere	*effugere*	*percutere*	*suscipere*
aspicere	*ēicere*	*perficere*	*suspicere*
aufugere	*ēripere*	*prōicere*	
capere	*facere*	*prōspicere*	
cōnficere	*fugere*	*quatere*	

Deponent verbs

ēgredī	*morī*	*patī*	*prōgredī*

4th Conjugation

Inf. pres. act. *-īre*, pass. *-īrī*

advenīre	*exaudīre*	*oboedīre*	*scīre*
aperīre	*exhaurīre*	*operīre*	*sentīre*
audīre	*finīre*	*pervenīre*	*servīre*
circumsilīre	*haurīre*	*prōsilīre*	*vāgīre*
convenīre	*invenīre*	*pūnīre*	*venīre*
cūstōdīre	*mollīre*	*reperīre*	*vestīre*
dēsilīre	*mūnīre*	*revenīre*	*vincīre*
dormīre	*nescīre*	*salīre*	

Deponent verbs

largīrī	*opperīrī*	*mentīrī*	*orīrī*
partīrī			

GRAMMATICAL TERMS

LATIN	ABBREVIATIONS	ENGLISH
ablātīvus (cāsus)	*abl*	ablative
accūsātīvus (cāsus)	*acc*	accusative
āctīvum (genus)	āct	active
adiectīvum (nōmen)	*adi*	adjective
adverbium ī *n*	*adv*	adverb
appellātīvum (nōmen)		appellative
cāsus ūs *m*		case
comparātiō ōnis *f*		comparison
comparātīvus (gradus)	*comp*	comparative
coniugātiō ōnis *f*		conjugation
coniūnctiō ōnis *f*	*coni*	conjunction
coniūnctīvus (modus)	*coni*	subjunctive
datīvus (cāsus)	*dat*	dative
dēclīnātiō ōnis *f*	*dēcl*	declension
dēmōnstrātīvum (prōnōmen)		demonstrative
dēpōnentia (verba)	*dēp*	deponent
fēminīnum (genus)	*f, fēm*	feminine
futūrum (tempus)	*fut*	future
futūrum perfectum (tempus)	*fut perf*	future perfect
genetīvus (cāsus)	*gen*	genitive
genus (nōminis/verbī)		gender/voice
gerundium ī *n*/ **gerundīvum** ī *n*		gerund/gerundive
imperātīvus (modus)	*imp, imper*	imperative
imperfectum (tempus praeteritum)	*imperf*	imperfect
indēclinābile (vocābulum)	*indēcl*	indeclinable
indēfīnītum (prōnōmen)		indefinite
indicātīvus (modus)	*ind*	indicative
īnfīnītīvus (modus)	*īnf*	infinitive
interiectiō ōnis *f*		interjection
interrogātīvum (prōnōmen)		interrogative
locātīvus (cāsus)	*loc*	locative
masculīnum (genus)	*m, masc*	masculine

modus (verbī)		mode
neutrum (genus)	*n, neutr*	neuter
nōminātīvus (cāsus)	*nōm*	nominative
optātīvus (modus)		optative
pars ōrātiōnis		part of speech
participium ī *n*	*part*	participle
passīvum (genus)	*pass*	passive
perfectum (tempus praeteritum)	*perf*	perfect
persōna ae *f*	*pers*	person
persōnāle (prōnōmen)		personal
plūrālis (numerus)	*pl, plūr*	plural
plūsquamperfectum (tempus praet.)	*plūsqu*	pluperfect
positīvus (gradus)	*pos*	positive
possessīvum (prōnōmen)		possessive
praepositiō ōnis *f*	*prp, praep*	preposition
praesēns (tempus)	*praes*	present
praeteritum (tempus)	*praet*	preterite, past tense
prōnōmen inis *n*	*prōn*	pronoun
proprium (nōmen)		proper name
relātīvum (prōnōmen)	*rel*	relative
singulāris (numerus)	*sg, sing*	singular
superlātīvus (gradus)	*sup*	superlative
supīnum		supine
tempus (verbī)		tense
verbum	*vb*	verb
vocātīvus (cāsus)	*voc*	vocative

Index